Houghton Mifflin Company Boston

New York Atlanta Geneva, Illinois Dallas Palo Alto

Houghton Mifflin Company   Boston

New York   Atlanta   Geneva, Illinois   Dallas   Palo Alto

Tragedy:

A Critical Anthology

Edited and with an introduction by
Robert W. Corrigan
California Institute of the Arts

Headnotes by
Glenn M. Loney
Brooklyn College

Library of Congress Catalog Card Number: 70–150135

ISBN: 0–395–04326–3

Oedipus the King by Sophocles as translated by Kenneth Cavander pub-
lished by Chandler Publishing Company, San Francisco. Copyright ©
1961 by Chandler Publishing Company. Reprinted by permission.
WARNING: For performing rights, please apply to Mrs. Janet Brooks,
International Famous Agency, Inc., 1301 Avenue of the Americas,
New York, New York 10019.

The Bacchae by Euripides, translated by Kenneth Cavander. Copyright
© 1966 by Kenneth Cavander. Reprinted by permission. WARNING:
For performing rights, please apply to Mrs. Janet Brooks, International
Famous Agency, Inc., 1301 Avenue of the Americas, New York, New
York 10019.

Doctor Faustus by Christopher Marlowe, edited by Roma Gill. Copyright © 1965 by Ernest Benn Limited. Reprinted by permission of
Hill and Wang, Inc., and Ernest Benn Limited.

The Tragedy of King Lear by William Shakespeare from *The Complete
Plays and Poems of William Shakespeare*, edited by William Allan
Neilson and Charles Jarvis Hill. Copyright 1942 by William Allan
Neilson and Charles Jarvis Hill. Reprinted by permission of Houghton
Mifflin Company.

Phaedra by Jean Racine as translated by Wesley Goddard published by
Chandler Publishing Company, San Francisco. Copyright © 1961 by
Chandler Publishing Company. Reprinted by permission.

Miss Julie by August Strindberg as translated by Evert Sprinchorn published by Chandler Publishing Company, San Francisco. Copyright ©
1961 by Chandler Publishing Company. Reprinted by permission.

The Master Builder by Henrik Ibsen translated by Kjell Amble published
by Literary Discoveries, Inc., San Francisco. Copyright © 1967 by
Literary Discoveries, Inc. Reprinted by permission. Application to

Contents

Tragedy and the Tragic Spirit

The facts of tragedy have haunted the spirit of every man in all ages, and for this reason the subject of tragedy has usually interested those who feel the need for a more intelligent awareness of themselves and the world in which they live. This has always been true, but never more so than it is today when we feel that our lives are perched precariously on the brink of continual disaster. The number of books and articles on tragedy and the tragic written in the past quarter of a century is overwhelming, and the very fact of their existence indicates that the conditions of our world have forced our imaginations to dwell once again on the facts of suffering, failure, and death.

Until World War II, "tragedy" was a dirty word in public parlance (we destroyed its power by indiscriminately using it to describe any kind of painful experience), and in academic circles it had become an honorific term reeking with a musty nostalgia for past ages of glory. It was argued that tragedy, the great flower of aristocratic societies, was dead and that all attempts to revive it in a democratic and egalitarian age were doomed to failure. Even the mighty Ibsen seemed small when placed next to Aeschylus, Sophocles, and Euripides, or Marlowe, Shakespeare, Corneille, and Racine. So said the professors. On the surface the students agreed and they read their Sophocles with dutiful respect, but they really liked O'Neill, no matter how tin his ear was supposed to have been. In fact, it is now clear that tragedy hadn't died at all, it had just gone underground for a couple of centuries. Dostoevsky, Nietzsche, and Kierkegaard had told us so, but most people were not convinced. Dunkirk, Belsen, and Hiroshima changed all this, and once again tragedy has taken its place as an accepted part of our lives.

Looking back, it is easy to see how and why the subversion of tragedy occurred. After the Restoration and on into the eighteenth century, England had a new deal in politics and religion; the emerging middle-class economy was burgeoning and creating a new prosperity; a growing confidence in the methods of empirical science tended to dispel personal doubts; and the bright flame of the Enlightenment cast its light on all that had been dark and mysterious. Man may have been "Born but to die, and reasoning but to err," but as Pope went on, there *was* a plan, for those who would but look:

All nature is but Art, unknown to thee;
All Chance, Direction, which thou canst not see;

> All Discord, Harmony not understood;
> All partial evil, universal Good . . .

On the Continent, the romanticism of Rousseau and his followers had a similar effect on popular attitudes about tragedy. The Curse of Adam was a social blight, not an innate quality of man. Individual man was born good and was then corrupted by his society. But society could be changed, and it was the duty of all men of goodwill to work for its improvement. In reducing Evil to evils, catastrophe was institutionalized and therefore made remediable. Thus, by insisting that human suffering and failure are not so much the result of our essentially divided nature as the effects of impersonal and external social forces, Rousseauian romanticism tended to dissolve tragic guilt — although it should be noted that it was also largely responsible for creating the psychology of victimization.

The nineteenth century was more or less officially the century of progress, and tragedy was given little place in either official life or official art. The "Cult of Life" emerged victorious (in theory at least), and the tragic view of life was seen as the great enemy which had to be suppressed at all costs. Victorianism, with its sturdy morality, its conservatism, its willingness to compromise, and its ability to assimilate alien' views into its unique brand of optimism, was riding high on the crest of a wave of material expansion and unthought-of prosperity. The voices of doubt and dissent were there, of course, but they were seldom heard. And in America we were too busy getting the land settled to worry much about aesthetic abstractions like tragedy.

At the turn of the present century, rumblings from the underground and occasional eruptions could be heard. The theatre especially had begun to change. We see it first in the later plays of Ibsen, such as *The Master Builder*, and in Strindberg's *Miss Julie* and his post-inferno plays; it rises to a frenzy in the works of the German Expressionists. Even a Fabian optimist like Shaw, who for so long had an answer for everything, began to come up with the most improbable solutions to the question of "What's to be done?" And as the final curtain descends with Saint Joan crying out, "O God that madest this beautiful earth, when will it be ready to receive thy saints? How long, O Lord, how long?" we know that the answer is, "Never!" So we pass through the era of Maxwell Anderson and Clifford Odets and enter the Age of the Bomb. All the debates about the common man being tragic (invariably any discussion of tragedy will sooner than later evoke the question: "Is *Death of a Salesman* a tragedy?") are ample, if not always eloquent, testimony that tragedy is once more a central concern of many thoughtful people.

But as soon as we acknowledge the renewed possibility of tragedy, we invariably exclaim: "Where is it?" People turn feverishly to the giants, of the past or to Aristotle's *Poetics* and bemoan the fact that while our world may certainly be tragic, it is not very hospitable to the nobility and grandeur that we tend to associate with tragedy as a dramatic form. In our lament we reveal that for all of our interest in the subject we really do not understand it very well. We reveal the commonplace assumption that there is in Western culture a persisting "idea of tragedy" that can be defined in terms of certain formal or structural characteristics. The history of the Western theatre documents the fact that nothing could be further from the truth.

It seems to me that a much more effective way of dealing with the subject would be to distinguish between *the form of tragedy*, which constantly changes — even in the work of a single dramatist — and *the tragic*, which is a way of looking at experience that has persisted more or less unchanged in the Western world from the time of Homer to the present. Santayana once wrote: "Everything in nature is lyrical in its ideal essence, tragic in its fate, and comic in its existence." The tragic writer in all ages has always been chiefly concerned with man's fate, and a man's fate is that he is ultimately doomed to defeat because he is born to die. Sophocles, Shakespeare, and Ibsen were tragedians because they were, in large measure, concerned with the individual's struggle with fate; and for them, as for all writers of tragedy, this struggle is seen as a conflict with necessity, or what the Greeks referred to as *ananke*. Necessity is not some kind of social disease that those who would change the world can ignore, soften, or legislate out of existence. Necessity is the embodiment of life's smallness, absurdity, and fragility; it is the acknowledgment of the limitation and mortality of all human experience. Man's struggle with necessity has been expressed in many forms and in varying contexts throughout history, but it is the constant of tragic drama, and it is the bond that links each of the writers represented in this volume insofar as they can be related. But such a view of life does not necessarily have anything to do with artistic form; one need not be an artist at all to hold such a view (certainly Adlai Stevenson saw the world in this way); and it is a view that is as compatible with the lyric poem or the novel as it is with drama. Thus, in referring to Euripides as "the most tragic of poets," Aristotle was saying nothing about him as a playwright or about the form of his plays.

The tragic view of life, then, begins by insisting that we accept the inevitable doom of our fate, and this fact is the mainspring of all tragic drama. However, our experience of tragedy tells us that it is more than this. The great tragedies of history also — and with equally compelling force — celebrate the fact that, while a man may have to learn to face and accept the reality of necessity, he also has an overpowering need to give a meaning to his fate. If man's fate, no matter how frightening, has no meaning, then why struggle? "If," as Kierkegaard wrote in *Fear and Trembling*,

> . . . there were no eternal consciousness in a man, if at the foundation of all there lay only a wildly seething power which writhing with obscene passions produced everything that is great and every-

thing that is insignificant, if a bottomless void never satiated lay
hidden beneath all — what then would life be but despair?

But, like Prospero, we tend to trust that our ending is not despair, and
our experience with tragic drama is sufficient testimony to our capacity
to give meaning to our fate.

The spirit of tragedy, then, is not quietistic; it is a grappling spirit.
And while the nature and terms of the struggle vary in direct relationship
to the individual dramatist's belief in the meaning of the struggle, in
every great tragedy we sense the validity of a meaningful struggle and
the real possibility of it. Thus, tragic characters may win or lose; or
more precisely, they win in the losing and lose in the winning. But it
is the struggle itself that is the source of the dramatic significance, and
it is out of this struggle with necessity that heroism is born.

When we think of tragic heroes, we usually think first of their great
nobility of spirit. Oedipus, Faustus, Lear, or Solness may be right or
wrong; they may suffer and be destroyed; but the emotional depth and
intellectual capacity each of them brings to his suffering condition
stamps him with the mark of greatness. We admire the hero because
he resists the forces of Fate.

In this regard, as has so often been the case, Aristotle — or at least the
usual interpretations of *The Poetics* — has misled us. That quality of
human will which dares to stand up against the universe and struggle
with necessity is called *hubris* by Aristotle, a flaw and therefore undesirable. We must never forget that this interpretation of *hubris* is an
expression of the fourth-century Greek's admiration (or need) for moderation in all its forms. While the turmoils of the preceding century may
have prompted the widespread acceptance of this Aristotelian attitude,
to apply it as a judgment or think of it as describing what happens in
tragedy is nonsensical. Each play in this volume reveals that *hubris* is
that quality in man which defies the *status quo* of being human: it is the
protest against the limitations of being a man. Whether this resistance
takes the form of an inordinate and monomaniacal pursuit of a finite goal
or is an arrogant and suicidal aspiration toward the infinite, it cannot
be considered as only a character defect. Rather, it is an integral part of
human nature; it is the necessary counterpart of man's capacity as a
feeling and thinking being. This explains why the action of tragedy
seems creative and destructive at the same time, why the spirit of tragedy
is the spirit of achievement. It is an end (usually death) and it is a
fulfillment, a complete realization filled with a heightened sense of life.

It is the paradoxical nature of this confrontation with fate which leads
the hero into what Karl Jaspers has called "boundary situations," those
areas of experience where man is shown at the limits of his sovereignty.
"Here," as Richard B. Sewall puts it in his *The Vision of Tragedy*, "with
all the protective coverings stripped off, the hero faces as if no man ever
faced it before the existential question — Job's question, 'What is man?'
or Lear's 'Is man no more than?' " At this frontier, the hero with faith

and those generalizations derived from his experience attempts to map his universe. What happens finally in tragedy is a failure of maps; in the tragic situation, man finds himself in a primitive country that he had believed his forefathers had tamed, civilized, and charted, only to discover they had not. One of the great holds that tragedy has always had on the imagination is that it brings us into direct touch with the naked landscape. The playwright begins by moving the hero into the destructive element, and then he presses these boundary situations to their fullest yield. In the midst of "the blight man was born for," the tragic dramatist demands of his hero what Hamlet demanded of himself: "How to be!" Thus, in carrying the action to the uttermost limits, the playwright is able to explore the farthest reaches of human possibility.

Man's tragic condition is that he is doomed by fate to defeat. The affirmation of tragedy is that man's spirit triumphs over his fate. This mortal encounter between the tragic and tragedy — between life and form — is the chief source of tension and turbulence in what we call tragic drama. Paradoxically, death in some form usually triumphs, but heroism is born out of that moral struggle and its spirit lives on long after the corpse has been interred.

Finally, however, the real key to the understanding of tragedy lies in recognizing that all tragedy has its roots in human struggles and springs from the basic dividedness of man's nature. All drama is built upon catastrophe (literally, a shift in direction) — any event which overturns the previously existing order or system of things. As such, catastrophe itself lacks moral meanings; it is equally capable of producing joy and happiness or sadness and grief, depending on the context in which it occurs. The most important characteristic of tragedy — the one distinguishing it from all other dramatic forms, especially melodrama — is that all significant "catastrophic" events are caused by the inner dividedness of the protagonist and not by some external force. *King Lear* and *The Duchess of Malfi* have many things in common, but because Lear is clearly brought low by the dividedness of his own nature while the Duchess, in spite of her inner conflicts, is ultimately destroyed by forces not of her own making and over which she has never had any control, we consider Shakespeare's play a tragedy and Webster's a melodrama. A similar distinction can be found in classical Greek drama: certainly there is as much suffering in *The Trojan Women* as in *Oedipus the King* — probably more. But because the King of Thebes is responsible for his own suffering in a way that the victimized women of Troy are not, we correctly believe that the difference between the two dramas is one of kind and not degree. This is an important distinction, because if the catastrophes of experience are considered to be the result of an external force — whether it be a divinity, a power of nature, or some societal pressure — then the individual is ultimately not responsible for them no matter how much he might suffer because of them. Tragedy cannot exist if the protagonist does not eventually come to recognize that he is morally responsible for his deeds and that his acts are the direct offspring of choices he has made. Professor Robert B. Heilman, in his very important book *Tragedy and Melodrama: Versions of Experience,* argues that the tragic character is one in whom is incorporated "the dividedness of a humanity whose values, because they naturally elude the confines of formal logic, create an apparently insoluble situation." These divisions may and do take many forms, but they always present alternatives and demand that man choose between them. And choice implies consciousness, for alternatives are not really alternatives if they do not in some way live in the hero's consciousness. Thus division is not only the occasion of self-knowledge, it is the very material of self-knowing. And self-knowledge derived from the irreconcilable conflicts within us is the very stuff of tragedy.

Such is the turbulence of the tragic, and if we are to rescue those plays which celebrate these abiding conflicts from those dusty repositories where most materpieces of culture are usually stored, we must find ways to rediscover that tension of struggle against struggle which is inevitable when men try vainly but nobly to impose a meaning on their own lives and on the world around them. If we are to succeed in this we must recognize that the constant in tragedy is the tragic view of life or the tragic spirit: that sense that life is, as Scott Fitzgerald once put it, "essentially a cheat and its conditions are those of defeat." This spirit can and does take many forms — both in drama and life — but it is always there as a backdrop to man's fate. Tragedy has always been both a celebration and a protest of this condition, and it is as possible in our day as it ever was. If only we would stop looking for another Shakespeare or Sophocles we might discover that *Mother Courage* is as much a tragedy as is *Coriolanus* or *Ajax,* or that *Waiting For Godot* or *Death of a Salesman* say as much to our time about the tragic nature of our existence as does *Oedipus the King.*

And this is the chief reason for this book. The fact that tragedy is being taught in more and more of our colleges and schools is a sign of our cultural maturity. But this growth brings with it a new responsibility: what ideas will be transmitted in the process? This is not just an academic quibble. A failure to understand what tragedy is about can have important and undesirable consequences for our grasp of reality; confusion in this subject may result in our losing touch with certain ideas that are an indispensable means of contemplating and understanding and experiencing the human catastrophes that surround us everywhere. This volume is an attempt to bring together a number of plays and essays which deal with such catastrophes of body and spirit with clarity, understanding, and compassion.

PART ONE

THE PLAYS

Sophocles · *Oedipus the King*

Euripides · *The Bacchae*

Marlowe · *Doctor Faustus*

Shakespeare · *The Tragedy of King Lear*

Racine · *Phaedra*

Dryden · *All for Love*

Strindberg · *Miss Julie*

Ibsen · *The Master Builder*

Shaw · *Saint Joan*

Miller · *Death of a Salesman*

Coxe and Chapman · *Billy Budd*

MacLeish · *J. B.*

The grandeur of the poetry of Sophocles (c. 467–406 B.C.), the elevation of his tragedies, and the remarkable insight he showed into man's fundamental fears have made his plays venerated for as long as men have read them. *Oedipus the King* (c. 429 B.C.), generally regarded as one of the finest if not *the* finest of Greek tragedies, presents some challenging problems in interpretation, but these deliberate poetical ambiguities contribute much to its dramatic interest and excitement. If *Oedipus* were easily understood, would readers and audiences find it quite so fascinating?

The central issues of the play have become obscured by discussions about peripheral ambiguities like the Freudian concept of the Oedipus complex. Any preoccupation with this question probably reveals more about modern problems than Oedipus' domestic difficulties. To be subconsciously in love with one's mother is one thing; to marry and sire children by a beloved woman is quite another.

Another peripheral ambiguity our factual, reasonable, twentieth-century minds exaggerate is the mysterious dearth of concrete motivations for the characters' actions. If Oedipus could solve the riddle of the Sphinx, why couldn't he answer some other questions which must have occurred to him? Why did he not inquire more into the death of Laius when he first arrived in Thebes; why did he not insist on interrogating the one servant who escaped alive from Laius' slaying? Why did Jocasta herself not ask the man why he was so upset on seeing Oedipus arrive in Thebes, and why did she allow him to rush to a remote mountain exile? These are provocative questions, to be sure, but we must remember that *Oedipus* was written for an audience not so apt to question these points as we are today. They knew the outcome of the play before it began; they were watching a drama of ritual actions which had never needed explanation, not a realistic twentieth-century play.

The most debated ambiguity and certainly the most valid one is whether *Oedipus* is a tragedy of fate or free will. Fate was accepted in classic times, as it often is now, as strange chance events, either miracles or disasters, changing the course of man's life without his being able to foresee or forestall them. We can argue that everything that happens in *Oedipus* is foreordained by fate. But, as Sophocles makes repeatedly clear, Jocasta, Laius, and Oedipus exercise free will to beat the rap of fate, as it has been plainly forecast to Jocasta and Oedipus by the Oracle at Delphi. In trying to destroy the child who is fated to kill Laius and marry her, Jocasta deliberately attempted to circumvent what had been ordained. Less is known about Laius' attitudes and actions, but apparently, by willfully refusing to let his unknown son pass by his chariot and thus provoking Oedipus' rash temper, he helped bring on his own predicted death. Oedipus, himself having heard a prophecy of patricide and incestuous marriage, abruptly left his "parents," Polybus and Merope, much as he respected and loved them. He wills that the oracle be

3

proven wrong; he tries to cheat fate. Even when he heard that Polybus had died a natural death, he refused to return to Corinth and accept the crown he inherited for fear of fulfilling at least half the prediction by marrying Merope.

If the downfall of the tragic hero — and Oedipus, according to Aristotle, is an excellent example of such a figure — comes through a character flaw which causes him to make a wrong decision or an unwise action, then the wrong decision or the unwise action is not a willful attempt to thwart fate. In its way, it shows nobility in the highest degree. Rather than kill his father and marry his mother, Oedipus is willing to be a wandering exile; rather than live in ignorant bliss as husband of Jocasta and king of Thebes, he has to find out who he is. These decisions and actions are rash — Oedipus is a proud, impetuous man, easily moved to harsh anger on little justification. *That* is his flaw and that is his fate. It causes him to leave Corinth and go to Thebes; it causes him to slay a prosperous traveler who has impeded his progress; it causes him to answer the riddle of the Sphinx; it causes him to keep seeking the truth about himself, with no thought of self-preservation. In short, it causes him to make wrong decisions and unwise actions at every turn. And it would have caused him to exercise free will and try to elude his destiny even if he had made and acted on an entirely different set of decisions.

This intentional ambiguity — fate or free will? — allows the play its most fascinating and agonizing feature: unrelenting irony. Sophocles projects Oedipus' whole tragedy through irony: his blindness to his own condition is made ironic and tragic through Teiresias' real blindness; then he mocks his eventual ability to see himself clearly by virtually blinding himself; in cursing Laius' murderer he curses himself; he is not smart enough to apply the answer to himself; his justness as a ruler and desire for truth bring on his salvation as a man — knowledge of himself — but also his downfall as a king. And these smaller ironies contribute to the larger one that involves the initial ambiguity: Oedipus' magnificent acts of free will only hasten his prophesied fate. We are led back in a circle to the main ambiguity; the effect is a chicken-and-the-egg paradox: which is operative, fate or free will?

G.L.

SOPHOCLES

Oedipus the King

TRANSLATED BY KENNETH CAVANDER

Characters

OEDIPUS, *King of Thebes*
PRIEST
CREON, *brother of Jocasta*
TEIRESIAS, *an old blind prophet*
JOCASTA, *wife of Oedipus*
MESSENGER
SHEPHERD
SERVANT

(In front of the palace of OEDIPUS *at Thebes. Near the altar stands the* PRIEST *with a large crowd of supplicants.*

Enter OEDIPUS.)

OEDIPUS.   My children, why do you crowd and wait at my altars?
Olive branches . . . and wreaths of sacred flowers —
Why do you bring these, my people of Thebes? Your streets
Are heavy with incense, solemn with prayers for healing,
And when I heard your voices, I would not let
My messengers tell me what you said. I came
To be your messenger myself, Oedipus, whose name
Is greatest known and greatest feared.
(To PRIEST.)   Will you tell me, then? You have dignity enough
To speak for them all — is it fear that makes you kneel
Before me, or do you need my help? I am ready,
Whatever you ask will be done . . . Come, I am not cold
Or dead to feeling — I will have pity on you.
PRIEST.   King Oedipus, our master in Thebes, if you will look
At your altars, and at the ages of those who kneel there,
You will see children, too small to fly far from home;
You will see old men, slow with the years they carry,
And priests — I am a priest of Zeus; and you will see
The finest warriors you have; the rest of your people
Kneel, praying, in the open city, in the temples
Of Athene, and in the shrine where we keep a flame

5

Always alive and the ash whispers the future.
Look about you. The whole city drowns
And cannot lift its hand from the storm of death
In which it sinks: the green corn withers
In the fields, cattle die in the meadows,
Our wives weep in agony, and never give birth!
Apollo brings his fire like a drover and herds us
Into death, and nature is at war with herself.
Thebes is sick, every house deserted, and the blind
Prison of the dead grows rich with mourning
And our dying cries.
Eternal powers control our lives, and we do not
Think you are their equal; yet we pray to you, as your children,
Believing that you, more than any man, may direct
Events, and come to terms with the powers beyond us.
When the savage riddle of the Sphinx enslaved
Thebes, you came to set us free. We
Were powerless, we could not tell you how to answer her.
And now they say, and it is believed, that you
Were close to God when you raised our city from the dead.
Oedipus, we pray to your power, which can overcome
Sufferings we do not understand; guard us
From this evil. In heaven and earth there must
Be some answer to our prayer, and you may know it.
You have struggled once with the powers above us and been
Victorious; we trust that strength and believe your words.
Oedipus, you are the royal glory of Thebes —
Give us life; Oedipus — think. Because
You overpowered the evil in the Sphinx
We call you saviour still. Must we remember
Your reign for the greatness in which you began, and the sorrow
In which you ended? The country is sick, and you
Must heal us. You were once our luck, our fortune, the augury
Of good we looked for in the world outside. Fulfil
That augury now. You are king of Thebes, but consider:
Which is it better to rule — a kingdom? Or a desert?
What is a castle or a ship if there are
No men to give it life? Emptiness! Nothing!

    OEDIPUS. My children, I know your sorrows, I know why
You have come, and what you ask of me. I see
The pain of sickness in you all, and yet in all
That sickness, who is so sick as I? Each
Of you has one sorrow, his grief is his own —
But I must feel for my country, for myself,
And for you. That is why you did not find me
Deaf or indifferent to your prayers. No,
I have spent many tears, and in my thoughts

Travelled long journeys. And then I saw
That we could be saved in one way only;
I took that way and sent Creon, my brother-
In-law, to the Oracle of Apollo; there
The god will tell him how I can save the city —
The price may be an act of sacrifice, or perhaps
A vow, a prayer, will be enough . . . But the days
Run on and the measure of time keeps pace with them
And I begin to fear. What is he doing?
I did not think he would stay so long — he should not
Stay so long! . . . But when he comes I will do
Whatever the god commands; if I disobeyed
It would be a sin.

PRIEST.　　　　Heaven listened then;
This messenger says that Creon is returning.

OEDIPUS.　My lord Apollo, let his news be the shining sun
That answers our prayers and guides us out of death!

PRIEST.　I can see him now . . . the news must be good.
Look, there is a crown of bay thick with flowers
Covering his hair.

OEDIPUS.　　　　At last we shall know the truth.
If I shout, he will hear me . . . Creon!
My brother, son of Menoeceus, Lord of Thebes,
What answer does Apollo send to us? Do you bring
An answer?

(*Enter* CREON.)

CREON.　Our danger is gone. This load of sorrow
Will be lifted if we follow the way
Where Apollo points.

OEDIPUS.　　　　What does this mean? I expected
Hope, or fear, but your answer gives me neither.

CREON.　I am ready to tell you my message now, if you wish;
But they can hear us, and if we go inside . . .

OEDIPUS.　Tell me now and let them hear! I must not think
Of myself; I grieve only when my people suffer.

CREON.　Then this is what I was told at Delphi:
Our land is tainted. We carry the guilt in our midst.
A foul disease, which will not be healed unless
We drive it out and deny it life.

OEDIPUS.　　　　　　But how
Shall we be clean? How did this happen to us?

CREON.　The crime of murder is followed by a storm.
Banish the murder and you banish the storm, kill
Again and you kill the storm.

OEDIPUS.　　　　　　But Apollo means
One man — who is this man?

CREON.   My lord,
There was once a king of Thebes; he was our master
Before you came to rule our broken city.

OEDIPUS.   I have heard of him . . . I never saw your king.

CREON.   Now that he is dead your mission from the god
Is clear: take vengeance on his murderers!

OEDIPUS.   But where are they now? The crime is old,
And time is stubborn with its secrets. How
Can you ask me to find these men?

CREON.   The god said
You must search in Thebes; what is hunted can
Be caught, only what we ignore escapes.

OEDIPUS.   Where was the murder? Was Laius killed in the city?
Or did this happen in another country?

CREON.   He was travelling
To Delphi, he said. But he never returned to the palace
He left that day.

OEDIPUS.   Did no one see this?
A messenger? The guard who watched his journey? You could
Have questioned them.

CREON.   They were all killed, except
One. He ran home in terror, and could only
Repeat one thing.

OEDIPUS.   What did he repeat?
Once we have learnt one thing, we may learn the rest.
This hope is the beginning of other hopes.

CREON.   He said they met some robbers who killed the king.
He talked of an army, too strong for the servants of Laius.

OEDIPUS.   Robbers would not dare to kill a king — unless
They had bribes. They must have had bribes from the city!

CREON.   We suspected that, but with Laius dead
We were defenceless against our troubles.

OEDIPUS.   Were
Your troubles so great that they prevented you
From knowing the truth? Your king had been murdered . . . !

CREON.   But the Sphinx
Had a riddle to which there was no answer, and we thought
Of our closest sorrows. We had no time for other
Mysteries.

OEDIPUS.   But I will begin again, and make your mysteries
Plain. Apollo was right, and you were right,
To turn my thoughts to the king who died. Now
You will see the measure of my power; I come to defend you,
Avenging your country and the god Apollo.
(aside) If I can drive out this corruption and make the city
Whole, I shall do more than save my people,
Who are my friends, but still my subjects — I shall save

Myself. For the knife that murdered Laius may yet
Drink from my heart, and the debt I pay to him
Lies to my own credit.
My children, quickly, leave this altar and take
Your branches. I will have the people of Thebes assembled
To hear that I shall do all the god commands.
And in the end we shall see my fortune smiling
From heaven, or my fall. (*Exit.*)

PRIEST. Let us go, my sons; our king has given the order
We came to hear. May Apollo, who sent this answer
From his oracle, come to lay our sickness
To rest, and give us life.

(*Exeunt* PRIEST, CREON, *and some of the elders. Enter* CHORUS.)

CHORUS. From golden Delphi Apollo replies to Thebes
And the words of heaven send a warning.
As a lyre is strung and tightened, so we
Are tightened by fear.
As a lyre trembles, so we tremble at the touch of fear.
Apollo, god of healing, god of newness,
We fear you, and the commands you send to humble us.
Do you ask a new submission? Or is your command
The same as we hear in every wind, and every season, and every year?
Only the child of golden hope, whose voice
Will never die, only the spirit of truth can tell us.
First in my prayers is the goddess Athene, the daughter of Zeus;
Second, her sister Artemis, who is queen in Thebes,
For she sits at our country's heart, pure and honoured,
In a temple like the sun. And third in our prayer
Is Phoebus Apollo, whose arm reaches over all the world.
Come three times to drive our wrongs before you!
If ever in the past, when evil and blindness
Rose like a wave, when grief was burning in our city,
If ever you banished that grief,
Come now to help us.
There is no numbering our sorrows;
The whole country is sick, and mortal will and human mind
Are no weapons to defend us.
The great earth whom we call our mother
Is barren and dead; women weep in the pain of childbirth
But they fall sick and die.
Look, can you see the dying go following each other,
Gliding like gentle birds, quicker
Than the restless flash of fire that will never sleep,
The dying on their flight to the shore
Where evening sits like a goddess?

The city of the dying goes countless away
And the children of life fall to the earth,
The toys of death,
With no pity and no remembering tears.
   In the rest of our city wives and mothers
Stand grey at the altars,
Which tell us of a certainty resisting the seas of doubt;
They weep, pray, plead for release
From the harsh revenge which heaven brings.
A cry for healing rises and burns above the still crowd
That mourns in the city.
Send us strength that will look kindly on us,
Golden daughter of Zeus.
Ares, the god of war, confronts us, bitter in his cruelty,
And his shout burns like fire;
But his war is fought with no armour, and Ares
Carries no shield, for he brings his conflict
Into the moment of our birth and death.
Oh turn him flying down the winds, turn him
Back and dash him from our country
Into the wide chambers where Amphitrite sleeps,
Or to the lonely cliffs of Thrace where the seas
Allow no guests. For Ares comes to finish
The deadly work left undone by the night.
Zeus, you are the lord of lightning, lord of fire,
Destroy him with your thunder, crush our enemy!
   Lord Apollo, god in the sun, we pray for your light;
Strike with your golden spears and your hands of fire,
Strike to protect us.
We pray for Artemis to bring her chaste fires,
Which we see her carry like a shining torch across
The mountains where the wolf runs.
I call you, the god with the golden crown,
Born in our country, Bacchus,
With the fire of wine in your cheek,
And the voice of wine in your shout,
Come with your pine branch burning, and your Maenads
Following the light, the fire of heaven's madness
In their eyes, come to guard us against the treacherous power
Who goes to war with justice and the harmony of heaven!

   (Enter OEDIPUS.)

OEDIPUS.   You have told me of your need. Are you content
To hear me speak, obey my words, and work
To humour the sickness? . . . Then you will thrust away
The weight with which you struggle, and fulfil

Your need. I am a stranger to this story,
And to the crime; I have no signs to guide me,
And so if I am to trap this murderer, my hunt
Must follow every hope. I am speaking, then,
To every citizen of Thebes, and I shall not
Exempt myself, although I am a citizen only
In name, and not in blood.
Whoever knows the murderer of Laius, son
Of Labdacus, must make his knowledge mine.
It is the king's command! And if he is afraid,
Or thinks he will escape, I say to him, "Speak!
You will go into exile, but you will go unharmed —
Banishment is all you have to fear."
Or if you know the assassin comes from another
Country, you must not be silent. I shall pay
The value of your knowledge, and your reward
Will be more than gratitude.
But if I find only silence, if you are afraid
To betray a friend or reveal yourself, and lock
The truth away, listen, this is my decree:
This murderer, no matter who he is, is banished
From the country where my power and my throne
Are supreme. No one must shelter him or speak to him;
When you pray to heaven, he must not pray with you;
When you sacrifice, drive him away, do not
Give him holy water, beat him from your doors!
He carries the taint of corruption with him — for so
The god Apollo has revealed to me . . . You see
How I serve the god and revenge the king who died!
I curse that murderer; if he is alone, I curse him!
If he shares his guilt with others, I curse him! May
His evil heart beat out its years in sorrow,
Throughout his life may he breathe the air of death!
If I give him shelter, knowing who
He is, and let him feel the warmth of my fire,
I ask this punishment for myself.
This must be done! In every word I speak
I command obedience, and so does the god Apollo,
And so does your country, which a barren sickness
And an angry heaven drag to death. But even
If it is not a god that comes to punish you
It would be shame to leave your land impure.
Your king was killed — he was a royal and noble
Man; hunt his murderer down!
I live in Laius' palace, my queen was once
The queen of Laius, and if his line had prospered
His children would have shared my love.

But now time has struck his head to earth
And in revenge I will fight for him as I
Would fight for my own father. My search will never
End until I take in chains the murderer
Of Laius, son of Labdacus. I pray heaven
That those who will not help me may watch the soil
They have ploughed crumble and turn black, let them see
Their women barren, let them be destroyed by the fury
That scourges us, but may it rage more cruelly!
And for all the Thebans who will obey me gladly
I ask the strength of justice, and the power of heaven.
So we shall live in peace; so we shall be healed.

    CHORUS. Your curse menaces me, my lord, if I lie.
I swear I did not kill him, nor can I tell
Who did. Apollo sent the reply, and Apollo
Should find the murderer.

    OEDIPUS.   Yes, we believe
It is Apollo's task — but we cannot make
The gods our slaves; we must act for ourselves.

    CHORUS.   Our next
Hope then, must be . . .

    OEDIPUS.   And every hope
You have. When I search, nothing escapes.

    CHORUS. We know a lord who sees as clearly as the lord
Apollo — Teiresias; we could ask Teiresias, my king,
And be given the truth.

    OEDIPUS.   Creon told me, and his advice
Did not lie idle for want of action. I have sent
Two servants . . . It is strange they are not here.

    CHORUS. And there are the old rumours — but they tell us nothing . . .

    OEDIPUS. What do these rumours say? I must know
Everything.

    CHORUS. They say some travellers killed him.

    OEDIPUS. I have heard that too. But the man who saw those travellers
Was never seen himself.

    CHORUS.   The murderer will leave our country;
There is a part of every man that is ruled
By fear, and when he hears your curse . . .

    OEDIPUS.   A sentence
Holds no terror for the man who is not afraid
To kill.

    CHORUS. But now he will be convicted. Look,
They are leading your priest to you; Teiresias comes.
When he speaks, it is the voice of heaven
That we hear.

    (*Enter* TEIRESIAS, *guided by a boy.*)

OEDIPUS. Teiresias, all things lie
In your power, for you have harnessed all
Knowledge and all mysteries; you know what heaven
Hides, and what runs in the earth below, and you
Must know, though you cannot see, the sickness with which
Our country struggles. Defend us, my lord, and save us —
We shall find no other defence or safety.
For Apollo — and yet you must have heard the message —
Apollo, whom we asked in our doubt, promised release —
But on one condition: that we find the murderers
Of Laius, and banish them, or repay the murder.
Teiresias, the singing birds will tell you of the future,
You have many ways of knowing the truth. Do not grudge
Your knowledge, but save yourself and your city, save me,
For murder defiles us all. Think of us
As your prisoners, whose lives belong to you!
To have the power and use that power for good
Is work to bring you honour.

TEIRESIAS. When truth cannot help
The man who knows, then it brings terror. I knew
That truth, but I stifled it. I should not have come.

OEDIPUS. What is it? You come as sadly as despair.

TEIRESIAS. Send me away, I tell you! Then it will be easy
For you to play the king, and I the priest.

OEDIPUS. This is no reply. You cannot love Thebes — your own
Country, Teiresias — if you hide what the gods tell you.

TEIRESIAS. I see your words guiding you on the wrong
Path; I pray for my own escape.

OEDIPUS. Teiresias!
You do not turn away if you know the truth; we all
Come like slaves to a king with our prayers to you.

TEIRESIAS. But you come without the truth, and I can never
Reveal my own sorrows, lest they become
Yours.

OEDIPUS. You cannot? Then you know and will not tell us!
Instead, you plan treason and the city's death.

TEIRESIAS. I mean to protect us both from pain. You search
And probe, and it is all wasted. I will not tell you!

OEDIPUS. You demon! You soul of evil! You would goad
A thing of stone to fury. Will you never speak?
Can you feel, can you suffer? Answer me, and end this!

TEIRESIAS. You see wrong in my mood, you call me evil — blind
To the mood that settles in you and rages there.

OEDIPUS. Rages! Yes, that is what your words
Have done, when they shout your contempt for Thebes.

TEIRESIAS. The truth will come; my silence cannot hide it.

OEDIPUS. And what must come is what you must tell me.

TEIRESIAS.   I can tell you no more, and on this answer let
Your fury caper like a beast.

OEDIPUS.   It is
A fury that will never leave me. Listen, I know
What you are. I see now that you conspired to plan
This murder, and you committed it — all but the stroke
That killed him. If you had eyes, I would have said
The crime was yours alone.

TEIRESIAS.   Oedipus, I warn you!
Obey your own decree and the oath you swore.
Never from this day speak to me, or to these nobles;
You are our corruption, the unholiness in our land.

OEDIPUS.   How you must despise me to flaunt your scorn like this,
Thinking you will escape. How?

TEIRESIAS.   I have escaped.
I carry the truth: it is my child, and guards me.

OEDIPUS.   Truth! Who taught you? Heaven never taught you!

TEIRESIAS.   You taught me; you forced me to the point of speech.

OEDIPUS.   Repeat your words, I do not remember this speech.

TEIRESIAS.   You did not understand? Or do you try to trap me?

OEDIPUS.   I know nothing! Repeat your truth!

TEIRESIAS.   I said, you are the murderer you are searching for.

OEDIPUS.   Again you attack me, but I will not forgive you again!

TEIRESIAS.   Shall I say more to make your anger sprawl?

OEDIPUS.   All you have breath for — it will all be useless.

TEIRESIAS.   Then . . . you live with your dearest one in burning
Shame, and do not know it; nor can you see
The evil that surrounds you.

OEDIPUS.   Do you think
You will always smile in freedom if you talk like this?

TEIRESIAS.   If truth can give strength, I will.

OEDIPUS.   It can —
But not to you; you have no truth. Your senses
Have died in you — ears: deaf! eyes: blind!

TEIRESIAS.   Yes, be bitter, mock at me, poor Oedipus.
Soon they will all mock as bitterly as you.

OEDIPUS.   You live in perpetual night; you cannot harm
Me, nor anyone who moves in the light.

TEIRESIAS.   Your downfall
Will come, but I will not be the cause. Apollo
Is a great power; he watches over the end.

OEDIPUS.   Did you or Creon plan this?

TEIRESIAS.   Creon is not
Your enemy; you carry your enemy with you — in your soul.

OEDIPUS.   We have wealth and power, the mind reaches higher, grows,
Breaks its own fetters, our lives are great and envied,
And the world rewards us — with spitefulness and hate!

Consider my power — I did not come begging, the city
Laid its submission in my hands as a gift.
Yet, for this power, Creon, my trusted, my first
Friend, goes like a thief behind my back,
Tries to exile me, and sends this wizard,
This patcher of threadbare stories, this cunning peddler
Of the future, with no eyes except
For money, and certainly no eyes for mysteries.
Tell me, tell me, when did you ever foretell the truth?
When the Sphinx howled her mockeries and riddles
Why could you find no answer to free the city?
Her question was too hard for the simple man,
The humble man; only heaven's wisdom could find
A reply. But you found none! Neither your birds
Above you, nor the secret voice of your inspiration
Sent you knowledge — then we saw what you were!
But I came, ignorant Oedipus, and silenced her,
And my only weapon was in my mind and my will;
I had no omens to teach me. And this is the man
You would usurp! You think, when Creon is king
You will sit close to the throne; but I think
Your plans to drive the accursed away will return
To defeat you, and to defeat their architect.
You are old, Teiresias, or else your prophetic wisdom
Would have been your death.

    CHORUS.   Your majesty, what he has said
And your reply — they were both born in anger.
We do not need this wildness; we ask the best
Fulfilment of Apollo's commands. This must be the search.

    TEIRESIAS (to OEDIPUS).   You flourish your power; but you must give
        me the right
To make my reply, and that will have equal power.
I have not lived to be your servant, but Apollo's;
Nor am I found in the list of those whom Creon
Protects. You call me blind, you jeer at me —
I say your sight is not clear enough to see
Who shares your palace, nor the rooms in which you walk,
Nor the sorrow about you. Do you know who gave you birth?
You are the enemy of the dead, and of the living,
And do not know it. The curse is a two-edged sword,
From your mother, from your father; the curse will hunt you,
Like a destruction, from your country. Now
You have sight, but then you will go in blindness;
When you know the truth of your wedding night
All the world will hear your crying to rest,
Every hill a Cithaeron to echo you.
You thought that night was peace, like a gentle harbour —

But there was no harbour for that voyage, only grief.
Evil crowds upon you; you do not see
How it will level you with your children and reveal
Yourself as you truly are. Howl your abuse
At Creon and at me . . . All men must suffer,
Oedipus, but none will find suffering more terrible
Than you.

    OEDIPUS.   Must I bear this? Must I be silent?
Die! Go to your death! Leave my palace now!
Get away from me!

    TEIRESIAS.   Yet you called me here, or I would not have come.

    OEDIPUS.   If I had known you would talk in the raving language
Of a madman, I would never have sent for you.

    TEIRESIAS.   I am no more than you see. You see a madman,
The parents who gave you life saw a prophet.

    OEDIPUS.   My parents? Wait! Who were my parents?

    TEIRESIAS.   Today will be your parent, and your murderer.

    OEDIPUS.   Always riddles, always lies and riddles!

    TEIRESIAS.   You were best at solving riddles, were you not?

    OEDIPUS.   When you think of my greatness, it inspires your mockery.

    TEIRESIAS.   That greatness has conspired to be your traitor.

    OEDIPUS.   I saved this country, I care for nothing else.

    TEIRESIAS.   Then I shall go . . . (*To his guide.*) Boy, lead me away.

    OEDIPUS.   Yes, lead him . . . You come and trouble me — you are
      nothing
But hindrance to my plans. Go, and I shall be safe.

    TEIRESIAS.   I came to speak, and I shall not leave until I speak.
I need not cower at your frown, you cannot
Harm me. This man for whom you search,
Whom you threaten, and to the people call "the murderer
Of Laius," this man is here, a stranger, a foreigner;
But he will see his Theban blood, though he will not
Have any joy at the discovery.
He will be blind — though now he sees; a beggar —
Though now he is rich, and he will go feeling
Strange ground before him with a stick.
He is a father to children — then he will
Be called their brother; he is his mother's son —
Then he will be called her husband, then
He will be called his father's murderer.
Consider this when you walk between your palace walls;
If you find I have been false to you, then say
That all my prophetic wisdom is a lie.

    (*Exeunt all but the* CHORUS.)

    CHORUS.   In the rock at Delphi there is a cave
Which is the mouth of heaven; now

The cave warns us of one man, whose hands are red
With murder, and whose actions
Break the unspoken laws that shackle us.
Time tells him now to escape,
Faster than the jostling horses of the storm,
For Apollo, the son of Zeus, leaps down on him,
Armed with lightning, dressed in fire,
And the terrible avengers follow where he goes,
The Furies who never mistake and are never cheated.
From the snow of Parnassus over Delphi the message
Gleamed and came shining to Thebes.
We must all hunt the murderer
Who hides from justice. Like a lonely bull
He crosses and crosses our country, through the harsh forests,
The hollows of the mountains, and the rocks.
Sadly thinking and alone,
Sadly trying to escape
The words that came from Delphi, the heart of the world.
But their wings are always beating in his head.

The wisdom of the priest sets fear, fear, beating in our blood;
Truth or lies, nothing comforts, nothing denies.
The world is built out of our beliefs,
And when we lose those beliefs in doubt,
Our world is destroyed, and the present and the past
Vanish into night.
We must have proof, a certainty that we can touch
And feel, before we turn against Oedipus.
The land is peopled with rumours and whispers —
They cannot make us avenge King Laius,
Whose death is guarded by such mystery.

All that men may do is watched and remembered
By Zeus, and by Apollo. But they are gods;
Can any man, even the prophet, the priest,
Can even he know more than us?
And if he can, who will be judge of him, and say he lied
Or spoke the truth?
Yet wisdom may come to us, not the wisdom that sees
How the world is ruled, but the wisdom that guides
The modest life. In this alone we may excel.
But the proof must be clear and certain,
Before I can accuse Oedipus.
Remember that the Sphinx came flying
To meet him, evil beyond our comprehension,
And we saw his wisdom then, we knew and felt
The goodness of his heart towards our country.
Thoughts cannot be guilty traitors to such a man.

(*Enter* CREON.)

CREON.   Lords of Thebes, this message has called me here
In terror . . . These crimes of which our king accuses me —
No one would dare to think of them! If he
Believes I could wrong him, or even speak of wrong,
At such a time, when we are in such sorrow,
Let me die! I have no wish to live out my years
If I must live them suspected and despised.
I will not bear this slander, which is no trifle
To forget, but the greatest injury — the name
Of traitor. The people will call me that, even
You will call me that!
CHORUS.   His fury mastered him;
Perhaps he did not mean the charge.
CREON.   He said
To you all — you all heard — that the priest
Had been told to lie, and that I had planned the answer?
CHORUS.   He said that, but I know he did not mean it.
CREON.   And when he
Accused me, he seemed master of his thoughts, and there was
Reason in his voice?
CHORUS.   I cannot remember,
I do not observe my king so closely . . . But here
He comes from the palace himself to meet you.

(*Enter* OEDIPUS.)

OEDIPUS.   So,
My citizen, you have come to your king? Your eyes have great
Courage — they can look on my palace out of a murderer's
Face, a robber's face! Yes, I know you;
You blaze, you thief of power . . . In heaven's name
Tell me: when you planned to kill me, did you think I had
Become a coward or a fool? Did you think I would not
Notice your treason stalking me? Or were you sure
That if I knew, I would not dare defence?
See your insane attempt! You try to capture
Power, which must be hunted with armies and gold;
But no one will follow you, no one will make
You rich!
CREON.   Wait! You have accused, but you must not judge
Until you have heard my defence; I can reply.
OEDIPUS.   You talk with the fangs of cleverness; but how
Can I understand? I understand only
That you are my enemy, and dangerous.
CREON.   There is one thing I must say; hear it first.

OEDIPUS.   One thing you must not say: "I am innocent."

CREON.   You are stubborn, Oedipus, your will is too hard;
It is nothing to treasure, and you are wrong to think it is.

OEDIPUS.   Treason, crimes against a brother, will not
Escape justice: you are wrong to think they will.

CREON.   I do not quarrel with your talk of justice.
But tell me how I have harmed you: what is my crime?

OEDIPUS.   Did you persuade me — perhaps you did not — to send for
The priest whom we used to worship for his wisdom?

CREON.   And I still have faith in that advice.

OEDIPUS.   How long
Is it since Laius . . .

CREON.   What has Laius to do
With this? I do not see . . .

OEDIPUS.   Since he was hidden
From the living sun, since he was attacked and killed?

CREON.   The years are old and the time is long since then.

OEDIPUS.   Was Teiresias already a priest and prophet then?

CREON.   As wise as now, and no less honoured and obeyed.

OEDIPUS.   But at the time he did not mention me?

CREON.   I did not hear him . . .

OEDIPUS.   But surely you tried to find
The murderer?

CREON.   We searched, of course, we could discover
Nothing.

OEDIPUS.   If I was guilty, why did Teiresias
Not accuse me then? He must have known, for he is wise.

CREON.   I do not know. If I cannot know the truth
I would rather be silent.

OEDIPUS.   But there is one truth
You will confess to; none knows it better . . . ?

CREON.   What is that? I shall deny nothing . . .

OEDIPUS.   That only by some insidious plan of yours
Could Teiresias ever say I murdered Laius!

CREON.   If he says that, I cannot unsay it for him;
But give me an answer in return for mine.

OEDIPUS.   Question till you have no questions left;
You cannot prove me a murderer.

CREON.   Now,
You have married my sister?

OEDIPUS.   I do not deny it; the truth
Was in your question.

CREON.   You and she rule
This country, you are equal?

OEDIPUS.   If she has a wish
I grant it all to her.

CREON.   And am I not
Considered equal to you both?

OEDIPUS.   Yes, there your friendship
Shows the face of evil is concealed.

CREON.   No, reason to yourself as I have reasoned.
First, imagine two ways of ruling, each
Bringing equal power. With one of these fear
Never leaves you, but with the other you sleep
Calm in the night. Who do you think
Would not choose the second? I feel no ambition
To be the king, when I have the power of a king.
For I have my place in the world, I know it, and will not
Overreach myself. Now, you give me all
I wish, and no fear comes with the gift;
But if I were king myself, much more would be forced
Upon me. Why should I love the throne better
Than a throne's power and a throne's majesty
Without the terrors of a throne? Now,
I may smile to all, and all will bow to me;
Those who need you petition me,
For I am their hopes of success. Is this such a worthless
Life that I should exchange it for yours? Treason
Is for those who cannot value what they have.
I have never had longing thoughts about your power,
Nor would I help a man who had. Send
To Delphi, make a test of me, ask the god
Whether my message was true, and if you find
I have plotted with your priest, then you may kill me —
I will be your authority, I will assent
When you decree my death. But do not accuse me
Yet, when you know nothing. You wrong your friends
To think them enemies, as much as you do wrong
To take enemies for friends. Think, be sure!
You banish life from your body — and life you love
Most dearly — by banishing a good friend.
Time will set this knowledge safely in your heart;
Time alone shows the goodness in a man —
One day is enough to tell you all his evil.

CHORUS.   My king, a cautious man would listen; beware
Of being convinced too quickly. Suddenness is not safety.

OEDIPUS.   When the attack is quick and sudden, and the plot
Runs in the darkness, my thoughts must be sudden
In reply. If I wait, sitting in silence,
He will have done his work, and I lost
My chance to begin.

CREON.   Your decision then! Will you
Banish me?

OEDIPUS. No, not banishment; I
Will have your life! You must teach men the rewards
That I keep for the envious and the cruel.

CREON. Will you not listen to persuasion and the truth?

OEDIPUS. You will never persuade me that you speak the truth.

CREON. No, I can see you are blind to truth.

OEDIPUS. I see
Enough to guard my life.

CREON. My life is as precious
To me.

OEDIPUS. But you are a traitor!

CREON. You know nothing!

OEDIPUS. Yet the king must rule.

CREON. Not when the king is evil.

OEDIPUS. My city! My city!

CREON. It is my city too, do not forget that!

CHORUS. Stop, my lords! Look, here is Jocasta coming to you
From the palace, at the moment when she may help you
To bring this quarrel to rest.

(*Enter* JOCASTA.)

JOCASTA. My lords, it is pitiful to hear your senseless voices
Shouting and wrangling. Have you no shame? Our country
Is sick, and you go bustling about your private
Quarrels. My king, you must go inside, and you,
Creon, go to the palace. At this time
We have no troubles except the plague; all
Others are pretence.

CREON. My sister, your sovereign, Oedipus,
Condemns me cruelly in his efforts to be just.
He will banish me, or murder me; in both he does wrong.

OEDIPUS. No, I have found a traitor, my queen, who plots
Against my life.

CREON. Never let me breathe
In freedom again, let me die under your curse,
If I am guilty of those crimes!

JOCASTA. Oh, Oedipus,
Believe him. Believe him for the sake of those words
That heaven witnessed; you have a duty to that oath,
And to me, and to your people.

CHORUS. Obey her, my lord, I beg you; do not be harsh,
Be wise.

OEDIPUS. Must I be ruled by you?

CHORUS. Creon was always wise and faithful in the past; his oath was
    great
And you must respect it.

OEDIPUS.   You know what you are asking?
CHORUS.   I know.
OEDIPUS.   Tell me, what do you advise?
CHORUS.   He is your friend — that is a truth
As simple as the light of day;
But only confused and uncertain rumours call him traitor;
No cause to rob him of his honour.
OEDIPUS.   But listen, in asking this, you ask
For my banishment, or for my death.
CHORUS.   No! By the sun who is prince of the sky!
If that was ever my intention,
I pray for death, without friends on earth,
Without love in heaven,
Death in pain and misery.
Now, now, when the decaying earth eats our lives
Away, will you add your quarrels to all
That we already suffer?
OEDIPUS.   Let him go then; I shall die, I do not care;
I shall be driven into banishment and disgrace.
I do this for love and pity of you. For him, I feel none;
Wherever he goes, he cannot escape my hatred.
CREON.   For you submission is a torment — you do not hide it.
And when you force your way against the world
You crush us all beneath you. Such natures
Find their own company most terrible to bear.
It is their punishment.
OEDIPUS.   Leave my sight, then! Leave me to myself!
CREON.   I shall leave you. In all the time you knew me,
You never understood me . . . They see my innocence. (*Exit.*)
CHORUS.   My queen, take our king to the palace now.
JOCASTA.   I must know what has happened.
CHORUS.   Doubt and suspicion. Oedipus spoke without thinking;
He was unjust, and Creon cannot bear injustice.
JOCASTA.   Both were to blame?
CHORUS.   Yes.
JOCASTA.   What was said?
CHORUS.   The country is weary with sickness already;
I am content, content to go no further
And let the evil rest.
OEDIPUS.   You see what you have done, you good,
Good adviser? My temper was a spear
And you have turned the edge and blunted it.
CHORUS.   Your majesty, I have repeated many times —
But I tell you again;
I would have been robbed of all my senses,
Emptied of all my reason,

If I caused your death.
You came like the wind we pray for in danger,
When the storm was conquering us with sorrows,
And carried our country into safety. Again
You may bring a spirit to guide us.
    JOCASTA.   But I still do not know why you were quarrelling, my king,
And I must know, for they talked of your death.
    OEDIPUS.   Jocasta,
You may command me when even my people may not,
And I let Creon go. But he had conspired
Against me . . .
    JOCASTA.   Treason! Is this true? Can you prove it?
    OEDIPUS.   He says I am Laius' murderer.
    JOCASTA.   How
Can he know? Has he always known, or has someone told him?
    OEDIPUS.   He sent that priest Teiresias, the wicked Teiresias.
Creon's lips do not commit themselves to words!
    JOCASTA.   Then set all this talk aside and listen. I
Will teach you that no priest, no holy magic
Can know your future or your destiny. And my proof
Is as short as the stroke of a knife. Once, an oracle
Came to Laius — I will not say it was from
Apollo — but from Apollo's priests. It told him
He was destined to be murdered by the son that I
Would bear to him. But Laius, so they say,
Was murdered by robbers from another country at a place
Where three roads meet. A son was born
To us, but lived no more than three days. Yes,
Laius pinned his ankles together and sent him
Away to die on a distant, lonely mountain.
Once he was there, no power could make him a murderer,
Nor make Laius die at the hands of his son —
And he feared that above anything in the world.
You see how you may rely upon priests and their talk
Of the future. Never notice them! When God wishes
The truth discovered, he will easily work his will.
    OEDIPUS.   As I listened, my queen, my thoughts went reaching out
And touched on memories that make me shudder . . .
    JOCASTA.   What memories? You stare as if you were trapped.
    OEDIPUS.   You said — I heard you say — that Laius' blood
Was spilt at a place where three roads meet.
    JOCASTA.   We were all told that, and no one has denied it.
    OEDIPUS.   And where is the place where this happened?
    JOCASTA.   The country
Is called Phocis; the road splits, to Delphi
And to Daulia.

OEDIPUS.   When did all this happen?

JOCASTA.   The city was given the news a little before
You became king of Thebes.

OEDIPUS.   God,
What do you hold prepared for me?

JOCASTA.   Oedipus!
What made you frown when I talked of your becoming king?

OEDIPUS.   Do not ask me yet . . . Laius — what was he like?
His appearance, his age, describe them to me.

JOCASTA.   He was tall, his hair beginning to be flecked with a down
Of white; he was built like you . . .

OEDIPUS.   Stop! You torture me!
I have hurled myself blindly against unthinking
Fury and destruction!

JOCASTA.   How? I cannot bear
To watch you, my lord.

OEDIPUS.   So little hope is frightening.
Listen, Teiresias the priest was not blind!
But one more answer, one more, will be better proof.

JOCASTA.   I dare not answer; but if my answers help you,
Ask.

OEDIPUS.   When he left Thebes, was he alone,
Or did he have a company of men at arms
So that all could recognize he was a king?

JOCASTA.   No, five were all the travellers, and one
Was a herald. A single chariot carried Laius . . .

OEDIPUS.   Yes! Now I see the truth . . . Who told you this?

JOCASTA.   A servant, the only man who returned alive.

OEDIPUS.   Is he still in the palace with us?

JOCASTA.   No, after
He escaped, and found that you were king, and Laius
Dead, he implored me by my duty to a suppliant
To send him away. To the country, he said, herding
Sheep on the hillsides, where he could never see
The city he had left . . . And I let him go; he was
A good servant, deserving more than this
Small favour.

OEDIPUS.   He must be found at once;
Can this be done?

JOCASTA.   Yes, but why do you want him?

OEDIPUS.   My queen, as I look into myself I begin to fear;
I had no right to say those things, and so
I must see this man.

JOCASTA.   He will come. But I
Expect to be told your sorrows, my king, when they weigh
So heavily.

OEDIPUS.   And I will not refuse you, Jocasta.

I have come to face such thoughts, and who should hear
Of them before you? I walk among
Great menaces.
My father is king of Corinth — Polybus; my mother —
Merope from Doris. In Corinth I was called
Their prince, their greatest noble, until
This happened to me — it was strange, yet not
So strange as to deserve my thoughts so much.
A man, stuffed with wine at a feast, called out
To me as he drank. He said I was a son only
In the imagination of my father. Anger
And pain would not let me rest that day; the next
I went to my parents and questioned them. They answered
The drunkard harshly for his insulting story,
And for their sakes I was glad he lied. Yet I always
Felt the wound, and the story spread in whispers.
At last I went to Delphi — my parents did not know —
But Apollo thought me unworthy of an answer
To that question. Instead he foretold many trials,
Many dangers, many sorrows. I was to be
My mother's husband, I was to murder my own
Father, my children would carry the guilt and none
Would dare look on them. When I heard this
I ran from my home and afterwards knew the land
Only by the stars that stood above it.
Never must I see the shame of that evil prophecy
Acted out by me in Corinth. I travelled
Until I came to this place where you say your king
Was killed . . . My wife, this is the truth . . . I will tell you . . .
My journey brought me to the meeting of three roads;
And there a herald, and an old man who rode
A chariot drawn by mares, came towards me . . .
Jocasta, the rider was like the man you described!
He and the herald, who went in front, tried
To force me out of their path. In a rage I struck
The one who touched me, the servant at the wheel.
The old man watched me, and waited till I was passing;
Then from the chariot he aimed at the crown of my head
With the twin prongs of his goad. It was a costly
Action! Slashing with my stick I cut at him
And my blow tumbled him backwards out of the chariot —
Then I killed them all! If this man I met may be said
To resemble Laius, to be, perhaps, Laius,
I stand condemned to more sorrows than any man,
More cursed by an evil power than any man.
No one in Thebes, no stranger, may shelter me
Or speak to me; they must hunt me from their doors.

And I, it was I, who cursed myself, cursed myself!
And the dead king's pillow is fouled by the touch
Of my murdering hands. Is the evil in my soul?
Is my whole nature tainted? Must I go into exile,
Never see my people again, nor turn home
And set foot in Corinth? — for if I do, I must wed
My mother, and kill my father — Polybus, who gave me
Life and youth. Can you see this happen, and then
Deny that a cruel power has come to torture me?
No! You heavens, you pure light and holiness!
Let me die before that day, hide me before
I feel that black corruption in my soul!

    CHORUS.   My king, this is a frightening story. But hope,
Until you hear from the man who saw what happened.

    OEDIPUS.   Yes, that is all the hope I have. Oedipus
Waits for one man, and he is a shepherd.

    JOCASTA.   What makes you so eager for him to come?

    OEDIPUS.   I reason like this. We may find that his story
Matches yours. Then I shall be as free
As if this had never happened.

    JOCASTA.   Was there anything in what
I said that could have such power?

    OEDIPUS.   You said
He told you robbers murdered Laius. If he still
Says "robbers" and not "a robber," I am innocent.
One man cannot be taken for many.
But if he says a murderer, alone,
The guilt comes to rest on me.

    JOCASTA.   . . . . But we all
Heard him say "robbers"; that is certain. He cannot
Unsay it. I am not alone, for the whole city heard.
But even if he swerves a little from his old account,
That will not prove you Laius' murderer,
Not in truth, not in justice. For Apollo said
He was to be killed by a son that was born to me . . .
And yet my son, poor child, could not have killed him,
For he died first . . . but that shows the deceit
Of prophecies. They beckon at you, but I
Would fix my eyes ahead, and never look at them!

    OEDIPUS.   You are right. Nevertheless send someone
To bring me that servant; do not forget.

    JOCASTA.   Yes,
I will send now. Let us go to the palace;
I would do nothing that could harm or anger you.

    (*Exeunt all but the* CHORUS.)

CHORUS. All actions must beware of the powers beyond us, and each
    word
Must speak our fear of heaven. I pray
That I may live every hour in obedience.
The laws that hold us in subjection
Have always stood beyond our reach, conceived
In the high air of heaven. Olympus
Was their sire, and no woman on earth
Gave them life. They are laws
That will never be lured to sleep in the arms of oblivion,
And in their strength heaven is great and cannot grow old.
Yet man desires to be more than man, to rule
His world for himself.
This desire, blown to immensity
On the rich empty food of its ambition,
Out of place, out of time,
Clambers to the crown of the rock, and stands there,
Tottering; then comes the steepling plunge down to earth,
To the earth where we are caged and mastered.
But this desire may work for good
When it fights to save a country, and I pray
That heaven will not weaken it then.
For then it comes like a god to be our warrior
And we shall never turn it back.
    Justice holds the balance of all things,
And we must fear her.
Do not despise the frontiers in which we must live,
Do not cross them, do not talk of them,
But bow before the places where the gods are throned.
Time will come with cruel vengeance on the man
Who disobeys; that is the punishment
For those who are proud and are more than men —
They are humbled.
If a man grows rich in defiance of this law,
If his actions trespass on a world that he should fear,
If he reaches after mysteries that no man should know,
No prayer can plead for him when the sword of heaven is raised.
If he were to glory in success
All worship would fall dumb.
    Delphi is the heart of the world and holds its secrets;
The temple of Zeus, and Olympia, command our prayers;
But we shall never believe again
Until the truth of this murder is known.
Let us be sure of our beliefs, give us proof.
Zeus, you may do your will; do not forget that you are immortal,
Your empire cannot die; hear our prayers.

For the oracle given to Laius in the years of the long past
Is dying and forgotten, wiped from the memory,
Apollo's glory turns to shadows,
And all divinity to ruin.

(*Enter* JOCASTA.)

JOCASTA.   My lords, I have been summoned by my thoughts
To the temples of the gods, and I have brought
These garlands and this incense for an offering.
Oedipus is like a lonely bird among
The terrors that flock about his mind. He forgets
His wisdom, and no longer thinks the past will guide him
When he tries to foresee the future. Instead, he is
The slave of any word that talks of fear.
I try to reach him, to make him see that there is hope,
But it is useless; I have failed. And so I turn
To you, Apollo, nearest to us in Thebes,
A suppliant with prayers and gifts. Resolve this doubt
By sending the truth. He is the guide and master
Of our ship. What shall we do when even he
Is struck into bewilderment?

(*Enter* MESSENGER.)

MESSENGER.   I do not know this country. Will you show me the palace
Of King Oedipus? I must find King Oedipus ...
Do you know where he is?
CHORUS.   This is his palace, sir.
He is inside, and you see his queen before you.
MESSENGER.   Heaven give her and all she loves riches
And happiness if she is the queen of such a king.
JOCASTA.   I return your greeting. You have spoken well and deserve
Well wishing. But what do you want with Oedipus?
Or do you bring a message for us?
MESSENGER.   A message
Of good, for your palace and your husband, my queen.
JOCASTA.   What is it? Who sent you here?
MESSENGER.   I come from Corinth.
My story may be quickly told. You will be glad, of course,
For the news is glad, and yet ... yet you may grieve.
JOCASTA.   Well, what is this story with a double meaning?
MESSENGER.   The people of Corinth — it was already announced
There — will make Oedipus their king.
JOCASTA.   But why?
Your king is Polybus. He is wise, revered ...
MESSENGER.   But no longer our king. Death hugs him to the earth.

JOCASTA.   Is this true? Polybus is dead?
MESSENGER.   By my hopes of living out my years, it is true.
JOCASTA.   Servant, go, tell this to your master. Run!

(*Exit* SERVANT.)

Where are the prophecies of heaven now? Always
Oedipus dreaded to kill this man, and hid
From him. But look, Polybus has been murdered
By the careless touch of time, and not by Oedipus.

(*Enter* OEDIPUS.)

OEDIPUS.   Dear Jocasta, dear wife, why have you called me
Here from the palace?
JOCASTA.   This man brings a message;
Listen, and then ask yourself what comes
Of the oracles from heaven that used to frighten us.
OEDIPUS.   Who is this man? What has he to say to me?
JOCASTA.   He comes from Corinth, and his message is the death
Of Polybus. You will never see Polybus again!
OEDIPUS.   You said that, stranger? Let me hear you say that plainly.
MESSENGER.   Since you force me to give that part of my message first,
I repeat, he walks among the dead.
OEDIPUS.   A plot?
Or did sickness conspire to kill him?
MESSENGER.   A small
Touch on the balance sends old lives to sleep.
OEDIPUS.   So, my poor father, sickness murdered you.
MESSENGER.   And many years had measured out his life.
OEDIPUS.   Oh look, look, who would listen to Apollo
Talking in his shrine at Delphi, or notice birds
That clamour to the air? They were the signs
That told me — and I believed — that I would kill
My father. But now he has the grave to protect him,
While I stand here, and I never touched a sword . . .
Unless he died of longing to see me —
Then perhaps he died because of me. No!
Polybus lies in darkness, and all those prophecies
Lie with him, chained and powerless.
JOCASTA.   I told you long ago how it would happen . . .
OEDIPUS.   Yes, but I was led astray by fears.
JOCASTA.   Then think no more of them; forget them all.
OEDIPUS.   Not all. The marriage with my mother — I think of it.
JOCASTA.   But is there anything a man need fear, if he knows
That chance is supreme throughout the world, and he cannot
See what is to come? Give way to the power

Of events and live as they allow! It is best.
Do not fear this marriage with your mother. Many
Men have dreams, and in those dreams they wed
Their mothers. Life is easiest, if you do not try
To oppose these things that seem to threaten us.

OEDIPUS.   You are right, and I would agree with all
You say, if my mother were not alive. And though
You are right, I must fear. She is alive.

JOCASTA.   Think of your father, and his grave.
There is a light to guide you.

OEDIPUS.   It does guide me!
I know he . . . But she is alive and I am afraid.

MESSENGER.   You are afraid of a woman, my lord?

OEDIPUS.   Yes,
Merope — Polybus was her husband.

MESSENGER.   How can you be afraid of her?

OEDIPUS.   A prophecy warned me.
To beware of sorrow . . .

MESSENGER.   Can you speak of it, or are you
Forbidden to talk of these things to others?

OEDIPUS.   No,
I am not forbidden. The Oracle at Delphi
Has told me my destiny — to be my mother's husband
And my father's murderer. And so I left
Corinth, many years ago and many
Miles behind me. The world has rewarded me richly,
And yet all those riches are less than the sight
Of a parent's face.

MESSENGER.   And you went into exile because
You feared this marriage?

OEDIPUS.   And to save myself from becoming
My father's murderer.

MESSENGER.   Then, my king,
I ought to have freed you from that fear since I
Wished to be thought your friend.

OEDIPUS.   Your reward
Will be measured by my gratitude.

MESSENGER.   I had hoped for reward
When you returned as king of your palace in Corinth.

OEDIPUS.   I must never go where my parents are.

MESSENGER.   My son,
You do not know what you say; I see you do not.

OEDIPUS.   How, sir? Tell me quickly.

MESSENGER.   . . . If you live in exile
Because of Polybus and Merope.

OEDIPUS.   Yes, and I live
In fear that Apollo will prove he spoke the truth.

MESSENGER. And it is from your parents that the guilt is to come?

OEDIPUS. Yes, stranger, the fear never leaves my side.

MESSENGER. You have no cause to be afraid — do you know that?

OEDIPUS. No cause? But they were my parents — that is the cause!

MESSENGER. No cause, because they were not your parents, Oedipus.

OEDIPUS. What do you mean? Polybus was not my father?

MESSENGER. As much as I, and yet no more than I am.

OEDIPUS. How could my father be no more than nothing?

MESSENGER. But Polybus did not give you life, nor did I.

OEDIPUS. Then why did he call me son?

MESSENGER.   Listen, you were
A gift that he took from my hands.

OEDIPUS.   A child
Given him by a stranger? But he loved me
Dearly.

MESSENGER. He had no children, and so consented.

OEDIPUS. So you gave me to . . . Had you bought me for your slave?
Where did you find me?

MESSENGER.   You were lying beneath the trees
In a glade upon Cithaeron.

OEDIPUS.   What were you doing on Cithaeron?

MESSENGER. My flocks were grazing in the mountains;
I was guarding them.

OEDIPUS.   Guarding your flocks — you were
A shepherd, a servant?

MESSENGER.   It was in that service that I saved
Your life, my child.

OEDIPUS.   Why? Was I hurt or sick
When you took me home?

MESSENGER.   Your ankles will be my witness
That you would not have lived.

OEDIPUS.   Why do you talk
Of that? The pain is forgotten!

MESSENGER.   Your feet were pierced
And clamped together. I set you free.

OEDIPUS.   The child
In the cradle had a scar — I still carry
The shame of it.

MESSENGER. You were named in remembrance
Of that scar.

OEDIPUS. In heaven's name, who did this?
My mother? My father?

MESSENGER.   I do not know. The man
Who gave you to me knows more of the truth.

OEDIPUS. But you said you found me! Then it was not true . . .
You had me from someone else?

MESSENGER.   Yes, another
Shepherd gave me the child.
    OEDIPUS.   Who? Can you
Describe him?
    MESSENGER.   They said he was a servant of Laius.
    OEDIPUS.   Laius, who was once king of Thebes?
    MESSENGER.   Yes,
This man was one of his shepherds.
    OEDIPUS.   Is he still
Alive; could I see him?
    MESSENGER.   Your people here
Will know that best.
    OEDIPUS.   Do any of you,
My friends, know the shepherd he means? Has he
Been seen in the fields, or in the palace? Tell me,
Now! It is time these things were known!
    CHORUS.   I think
He must be the man you were searching for, the one
Who left the palace after Laius was killed.
But Jocasta will know as well as I.
    OEDIPUS.   My wife, you remember the man we sent for a little
Time ago? Is he the one this person means?
    JOCASTA.   Perhaps . . . But why should he . . . Think nothing of this!
Do not idle with memories and stories . . .
    OEDIPUS.   No, I have been given these signs, and I must
Follow them, until I know who gave me birth.
    JOCASTA.   No! Give up this search! I am tortured and sick
Enough. By the love of heaven, if you value life . . .
    OEDIPUS.   Courage! You are still a queen, though I discover
That I am three times three generations a slave.
    JOCASTA.   No, listen to me, I implore you! You must stop!
    OEDIPUS.   I cannot listen when you tell me to ignore the truth.
    JOCASTA.   But I know the truth, and I only ask you to save
Yourself.
    OEDIPUS.   I have always hated that way to safety!
    JOCASTA.   But evil lies in wait for you . . . Oh, do not let him
Find the truth!
    OEDIPUS.   Bring this shepherd to me,
And let her gloat over the riches of her ancestry.
    JOCASTA.   My poor child! Those are the only words
I shall ever have for you . . . I can speak no others! (*Exit.*)
    CHORUS.   What is the torment that drives your queen so wildly
Into the palace, Oedipus? Her silence threatens
A storm. I fear some wrong . . .
    OEDIPUS.   Let the storm
Come if it will. I must know my birth,
I must know it, however humble. Perhaps she,

For she is a queen, and proud, is ashamed
That I was born so meanly. But I consider
Myself a child of Fortune, and while she brings me
Gifts, I shall not lack honour. For she has given me
Life itself; and my cousins, the months, have marked me
Small and great as they marched by. Such
Is my ancestry, and I shall be none other —
And I will know my birth!

    CHORUS.   There are signs
Of what is to come, and we may read them,
Casting our thoughts into the future,
And drawing in new knowledge.
For we have seen how the world goes
And we have seen the laws it obeys.
Cithaeron, mountain of Oedipus, the moon
Will not rise in tomorrow's evening sky
Before our king calls you his true father,
His only nurse and mother — and then
You will have your greatest glory.
You will be honoured with dances and choirs
For your gentle kindness to our king — Hail
To the god Apollo! May he be content
With all our words.

    Pan walks among the mountains, and one
Of the immortal nymphs could have lain with him;
Who was the goddess who became your mother, Oedipus?
Or was she the wife of Apollo, for he loves
The wild meadows and the long grass.
Or was it the prince of Cyllene, Hermes?
Or Bacchus, whose palace is the mountain top?
Did he take you as a gift from the nymphs of Helicon,
With whom he plays through all his immortal years?

    OEDIPUS.   I never knew the shepherd or encountered him,
My people, but the man I see there must be
The one we have been seeking. His age answers
My riddle for me; it holds as many years
As our messenger's. And now I see that those
Who lead him are my servants. But you have known him
Before, you can tell me whether I am right.

    CHORUS.   Yes, we recognise him — the most faithful
Of Laius' shepherds.

    OEDIPUS.   And you, Corinthian,
You must tell me first. Is this the man you mean?

    MESSENGER.   It is; you see him there.

(*Enter* SHEPHERD.)

OEDIPUS.   You, sir, come to me,
Look me in the eyes, and answer all my questions!
Did you once serve Laius?
    SHEPHERD.   Yes, and I was born
In his palace; I was not brought from another country . . .
    OEDIPUS.   Your life? How were you employed?
    SHEPHERD.   Most
Of my life I watched his flocks.
    OEDIPUS.   And where
Was their pasture? They had a favourite meadow?
    SHEPHERD.   Sometimes Cithaeron, sometimes the places near.
    OEDIPUS.   Do you recognise this man? Did you see him on Cithaeron?
    SHEPHERD.   Why should anyone go there? Whom do you mean?
    OEDIPUS.   Here! Standing beside me. Have you ever met him?
    SHEPHERD.   I do not think so . . . My memory is not quick.
    MESSENGER.   We should not wonder at this, your majesty;
But I shall remind him of all he has forgotten.
I know that he remembers when for three
Whole years I used to meet him near Cithaeron,
Six months, from each spring to the rising of the Bear;
I had a single flock and he had two.
Then, in the winters, I would take my sheep to their pens
While he went to the fields of Laius . . . Did this happen?
Have I told it as it happened, or have I not?
    SHEPHERD.   The time is long since then . . . yes, it is the truth.
    MESSENGER.   Good; now, tell me: you know the child you gave
me . . . ?
    SHEPHERD.   What is happening? What do these questions mean?
    MESSENGER.   Here is the child, my friend, who was so little then.
    SHEPHERD.   Damnation seize you! Can you not keep your secret?
    OEDIPUS.   Wait, Shepherd! Do not find fault; as I listened
I found more fault in you than in him.
    SHEPHERD.   What
Have I done wrong, most mighty king?
    OEDIPUS.   You will not
Admit the truth about that child.
    SHEPHERD.   He wastes
His time. He talks, but it is all lies.
    OEDIPUS.   When it would please me, you will not speak; but you will
When I make you cry for mercy . . .
    SHEPHERD.   No, my king,
I am an old man — do not hurt me!
    OEDIPUS (to guards).   Take his arms and tie them quickly!
    SHEPHERD.   But why,
Poor child? What more do you want to know?
    OEDIPUS.   You gave
The boy to this Corinthian?

SHEPHERD.   Yes, I did . . .
And I should have prayed for death that day.
   OEDIPUS.   Your prayer will be answered now if you lie to me!
   SHEPHERD.   But you will surely kill me if I tell the truth.
   OEDIPUS.   He will drive my patience to exhaustion!
   SHEPHERD.   No!
I told you now, I did give him the child.
   OEDIPUS.   Where did it come from? Your home? Another's?
   SHEPHERD.   It was not mine, it was given to me.
   OEDIPUS.   By someone
In the city? . . . I want to know the house!
   SHEPHERD.   By all that is holy,
No more, your majesty, no more questions!
   OEDIPUS.   You die
If I have to ask again!
   SHEPHERD.   The child was born
In the palace of King Laius.
   OEDIPUS.   By one of his slaves?
Or was it a son of his own blood?
   SHEPHERD.   My king,
How shall I tell a story of such horror?
   OEDIPUS.   And how shall I hear it? And yet I must, must hear.
   SHEPHERD.   The child was called his son. But your queen in the palace
May tell you the truth of that most surely.
   OEDIPUS.   Jocasta gave you the child?
   SHEPHERD.   Yes, my king.
   OEDIPUS.   Why? What were you to do?
   SHEPHERD.   I was to destroy him.
   OEDIPUS.   The poor mother asked that?
   SHEPHERD.   She was afraid.
A terrible prophecy . . .
   OEDIPUS.   What?
   SHEPHERD.   There was a story
That he would kill his parents.
   OEDIPUS.   Why did you give
The child away to this stranger?
   SHEPHERD.   I pitied it,
My lord, and I thought he would take it to the far land
Where he lived. But he saved its life only for
Great sorrows. For if you are the man he says,
You must know your birth was watched by evil powers.
   OEDIPUS.   All that was foretold will be made true! Light,
Now turn black and die; I must not look on you!
See, this is what I am; son of parents
I should not have known, I lived with those
I should not have touched, and murdered those
A man must not kill! (*Exit.*)

CHORUS.   Every man who has ever lived
Is numbered with the dead; they fought with the world
For happiness, yet all they won
Was a shadow that slipped away to die.
And you, Oedipus, are all those men. I think of the power
Which carried you to such victories and such misery
And I know there is no joy or triumph in the world.
    Oedipus aimed beyond the reach of man
And fixed with his arrowing mind
Perfection and rich happiness.
The Sphinx's talons were sharp with evil, she spoke in the mysteries
Of eternal riddles, and he came to destroy her,
To overcome death, to be a citadel
Of strength in our country.
He was called our king, and was
The greatest noble in great Thebes.
And now his story ends in agony.
Death and madness hunt him,
Destruction and sorrow haunt him.
Now his life turns and brings the reward of his greatness . . .
Glorious Oedipus, son, and then father,
In the same chamber, in the same silent room,
Son and father in the same destruction;
Your marriage was the harvesting of wrong.
How could it hold you where your father lay,
And bear you in such silence for such an end?
    Child of Laius, I wish, I wish I had never known you,
For now there is only mourning, sorrow flowing
From our lips.
And yet we must not forget the truth;
If we were given hope and life, it was your work.

    (*Enter* SERVANT.)

SERVANT.   My lords of Thebes, on whom rest all the honours
Of our country, when you hear what has happened,
When you witness it, how will you bear your grief
In silence? Weep, if you have ever loved
The royal house of Thebes. For I do not think
The great streams of the Phasis or the Ister
Could ever wash these walls to purity. But all
The crimes they hide must glare out to the light,
Crimes deliberate and considered. The sorrows
We choose ourselves bring the fiercest pain!
    CHORUS.   We have seen great wrongs already, and they were fright-
        ening.
Do you bring new disasters?
    SERVANT.   I bring a message

That I may tell, and you may hear, in a few
Swift words. Jocasta is dead.
   CHORUS.   Then she died in grief. What caused her death?
   SERVANT.   It was her own will. Of that terrible act
The worst must remain untold, for I did not watch it.
Yet you will hear what happened to our poor queen
As far as memory guides me. When she went
Into the domed hall of the palace, whirled
On the torrent of her grief, she ran straight
To her marriage chamber, both hands clutched at her hair,
Tearing like claws. Inside, she crashed shut the door
And shrieked the name Laius, Laius who died
So long ago. She talked to herself of the son
She once bore, and of Laius murdered by that son;
Of the mother who was left a widow, and became
Wife and mother again in shame and sorrow.
She wept for her marriage, in which her husband gave
To her a husband, and her children, children.
How her death followed I cannot tell you . . .
We heard a shout, and now Oedipus blazed
And thundered through the door. I could not see
How her sorrow ended, because he was there,
Circling in great mad strides, and we watched
Him. He went round begging to each
Of us; he asked for a sword, he asked to go
To his wife who was more than a wife, to his mother in whom
His birth and his children's birth, like two harvests
From the same field, had been sown and gathered. His grief
Was a raging madness, and some power must have guided him —
It was none of us who were standing there. He gave
A cry full of fear and anguish, then, as if
A ghost was leading him, he leaped against the double
Doors of Jocasta's room. The hinges tilted
Full out of their sockets, and shattered inside
The chamber — and there we saw his wife, hanging
By her throat in the grip of a tall rope. And when
He saw her, he shrieked like a wounded beast, wrenched loose
The knot that held her, and laid her on the ground.
What followed was terrible to watch. He ripped
The gold-worked brooches from her robes — she wore them
As jewels — and raised them above his head. Then he plunged them
Deep into the sockets of his eyes, shouting
That he would never look upon the wrongs
He had committed and had suffered. Now
In his blackness he must see such shapes as he deserved
And never look on those he loved. Repeating
This like a chant, he lifted his hands and stabbed

His eyes, again and again. We saw his eyeballs
Fill with tears of blood that dyed his cheeks,
And a red stream pouring from his veins, dark
As the blood of life, thick as storming hail.
Yes, this is a storm that has broken, a storm
That holds the queen and the king in its embrace.
They were rich and fortunate, and they were so
As we should wish to be. Now, in one day,
See how we must mourn them. The blind rush
To death, the shame, all the evils that we
Have names for — they have escaped none!

    CHORUS. Has our poor king found ease for his sorrow yet?
    SERVANT. He shouts at us to open the doors and show
To all Thebes the murderer of his father
And his mother's . . . his words are blasphemous,
I dare not speak them . . . He will be driven from Thebes,
Will not stay beneath this curse that he called upon
Himself. Yet he needs help and a guide. No one
Could bear that agony . . . But he comes himself to show you;
The great doors of the palace open, and what you will see
Will turn you away in horror — yet will ask for pity.

    (*Enter* OEDIPUS.)

    CHORUS. This suffering turns a face of terror to the world.
There is no story told, no knowledge born
That tells of greater sorrow.
Madness came striding upon you, Oedipus,
The black, annihilating power that broods
And waits in the hand of time . . .
I cannot look!
We have much to ask and learn and see.
But you blind us with an icy sword of terror.

    OEDIPUS. Where will you send this wreckage and despair of man?
Where will my voice be heard, like the wind drifting emptily
On the air. Oh you powers, why do you drive me on?
    CHORUS. They drive you to the place of horror,
That only the blind may see,
And only the dead hear of.
    OEDIPUS. Here in my cloud of darkness there is no escape,
A cloud, thick in my soul, and there it dumbly clings;
That cloud is my own spirit
That now wins its fiercest battle and turns back
To trample me . . . The memory of evil can tear
Like goads of molten fire, and go deep,
Infinity could not be so deep.
    CHORUS. More than mortal in your acts of evil.
More than mortal in your suffering, Oedipus.

OEDIPUS.   You are my last friend, my only help; you have
Waited for me, and will care for the eyeless body
Of Oedipus.   I know you are there . . . I know . . .
Through this darkness I can hear your voice.
    CHORUS.   Oedipus, all that you do
Makes us draw back in fear.   How could you take
Such vivid vengeance on your eyes?   What power lashed you on?
    OEDIPUS.   Apollo, my lords, Apollo sent this evil on me.
I was the murderer; I struck the blow.   Why should I
Keep my sight?   If I had eyes, what could delight them?
    CHORUS.   It is so; it is as you say.
    OEDIPUS.   No, I can look on nothing . . .
And I can love nothing — for love has lost
Its sweetness, I can hear no voice — for words
Are sour with hate . . . Take stones and beat me
From your country.   I am the living curse, the source
Of sickness and death!
    CHORUS.   Your own mind, reaching after the secrets
Of gods, condemned you to your fate.
If only you had never come to Thebes . . .
    OEDIPUS.   But when my feet were ground by iron teeth
That bolted me in the meadow grass.
A man set me free and ransomed me from death.
May hell curse him for that murderous kindness!
I should have died then
And never drawn this sorrow on those I love
And on myself . . .
    CHORUS.   Our prayers echo yours.
    OEDIPUS.   Nor killed my father,
Nor led my mother to the room where she gave me life.
But now the gods desert me, for I am
Born of impurity, and my blood
Mingles with those who gave me birth.
If evil can grow with time to be a giant
That masters and usurps our world,
That evil lords its way through Oedipus.
    CHORUS.   How can we say that you have acted wisely?
Is death not better than a life in blindness?
    OEDIPUS.   Do not teach me that this punishment is wrong ⟶
I will have no advisers to tell me it is wrong!
Why choke my breath and go among the dead
If I keep my eyes?   For there I know I could not
Look upon my father or my poor mother . . .
My crimes have been too great for such a death.
Or should I love my sight because it let me
See my children?   No, for then I would
Remember who their father was.   My eyes

Would never let me love them, nor my city,
Nor my towers, nor the sacred images
Of gods. I was the noblest lord in Thebes,
But I have stripped myself of Thebes, and become
The owner of all miseries. For I commanded
My people to drive out the unclean thing, the man
Heaven had shown to be impure in the house
Of Laius.
I found such corruption in me — could I see
My people and not turn blind for shame? . . .
My ears are a spring, and send a river
Of sound through me; if I could have dammed that river
I would have made my poor body into a bolted prison
In which there would be neither light nor sound.
Peace can only come if we shut the mind
Away from the sorrow in the world outside.
Cithaeron, why did you let me live? Why
Did you not kill me as I lay there? I would
Have been forgotten, and never revealed the secret
Of my birth. Polybus, Corinth, the palace
They told me was my father's, you watched over
My youth, but beneath that youth's nobility lay
Corruption — you see it in my acts, in my blood!
There are three roads, a hidden valley, trees,
And a narrow place where the roads meet — they
Drink my blood, the blood I draw from my father —
Do they remember me, do they remember what I did?
Do they know what next I did? . . . The room, the marriage
Room — it was there I was given life, and now
It is there I give the same life to my children.
The blood of brothers, fathers, sons, the race
Of daughters, wives, mothers, all the blackest
Shame a man may commit . . . But I must not name
Such ugly crimes. Oh, you heavens, take me
From the world and hide me, drown me in oceans
Where I can be seen no more! Come, do not fear
To touch a single unhappy man. Yes, a man,
No more. Be brave, for my sufferings can fall to no one
But myself to bear!
    CHORUS.   Oedipus, Creon came
While you were praying; he brings advice and help.
You can protect us no more, and we turn to him.
    OEDIPUS.   What can I say to Creon? I have given him
No cause to trust me or to listen. In all I said
Before, he has seen that I was wrong.

(*Enter* CREON *with* ANTIGONE *and* ISMENE.)

CREON.   I have not come scorning or insulting you, Oedipus,
For those wrongs. (*To servants.*) Have you no shame before
Your countrymen? At least show reverence to the sun's
Flame that sends us life, and do not let
This curse lie open to disfigure heaven.
Neither earth, nor the pure falling rain, nor light
May come near it. Take him to the palace now!
When evil grows in the family, only the family
May hear of it and look without pollution.
   OEDIPUS.   Creon, I thought . . . but now you have struck those fears
Away — you will be a gentle king.
But I ask one thing, and I ask it to help you,
Not myself, for I am hated by powers too strong
For us.
   CREON.   What do you ask so eagerly?
   OEDIPUS.   Banish me from the country now. I must go
Where no one can see or welcome me again.
   CREON.   I would have done so, Oedipus, but first
I must know from Apollo what he commands.
   OEDIPUS.   But we have heard all his answer — destroy the
Parricide, the unholiness, destroy me!
   CREON.   So it was said . . . And yet we are in such danger;
It is better to hear what we must do.
   OEDIPUS.   Why need you
Go to Delphi for my poor body?
   CREON.   Delphi will never deceive us; you know it speaks
The truth.
   OEDIPUS.   But Creon, I command you! . . . I will kneel
And pray to you . . . Bury my queen as you wish
In her royal tomb; she is your sister
And it is her right. But as for myself, I
Must never think of entering my father's city
Again, so long as its people live. Let me
Have no home but the mountains, where the hill
They call Cithaeron, my Cithaeron, stands.
There my mother and my father, while
They lived, decreed I should have my grave.
My death will be a gift from them, for they
Have destroyed me . . . And yet I know that sickness
Cannot break in and take my life, nothing
May touch me. I am sure of this, for each moment
Is a death, and I am kept alive only
For the final punishment . . . But let it go,
Let it go, I do not care what is done with me.
Creon, my sons will ask nothing more from you;
They are men, wherever they go they will take what they need
From life. But pity my two daughters, who will have

No love. All that was owned by me, they shared,
And when I banqueted, they were always beside me.
You must become their father . . . But let me touch them
And talk to them of our sorrows. Come, my lord,
Come, my noble kinsman, let me feel them
In my arms and believe they are as much my own
As when I saw . . . I cannot think . . . Their weeping,
Their dear voices are near. Creon has pitied me
And given me my children. Is this true?

CREON. I sent for them; I know what joy they would give you
And how you loved them once. Yes, it is true.

OEDIPUS. May heaven bless your life, and may the power
Watching us, guard you more safely on the throne
Than me. My children, where are you? Come near, come
To my hands; they are your brother's hands and they
Went searching out and took your father's seeing
Eyes to darkness. I did not know my children,
And did not ask, but now the world may see
That I gave you life from the source that gave me mine.
Why is there no light? I cannot see you! . . . And tears
Come when I think of the years you will have to live
In a cruel world. In the city they will shun you,
Fear your presence; when they feast and dance in the streets
You will not be allowed to watch, and they
Will send you weeping home. And when you come
To the years of marriage, children, who will there be
So careless of his pride as to accept the shame
That glares on my birth and on yours? "Your father
Killed his father!" "Your father gave life where he
Was given life, you are children where he was once
A child." That will be your humiliation!
And who will wed you?
No one, my daughters, there will be no one, and I see
You must pine to death in lonely childlessness.
Creon, you are their father, you alone.
For they have lost their parents. Do not let them go
Into beggary and solitude — their blood is yours.
I have nothing, but do not afflict them with
My poverty. Have pity on them. See, so young
And robbed of all except your kindliness.
Touch me once, my lord, and give your consent.
My children, I would have said much to comfort
And advise you — but how could you understand?
But pray, you must pray to live as the world allows
And find a better life than the father whom you follow.

CREON. No more now. Go inside the palace.

OEDIPUS. It is hard, but I must obey.

CREON.   All things are healed
By time.

OEDIPUS.   But Creon, I demand one thing before
I go.

CREON.   What do you demand?

OEDIPUS.   Banishment!

CREON.   Only heaven can answer your prayer. When Apollo . . .

OEDIPUS.   But Apollo can only detest me.

CREON.   Then your prayer will be
The sooner heard.

OEDIPUS.   You mean what you say?

CREON.   I cannot
Promise, when I see nothing certain.

OEDIPUS.   Now!
Exile me now!

CREON.   Go then, and leave your children.

OEDIPUS.   You must not take them from me!

CREON.   You give
Commands as if you were king. You must remember
Your rule is over, and it could not save your life.

CHORUS.   Men of Thebes, look at the king who ruled
Your country; there is Oedipus.
He knew how to answer the mystery
Of evil in the Sphinx, and was our greatest lord.
We saw him move the world with his will, and we envied him.
But look, the storm destroys him, the sea
Has come to defeat him.
Remember that death alone can end all suffering;
Go towards death, and ask for no greater
Happiness than a life
In which there has been no anger and no pain.

Curtain

Possibly one of the most enigmatic and compelling of the surviving Greek tragedies, *The Bacchae* (*c*. 405 B.C.) has fascinated and baffled both commentators and directors. Even the surface conflicts are perplexing. Is not Pentheus completely justified in wanting to suppress a violently sensual cult which apparently runs counter to the relatively restrained social codes and the Olympian religion? In its excesses, it deranges its devotees and frequently disrupts peace and order. Pentheus speaks with the voice of reason. Dionysus, on the other hand, is calling his followers forth to unbridled ecstasy. Intellectually, the modern reader or spectator is apt to sympathize with Pentheus.

But there *is* the other side of the coin. Pentheus is a young ruler, and he is really somewhat unsure of himself. The very model of a modern conservative moralist, he is no more moderate than Dionysus. His insecurity gives him away and leads him to repressive measures. He has an unspoken fear of his cousin, Dionysus. He does not want to give in to the claims of the flesh, nor does he want anyone else to do so. Under pressure, he is ordering a total restraint as contrary to the human spirit as total debauchery. Without Dionysus, there will be no harvests, no children; without Pentheus, there will be no humanity, no civilization. But neither will be denied totality, so they can reach no compromise.

The play may well be viewed as a parable of the eternal internal human struggle between the claims of the flesh and the claims of the spirit. Euripides (480–406 B.C.), by indirection and example, makes an important point which has been willfully and dangerously ignored for centuries: *moderation* is the key. Sexual moderation has often been urged by both philosophers of ethics and Christian theologians — but they have not really meant moderation at all, but abstinence. Euripides seems to suggest that a man cannot deny or hide parts of what he is. He must come to terms with the All of his being. To "Know Thyself," one must do more than search the caverns of the mind; one must know the darker corridors of the heart as well. Dionysian desire, passion, and lust are as much a part of us as reason. When they are forgotten, ignored, or suppressed, a reservoir of unfulfilled longing builds up which may burst the dam of self-control in ways quite shocking even to their seemingly helpless servant. Only moderation between the extremes of reason and passion will serve.

Pentheus is punished for his lack of moderation. When Dionysus finally reaches him, he is able to transform this young ruler's cold reason into feminine coquettishness. From being masculinely hard, tough, unyielding, he finds himself going just as far in the opposite direction, becoming silly, soft, pliant, even weak. What this implies is not anything so trite as that Pentheus was a latent homosexual. Instead, it is an example showing what happens when one lives by extremes. Just as reason and passion are matched opposites which may be kept in balance by moderation, so also are the masculine and feminine qualities in a human being.

Still, *The Bacchae* is far more complex than a morality play. Like the other great Greek tragic dramas, it may at the same time be viewed as a religious ritual, seen in the framework of the annual Athenian festival of Dionysus. But viewing the play as a ritual in no way makes it easier to deal with. In a sense, the play asks more questions than it answers. The largest is: If no men are allowed to take part in the Bacchic ecstasies — or even view them, on peril of death — what is the actual nature of the mythically erotic rites the female Bacchantes celebrate in the woods? Pentheus has a sordid notion; a herdsman has quite a different view: benevolent generosity, womanly grace and power, wild beauty, and the strange and dangerous in nature suddenly bent to the Bacchic will in the most benign ways.

Pentheus is afraid to admit publicly that he wants to find out what it is all about, and he masks his curiosity with repression. The determination — even hysteria — with which he tries to root out the worship of Dionysus by his special devotees may be viewed as ample justification for the awful severity of the revenge the god takes on him. Not for Dionysus was it enough merely to drive him mad: his retaliation is total and imposed in degrees of subtle cruelty. Since, at the end, Pentheus is horribly destroyed, it might be argued that the lesson has not done him much good. He will scarcely be able to apply what he has learned to future conduct of the state and himself. That is hardly the point. His death is his payment for violating the natural laws of balance, and it serves as an example to those who will come after him and hear his tragic tale recited over and over.

It may seem harsh to readers that the judgment of Dionysus also falls on old Kadmos — to be turned into a dragon of war — and on his wife Harmony — to be transformed into a snake — together with her husband eternally condemned to bring war to Greece and the world. But, say Dionysus and Euripides, Kadmos and Harmony denied the life principle as much as Pentheus or Agave, and for that they must know and bring death. Could Euripides have been indirectly referring to the Greek generals who were then prosecuting a war that was to destroy Athens?

G.L.

EURIPIDES

The Bacchae

TRANSLATED BY KENNETH CAVANDER[1]

Characters

DIONYSOS
CHORUS
TEIRESIAS, *a prophet*
KADMOS, *ex-King of Thebes*
PENTHEUS, *King of Thebes, grandson of Kadmos*
GUARD
HERDSMAN
SERVANT
AGAVE, *mother of Pentheus*
GUARDS, SOLDIERS, SERVANTS, PEOPLE OF THEBES

(DIONYSOS *and* CHORUS.)

DIONYSOS.   Dionysos has come.
Here, in Thebes, Zeus came swooping down and took
A woman of the earth. Lightning made
Her labour quick, and out of her burning thighs
I was born.

Today I walk on the piece of land enclosed
By two rivers — Dirce and Ismenos —
The land they call . . . Thebes.
Today I look like a man, but I am more.

Here was the lightning blast that killed my mother,
Semele, here was her room and . . .
There's something alive! Smoke in the rubble, the fire
Of Zeus . . . still. So, something alive
Still . . .

Yes, Kadmos has said: "On this ground
No man walks!" to remind Thebes

---

[1] This version of *The Bacchae* was originally commissioned by the BBC and later rewritten for production at the Mermaid Theatre in London. It is an acting version. In a few places, for the sake of a twentieth-century audience, it is interpretative rather than literal. Nevertheless, the script stays close to Euripides' own words at all times, and the intentions of the lines are invariably based on the suggestive power of the original. — K. C.

Of Semele, his daughter, to keep her alive in the heart
Of Thebes. I am glad. He was right.
The vines that cover that wall are mine. They flush,
And cluster . . .
And swell . . .
    Behind me — Lebanon and its golden plains,
Iraq, the sun-struck steppes of Persia,
The fortresses of Syria, the harsh country
Where the Afghans live, Arabia drugged,
And all the eastern coasts, where Greece and Asia
Merge, and towers fringe the teeming cities;
Behind me — dance swaying bodies, intoxication,
Life.
    Here — Greece. And first in Greece — Thebes.
My own country, where I will be known,
Where I must be known.
There is a reason why Thebes comes first.
I made this city wild with women shrilling
My name, I slung hide on their backs, I stuck
Branches in their hands, spears tipped
With ivy — for a reason.
Because my mother's sisters denied I was
The son of Zeus; because they said Semele
Lost her virginity to a man here in Thebes,
Then blamed the result on Zeus; because they swore
Kadmos invented it all; because they claimed
Zeus killed Semele for lying about
Her husband.
They shouldn't have said that. They,
Particularly, should not have said all that.
Because now, they hurtle out of their homes, possessed,
Scatter to the hills, and they all wear my uniform,
They all know how to bring me to life. . . .
    I willed it, and they must.
Every woman in this city is mine,
Totally.
They have abandoned Thebes, and now they have joined
My mother's sisters in the green pine shades,
Among the cliffs and hollows. Mad. Bacchae.
This place must find out what it means
To be half-born, to have no
Dionysos, never to have tried me or tasted me,
This place must take account of my birth
In Semele, my descent from Zeus, my presence here,
And my power over man. This place
May wish it did not have to, but it must learn.
    Kadmos has given way to Pentheus, his grandson.

Authority, decision, are now all Pentheus,
Who resists me and my power, keeps me
Clear out of thought. When he looks outside
Himself for help, he never looks to me.
I am despised, pushed aside, stamped upon.
And therefore I'll turn him round to face me. Show
Myself in Thebes, show them they are small
And I am great.
  This one matter set to rights I pack up
And move on, to make myself known
Elsewhere.
If Thebes recklessly tries to bring the women
Back from the hills and their madness by force, you
Will see a fight — the army versus Bacchae —
Arranged by me.
  And so I have dressed myself in flesh today.
I have the body and blood of a man, but
My real nature is . . . still my own.
(To CHORUS.) Friends, you have been loyal, you have followed me
From countries far across the sea, travelled
Beside me, never deserted me. Lift your drums
Now. Let these proud walls of Pentheus,
The king, hear the sound of the east, the creation
Of Earth, my mother, and myself. The beat!
The beat! Let the city open its eyes.
I will go to the heights of Kithairon where
The women are dancing on the slopes, and join
The Bacchae. (Exit.)
  CHORUS. Look — the hills of
The East, where new life leaps —
We came from there.
Our work . . . !
It's easy,
It's singing work,
It's dancing labour,
It's laughing drudgery.
I never stop, I never tire,
Letting myself run free for Dionysos.
Clear the streets —
We're here.
Clear the streets —
We've come.
Room! Room! Stay at home, lips closed, because . . .
A word spilled can make a stain.
The only words allowed here are the words for
Dionysos.
And I sing them

Over and over,
I sing them . . .
Who is alive? Who is happy?
The one who knows . . .
Knows?
Knows the secret . . .
The secret?
The secret of the night
When his whole life begins again
And he's all one with the friends of Dionysos,
The pure lovers of the mountains,
Bedded in the earth's grasp
Plunged in forgetfulness,
Buried
. . . Living!
Like green leaves in winter, woodsap in snow,
Ivy crowns make you King
And from the pine tree stems your power.
Dionysos, my lord,
Dionysos, my dear harsh master.
Run on, run on! Bring him here, fill the streets
With the young life, the new life —
Dionysos!
Flood Greece with his fresh blood,
Beat, beat, beat him into the heart like thunder —
Dionysos!
     Burst from fire, gashed by thunderbolt.
He was flung into life by flame.
His mother screamed, the pain rending her,
And let him go to the lightning.
She died then . . .
But he lived! Hatched in a golden clasp,
In the storehouse of life in the body of Zeus.
And Hera never knew!
Then out into the world —
When the time was ready for him,
And he for the time.
He had bull horns empowering him.
He had snake hair crowning him.
And we will wear crowns like that —
We'll catch them, and tame them, and wear them —
Snakes!
     Thebes — mother land of Semele —
Wear a crown too — coiled-within-coil ivy.
Let the never-dying blossoms,
Flower in you, drench you in greenery, Thebes!
Oak-leaf mad,

Fir-branch crazy,
Fawn-skin clothed,
And white-wool jewelled —
Then you're dressed.
Hold the branch in your hand,
Power in the thick wood, feel it pulsing,
The whole land will rock,
The whole land will jump —
He stirs, yes, now — the power Dionysos.
And then we go up to the hills, to the hills,
Where the women who lived indoors at a loom,
Or a spindle, wait for him now
Packed, trembling, his thorn in their blood.
    Crete holds caves where Zeus was nursed,
And there the drum, the drum, the drum was born.
When the dance comes over you, and the strain drags tight,
The singing woodwind cools
The drum-beat,
The singing wind softens the drum
And together they make the dance, they make it, till . . .
The mind splits open,
The world falls in —
And Dionysos is glad.
    Then you're tired of the running, and at last, at last
You fling yourself on the ground —
Your only cover the flakes of sunlight on the skin of a fawn;
This is the moment, sacred and secret, in the mountains,
When your hands search for the goat,
Hands grope for its blood,
And you drink,
As it comes from the goat,
The fresh red juice, the joy of . . .
That's the way Dionysos has led you
In the hills of the east, the morning sun . . . (CHORUS makes a sound —
      of joy, ecstasy, praise.)
    Earth gushing milk
Gushing wine,
Gushing rivers of honey,
You hold the flame
High, it smells like a scent from Syria,
Its pine wood flaring,
Smoke streaming as you hurl your body
Down through dances
Shouting, and raving, and reddening the torch
With your speed
Your hair floods down, the wind-gusts flourish it . . .
And among the shrilling, the shouting, the singing a voice

Blares,
"Run on, run on,
My Bacchae,
Like a stream of gold from the lavish east
Sing, sing, sing!
Let the drum stamp loud,
Shout for him,
Throat, tongue, breath,
Blaze for him,
Let the leaping flute
Lure and tempt,
Calling out the powers of life
To join us, and play
In the hills,
In the hills."
Then, freedom!
Joy of a foal
In the meadows with its mother.
Bacchae, dart!
Bacchae, run!
Bacchae, *dance!*

(*Enter* TEIRESIAS.)

TEIRESIAS (*knocks at door of palace*). Answer the door! Answer it!
    Call Kadmos
Out, Kadmos, the man from Phoenicia who built
A towering city here at Thebes. Go,
Someone, tell him Teiresias wants him.
He knows why I've come . . .

(*A* GUARD *goes.*)

We are collaborating and we have
This pact. We take branches, we twist ivy
Leaves round them, we weave more ivy in
Our hair, like crowns, but live, and then we take
Skins of young deer . . . Well, I may
Be old, but he is older . . .

(*Enter* KADMOS.)

KADMOS. Teiresias, my dear friend, I knew
It was you when I heard your voice.
(*To* GUARDS.) Pay attention.
This is a wise, wise man.
(*To* TEIRESIAS.) Look, I am ready. I found the things. We

Must give him all we can, build
Respect for him. He is a power, a wonder,
And he is the child of my own daughter.
Do we dance now? Where do we go? (*Shaking his head.*)
One — two — *back!* One — two — *back!*
Is this right, Teiresias? We are both old
But you know things, you see more.
All day and all night, I won't
Need rest — down, down — (*He thumps his stick on the ground.*)
Forget the years, we are born again, and it's beautiful.

TEIRESIAS. Yes, do you feel it? Young again.
I'll dance too, I can, I'm ready . . .

KADMOS.   We climb
To the hills, then, we don't ride there?

TEIRESIAS. No. We need to go *simply* into the presence
Of this being.

KADMOS.   An old blind prophet
And I shall take you by the hand like a child . . .

TEIRESIAS. The one who calls us will lead us there. And we
Shall never notice the journey.

KADMOS.   Are we the only
Two in Thebes to worship this way, dancing?

TEIRESIAS. We are the only two in Thebes with our senses left
Intact. The rest of the city has fallen apart.

KADMOS. I want to go. Hurry. Take my hand.

TEIRESIAS. Here, hold on to me, don't let me lose you.

KADMOS. I look at the world, the power in it, and I
Feel lost, mortal, small, small . . .

TEIRESIAS.   Yes,
You feel those forces working in you. To them
All our intellect is a joke. There are things
Not measured in time, a birthright, an inheritance.
They exist. You can't reason them away,
You can't talk them, define them, describe them away,
Yes, I'm old, but I mean to go dancing,
Put vine leaves in my hair, and I'm not ashamed.
This power does not
Tell men apart. When they dance it can't distinguish
Young from old. It needs to be recognized
By everyone in the world — that is how
It lives — but it doesn't keep score. No one comes
Before anyone else . . .

KADMOS.   Teiresias,
You have sight, but no eyes. You need
Mine to light your way for you. Listen,
Pentheus is here, the youth I gave my power to.

How he drives himself!
What's happened? What is new now?

(*Enter* PENTHEUS *with* SOLDIERS.)

PENTHEUS.   I leave my country, I just go away,
And the result — chaos, the city in uproar. I hear
All our women have left home, and the new
Fashion is to be Bacchae, to mob
The mountains — more shadows there, of course —
And all in honour of someone, some moving spirit
They've just discovered — Dionysos. Who
Is he? What is Dionysos?
And this dancing . . . ? Dancing! . . . I was told
There are gatherings where they drink so much
You could never see the cups for the wine.
The women creep away, one here, one there,
Into the bushes — and there a man is waiting
And they copulate. They say it's all
Part of the service for this divine power.
Service! All they care about is being
Serviced.
I caught a few and my men have them chained
To the wall in the city gaol. The rest escaped,
They're in the hills, but I shall hunt them down.
Yes, that's how they'll end, in a cage,
Behind bars. No more drunken
Dancing then, no more orgies,
No more Bacchae!
    They say a stranger has come to my country —
Some sorcerer, hypnotist, from the East,
From Lydia or somewhere, all curly blonde
Hair stinking of scent, cheeks hot
With wine, and flashing eyes — a real seducer —
Who spends all his days — and his nights —
With the girls from my city. He calls it initiation.
If I get this initiator inside
My palace, I'll finish his thumping, jumping,
Hair-shaking, snaking game, I'll initiate
That head away from that body.
He claims Dionysos still exists,
Never died, got life from eternal
Powers. Very likely — since Dionysos was roasted
In his mother's womb, after she told
Everyone Zeus was father of her child.
That myth was exploded in a blast of lightning.

But this new boy has the gall
To foist it back on us. Whoever he is
He deserves a reward for that — a rope around
His neck . . . (*He sees* KADMOS *and* TEIRESIAS.)
No, I can't believe it! My prophet, Teiresias,
In a fawn skin . . . And my own grandfather playing
With a woolly stick. Ridiculous!
(*To* KADMOS.) Grandfather, you disgust me. Look at you,
An old man, clowning. Throw away
That ivy, drop those toys, don't touch them . . .
(*To* TEIRESIAS.) Teiresias, this is you. You talked him into it.
You want to drag this new obsession across
Our lives, so that you can squint up
At a few birds, burn a few sacrifices,
And make yourself more of a profit than ever.
If you weren't already mouldering in senility
You'd be rattling your chains with all the other Bacchae
For smuggling in this pernicious, lecherous gospel.
When women drink, and their eyes light up like the wine
Itself, then I say, Goodbye to decency,
The animals are out!

    CHORUS.   You — King of this place, be careful,
You, stranger, you dirty something pure,
That's dangerous.
Remember — you're born out of the earth yourself.
Kadmos planted dragon's teeth in soil, and harvested men.
To those men you are a living insult.

    TEIRESIAS.   Easy for some to make speeches. They're clever,
They pick an easy target, and the words sound good.
Now you — your tongue races along
And makes a plausible sound, which might
Almost be mistaken for sense, except
That you have none. Arrogant, self-confident, with a gift
For phrases — that kind of man is useless, a danger
To his fellows, while his mind stays closed.
This new life in our midst, which you
Sneer at, is going to be so powerful all
Over Greece, so vast, I . . . I can't
Describe it.
    You are a young man. Here are two
Principles for you, the two supreme principles
In life.
First the principle of earth, Demeter,
Goddess of the soil, or whatever else
You like to call it. This provides the firm
Solid base in man. Second, the opposite

Principle, Dionysos, who found the living
Juice in the grape, and gave it to us all,
To slake our parched, aching souls, wash us
In streams of wine. When living is a struggle
He is the only drug for our pain, he gives us
Sleep and oblivion. We drink him down, we swallow
His power, and he comes alive in us. Then
We soar, we fly, we are free, and through his agency
Man can know some happiness. You laugh at him.
You laugh at the story that he was sewn in the loins
Of Zeus. Let me show you how to interpret
That — it makes sense.
    Zeus snatched the unborn child out
Of the blazing thunderbolt, took him back
To where he came from, Olympos. Hera, the bride
Of Zeus, wanted her rival's child to die.
But Zeus, like the wise power he is, found
A way out of the dilemma. He broke off
A part of the earth's envelope, the atmosphere,
And made a *loan* of it to Hera, to protect
The real Dionysos from her jealousy.
In time people confused "loan" with "loin" —
Told some story of how he was sewn in the loins
Of Zeus, and made a new version.
    And there is more. The power of Dionysos can break
Out of time. When he invades the mind
And puts reason to sleep, we have sight
Of things to come. If he takes full possession
He makes those who give themselves to him
Tell the future . . . What else? . . . War! He is even
There in war, yes . . . An army is in
The field, marching into battle. Then,
Before the weapons have touched, panic! That
Is Dionysos . . . Delphi too, home
Of Apollo, sanctuary of reason. But look
Up at the rocks. Who do you see bounding
Over the high plateau between the peaks,
Through the pine forests, shaking winter
Into life with green branches? — Dionysos!
Yes, he is everywhere.
Believe me, Pentheus, never boast
That you have any power to rule your life.
You may think you do, but thought is impotent,
Your certainty an illusion. Dionysos is here,
In your country, at work.
Accept him,

Pour wine for him,
Put vine leaves in your hair for him,
Dance for him.
   Dionysos will not restrain desire
In women. Restraint is something they must practise
For themselves. It cannot be imposed. But those
Who have control already will not lose it
Merely because they lose themselves
To Dionysos.
   Look, you are glad when crowds at the city
Gates cheer, shout, "Pentheus! Pentheus!"
Till every street rings with your name. Well,
Dionysos, too, I imagine, enjoys
Some recognition.
   And so Kadmos and myself — yes,
You can laugh — but we'll take our ivy branches
And we shall dance, we shall partner each other,
Old and grey as we are. Nevertheless
Dance we must. We shall not fight this power;
We shall not listen to your talk, which is
The most terrible madness of all. I pity you,
Pentheus. You'll get no relief from medicine,
Nor can you cure yourself.

    CHORUS. The old man understands. He leaves reason where it is,
Apollo has his place, and so has Dionysos . . .
You are safe. Dionysos has power — and you
Have granted it.

    KADMOS. Listen to Teiresias. You are still young,
And he is right. Your place is here, beside us.
Don't close doors on the past. This moment
You're nowhere, suspended in a void. Your brain
Works, but only against yourself.
You may be right. Dionysos may have
No special powers, but even so,
Why not pretend he does? It may be a lie,
But it's a useful one. If we can say
That Semele gave birth to a superior
Being, to something undying, it will be
A tremendous honour to our family.
Remember how your cousin, Akteon, died.
That was a horrible end. The hounds from his own
Kennels turned man-eater and tore him apart.
He had boasted he was a greater hunter than Artemis
Herself. And so he died in a velvet glade.
It could happen to you, unless you change! Come here,
I'll put some leaves on your head . . . Ivy . . . Be

With us. Acknowledge him. He is a great
Power. Let me . . .
   PENTHEUS.   Don't touch me!
Go and play Bacchae, but don't smear
Your idiocy onto me! Just don't
Come near me!
   And now, for your teacher, Teiresias, who fed you this drivel,
Punishment!
(*To* GUARD.) One of you, here!
He has a place where he sits hoping for some
Revelation out of birdsong. Go. Take
A crowbar with you, and destroy that place.
Level it to the ground, all of it,
Throw his bits of wool to the winds, and let
The storms have them. *Hurry!*
   This is the one thing I can do to him
That will really hurt.
And you, you go into the city
And bring me this foreigner, this thing
Of doubtful gender, spreading his sick notions
Amongst our women, dragging our marriages
Through the filth.
When you find him, chain him up, and fetch him
Here. And then he'll have justice, because we'll stone him,
(*To* GUARDS.) Stone him till he's dead. He'll find Thebes
A hard, hard place for Bacchae!
   TEIRESIAS.   You fiend! Do you realise what you're saying?
No, you're mad. You had little enough sense
Before, but now . . . !
(*To* KADMOS.) Kadmos, let's go. And let us pray
For him. Yes, he's a monster, but for the sake
Of the rest of us, let us pray this
Is overlooked. Bring your ivy branches
And follow me. Try to help me, hold me
Upright, and I'll help you. We are old
But we must stand by ourselves. Take pride in it . . .
Don't think of him!
We have work to do for this great power, this supreme
Power . . .
   Kadmos — in Greek the name Pentheus signifies
Sorrow. Does that mean anything? . . .
I hope not.
I don't talk of things to come — this is happening
Now (*meaning to* PENTHEUS) . . . Only a fool blurts out his folly!

  (*Exeunt* KADMOS *and* TEIRESIAS.)

CHORUS.   Back!
Keep away!
This is filth — stain — smear — decay —
Keep away! He turns pure gold black.
    Did you hear him?
The scorn that drips,
From his mouth, fouling Dionysos, child of his own city.
Doesn't know happiness, or the pure-drained drink of joy.
But Dionysos is the one
Who sends you dancing out of your mind,
Flings you laughing out of yourself to the flute-song,
Stops your crying, stops your caring,
And when the bright wine dazes you
Life can't end, ivy glows on your brow
And you swallow thick sleep by the mouthful.
When reason forgets its place, wanders, and starts an invasion,
And words go mad and run away with their master,
The end has come —
The man is doomed.
Live easy, live calm, and the storm can't wreck you —
That way you stay whole.
There are powers in the world, who oversee life;
It's not so wise to be clever.
Life is short, and since it is,
Why chase more, more, more?
Can't you bear what is here?
Let others go mad, draw up the plans for destruction —
But don't let them take us with them!
I want to go back to Cyprus, island of Aphrodite,
Where desire blows warm and breathes away thought;
I want to lie in the fields of Paphos,
Where the distant Nile feeds a hundred wells
And gives fruit to the land without rain.
I want to see Pieria, because music is first there,
And the slope of Olympos leads straight to the sky.
Take me there, Dionysos, I'm calling you —
Hear me, come and lead me away. . . .
Then I can hand over my seeing,
Hand over my striving
And dance to my heart-beats,
And no one can say no.
Dionysos, child of the universe, comes to life in my laughter.
His great love is Peace,
Lavish with her treasures, careful of youth.
He sends the poor, he sends the rich, his one gift — wine.
So that the whole world can know
Where pain stops, and where joy starts.

He hates the man who says no.
No to the day,
No to the night,
No to life, and no to all love —
Keep away from that kind,
They are too much for you, they will consume you.
There is another way, never named, never mapped.
But the unheard-of, untalked-of people follow it.
That way I choose — I say yes to it.

(*Enter a* GUARD, *with* DIONYSOS, *chained.*)

GUARD.   Pentheus, we caught him. The hunt is over, and here
Is the animal you sent us after . . .
A gentle animal, we found, made
No attempt to escape, handed himself
Over without a murmur, never went pale,
That wine-stain flush never left his cheek, and he smiled.
He told us to put on the chains and take him away.
He waited for us, making it so simple
I was embarrassed. So I said, "Stranger," I said,
"I only obey orders here. I am taking you
Now, on instructions from Pentheus. Pentheus
Sends for you. *Pentheus*. Not me."
But the women you captured and had locked up in prison,
The ones who were dancing,
They're out.
They're free, and they're away in the forest, running
Like deer, calling on Bromios — he's their master,
And governs them completely.
The chains all fell from their limbs of their own
Accord, keys turned, doors opened,
Without a hand touching them. This man
Is an amazing . . .
He is full of . . .
I don't understand what it is he has brought to Thebes
But it is your concern now, all of it.
        PENTHEUS.   Let him go. He is inside the cage and he can't
Escape from me now. He doesn't move
So fast.
Well, stranger, you're not at all bad-looking,
Are you? At least, to the women . . . Which is why
You have come to Thebes, I suppose . . . Long hair,
Crinkling down your cheeks — you've never wrestled,
I presume — very desirable . . . White
Skin — you keep out of the sun, you cultivate
The shadows, where you hunt down love

With your handsome profile. Yes?
Who are you? Where do you come from?
   DIONYSOS.   I am no one . . .
But I will give you an easier answer.
Have you heard of a river called Tmolos? It runs
Through fields of flowers . . .
   PENTHEUS.   Yes, I know that river, it circles the town
Of Sardis.
   DIONYSOS.   I come from there. My country is Lydia.
   PENTHEUS.   And these
Activities. How is it you bring them to Greece?
   DIONYSOS.   Dionysos inspired me. Dionysos . . . He
Is the son of Zeus.
   PENTHEUS.   So you have a Zeus
Over there, who fathers new powers
On the world.
   DIONYSOS.   No. Zeus was united
With Semele in Thebes, and gave her the child
Here.
   PENTHEUS.   Did this irresistible urge
Come to you at night, or were you
"Inspired" in the daytime?
   DIONYSOS.   I saw him.
He saw me. And he gave me the secret
Means to summon his presence.
   PENTHEUS.   And this secret —
What is it like? Can you tell me?
   DIONYSOS.   It must not
Be revealed to someone in whom Dionysos
Has not been born.
   PENTHEUS.   Those who share this secret —
Do they benefit — and how?
   DIONYSOS.   I am forbidden to tell.
But it is worth knowing.
   PENTHEUS.   You're clever, but
You're a fake! You want to make me curious.
   DIONYSOS.   For a man who is so sure of what he knows
There are no other powers, there is no other
Life. It simply escapes him.
   PENTHEUS.   You say you saw
Dionysos clearly . . . What did he look like?
   DIONYSOS.   Whatever
He wished. I didn't arrange it.
   PENTHEUS.   Very good.
But once more you evade the issue,
Your statement was meaningless.

DIONYSOS.   The greatest truths often sound like babblings
Of madmen — till they are understood.

PENTHEUS.   Are we
The first to be visited by you and your offer
Of supernatural aid?

DIONYSOS.   No. All
The people of the east are awake. They dance.
They live . . .

PENTHEUS.   They're out of their minds, we in Greece
Have more sense.

DIONYSOS.   No, in this case, less.
Their way is different, that is all.

PENTHEUS.   And these practices you claim are sacred —
Do they take place at night, or in the day?

DIONYSOS.   Mostly at night. Darkness has dignity.

PENTHEUS.   For women the night hours are dangerous,
Lascivious hours . . .

DIONYSOS.   People have been known
To sin during the day.

PENTHEUS.   You play with words!
You'll be punished for that.

DIONYSOS.   You soil mysteries
With your ignorant sneers. You'll be punished
For that.

PENTHEUS.   He's so sure. The drunken dancer
Has been in training — for argument.

DIONYSOS.   Come,
Pronounce sentence. What terrible fate have you
In store for me?

PENTHEUS.   First, I'll clip those flowing
Locks . . .

DIONYSOS.   My hair must not be touched. I grow it
For Dionysos.

PENTHEUS.   Next, you will hand over
Your wand, that branch you carry . . .

DIONYSOS.   Take it from me
Yourself. I carry it for Dionysos.

PENTHEUS.   Then
We shall lock you in prison, and you will never get out.

DIONYSOS.   Dionysos will free me, when I wish him to.

PENTHEUS.   Yes, when you get your followers round you and "summon
His presence."

DIONYSOS.   He sees. He's here. This minute he knows
What is being done to me.

PENTHEUS.   Where is he, then?
I can't see him. Why doesn't he show himself?

DIONYSOS.   He's here, where I stand. You, being crass
And proud, see nothing.
    PENTHEUS.   You're raving.
(*To* GUARDS.) He insults me!
He insults you all!
    DIONYSOS.   I am sane. You
Are not. I say to you, set me free.
    PENTHEUS.   And I say you go to prison, because
I am master here, I have the power.
    DIONYSOS.   You don't know what your life is, what
You are doing, who you are . . .
    PENTHEUS.   I am Pentheus,
Son of Echion and Agave.
    DIONYSOS.   Pentheus;
A very convenient name for a doomed man.
    PENTHEUS.   Go away, go on! Go!
(*To* GUARDS.) Lock him up somewhere near — in the stables.
Leave him to stare at the darkness,
Darkness all the time.
(*To* DIONYSOS.) Dance in there!
And these creatures you have brought here, these
Accessories,
We'll either sell them, or we'll give their hands work
To do — not this banging, thumping on pieces of skin,
But *work*. Spinning. Weaving. They'll belong to us.
    DIONYSOS.   I leave you now. But I shall not suffer
What I have no need to suffer. Dionysos
Will punish you for your gross contempt. You
Say he does not exist. But when you send
Me to prison
It is you
Who commit the crime . . .
Against him.

(*The* GUARDS *lead* DIONYSOS *away*.)

    CHORUS.   Gently flowing Dirce,
Life-stream to these fields,
Innocent waters,
Banks that were a cradle for the newborn Dionysos
The day his father saved him from the blazing thunderbolt,
The day Zeus shouted:
"Welcome, my son, welcome to the world!
My man's loins shall be your womb.
You'll have a name, and Thebes will know you by it
Because I will open their eyes."

But now this same river they all live by here,
She doesn't want us.
"Don't come near," she cries,
"No ivy crowns on my banks,
No gatherings, no dancing near me!"
    Why?
Why turn away from us?
Why say no to us?
Some day you will long for . . . ache for . . .
. . . dry . . .
Ask for . . . parched . . .
Wine.
You'll thirst! Yes, some day,
You'll thirst for Dionysos.
    Never seen such fury like the fury staring out of
Pentheus.
That's not a man. It's a beast run wild.
He's one of the crop, the dragon-toothed flowers,
Who gnashed the soil to get spawned in the world —
A snarling freak,
A monster,
A fiend, murderous to the bone.
He means to shut me away,
Rope me in darkness,
But I'm not his. I belong to Dionysos.
Already, in there, in a dungeon, a sightless pit,
He buries our leader . . .
Dionysos . . . can you see this?
We can't move,
We can't breathe,
The only ones who speak for you, crushed.
Down . . .
. . . With a tree in one hand . . .
Down . . .
. . . like a tower of gold
Down from Olympos . . .
DIONYSOS!
And tame him.
Dionysos — we are calling you
Wherever you are,
Come . . .
Come from the mountain forests,
Glide from the wild beasts' lairs,
Spring from a cruel snow peak,
Leap from a whirlwind dance,
Grow from a thousand branches,

Rise from a sleeping valley,
Descend from Olympos,
Tree-leaved and silent,
Fly on the air,
In the grass that Orpheus tamed,
Over animals silenced by his music
Nearer and nearer —
The drumming of feet heralds you —
Dance out of mountain torrents,
Swing over eastern rivers,
Surge over waves towards us,
Driving a storm of souls,
Now he's coming, he's coming into Greece!
    He's over the land now,
In the green plains alive with horses,
In the streams that water the fields,
He's coming.
    YES! YES!
DIONYSOS! DIONYSOS! DIONYSOS!

(*As the* CHORUS *ends, the voice of* DIONYSOS *comes from offstage all round.*)

    DIONYSOS (*stereo*).   Aaaaaouoooooowah! Hark!
I got life!
I have a voice!
Hark! Aaaaoooouwah! Take me!
Aaaooouwah! Take me!
    CHORUS.   Has it come? . . . Hear it? . . . Feel it? . . .
The call! The call! . . . Where? . . . Is it here?
    DIONYSOS (*stereo*).   Yes! Coming to life . . . Yes! Coming
To life . . . Aaaooowah! . . . Born in the ground, born in
The sky . . . !
    CHORUS.   Master! Master!
Come close, come close. Come into us . . . In . . . In . . .
NOW . . . Closer, closer . . .
    DIONYSOS (*stereo*).   The earth — SHAKE.
The earth's floor — MOVE.
Move, nothing stand still, *move!*
    CHORUS.   Look, the palace of Pentheus bulges, quivers . . . It will
Fall, fall . . . It's got into the palace . . . It's in,
It's *in!* . . . See, pillars melt, marble streams,
Trembles . . . It's inside now, it's taken, it's taken.
    DIONYSOS (*stereo*).   Touch off the fire, flames and thunder!
Burn, burn, house of Pentheus.

(*During the following speech of* CHORUS, *darkness, thunder, flames, roar of collapsing masonry, triumph noise of* DIONYSOS.)

CHORUS.   Fire! Watch the fever-fire dance round the grave
Of Semele, charred earth no one walks on, the lightning
Left a living flame there . . .
Down, down! Everyone down to the ground . . .
Dionysos is . . .
. . . don't move . . .
In possession of . . .
. . . don't look . . .
The palace
. . . don't breathe!
    DIONYSOS.   Afraid, my friends? After all our journeys
Together . . .? Look at you, hugging the earth,
Terrorstruck . . . Yes, you saw the house
Of Pentheus split and sundered by the presence
Of Dionysos. But now . . . look up at me,
You're safe . . . Don't flinch . . . All is well . . .
    CHORUS.   You're dawn for us, our life-light, and calm rose
In the depths of the mind . . . The sight of you is comfort . . .
We'd lost you, we were alone.
    DIONYSOS.   So you surrendered, gave in to despair. When I was taken
In there you thought I would be buried in the death
Cells of Pentheus' darkness?
    CHORUS.   Yes, yes.
Who was to protect us if you were harmed?
But now you're free.
    DIONYSOS.   As always . . .
    CHORUS.   And safe . . .
    DIONYSOS.   I saved myself.
    CHORUS.   How? The man was in a killing mood . . .
    DIONYSOS.   Easy. I had no trouble with him.
    CHORUS.   But you couldn't move. He lashed your hands
Together.
    DIONYSOS.   He thought he did, but he never touched them, never came
near me. He thought he had me, but he breakfasted on lies this morning and I laughed — because I had him . . . He took me to the stables to
be locked up, and found a bull there. This bull he loaded with chains —
on its knees, on its hooves — gasping with rage, streaming sweat all over
his body, chewing his lips . . . I waited close beside him, did nothing, said
nothing, just sat there and watched. Meanwhile the palace quivered.
Dionysos had come, and fire spurted from Semele's grave . . . When
Pentheus saw it he decided his house was on fire. He rushed from end
to end of the palace, screaming at his servants to pump water, more water,
on the flames, till every slave was working — over nothing. The fire
existed only in his mind. All at once he left it — snatched up a long
steel sword and hurled himself indoors — his prisoner, me, had escaped.
Then Dionysos — or so I think, because I only tell you what I think —
created a phantom figure. Because Pentheus charged at something in the

courtyard, stabbing and lunging as if it was me on the end of his blade.
But there was nothing there, only clear bright air. More havoc followed.
Dionysos shattered the palace. Inside now is nothing but a heap of
rubble. My spell in prison was hard on Pentheus. Finally, spent and
limp, he threw away his sword . . . Well, he is a man, and he fought a
god. He expected too much . . . Quietly I left his house, and came back
here to you. Pentheus never troubled me . . . Listen. I hear footsteps.
This will be him . . . Watch that door. He'll come out and say . . . but
what can he say now? Let him explode — I'll manage him easily anyhow. The secret of life is balance, tolerance . . .

(*Enter* PENTHEUS.)

PENTHEUS.   I've been cheated! I had that foreigner. I had him
So trussed up he couldn't move — and still
He got away! (*Sees* DIONYSOS *and gives a shout.*)
There he is! That's the man. Look,
He stands there, on the doorstep of my palace,
Out in the open . . .
Look at him!
    DIONYSOS.   Stay where you are!
Calm yourself . . .
Anger's going . . . going . . .
Now . . .
    PENTHEUS.   How did you get out? You were locked in, chained . . .
    DIONYSOS.   Didn't I tell you — or didn't you hear? — someone
Would free me?
    PENTHEUS.   Free you? Who? You always produce
A new riddle.
    DIONYSOS.   The grape-gardener, the wine-grower
To mankind.
    PENTHEUS.   The planter of all drunkenness
And disorder.
    DIONYSOS.   Insults from you would make him proud.
    PENTHEUS (*to* GUARD). Surround the palace. Close every gate in the
        city.
Shut him in!
    DIONYSOS.   Come, come, if such powers
Exist, surely they move on a higher plane
Than your city walls.
    PENTHEUS.   So clever, so
Clever. All that cleverness misused!
    DIONYSOS.   I use it where I need it most . . . Look,
Someone is coming with a message for you. Listen
To him first . . . Of course we'll wait for you —

We are in no hurry to go . . . You
Hear what he has to say. He comes from the mountains.

(*Enter* HERDSMAN.)

HERDSMAN.   Pentheus, I am one of your subjects here
In Thebes. I come from Kithairon. There's still snow
There, it dazzles you, the hills are all white . . .
  PENTHEUS.   And what is your news? How urgent is it?
  HERDSMAN.   I have seen
The Bacchae . . . those women, strange women, they fling
Their white limbs like a storm of javelins across
The fields. I came to tell you and everyone here . . .
I want you to know, master, what marvellous things
They do . . . beyond anything you could imagine.
But first I would like your word that I can speak
Freely about what happened there. Or must I
Trim the facts a little . . . ? It's your temper, you see,
Master, your very quick temper, which rules us
All so harshly . . . too harshly.
  PENTHEUS.   Tell me, I give my word, nothing will happen
To you. Do your duty, and no one will be angry.
The worse you make the Bacchae sound, the more
Firmly shall I crush their ringmaster, as he deserves.
  HERDSMAN.   Our herds of cattle are topping the rise of the hills,
Grazing as they go, and the sun's rays are just
Beginning to warm the grass, when I see three
Circles of women — the dancers!
One of them is round Autonoë,
The second with Agave, your mother,
And the third is with Ino.
They are all asleep, lying every way,
Some propped against pine-tree trunks,
Others curled up modestly on a pile
Of oak leaves, pillowed on the earth —
None of the drunkenness you talked about,
None of the obscene abandon, or the wild
Music — no love among the bushes.
All at once, your mother stands up. She cries out
And wakes the rest of the women, says she can hear
The lowing of cattle. They shake the sleep petals
From their eyes, and all stand upright,
A marvel of calm and order . . . Young girls,
Old women, maidens who have never slept
With a man. First, they let their hair tumble
Down their shoulders. Then, the ones whose fawn-skins

Have come loose from the brooches pinning them, fasten them
Back on their shoulders, and belt the spotted hides
With snakes —
And those snakes were live — I saw their tongues
Flicker . . .
One of them might carry a fawn, cradled
In her arms, or a wild wolf cub, and gives it her own
Milk —
You see, some had left newborn babies at home
And so their breasts were full . . .
They all weave strands of ivy, oak leaves,
Tendrils of flowering briony in their hair.
Then one of them winds ivy on a branch,
Taps a rock, and out of that rock spouts
Water — running water! Fresh as dew!
Another drops her wand, a little twig,
On to the earth, and where she drops it some force
Sends up a spring — a wine-spring! Some
Feel they'd like to drink fresh milk.
They scrape the tips of their fingers on the earth
And they have milk — fountains of milk! From all
Their ivy-covered branches sweet honey
Drips, cascades down . . . Oh, if you
Had been there and seen all this, you would have been
On your knees, praying — not criticising — but praying
For help and guidance.
      All we herdsmen and shepherds hold
A meeting, we begin to talk, we compare
Stories —
Because these were fantastic things the women were doing,
We could hardly believe our eyes . . .
Someone who knows his way in the city, knows
How they make speeches there, he stands up
And makes one himself:
"You inhabitants of the majestic mountain acres, allow me to propose to
you that we hunt down Agave, mother of Pentheus, from the midst of her
Dionysiac festivities, and thereby do our royal master in Thebes . . . a
great good turn . . ."
Applause!
      We decide to lay an ambush for the women
In the undergrowth,
We hide in the leaves,
We wait.
The hour for their rites approaches . . .
The sticks with ivy begin to beat out a rhythm.
It gets in your blood, that rhythm.

"Iacchos!" they howl in unison,
"Bromios!"
"Son of Zeus!"
  The whole mountain sways to that one beat, beat, beat:
The wild beasts join in,
Everything moves,
Everything's running, running, Agave is racing towards me, she's coming
near, nearer, almost touches me, I leap out — I wanted to catch her, you
see — I jump from my safe hiding place and —
She gives a screech:
"Look, my swift hounds, we are being hunted
By these men. Follow me!
Follow me!
Branches — get branches and arm yourselves!"
  We turn and run —
If we hadn't we would have been torn to shreds
By the Bacchae . . .
  As it is, they descend on our heifers grazing
In the long grass. They have nothing in their hands,
Those women — nothing metal. But imagine you see
One of them, just with her hands, tearing a young
Well-grown heifer in two, while it screams . . .
Others have found full-grown cows and are wrenching them
Limb from limb. Ribs, hooves, toss
Up in the air, drop to the ground. Parts
Of our animals hang from the branches of pine trees,
Dripping there, blood spattering the leaves.
Bulls with surging horns, invincible
Till now, are tripped, sprawl full length
On the ground, while a mob of hands, girls'
Hands, rip them apart. Faster than you can
Blink your royal eyes the flesh is peeled
Off their bones.
  Then down, like flocks of birds, so fast
Their feet never touch the ground, they sweep to the Valley
Sleeping between the hills. Here, on the banks
Of the Asopos, the grain grows deep in the farmlands,
Little towns, Hysiai, Erythrai, snuggle
Beneath the slopes of Kithairon . . .
Like an invading army those women mill
Through the valley, they tear it apart, chaos! Children
Snatched from their beds . . . Anything they can pick up,
And carry on their backs, stays there — nothing
Holds it on, but it never slips to the ground,
Even the bronze, the iron, — they put live coals
In their hair — and nothing burns them!

The people are furious, being plundered by these women,
And rush to defend themselves. Then what happens?
    — It was a terrible sight to see, master . . .
    No spear, no weapon, nothing so much as scratches
The Bacchae. But one of those wooden sticks they carry
Draws blood at once. They throw them — and men run
For their lives — that isn't human, there's some other power
At work . . . At last, they go, back to the mountains
Where they came from, back to the springs of water
Which Dionysos sent them. They wash away
The blood . . . and the snakes lick off the dirt and gore
From the womens' cheeks with their tongues . . .
    This power, master, whoever he is, whatever
He is . . . let him into Thebes! He
Is great. And one thing above all they say
He has done, I've heard that he gave mankind
The grape . . . And the grape is the best grave — for grief.
If there were no wine
There would be no love,
There would be no joy in life.
    CHORUS.   In this king's company, honesty is a dangerous pastime
Yet I must speak . . .
    . . . Say it, say it . . . !
Of all the powers in life the greatest is Dionysos.
    PENTHEUS.   Now, I see . . . yes! Nearer . . . nearer!
This insufferable craze is like a fire, and it's spreading!
All Greece despises us. But we must
Be firm, not give way . . .
(To GUARDS.) Go to the gates of Electra, get every man
Under arms. I want all the cavalry, every
Spearman, every bowman, mobilised.
We attack the Bacchae at once . . .
I have been too patient. But my patience
Is finished, we are being governed by a pack of women.
    DIONYSOS.   I told you, Pentheus, but you never listen.
You have not been good to me. All the same
I am going to warn you. You must not use force against
Dionysos.
End the war in yourself. He will not
Allow you to disturb his Bacchae. Leave them
In the mountains where they are happy.
    PENTHEUS.   Don't preach
To me. You were in prison and you escaped.
Well, look after your freedom or I may remind
Myself that you have been judged and condemned.

DIONYSOS.   I
Would sacrifice to him . . . not rage and struggle
And kick. This is an eternal power —
You are a man.
    PENTHEUS. *I'll* sacrifice to him!
A blood sacrifice, a woman sacrifice —
That is all they are fit for. I will be lavish —
There will be carnage in the glades of Kithairon.
    DIONYSOS. You'll lose. It will be an ignominious rout.
Your bronze shields won't hold off wooden sticks
And women's hands.
    PENTHEUS.   Will someone tell me how
To get rid of this man? Extricate me, someone!
Whatever I do to him, whatever he does
To me, it's the same. Talk, talk, talk!
    DIONYSOS. Excuse me — but you can settle all this,
No trouble . . . It is still possible.
    PENTHEUS.   How? What
Do I do? Make myself lower than the lowest
In this country?
    DIONYSOS. I will bring the women
Here, without the use of force.
    PENTHEUS.   Yes,
I see, thank you. This is the great master
Plan — the great deception.
    DIONYSOS.   How can you call it
That? I want to keep you whole. I work
For nothing else.
    PENTHEUS. You arranged this with your friends.
Licence to dance, disorder in perpetuity.
    DIONYSOS. Certainly I arranged it, quite true —
With Dionysos.
    PENTHEUS (to GUARDS). Bring out my armour . . . (To DIONYSOS.)
        You —
Keep quiet!
    DIONYSOS (to GUARDS). Wait! (To PENTHEUS.) Do you want to see
        them . . .
In their nests up there in the hills. See
The women . . . ?
    PENTHEUS. Yes, yes, I do. Yes,
I'll pay if I have to. Gold. How much? A thousand?
Ten thousand?
    DIONYSOS. You've fallen in love with my idea.
You can't wait. Why?
    PENTHEUS.   I'll see them drunk,
Hopelessly drunk. It revolts me, but . . . I . . .

DIONYSOS. But you really want to. That disgusting sight
Lures you there . . . ?
PENTHEUS. Yes, I told you, it does.
I won't say anything, I'll be quiet, I'll stay
Among the pine-trees.
DIONYSOS. You can try to hide
But they'll pick up your scent.
PENTHEUS. Good point. I'd forgotten.
I'll go openly.
DIONYSOS. I'll take you there. Would you like that?
The way is before you. Will you dare?
PENTHEUS. Now!
Take me there now. I hate every minute
We lose.
DIONYSOS. Then you must be covered. Find a linen
Dress to wear . . .
PENTHEUS. Wait, now what is
This? I'm a man, I don't change places
With any woman. Why should I?
DIONYSOS. In case
They kill you. Suppose you, a man, are discovered
There — you die.
PENTHEUS. Right again. I understand.
There is some intelligence in you. I should have seen it
Before.
DIONYSOS. Dionysos came alive in me.
All I know is him.
PENTHEUS. Yes, yes . . .
Now, this good advice of yours, how
Do we carry it out?
DIONYSOS. We go inside, and there
I prepare you for your journey.
PENTHEUS. How — prepare me?
Dress me up as a woman? Oh no, no,
I would be ashamed.
DIONYSOS. Have you lost heart? The sight
Of those possessed and demented women, it no longer
Interests you?
PENTHEUS. What kind of clothing did you say
I have to wear?
DIONYSOS. Long hair to your shoulders.
You must have a wig . . .
PENTHEUS. And then what else? Is there more
To this costume?
DIONYSOS. A full length robe.
And for the head — a scarf.

PENTHEUS.   Anything else
You want to drape me in?
    DIONYSOS.   We'll give you a stick
Covered with ivy to hold, and wrap a spotted
Fawn-skin round you . . .
    PENTHEUS.   No, I could never put on
Woman's clothing.
    DIONYSOS.   What will you do — fight them?
It's a waste of your blood.
    PENTHEUS.   You're right. First we must go
And watch. Nothing more yet.
    DIONYSOS.   That
Makes better sense than hunting down evil
With more evil.
    PENTHEUS.   How can I get through the streets
Of Thebes and not be seen?
    DIONYSOS.   We'll find a secret
Way. I'll lead you.
    PENTHEUS.   Anything — but I will not
Be entertainment for that herd of females. Let's go
Inside. I want to consider this plan.
    DIONYSOS.   Decide,
I'm ready for you. Nothing will be too much trouble . . .
    PENTHEUS.   No, inside . . . I may call out my army
And march up there . . . Or I may follow
Your advice. We shall see. (*Exit.*)
    DIONYSOS (*to* CHORUS). Friends, the man stands in the gate of the
        trap.
He'll find the Bacchae and he'll answer to them with his life.
Dionysos, now your work begins.
You are not too far away, I hope. Let us
Reward this man for his attentions. First,
Dislodge his thoughts, make his reason slither.
If he were sane, he would not agree to put on
Woman's clothing. But when he edges out
Of his mind then, yes, then he'll wear it.
I want him to raise a howl of derision all
Through Thebes when he minces along the streets
In skirts. Once he mouthed fearsome threats,
And now . . .
Now to Pentheus, to disguise him, dress him for
His journey into death. His mother's hands
Will caress him roughly to his grave, and he'll see
Dionysos face to face, know that power,
Know its nature, its ferocious gentle nature
Alive in man, an undeniable *god!* (*Exit.*)

CHORUS. Night — will it ever come?
And my flying feet,
Flash of white thighs in the hills,
Head flung back,
And the dew-soaked air kissing my throat —
  And running, running —
Oh, when will it come?
  I want to be free and play and be happy again
Like a young deer, swathed in an emerald meadow,
When he runs in stark terror of the hunt,
And the knotted nets close in —
Then he leaps up and over them,
While the hunter shrieks to his hounds to keep racing,
Pacing behind.
But the deer strains his flashing legs taut.
He skims and spurts across open stretches
Where the river winds
Till he comes to a wood,
And the deep shade lulls him,
The green branches soothe him,
And he rests where no man is.
  What does it mean to live a life?
Can you hope for better than to rise above all warring,
Control what threatens you,
Defeat what oppresses you?
To be strong —
No, nothing is better.
I choose that.
There are forces not ruled by us,
And we obey them.
Trust them — though they travel inch by inch,
They arrive.
Self-swollen and calloused,
Soul, tumoured and hard,
All the malignant growths of thought,
They level, and pare, and crop,
They move in the dark with a subtle glitter
So that no one times their work,
But always the hunt goes on —
For the man who has turned his back on them.
Their rules cannot be overruled —
It is your peril, and your death that follows.
But if you grant their power — what does it cost?
Nothing.
Not even a word — because
These forces lack a name.
Call them whatever you like —

Spirits —
Gods —
Principles —
Elements —
Currents —
Laws —
Anything, anything you like.
But they are born in your blood
They have been observed and preserved since before time.
    What does it mean to live a life?
Can you hope for better than to rise above all warring,
Control what threatens you,
Defeat what oppresses you?
To be strong —
No, nothing is better
I choose that.
Life is a stormy sea,
Happiness is a harbour.
Finding your harbour is your life-work.
He is truly happy who succeeds in that life-work.
Some end rich, some poor,
Some are strong, some achieve nothing.
There are ten thousand hopes, ten thousand dreams,
They may all come true — they may all vanish,
But happiness —
A man finds happiness when he lives every day
With those forces of the world on his side.
All hail to that man!

    (*Enter* DIONYSOS.)

    DIONYSOS (*into palace*).   You! You with a white-hot wish for a peep
At the forbidden. You, reaching out for the out-of-reach,
You — I'm talking to you — Pentheus! Come
Out here, in front of your palace, let me
See you, dressed a woman of the wild wine
Nights of Dionysos. Are you ready to spy?
Your mother is there . . .
All the women are there . . .

    (*Enter* PENTHEUS.)

Perfect! You are a daughter of Kadmos to the life.
    PENTHEUS.   No, listen. I think I see two suns,
And two Thebes. The seven-gated city
Has doubled . . . and you, you look
Like a bull, leading me — horns sprout from your head . . .

All the time, were you that beast?
Are you the bull now . . . ?

DIONYSOS.   Dionysos favours you. He is bound to us
For the wine-gifts we gave him. Before he was not
Pleased. But now he is. And you see
What you ought to see.

PENTHEUS.   How do I look to you?
My aunt . . . isn't this how she walks? . . . Or this . . . My mother
Agave, — isn't it? Isn't it Agave?

DIONYSOS.   It's them! When I look at you it's them I see . . .
Wait — a wisp of hair has come away.
It isn't lying where I set it, under the scarf.

PENTHEUS.   Inside, I went this way with my head,
That way — back, forward, back — I was being
A woman in a trance. And I made the hair
Come loose . . .

DIONYSOS.   We must keep you groomed. I'll put it in place
Again. Here . . . lift your head up straight.

PENTHEUS.   Look . . . there . . . you do it. Make me pretty.
I am yours to play with. Take me.

DIONYSOS.   Your sash is loose —
Look. And your dress is wrong. The pleats should hang
The same length round your ankles.

PENTHEUS.   Yes,
I see . . . a little too long by the right foot.
But on this side it seems all right, touching
My heel just there . . .

DIONYSOS.   Who is your best friend?
I am . . . You don't believe me? Wait till you see
Bacchae, how modest they are, how pure, how sane —
Astonishing.

PENTHEUS.   This branch with ivy — in my right
Hand — or my left? Which makes me
More like a genuine wild woman of the hills?

DIONYSOS.   Hold it in your right hand, and raise it
In time with your right foot . . . Very good.
I see a change, a new mind, in you . . .

PENTHEUS.   Now I could . . . I could hoist the whole of Kithairon
On my shoulder — valleys full of women
Dancing, madness and all! . . . Yes?

DIONYSOS.   Of course,
If you will it. Your mood was before most unhealthy,
Now it is all it should be.

PENTHEUS.   Shall we bring iron bars, or shall I delve it
Up with my own bare hands, wedge
One shoulder or one arm under the hill-top . . . ?

DIONYSOS.   And destroy the homes of the nymphs? No, no.
Pan lives there too. Let him go on playing
His pipes.
PENTHEUS.   You're right. One should not coerce women.
I shall hide myself in the boughs of a pine tree.
DIONYSOS.   You find
The hiding place that suits you best. You're a spy,
A secret witness of secret rites.
PENTHEUS.   Yes,
Imagine, they are nestling like birds in the thick leaves,
Locked in their lust, enjoying it . . .
DIONYSOS.   You must break in
And prevent them. Perhaps you will find them in the act . . .
Unless they find you first.
PENTHEUS.   Take me through Thebes,
Right through the centre. I am the only man
Here who has any courage.
DIONYSOS.   Yes, you alone
Make sacrifices for your people, you alone.
And so — the test. It has always been there, waiting
For you. Follow me. I am your
Protector, your escort . . . as far as Kithairon —
Someone else will bring you back.
PENTHEUS.   Yes, my mother . . .
DIONYSOS.   In full view of everyone . . .
PENTHEUS.   That's why I'm going . . .
DIONYSOS.   You will be borne back on high.
PENTHEUS.   Yes, in triumph, you mean my great triumph!
DIONYSOS.   In the hands of your mother . . .
PENTHEUS.   You'll spoil me — all this pampering!
DIONYSOS.   Yes, I'll spoil you, I'll spoil you utterly.
PENTHEUS.   Still, I deserve it, and I shall have it! (*Exit.*)
DIONYSOS.   Headstrong, headstrong — you go walking
To your headlong end — which will make you
Famous, far beyond this life, beyond
This time.
Agave, fling open your arms.
Prepare, you sisters, daughters of Kadmos.
I bring this young man to you —
Prepare for a great contest.
The victor shall be myself — and Dionysos.
As for the rest — wait, watch, and listen. (*Exit.*)
CHORUS.   Go, track to the mountains
Dogs of madness,
Run, dogs, run,
Find the daughters of Kadmos,

Snap at their dancing heels, sink your fangs in their brains,
Then turn them loose on the would-be woman,
The spy in the flapping skirts,
Who goes mad for the secret of the possessed.
   His mother will see him first,
As he peers from a rock-wall or cliff-steeple.
She'll scream to the women:
"Look! See what creeps sniffing up to our mountain,
Our mountain, my friends —
This creature crawling across the hillside!
What mothered such a thing?
Not a woman, no — it got life from a lioness
Or a beast heaved up out of African sands."
Now we shall see balance restored.
We shall see it, sharp, clear, a sword
With blood on its edge, driving deep
To the gullet of Pentheus, the blossom of the dragon's jawbone,
Who enforces his will on the forces of life,
Outlaws law,
Orders all other order out of existence.
   And now —
With insane and petty determination,
With intent sick passion,
All his thought corrupted,
All his mind a sewer,
He smells his way to the living heart
Of the mysteries, where Dionysos is born and re-born.
He wants to master with violence that forever-free spirit.
   The laws of all life admit no excuses,
Live by them, live as a man —
That is the way of no pain.
   I don't grudge man his search for knowledge,
I acclaim it, applaud it,
But there is more, there are great things
That must be brought to the daylight,
Made part of our waking and sleeping.
Calmly accept them, peacefully weave them
Into your life — and it will be a good life,
Freeing you.
   Now we shall see balance restored,
We shall see it, sharp, clear, a sword
With blood on its edge, driving deep
To the gullet of Pentheus, the blossom of the dragon's jawbone,
Who enforces his will on the forces of life,
Outlaws law,
Orders all other order out of existence.

Now Dionysos, into the open!
Let him see you . . .
As a BULL!
A dragon, with swarming heads!
A lion, vomiting flames!
Come, Dionysos, come sweetly smiling
And string your noose round the throat of this hunter.
Bring the one-minded women in a pack
To trip him,
Smother him,
Kill him!

(*Enter* PENTHEUS' *own* SERVANT.)

SERVANT.   In this house lived people who were the envy
Of all Greece . . . once. A family begun
In dragon's teeth, a summer harvest reaped
By Kadmos, the great traveller and merchant
Of the western seas. And I am nothing,
An obscure someone who takes orders. And yet
I pity *them.*
　　CHORUS.   What is it? Have you news? Have you been in the hills?
　　SERVANT.   Pentheus is dead, King Pentheus, son of Echion, is dead.
　　CHORUS.   Victory! The first day of Dionysos — now they see you,
　　　now you live, now you face them . . .
　　SERVANT.   What do you mean? How can you say that?
My master is dead. Are you glad? He is dead, *dead!*
　　CHORUS.   Not my master. I've another home, I've another
Life . . . No more fear, no more prison, no more terror . . .
Free, free!
　　SERVANT.   There are still men in Thebes who can . . .
　　CHORUS.   Thebes can't touch me, Thebes has no power . . . Dionysos,
　　　Dionysos comes first for me.
　　SERVANT.   I can forgive the rest, but not this. Terrible things have
　　　happened, and you gloat. It's ugly.
　　CHORUS.   Terrible things? Describe them, tell us, how did the man
　　　die, the wrong-headed master-fool . . .
　　SERVANT.   Behind us were the last houses of Thebes —
We had come out at the river Asopos. Then
We began to climb, mounting the slopes of Kithairon,
Pentheus and I — he was my master, so
I followed him — and this stranger, who
Was to be the guide of our expedition.
Treading very softly, and never speaking,
So that we could see without being seen, we came
First to a glade thick with grass and rested

There . . . It was in a little valley, overhung
On each side with cliffs, and fed by rills
Of water. Pine trees leant over to shade it,
And somewhere in this valley were the women,
The mad women, the Bacchae.
   Then we saw them.
   They're sitting, quietly working and happy. Some
Are re-winding the ivy that slipped off
The tips of their branches. Others, like young mares
Unharnessed from their painted chariots, are playing.
They sing — the tunes sound strange to me, but they
Pick them up and echo each other.
   Though they are everywhere, poor Pentheus sees nothing,
Not one woman. "Stranger," he says, "from where
I stand I can't get a sight of these whores
Who call themselves Bacchae. Perhaps if I went
Up that slope and climbed the trunk of a pine tree
I could have a direct view of their filthy games."
And then — a miracle. There is a pine-tree there
That tickles heaven. As I watch, the stranger
Takes the topmost branch and . . .
Down . . . down . . . down he draws it towards us
Out of the sunlight, into the deep shade
Where we stand. It bends like a bow — or like
A wheel, when its rim is marked out with a compass and traces
A full circle — that's how the stranger, with his bare
Hands, made the mountain pine curve to the ground —
Something no man born of woman
Could have done.
He seats Pentheus on the topmost shoots, then gently
Lets the trunk uncoil, from his grip, being
Very careful not to shake our king from his new throne
Among the leaves, till it towers straight in the air
Again with Pentheus perched astride it . . . Now
It is he who is in view, rather than having
A view himself . . . He is just rising into sight
Above the surrounding trees, when the stranger vanishes,
And out of the air a voice comes —
My belief is — Dionysos spoke then.
"Young women, I bring you this man who intends
To amuse himself with me and my deepest mysteries.
Punish him!"
   While these words still echo in the hills
A pillar of fierce fire is planted between
Earth and heaven . . .
   The air is still now . . .
Silence.

In the cloistered trees not a leaf moves,
The noises of animals cease . . .
The women, not sure what it is they've heard, stand
On tiptoe, glancing this way and that. So,
Once again, he brands the air with his voice.
This time there is no doubt. The daughters
Of Kadmos know their master, and obey.
They begin to run — they dart, they flash, like pigeons
In flight, his mother, Agave, all her sisters,
And the rest of the women, Bacchae! Down through the glade,
Across the stream,
Over the rocks,
Whirled in the tempest of Dionysos' power
They rush — then they see my master sitting
On the pine-tree. First they clamber onto
A rock face opposite and try pelting him
With volleys of sharp stones and javelins made
From pine branches, while others fling
Their ivy-covered sticks . . . Poor man,
He can only be a target . . . But they can't reach him.
Their victim is sitting too high, even for their
Terrible urgency. All the same,
He's trapped. There's nothing he can do. At last
They snap off great oak boughs — a thunderbolt
Could not do it more cleanly, and using the raw
Wood as levers they try to wrench the tree
Up by its roots — and still they can't do it.
They struggle but they can't . . . they can't . . .
"Here," says Agave, "make a circle and take
Hold of the stem, my friends, and we'll catch this agile
Beast. He must never betray the secret of our dancing
For Dionysos!"
    A flurry of hands reach out to the pine tree and tug.
It comes clean out of the earth.
Down from the height where he sits, falling, falling,
Screaming all the time till he dashes against
The rocks, comes Pentheus.
He knows his end is near, knows it will
Be hideous . . .
    His mother is first, chief priestess of the slaughter,
She descends on him. He rips off
The scarf around his head, hoping she'll recognize him,
And spare him, he touches her cheeks, he says, "Mother,
It's your son, Pentheus, the son
You bore in the house of Echion. Mother, pity me,
Have mercy, I have sinned, but don't murder me,
Your own son, for what I've . . . "

But she can't help herself. There's froth on her lips,
Her eyes are rolling, staring, her mind's gone,
She's been seized by a greater power, Dionysos,
And doesn't listen to her son. She grips
His left arm, just below the elbow,
Rams her foot against the poor man's ribs,
And pulls. His arm comes away at the shoulder . . .
That strength didn't come from her — it came
From Dionysos.

Meanwhile, Ino is gouging the other side,
Rending the flesh from his bones, whilst Autonoë
And the whole crowd of the Bacchae press down
On him. His shrieking — so long as there's breath
In his lungs — and their howls of triumph merge
Into one great din. One woman carries
An arm, another, one of his feet, with a sandal
Still on it. His ribs are stripped of skin, the flesh
Hangs in rags. They play with it, they toss
Pieces of Pentheus from hand to bloodstained hand
Like a ball, until the mountain is strewn with fragments
Of his body — some of it under the sheer
Rock-faces, some under the green
Leaves in the depths of the wood. I don't know
How you could find it all again . . .

His mother was left holding his destroyed head.
She impaled it on a wooden spike, as if
It was some mountain lion she had caught in the heart
Of Kithairon, and left her sisters amongst the still-dancing
Women. Now, she's running this way, to the city,
Exulting in her terrible kill. She's praising
Dionysos as her fellow huntsman, the one
Who helps her in the chase, the bringer of bright
Victory . . . But she'll thank him with her tears.

I want to go. I hate suffering. I don't
Want to see Agave come home. The best
And safest thing is to keep a balance in your life,
And acknowledge the great powers around us and in us.
I think that is the meaning of wisdom. If you have
That, and can live that way, you really are
A wise man. (*Exit.*)

CHORUS. Dance him into life!
Move like one,
Shout like one!
The last of the dragon is dead,
Pentheus is dead.
He took woman's clothing,
Picked up a twig, made it live with ivy,

He trusted it —
And it killed him.
And heading him into death was a bull.
Daughters of Kadmos — Bacchae — now you are famous.
The prize —
— and the price —
Of your victory is tears, mourning.
You won the contest at a cost —
Your hands are slippery with your child's
flowing life.

(*Looking offstage.*) Look! She's coming . . . Agave . . .
. . . His mother . . .
Running home . . . her eyes, look at her eyes . .
They're staring, they're mad . . .
Take her into our midst . . . she belongs to the god . . .
And to his happiness.

(*Enter* AGAVE, *carrying the head of* PENTHEUS.)

AGAVE. Women of the east — Bacchae . . .
CHORUS. Why do you use that word? What do you want?
AGAVE. I'm bringing this branch with trailing leaves, I cut it just now
in the mountains, and look — I'm bringing it back home — I had to hunt
— but I tracked it down . . . and now I'm happy . . .
CHORUS. I see . . . join us . . . become one of us . . .
AGAVE. It's a lion cub. I caught it. I didn't need nets. You can see
— look . . .
CHORUS. Where — where did it happen? Where did you find it?
AGAVE. Kithairon . . .
CHORUS. Kithairon?
AGAVE. . . . was the killer.
CHORUS. Who struck first?
AGAVE. I struck first. I. I did it, no one else. When we meet in the
hills, I am the one they envy — I am so lucky.
CHORUS. And who else?
AGAVE. Kadmos, Kadmos . . .
CHORUS. How, Kadmos . . . ?
AGAVE. Had children . . . those children were there,
Shared the hunt — but I was first, I was first.
Happy . . . chasing the beast . . . Come with me
Now . . . to the meal . . .
CHORUS. How can we come . . . What meal?
AGAVE. It's a young bull . . . Here, on his
Cheek, the hair is soft . . .
Just below the crest . . . It grows . . . so sleek.
CHORUS. Yes, that hair could belong to a beast.
It looks like an animal.

AGAVE.   The hounds were whipped on by Dionysos . . .
He sent us hurtling after the prey . . .
He knew its ways, he knows
Us all . . .
    CHORUS.   Yes, our prince leads the hunt.
    AGAVE.   You praise him?
    CHORUS.   I praise him.
    AGAVE.   Then soon all Thebes will.
    CHORUS.   Yes . . . and Pentheus? . . . Your son?
    AGAVE.   Pentheus . . . Yes, he will praise his mother because she
caught this young wild lion.
    CHORUS.   But think what it is.
    AGAVE.   No! Think how I did it.
    CHORUS.   You're proud?
    AGAVE.   I'm happy. We did great, great things — as all the world
will see — when we hunted today.
    CHORUS.   Then show your trophy, poor woman, show it to everyone.
Let people see what you brought home from the day's hunting.
    AGAVE.   Men and women of Thebes, our city of high
Towers, so well defended, come and see
What I brought home from the wild country for you. —
    A beast . . . We tracked him down, we daughters of Kadmos.
We used no snares, no traps,
No spears forged in the workshops of Thessaly —
Only our hands we used, our soft, white,
Delicate hands — they were our spears.
And hunters boast of their machines, their useless
Contraptions of steel and wire . . . we caught this beast
And tore it limb from limb with only our hands . . .
Where is my father? I want him here. And where
Is Pentheus, where's my son? . . .
    Go, someone, find a ladder, and lean it
Against the palace and nail this trophy against
The beam ends. I want everyone to see
What I have brought home from the hunt . . .

    (*Enter* KADMOS, *helping* SERVANTS *to carry the body of* PENTHEUS.)

    KADMOS.   This way . . . Stay close to me . . . This way . . .
He seems so heavy . . . like my grief — now,
Lay him down — there . . .
    Pentheus has come home.
    I searched, hoping and looking, hoping and looking —
It was so hard to see them, scattered among the trees —
No two parts together, all over Kithairon . . .
Those steep paths! — I have no strength left . . .
Well, here is his body, I found it.

I had just reached the city with Teiresias
After paying our tribute to Dionysos when
I heard of the monstrous thing my daughters had done.
Back I went, back, back to the mountainside
To bring home my grandson — or what remained
After the women . . . What was in their minds then? . . .
I saw Akteon's mother in the forest,
Autonoë, and Ino with her — it was hideous . . .
Their contorted bodies, writhing, jerking . . .
Then someone told me the same driving force
Had guided Agave here . . . Yes, they were right . . .
There she is . . . I see . . .
No, no . . . I don't want to see!
    AGAVE.   Father, be proud, you should be — especially now —
The proudest man alive. You have such daughters
No one, no one in the world, could
Surpass them . . . I speak for us all, but I have gone
Far beyond the others. I don't spin.
And weave now. I have progressed.
Now I hunt — with my bare hands — wild beasts!
And look . . . the pickings of my success.
Here — for you — my newborn glory;
Hang him against your palace wall — take him,
Father — here . . . Can't you feel the joy, the glory
Of my kill too? Tell your friends to come,
To celebrate with you — because you have much
To be thankful for, much to celebrate.
Think of the great things we have done today.
    KADMOS.   Can I measure hurt like this . . . No, no way of . . .
I can't even look . . . The great things you've done — yes,
The great murders, the blood, the . . . !
Oh, fling your thanksgiving before some deity.
He'll love it!
And you tell the people they must celebrate . . .
You tell me!
Celebrate! . . . (He weeps.)
For you, my child, this is for you . . .
And for me. Oh, Dionysos is right,
But he is not fair!
Being so right, he has broken us . . . But then
He was born here, this is his home . . .
    AGAVE.   Old men! All they do is grumble.
And they always look so grim. I wish my son
Was happy hunting. I wish he was like his mother.
She goes out and runs with the young women
Of Thebes till they track down an animal. But all
He can do is oppose the forces from which

We draw life. You should speak to him, father,
You should advise him . . . Someone — go and fetch him.
I want him to see me in the full flood of my joy.

    KADMOS (*a cry is wrenched from him*). You'll know — you must!
        You'll see
What you've done, and the pain will wring tears
From you . . .
And yet, if you never wake from the dream you're in . . .
Well, it won't be happiness — but you'll feel no pain.

    AGAVE.   Is something wrong? Are you angry with me, father?

    KADMOS.   Look up at the sky.

    AGAVE.   There . . . What do you expect me to see?

    KADMOS.   Does it look the same to you, or do you see
A change?

    AGAVE.   It looks brighter than before,
Not so blurred.

    KADMOS.   And inside you —
Do you still feel this sense of flying?

    AGAVE.   I don't . . .
Understand . . . Wait. Something's happening.
My head! . . . There's a change . . . somewhere
Inside, the mind shifts . . . Yes, I feel . . .

    KADMOS.   Listen to me.
Do you know what I'm saying? Can you answer me?

    AGAVE.   I've forgotten . . . What were we talking about,
Father?

    KADMOS.   When you were married, do you remember whose house
you came to?

    AGAVE.   You . . . gave me to . . .
Didn't they say his name was . . . Echion of the
Dragon's seed?

    KADMOS.   And you had a son.
Your husband gave you a son. What was his name?

    AGAVE.   Pentheus — child of our true married love.

    KADMOS.   Now look at the face that lies between your
Hands. Whose is it?

    AGAVE.   It's a lion . . . You see . . . they . . . they told me
So — the hunters . . . the women.

    KADMOS.   Look! Look properly. It won't take long.
It's easy.

    AGAVE (*obeys, gives a shriek*). What is it — this . . . thing! I'm
        carrying?
Oh, dear God! What is this?

    KADMOS.   Open your eyes, and see. You can't mistake
The face.

    AGAVE.   This foul wound, this foul . . . object!
I can't bear it . . . !

KADMOS.   Does it look like a lion
To you?
    AGAVE.   No . . . It's Pentheus . . . My son . . .
Your head . . . your poor . . .
    KADMOS.   My tears flowed for him long before
You knew who he was.
    AGAVE.   Who killed him? How
Did he come here? How am I holding him?
    KADMOS.   You will have to hear something . . . abominable.
Perhaps you are not ready . . .
    AGAVE.   Tell me! I'll choke,
My heart's bursting — I must know!
    KADMOS.   You,
And your sisters with you, murdered him.
    AGAVE.   Where?
Where did he die? Here in the palace?
    KADMOS.   No.
You remember where, long ago, Akteon
Was savaged by his hounds . . .
    AGAVE.   On Kithairon!
But why did the poor fool go there?
    KADMOS.   He went to jeer at Dionysos, and your dancing
In his honour.
    AGAVE.   And we destroyed him . . . But what happened?
    KADMOS.   You have no minds left. The whole city
Was convulsed. Dionysos was in possession.
    AGAVE.   Dionysos took us and laid us waste. Now
I see it.
    KADMOS.   He was displaced. He was usurped.
You did not believe he had power.
    AGAVE.   Where
Is my child's body? . . . Father, I loved him . . . Where is he?
    KADMOS.   I brought him home. It was hard — but I found him.
    AGAVE.   Are the limbs . . . is his body . . . a body . . . or . . . ?
    KADMOS.   He lies there.
    AGAVE.   Pentheus, Pentheus — my only son — my child.
    KADMOS.   Yes, your son — and your heir . . .
Heir to your madness.
    AGAVE.   But how could that touch Pentheus? How
Could he inherit that from me?
    KADMOS.   He took
From you his stubbornness. He would not open
Himself to Dionysos — and we all suffered
For his fault. In a sense, he united us,
The whole family, because now we are all, like him,
Shattered fragments.
    And I, who never had a son, only

This grandson, your boy, I'm left with nothing,
Just a carcass, a shamefully mutilated
Corpse . . . That was once the hope, the new
Life of my family . . . Pentheus, my child,
You were our centre, you gave us permanence,
Child of my child, and you were strict with them all
In Thebes. I was an old man, but people
Took notice of me, they respected me, so long as
You were there. If they did not, you would pick out
The culprit and punish him. But now I,
Kadmos, Kadmos the great, I'll be banished —
No home, no rights — and I was the man who sowed
The seed of Thebes, and the harvest I reaped was the greatest
Of our time. Child I loved best —
And now I can no longer say that.
There's nothing left — never again will you touch
My beard, put your arm round me, and say, "Father
Of my mother, who has hurt you, who denies you
Your rights? Come, grandfather, who troubles you,
Who is unkind to you? Tell me. If anyone
Has done you wrong I will have him whipped!"
     I have only my grief now, and you are a memory.
If anyone thinks that his own mind alone
Can govern the world, he should see Pentheus here
And believe, believe there are other powers,
Ones he does not dominate.
     CHORUS. I grieve for you, Kadmos. Your grandson died for a good
reason, but it hurt you.
     AGAVE. Father, you see how all my daylight reason
Dawns again in me. I see, I think,
I feel, and as clearly as you,
I know that I am a murderer for my sacrifice
To Dionysos. The victim is dead; the priestess
Lives polluted.
But Pentheus is my son in my heart still,
The son I gave life to and watched over. I want to
Give him one last gift.
I want to arrange his body for the grave,
Though he'll never know of it — the dead feel no
Gratitude for favours to their unfeeling limbs.
     KADMOS. He was your child; I can't refuse you. Be gentle
With his body — you were not before. I have laid him there
As if he were asleep. Do not disturb him.
     AGAVE. Pentheus, my son . . .
My baby . . .
You lay in my arms so often, so helpless,
And now again you need my loving care,

My dear, dear child . . .
I killed you.
No! I will not say that. I was not there. I was . . .
I was in some other place . . .
It was Dionysos. Dionysos took me, Dionysos
Used me, and Dionysos murdered you!
   DIONYSOS.   No! (DIONYSOS *as a god now becomes visible above them*
     all.)
Accuse yourselves, accept the guilt,
You let Pentheus rule you, you were happy being ruled,
And for his sake you locked me out of your city.
And so Thebes will have new masters,
An army from the east will live in your homes,
Walk your streets, plough your fields.
Agave — you and your sisters have no place here.
Your home now is . . . wherever a murderer
Can find rest or peace — but not in Thebes.
And you — Kadmos — you must begin again. You must
Forfeit your human shape, and become a dragon.
Your wife, daughter of the spirit of war, Harmony,
Will also be transfigured — into a snake. Then,
With your bride, you'll drive in a chariot hauled
By young bulls, at the head of an army from
The east. With countless men at your command
You will plunder city after city. But once they
Have wrecked the sanctuary where Apollo speaks
Of things to come — their luck will change, they
Will be defeated, and then disperse. The war-spirit, however,
Will rescue you and Harmony, and keep you both alive
In the world of the undying . . .
This is the universal will of Zeus and
I tell you these things with authority from him. I am
Dionysos, his son — I will always return to life.
   If you had understood what wholeness is, you
Would now be happy, the son of Zeus would be
Helping you, a friend, an ally.
But you did not want that.
   KADMOS.   Dionysos, listen to us, we have been wrong . . .
   DIONYSOS.   Now you understand, but now is too late.
When you should have seen, you were blind.
   KADMOS.   We know that.
But you are like a tide that turns and drowns us.
   DIONYSOS.   Because I was born with dominion over you
And you dispossessed me.
   KADMOS.   Then you should not
Be like us, your subjects. You should have no passions.

DIONYSOS. And I don't. But these are laws of life. I cannot
Change them.

AGAVE (weeps). It is decided, father. We must leave
And take our sorrow with us.

DIONYSOS. Why delay?
You can change nothing now. (*He vanishes.*)

KADMOS. My child, we have suffered cruelly, all of us —
I did not escape . . .
I am an old man, and I must leave my home,
Go to a foreign country. And then, I am told,
My destiny is to lead this strange army
Into Greece.
I shall be a dragon, my wife, a dragon; myself
And Harmony, beasts, no longer human, will bring
War to the calm altars and graves of Greece.
There will be no end to the suffering, not even in the country
Of the dead; I am to be allowed no peace.

AGAVE. Father, I shall lose you, never see my home again . . .

KADMOS. No, don't hold me, my poor child . . . Why?
I'm old, a grey, dying swan — the young
Bird can't protect it . . .

AGAVE. Where shall I go?
I have no country. What will happen to me? . . .

KADMOS. I don't know, my daughter, your father is weak.
He is tired, he is no use.

AGAVE. Goodbye, my home,
Goodbye, my city. I am leaving you. I have no
Place here. I am cursed.

KADMOS. Go now, Agave . . .

AGAVE. Father! Come here! . . . I want to hold you . . .

KADMOS. Look, my tears . . . for you and for your sisters.

AGAVE. In our lives Dionysos has been a spirit
Of havoc, cruel, relentless . . .

KADMOS. But only because
He was thrust aside, and no one let him in
Here. The cruelty was yours.

AGAVE. Goodbye, father . . .

KADMOS. Goodbye — daughter — though what is there good in it?

AGAVE (*to* PEOPLE OF THEBES). Please, my friends, will you help me?
Take me to my sisters, who will share my exile
And the years of sorrow with me.
I want to be where Kithairon can't shadow my life —
Where I don't even have to see its distant slopes . . .
Take me where branches wound with ivy
Can't remind me of what has happened.
Let someone else be possessed.
I have withered.

CHORUS.   The forces of life are seen in disguise,
A thousand disguises.
They make all things possible,
They guarantee nothing,
What you thought was forgotten, buried,
They conceive, and bring to birth again.
Today you have watched their power at work —
It never ends.

Curtain

Whether Christopher Marlowe (1564–1593) was the real author of Shakespeare's plays, as some claim, or not, he was in his own right a brilliant, vibrant personality, a poet-dramatist of genuine importance. That he died, according to tradition, in a tavern brawl when he was only twenty-nine was clearly a loss to English literature. What might he have written after such works as *Tamburlaine the Great* (1587–1588) or *Edward II* (1591–1593)? His fantasy, his command of imagery, his talent for dramatic effects indicate that he probably would have developed into an even more considerable literary figure than Shakespeare.

Marlowe, like Shakespeare and indeed most of the Elizabethan dramatists, based *Doctor Faustus* (1588–1592) on another work, a German original, *Historia von D. Johann Fausten* (1587), which he may have known from an English translation. The Faust legend is an old one, and it was useful in the medieval Christian tradition not only for maintaining a strong fear of evil and damnation but also for discouraging too much thirst for knowledge and power. Earlier versions than Marlowe's were frankly offered as admonitions against seeking forbidden things. Only in Marlowe's version (and much later in Goethe's) is the great spirit of Man, striving for ever more wisdom and mastery — not so much for his own gain as for a better understanding of what or who he is — the vital center of the drama. Marlowe's Faustus is the epitome of the learned Renaissance man, and his vanity and curiosity drive him to pay any price to acquire more knowledge and the power that goes with it. Although he shows passing interest in riches, fame, women, and other luxuries, his restless spirit is always thrusting out to understand more about the world and its history.

The seeming emphasis on the magical and the wonderful in *Doctor Faustus* may present a problem to some readers. But the Good Angel and the Bad Angel, for instance, Marlovian borrowings from the medieval theatre tradition which had but recently been suppressed in England along with Roman Catholicism, are not merely simplistic devices in Marlowe's play. They externalize the terrible debate raging inside Faustus and point it up for those who may be more attracted to theatrical tricks than to thought. They heighten tension; they define conflict; they offer competing rewards and threats. Since they appear more than once, they also lend some unity to the relatively episodic plot and intensify Faust's inner struggle by repeating their offers, like T. S. Eliot's four tempters in *Murder in the Cathedral*.

Even today, productions tend to emphasize the magic and the spectacle, perhaps in the mistaken belief that audiences who may have either lost or never had a faith cannot understand the credos and taboos of Faustus' world or empathize with his emotional and intellectual turmoil. The scene with the Pope often proves the most successful with audiences. Mephistophilis often makes his entrances and exits in a colored cloud from a smokepot. The procession of the Seven Deadly Sins is heightened with surrealistic lighting and fantastic costumes. At Stratford-upon-Avon a few years ago, Helen appeared naked.

There is evidence that some of the visual hi-jinx written into the play are not Marlowe's work at all but inserted by others, who, like Shakespeare, were well aware of what the ignorant groundlings wanted in the Elizabethan theatre. The farcical scene with the Pope, for instance, may not be Marlowe's (he was, in fact, charged with being a secret Catholic shortly before his death). Nonetheless, it must have appealed enormously to audiences in the late sixteenth century. Elizabeth I was on the throne, and her own father had but recently broken with Rome. Recent converts and Anglican leaders alike must have welcomed this hilarious repudiation of the Italianate Catholic Church.

Faustus' fantastic bargain with Mephistophilis has great dramatic meaning only within the religious conventions of a believing society, and the Londoners of that period were fervent believers for the most part. Faustus has real courage to pawn his soul for more knowledge and power. In a world but slowly emerging from the medieval theocracy which had, despite the many separate feudal domains, imposed an intellectual and spiritual unity on Europe, such a thing was almost unthinkable.

Analogically, it is Faustus' search for mastery, understanding, and power that is important. It is daily repeated in modern life, just as it was four hundred years ago, though the price paid by such searchers as astronauts, heart surgeons, or revolutionaries may be quite different. Figuratively, man is still giving up his soul for gifts and secrets he feels he must have — only to find that his winnings are ashes and his inner losses catastrophes.

Marlowe's aim is hardly to discourage the search for knowledge or discredit learned men. Rather, he seems fascinated by the heroic, tragic daring of Faustus' blasphemy. If magical power or sensual gratification were Faustus' only goals, he would still have been a forbiddingly fascinating character, but his serious pursuit of knowledge makes him something more — it gives him nobility and dignity even in his failure. It also sets him apart from the simple, god- and law-fearing folk who do not challenge or threaten the established order, who accept the world in which they find themselves and do not ask embarrassing questions about life after death or government in this.

G.L.

CHRISTOPHER MARLOWE

Doctor Faustus[1]

Characters

CHORUS

DR. JOHN FAUSTUS

WAGNER, *his servant, a student*

VALDES,
CORNELIUS, } *his friends, magicians*

THREE SCHOLARS, *students under Faustus*

AN OLD MAN

POPE ADRIAN

RAYMOND, *King of Hungary*

BRUNO, *the rival pope*

CARDINALS OF FRANCE and PADUA

THE ARCHBISHOP OF RHEIMS

CHARLES V, *Emperor of Germany*

MARTINO,
FREDERICK, } *knights at the Emperor's court*
BENVOLIO,

DUKE OF SAXONY

DUKE OF VANHOLT

DUCHESS OF VANHOLT

ROBIN, *also called the* CLOWN

DICK

A VINTNER

A HORSE-COURSER

A CARTER

THE HOSTESS *at an inn*

THE GOOD ANGEL

THE BAD ANGEL

MEPHOSTOPHILIS

LUCIFER

BELZEBUB

SPIRITS *presenting* THE SEVEN DEADLY SINS
　　　　　　　　ALEXANDER THE GREAT
　　　　　　　　ALEXANDER'S PARAMOUR
　　　　　　　　DARIUS, *King of Persia*
　　　　　　　　HELEN OF TROY

DEVILS, BISHOPS, MONKS, SOLDIERS *and* ATTENDANTS

[1] This edition is based on the quarto of 1616, known as the B1 text, with some readings from the A texts of 1604, 1609, and 1611.

Lines have been renumbered for this edition.

PROLOGUE

(*Enter* CHORUS.)

CHORUS. Not marching in the fields of Thrasimene,
Where Mars did mate the warlike Carthagens,
Nor sporting in the dalliance of love
In courts of kings, where state is overturned,
Nor in the pomp of proud audacious deeds,   5
Intends our Muse to vaunt his heavenly verse:
Only this, Gentles — we must now perform
The form of Faustus' fortunes, good or bad.
And now to patient judgements we appeal,
And speak for Faustus in his infancy.   10
Now is he born, of parents base of stock,
In Germany, within a town called Rhode:
At riper years to Wittenberg he went,
Whereas his kinsmen chiefly brought him up;
So much he profits in divinity,   15
The fruitful plot of scholarism graced,
That shortly he was graced with doctor's name,
Excelling all, whose sweet delight disputes
In th' heavenly matters of theology.
Till, swollen with cunning, of a self-conceit,   20
His waxen wings did mount above his reach,
And, melting, heavens conspired his overthrow:
For, falling to a devilish exercise,
And glutted now with learning's golden gifts,
He surfeits upon cursed necromancy: 25
Nothing so sweet as magic is to him,
Which he prefers before his chiefest bliss:
And this the man that in his study sits. (*Exit.*)

ACT ONE

Scene 1

(FAUSTUS *in his study.*)

FAUSTUS. Settle thy studies, Faustus, and begin
To sound the depth of that thou wilt profess;

Prologue, line 14. **Whereas:** where. 17. **graced:** at Cambridge a new Doctor
of Divinity was enrolled in the Book of Grace. 20. **cunning:** knowledge (usually
knowledge misapplied). **self-conceit:** pride in his own abilities. 21–22. **His . . .
overthrow:** Icarus flew too near the sun on wings of wax; they melted and he fell
into the sea. 27. **chiefest bliss:** *i.e.*, hope of salvation.

Act I, Scene i, 2. **profess:** specialize in, study and teach.

Having commenced, be a divine in show,
Yet level at the end of every art,
And live and die in Aristotle's works.   5
Sweet *Analytics*, 'tis thou hast ravished me:
Bene disserere est finis logices.
Is to dispute well logic's chiefest end?
Affords this art no greater miracle?
Then read no more, thou hast attained that end;   10
A greater subject fitteth Faustus' wit.
Bid *on kai me on* farewell; Galen come:
Seeing, *ubi desinit philosophus, ibi incipit medicus.*
Be a physician Faustus, heap up gold,
And be eternized for some wondrous cure.   15
Summum bonum medicinae sanitas:
The end of physic is our body's health.
Why Faustus, hast thou not attained that end?
Is not thy common talk sound aphorisms?
Are not thy bills hung up as monuments,   20
Whereby whole cities have escaped the plague,
And thousand desperate maladies been cured?
Yet art thou still but Faustus, and a man.
Couldst thou make men to live eternally,
Or, being dead, raise them to life again,   25
Then this profession were to be esteemed.
Physic farewell! Where is Justinian?
Si una eademque res legatur duobus,
Alter rem, alter valorem rei etc.
A petty case of paltry legacies!   30
Exhereditare filium non potest pater nisi ...
Such is the subject of the Institute,
And universal body of the law.
This study fits a mercenary drudge,
Who aims at nothing but external trash,   35
Too servile and illiberal for me.
When all is done, divinity is best:

3. **commenced:** graduated (a Cambridge term). **in show:** in appearance; show that you are indeed a student of theology. 4. **level ... art:** consider the purpose of every discipline. 12. **on kai me on:** being and not being. 13. **ubi ... medicus:** since the doctor starts where the philosopher leaves off (Aristotle, *de sensu*, 436a). 15. **eternized:** immortalized. 16. **Summum . . . sanitas** (Aristotle, *Nichomachean Ethics*, 1094.a.8). 19. **aphorisms:** medical precepts; after the Aphorisms of Hippocrates. 20. **bills:** prescriptions. 28–29. **Si . . . rei:** if one and the same thing is bequeathed to two persons, one should have the thing itself, the other the value of the thing (Justinian, *Institutes*, ii.20). 31. **Exhereditare ... nisi:** a father cannot disinherit his son unless ... (Justinian, ii.13).

Jerome's Bible Faustus, view it well:
Stipendium peccati mors est: ha! *Stipendium, etc.*
The reward of sin is death? That's hard.   40
Si peccasse negamus, fallimur, et nulla est in nobis veritas:
If we say that we have no sin, we deceive ourselves, and there is no truth
in us. Why then, belike, we must sin, and so consequently die.
Ay, we must die an everlasting death.
What doctrine call you this? *Che sarà, sarà:*   45
What will be, shall be. Divinity adieu!
These metaphysics of magicians,
And necromantic books are heavenly;
Lines, circles, signs, letters and characters!
Ay, these are those that Faustus most desires.   50
O what a world of profit and delight,
Of power, of honour, of omnipotence,
Is promised to the studious artisan!
All things that move between the quiet poles
Shall be at my command: emperors and kings,   55
Are but obeyed in their several provinces,
Nor can they raise the wind, or rend the clouds;
But his dominion that exceeds in this,
Stretcheth as far as doth the mind of man:
A sound magician is a mighty god;   60
Here Faustus, try thy brains to gain a deity.

(*Enter* WAGNER.)

Wagner, commend me to my dearest friends,
The German Valdes and Cornelius,
Request them earnestly to visit me.
   WAGNER.   I will sir. (*Exit.*)   65
   FAUSTUS.   Their conference will be a greater help to me,
Than all my labours, plod I ne'er so fast.

(*Enter the* ANGEL *and* SPIRIT.)

   GOOD ANGEL.   O Faustus, lay that damned book aside,
And gaze not on it lest it tempt thy soul,
And heap God's heavy wrath upon thy head: 70
Read, read the Scriptures; that is blasphemy.
   BAD ANGEL.   Go forward Faustus in that famous art
Wherein all nature's treasury is contained:

---

38. **Jerome's Bible:** the Vulgate, prepared mainly by St. Jerome; but the texts
Faustus quotes are not in the words of the Vulgate. 39. *Stipendium . . . est*
(Romans, vi, 23). 41. *Si . . . veritas* (I John, i, 8). 47. **metaphysics:** supernatural sciences. 53. **artisan:** craftsman. 54. **quiet poles:** the poles of the universe, quiet because unmoving. 56. **several:** respective. 58. **this:** this art, magic.

Be thou on earth as Jove is in the sky,
Lord and commander of these elements. 75

(*Exeunt* ANGELS.)

FAUSTUS. How am I glutted with conceit of this!
Shall I make spirits fetch me what I please?
Resolve me of all ambiguities?
Perform what desperate enterprise I will?
I'll have them fly to India for gold; 80
Ransack the ocean for orient pearl,
And search all corners of the new-found-world
For pleasant fruits, and princely delicates.
I'll have them read me strange philosophy,
And tell the secrets of all foreign kings: 85
I'll have them wall all Germany with brass,
And make swift Rhine, circle fair Wittenberg:
I'll have them fill the public schools with silk,
Wherewith the students shall be bravely clad.
I'll levy soldiers with the coin they bring, 90
And chase the Prince of Parma from our land,
And reign sole king of all our provinces.
Yea, stranger engines for the brunt of war,
Than was the fiery keel at Antwerp's bridge,
I'll make my servile spirits to invent. 95
Come German Valdes and Cornelius,
And make me blest with your sage conference.

(*Enter* VALDES *and* CORNELIUS.)

Valdes, sweet Valdes, and Cornelius!
Know that your words have won me at the last
To practise magic and concealed arts; 100
Yet not your words only, but mine own fantasy,
That will receive no object for my head,
But ruminates on necromantic skill.
Philosophy is odious and obscure;
Both law and physic are for petty wits; 105
Divinity is basest of the three,
Unpleasant, harsh, contemptible and vile.
'Tis magic, magic that hath ravished me.

---

76. **glutted with conceit:** drunk with the thought. 83. **delicates:** delicacies.
88. **public schools:** university lecture rooms. **silk:** in Marlowe's day undergraduates were ordered to dress soberly. 89. **bravely:** smartly. 91. **Prince of
Parma:** Spanish governor-general of the Netherlands, 1579–1592. 93. **engines:**
machines. **brunt:** assault. 94. **bridge:** a bridge across the Scheldt, constructed
by the Duke of Parma in the blockade of Antwerp; attacked and destroyed by a
fire-ship in April, 1585. 100. **concealed:** occult.

Then gentle friends, aid me in this attempt,
And I, that have with concise syllogisms   110
Gravelled the pastors of the German church
And made the flowering pride of Wittenberg
Swarm to my problems, as th'infernal spirits
On sweet Musaeus when he came to hell,
Will be as cunning as Agrippa was,   115
Whose shadows made all Europe honour him.

    VALDES.   Faustus, these books, thy wit, and our experience
Shall make all nations to canonise us.
As Indian Moors obey their Spanish lords
So shall the spirits of every element   120
Be always serviceable to us three;
Like lions shall they guard us when we please,
Like Almaine rutters with their horsemen's staves,
Or Lapland giants trotting by our sides;
Sometimes like women or unwedded maids,   125
Shadowing more beauty in their airy brows,
Than have the white breasts of the Queen of Love.
From Venice shall they drag huge argosies,
And from America the golden fleece,
That yearly stuffs old Philip's treasury,   130
If learned Faustus will be resolute.

    FAUSTUS.   Valdes, as resolute am I in this,
As thou to live, therefore object it not.

    CORNELIUS.   The miracles that magic will perform,
Will make thee vow to study nothing else.   135
He that is grounded in astrology,
Enriched with tongues, well seen in minerals,
Hath all the principles magic doth require:
Then doubt not Faustus but to be renowned,
And more frequented for this mystery,   140
Than heretofore the Delphian oracle.

---

110. **concise syllogisms**: trenchant argument. 111. **Gravelled**: confounded, perplexed. 113. **problems**: topics of scholarly debate. 114. **Musaeus**: a legendary pre-Homeric bard often confused (as perhaps here) with Orpheus. (*Aeneid* vi.667–668 describes Musaeus in the Elysian fields and *Georgics* iv tells of spirits swarming round Orpheus in the Underworld.) 115. **Agrippa**: Henry Cornelius Agrippa von Nettesheim (1486–1535), magician and necromancer, famous for his reputed power of invoking shades of the dead. 119. **Moors**: dark-skinned natives (here specifically American Indians). 123. **Like . . . staves**: like German cavalry with lances. 128. **argosies**: treasure ships. 129–130. **America . . . treasury**: America, whose richness is compared to the golden fleece sought by Jason and the Argonauts, paid annual tribute to Philip of Spain. 133. **object it not**: don't raise such objections. 136. **grounded in**: well schooled in. 137. **well seen in minerals**: informed about the properties of minerals. 140. **more . . . mystery**: more sought after for practising this art. 141. **Delphian oracle**: the oracle of Apollo at Delphi.

The spirits tell me they can dry the sea,
And fetch the treasure of all foreign wrecks;
Yea, all the wealth that our forefathers hid,
Within the massy entrails of the earth: 145
Then tell me, Faustus, what shall we three want?
    FAUSTUS.   Nothing Cornelius! O this cheers my soul!
Come, show me some demonstrations magical,
That I may conjure in some lusty grove,
And have these joys in full possession.   150
    VALDES.   Then haste thee to some solitary grove,
And bear wise Bacon's and Abanus' works,
The Hebrew Psalter, and New Testament;
And whatsoever else is requisite,
We will inform thee ere our conference cease.   155
    CORNELIUS.   Valdes, first let him know the words of art,
And then, all other ceremonies learnt,
Faustus may try his cunning by himself.
    VALDES.   First I'll instruct him in the rudiments,
And then wilt thou be perfecter than I.   160
    FAUSTUS.   Then come and dine with me, and after meat
We'll canvass every quiddity thereof:
For ere I sleep, I'll try what I can do:
This night I'll conjure though I die therefore.

        (Exeunt omnes.)

                        Scene 2

(Enter two SCHOLARS.)

    FIRST SCHOLAR.   I wonder what's become of Faustus, that was wont to
make our schools ring with *sic probo*.
    SECOND SCHOLAR.   That shall we presently know; here comes his boy.

(Enter WAGNER.)

    FIRST SCHOLAR.   How now sirra, where's thy master?
    WAGNER.   God in heaven knows.
    SECOND SCHOLAR.   Why, dost not thou know then?   6
    WAGNER.   Yes, I know, but that follows not.
    FIRST SCHOLAR.   Go to sirra, leave your jesting, and tell us where he is.

---

145. massy: solid.   162. canvass every quiddity: explore every detail.   quiddity:
a scholastic term denoting the essence of a thing, that which makes it what it is.
    Scene ii, 2. *sic probo:* I prove it thus (a term from scholastic disputation).
3. presently: at once.

WAGNER. That follows not by force of argument, which you, being licentiates, should stand upon, therefore acknowledge your error, and be attentive.

SECOND SCHOLAR. Then you will not tell us? 12

WAGNER. You are deceived, for I will tell you: yet if you were not dunces, you would never ask me such a question. For is he not *corpus naturale?* And is not that *mobile?* Then wherefore should you ask me such a question? But that I am by nature phlegmatic, slow to wrath, and prone to lechery — to love, I would say — it were not for you to come within forty foot of the place of execution, although I do not doubt but to see you both hanged the next sessions. Thus having triumphed over you, I will set my countenance like a precisian, and begin to speak thus: Truly my dear brethren, my master is within at dinner, with Valdes and Cornelius, as this wine, if it could speak, would inform your worships: and so the Lord bless you, preserve you, and keep you, my dear brethren. (*Exit.*) 24

FIRST SCHOLAR. Nay then, I fear he is fallen into that damned art, for which they two are infamous through the world.

SECOND SCHOLAR. Were he a stranger, and not allied to me, yet should I grieve for him. But come, let us go and inform the Rector, and see if he by his grave counsel can reclaim him.

FIRST SCHOLAR. I fear me, nothing will reclaim him now. 30

SECOND SCHOLAR. Yet let us see what we can do.

(*Exeunt.*)

Scene 3

(*Thunder. Enter* LUCIFER *and four* DEVILS *above.* FAUSTUS *to them, with this speech.*)

FAUSTUS. Now that the gloomy shadow of the earth,
Longing to view Orion's drizzling look,
Leaps from th'antarctic world unto the sky,
And dims the welkin, with her pitchy breath:
Faustus, begin thine incantations, 5
And try if devils will obey thy hest,
Seeing thou hast prayed and sacrificed to them.

10. **licentiates:** graduates; holders of a degree permitting them to study for higher (master's or doctor's) degrees. 14–15. *corpus . . . mobile:* a natural body and as such capable of movement. Aristotle's *corpus naturale seu mobile* was the current scholastic definition of the subject matter of physics. 18. **place of execution:** the dining room; Wagner continues to make comic capital out of the phrase. 20. **precisian:** Puritan. 28. **Rector:** head of the university.

Scene iii, 7. **prayed and sacrificed:** a period of prayer and sacrifice, a kind of spiritual preparation, was a prerequisite for conjuring.

Within this circle is Jehovah's name,
Forward and backward anagrammatised:
Th'abbreviated names of holy saints,   10
Figures of every adjunct to the heavens,
And characters of signs and erring stars,
By which the spirits are enforced to rise:
Then fear not Faustus, but be resolute
And try the uttermost magic can perform.   15

(*Thunder.*)

*Sint mihi dei Acherontis propitii, valeat numen triplex Jehovae; ignei,
aerii, aquatici, terreni spiritus salvete! Orientis princeps, Belzebub inferni
ardentis monarcha, et Demogorgon, propitiamus vos, ut appareat, et surgat
Mephostophilis.*   19

(*Dragon.*)

*Quid tu moraris? Per Jehovam, Gehennam, et consecratam aquam, quam
nunc spargo; signumque crucis quod nunc facio; et per vota nostra, ipse
nunc surgat nobis dicatus Mephostophilis.*   22

(*Enter a* DEVIL.)

I charge thee to return, and change thy shape,
Thou art too ugly to attend on me:
Go and return an old Franciscan friar,   25
That holy shape becomes a devil best.

(*Exit* DEVIL.)

8–13. **Within . . . rise:** before he began his conjuring the magician would draw
a circle round himself, inscribing on the periphery certain signs (of the zodiac, for
instance) and the tetragrammaton, the four Hebrew letters of the Divine Name.
This was not only part of the invocation; so long as the circle was unbroken and
the magician stayed inside it, no evil spirit could harm him.   11. **adjunct:** heavenly body fixed to the firmament.   12. **characters:** symbols.   **signs and erring
stars:** signs of the zodiac and planets.   16–22. *Sint . . . Mephostophilis:* May the
gods of Acheron look with favour upon me. Away with the spirit of the threefold
Jehovah. Welcome, spirits of fire, air, water and earth. We ask your favour, O
prince of the East, Belzebub, monarch of burning hell, and Demogorgon, that
Mephostophilis may appear and rise. Why do you delay? By Jehovah, Gehenna,
and the holy water which I now sprinkle, and the sign of the cross which I now
form, and by our vows, may Mephostophilis himself now rise, compelled to obey
us.   17. *Belzebub:* Marlowe's form of the name has been retained because at certain points (*e.g.*, II.i.12) this suits better with the metre than the more commonly used Hebraic *Beëlzebub.*   23–24. **I . . . me:** the wary magician always
stipulated from the beginning that a pleasing shape would be assumed.

I see there's virtue in my heavenly words!
Who would not be proficient in this art?
How pliant is this Mephostophilis,
Full of obedience and humility,   30
Such is the force of magic and my spells.
Now Faustus, thou art conjuror laureate
That canst command great Mephostophilis.
Quin redis, Mephostophilis, fratris imagine!

(*Enter* MEPHOSTOPHILIS.)

MEPHOSTOPHILIS.   Now Faustus, what wouldst thou have me do?   35
FAUSTUS.   I charge thee wait upon me whilst I live
To do whatever Faustus shall command:
Be it to make the moon drop from her sphere,
Or the ocean to overwhelm the world.
MEPHOSTOPHILIS.   I am a servant to great Lucifer,   40
And may not follow thee without his leave;
No more than he commands, must we perform.
FAUSTUS.   Did not he charge thee to appear to me?
MEPHOSTOPHILIS.   No, I came now hither of mine own accord.
FAUSTUS.   Did not my conjuring speeches raise thee? Speak!   45
MEPHOSTOPHILIS.   That was the cause, but yet *per accidens*:
For when we hear one rack the name of God,
Abjure the Scriptures, and his saviour Christ,
We fly in hope to get his glorious soul;
Nor will we come unless he use such means,   50
Whereby he is in danger to be damned:
Therefore the shortest cut for conjuring
Is stoutly to abjure the Trinity,
And pray devoutly to the prince of hell.
FAUSTUS.   So Faustus hath already done, and holds this principle: 55
There is no chief but only Belzebub,
To whom Faustus doth dedicate himself.
This word 'damnation' terrifies not him,
For he confounds hell in Elysium:
His ghost be with the old philosophers.   60
But leaving these vain trifles of men's souls,
Tell me, what is that Lucifer thy lord?
MEPHOSTOPHILIS.   Arch-regent and commander of all spirits.
FAUSTUS.   Was not that Lucifer an angel once?
MEPHOSTOPHILIS.   Yes Faustus, and most dearly loved of God.   65
FAUSTUS.   How comes it then that he is prince of devils?

34. *Quin . . . imagine!* Why do you not return, Mephostophilis, in the likeness
of a friar! 46. *per accidens*: as it appeared (what the conjuring represented was
the real cause). 47. rack: violate.

MEPHOSTOPHILIS.   O, by aspiring pride and insolence,
For which God threw him from the face of heaven.
    FAUSTUS.   And what are you that live with Lucifer?
    MEPHOSTOPHILIS.   Unhappy spirits that fell with Lucifer,   70
Conspired against our God with Lucifer,
And are for ever damned with Lucifer.
    FAUSTUS.   Where are you damned?
    MEPHOSTOPHILIS.   In hell.
    FAUSTUS.   How comes it then that thou art out of hell?   75
    MEPHOSTOPHILIS.   Why this is hell, nor am I out of it.
Think'st thou that I, who saw the face of God,
And tasted the eternal joys of heaven,
Am not tormented with ten thousand hells,
In being deprived of everlasting bliss?   80
O Faustus, leave these frivolous demands,
Which strike a terror to my fainting soul.
    FAUSTUS.   What, is great Mephostophilis so passionate
For being deprived of the joys of heaven?
Learn thou of Faustus manly fortitude,   85
And scorn those joys thou never shalt possess.
Go bear these tidings to great Lucifer,
Seeing Faustus hath incurred eternal death,
By desperate thoughts against Jove's deity:
Say he surrenders up to him his soul,   90
So he will spare him four and twenty years,
Letting him live in all voluptuousness,
Having thee ever to attend on me,
To give me whatsoever I shall ask;
To tell me whatsoever I demand: 95
To slay mine enemies, and aid my friends,
And always be obedient to my will.
Go, and return to mighty Lucifer,
And meet me in my study, at midnight,
And then resolve me of thy master's mind.   100
    MEPHOSTOPHILIS.   I will Faustus. (*Exit.*)
    FAUSTUS.   Had I as many souls as there be stars
I'd give them all for Mephostophilis.
By him, I'll be great conqueror of the world,
And make a bridge through the moving air   105
To pass the ocean with a band of men;
I'll join the hills that bind the Afric shore,
And make that country continent to Spain,
And both contributory to my crown.

91. **So:** on condition that.   107. **hills . . . shore:** the hills on either side of the
Straits of Gibraltar which, if joined, would unite Africa and Europe into a single
continent.

The emperor shall not live, but by my leave,   110
Nor any potentate of Germany.
Now that I have obtained what I desired
I'll live in speculation of this art
Till Mephostophilis return again. (*Exit.*)

Scene 4

(*Enter* WAGNER *and the* CLOWN.)

WAGNER.   Come hither sirra boy.

CLOWN.   Boy? O disgrace to my person! Zounds, boy in your face!
You have seen many boys with such pickadevants, I am sure.

WAGNER.   Sirra, hast thou no comings in?

CLOWN.   Yes, and goings out too, you may see sir.   5

WAGNER.   Alas poor slave, see how poverty jests in his nakedness. The
villain is bare and out of service, and so hungry, that I know he would
give his soul to the devil, for a shoulder of mutton, though it were blood-
raw.

CLOWN.   Not so neither! I had need to have it well roasted, and good
sauce to it, if I pay so dear, I can tell you.   11

WAGNER.   Sirra, wilt thou be my man and wait on me? And I will
make thee go, like *Qui mihi discipulus*.

CLOWN.   What, in verse?

WAGNER.   No slave, in beaten silk, and stavesacre.   15

CLOWN.   Stavesacre? That's good to kill vermin; then, belike, if I
serve you, I shall be lousy.

WAGNER.   Why, so thou shalt be, whether thou dost it or no: for sirra,
if thou dost not presently bind thyself to me for seven years, I'll turn all
the lice about thee into familiars, and make them tear thee in pieces. 20

CLOWN.   Nay sir, you may save yourself a labour, for they are as
familiar with me, as if they paid for their meat and drink, I can tell you.

WAGNER.   Well sirra, leave your jesting, and take these guilders.

CLOWN.   Gridirons, what be they?

WAGNER.   Why, French crowns.   25

CLOWN.   Mass, but for the name of French crowns a man were as good
have as many English counters.

Scene iv, 3. **pickadevants:** beards fashionably cut to a small point (French
pic à devant).   4. **comings in:** earnings, income.   5. **goings out:** expenses; but the
Clown makes the word serve two functions, pointing also to his tattered clothing.
7. **out of service:** out of a job.   13. *Qui mihi discipulus:* you who are my pupil
(the opening words of a didactic Latin poem by the schoolmaster William Lily
which would be familiar to every grammar-school boy).   20. **familiars:** familiar
spirits, diabolical personal attendants.   21–22. **they . . . drink:** they treat me as
contemptuously as if they were customers at an inn who pay for what they consume.   27. **counters:** worthless tokens.

WAGNER. So, now thou art to be at an hour's warning, whensoever, and wheresoever the devil shall fetch thee.

CLOWN. Here, take your guilders again, I'll none of 'em. 30

WAGNER. Not I, thou art pressed, prepare thyself, for I will presently raise up two devils to carry thee away: Baliol and Belcher!

CLOWN. Let your Balio and your Belcher come here, and I'll knock them, they were never so knocked since they were devils. Say I should kill one of them, what would folks say? 'Do ye see yonder tall fellow in the round slop, he has killed the devil!' So I should be called kill-devil all the parish over. 37

(*Enter two* DEVILS *and the* CLOWN *runs up and down crying.*)

WAGNER. How now sir, will you serve me now?

CLOWN. Ay good Wagner, take the devils away then.

WAGNER. Spirits away!

(*Exeunt* DEVILS.)

Now sirra, follow me. 40

CLOWN. I will sir; but hark you master, will you teach me this conjuring occupation?

WAGNER. Ay sirra, I'll teach thee to turn thyself to a dog, or a cat, or a mouse, or a rat, or anything.

CLOWN. A dog, or a cat, or a mouse, or a rat? O brave, Wagner. 45

WAGNER. Villain, call me Master Wagner, and see that you walk attentively, and let your right eye be always diametrally fixed upon my left heel, that thou may'st *quasi vestigias nostras insistere*.

CLOWN. Well sir, I warrant you.

(*Exeunt.*)

ACT TWO

Scene 1

(*Enter* FAUSTUS *in his study.*)

FAUSTUS. Now Faustus must thou needs be damned
And canst thou not be saved?
What boots it then to think on God or heaven?

---

31. **pressed:** enlisted; the taking of money was a token of enrolment for military service. 32. **Baliol:** probably a corruption of Belial. 33. **knock:** thump, beat. 35. **tall:** brave. 36. **round slop:** baggy trousers. 47. **diametrally:** diametrically. 48. *quasi . . . insistere:* as it were tread in our footsteps; the construction is false (for *vestigiis nostris*) but this may be intentional.

Away with such vain fancies and despair,
Despair in God, and trust in Belzebub.   5
Now go not backward: no, Faustus, be resolute,
Why waverest thou? O, something soundeth in mine ears:
'Abjure this magic, turn to God again'.
Ay, and Faustus will turn to God again.
To God? He loves thee not: 10
The God thou servest is thine own appetite
Wherein is fixed the love of Belzebub:
To him, I'll build an altar and a church,
And offer luke-warm blood of new-born babes.

(*Enter the two* ANGELS.)

GOOD ANGEL.   Sweet Faustus, leave that execrable art.   15
FAUSTUS.   Contrition, prayer, repentance — what of these?
GOOD ANGEL.   O they are means to bring thee unto heaven.
BAD ANGEL.   Rather illusions, fruits of lunacy,
That make men foolish that do trust them most.
GOOD ANGEL.   Sweet Faustus, think of heaven, and heavenly things.
BAD ANGEL.   No Faustus, think of honour and of wealth.   21

(*Exeunt* ANGELS.)

FAUSTUS.   Wealth!
Why, the signory of Emden shall be mine:
When Mephostophilis shall stand by me
What god can hurt me? Faustus thou art safe.   25
Cast no more doubts; Mephostophilis, come
And bring glad tidings from great Lucifer.
Is't not midnight? Come Mephostophilis,
Veni, veni Mephostophilis.

(*Enter* MEPHOSTOPHILIS.)

Now tell me what saith Lucifer thy lord?   30
MEPHOSTOPHILIS.   That I shall wait on Faustus whilst he lives,
So he will buy my service with his soul.
FAUSTUS.   Already Faustus hath hazarded that for thee.
MEPHOSTOPHILIS.   But now thou must bequeath it solemnly,
And write a deed of gift with thine own blood;   35
For that security craves Lucifer.
If thou deny it I must back to hell.

Act II, Scene i, 23. **signory of Emden:** governorship of Emden, a port on the
mouth of the Ems, at this time trading extensively with England.   29. **Veni . . .**
Mephostophilis: come, O Mephostophilis.   33. **hazarded:** jeopardized.

FAUSTUS.   Stay Mephostophilis, and tell me,
What good will my soul do thy lord?
MEPHOSTOPHILIS.   Enlarge his kingdom.   40
FAUSTUS.   Is that the reason why he tempts us thus?
MEPHOSTOPHILIS.   *Solamen miseris, socios habuisse doloris.*
FAUSTUS.   Have you any pain that torture others?
MEPHOSTOPHILIS.   As great as have the human souls of men.
But tell me Faustus, shall I have thy soul?   45
And I will be thy slave and wait on thee,
And give thee more than thou hast wit to ask.
FAUSTUS.   Ay Mephostophilis, I'll give it him.
MEPHOSTOPHILIS.   Then Faustus, stab thine arm courageously,
And bind thy soul, that at some certain day   50
Great Lucifer may claim it as his own,
And then be thou as great as Lucifer.
FAUSTUS.   Lo Mephostophilis, for love of thee (*stabs his arm*)
Faustus hath cut his arm, and with his proper blood
Assures his soul to be great Lucifer's,   55
Chief lord and regent of perpetual night.
View here this blood that trickles from mine arm,
And let it be propitious for my wish.
MEPHOSTOPHILIS.   But Faustus,
Write it in manner of a deed of gift.   60
FAUSTUS.   Ay, so I will. (*Writes.*) But Mephostophilis,
My blood congeals, and I can write no more.
MEPHOSTOPHILIS.   I'll fetch thee fire to dissolve it straight. (*Exit.*)
FAUSTUS.   What might the staying of my blood portend?
Is it unwilling I should write this bill?   65
Why streams it not, that I may write afresh?
'Faustus gives to thee his soul': ah, there it stayed!
Why should'st thou not? Is not thy soul thine own?
Then write again: 'Faustus gives to thee his soul'.

(*Enter* MEPHOSTOPHILIS *with the Chafer of Fire.*)

MEPHOSTOPHILIS.   See Faustus here is fire, set it on.   70
FAUSTUS.   So, now the blood begins to clear again (*writes again*):
Now will I make an end immediately.
MEPHOSTOPHILIS.   What will not I do to obtain his soul!
FAUSTUS.   *Consummatum est:* this bill is ended,
And Faustus hath bequeathed his soul to Lucifer.   75
But what is this inscription on mine arm?

42. *Solamen . . . doloris:* in Chaucer's version, 'Men seyn, "to wrecche is con-
solacioun To have an-other felawe in his peyne"' (*Troilus and Criseyde*, i.708–
709). 54. **proper:** own. 69. S.D. *Chafer:* portable grate. 70. **set it on:** set
his blood in a saucer on warm ashes. 74. *Consummatum est:* it is finished; the
last words of Christ on the cross (St. John, xix, 30).

Homo fuge! Whither should I fly?
If unto God, he'll throw me down to hell.
My senses are deceived, here's nothing writ:
O yes, I see it plain, even here is writ   80
Homo fuge! Yet shall not Faustus fly.
  MEPHOSTOPHILIS. I'll fetch him somewhat to delight his mind. (*Exit.*)

  (*Enter* DEVILS, *giving crowns and rich apparel to* FAUSTUS: *they dance, and then depart. Enter* MEPHOSTOPHILIS.)

  FAUSTUS. What means this show? Speak Mephostophilis.
  MEPHOSTOPHILIS. Nothing Faustus, but to delight thy mind,
And let thee see what magic can perform.   85
  FAUSTUS. But may I raise such spirits when I please?
  MEPHOSTOPHILIS. Ay Faustus, and do greater things than these.
  FAUSTUS. Then Mephostophilis, receive this scroll.
A deed of gift, of body and of soul:
But yet conditionally, that thou perform   90
All covenants and articles between us both.
  MEPHOSTOPHILIS. Faustus, I swear by hell and Lucifer,
To effect all promises between us made.
  FAUSTUS. Then hear me read it Mephostophilis.
On these conditions following: 95

  First, that Faustus may be a spirit in form and substance.
  Secondly, that Mephostophilis shall be his servant, and at his command.
  Thirdly, that Mephostophilis shall do for him, and bring him whatsoever.
  Fourthly, that he shall be in his chamber or house invisible.   100
  Lastly, that he shall appear to the said John Faustus, at all times, in what form or shape soever he please.
  I, John Faustus of Wittenberg, doctor, by these presents, do give both body and soul to Lucifer, Prince of the East, and his minister Mephostophilis, and furthermore grant unto them, that four and twenty years being expired, the articles above written inviolate, full power to fetch or carry the said John Faustus, body and soul, flesh, blood, or goods, into their habitation wheresoever.   108
                  By me John Faustus.

  MEPHOSTOPHILIS. Speak Faustus, do you deliver this as your deed?
  FAUSTUS. Ay, take it, and the devil give thee good on't.
  MEPHOSTOPHILIS. Now Faustus, ask what thou wilt.
  FAUSTUS. First will I question with thee about hell:
Tell me, where is the place that men call hell?

---

77. *Homo fuge!* Fly, O man! **96. spirit:** a spirit, to the Elizabethans, was usually an evil one, a devil (see Shakespeare, Sonnet CXLIV); according to some theologians, who followed Aquinas, God could have no mercy on a devil who was *ipso facto* incapable of repenting (see II.ii.13–15). **103. these presents:** the legal articles.

MEPHOSTOPHILIS.   Under the heavens.   115
FAUSTUS.   Ay, so are all things else; but whereabouts?
MEPHOSTOPHILIS.   Within the bowels of these elements,
Where we are tortured, and remain for ever.
Hell hath no limits, nor is circumscribed
In one self place; but where we are is hell,   120
And where hell is, there must we ever be.
And to be short, when all the world dissolves,
And every creature shall be purified,
All places shall be hell that is not heaven.
FAUSTUS.   I think hell's a fable.   125
MEPHOSTOPHILIS.   Ay, think so still, till experience change thy mind.
FAUSTUS.   Why, dost thou think that Faustus shall be damned?
MEPHOSTOPHILIS.   Ay, of necessity, for here's the scroll
In which thou hast given thy soul to Lucifer.
FAUSTUS.   Ay, and body too, but what of that?   130
Think'st thou that Faustus is so fond to imagine,
That after this life there is any pain?
No, these are trifles, and mere old wives' tales.
MEPHOSTOPHILIS.   But I am an instance to prove the contrary:
For I tell thee I am damned, and now in hell.   135
FAUSTUS.   Nay, and this be hell, I'll willingly be damned.
What, sleeping, eating, walking and disputing?
But leaving this, let me have a wife, the fairest maid in Germany, for I am
wanton and lascivious, and cannot live without a wife.   139
MEPHOSTOPHILIS.   How, a wife? I prithee Faustus, talk not of a wife.
FAUSTUS.   Nay sweet Mephostophilis, fetch me one, for I will have one.
MEPHOSTOPHILIS.   Well, thou wilt have one; sit there till I come;
I'll fetch thee a wife in the devil's name. (*Exit.*)

(*Enter with a* DEVIL *dressed like a woman, with fireworks.*)

MEPHOSTOPHILIS.   Tell me Faustus, how dost thou like thy wife?
FAUSTUS.   A plague on her for a hot whore! No, I'll no wife.   145
MEPHOSTOPHILIS.   Marriage is but a ceremonial toy,
And if thou lovest me think no more of it.
I'll cull thee out the fairest courtesans,
And bring them every morning to thy bed:
She whom thine eye shall like, thy heart shall have,   150
Were she as chaste as was Penelope,
As wise as Saba, or as beautiful
As was bright Lucifer before his fall.

117. **these elements**: the four elements below the sphere of the moon.   120. **one
self place**: one particular place.   131. **fond**: foolish.   148. **cull**: pick.   151.
Penelope: wife of Ulysses, renowned for her fidelity to a lost husband.   152. **Saba**:
the Queen of Sheba, who confronted Solomon with 'hard questions' (I Kings, x).

Hold, take this book, peruse it thoroughly:
The iterating of these lines brings gold; 155
The framing of this circle on the ground
Brings thunder, whirlwinds, storm and lightning:
Pronounce this thrice devoutly to thyself,
And men in harness shall appear to thee,
Ready to execute what thou command'st. 160
FAUSTUS. Thanks Mephostophilis; yet fain would I have a book
wherein I might behold all spells and incantations, that I might raise up
spirits when I please. 163
MEPHOSTOPHILIS. Here they are in this book. (*There turn to them.*)
FAUSTUS. Now would I have a book where I might see all characters
and planets of the heavens, that I might know their motions and disposi-
tions.
MEPHOSTOPHILIS. Here they are too. (*Turn to them.*) 168
FAUSTUS. Nay, let me have one book more, and then I have done,
wherein I might see all plants, herbs and trees that grow upon the earth.
MEPHOSTOPHILIS. Here they be.
FAUSTUS. O thou art deceived.
MEPHOSTOPHILIS. Tut I warrant thee. (*Turn to them.*) 173

(*Exeunt.*)

Scene 2

(*Enter* FAUSTUS *in his study and* MEPHOSTOPHILIS.)

FAUSTUS. When I behold the heavens then I repent
And curse thee wicked Mephostophilis,
Because thou hast deprived me of those joys.
MEPHOSTOPHILIS. 'Twas thine own seeking Faustus, thank thyself:
But think'st thou heaven is such a glorious thing? 5
I tell thee Faustus, it is not half so fair
As thou, or any man that breathes on earth.
FAUSTUS. How prov'st thou that?
MEPHOSTOPHILIS. 'Twas made for man; then he's more excellent.
FAUSTUS. If heaven was made for man, 'twas made for me: 10
I will renounce this magic and repent.

(*Enter the two* ANGELS.)

GOOD ANGEL. Faustus repent, yet God will pity thee.
BAD ANGEL. Thou art a spirit, God cannot pity thee.
FAUSTUS. Who buzzeth in mine ears I am a spirit?

159. harness: armour. 166–167. dispositions: situations.
Scene ii, 14. buzzeth: whispers.

Be I a devil yet God may pity me,   15
Yea, God will pity me if I repent.
   EVIL ANGEL.   Ay, but Faustus never shall repent.

(*Exeunt* ANGELS.)

   FAUSTUS.   My heart's so hardened I cannot repent!
Scarce can I name salvation, faith, or heaven,
But fearful echoes thunders in mine ears,   20
'Faustus, thou art damned': then swords and knives,
Poison, guns, halters and envenomed steel
Are laid before me to dispatch myself:
And long ere this, I should have done the deed,
Had not sweet pleasure conquered deep despair.   25
Have not I made blind Homer sing to me
Of Alexander's love, and Oenon's death?
And hath not he, that built the walls of Thebes
With ravishing sound of his melodious harp,
Made music with my Mephostophilis?   30
Why should I die then, or basely despair?
I am resolved! Faustus shall not repent.
Come Mephostophilis let us dispute again,
And reason of divine astrology.
Speak, are there many spheres above the moon?   35
Are all celestial bodies but one globe,
As is the substance of this centric earth?
   MEPHOSTOPHILIS.   As are the elements, such are the heavens,
Even from the moon unto the empyreal orb,
Mutually folded in each other's spheres,   40
And jointly move upon one axletree,
Whose termine is termed the world's wide pole.
Nor are the names of Saturn, Mars or Jupiter,
Feigned, but are erring stars.
   FAUSTUS.   But have they all one motion, both *situ et tempore?*   45
   MEPHOSTOPHILIS.   All move from east to west in four and twenty
hours, upon the poles of the world, but differ in their motions upon the
poles of the zodiac.
   FAUSTUS.   These slender questions Wagner can decide!
Hath Mephostophilis no greater skill?   50

15. **Be I**: this could mean either 'even if I am' or else 'even though I were.'
22. **halters**: hangman's ropes.   27. **Alexander . . . death**: Alexander, Homer's
name for Paris, son of Priam, fell in love with Oenone before he encountered
Helen; wounded in the Trojan War, he was carried to Oenone and died at her
feet, whereupon she stabbed herself.   28–29. **he . . . harp**: at the sound of
Amphion's harp the stones were so affected that they rose of their own accord to
form the walls of Thebes.   42. **termine**: boundary (astronomical).   45. *situ et
tempore*: in direction and in time.

Who knows not the double motion of the planets?
That the first is finished in a natural day, the second thus:
Saturn in thirty years; Jupiter in twelve; Mars in four; the Sun, Venus and
Mercury in a year; the Moon in twenty-eight days. These are freshmen's
suppositions. But tell me, hath every sphere a dominion or intelligentia?

MEPHOSTOPHILIS. Ay. 56

FAUSTUS. How many heavens, or spheres, are there?

MEPHOSTOPHILIS. Nine: the seven planets, the firmament, and the
empyreal heaven.

FAUSTUS. But is there not *coelum igneum? et cristallinum?* 60

MEPHOSTOPHILIS. No Faustus, they be but fables.

FAUSTUS. Resolve me then in this one question: why are not con-
junctions, oppositions, aspects, eclipses, all at one time, but in some years
we have more, in some less?

MEPHOSTOPHILIS. *Per inaequalem motum, respectu totius.* 65

FAUSTUS. Well, I am answered. Now tell me who made the world?

MEPHOSTOPHILIS. I will not.

FAUSTUS. Sweet Mephostophilis, tell me.

MEPHOSTOPHILIS. Move me not Faustus.

FAUSTUS. Villain, have not I bound thee to tell me anything? 70

MEPHOSTOPHILIS. Ay, that is not against our kingdom.
This is: thou art damned, think thou on hell.

FAUSTUS. Think, Faustus, upon God, that made the world.

MEPHOSTOPHILIS. Remember this! (*Exit.*)

FAUSTUS. Ay, go accursed spirit to ugly hell: 75
'Tis thou hast damned distressed Faustus' soul.
Is't not too late?

(*Enter the two* ANGELS.)

BAD ANGEL. Too late.

GOOD ANGEL. Never too late, if Faustus will repent.

BAD ANGEL. If thou repent, devils will tear thee in pieces. 80

GOOD ANGEL. Repent, and they shall never raze thy skin.

(*Exeunt* ANGELS.)

FAUSTUS. O Christ my saviour, my saviour,
Help to save distressed Faustus' soul.

(*Enter* LUCIFER, BELZEBUB, *and* MEPHOSTOPHILIS.)

LUCIFER. Christ cannot save thy soul, for he is just;
There's none but I have interest in the same. 85

55. **suppositions:** elementary facts given to first-year undergraduates for them to
build an argument on. 69. **Move:** vex. 81. **raze:** graze. 85. **interest in:** legal
claim on.

FAUSTUS.   O what art thou that look'st so terribly?
LUCIFER.   I am Lucifer, and this is my companion prince in hell.
FAUSTUS.   O Faustus, they are come to fetch thy soul!
BELZEBUB.   We are come to tell thee thou dost injure us.
LUCIFER.   Thou call'st on Christ contrary to thy promise.   90
BELZEBUB.   Thou should'st not think on God.
LUCIFER.   Think on the devil.
BELZEBUB.   And his dam too.
FAUSTUS.   Nor will I henceforth: pardon me for this,
And Faustus vows never to look to heaven,   95
Never to name God, or to pray to him,
To burn his scriptures, slay his ministers,
And make my spirits pull his churches down.
LUCIFER.   So shalt thou show thyself an obedient servant,
And we will highly gratify thee for it.   100
BELZEBUB.   Faustus, we are come from hell in person to show thee
some pastime: sit down and thou shalt behold the Seven Deadly Sins
appear to thee in their proper shapes and likenesses.
FAUSTUS.   That sight will be as pleasing unto me as Paradise was to
Adam the first day of his creation.   105
LUCIFER.   Talk not of Paradise or creation, but mark the show. Go
Mephostophilis, fetch them in.

(*Enter the* SEVEN DEADLY SINS.)

BELZEBUB.   Now Faustus, examine them of their several names and
dispositions.
FAUSTUS.   That shall I soon: what art thou, the first?   110
PRIDE.   I am Pride; I disdain to have any parents: I am like to Ovid's
flea, I can creep into every corner of a wench: sometimes, like a periwig,
I sit upon her brow; next, like a necklace, I hang about her neck; then,
like a fan of feathers, I kiss her lips; and then, turning myself to a
wrought smock, do what I list. But fie, what a smell is here! I'll not
speak another word unless the ground be perfumed, and covered with
cloth of arras.   117
FAUSTUS.   Thou art a proud knave indeed: what art thou, the second?
COVETOUSNESS.   I am Covetousness, begotten of an old churl in a
leather bag; and might I now obtain my wish, this house, you and all
should turn to gold, that I might lock you safe into my chest. O my
sweet gold!
FAUSTUS.   And what art thou, the third?   123

111–112. **Ovid's flea:** the poet of 'The Song of the Flea' (probably medieval but
attributed to Ovid) envies the flea for its freedom of movement over his mistress' body.   115. **wrought:** embroidered.   117. **cloth of arras:** tapestry woven at
Arras in Flanders and used for wall hangings.   120. **leather bag:** the miser's purse.

ENVY.   I am Envy, begotten of a chimney-sweeper, and an oyster-wife: I cannot read, and therefore wish all books burnt. I am lean with seeing others eat: O that there would come a famine over all the world, that all might die, and I live alone, then thou shouldst see how fat I'd be. But must thou sit, and I stand? Come down, with a vengeance.

FAUSTUS.   Out, envious wretch! But what art thou, the fourth?   129

WRATH.   I am Wrath: I had neither father nor mother; I leapt out of a lion's mouth when I was scarce an hour old, and ever since have run up and down the world with these case of rapiers, wounding myself when I could get none to fight withal: I was born in hell, and look to it, for some of you shall be my father.

FAUSTUS.   And what art thou, the fifth?   135

GLUTTONY.   I am Gluttony; my parents are all dead, and the devil a penny they have left me, but a small pension, and that buys me thirty meals a day, and ten bevers: a small trifle to suffice nature. I come of a royal pedigree: my father was a gammon of bacon, and my mother was a hogshead of claret wine. My godfathers were these: Peter Pickled-Herring and Martin Martlemass-Beef: O but my godmother, she was a jolly gentlewoman, and well loved in every good town and city; her name was Mistress Margery March-Beer. Now Faustus, thou hast heard all my progeny, wilt thou bid me to supper?   144

FAUSTUS.   No, I'll see thee hanged, thou wilt eat up all my victuals.

GLUTTONY.   Then the devil choke thee.

FAUSTUS.   Choke thyself, Glutton; what art thou, the sixth?

SLOTH.   Hey ho! I am Sloth: I was begotten on a sunny bank, where I have lain ever since, and you have done me great injury to bring me from thence; let me be carried thither again by Gluttony and Lechery. Hey ho, I'll not speak a word more for a king's ransom.   151

FAUSTUS.   And what are you Mistress Minx, the seventh and last?

LECHERY.   Who I? I sir? I am one that loves an inch of raw mutton, better than an ell of fried stockfish: and the first letter of my name begins with Lechery.

LUCIFER.   Away to hell, away, on piper.   156

(*Exeunt the* SEVEN SINS.)

FAUSTUS.   O how this sight doth delight my soul.

LUCIFER.   But Faustus, in hell is all manner of delight.

FAUSTUS.   O might I see hell, and return again safe, how happy were I then.   160

---

132. **these case**: a case of rapiers is in fact a pair. 138. **bevers**: snacks. 141. **Martlemass-Beef**: meat, salted to preserve it for winter, hung up at Martin-mas (November 11). 143. **March-Beer**: a rich ale, made in March and left to mature for at least two years. 144. **progeny**: lineage (obsolete). 154–155. **begins with Lechery**: a common form of jest: 'Her name begins with Mistress Purge' (Middleton, *The Family of Love*, II.iii.53).

LUCIFER.   Faustus, thou shalt, at midnight I will send for thee;
Meanwhile peruse this book, and view it throughly,
And thou shalt turn thyself into what shape thou wilt.
FAUSTUS.   Thanks mighty Lucifer:
This will I keep as chary as my life.   165
LUCIFER.   Now Faustus, farewell.
FAUSTUS.   Farewell, great Lucifer: come Mephostophilis.

(*Exeunt omnes, several ways.*)

Scene 3

(*Enter the* CLOWN [ROBIN].)

CLOWN.   What, Dick, look to the horses there till I come again. I
have gotten one of Doctor Faustus' conjuring books, and now we'll have
such knavery, as't passes.

(*Enter* DICK.)

DICK.   What, Robin, you must come away and walk the horses.   4
ROBIN.   I walk the horses! I scorn't, 'faith, I have other matters in
hand, let the horses walk themselves and they will. (*Reads.*) 'A per se a;
t. h. e. the; o per se o; deny orgon, gorgon.' Keep further from me, O
thou illiterate and unlearned ostler.
DICK.   'Snails, what hast thou got there? A book? Why, thou canst
not tell ne'er a word on't.   10
ROBIN.   That thou shalt see presently: keep out of the circle, I say, lest
I send you into the hostry with a vengeance.
DICK.   That's like, 'faith: you had best leave your foolery, for an my
master come, he'll conjure you, 'faith.   14
ROBIN.   My master conjure me? I'll tell thee what, an my master
come here, I'll clap as fair a pair of horns on's head as e'er thou sawest in
thy life.
DICK.   Thou needest not do that, for my mistress hath done it.
ROBIN.   Ay, there be of us here, that have waded as deep into matters,
as other men, if they were disposed to talk.   20
DICK.   A plague take you, I thought you did not sneak up and down
after her for nothing. But I prithee tell me, in good sadness, Robin, is
that a conjuring book?

162. **throughly:** thoroughly.   165. **chary:** carefully.   167. S.D. *several ways:* in
different directions.

Scene iii, 3. **as't passes:** as beats everything.   6. *per se:* by itself (a *by itself*
spells a).   7. **deny orgon, gorgon:** Robin is struggling to read the 'Demogorgon'
of Faustus' invocation.   9. **'Snails:** by God's nails.   12. **hostry:** hostelry, inn.
13. **That's like:** a likely chance.   19. **matters:** affairs; 'I meddle with no trades-
man's matters, nor women's matters' (*Julius Caesar*, I.i.23).   22. **in good sadness:** seriously.

ROBIN.   Do but speak what thou'lt have me to do, and I'll do't: if thou'lt dance naked, put off thy clothes, and I'll conjure thee about presently; or if thou'lt go but to the tavern with me, I'll give thee white wine, red wine, claret wine, sack, muscadine, malmsey and whippincrust, hold belly hold, and we'll not pay one penny for it.   28

DICK.   O brave! Prithee, let's to it presently, for I am as dry as a dog.

ROBIN.   Come then, let's away.

(*Exeunt.*)

Chorus I

(*Enter the* CHORUS.)

CHORUS.   Learned Faustus,
To find the secrets of astronomy,
Graven in the book of Jove's high firmament,
Did mount him up to scale Olympus' top;
Where sitting in a chariot burning bright,   5
Drawn by the strength of yoked dragons' necks,
He views the clouds, the planets, and the stars,
The tropics, zones, and quarters of the sky,
From the bright circle of the horned moon,
Even to the height of *Primum Mobile:*   10
And whirling round with this circumference,
Within the concave compass of the pole,
From east to west his dragons swiftly glide,
And in eight days did bring him home again.
Not long he stayed within his quiet house,   15
To rest his bones after his weary toil,
But new exploits do hale him out again,
And mounted then upon a dragon's back,
That with his wings did part the subtle air,
He now is gone to prove cosmography,   20
That measures coasts and kingdoms of the earth:
And as I guess will first arrive at Rome,
To see the Pope and manner of his court,
And take some part of holy Peter's feast,
The which this day is highly solemnized. (*Exit.*)   25

27. **sack:** strong, light-coloured wine from Spain. **muscadine:** muscatel, a strong sweet wine from the muscat grape. **malmsey:** another strong sweet wine. **whippincrust:** a spiced wine (corruption of hippocras).   28. **hold belly hold:** a belly-full.

Chorus I, 8. **tropics:** *i.e.,* of Cancer and Capricorn. **zones:** four circles (the two tropics and two polar circles) divide the world into five zones; this technical word is used by La Primaudaye (*French Academy*, III.xvii).   9–10. **From . . . mobile:** from the innermost to the outermost sphere; everywhere, that is, except to the empyrean.   11. **this circumference:** *i.e.,* the Primum Mobile.   25. **this day:** June 29 is the Feast of St. Peter.

ACT THREE

Scene 1

(*Enter* FAUSTUS *and* MEPHOSTOPHILIS.)

FAUSTUS.   Having now, my good Mephostophilis,
Passed with delight the stately town of Trier,
Environed round with airy mountain tops,
With walls of flint, and deep entrenched lakes,
Not to be won by any conquering prince;   5
From Paris next, coasting the realm of France,
We saw the river Main fall into Rhine,
Whose banks are set with groves of fruitful vines.
Then up to Naples, rich Campania,
With buildings fair, and gorgeous to the eye,   10
Whose streets straight forth, and paved with finest brick,
Quarter the town in four equivalents;
There saw we learned Maro's golden tomb,
The way he cut an English mile in length
Thorough a rock of stone in one night's space: 15
From thence to Venice, Padua and the rest,
In midst of which a sumptuous temple stands,
That threats the stars with her aspiring top,
Whose frame is paved with sundry coloured stones,
And roofed aloft with curious work in gold.   20
Thus hitherto hath Faustus spent his time.
But tell me now, what resting place is this?
Hast thou, as erst I did command,
Conducted me within the walls of Rome?
MEPHOSTOPHILIS.   I have my Faustus, and for proof thereof,   25
This is the goodly palace of the Pope:
And 'cause we are no common guests,
I choose his privy chamber for our use.
FAUSTUS.   I hope his holiness will bid us welcome.
MEPHOSTOPHILIS.   All's one, for we'll be bold with his venison.   30
But now my Faustus, that thou may'st perceive,
What Rome contains for to delight thine eyes,
Know that this city stands upon seven hills,
That underprop the groundwork of the same:

Act III, Scene i, 9. **Campania:** The English *Faust Book* led Marlowe into
this erroneous identification of Naples with Campagna.   11. **straight forth:** in
straight lines.   13–15. **There . . . space:** Virgil (Publius Virgilius Maro) was
buried in Naples in 19 B.C. and posthumously acquired some reputation as a
magician. His tomb stands at the end of the promontory of Posilippo between
Naples and Pozzuoli and legend ascribes the tunnel running through this promontory to his magic art.   23. **erst:** earlier.

Just through the midst runs flowing Tiber's stream,   35
With winding banks that cut it in two parts;
Over the which four stately bridges lean,
That make safe passage to each part of Rome.
Upon the bridge called Ponte Angelo
Erected is a castle passing strong,   40
Where thou shalt see such store of ordinance,
As that the double cannons forged of brass
Do match the number of the days contained
Within the compass of one complete year:
Besides the gates, and high pyramides   45
That Julius Caesar brought from Africa.
    FAUSTUS.   Now by the kingdoms of infernal rule,
Of Styx, of Acheron, and the fiery lake
Of ever-burning Phlegethon, I swear,
That I do long to see the monuments   50
And situation of bright-splendent Rome.
Come therefore, let's away.
    MEPHOSTOPHILIS.   Nay, stay my Faustus, I know you'd see the Pope,
And take some part of holy Peter's feast,
The which in state and high solemnity,   55
This day is held through Rome and Italy,
In honour of the Pope's triumphant victory.
    FAUSTUS.   Sweet Mephostophilis, thou pleasest me;
Whilst I am here on earth, let me be cloyed
With all things that delight the heart of man.   60
My four and twenty years of liberty
I'll spend in pleasure and in dalliance,
That Faustus' name, whilst this bright frame doth stand,
May be admired through the furthest land.
    MEPHOSTOPHILIS.   'Tis well said Faustus, come then stand by me   65
And thou shalt see them come immediately.
    FAUSTUS.   Nay stay my gentle Mephostophilis,
And grant me my request, and then I go.
Thou knowest within the compass of eight days,
We viewed the face of heaven, of earth and hell: 70
So high our dragons soared into the air,
That, looking down, the earth appeared to me
No bigger than my hand in quantity.
There did we view the kingdoms of the world,

---

39. **Ponte Angelo:** bridge built in 135 A.D. by Hadrian; his mausoleum faces
the bridge but never stood on it.   42. **double cannons:** cannons of very high
calibre.   45–46. **pyramides . . . Africa:** the obelisk; in fact this was brought
from Heliopolis by the Emperor Caligula in the first century A.D. The plural form
pyramides (here stressing the need to pronounce the final syllable) is also used
as a singular by Marlowe in *The Massacre at Paris*, ii.43–46.   51. **situation:** lay-
out.   64. **admired:** wondered at.

And what might please mine eye, I there beheld.   75
Then in this show let me an actor be,
That this proud Pope may Faustus' cunning see.
    MEPHOSTOPHILIS.   Let it be so my Faustus, but first stay,
And view their triumphs, as they pass this way;
And then devise what best contents thy mind,   80
By cunning in thine art to cross the Pope,
Or dash the pride of this solemnity;
To make his monks and abbots stand like apes,
And point like antics at his triple crown:
To beat the beads about the friars' pates,   85
Or clap huge horns upon the cardinals' heads:
Or any villainy thou canst devise,
And I'll perform it Faustus: hark, they come:
This day shall make thee be admired in Rome.

(Enter the CARDINALS and BISHOPS, some bearing crosiers, some the
pillars; MONKS and FRIARS singing their procession; then the POPE, and
RAYMOND King of Hungary, with BRUNO led in chains.)

    POPE.   Cast down our footstool.
    RAYMOND.   Saxon Bruno stoop,   90
Whilst on thy back his holiness ascends
Saint Peter's chair and state pontifical.
    BRUNO.   Proud Lucifer, that state belongs to me:
But thus I fall to Peter, not to thee.
    POPE.   To me and Peter shalt thou grovelling lie,   95
And crouch before the papal dignity:
Sound trumpets then, for thus Saint Peter's heir,
From Bruno's back ascends Saint Peter's chair.

(A Flourish while he ascends.)

Thus, as the gods creep on with feet of wool,
Long ere with iron hands they punish men,   100
So shall our sleeping vengeance now arise,
And smite with death thy hated enterprise.
Lord Cardinals of France and Padua,
Go forthwith to our holy consistory,
And read amongst the statutes decretal,   105
What by the holy council held at Trent,
The sacred synod hath decreed for him

---

79. **triumphs:** procession.   84. **antics:** clowns.   89. S.D. *pillars:* Wolsey substi-
tuted portable pillars for the silver maces usually carried by cardinals.   *procession:*
office sung in a religious procession.   99–100. **Thus . . . men:** proverb: 'God
comes with leaden (woolen) feet but strikes with iron hands.'   104. **consistory:**
meeting place of the papal senate.   106. **holy . . . Trent:** the Council of Trent
met, with interruptions, between 1545 and 1563.   107. **synod:** general council.

That doth assume the papal government,
Without election and a true consent:
Away, and bring us word with speed.   110
　FIRST CARDINAL.　We go my Lord.

(*Exeunt* CARDINALS.)

POPE.　Lord Raymond!

(*The* POPE *and* RAYMOND *converse.*)

　FAUSTUS.　Go, haste thee gentle Mephostophilis,
Follow the cardinals to the consistory;
And as they turn their superstitious books,   115
Strike them with sloth, and drowsy idleness;
And make them sleep so sound, that in their shapes,
Thyself and I may parley with this Pope,
This proud confronter of the Emperor,
And in despite of all his holiness   120
Restore this Bruno to his liberty,
And bear him to the states of Germany.
　MEPHOSTOPHILIS.　Faustus, I go.
　FAUSTUS.　　　　　　　　　Dispatch it soon:
The Pope shall curse that Faustus came to Rome.

(*Exeunt* FAUSTUS *and* MEPHOSTOPHILIS.)

　BRUNO.　Pope Adrian, let me have some right of law: 125
I was elected by the Emperor.
　POPE.　We will depose the Emperor for that deed,
And curse the people that submit to him;
Both he and thou shalt stand excommunicate,
And interdict from Church's privilege,   130
And all society of holy men:
He grows too proud in his authority,
Lifting his lofty head above the clouds,
And like a steeple overpeers the Church.
But we'll pull down his haughty insolence;   135
And as Pope Alexander, our progenitor,
Trod on the neck of German Frederick,
Adding this golden sentence to our praise:
That Peter's heirs should tread on emperors,
And walk upon the dreadful adder's back,   140

---

130. **interdict:** officially debarred.　136. **progenitor:** predecessor.　**136–137. Pope
. . . Frederick:** Pope Alexander III (1159–1181) compelled the Emperor Frederick Barbarossa to accept his supremacy.

Treading the lion, and the dragon down,
And fearless spurn the killing basilisk:
So will we quell that haughty schismatic,
And by authority apostolical
Depose him from his regal government.   145

   BRUNO.   Pope Julius swore to princely Sigismund,
For him, and the succeeding popes of Rome,
To hold the emperors their lawful lords.

   POPE.   Pope Julius did abuse the Church's rites,
And therefore none of his decrees can stand.   150
Is not all power on earth bestowed on us?
And therefore though we would we cannot err.
Behold this silver belt, whereto is fixed
Seven golden keys fast sealed with seven seals,
In token of our seven-fold power from heaven,   155
To bind or loose, lock fast, condemn, or judge,
Resign, or seal, or whatso pleaseth us.
Then he, and thou, and all the world shall stoop,
Or be assured of our dreadful curse,
To light as heavy as the pains of hell.   160

(Enter FAUSTUS and MEPHOSTOPHILIS like the cardinals.)

   MEPHOSTOPHILIS.   Now tell me Faustus, are we not fitted well?

   FAUSTUS.   Yes, Mephostophilis, and two such cardinals
Ne'er served a holy pope as we shall do.
But whilst they sleep within the consistory,
Let us salute his reverend Fatherhood.   165

   RAYMOND.   Behold my Lord, the cardinals are returned.

   POPE.   Welcome grave fathers, answer presently,
What have our holy council there decreed
Concerning Bruno and the Emperor,
In quittance of their late conspiracy   170
Against our state, and papal dignity?

   FAUSTUS.   Most sacred patron of the Church of Rome,
By full consent of all the synod
Of priests and prelates, it is thus decreed:
That Bruno and the German Emperor   175
Be held as lollards and bold schismatics,
And proud disturbers of the Church's peace.
And if that Bruno by his own assent,
Without enforcement of the German peers,
Did seek to wear the triple diadem,   180

142. basilisk: a mythical beast whose glance was fatal.   154. keys: symbolic of
St. Peter's keys.   157. Resign: unseal (the word has the force of the Latin
resignare).   176. lollards: heretics (originally followers of Wyclif).   179. enforcement of: compulsion from.

And by your death to climb Saint Peter's chair,
The statutes decretal have thus decreed,
He shall be straight condemned of heresy,
And on a pile of faggots burnt to death.
    POPE.   It is enough: here, take him to your charge,   185
And bear him straight to Ponte Angelo,
And in the strongest tower enclose him fast.
Tomorrow, sitting in our consistory,
With all our college of grave cardinals,
We will determine of his life or death.   190
Here, take his triple crown along with you,
And leave it in the Church's treasury.
Make haste again, my good lord cardinals,
And take our blessing apostolical.
    MEPHOSTOPHILIS.   So, so, was never devil thus blessed before!   195
    FAUSTUS.   Away sweet Mephostophilis, be gone,
The cardinals will be plagued for this anon.

(*Exeunt* FAUSTUS *and* MEPHOSTOPHILIS *with* BRUNO.)

    POPE.   Go presently, and bring a banquet forth,
That we may solemnize Saint Peter's feast,
And with Lord Raymond, King of Hungary,   200
Drink to our late and happy victory.

(*Exeunt.*)

Scene 2

(*A Sennet while the Banquet is brought in; and then enter* FAUSTUS *and* MEPHOSTOPHILIS *in their own shapes.*)

    MEPHOSTOPHILIS.   Now Faustus come, prepare thyself for mirth,
The sleepy cardinals are hard at hand,
To censure Bruno, that is posted hence,
And on a proud-paced steed, as swift as thought,
Flies o'er the Alps to fruitful Germany,   5
There to salute the woeful Emperor.
    FAUSTUS.   The Pope will curse them for their sloth today,
That slept both Bruno and his crown away.
But now, that Faustus may delight his mind,
And by their folly make some merriment,   10
Sweet Mephostophilis, so charm me here,

---

189. **college:** official title for the body of cardinals forming the pope's council.
    Scene ii, 1. S.D. Sennet: a flourish on the trumpets, usually heralding a ceremonious entrance.

That I may walk invisible to all,
And do whate'er I please, unseen of any.
    MEPHOSTOPHILIS.   Faustus thou shalt, then kneel down presently:

> Whilst on thy head I lay my hand,   15
> And charm thee with this magic wand:
> First wear this girdle, then appear
> Invisible to all are here:
> The planets seven, the gloomy air,
> Hell, and the Furies' forked hair,   20
> Pluto's blue fire, and Hecat's tree,
> With magic spells so compass thee,
> That no eye may thy body see.

So Faustus, now for all their holiness,
Do what thou wilt, thou shalt not be discerned.   25
    FAUSTUS.   Thanks Mephostophilis: now friars take heed,
Lest Faustus make your shaven crowns to bleed.
    MESPHOSTOPHILIS.   Faustus no more: see where the cardinals come.

(Sound a sennet. Enter POPE *and all the* LORDS. *Enter the* CARDINALS *with a book.)*

    POPE.   Welcome Lord Cardinals: come sit down.
Lord Raymond, take your seat. Friars attend,   30
And see that all things be in readiness,
As best beseems this solemn festival.
    FIRST CARDINAL.   First, may it please your sacred Holiness,
To view the sentence of the reverend synod,
Concerning Bruno and the Emperor?   35
    POPE.   What needs this question? Did I not tell you,
Tomorrow we would sit i' th' consistory,
And there determine of his punishment?
You brought us word even now, it was decreed,
That Bruno and the cursed Emperor   40
Were by the holy council both condemned
For loathed lollards and base schismatics:
Then wherefore would you have me view that book?
    FIRST CARDINAL.   Your Grace mistakes; you gave us no such charge.
    POPE.   Deny it not, we all are witnesses   45
That Bruno here was late delivered you,
With his rich triple crown to be reserved,
And put into the Church's treasury.

---

20. **forked hair:** the forked tongues of the snakes which form the hair of the
Furies. 21. **Pluto's blue fire:** the sulphurous smoke of hell. **Hecat's tree:** perhaps the gallows tree, since Hecate was also Trivia, goddess of crossroads where
the gallows was set up.

AMBO CARDINALS.   By holy Paul we saw them not.

POPE.   By Peter, you shall die,   50
Unless you bring them forth immediately:
Hale them to prison, lade their limbs with gyves:
False prelates, for this hateful treachery,
Cursed be your souls to hellish misery.

(*Exeunt* CARDINALS *with some* FRIARS.)

FAUSTUS.   So, they are safe: now Faustus, to the feast;   55
The Pope had never such a frolic guest.

POPE.   Lord Archbishop of Rheims, sit down with us.

ARCHBISHOP.   I thank your Holiness.

FAUSTUS.   Fall to! The devil choke you an you spare.

POPE.   Who's that spoke? Friars, look about!   60
Lord Raymond, pray fall to; I am beholding
To the Bishop of Milan, for this so rare a present.

FAUSTUS.   I thank you sir. (*Snatch it.*)

POPE.   How now? Who snatched the meat from me?
Villains, why speak you not?   65
My good Lord Archbishop, here's a most dainty dish,
Was sent me from a cardinal in France.

FAUSTUS.   I'll have that too. (*Snatch it.*)

POPE.   What lollards do attend our Holiness,
That we receive such great indignity?   70
Fetch me some wine.

FAUSTUS.   Ay, pray do, for Faustus is a-dry.

POPE.   Lord Raymond, I drink unto your grace.

FAUSTUS.   I pledge your grace. (*Snatch cup.*)

POPE.   My wine gone too! Ye lubbers, look about   75
And find the man that doth this villainy,
Or by our sanctitude you all shall die.
I pray my lords have patience at this troublesome banquet.

ARCHBISHOP.   Please it your Holiness, I think it be some ghost crept
out of purgatory, and now is come unto your Holiness for his pardon.   80

POPE.   It may be so:
Go then command our priests to sing a dirge,
To lay the fury of this same troublesome ghost.
Once again my lord, fall to. (*The* POPE *crosseth himself.*)

FAUSTUS.   How now? Must every bit be spiced with a cross?   85
Nay then, take that. (FAUSTUS *hits him a box of the ear.*)

POPE.   O, I am slain! Help me my lords!
O come and help to bear my body hence:
Damned be this soul for ever for this deed.   89

(*Exeunt the* POPE *and his train.*)

49. AMBO: both.   82. dirge: corruption of *dirige*, the antiphon at Matins in the
Office for the dead, hence any requiem mass (correctly used here but not in line
102).

MEPHOSTOPHILIS.   Now Faustus, what will you do now? For I can tell you, you'll be cursed with bell, book and candle.

FAUSTUS.   Bell, book and candle; candle, book and bell,
Forward and backward, to curse Faustus to hell.   93

(*Enter the* FRIARS *with Bell, Book and Candle for the Dirge.*)

FIRST FRIAR.   Come brethren, let's about our business with good devotion. (*Sing this.*)   95

> Cursed be he that stole his Holiness' meat from the table.
>   *Maledicat Dominus.*
> Cursed be he that struck his Holiness a blow on the face.
>   *Maledicat Dominus.*
> Cursed be he that took Friar Sandelo a blow on the pate.   100
>   *Maledicat Dominus.*
> Cursed be he that disturbeth our holy dirge.
>   *Maledicat Dominus.*
> Cursed be he that took away his Holiness' wine.
>   *Maledicat Dominus.*   105

(FAUSTUS *and* MEPHOSTOPHILIS *beat the* FRIARS, *fling fireworks among
them, and Exeunt.*)

Scene 3

(*Enter* CLOWN [ROBIN] *and* DICK, *with a Cup.*)

DICK.   Sirra Robin, we were best look that your devil can answer the
stealing of this same cup, for the vintner's boy follows us at the hard heels.

ROBIN.   'Tis no matter, let him come; an he follow us, I'll so conjure
him, as he was never conjured in his life, I warrant him: let me see the cup.

(*Enter* VINTNER.)

DICK.   Here 'tis — yonder he comes! Now Robin, now or never show
thy cunning.   6

VINTNER.   O, are you here? I am glad I have found you. You are a
couple of fine companions! Pray, where's the cup you stole from the
tavern?

ROBIN.   How, how? We steal a cup! Take heed what you say; we look
not like cup-stealers, I can tell you.   11

VINTNER.   Never deny't, for I know you have it, and I'll search you.

ROBIN.   Search me? Ay, and spare not — hold the cup Dick — come,
come, search me, search me.

(VINTNER *searches* ROBIN.)

97. *Maledicat Dominus:* may the Lord curse him.
   Scene iii, 2. **at the hard heels:** close on our heels.

VINTNER.   Come on sirra, let me search you now.   15
DICK.   Ay, ay, do, do — hold the cup Robin — I fear not your searching; we scorn to steal your cups, I can tell you.

(VINTNER *searches* DICK.)

VINTNER.   Never outface me for the matter, for sure the cup is between you two.
ROBIN.   Nay, there you lie, 'tis beyond us both.   20
VINTNER.   A plague take you, I thought 'twas your knavery to take it
away. Come, give it me again.
ROBIN.   Ay much! When, can you tell? Dick, make me a circle, and
stand close at my back, and stir not for thy life. Vintner, you shall have
your cup anon — say nothing Dick! O per se, o; Demogorgon, Belcher
and Mephostophilis!   26

(*Enter* MEPHOSTOPHILIS.)

MEPHOSTOPHILIS.   You princely legions of infernal rule,
How am I vexed by these villains' charms!
From Constantinople have they brought me now,
Only for pleasure of these damned slaves.   30

(*Exit* VINTNER.)

ROBIN.   By lady sir, you have had a shrewd journey of it. Will it please
you to take a shoulder of mutton to supper, and a tester in your purse,
and go back again?
DICK.   Ay, I pray you heartily sir, for we called you but in jest, I
promise you.   35
MEPHOSTOPHILIS.   To purge the rashness of this cursed deed,
First, be thou turned to this ugly shape,
For apish deeds transformed to an ape.
ROBIN.   O brave, an ape! I pray sir, let me have the carrying of him
about to show some tricks.   40
MEPHOSTOPHILIS.   And so thou shalt: be thou transformed to a dog,
and carry him upon thy back. Away, be gone!
ROBIN.   A dog? That's excellent: let the maids look well to their
porridge-pots, for I'll into the kitchen presently: come Dick, come.

(*Exeunt the two* CLOWNS.)

MEPHOSTOPHILIS.   Now with the flames of ever-burning fire,   45
I'll wing myself, and forthwith fly amain
Unto my Faustus, to the great Turk's court. (*Exit.*)

18. **outface . . . matter:** brazen it out with me.   20. **beyond us both:** out of our
hands; the Clowns have succeeded in juggling with the cup so that neither holds it.
23. **Ay . . . tell:** derisive comments.   31. **shrewd:** tiresome.   32. **tester:** sixpence
(slang).

CHORUS II

(*Enter* CHORUS.)

CHORUS.　When Faustus had with pleasure ta'en the view
Of rarest things and royal courts of kings,
He stayed his course, and so returned home,
Where such as bare his absence but with grief —
I mean his friends and near'st companions —　　　　　　5
Did gratulate his safety with kind words;
And in their conference of what befell,
Touching his journey through the world and air,
They put forth questions of astrology,
Which Faustus answered with such learned skill,　　　　10
As they admired and wondered at his wit.
Now is his fame spread forth in every land:
Amongst the rest, the Emperor is one,
Carolus the fifth, at which palace now
Faustus is feasted 'mongst his noblemen.　　　　　　15
What there he did in trial of his art,
I leave untold, your eyes shall see performed.

ACT FOUR

Scene 1

(*Enter* MARTINO *and* FREDERICK *at several doors.*)

MARTINO.　What ho, officers, gentlemen,
Hie to the presence to attend the Emperor!
Good Frederick, see the rooms be voided straight,
His Majesty is coming to the hall;
Go back, and see the state in readiness.　　　　　　5
FREDERICK.　But where is Bruno, our elected Pope,
That on a fury's back came post from Rome?
Will not his grace consort the Emperor?
MARTINO.　O yes, and with him comes the German conjuror,
The learned Faustus, fame of Wittenberg,　　　　　　10
The wonder of the world for magic art;
And he intends to show great Carolus,
The race of all his stout progenitors;

Chorus II, 14. Carolus: Charles V, Emperor 1519–1556.
　Act IV, Scene i, 2. presence: audience chamber.　3. voided straight: cleared
instantly.　5. state: throne.

And bring in presence of his Majesty,
The royal shapes and warlike semblances   15
Of Alexander and his beauteous paramour.
 FREDERICK. Where is Benvolio?
 MARTINO. Fast asleep I warrant you.
He took his rouse with stoups of Rhenish wine
So kindly yesternight to Bruno's health,   20
That all this day the sluggard keeps his bed.
 FREDERICK. See, see, his window's ope; we'll call to him.
 MARTINO. What ho, Benvolio!

(*Enter* BENVOLIO *above at a window, in his nightcap; buttoning.*)

 BENVOLIO. What a devil ail you two?
 MARTINO. Speak softly sir, lest the devil hear you: 25
For Faustus at the court is late arrived,
And at his heels a thousand furies wait,
To accomplish whatsoever the doctor please.
 BENVOLIO. What of this?
 MARTINO. Come, leave thy chamber first, and thou shalt see   30
This conjuror perform such rare exploits,
Before the Pope and royal Emperor,
As never yet was seen in Germany.
 BENVOLIO. Has not the Pope enough of conjuring yet?
He was upon the devil's back late enough;   35
And if he be so far in love with him
I would he would post with him to Rome again.
 FREDERICK. Speak, wilt thou come and see this sport?
 BENVOLIO. Not I.
 MARTINO. Wilt thou stand in thy window, and see it then?   40
 BENVOLIO. Ay, and I fall not asleep i'th'meantime.
 MARTINO. The Emperor is at hand, who comes to see
What wonders by black spells may compassed be.   43
 BENVOLIO. Well, go you attend the Emperor; I am content for this
once to thrust my head out at a window: for they say, if a man be drunk
overnight, the devil cannot hurt him in the morning: if that be true, I
have a charm in my head, shall control him as well as the conjuror, I
warrant you.   48

(*Exeunt* FREDERICK *and* MARTINO.)

---

15. **warlike:** heroic. 19. **took his rouse:** had a heavy drinking session (cf. *Hamlet*, I.iv.8–10). **stoups:** measures. 23. S.D. **buttoning:** buttoning up his clothes (the intransitive use of the verb is rare).

Scene 2

(*A Sennet*. charles *the* German Emperor, bruno, saxony, faustus, mephostophilis, frederick, martino, *and* attendants. benvolio *remains in the window.*)

emperor.   Wonder of men, renowned magician,
Thrice-learned Faustus, welcome to our court.
This deed of thine, in setting Bruno free
From his and our professed enemy,
Shall add more excellence unto thine art,   5
Than if by powerful necromantic spells,
Thou could'st command the world's obedience:
For ever be beloved of Carolus.
And if this Bruno thou hast late redeemed,
In peace possess the triple diadem,   10
And sit in Peter's chair, despite of chance,
Thou shalt be famous through all Italy,
And honoured of the German Emperor.
   faustus.   These gracious words, most royal Carolus,
Shall make poor Faustus to his utmost power,   15
Both love and serve the German Emperor,
And lay his life at holy Bruno's feet.
For proof whereof, if so your grace be pleased,
The doctor stands prepared, by power of art,
To cast his magic charms, that shall pierce through   20
The ebon gates of ever-burning hell,
And hale the stubborn furies from their caves,
To compass whatsoe'er your grace commands.
   benvolio.   'Blood, he speaks terribly; but for all that, I do not
greatly believe him; he looks as like a conjuror as the Pope to a coster-
monger.   26
   emperor.   Then Faustus, as thou late didst promise us,
We would behold that famous conqueror,
Great Alexander, and his paramour,
In their true shapes, and state majestical,   30
That we may wonder at their excellence.
   faustus.   Your Majesty shall see them presently.
Mephostophilis, away!
And with a solemn noise of trumpets' sound,
Present before this royal Emperor,   35
Great Alexander and his beauteous paramour.
   mephostophilis.   Faustus I will. (*Exit.*)
   benvolio.   Well master doctor, an your devils come not away quickly,
you shall have me asleep presently: zounds, I could eat myself for anger,

Scene ii, 29.   **paramour**: Alexander's wife, Roxana.

to think I have been such an ass all this while, to stand gaping after the
devil's governor, and can see nothing.   41
    FAUSTUS. I'll make you feel something anon, if my art fail me not.
My lord, I must forewarn your Majesty,
That when my spirits present the royal shapes
Of Alexander and his paramour,   45
Your grace demand no questions of the king,
But in dumb silence let them come and go.
    EMPEROR. Be it as Faustus please, we are content.
    BENVOLIO. Ay, ay, and I am content too: and thou bring Alexander
and his paramour before the Emperor, I'll be Actaeon, and turn my self
to a stag.
    FAUSTUS. And I'll play Diana, and send you the horns presently.   52

(*Sennet. Enter at one door the* EMPEROR ALEXANDER, *at the other*
DARIUS: *they meet,* DARIUS *is thrown down,* ALEXANDER *kills him; takes
off his crown, and offering to go out, his* PARAMOUR *meets him, he em-
braceth her, and sets* DARIUS' *crown upon her head; and coming back,
both salute the* EMPEROR, *who leaving his state, offers to embrace them,
which* FAUSTUS *seeing, suddenly stays him. Then trumpets cease, and
music sounds.*)

My gracious lord, you do forget yourself;
These are but shadows, not substantial.
    EMPEROR. O pardon me, my thoughts are so ravished   55
With sight of this renowned emperor,
That in mine arms I would have compassed him.
But Faustus, since I may not speak to them,
To satisfy my longing thoughts at full,
Let me this tell thee: I have heard it said,   60
That this fair lady, whilst she lived on earth,
Had on her neck a little wart or mole;
How may I prove that saying to be true?
    FAUSTUS. Your Majesty may boldly go and see.
    EMPEROR. Faustus I see it plain,   65
And in this sight thou better pleasest me,
Than if I gained another monarchy.
    FAUSTUS. Away, be gone.

(*Exit* SHOW.)

See, see, my gracious lord, what strange beast is yon, that thrusts his head
out at window?   70

---

50. **Actaeon:** as punishment for coming upon Diana and her nymphs bathing,
Actaeon was turned into a stag, and his own hounds tore him to pieces.

EMPEROR.   O wondrous sight! See, Duke of Saxony,
Two spreading horns most strangely fastened
Upon the head of young Benvolio.
SAXONY.   What, is he asleep, or dead?
FAUSTUS.   He sleeps my lord, but dreams not of his horns.   75
EMPEROR.   This sport is excellent: we'll call and wake him.
What ho, Benvolio!
BENVOLIO.   A plague upon you, let me sleep awhile.
EMPEROR.   I blame thee not to sleep much, having such a head of
thine own.   80
SAXONY.   Look up Benvolio, 'tis the Emperor calls.
BENVOLIO.   The Emperor? Where? O zounds my head!
EMPEROR.   Nay, and thy horns hold, 'tis no matter for thy head, for
that's armed sufficiently.   84
FAUSTUS.   Why, how now sir knight? What, hanged by the horns?
This is most horrible! Fie, fie, pull in your head for shame, let not all
the world wonder at you.
BENVOLIO.   Zounds doctor, is this your villainy?
FAUSTUS.   O say not so sir: the doctor has no skill,
No art, no cunning, to present these lords,   90
Or bring before this royal Emperor
The mighty monarch, warlike Alexander.
If Faustus do it, you are straight resolved
In bold Actaeon's shape to turn a stag.
And therefore my lord, so please your Majesty,   95
I'll raise a kennel of hounds shall hunt him so,
As all his footmanship shall scarce prevail
To keep his carcase from their bloody fangs.
Ho, Belimote, Argiron, Asterote!   99
BENVOLIO.   Hold, hold! Zounds, he'll raise up a kennel of devils, I
think, anon: good my lord, entreat for me: 'sblood, I am never able to
endure these torments.
EMPEROR.   Then good master doctor,
Let me entreat you to remove his horns,
He has done penance now sufficiently.   105
FAUSTUS.   My gracious lord, not so much for injury done to me, as
to delight your Majesty with some mirth, hath Faustus justly requited
this injurious knight; which being all I desire, I am content to remove his
horns. Mephostophilis, transform him — and hereafter sir, look you
speak well of scholars.   110
BENVOLIO.   Speak well of ye! 'Sblood, and scholars be such cuckold-
makers to clap horns of honest men's heads o' this order, I'll ne'er trust
smooth faces and small ruffs more. But an I be not revenged for this,
would I might be turned to a gaping oyster, and drink nothing but salt
water.   115

97. **footmanship:** skill in running. 113. **smooth . . . ruffs:** beardless scholars in
academic dress.

EMPEROR.   Come Faustus, while the Emperor lives,
In recompense of this thy high desert,
Thou shalt command the state of Germany,
And live beloved of mighty Carolus.

(*Exeunt omnes.*)

Scene 3

(*Enter* BENVOLIO, MARTINO, FREDERICK, *and* SOLDIERS.)

MARTINO.   Nay sweet Benvolio, let us sway thy thoughts
From this attempt against the conjuror.
BENVOLIO.   Away, you love me not, to urge me thus.
Shall I let slip so great an injury,
When every servile groom jests at my wrongs,   5
And in their rustic gambols proudly say,
'Benvolio's head was graced with horns today'?
O may these eyelids never close again,
Till with my sword I have that conjuror slain.
If you will aid me in this enterprise,   10
Then draw your weapons, and be resolute:
If not, depart: here will Benvolio die,
But Faustus' death shall quit my infamy.
FREDERICK.   Nay, we will stay with thee, betide what may,
And kill that doctor if he come this way.   15
BENVOLIO.   Then gentle Frederick, hie thee to the grove,
And place our servants and our followers
Close in an ambush there behind the trees.
By this (I know) the conjuror is near,
I saw him kneel and kiss the Emperor's hand,   20
And take his leave, laden with rich rewards.
Then soldiers boldly fight; if Faustus die,
Take you the wealth, leave us the victory.
FREDERICK.   Come soldiers, follow me unto the grove;
Who kills him shall have gold and endless love.   25

(*Exit* FREDERICK *with the* SOLDIERS.)

BENVOLIO.   My head is lighter than it was by th'horns,
But yet my heart's more ponderous than my head,
And pants until I see that conjuror dead.
MARTINO.   Where shall we place ourselves Benvolio?

Scene iii, 6. proudly: insolently.   **13. But:** unless.   **18. Close:** hidden.
19. By this: by this time.

BENVOLIO.   Here will we stay to bide the first assault.   30
O were that damned hell-hound but in place,
Thou soon should'st see me quit my foul disgrace.

(*Enter* FREDERICK.)

FREDERICK.   Close, close, the conjuror is at hand,
And all alone, comes walking in his gown.
Be ready then, and strike the peasant down.   35
    BENVOLIO.   Mine be that honour then: now sword strike home,
For horns he gave, I'll have his head anon.

(*Enter* FAUSTUS *with the false head.*)

MARTINO.   See, see, he comes.
    BENVOLIO.   No words; this blow ends all,
Hell take his soul, his body thus must fall. (*Strikes* FAUSTUS.)
    FAUSTUS.   O!   40
    FREDERICK.   Groan you master doctor?
    BENVOLIO.   Break may his heart with groans: dear Frederick see,
Thus will I end his griefs immediately. (*Cuts off his head.*)
    MARTINO.   Strike with a willing hand; his head is off.
    BENVOLIO.   The devil's dead, the furies now may laugh.   45
    FREDERICK.   Was this that stern aspect, that awful frown,
Made the grim monarch of infernal spirits,
Tremble and quake at his commanding charms?
    MARTINO.   Was this that damned head, whose heart conspired
Benvolio's shame before the Emperor?   50
    BENVOLIO.   Ay, that's the head, and here the body lies,
Justly rewarded for his villainies.
    FREDERICK.   Come, let's devise how we may add more shame
To the black scandal of his hated name.
    BENVOLIO.   First, on his head, in quittance of my wrongs,   55
I'll nail huge forked horns, and let them hang
Within the window where he yoked me first,
That all the world may see my just revenge.
    MARTINO.   What use shall we put his beard to?
    BENVOLIO.   We'll sell it to a chimney-sweeper; it will wear out ten
birchen brooms, I warrant you.   61
    FREDERICK.   What shall eyes do?
    BENVOLIO.   We'll put out his eyes, and they shall serve for buttons to
his lips, to keep his tongue from catching cold.
    MARTINO.   An excellent policy: and now sirs, having divided him, what
shall the body do?   66

(FAUSTUS *stands up.*)

31. **in place:** on the spot.

BENVOLIO.   Zounds, the devil's alive again!
FREDERICK.   Give him his head for God's sake.
FAUSTUS.   Nay keep it: Faustus will have heads and hands,
Ay, all your hearts to recompense this deed.   70
Knew you not, traitors, I was limited
For four and twenty years to breathe on earth?
And had you cut my body with your swords,
Or hewed this flesh and bones as small as sand,
Yet in a minute had my spirit returned,   75
And I had breathed a man made free from harm.
But wherefore do I dally my revenge?
Asteroth, Belimoth, Mephostophilis!

(*Enter* MEPHOSTOPHILIS *and other* DEVILS.)

Go, horse these traitors on your fiery backs,
And mount aloft with them as high as heaven,   80
Thence pitch them headlong to the lowest hell:
Yet stay, the world shall see their misery,
And hell shall after plague their treachery.
Go Belimoth, and take this caitiff hence,
And hurl him in some lake of mud and dirt: 85
Take thou this other, drag him through the woods,
Amongst the pricking thorns and sharpest briers,
Whilst with my gentle Mephostophilis,
This traitor flies unto some steepy rock.
That, rolling down, may break the villain's bones,   90
As he intended to dismember me.
Fly hence, dispatch my charge immediately.
FREDERICK.   Pity us gentle Faustus, save our lives.
FAUSTUS.   Away!
FREDERICK.   He must needs go that the devil drives.   95

(*Exeunt* SPIRITS *with the* KNIGHTS. *Enter the ambushed* SOLDIERS.)

FIRST SOLDIER.   Come sirs, prepare yourselves in readiness,
Make haste to help these noble gentlemen;
I heard them parley with the conjuror.
SECOND SOLDIER.   See where he comes, dispatch, and kill the slave.
FAUSTUS.   What's here? An ambush to betray my life!   100
Then Faustus try thy skill: base peasants stand!
For lo, these trees remove at my command,
And stand as bulwarks 'twixt yourselves and me,
To shield me from your hated treachery:
Yet to encounter this your weak attempt,   105
Behold an army comes incontinent.

95. **He . . . drives:** a well known proverb.   106. **incontinent:** without delay.

(FAUSTUS *strikes the door, and enter a* DEVIL *playing on a drum, after him another bearing an ensign: and divers with weapons,* MEPHOSTOPHILIS *with fireworks; they set upon the* SOLDIERS *and drive them out. Exit* FAUSTUS.)

Scene 4

(*Enter at several doors,* BENVOLIO, FREDERICK, *and* MARTINO, *their heads and faces bloody, and besmeared with mud and dirt; all having horns on their heads.*)

MARTINO.   What ho, Benvolio!
BENVOLIO.   Here, what Frederick, ho!
FREDERICK.   O help me gentle friend; where is Martino?
MARTINO.   Dear Frederick here,
Half smothered in a lake of mud and dirt,   5
Through which the furies dragged me by the heels.
FREDERICK.   Martino see, Benvolio's horns again!
MARTINO.   O misery! How now, Benvolio?
BENVOLIO.   Defend me heaven! Shall I be haunted still?
MARTINO.   Nay, fear not man, we have no power to kill.   10
BENVOLIO.   My friends transformed thus! O hellish spite,
Your heads are all set with horns.
FREDERICK.   You hit it right,
It is your own you mean; feel on your head.
BENVOLIO.   Zounds, horns again!
MARTINO.   Nay, chafe not man, we all are sped.
BENVOLIO.   What devil attends this damned magician,   15
That spite of spite, our wrongs are doubled?
FREDERICK.   What may we do, that we may hide our shame?
BENVOLIO.   If we should follow him to work revenge,
He'd join long asses' ears to these huge horns,
And make us laughing-stocks to all the world.   20
MARTINO.   What shall we do then dear Benvolio?
BENVOLIO.   I have a castle joining near these woods,
And thither we'll repair and live obscure,
Till time shall alter these our brutish shapes:
Sith black disgrace hath thus eclipsed our fame,   25
We'll rather die with grief, than live with shame.

(*Exeunt omnes.*)

Scene 5

(*Enter* FAUSTUS *and the* HORSE-COURSER.)

HORSE-COURSER.   I beseech your worship accept of these forty dollars.

Scene iv, 10. kill: this suggests a pun on *haunted/hunted* in the preceding line.
Scene v, 1. S.D. HORSE-COURSER: horse-dealer; a reputation for dishonesty has always attached to such traders.

FAUSTUS. Friend, thou canst not buy so good a horse for so small a price: I have no great need to sell him, but if thou likest him for ten dollars more, take him, because I can see thou hast a good mind to him.

HORSE-COURSER. I beseech you sir, accept of this; I am a very poor man, and have lost very much of late by horse-flesh, and this bargain will set me up again.   7

FAUSTUS. Well, I will not stand with thee; give me the money. Now, sirra, I must tell you, that you may ride him o'er hedge and ditch, and spare him not; but: do you hear, in any case ride him not into the water.

HORSE-COURSER. How sir, not into the water? Why, will he not drink of all waters?   12

FAUSTUS. Yes, he will drink of all waters, but ride him not into the water; o'er hedge and ditch, or where thou wilt, but not into the water. Go bid the ostler deliver him unto you, and remember what I say.

HORSE-COURSER. I warrant you sir; O joyful day! Now am I a made man for ever. (*Exit.*)

FAUSTUS. What art thou, Faustus, but a man condemned to die?   18
Thy fatal time draws to a final end;
Despair doth drive distrust into my thoughts.
Confound these passions with a quiet sleep:
Tush, Christ did call the thief upon the cross;
Then rest thee, Faustus, quiet in conceit. (*He sits to sleep.*)   23

(*Enter the* HORSE-COURSER, *wet.*)

HORSE-COURSER. O what a cozening doctor was this! I riding my horse into the water, thinking some hidden mystery had been in the horse, I had nothing under me but a little straw, and had much ado to escape drowning. Well, I'll go rouse him, and make him give me my forty dollars again. Ho, sirra doctor, you cozening scab! Maister doctor awake, and rise, and give me my money again, for your horse is turned to a bottle of hay. Maister doctor — (*He pulls off his leg.*) Alas, I am un-done, what shall I do? I have pulled off his leg!   31

FAUSTUS. O help, help, the villain hath murdered me!

HORSE-COURSER. Murder or not murder, now he has but one leg, I'll out-run him, and cast this leg into some ditch or other. (*Exit.*)

FAUSTUS. Stop him, stop him, stop him! — ha, ha, ha, Faustus hath his leg again, and the horse-courser a bundle of hay for his forty dollars.

(*Enter* WAGNER.)

How now Wagner, what news with thee?   37

8. **stand with thee:** haggle over it. 10. **in any case:** whatever happens. **not into the water:** running water (but not the stagnant water of a ditch) dissolves a witch's spell. 13. **drink of all waters:** go anywhere; 'I am for all waters' (*Twelfth Night*, IV.ii.57). 23. **in conceit:** in this thought. 24. **cozening:** cheating. 30. **bottle:** truss. **Maister:** here, and in the succeeding comic scenes, the author attempts to indicate dialectal pronunciation.

WAGNER. If it please you, the Duke of Vanholt doth earnestly entreat your company, and hath sent some of his men to attend you with provision fit for your journey.

FAUSTUS. The Duke of Vanholt's an honourable gentleman, and one to whom I must be no niggard of my cunning. Come away. 42

(*Exeunt.*)

Scene 6

(*Enter* CLOWN [ROBIN], DICK, HORSE-COURSER, *and a* CARTER.)

CARTER. Come my masters, I'll bring you to the best beer in Europe. What ho hostess! Where be these whores?

(*Enter* HOSTESS.)

HOSTESS. How now, what lack you? What, my old guests, welcome.

ROBIN. Sirra Dick, dost thou know why I stand so mute?

DICK. No Robin, why is't? 5

ROBIN. I am eighteenpence on the score; but say nothing, see if she have forgotten me.

HOSTESS. Who's this, that stands so solemnly by himself? What, my old guest!

ROBIN. O hostess, how do you? I hope my score stands still. 10

HOSTESS. Ay, there's no doubt of that, for methinks you make no haste to wipe it out.

DICK. Why hostess, I say, fetch us some beer.

HOSTESS. You shall presently. Look up into th'hall there, ho! (*Exit.*)

DICK. Come sirs, what shall we do now till mine hostess comes? 15

CARTER. Marry sir, I'll tell you the bravest tale how a conjuror served me; you know Doctor Fauster?

HORSE-COURSER. Ay, a plague take him. Here's some on's have cause to know him. Did he conjure thee too? 19

CARTER. I'll tell you how he served me. As I was going to Wittenberg t'other day, with a load of hay, he met me, and asked me what he should give me for as much hay as he could eat. Now, sir, I, thinking that a little would serve his turn, bade him take as much as he would for three farthings. So he presently gave me my money, and fell to eating, and as I am a cursen man, he never left eating, till he had eat up all my load of hay.

Scene vi, 2. whores: 'A cup of ale without a wench, why alas, 'tis like an egg without salt, or a red herring without mustard' (*Looking Glass for London*, II.278–280). 14. Look . . . ho: the Hostess calls to her servants. 25. cursen: Christian (the dialectal form of *christened*).

ALL.   O monstrous, eat a whole load of hay!   26

ROBIN.   Yes, yes, that may be; for I have heard of one, that h'as eat a load of logs.   28

HORSE-COURSER.   Now sirs, you shall hear how villainously he served me: I went to him yesterday to buy a horse of him, and he would by no means sell him under forty dollars; so sir, because I knew him to be such a horse, as would run over hedge and ditch, and never tire, I gave him his money. So when I had my horse, Doctor Fauster bade me ride him night and day, and spare him no time; 'But', quoth he, 'in any case ride him not into the water'. Now sir, I, thinking the horse had had some quality that he would not have me know of, what did I but rid him into a great river, and when I came just in the midst, my horse vanished away, and I sat straddling upon a bottle of hay.   38

ALL.   O brave doctor!

HORSE-COURSER.   But you shall hear how bravely I served him for it. I went me home to his house, and there I found him asleep; I kept a-hallowing and whooping in his ears, but all could not wake him. I, seeing that, took him by the leg, and never rested pulling, till I had pulled me his leg quite off, and now 'tis at home in mine hostry.   44

ROBIN.   And has the doctor but one leg then? That's excellent, for one of his devils turned me, into the likeness of an ape's face.

CARTER.   Some more drink hostess!

ROBIN.   Hark you, we'll into another room and drink awhile, and then we'll go seek out the doctor.   49

(*Exeunt omnes.*)

Scene 7

(*Enter the* DUKE OF VANHOLT, *his* DUCHESS, FAUSTUS, *and* MEPHO-STOPHILIS.)

DUKE.   Thanks master doctor, for these pleasant sights. Nor know I how sufficiently to recompense your great deserts in erecting that enchanted castle in the air; the sight whereof so delighted me, as nothing in the world could please me more.   4

FAUSTUS.   I do think myself, my good lord, highly recompensed, in that it pleaseth your grace to think but well of that which Faustus hath performed. But gracious lady, it may be, that you have taken no pleasure in those sights; therefore I pray you tell me, what is the thing you most desire to have: be it in the world, it shall be yours. I have heard that great-bellied women do long for things are rare and dainty.   10

LADY.   True, master doctor, and since I find you so kind, I will make known unto you what my heart desires to have; and were it now summer,

27. h'as: he has.

as it is January, a dead time of the winter, I would request no better meat, than a dish of ripe grapes.

FAUSTUS.   This is but a small matter: go Mephostophilis, away.   15

(*Exit* MEPHOSTOPHILIS.)

Madam, I will do more than this for your content.

(*Enter* MEPHOSTOPHILIS *again with the grapes.*)

Here, now taste ye these; they should be good for they come from a far country, I can tell you.

DUKE.   This makes me wonder more than all the rest, that at this time of the year, when every tree is barren of his fruits, from whence you had these ripe grapes.   21

FAUSTUS.   Please it your grace, the year is divided into two circles over the whole world, so that when it is winter with us, in the contrary circle it is likewise summer with them, as in India, Saba, and such countries that lie far east, where they have fruit twice a year. From whence, by means of a swift spirit that I have, I had these grapes brought as you see.

LADY.   And trust me, they are the sweetest grapes that e'er I tasted.

(*The* CLOWNS *bounce at the gate, within.*)

DUKE.   What rude disturbers have we at the gate?   28
Go pacify their fury, set it ope,
And then demand of them, what they would have.

(*They knock again, and call out to talk with* FAUSTUS.)

A SERVANT.   Why, how now masters? What a coil is there! What is the reason you disturb the Duke?   32

DICK.   We have no reason for it, therefore a fig for him.

SERVANT.   Why saucy varlets, dare you be so bold?

HORSE-COURSER.   I hope sir, we have wit enough to be more bold than welcome.   36

SERVANT.   It appears so; pray be bold elsewhere, and trouble not the Duke.

DUKE.   What would they have?

SERVANT.   They all cry out to speak with Doctor Faustus.   40

CARTER.   Ay, and we will speak with him.

Scene vii, 22–25. year . . . year: the relevant circles would be the northern and southern hemispheres, but the author appears to be thinking in terms of east and west. 24. Saba: Sheba. 27. S.D. *bounce:* beat. 31. coil: din. 33. reason . . . fig: Dick makes the not uncommon pun on *reason/raisin.*

DUKE. Will you sir? Commit the rascals.

DICK. Commit with us! He were as good commit with his father, as commit with us.

FAUSTUS. I do beseech your grace let them come in,   45
They are good subject for a merriment.

DUKE. Do as thou wilt Faustus, I give thee leave.

FAUSTUS. I thank your grace.

(*Enter the* CLOWN [ROBIN], DICK, CARTER, *and* HORSE-COURSER.)

Why, how now my good friends?
'Faith, you are too outrageous, but come near,
I have procured your pardons: welcome all.   50

ROBIN. Nay sir, we will be welcome for our money, and we will pay for what we take: what ho! Give's half a dozen of beer here, and be hanged.

FAUSTUS. Nay, hark you, can you tell me where you are?

CARTER. Ay, marry can I, we are under heaven.   55

SERVANT. Ay, but sir sauce-box, know you in what place?

HORSE-COURSER. Ay, ay, the house is good enough to drink in. Zounds, fill us some beer, or we'll break all the barrels in the house, and dash out all your brains with your bottles.

FAUSTUS. Be not so furious: come, you shall have beer.   60
My lord, beseech you give me leave awhile,
I'll gage my credit, 'twill content your grace.

DUKE. With all my heart, kind doctor, please thyself:
Our servants, and our court's at thy command.

FAUSTUS. I humbly thank your grace: then fetch some beer.   65

HORSE-COURSER. Ay, marry, there spake a doctor indeed, and 'faith I'll drink a health to thy wooden leg for that word.

FAUSTUS. My wooden leg? What dost thou mean by that?

CARTER. Ha, ha, ha, dost thou hear him Dick? He has forgot his leg.

HORSE-COURSER. Ay, ay, he does not stand much upon that.   70

FAUSTUS. No 'faith, not much upon a wooden leg.

CARTER. Good Lord, that flesh and blood should be so frail with your worship! Do not you remember a horse-courser you sold a horse to?

FAUSTUS. Yes, I remember one I sold a horse.   74

CARTER. And do you remember you bid he should not ride into the water?

FAUSTUS. Yes, I do very well remember that.

42. **Commit:** take to prison; through frequent collocations such as 'commit adultery' the word came to have the sense of 'fornicate,' which Dick assumes in the next line. 51ff. The Clowns believe that, as they promised at the end of IV.vi, they have simply stepped into 'another room,' whereas it would appear that Faustus, by his magic spells, has brought them unawares to the court of Vanholt. 62. **gage:** stake.

CARTER.   And do you remember nothing of your leg?

FAUSTUS.   No, in good sooth.   79

CARTER.   Then I pray remember your curtsy.

FAUSTUS.   I thank you sir. (*He bows to the company.*)

CARTER.   'Tis not so much worth; I pray you tell me one thing.

FAUSTUS.   What's that?

CARTER.   Be both your legs bedfellows every night together?   84

FAUSTUS.   Would'st thou make a colossus of me, that thou askest me such questions?

CARTER.   No truly sir, I would make nothing of you, but I would fain know that.

(*Enter* HOSTESS *with drink.*)

FAUSTUS.   Then I assure thee certainly they are.

CARTER.   I thank you, I am fully satisfied.   90

FAUSTUS.   But wherefore dost thou ask?

CARTER.   For nothing sir — but methinks you should have a wooden bedfellow of one of 'em.

HORSE-COURSER.   Why, do you hear sir, did not I pull off one of your legs when you were asleep?   95

FAUSTUS.   But I have it again now I am awake: look you here sir.

ALL.   O horrible! Had the doctor three legs?

CARTER.   Do you remember sir, how you cozened me and eat up my load of —

(FAUSTUS *charms him dumb.*)

DICK.   Do you remember how you made me wear an ape's —   100

HORSE-COURSER.   You whoreson conjuring scab, do you remember how you cozened me with a ho —

ROBIN.   Ha' you forgotten me? You think to carry it away with your hey-pass and re-pass: do you remember the dog's fa —   104

(*Exeunt* CLOWNS.)

HOSTESS.   Who pays for the ale? Hear you maister doctor, now you have sent away my guests, I pray who shall pay me for my a — (*Exit* HOSTESS.)

LADY.   My lord,
We are much beholding to this learned man.

---

82. 'Tis . . . worth: Faustus' bow is not worth much as an indication of whether or not he has a wooden leg.   85. colossus: gigantic statue; the Colossus at Rhodes straddled the entrance to the harbour (cf. *Julius Caesar*, I.ii.135–136).
104. hey-pass and re-pass: abracadabra.

DUKE. So are we, madam, which we will recompense   110
With all the love and kindness that we may;
His artful sport drives all sad thoughts away.

(*Exeunt.*)

ACT FIVE

Scene 1

(*Thunder and lightning. Enter* DEVILS *with covered dishes:* MEPHO-
STOPHILIS *leads them into* FAUSTUS' *study. Then enter* WAGNER.)

WAGNER. I think my master means to die shortly,
For he hath given to me all his goods;
And yet, methinks, if that death were near,
He would not banquet, and carouse, and swill   4
Amongst the students, as even now he doth,
Who are at supper with such belly-cheer,
As Wagner ne'er beheld in all his life.
See where they come: belike the feast is ended. (*Exit.*)   8

(*Enter* FAUSTUS, MEPHOSTOPHILIS, *and two or three* SCHOLARS.)

FIRST SCHOLAR. Master Doctor Faustus, since our conference about
fair ladies, which was the beautifullest in all the world, we have determined with ourselves, that Helen of Greece was the admirablest lady that
ever lived: therefore, master doctor, if you will do us so much favour, as
to let us see that peerless dame of Greece, we should think ourselves much
beholding unto you.

FAUSTUS. Gentlemen,   15
For that I know your friendship is unfeigned,
And Faustus' custom is not to deny
The just requests of those that wish him well:
You shall behold that peerless dame of Greece,
No otherways for pomp and majesty,   20
Than when Sir Paris crossed the seas with her,
And brought the spoils to rich Dardania:
Be silent then, for danger is in words.

(*Music sound.* MEPHOSTOPHILIS *brings in* HELEN; *she passeth over the
stage.*)

Act V, Scene i, 22. Dardania: Troy; in fact the city built by Dardanus on the
Hellespont, but the name is often transferred to Troy.

SECOND SCHOLAR.   Too simple is my wit to tell her praise,
Whom all the world admires for majesty.   25
THIRD SCHOLAR.   No marvel though the angry Greeks pursued
With ten years' war the rape of such a queen,
Whose heavenly beauty passeth all compare.
FIRST SCHOLAR.   Since we have seen the pride of Nature's works,
And only paragon of excellence,   30
Let us depart, and for this glorious deed
Happy and blest be Faustus evermore.
FAUSTUS.   Gentlemen farewell; the same I wish to you.

(*Exeunt* SCHOLARS. *Enter an* OLD MAN.)

OLD MAN.   O gentle Faustus, leave this damned art,
This magic, that will charm thy soul to hell,   35
And quite bereave thee of salvation.
Though thou hast now offended like a man,
Do not persever in it like a devil;
Yet, yet, thou hast an amiable soul,
If sin by custom grow not into nature: 40
Then, Faustus, will repentance come too late,
Then thou art banished from the sight of heaven;
No mortal can express the pains of hell.
It may be this my exhortation
Seems harsh, and all unpleasant; let it not,   45
For, gentle son, I speak it not in wrath,
Or envy of thee, but in tender love,
And pity of thy future misery;
And so have hope, that this my kind rebuke,
Checking thy body, may amend thy soul.   50
FAUSTUS.   Where art thou Faustus, wretch, what hast thou done?
Damned art thou Faustus, damned; despair and die!

(MEPHOSTOPHILIS *gives him a dagger.*)

Hell claims his right, and with a roaring voice
Says 'Faustus come, thine hour is almost come,'
And Faustus now will come to do thee right. (FAUSTUS *goes to use the
    dagger.*)   55
OLD MAN.   O stay, good Faustus, stay thy desperate steps!
I see an angel hover o'er thy head,
And with a vial full of precious grace,

---

38. **persever:** accented on the second syllable.   39–40. **thou . . . nature:** your
soul is still capable of being loved, so long as sin does not become habitual and
thus part of your nature.

Offers to pour the same into thy soul;
Then call for mercy, and avoid despair.   60
    FAUSTUS.   O friend, I feel
Thy words to comfort my distressed soul:
Leave me awhile, to ponder on my sins.
    OLD MAN.   Faustus I leave thee, but with grief of heart,
Fearing the enemy of thy hapless soul. (*Exit.*)   65
    FAUSTUS.   Accursed Faustus, where is mercy now?
I do repent, and yet I do despair;
Hell strives with grace for conquest in my breast:
What shall I do to shun the snares of death?
    MEPHOSTOPHILIS.   Thou traitor Faustus, I arrest thy soul   70
For disobedience to my sovereign lord.
Revolt, or I'll in piecemeal tear thy flesh.
    FAUSTUS.   I do repent I e'er offended him;
Sweet Mephostophilis, entreat thy lord
To pardon my unjust presumption,   75
And with my blood again I will confirm
The former vow I made to Lucifer.
    MEPHOSTOPHILIS.   Do it then quickly with unfeigned heart,
Lest greater dangers do attend thy drift.
    FAUSTUS.   Torment, sweet friend, that base and crooked age, 80
That durst dissuade me from thy Lucifer,
With greatest torment that our hell affords.
    MEPHOSTOPHILIS.   His faith is great, I cannot touch his soul;
But what I may afflict his body with,
I will attempt, which is but little worth.   85
    FAUSTUS.   One thing, good servant, let me crave of thee,
To glut the longing of my heart's desire,
That I may have unto my paramour,
That heavenly Helen, which I saw of late,
Whose sweet embracings may extinguish clear   90
Those thoughts that do dissuade me from my vow,
And keep mine oath I made to Lucifer.
    MEPHOSTOPHILIS.   This, or what else my Faustus shall desire,
Shall be performed in twinkling of an eye.

   (*Enter* HELEN *again, passing over between two* CUPIDS.)

    FAUSTUS.   Was this the face that launched a thousand ships, 95
And burnt the topless towers of Ilium?
Sweet Helen, make me immortal with a kiss:
Her lips suck forth my soul, see where it flies!
Come Helen, come, give me my soul again.

---

72. **Revolt:** turn again to your allegiance. 79. **drift:** drifting; also *purpose.*
96. **Ilium:** Troy.

Here will I dwell, for heaven is in these lips, 100
And all is dross that is not Helena.

(*Enter* OLD MAN.)

I will be Paris, and for love of thee,
Instead of Troy shall Wittenberg be sacked;
And I will combat with weak Menelaus,
And wear thy colours on my plumed crest; 105
Yea, I will wound Achilles in the heel,
And then return to Helen for a kiss.
O, thou art fairer than the evening's air,
Clad in the beauty of a thousand stars:
Brighter art thou than flaming Jupiter, 110
When he appeared to hapless Semele;
More lovely than the monarch of the sky
In wanton Arethusa's azured arms;
And none but thou shalt be my paramour.

(*Exeunt* FAUSTUS *and* HELEN.)

OLD MAN.   Accursed Faustus, miserable man, 115
That from thy soul exclud'st the grace of heaven,
And fliest the throne of His tribunal seat!

(*Enter the* DEVILS.)

Satan begins to sift me with his pride,
As in this furnace God shall try my faith:
My faith, vile hell, shall triumph over thee! 120
Ambitious fiends, see how the heavens smiles
At your repulse, and laughs your state to scorn!
Hence hell, for hence I fly unto my God.

(*Exeunt.*)

Scene 2

(*Thunder. Enter* LUCIFER, BELZEBUB, *and* MEPHOSTOPHILIS.)

LUCIFER.   Thus from infernal Dis do we ascend
To view the subjects of our monarchy,
Those souls which sin seals the black sons of hell,
'Mong which as chief, Faustus, we come to thee,

Scene ii, 1. **Dis**: the Underworld; an alternative name for Pluto and extended
to his kingdom.

Bringing with us lasting damnation,   5
To wait upon thy soul; the time is come
Which makes it forfeit.
    MEPHOSTOPHILIS.   And this gloomy night,
Here in this room will wretched Faustus be.
    BELZEBUB.   And here we'll stay,
To mark him how he doth demean himself.   10
    MEPHOSTOPHILIS.   How should he, but in desperate lunacy?
Fond worldling, now his heart-blood dries with grief,
His conscience kills it, and his labouring brain,
Begets a world of idle fantasies,
To overreach the devil; but all in vain: 15
His store of pleasures must be sauced with pain.
He and his servant Wagner are at hand,
Both come from drawing Faustus' latest will.
See where they come.

    (*Enter* FAUSTUS *and* WAGNER.)

    FAUSTUS.   Say Wagner, thou hast perused my will,   20
How dost thou like it?
    WAGNER.   Sir, so wondrous well,
As in all humble duty, I do yield
My life and lasting service for your love.
    FAUSTUS.   Gramercies Wagner.

    (*Exit* WAGNER. *Enter the* SCHOLARS.)

                               Welcome gentlemen.
    FIRST SCHOLAR.   Now worthy Faustus, methinks your looks are
changed.   26
    FAUSTUS.   Ah, gentlemen!
    SECOND SCHOLAR.   What ails Faustus?
    FAUSTUS.   Ah my sweet chamber-fellow, had I lived with thee, then
had I lived still, but now must die eternally. Look sirs, comes he not,
comes he not?   31
    FIRST SCHOLAR.   O my dear Faustus, what imports this fear?
    SECOND SCHOLAR.   Is all our pleasure turned to melancholy?
    THIRD SCHOLAR.   He is not well with being over-solitary.
    SECOND SCHOLAR.   If it be so, we'll have physicians, and Faustus shall
be cured.   36
    THIRD SCHOLAR.   'Tis but a surfeit sir, fear nothing.
    FAUSTUS.   A surfeit of deadly sin, that hath damned both body and
soul.
    SECOND SCHOLAR.   Yet Faustus, look up to heaven, and remember
God's mercy is infinite.   41
    FAUSTUS.   But Faustus' offence can ne'er be pardoned. The serpent

that tempted Eve may be saved, but not Faustus. Ah gentlemen, hear
with patience, and tremble not at my speeches; though my heart pants
and quivers to remember that I have been a student here these thirty years
— O would I had never seen Wittenberg, never read book — and what
wonders I have done, all Germany can witness, yea, all the world — for
which Faustus hath lost both Germany and the world — yea, heaven
itself — heaven, the seat of God, the throne of the blessed, the kingdom
of joy; and must remain in hell for ever. Hell, ah hell, for ever! Sweet
friends, what shall become of Faustus, being in hell for ever?   51

SECOND SCHOLAR.   Yet Faustus, call on God.

FAUSTUS.   On God, whom Faustus hath abjured? On God, whom
Faustus hath blasphemed? Ah my God — I would weep, but the devil
draws in my tears. Gush forth blood instead of tears, yea, life and soul.
O, he stays my tongue; I would lift up my hands, but see, they hold 'em,
they hold 'em.   57

ALL.   Who Faustus?

FAUSTUS.   Why, Lucifer and Mephostophilis: ah gentlemen, I gave
them my soul for my cunning.

ALL.   God forbid!   61

FAUSTUS.   God forbade it indeed, but Faustus hath done it. For the
vain pleasure of four and twenty years hath Faustus lost eternal joy and
felicity. I writ them a bill with mine own blood: the date is expired, this
is the time, and he will fetch me.   65

FIRST SCHOLAR.   Why did not Faustus tell us of this before, that
divines might have prayed for thee?

FAUSTUS.   Oft have I thought to have done so, but the devil threatened
to tear me in pieces if I named God, to fetch me body and soul if I once
gave ear to divinity; and now 'tis too late. Gentlemen, away: lest you
perish with me.   71

SECOND SCHOLAR.   O what may we do to save Faustus?

FAUSTUS.   Talk not of me, but save yourselves and depart.

THIRD SCHOLAR.   God will strengthen me. I will stay with Faustus.

FIRST SCHOLAR.   Tempt not God, sweet friend, but let us into the next
room and there pray for him.   76

FAUSTUS.   Ay, pray for me, pray for me; and what noise soever you
hear, come not unto me, for nothing can rescue me.

SECOND SCHOLAR.   Pray thou, and we will pray, that God may have
mercy upon thee.   80

FAUSTUS.   Gentlemen, farewell. If I live till morning, I'll visit you:
if not, Faustus is gone to hell.

ALL.   Faustus, farewell.

(*Exeunt* SCHOLARS.)

MEPHOSTOPHILIS.   Ay Faustus, now thou hast no hope of heaven,
Therefore despair, think only upon hell;   85
For that must be thy mansion, there to dwell.

FAUSTUS.   O thou bewitching fiend, 'twas thy temptation,
Hath robbed me of eternal happiness.
MEPHOSTOPHILIS.   I do confess it Faustus, and rejoice:
'Twas I that, when thou wert i'the way to heaven,   90
Damned up thy passage; when thou took'st the book,
To view the Scriptures, then I turned the leaves
And led thine eye.
What, weep'st thou? 'Tis too late, despair, farewell:
Fools that will laugh on earth, must weep in hell. (*Exit.*)   95

(*Enter the* GOOD ANGEL, *and the* BAD ANGEL *at several doors.*)

GOOD ANGEL.   O Faustus, if thou hadst given ear to me,
Innumerable joys had followed thee.
But thou didst love the world.
BAD ANGEL.   Gave ear to me,
And now must taste hell's pains perpetually.
GOOD ANGEL.   O what will all thy riches, pleasures, pomps,   100
Avail thee now?
BAD ANGEL.   Nothing but vex thee more,
To want in hell, that had on earth such store.

(*Music while the throne descends.*)

GOOD ANGEL.   O thou hast lost celestial happiness,
Pleasures unspeakable, bliss without end.
Hadst thou affected sweet divinity,   105
Hell, or the devil, had had no power on thee.
Hadst thou kept on that way, Faustus behold,
In what resplendent glory thou hadst sat
In yonder throne, like those bright shining saints,
And triumphed over hell; that hast thou lost,   110
And now, poor soul, must thy good angel leave thee:
The jaws of hell are open to receive thee. (*Exit.*)

(*The throne ascends. Hell is discovered.*)

BAD ANGEL.   Now Faustus, let thine eyes with horror stare
Into that vast perpetual torture-house.
There are the furies tossing damned souls,   115
On burning forks; there bodies boil in lead:
There are live quarters broiling on the coals,
That ne'er can die: this ever-burning chair,
Is for o'er-tortured souls to rest them in:
These, that are fed with sops of flaming fire,   120
Were gluttons, and loved only delicates,
And laughed to see the poor starve at their gates:

But yet all these are nothing: thou shalt see
Ten thousand tortures that more horrid be.
    FAUSTUS.   O, I have seen enough to torture me.   **125**
    BAD ANGEL.   Nay, thou must feel them, taste the smart of all:
He that loves pleasure, must for pleasure fall.
And so I leave thee Faustus, till anon,
Then wilt thou tumble in confusion. (*Exit.*)

    (*The clock strikes eleven.*)

    FAUSTUS.   Ah Faustus,   **130**
Now hast thou but one bare hour to live,
And then thou must be damned perpetually.
Stand still, you ever-moving spheres of heaven,
That time may cease, and midnight never come.
Fair nature's eye, rise, rise again and make   **135**
Perpetual day; or let this hour be but
A year, a month, a week, a natural day,
That Faustus may repent, and save his soul.
O lente, lente currite noctis equi!
The stars move still, time runs, the clock will strike,   **140**
The devil will come, and Faustus must be damned.
O I'll leap up to my God! Who pulls me down?
See, see where Christ's blood streams in the firmament!
One drop would save my soul, half a drop. Ah my Christ —
Rend not my heart for naming of my Christ;   **145**
Yet will I call on him: O spare me Lucifer!
Where is it now? 'Tis gone, and see where God
Stretcheth out his arm, and bends his ireful brows:
Mountains and hills, come, come, and fall on me,
And hide me from the heavy wrath of God.   **150**
No, no!
Then will I headlong run into the earth:
Earth, gape! O no, it will not harbour me.
You stars that reigned at my nativity,
Whose influence hath allotted death and hell,   **155**
Now draw up Faustus like a foggy mist
Into the entrails of yon labouring cloud,
That when you vomit forth into the air,
My limbs may issue from your smoky mouths,
So that my soul may but ascend to heaven.   **160**

    (*The watch strikes.*)

139. *O . . . equi:* 'Gallop slowly, slowly, you horses of the night.' The final and
most famous irony of the play. The line is from Ovid's *Amores*, I.xiii.40, where
the poet longs for never-ending night in the arms of his mistress. **147. it:** the
vision of God; the momentary yielding to terror and the devil banishes even this
remote vision of mercy.

Ah, half the hour is past; 'twill all be past anon!
O God,
If thou wilt not have mercy on my soul,
Yet for Christ's sake, whose blood hath ransomed me,
Impose some end to my incessant pain: 165
Let Faustus live in hell a thousand years,
A hundred thousand, and at last be saved.
O, no end is limited to damned souls!
Why wert thou not a creature wanting soul?
Or why is this immortal that thou hast?   170
Ah, Pythagoras' *metempsychosis* — were that true,
This soul should fly from me, and I be changed
Unto some brutish beast.
All beasts are happy, for when they die,
Their souls are soon dissolved in elements;   175
But mine must live still to be plagued in hell.
Cursed be the parents that engendered me!
No Faustus, curse thyself, curse Lucifer,
That hath deprived thee of the joys of heaven.

    (*The clock striketh twelve.*)

It strikes, it strikes! Now body turn to air,   180
Or Lucifer will bear thee quick to hell.

    (*Thunder and lightning.*)

O soul, be changed into little water drops,
And fall into the ocean, ne'er be found.

    (*Enter the* DEVILS.)

My God, my God! Look not so fierce on me!
Adders, and serpents, let me breathe awhile!   185
Ugly hell gape not! Come not Lucifer;
I'll burn my books — ah Mephostophilis!

    (*Exeunt with him.*)

---

171. **Pythagoras'** *metempsychosis:* the theory of the transmigration of souls, attributed to Pythagoras, whereby the human soul at the death of the body took on some other form of life. 181. **quick:** living. 187. **I'll burn my books:** all magicians who renounced their art made a solemn act of disposing of their books of magic (cf. *The Tempest,* V.i.56–57).

Scene 3

(*Enter the* SCHOLARS.)

FIRST SCHOLAR.   Come gentlemen, let us go visit Faustus,
For such a dreadful night was never seen
Since first the world's creation did begin;
Such fearful shrieks, and cries were never heard.
Pray heaven the doctor have escaped the danger.   5
SECOND SCHOLAR.   O help us heaven! See, here are Faustus' limbs,
All torn asunder by the hand of death.
THIRD SCHOLAR.   The devils whom Faustus served have torn him thus:
For 'twixt the hours of twelve and one, methought
I heard him shriek and call aloud for help: 10
At which self time the house seemed all on fire,
With dreadful horror of these damned fiends.
SECOND SCHOLAR.   Well Gentlemen, though Faustus' end be such
As every Christian heart laments to think on;
Yet for he was a scholar, once admired   15
For wondrous knowledge in our German schools,
We'll give his mangled limbs due burial,
And all the students clothed in mourning black,
Shall wait upon his heavy funeral.

(*Exeunt.*)

EPILOGUE

(*Enter* CHORUS.)

CHORUS.   Cut is the branch that might have grown full straight,
And burned is Apollo's laurel bough,
That sometime grew within this learned man.
Faustus is gone: regard his hellish fall,
Whose fiendful fortune may exhort the wise   5
Only to wonder at unlawful things:
Whose deepness doth entice such forward wits,
To practise more than heavenly power permits. (*Exit.*)

Terminat hora diem, terminat author opus finis.

Scene iii, 16. **schools**: universities. 19. **heavy**: sorrowful.
Epilogue, 9. **Terminat . . . opus**: 'The hour ends the day, the author ends his work.' The origin is unknown, and it seems likely that the line was appended to the play by the printer and not by Marlowe.

Shakespeare (1564–1616) repeatedly demonstrates in his comedies, chronicle plays, and tragedies a remarkable ability to abstract plots, characters, or details from other plays, poems, and stories. *King Lear* (*c.* 1605) is no exception. The major plot line, it is believed, was taken from *The True Chronicle History of King Leir and His Three Daughters,* an anonymous play probably written around 1594. There are a number of other versions of the Lear story, all of which seem to be reflected in the text in one way or another. But the embellishments and richnesses are all Shakespeare's: the doubly tragic ending, the banishment of Kent, the addition of the Fool, the counterpoint of the subplot.

And the subplot, too, is derived from another source, a story in Sidney's *Arcadia* (1590). It is so intertwined with the main plot that it thickens the texture of the whole play, mirroring its theme, echoing its events, and clarifying its structure. Both Lear and Gloucester reject and are rescued by the children who love them, and they mistakenly trust the ones who are faithless. Both are physically ruined and spiritually saved by their mistakes. Edgar's false madness mirrors Lear's genuine delirium, with the Fool's professional madness weaving in and out between them. With so many emotions moving in so many different directions, *King Lear* is one of Shakespeare's richest and most provocative tragedies.

A recurrent strain in Sophocles is that no man should be called happy until he is dead — presumably finally free from earthly sufferings. Lear too, like a Sophoclean tragic hero, strives not so much against the necessity of death as to come to terms with life and himself. Shakespeare, however, did not tell his tale with the medieval simplicity of a morality play or the eloquent rituality of the Greek classics. The tragedy of Lear unfolds in a flourish of pageantry, with a wealth of plot and subplot detail and a large cast of characters who can be the source of confusion of interest if the central character and theme are not clearly kept in mind. Indeed, some critics have proposed that *Lear,* with a few readjustments, might successfully be performed as *The Tragedy of Goneril and Regan.* But a close reading of the latter portions of the text shows enough insufficiently motivated malice and villainy — as well as greed — in both Cordelia's sisters to suggest that they are really more appropriate candidates for melodrama than for tragedy. Viewing Cordelia as the tragic heroine, a saintly piece of innocent sweetness betrayed by father and sisters, is also the interpretation of melodrama. At the beginning of the play, after all, Cordelia is as unwise and unbending as her father; she is not all good by any means.

Certainly there are melodramatic elements in plenty in *King Lear*: the gory blinding of Gloucester, Lear's madness, the storm, the villainy of Edmund, the noble valor of Edgar, as well as the consummate evil of Goneril and Regan and the innocent, wounded love of Cordelia for her father. Stressing such elements heavily in performance may very well produce exciting romantic theatre, but Lear's tragedy and the point of the play will be diminished if not eclipsed entirely. If Goneril and Regan are shown to be correct and dutiful at the outset by those who play them, their growing impatience with and disaffection from their father, together with their growing lust for power, will seem more believable, less melodramatic. Cordelia's stubborn and unwise provocation of her father, too, must be shown honestly. This is Lear's tragedy, and the daughters merely contribute to it.

Once we accept the illogic of the first scene, Lear's troubles start. He was wrong to divide the kingdom at all. That way trouble always lies, for one of the rulers of a new division will usually try to restore the old kingdom under his own rule. If Cordelia had at least accepted the major third, she and her husband would have been a force for maintaining peace. But Lear's gravest fault, that which leads to his personal crisis, is his failure to understand who or what he has become by divesting himself of kingship. Used to autocratic rule, he demands all the comforts, honors, and prerogatives of a ruler. But he is fulfilling none of the obligations and does not see that he thus deserves the privileges no longer.

Lear moves from arrogance in power to self-pity in abused retirement; he is a cantankerous old man who is being treated shabbily. But nature's rebellious elements help define his true stature, and Poor Tom brings out his humanity. Self-pity is purged in his growing understanding of who he really is and what kind of mistakes he has made. His delirium is part of his progression in self-knowledge and knowledge of others, to whom he has previously given little thought, and when he again meets Cordelia, he is truly able to give and receive forgiveness. He has climbed the heights of human understanding, where one must forgive all. His death may seem the more cruel and sad because he has made his peace with Cordelia and himself and won his wisdom fairly. But it is his hard-won self-awareness that is truly important, not his death. In fact, Lear's death could even be viewed as a welcome release for a man who has suffered to find out at last what it is to be whole.

G.L.

WILLIAM SHAKESPEARE

The Tragedy of King Lear[1]

Characters

[LEAR, *King of Britain*
KING OF FRANCE
DUKE OF BURGUNDY
DUKE OF CORNWALL
DUKE OF ALBANY
EARL OF KENT
EARL OF GLOUCESTER
EDGAR, *son to Gloucester*
EDMUND, *bastard son to Gloucester*
GONERIL, ⎫
REGAN, ⎬ *daughters to Lear*
CORDELIA, ⎭
CURAN, *a courtier*
OLD MAN, *tenant to Gloucester*
DOCTOR
FOOL
OSWALD, *steward to Goneril*
CAPTAIN, *employed by Edmund*
GENTLEMAN, *attendant on Cordelia*
HERALD
Servants *to Cornwall,* Knights *of Lear's train,* Captains, Messengers, Soldiers, *and* Attendants

SCENE: *Britain.*]

---

[1] "The present text is based upon the Folio [1623] as the more accurately printed version, although the Quarto [1608] supplies not only its unique passages but numerous good readings." (Neilson and Hill, p. 1136.) Bracketed passages have been supplied from other sources with the suppliers recorded in the notes in parentheses: (Edwards), (Malone), etc. A capital F in the notes stands for "Folio," a capital Q for "Quarto."

Lines have been renumbered for this volume.

"Stage directions, if modern, are enclosed in [brackets]; when they are substantially those of editions not later than 1623, they are unbracketed, or are set aside by a single bracket only, or, when occurring within a line, are enclosed in (parentheses)." (Neilson and Hill, p.v.)

155

ACT ONE

Scene 1.   [King Lear's palace.]

Enter KENT, GLOUCESTER, *and* EDMUND.

KENT.   I thought the King had more affected the Duke of Albany than
Cornwall.

GLOUCESTER.   It did always seem so to us; but now, in the division of
the kingdom, it appears not which of the Dukes he values most; for qualities are so weigh'd, that curiosity in neither can make choice of either's
moiety.   6

KENT.   Is not this your son, my lord?

GLOUCESTER.   His breeding, sir, hath been at my charge. I have so
often blush'd to acknowledge him, that now I am braz'd to't.

KENT.   I cannot conceive you.   10

GLOUCESTER.   Sir, this young fellow's mother could; whereupon she
grew round-womb'd, and had, indeed, sir, a son for her cradle ere she had
a husband for her bed. Do you smell a fault?   13

KENT.   I cannot wish the fault undone, the issue of it being so proper.

GLOUCESTER.   But I have a son, sir, by order of law, some year elder
than this, who yet is no dearer in my account. Though this knave came
something saucily to the world before he was sent for, yet was his mother
fair; there was good sport at his making, and the whoreson must be acknowledged. Do you know this noble gentleman, Edmund?   19

EDMUND.   No, my lord.

GLOUCESTER.   My Lord of Kent. Remember him hereafter as my
honourable friend.

EDMUND.   My services to your lordship.

KENT.   I must love you, and sue to know you better.

EDMUND.   Sir, I shall study deserving.   25

GLOUCESTER.   He hath been out nine years, and away he shall again.
The King is coming.

Sennet. Enter one bearing a coronet, then KING LEAR, *then the* DUKES
OF ALBANY *and* CORNWALL, *next* GONERIL, REGAN, CORDELIA, *with followers.*

LEAR.   Attend the lords of France and Burgundy, Gloucester.

GLOUCESTER.   I shall, my lord.

*[Exeunt [*GLOUCESTER *and* EDMUND*].*

Act I, Scene i, line 1. **affected:** liked. 4–5. **qualities** F. *equalities* Q.
5. **weigh'd:** balanced. **curiosity:** careful scrutiny. 6. **moiety:** share. 9. **braz'd:**
brazened, hardened. 16. **account:** esteem. 26. **out:** in military service.
27. S.D. **Sennet:** set of notes on a trumpet.

LEAR.   Meantime we shall express our darker purpose.   30
Give me the map there. Know that we have divided
In three our kingdom; and 'tis our fast intent
To shake all cares and business from our age,
Conferring them on younger strengths, while we
Unburden'd crawl toward death. Our son of Cornwall,   35
And you, our no less loving son of Albany,
We have this hour a constant will to publish
Our daughters' several dowers, that future strife
May be prevented now. The Princes, France and Burgundy,
Great rivals in our youngest daughter's love,   40
Long in our court have made their amorous sojourn,
And here are to be answer'd. Tell me, my daughters, —
Since now we will divest us both of rule,
Interest of territory, cares of state, —
Which of you shall we say doth love us most,   45
That we our largest bounty may extend
Where nature doth with merit challenge? Goneril,
Our eldest-born, speak first.
       GONERIL.   Sir, I love you more than word can wield the matter;
Dearer than eye-sight, space, and liberty;   50
Beyond what can be valued, rich or rare;
No less than life, with grace, health, beauty, honour;
As much as child e'er lov'd, or father found;
A love that makes breath poor, and speech unable:
Beyond all manner of so much I love you.   55
       CORDELIA [aside].   What shall Cordelia speak? Love and be silent.
       LEAR.   Of all these bounds, even from this line to this,
With shadowy forests and with champains rich'd,
With plenteous rivers and wide-skirted meads,
We make thee lady. To thine and Albany's issues   60
Be this perpetual. What says our second daughter,
Our dearest Regan, wife of Cornwall? [Speak.]
       REGAN.   I am made of that self metal as my sister,
And prize me at her worth. In my true heart
I find she names my very deed of love;   65
Only she comes too short, that I profess
Myself an enemy to all other joys
Which the most precious square of sense [possesses],
And find I am alone felicitate
In your dear Highness' love.

44. Interest: possession.   47. Where . . . challenge? to the one whose nature
and deserts make the best claim.   58. champains: plains.   62. [Speak] Q.
Omitted in F.   64. prize . . . worth: estimate myself as her equal (in affection).
68. most . . . sense: most exquisite region of my senses. [possesses] Q. professes
F.   69. felicitate: made happy.

CORDELIA [aside].   Then poor Cordelia!   70
And yet not so; since, I am sure, my love's
More ponderous than my tongue.
    LEAR.   To thee and thine hereditary ever
Remain this ample third of our fair kingdom;
No less in space, validity, and pleasure,   75
Than that conferr'd on Goneril. Now, our joy,
Although our last and least, to whose young love
The vines of France and milk of Burgundy
Strive to be interess'd, what can you say to draw
A third more opulent than your sisters? Speak.   80
    CORDELIA.   Nothing, my lord.
    LEAR.   Nothing!
    CORDELIA.   Nothing.
    LEAR.   Nothing will come of nothing. Speak again.
    CORDELIA.   Unhappy that I am, I cannot heave   85
My heart into my mouth. I love your Majesty
According to my bond; no more nor less.
    LEAR.   How, how, Cordelia! Mend your speech a little,
Lest you may mar your fortunes.
    CORDELIA.   Good my lord,
You have begot me, bred me, lov'd me: I   90
Return those duties back as are right fit;
Obey you, love you, and most honour you.
Why have my sisters husbands, if they say
They love you all? Haply, when I shall wed,
That lord whose hand must take my plight shall carry   95
Half my love with him, half my care and duty.
Sure, I shall never marry like my sisters
[To love my father all].
    LEAR.   But goes thy heart with this?
    CORDELIA.   Ay, my good lord.
    LEAR.   So young, and so untender?   100
    CORDELIA.   So young, my lord, and true.
    LEAR.   Let it be so; thy truth, then, be thy dower!
For, by the sacred radiance of the sun,
The [mysteries] of Hecate and the night;
By all the operation of the orbs   105
From whom we do exist and cease to be;
Here I disclaim all my paternal care,
Propinquity and property of blood,
And as a stranger to my heart and me
Hold thee from this for ever. The barbarous Scythian,   110

75. **validity:** value.   77. **our . . . least** F. *the last not least* Q.   79. **be interess'd:**
establish a claim.   87. **bond:** duty.   95. **plight:** troth-plight.   98. **[To . . . all]**
Q. Om. F.   104. **[mysteries]** F₂. *miseries* F₁. *mistresse* Q. **Hecate:** goddess of
the infernal regions.   105. **operation:** influence.

Or he that makes his generation messes
To gorge his appetite, shall to my bosom
Be as well neighbour'd, piti'd, and reliev'd,
As thou my sometime daughter.
    KENT.   Good my liege, —
    LEAR.   Peace, Kent!   115
Come not between the dragon and his wrath.
I lov'd her most, and thought to set my rest
On her kind nursery. [*To* CORDELIA.] Hence, and avoid my sight! —
So be my grave my peace, as here I give
Her father's heart from her! Call France. — Who stirs?   120
Call Burgundy. Cornwall and Albany,
With my two daughters' dowers digest the third;
Let pride, which she calls plainness, marry her.
I do invest you jointly with my power,
Pre-eminence, and all the large effects   125
That troop with majesty. Ourself, by monthly course,
With reservation of an hundred knights
By you to be sustain'd, shall our abode
Make with you by due turn. Only we shall retain
The name, and all th' addition to a king;   130
The sway, revenue, execution of the rest,
Beloved sons, be yours; which to confirm,
This coronet part between you.
    KENT.   Royal Lear,
Whom I have ever honour'd as my king,
Lov'd as my father, as my master follow'd,   135
As my great patron thought on in my prayers, —
    LEAR.   The bow is bent and drawn; make from the shaft.
    KENT.   Let it fall rather, though the fork invade
The region of my heart: be Kent unmannerly
When Lear is mad. What wouldst thou do, old man?   140
Thinkest thou that duty shall have dread to speak
When power to flattery bows? To plainness honour's bound
When majesty falls to folly. Reserve thy state;
And in thy best consideration check
This hideous rashness. Answer my life my judgement,   145
Thy youngest daughter does not love thee least;
Nor are those empty-hearted whose low sounds
Reverb no hollowness.
    LEAR.   Kent, on thy life, no more.
    KENT.   My life I never held but as a pawn
To wage against thine enemies, [nor] fear to lose it,   150
Thy safety being motive.

111. **generation:** children. But Herodotus says the Scythians ate the aged. 117.
set my rest: stake my all. 118. **nursery:** cherishing. 122. **digest:** absorb. 130.
addition: title. 138. **fork:** barb. 150. [nor] Q. *nere* F.

LEAR.   Out of my sight!

KENT.   See better, Lear; and let me still remain
The true blank of thine eye.

LEAR.   Now, by Apollo, —

KENT.   Now, by Apollo, king,
Thou swear'st thy gods in vain.

LEAR.   O, vassal! miscreant! [*Laying his hand on
his sword.*]   155

ALBANY.   ⎱
CORNWALL.   ⎰ Dear sir, forbear.

KENT.   Kill thy physician, and thy fee bestow
Upon the foul disease. Revoke thy gift,
Or, whilst I can vent clamour from my throat,
I'll tell thee thou dost evil.

LEAR.   Hear me, recreant!   160
On thine allegiance, hear me!
That thou hast sought to make us break our vows,
Which we durst never yet, and with strain'd pride
To come betwixt our sentence and our power,
Which nor our nature nor our place can bear,   165
Our potency made good, take thy reward.
Five days we do allot thee, for provision
To shield thee from disasters of the world;
And on the sixth to turn thy hated back
Upon our kingdom. If, on the tenth day following,   170
Thy banish'd trunk be found in our dominions,
The moment is thy death. Away! By Jupiter,
This shall not be revok'd.

KENT.   Fare thee well, king! Sith thus thou wilt appear,
Freedom lives hence, and banishment is here.   175
[*To* CORDELIA.] The gods to their dear shelter take thee, maid,
That justly think'st and hast most rightly said!
[*To* REGAN *and* GONERIL.] And your large speeches may your deeds ap-
prove,
That good effects may spring from words of love.
Thus Kent, O princes, bids you all adieu;   180
He'll shape his old course in a country new. [*Exit.*

Flourish. Re-enter GLOUCESTER, *with* FRANCE, BURGUNDY, *and* Attendants.

GLOUCESTER.   Here's France and Burgundy, my noble lord.

LEAR.   My Lord of Burgundy,
We first address toward you, who with this king
Hath rivall'd for our daughter. What, in the least,   185

153. **blank:** center of the target. 163. **strain'd:** exaggerated. 166. **Our . . .**
good: to prove my power. 174. **Sith:** since. 178. **approve:** justify.

Will you require in present dower with her,
Or cease your quest of love?
  BURGUNDY.   Most royal Majesty,
I crave no more than what your Highness offer'd,
Nor will you tender less.
  LEAR.   Right noble Burgundy,
When she was dear to us, we did hold her so;   190
But now her price is fall'n. Sir, there she stands:
If aught within that little-seeming substance,
Or all of it, with our displeasure piec'd,
And nothing more, may fitly like your Grace,
She's there, and she is yours.
  BURGUNDY.   I know no answer.   195
  LEAR. Will you, with those infirmities she owes,
Unfriended, new-adopted to our hate,
Dower'd with our curse, and stranger'd with our oath,
Take her, or leave her?
  BURGUNDY.   Pardon me, royal sir;
Election makes not up in such conditions.   200
  LEAR. Then leave her, sir; for, by the power that made me,
I tell you all her wealth. [*To* FRANCE.] For you, great king,
I would not from your love make such a stray
To match you where I hate; therefore beseech you
T'avert your liking a more worthier way   205
Than on a wretch whom Nature is asham'd
Almost t' acknowledge hers.
  FRANCE.   This is most strange,
That she, whom even but now was your [best] object,
The argument of your praise, balm of your age,
The best, the dearest, should in this trice of time 210
Commit a thing so monstrous, to dismantle
So many folds of favour. Sure her offence
Must be of such unnatural degree
That monsters it, or your fore-vouch'd affection
Fallen into taint; which to believe of her,   215
Must be a faith that reason without miracle
Should never plant in me.
  CORDELIA.   I yet beseech your Majesty, —
If for I want that glib and oily art
To speak and purpose not, since what I [well] intend,
I'll do't before I speak, — that you make known 220
It is no vicious blot, murder, or foulness,
No unchaste action, or dishonoured step,

---

189. **tender:** offer. 194. **like:** please. 196. **owes:** owns. 200. **Election . . .
conditions:** one cannot make a choice on these terms. 203. **stray:** departure.
208. **[best]** Q. Om. F. 209. **argument:** theme. 214. **monsters:** makes monstrous. 215. **Fallen into taint:** must have decayed. 219. **[well]** Q. *will* F.

That hath depriv'd me of your grace and favour;
But even for want of that for which I am richer,
A still-soliciting eye, and such a tongue   225
That I am glad I have not, though not to have it
Hath lost me in your liking.

    LEAR.   Better thou
Hadst not been born than not t' have pleas'd me better.

    FRANCE.   Is it but this, — a tardiness in nature
Which often leaves the history unspoke   230
That it intends to do? My Lord of Burgundy,
What say you to the lady? Love's not love
When it is mingled with regards that stands
Aloof from th' entire point. Will you have her?
She is herself a dowry.

    BURGUNDY.   Royal king,   235
Give but that portion which yourself propos'd,
And here I take Cordelia by the hand,
Duchess of Burgundy.

    LEAR.   Nothing. I have sworn; I am firm.

    BURGUNDY.   I am sorry, then, you have so lost a father   240
That you must lose a husband.

    CORDELIA.   Peace be with Burgundy.
Since that respect and fortunes are his love,
I shall not be his wife.

    FRANCE.   Fairest Cordelia, that art most rich being poor,
Most choice forsaken, and most lov'd despis'd!   245
Thee and thy virtues here I seize upon,
Be it lawful I take up what's cast away.
Gods, gods! 'tis strange that from their cold'st neglect
My love should kindle to inflam'd respect.
Thy dowerless daughter, king, thrown to my chance,   250
Is queen of us, of ours, and our fair France.
Not all the dukes of waterish Burgundy
Can buy this unpriz'd precious maid of me.
Bid them farewell, Cordelia, though unkind;
Thou losest here, a better where to find.   255

    LEAR.   Thou hast her, France. Let her be thine: for we
Have no such daughter, nor shall ever see
That face of hers again. — [To CORDELIA.] Therefore be gone
Without our grace, our love, our benison. —
Come, noble Burgundy.   260

[*Flourish. Exeunt* [all but FRANCE, GONERIL, REGAN, and CORDELIA.]

233. **regards:** considerations.   242. **respect and:** consideration of.   250. **thrown
. . . chance:** fallen to my lot.   252. **waterish:** (1) well-watered, (2) poor.
255. **where:** place.

FRANCE. Bid farewell to your sisters.

CORDELIA. The jewels of our father, with wash'd eyes
Cordelia leaves you. I know you what you are;
And like a sister am most loath to call
Your faults as they are nam'd. Love well our father.   265
To your professed bosoms I commit him;
But yet, alas, stood I within his grace,
I would prefer him to a better place.
So, farewell to you both.

REGAN. Prescribe not us our duty.

GONERIL.   Let your study   270
Be to content your lord, who hath receiv'd you
At fortune's alms. You have obedience scanted,
And well are worth the want that you have wanted.

CORDELIA. Time shall unfold what plighted cunning hides;
Who covers faults, at last shame [them] derides.   275
Well may you prosper!

FRANCE.   Come, my fair Cordelia.

*[Exeunt [*FRANCE *and* CORDELIA.*]*

GONERIL. Sister, it is not little I have to say of what most nearly ap-
pertains to us both. I think our father will hence to-night.

REGAN. That's most certain, and with you; next month with us.   279

GONERIL. You see how full of changes his age is; the observation we
have made of it hath [not] been little. He always lov'd our sister most;
and with what poor judgement he hath now cast her off appears too
grossly.

REGAN. 'Tis the infirmity of his age; yet he hath ever but slenderly
known himself.   285

GONERIL. The best and soundest of his time hath been but rash; then
must we look from his age to receive not alone the imperfections of long-
engraffed condition, but therewithal the unruly waywardness that infirm
and choleric years bring with them.

REGAN. Such unconstant starts are we like to have from him as this of
Kent's banishment.   291

GONERIL. There is further compliment of leave-taking between France
and him. Pray you, let['s hit] together; if our father carry authority with
such disposition as he bears, this last surrender of his will but offend us.

---

262. **wash'd:** tear-washed. 266. **professed:** making professions (of love).
272. **scanted:** come short in. 273. **And . . . wanted:** And have well deserved
the loss of that affection in which you were lacking. 274. **plighted:** folded,
complicated. 275. **shame [them]** Q. *with shame* F. 281. **[not]** Q. Om. F.
283. **grossly:** obviously. 290. **starts:** impulsive actions. 293. **let['s hit]** Q: let
us agree. *let us sit* F.

REGAN.   We shall further think of it.   295
GONERIL.   We must do something, and i' th' heat.

[*Exeunt.*

SCENE 2.   [*The Earl of Gloucester's castle.*]

Enter Bastard [EDMUND *with a letter.*]

EDMUND.   Thou, Nature, art my goddess; to thy law
My services are bound. Wherefore should I
Stand in the plague of custom, and permit
The curiosity of nations to deprive me,
For that I am some twelve or fourteen moonshines   5
Lag of a brother? Why bastard? Wherefore base?
When my dimensions are as well compact,
My mind as generous, and my shape as true,
As honest madam's issue? Why brand they us
With base? with baseness? bastardy? base, base?   10
Who, in the lusty stealth of nature, take
More compositon and fierce quality
Than doth, within a dull, stale, tired bed,
Go to the creating a whole tribe of fops,
Got 'tween asleep and wake? Well, then,   15
Legitimate Edgar, I must have your land.
Our father's love is to the bastard Edmund
As to th' legitimate. Fine word, "legitimate!"
Well, my legitimate, if this letter speed
And my invention thrive, Edmund the base   20
Shall [top] th' legitimate. I grow; I prosper.
Now, gods, stand up for bastards!

Enter GLOUCESTER.

GLOUCESTER.   Kent banish'd thus! and France in choler parted!
And the King gone tonight! [subscrib'd] his power!
Confin'd to exhibition! All this done   25
Upon the gad! Edmund, how now! what news?
    EDMUND.   So please your lordship, none. [*Putting up the letter.*]
GLOUCESTER.   Why so earnestly seek you to put up that letter?
    EDMUND.   I know no news, my lord.

296. **i' th' heat:** while the iron is hot.
    Scene ii, 3. plague: vexation. 4. **curiosity of nations:** *i.e.,* the absurd law
favoring the first-born. 6. **Lag of:** younger than. 19. **speed:** succeed. 21.
[**top**] (Edwards conjecture). *to'* F. 24. [**subscrib'd**] Q: surrendered. *prescrib'd*
F. 25. **exhibition:** an allowance. 26. **gad:** spur of the moment.

GLOUCESTER.   What paper were you reading?   30

EDMUND.   Nothing, my lord.

GLOUCESTER.   No? What needed, then, that terrible dispatch of it into your pocket? The quality of nothing hath not such need to hide itself. Let's see. Come, if it be nothing, I shall not need spectacles.   34

EDMUND.   I beseech you, sir, pardon me. It is a letter from my brother that I have not all o'er-read; and for so much as I have perus'd, I find it not fit for your o'er-looking.

GLOUCESTER.   Give me the letter, sir.

EDMUND.   I shall offend either to detain or give it. The contents, as in part I understand them, are to blame.   40

GLOUCESTER.   Let's see, let's see.

EDMUND.   I hope, for my brother's justification, he wrote this but as an essay or taste of my virtue.   43

GLOUCESTER (*reads*).   "This policy and reverence of age makes the world bitter to the best of our times; keeps our fortunes from us till our oldness cannot relish them. I begin to find an idle and fond bondage in the oppression of aged tyranny; who sways, not as it hath power, but as it is suffer'd. Come to me, that of this I may speak more. If our father would sleep till I wak'd him, you should enjoy half his revenue for ever, and live the beloved of your brother, EDGAR."   50

Hum — conspiracy! — "Sleep till I wake him, you should enjoy half his revenue!" — My son Edgar! Had he a hand to write this? a heart and brain to breed it in? — When came this to you? Who brought it?

EDMUND.   It was not brought me, my lord; there's the cunning of it. I found it thrown in at the casement of my closet.

GLOUCESTER.   You know the character to be your brother's?   56

EDMUND.   If the matter were good, my lord, I durst swear it were his; but, in respect of that, I would fain think it were not.

GLOUCESTER.   It is his.

EDMUND.   It is his hand, my lord; but I hope his heart is not in the contents.   61

GLOUCESTER.   Has he never before sounded you in this business?

EDMUND.   Never, my lord; but I have heard him oft maintain it to be fit that, sons at perfect age and fathers declin'd, the father should be as ward to the son, and the son manage his revenue.   65

GLOUCESTER.   O villain, villain! His very opinion in the letter! Abhorred villain! Unnatural, detested, brutish villain! worse than brutish! Go, sirrah, seek him; I'll apprehend him. Abominable villain! Where is he?   69

EDMUND.   I do not well know, my lord. If it shall please you to suspend your indignation against my brother till you can derive from him better testimony of his intent, you should run a certain course; where, if

43. **essay or taste:** trial or test.   44. **policy and reverence:** policy of revering.
45. **times:** lives.   46. **fond:** foolish.   56. **character:** handwriting.   64. **declin'd:** failed.   72. **where:** whereas.

you violently proceed against him, mistaking his purpose, it would make a great gap in your own honour and shake in pieces the heart of his obedience. I dare pawn down my life for him that he hath writ this to feel my affection to your honour, and to no other pretence of danger.

GLOUCESTER.   Think you so?   77

EDMUND.   If your honour judge it meet, I will place you where you shall hear us confer of this, and by an auricular assurance have your satisfaction; and that without any further delay than this very evening.

GLOUCESTER.   He cannot be such a monster —

[EDMUND.   Nor is not, sure.   82

GLOUCESTER.   To his father, that so tenderly and entirely loves him. Heaven and earth!] Edmund, seek him out; wind me into him, I pray you. Frame the business after your own wisdom. I would unstate myself to be in a due resolution.

EDMUND.   I will seek him, sir, presently; convey the business as I shall find means, and acquaint you withal.   88

GLOUCESTER.   These late eclipses in the sun and moon portend no good to us. Though the wisdom of nature can reason it thus and thus, yet nature finds itself scourg'd by the sequent effects. Love cools, friendship falls off, brothers divide: in cities, mutinies; in countries, discord; in palaces, treason; and the bond crack'd 'twixt son and father. This villain of mine comes under the prediction; there's son against father: the King falls from bias of nature; there's father against child. We have seen the best of our time; machinations, hollowness, treachery, and all ruinous disorders, follow us disquietly to our graves. Find out this villain, Edmund; it shall lose thee nothing; do it carefully. And the noble and true-hearted Kent banish'd! his offence, honesty! 'Tis strange. [Exit.   99

EDMUND.   This is the excellent foppery of the world, that, when we are sick in fortune, — often the surfeits of our own behaviour, — we make guilty of our disasters the sun, the moon, and stars, as if we were villains on necessity, fools by heavenly compulsion, knaves, thieves, and treachers by spherical predominance, drunkards, liars, and adulterers by an enforc'd obedience of planetary influence, and all that we are evil in, by a divine thrusting on. An admirable evasion of whoremaster man, to lay his goatish disposition on the charge of a star! My father compounded with my mother under the dragon's tail, and my nativity was under Ursa major; so that it follows, I am rough and lecherous. Fut, I should have been that I am, had the maidenliest star in the firmament twinkled on my bastardizing. [Edgar —]   111

Enter EDGAR.

76. feel: sound.   pretence of danger: dangerous intent.   82–84. [EDMUND . . . earth!] Q. Om. F.   84. wind . . . him: gain his confidence.   85–86. unstate . . . resolution: forfeit my position to be properly assured.   87. presently: at once. convey: carry on.   95. falls . . . nature: acts against his natural disposition. 100. foppery: foolishness.   103. treachers: traitors.   104. spherical predominance: influence of the planets.   111. [Edgar —] Q. Om. F.

pat he comes like the catastrophe of the old comedy. My cue is villanous melancholy, with a sigh like Tom o' Bedlam. — O, these eclipses do portend these divisions! *fa, sol, la, mi.*   114

EDGAR.   How now, brother Edmund! what serious contemplation are you in?

EDMUND.   I am thinking, brother, of a prediction I read this other day, what should follow these eclipses.

EDGAR.   Do you busy yourself with that?   119

EDMUND.   I promise you, the effects he writes of succeed unhappily; [as of unnaturalness between the child and the parent; death, dearth, dissolutions of ancient amities; divisions in state, menaces and maledictions against king and nobles; needless diffidences, banishment of friends, dissipation of cohorts, nuptial breaches, and I know not what.

EDGAR.   How long have you been a sectary astronomical?   125

EDMUND.   Come, come;] when saw you my father last?

EDGAR.   The night gone by.

EDMUND.   Spake you with him?

EDGAR.   Ay, two hours together.   129

EDMUND.   Parted you in good terms? Found you no displeasure in him by word nor countenance?

EDGAR.   None at all.

EDMUND.   Bethink yourself wherein you may have offended him; and at my entreaty forbear his presence until some little time hath qualified the heat of his displeasure, which at this instant so rageth in him, that with the mischief of your person it would scarcely allay.

EDGAR.   Some villain hath done me wrong.   137

EDMUND.   That's my fear. I pray you, have a continent forbearance till the speed of his rage goes slower; and, as I say, retire with me to my lodging, from whence I will fitly bring you to hear my lord speak. Pray ye, go; there's my key. If you do stir abroad, go arm'd.

EDGAR.   Arm'd, brother!   142

EDMUND.   Brother, I advise you to the best; I am no honest man if there be any good meaning toward you. I have told you what I have seen and heard; but faintly, nothing like the image and horror of it. Pray you, away.

EDGAR.   Shall I hear from you anon?   147

EDMUND.   I do serve you in this business.

[*Exit* EDGAR.

A credulous father and a brother noble,
Whose nature is so far from doing harms   150
That he suspects none; on whose foolish honesty

---

113. **Tom o' Bedlam:** a lunatic beggar.   121–126. [as . . . come;] Q. Om. F.
123. **diffidences:** suspicions.   125. **sectary astronomical:** student of astrology.
134. **qualified:** moderated.   136. **mischief:** injury.

My practices ride easy. I see the business.
Let me, if not by birth, have lands by wit:
All with me 's meet that I can fashion fit. [*Exit.*

SCENE 3. [*The Duke of Albany's palace.*]

Enter GONERIL, *and* [OSWALD, *her*] *steward.*

GONERIL. Did my father strike my gentleman for chiding of his Fool?
OSWALD. Ay, madam.
GONERIL. By day and night he wrongs me; every hour
He flashes into one gross crime or other
That sets us all at odds. I'll not endure it.   5
His knights grow riotous, and himself upbraids us
On every trifle. When he returns from hunting
I will not speak with him; say I am sick.
If you come slack of former services,
You shall do well; the fault of it I'll answer.   10
OSWALD. He's coming, madam; I hear him.

[*Horns within.*]

GONERIL. Put on what weary negligence you please,
You and your fellows; I'd have it come to question.
If he distaste it, let him to my sister,
Whose mind and mine, I know, in that are one,   15
[Not to be over-rul'd. Idle old man,
That still would manage those authorities
That he hath given away! Now, by my life,
Old fools are babes again, and must be us'd
With checks as flatteries, when they are seen abus'd.]   20
Remember what I have said.
OSWALD.   Well, madam.
GONERIL. And let his knights have colder looks among you;
What grows of it, no matter. Advise your fellows so.
[I would breed from hence occasions, and I shall,
That I may speak.] I'll write straight to my sister   25
To hold my [very] course. Prepare for dinner.

[*Exeunt.*

152. **practices**: plots.
   Scene iii, 13. question: discussion.   16–20. [**Not . . . abus'd.**] Q. Om. F.
20. **as**: as well as. **abus'd**: misled.   24–25. [**I . . . speak.**] Q. Om. F.   26. [**very**]
Q: identical. Om. F.

SCENE 4. [*A hall in the same.*]

Enter KENT [*disguised*].

KENT. If but as well I other accents borrow,
That can my speech defuse, my good intent
May carry through itself to that full issue
For which I raz'd my likeness. Now, banish'd Kent,
If thou canst serve where thou dost stand condemn'd,   5
So may it come, thy master, whom thou lov'st,
Shall find thee full of labours.

Horns within. Enter LEAR, [*Knights*] *and* Attendants.

LEAR. Let me not stay a jot for dinner; go get it ready.

[*Exit an* Attendant.]

How now! what art thou?
KENT. A man, sir.   10
LEAR. What dost thou profess? What wouldst thou with us?
KENT. I do profess to be no less than I seem; to serve him truly that
will put me in trust; to love him that is honest; to converse with him that
is wise and says little; to fear judgement; to fight when I cannot choose;
and to eat no fish.   15
LEAR. What art thou?
KENT. A very honest-hearted fellow, and as poor as the King.
LEAR. If thou be'st as poor for a subject as he's for a king, thou art
poor enough. What wouldst thou?
KENT. Service.   20
LEAR. Who wouldst thou serve?
KENT. You.
LEAR. Dost thou know me, fellow?
KENT. No, sir; but you have that in your countenance which I would
fain call master.   25
LEAR. What's that?
KENT. Authority.
LEAR. What services canst thou do?
KENT. I can keep honest counsel, ride, run, mar a curious tale in tell-
ing it, and deliver a plain message bluntly. That which ordinary men are
fit for, I am qualified in; and the best of me is diligence.   31
LEAR. How old art thou?
KENT. Not so young, sir, to love a woman for singing, nor so old to
dote on her for anything. I have years on my back forty-eight.

Scene iv, 2. **defuse:** disguise.   4. **raz'd my likeness:** changed my appearance.
15. **eat no fish:** be a Protestant.

LEAR.   Follow me; thou shalt serve me. If I like thee no worse after
dinner, I will not part from thee yet. Dinner, ho, dinner! Where's my
knave? my Fool? Go you, and call my Fool hither.   37

[*Exit an* Attendant. *Enter steward* [OSWALD].]

You, you, sirrah, where's my daughter?
OSWALD.   So please you, — [*Exit.*
LEAR.   What says the fellow there? Call the clotpoll back.   40

[*Exit a* Knight.]

Where's my Fool, ho? I think the world's asleep.

[*Re-enter* Knight.]

How now! where's that mongrel?
KNIGHT.   He says, my lord, your daughter is not well.
LEAR.   Why came not the slave back to me when I call'd him?   44
KNIGHT.   Sir, he answered me in the roundest manner, he would not.
LEAR.   He would not!
KNIGHT.   My lord, I know not what the matter is; but, to my judge-
ment, your Highness is not entertain'd with that ceremonious affection
as you were wont. There's a great abatement of kindness appears as well
in the general dependants as in the Duke himself also and your daughter.
LEAR.   Ha! say'st thou so?   51
KNIGHT.   I beseech you, pardon me, my lord, if I be mistaken; for my
duty cannot be silent when I think your Highness wrong'd.
LEAR.   Thou but remem'brest me of mine own conception. I have
perceived a most faint neglect of late, which I have rather blamed as mine
own jealous curiosity than as a very pretence and purpose of unkindness.
I will look further into't. But where's my Fool? I have not seen him this
two days.   58
KNIGHT.   Since my young lady's going into France, sir, the Fool hath
much pined away.
LEAR.   No more of that; I have noted it well. Go you, and tell my
daughter I would speak with her.   62

[*Exit an* Attendant.]

Go you, call hither my Fool.

[*Exit an* Attendant.] *Re-enter steward* [OSWALD].

O, you sir, you, come you hither, sir. Who am I, sir?

40. clotpoll: blockhead. 56. jealous curiosity: suspicious fussiness. very pretence: real intention.

OSWALD.   My lady's father.   65

LEAR.   "My lady's father"! My lord's knave! You whoreson dog! you slave! you cur!

OSWALD.   I am none of these, my lord; I beseech your pardon.

LEAR.   Do you bandy looks with me, you rascal? [*Striking him.*]

OSWALD.   I'll not be strucken, my lord.   70

KENT.   Nor tripp'd neither, you base foot-ball player. [*Tripping up his heels.*]

LEAR.   I thank thee, fellow. Thou serv'st me, and I'll love thee.

KENT.   Come, sir, arise, away! I'll teach you differences. Away, away! If you will measure your lubber's length again, tarry; but away! go to. Have you wisdom? So. [*Pushes* OSWALD *out.*]   76

LEAR.   Now, my friendly knave, I thank thee. There's earnest of thy service. [*Giving* KENT *money.*]

Enter FOOL.

FOOL.   Let me hire him too; here's my coxcomb. [*Offering* KENT *his cap.*]

LEAR.   How now, my pretty knave! how dost thou?

FOOL.   Sirrah, you were best take my coxcomb.   82

[KENT.   Why, Fool?]

FOOL.   Why? For taking one's part that's out of favour. Nay, an thou canst not smile as the wind sits, thou'lt catch cold shortly. There, take my coxcomb. Why, this fellow has banish'd two on 's daughters, and did the third a blessing against his will; if thou follow him, thou must needs wear my coxcomb. — How now, nuncle! Would I had two coxcombs and two daughters!   89

LEAR.   Why, my boy?

FOOL.   If I gave them all my living, I'd keep my coxcombs myself. There's mine; beg another of thy daughters.

LEAR.   Take heed, sirrah; the whip.

FOOL.   Truth's a dog must to kennel; he must be whipp'd out, when [Lady the] brach may stand by the fire and stink.   95

LEAR.   A pestilent gall to me!

FOOL.   Sirrah, I'll teach thee a speech.

LEAR.   Do.

FOOL.   Mark it, nuncle:

> "Have more than thou showest,   100
> Speak less than thou knowest,
> Lend less than thou owest,
> Ride more than thou goest,

---

77. **earnest:** advance payment.   83. [KENT. . . . Fool?] Q. *Lear. Why my Boy?* F.   95. [**Lady the**] (Malone). *The Lady* F. **brach:** bitch.   102. **owest:** ownest. 103. **goest:** walkest.

> Learn more than thou trowest,
> Set less than thou throwest;   105
> Leave thy drink and thy whore,
> And keep in-a-door,
> And thou shalt have more
> Than two tens to a score."

KENT.   This is nothing, Fool.   110

FOOL.   Then 'tis like the breath of an unfee'd lawyer; you gave me nothing for't. Can you make no use of nothing, nuncle?

LEAR.   Why, no, boy; nothing can be made out of nothing.

FOOL [to KENT].   Prithee, tell him so much the rent of his land comes to. He will not believe a Fool.   115

LEAR.   A bitter fool!

FOOL.   Dost thou know the difference, my boy, between a bitter fool and a sweet one?

LEAR.   No, lad; teach me.

> [FOOL.   "That lord that counsell'd thee   120
>   To give away thy land,
>   Come place him here by me,
>   Do thou for him stand:
>   The sweet and bitter fool
>   Will presently appear;   125
>   The one in motley here,
>   The other found out there."

LEAR.   Dost thou call me fool, boy?

FOOL.   All thy other titles thou hast given away; that thou wast born with.   130

KENT.   This is not altogether fool, my lord.

FOOL.   No, faith, lords and great men will not let me; if I had a monopoly out, they would have part on't. And ladies, too, they will not let me have all the fool to myself; they'll be snatching.] Nuncle, give me an egg, and I'll give thee two crowns.   135

LEAR.   What two crowns shall they be?

FOOL.   Why, after I have cut the egg i' th' middle and eat up the meat, the two crowns of the egg. When thou clovest thy crown i' th' middle and gav'st away both parts, thou bor'st thine ass on thy back o'er the dirt. Thou hadst little wit in thy bald crown when thou gav'st thy golden one away. If I speak like myself in this, let him be whipp'd that first finds it so.

> "Fools had ne'er less grace in a year;   142
>   For wise men are grown foppish,
> And know not how their wits to wear,
>   Their manners are so apish."

---

105. Set: stake. throwest: win at a throw of the dice. 120–134. [FOOL. . . . snatching.] Q. Om. F.

LEAR.   When were you wont to be so full of songs, sirrah?   146
FOOL.   I have used it, nuncle, e'er since thou mad'st thy daughters thy
mothers; for when thou gav'st them the rod, and puttest down thine own
breeches,

> "Then they for sudden joy did weep,   150
>   And I for sorrow sung,
>   That such a king should play bo-peep,
>   And go the fools among."

Prithee, nuncle, keep a schoolmaster that can teach thy Fool to lie. I
would fain learn to lie.   155
LEAR.   And you lie, sirrah, we'll have you whipp'd.
FOOL.   I marvel what kin thou and thy daughters are. They'll have me
whipp'd for speaking true, thou'lt have me whipp'd for lying; and sometimes I am whipp'd for holding my peace. I had rather be any kind o'
thing than a Fool; and yet I would not be thee, nuncle; thou hast pared
thy wit o' both sides, and left nothing i' th' middle. Here comes one o'
the parings.   162

Enter GONERIL.

LEAR.   How now, daughter! what makes that frontlet on? [Methinks]
you are too much of late i' th' frown.
FOOL.   Thou wast a pretty fellow when thou hadst no need to care for
her frowning; now thou art an O without a figure. I am better than thou
art now; I am a Fool, thou art nothing. [*To* GONERIL.] Yes, forsooth, I
will hold my tongue; so your face bids me, though you say nothing. Mum,
mum,   169

> "He that keeps nor crust nor crumb,
>   Weary of all, shall want some."

[*Pointing to* LEAR.] That's a sheal'd peascod.
GONERIL.   Not only, sir, this your all-licens'd Fool,
But other of your insolent retinue
Do hourly carp and quarrel, breaking forth   175
In rank and not-to-be-endured riots. Sir,
I had thought, by making this well known unto you,
To have found a safe redress; but now grow fearful,
By what yourself, too, late have spoke and done,
That you protect this course and put it on   180
By your allowance; which if you should, the fault
Would not scape censure, nor the redresses sleep,
Which, in the tender of a wholesome weal,

---

163. **frontlet:** frown (literally, a forehead band). [**Methinks**] Q. Om. F.   172.
sheal'd: empty.   180. **put it on:** encourage it.   181. **allowance:** approval.   183.
tender of: care for.   **weal:** commonweal.

Might in their working do you that offence,
Which else were shame, that then necessity   185
Will call discreet proceeding.
    FOOL.   For, you know, nuncle,

        "The hedge-sparrow fed the cuckoo so long,
        That it had it head bit off by it young."

So, out went the candle, and we were left darkling.   190
    LEAR.   Are you our daughter?
    GONERIL.   [Come, sir,]
I would you would make use of your good wisdom,
Whereof I know you are fraught, and put away
These dispositions which of late transport you   195
From what you rightly are.
    FOOL.   May not an ass know when the cart draws the horse? "Whoop,
Jug! I love thee."
    LEAR.   Doth any here know me? This is not Lear.
Doth Lear walk thus? speak thus? Where are his eyes?   200
Either his notion weakens, his discernings
Are lethargied — Ha! waking? 'Tis not so.
Who is it that can tell me who I am?
    FOOL.   Lear's shadow.
    [LEAR.   I would learn that; for, by the marks of sovereignty, knowledge,
and reason, I should be false persuaded I had daughters.   206
    FOOL.   Which they will make an obedient father.]
    LEAR.   Your name, fair gentlewoman?
    GONERIL.   This admiration, sir, is much o' the savour
Of other your new pranks. I do beseech you   210
To understand my purposes aright.
As you are old and reverend, should be wise.
Here do you keep a hundred knights and squires,
Men so disorder'd, so debosh'd and bold,
That this our court, infected with their manners,   215
Shows like a riotous inn. Epicurism and lust
Makes it more like a tavern or a brothel
Than a grac'd palace. The shame itself doth speak
For instant remedy. Be then desir'd
By her, that else will take the thing she begs,   220
A little to disquantity your train;
And the remainders that shall still depend
To be such men as may besort your age,
Which know themselves and you.

189. it: its. 190. darkling: in the dark. 192. [Come, sir,] Q. Om. F.
194. fraught: furnished with. 201. notion: mental power. 205–207. [Lear....
father.] Q. Om. F. 205. by . . . of: tested by. 209. admiration: (pretended)
surprise. 214. debosh'd: debauched. 216. Epicurism: gluttony. 221. disquantity: reduce. 222. depend: be your dependents. 223. besort: suit.

LEAR.   Darkness and devils!
Saddle my horses; call my train together!   225
Degenerate bastard! I'll not trouble thee;
Yet have I left a daughter.
   GONERIL.   You strike my people; and your disorder'd rabble
Make servants of their betters.

Enter ALBANY.

   LEAR.   Woe, that too late repents! — [O, sir, are you come?]   **230**
Is it your will? Speak, sir. — Prepare my horses. —
Ingratitude, thou marble-hearted fiend,
More hideous when thou show'st thee in a child
Than the sea-monster!
   ALBANY.   Pray, sir, be patient.
   LEAR [*to* GONERIL].   Detested kite! thou liest.   235
My train are men of choice and rarest parts,
That all particulars of duty know,
And in the most exact regard support
The worships of their name. O most small fault,
How ugly didst thou in Cordelia show!   240
Which, like an engine, wrench'd my frame of nature
From the fix'd place; drew from my heart all love
And added to the gall. O Lear, Lear, Lear!
Beat at this gate, that let thy folly in [*striking his head*]
And thy dear judgement out! Go, go, my people.   245
   ALBANY.   My lord, I am guiltless as I am ignorant
Of what hath moved you.
   LEAR.   It may be so, my lord.
Hear, Nature! hear, dear goddess, hear!
Suspend thy purpose, if thou didst intend
To make this creature fruitful!   250
Into her womb convey sterility!
Dry up in her the organs of increase,
And from her derogate body never spring
A babe to honour her! If she must teem,
Create her child of spleen, that it may live   255
And be a thwart disnatur'd torment to her!
Let it stamp wrinkles in her brow of youth,
With cadent tears fret channels in her cheeks,
Turn all her mother's pains and benefits
To laughter and contempt, that she may feel   260
How sharper than a serpent's tooth it is
To have a thankless child! — Away, away! [*Exit.*

230. [O . . . come?] Q. Om. F.   239. **worships . . . name:** their honorable
reputation.   241. **engine:** rack.   253. **derogate:** debased.   256. **thwart:** dis-
torted, perverse. **disnatur'd:** unnatural.   258. **cadent:** falling.

ALBANY.   Now, gods that we adore, whereof comes this?

GONERIL.   Never afflict yourself to know more of it,
But let his disposition have that scope   265
As dotage gives it.

Re-enter LEAR.

LEAR.   What, fifty of my followers at a clap!
Within a fortnight!

ALBANY.   What's the matter, sir?

LEAR.   I'll tell thee. [*To* GONERIL.] Life and death! I am asham'd
That thou hast power to shake my manhood thus;   270
That these hot tears, which break from me perforce,
Should make thee worth them. Blasts and fogs upon thee!
Th' untented woundings of a father's curse
Pierce every sense about thee! Old fond eyes,
Beweep this cause again, I'll pluck ye out,   275
And cast you, with the waters that you loose,
To temper clay. Ha! [is it come to this?]
Let it be so: I have another daughter,
Who, I am sure, is kind and comfortable.
When she shall hear this of thee, with her nails   280
She'll flay thy wolvish visage. Thou shalt find
That I'll resume the shape which thou dost think
I have cast off for ever. [Thou shalt, I warrant thee.]

[*Exeunt* [LEAR, KENT, *and* Attendants].

GONERIL.   Do you mark that?

ALBANY.   I cannot be so partial, Goneril,   285
To the great love I bear you, —

GONERIL.   Pray you, content. — What, Oswald, ho!
[*To the* FOOL.] You, sir, more knave than fool, after your master.

FOOL.   Nuncle Lear, nuncle Lear, tarry! Take the Fool with thee.

> A fox, when one has caught her,   290
> And such a daughter,
> Should sure to the slaughter,
> If my cap would buy a halter.
> So the Fool follows after. [*Exit.*

GONERIL.   This man hath had good counsel, — a hundred knights!
'Tis politic and safe to let him keep   296
At point a hundred knights; yes, that, on every dream,
Each buzz, each fancy, each complaint, dislike,

264. **more of it** F. *the cause* Q.   273. **untented:** not to be probed.   277. **[is it come to this?]** Q. Om. F.   279. **comfortable:** comforting.   283. **[Thou . . . thee.]** Q. Om. F.   297. **At point:** armed.

He may enguard his dotage with their powers,
And hold our lives in mercy. Oswald, I say!   300
  ALBANY.   Well, you may fear too far.
  GONERIL.   Safer than trust too far.
Let me still take away the harms I fear,
Not fear still to be taken. I know his heart.
What he hath utter'd I have writ my sister.
If she sustain him and his hundred knights,   305
When I have show'd th' unfitness, —

  Re-enter steward [OSWALD].

                         How now, Oswald!
What, have you writ that letter to my sister?
  OSWALD.   Ay, madam.
  GONERIL.   Take you some company, and away to horse.
Inform her full of my particular fear;   310
And thereto add such reasons of your own
As may compact it more. Get you gone;
And hasten your return.

  [*Exit* OSWALD.]

                      No, no, my lord,
This milky gentleness and course of yours
Though I condemn not, yet, under pardon,   315
You are much more at task for want of wisdom
Than prais'd for harmful mildness.
  ALBANY.   How far your eyes may pierce I cannot tell.
Striving to better, oft we mar what's well.
  GONERIL.   Nay, then —   320
  ALBANY.   Well, well; th' event.

  [*Exeunt.*

                 SCENE 5.   [*Court before the same.*]

  Enter LEAR, KENT, *and* FOOL.

  LEAR.   Go you before to Gloucester with these letters. Acquaint my
daughter no further with anything you know than comes from her demand out of the letter. If your diligence be not speedy, I shall be there
afore you.   4
  KENT.   I will not sleep, my lord, till I have delivered your letter. [*Exit.*

300. **in mercy:** at his mercy.   312. **compact:** confirm.   316. **at task:** to be
blamed.   321. **th' event:** (we'll see) the outcome.
  Scene v, 1. Gloucester: the city.

FOOL.　If a man's brains were in 's heels, were't not in danger of kibes?

LEAR.　Ay, boy.

FOOL.　Then, I prithee, be merry; thy wit shall not go slip-shod.

LEAR.　Ha, ha, ha!　　　　　　　　　　　　　　　　　　　9

FOOL.　Shalt see thy other daughter will use thee kindly; for though she's as like this as a crab's like an apple, yet I can tell what I can tell.

LEAR.　What canst tell, boy?

FOOL.　She will taste as like this as a crab does to a crab. Thou canst tell why one's nose stands i' th' middle on 's face?

LEAR.　No.　　　　　　　　　　　　　　　　　　　　15

FOOL.　Why, to keep one's eyes of either side 's nose, that what a man cannot smell out, he may spy into.

LEAR.　I did her wrong —

FOOL.　Canst tell how an oyster makes his shell?

LEAR.　No.　　　　　　　　　　　　　　　　　　　　20

FOOL.　Nor I neither; but I can tell why a snail has a house.

LEAR.　Why?

FOOL.　Why, to put 's head in; not to give it away to his daughters and leave his horns without a case.　　　　　　　　　　　24

LEAR.　I will forget my nature. So kind a father! Be my horses ready?

FOOL.　Thy asses are gone about 'em. The reason why the seven stars are no moe than seven is a pretty reason.

LEAR.　Because they are not eight?

FOOL.　Yes, indeed. Thou wouldst make a good Fool.

LEAR.　To take 't again perforce! Monster ingratitude!　　　30

FOOL.　If thou wert my Fool, nuncle, I'd have thee beaten for being old before thy time.

LEAR.　How's that?

FOOL.　Thou shouldst not have been old till thou hadst been wise.

LEAR.　O, let me not be mad, not mad, sweet heaven!　　　35
Keep me in temper; I would not be mad!

[Enter GENTLEMAN.]

How now! are the horses ready?

GENTLEMAN.　Ready, my lord.

LEAR.　Come, boy.

FOOL.　She that's a maid now, and laughs at my departure,　　40
Shall not be a maid long, unless things be cut shorter.

[Exeunt.

---

6. **kibes:** chilblains.　8. **thy . . . slip-shod:** *i.e.,* because there is no sense in your proposed journey.　10. **kindly:** (1) in friendly fashion, (2) according to her nature.

ACT TWO

Scene 1.   [*The Earl of Gloucester's castle.*]

Enter Bastard [EDMUND] *and* CURAN, *severally.*

EDMUND.   Save thee, Curan.

CURAN.   And you, sir. I have been with your father, and given him notice that the Duke of Cornwall and Regan his duchess will be here with him this night.

EDMUND.   How comes that?   5

CURAN.   Nay, I know not. You have heard of the news abroad; I mean the whisper'd ones, for they are yet but ear-kissing arguments?

EDMUND.   Not I. Pray you, what are they?

CURAN.   Have you heard of no likely wars toward, 'twixt the Dukes of Cornwall and Albany?   10

EDMUND.   Not a word.

CURAN.   You may do, then, in time. Fare you well, sir. [*Exit.*

EDMUND.   The Duke be here to-night? The better! best!
This weaves itself perforce into my business.
My father hath set guard to take my brother;   15
And I have one thing, of a queasy question,
Which I must act. Briefness and fortune, work!

Enter EDGAR.

Brother, a word; descend. Brother, I say!
My father watches; O sir, fly this place;
Intelligence is given where you are hid;   20
You have now the good advantage of the night.
Have you not spoken 'gainst the Duke of Cornwall?
He's coming hither, now, i' th' night, i' th' haste,
And Regan with him. Have you nothing said
Upon his party 'gainst the Duke of Albany?   25
Advise yourself.

EDGAR.   I am sure on't, not a word.

EDMUND.   I hear my father coming. Pardon me,
In cunning I must draw my sword upon you.
Draw; seem to defend yourself; now quit you well.
Yield! Come before my father. Light, ho, here! —   30
Fly, brother. — Torches, torches! — So, farewell.

[*Exit* EDGAR.

Act II, Scene i, 7. ear-kissing arguments: whispered topics.   **9. toward:** imminent.   **16. of . . . question:** requiring delicate handling.   **26. Advise yourself:** consider.

Some blood drawn on me would beget opinion [*wounds his arm*]
Of my more fierce endeavour. I have seen drunkards
Do more than this in sport. — Father, father! —
Stop, stop! — No help?   35

    Enter GLOUCESTER, *and* Servants *with torches.*

  GLOUCESTER.   Now, Edmund, where's the villain?
  EDMUND.   Here stood he in the dark, his sharp sword out,
Mumbling of wicked charms, conjuring the moon
To stand ['s] auspicious mistress, —
  GLOUCESTER.   But where is he?
  EDMUND.   Look, sir, I bleed.
  GLOUCESTER.   Where is the villain, Edmund?   40
  EDMUND.   Fled this way, sir. When by no means he could —
  GLOUCESTER.   Pursue him, ho! Go after.

    [*Exeunt some Servants.*]

                                 By no means what?
  EDMUND.   Persuade me to the murder of your lordship;
But that I told him, the revenging gods
'Gainst parricides did all the thunder bend;   45
Spoke, with how manifold and strong a bond
The child was bound to th' father; sir, in fine,
Seeing how loathly opposite I stood
To his unnatural purpose, in fell motion,
With his prepared sword he charges home   50
My unprovided body, latch'd mine arm;
And when he saw my best alarum'd spirits,
Bold in the quarrel's right, rous'd to th' encounter,
Or whether gasted by the noise I made,
Full suddenly he fled.
  GLOUCESTER.   Let him fly far.   55
Not in this land shall he remain uncaught;
And found, — dispatch. The noble Duke my master,
My worthy arch and patron, comes to-night.
By his authority I will proclaim it,
That he which finds him shall deserve our thanks,   60
Bringing the murderous coward to the stake;
He that conceals him, death.
  EDMUND.   When I dissuaded him from his intent,
And found him pight to do it, with curst speech

39. **stand . . . mistress:** to shed favorable influence on him. ['s] Q: his. Om. F.
49. **in fell motion:** with a fierce stab. 51. **latch'd:** caught. 54. **gasted:** scared.
58. **arch:** chief. 63. **dissuaded:** tried to dissuade. 64. **pight:** pitched, determined.

I threaten'd to discover him; he replied,   65
"Thou unpossessing bastard! dost thou think,
If I would stand against thee, would the reposal
Of any trust, virtue, or worth in thee
Make thy words faith'd? No! what [I should] deny, —
As this I would; [ay,] though thou didst produce   70
My very character, — I'd turn it all
To thy suggestion, plot, and damned practice;
And thou must make a dullard of the world
If they not thought the profits of my death
Were very pregnant and potential [spurs]   75
To make thee seek it."
    GLOUCESTER.   O strange and fast'ned villain!
Would he deny his letter? [I never got him.]

    [*Tucket within.*

Hark, the Duke's trumpets! I know not [why] he comes.
All ports I'll bar, the villain shall not scape;
The Duke must grant me that. Besides, his picture   80
I will send far and near, that all the kingdom
May have due note of him; and of my land,
Loyal and natural boy, I'll work the means
To make thee capable.

    Enter CORNWALL, REGAN, *and* Attendants.

    CORNWALL.   How now, my noble friend! since I came hither,   85
Which I can call but now, I have heard [strange news].
    REGAN.   If it be true, all vengeance comes too short
Which can pursue th' offender. How dost, my lord?
    GLOUCESTER.   O, madam, my old heart is crack'd, it's crack'd!
    REGAN.   What, did my father's godson seek your life?   90
He whom my father nam'd? your Edgar?
    GLOUCESTER.   O, lady, lady, shame would have it hid!
    REGAN.   Was he not companion with the riotous knights
That tended upon my father?
    GLOUCESTER.   I know not, madam. 'Tis too bad, too bad.   95
    EDMUND.   Yes, madam, he was of that consort.
    REGAN.   No marvel, then, though he were ill affected:
'Tis they have put him on the old man's death,
To have th' expense and waste of his revenues.

65. **discover:** reveal.   69. **faith'd:** trusted.   [**I should**] Q. *should I* F.   70. [**ay**]
I Q. Om. F.   72. **practice:** conspiracy.   75. [**spurs**] Q. *spirits* F.   76. **fast'ned:**
hardened.   77. [**I . . . him**] Q. *said he?* F. S.D. *Tucket:* flourish on a trumpet.
78. [**why**] Q. *wher* F.   84. **capable:** able to inherit.   86. [**strange news**] Q.
strangeness F.   99. **expense and waste:** power of spending and wasting.

I have this present evening from my sister　　　　　　100
Been well inform'd of them; and with such cautions,
That if they come to sojourn at my house,
I'll not be there.

  CORNWALL. Nor I, assure thee, Regan.
Edmund, I hear that you have shown your father
A child-like office.

  EDMUND. 'Twas my duty, sir.   105

  GLOUCESTER. He did bewray his practice; and receiv'd
This hurt you see, striving to apprehend him.

  CORNWALL. Is he pursued?

  GLOUCESTER.   Ay, my good lord.

  CORNWALL. If he be taken he shall never more
Be fear'd of doing harm. Make your own purpose,　　　110
How in my strength you please. For you, Edmund,
Whose virtue and obedience doth this instant
So much commend itself, you shall be ours.
Natures of such deep trust we shall much need;
You we first seize on.

  EDMUND.   I shall serve you, sir,　　　115
Truly, however else.

  GLOUCESTER. For him I thank your Grace.

  CORNWALL. You know not why we came to visit you, —

  REGAN. Thus out of season, threading dark-ey'd night?
Occasions, noble Gloucester, of some [poise],
Wherein we must have use of your advice.　　　　　　120
Our father he hath writ, so hath our sister,
Of differences, which I best thought it fit
To answer from our home; the several messengers
From hence attend dispatch. Our good old friend,
Lay comforts to your bosom; and bestow　　　　　　125
Your needful counsel to our businesses,
Which craves the instant use.

  GLOUCESTER.   I serve you, madam.
Your Graces are right welcome.

   [Exeunt. Flourish.

    SCENE 2. [Before Gloucester's castle.]

Enter KENT and steward [OSWALD], severally.

  OSWALD. Good dawning to thee, friend. Art of this house?

  KENT. Ay.

105. **child-like:** filial. 106. **bewray:** reveal. 111. **strength:** authority. 119.
[**poise**] Q: weight. *prize* F. 124. **From:** away from.

OSWALD.   Where may we set our horses?
KENT.   I' th' mire.
OSWALD.   Prithee, if thou lov'st me, tell me.
KENT.   I love thee not.   6
OSWALD.   Why, then, I care not for thee.
KENT.   If I had thee in Lipsbury pinfold, I would make thee care
for me.
OSWALD.   Why dost thou use me thus? I know thee not.
KENT.   Fellow, I know thee.
OSWALD.   What dost thou know me for?   12
KENT.   A knave; a rascal; an eater of broken meats; a base, proud,
shallow, beggarly, three-suited, hundred-pound, filthy, worsted-stocking
knave; a lily-livered, action-taking, whoreson, glass-gazing, superservice-
able, finical rogue; one-trunk-inheriting slave; one that wouldst be a
bawd in way of good service, and art nothing but the composition of a
knave, beggar, coward, pandar, and the son and heir of a mongrel bitch;
one whom I will beat into clamorous whining, if thou deni'st the least
syllable of thy addition.   20
OSWALD.   Why, what a monstrous fellow art thou, thus to rail on one
that is neither known of thee nor knows thee!
KENT.   What a brazen-fac'd varlet art thou, to deny thou knowest me!
Is it two days since I tripp'd up thy heels, and beat thee before the King?
Draw, you rogue; for, though it be night, yet the moon shines. I'll make
a sop o' th' moonshine of you, you whoreson cullionly barber-monger!
Draw! [*Drawing his sword.*]   27
OSWALD.   Away! I have nothing to do with thee.
KENT.   Draw, you rascal! You come with letters against the King; and
take Vanity the puppet's part against the royalty of her father. Draw, you
rogue, or I'll so carbonado your shanks, — draw, you rascal! Come your
ways.   32
OSWALD.   Help, ho! murder! help!
KENT.   Strike, you slave! Stand, rogue, stand! You neat slave, strike.
[*Beating him.*]
OSWALD.   Help, ho! murder! murder!   36

Enter Bastard [EDMUND] *with his rapier drawn,* CORNWALL, REGAN,
GLOUCESTER, *and Servants.*

EDMUND.   How now! What's the matter? Part.
KENT.   With you, goodman boy, if you please. Come, I'll flesh ye;
come on, young master.
GLOUCESTER.   Weapons! arms! What's the matter here?   40

Scene ii, 8. Lipsbury pinfold: my teeth(?). **15. lily-livered:** cowardly. **action-taking:** preferring going to law to fighting. **glass-gazing:** vain. **15–16. super-
serviceable:** officious. **17. composition:** combination. **20. thy addition:** the
titles I have given you. **26. cullionly:** rascally. **barber-monger:** frequenter of
barbershops. **31. carbonado:** slash. **34. neat:** foppish.

CORNWALL.   Keep peace, upon your lives!
He dies that strikes again. What is the matter?

REGAN.   The messengers from our sister and the King.

CORNWALL.   What is your difference? Speak.

OSWALD.   I am scarce in breath, my lord.   45

KENT.   No marvel, you have so bestirr'd your valour. You cowardly rascal, Nature disclaims in thee. A tailor made thee.

CORNWALL.   Thou art a strange fellow. A tailor make a man?

KENT.   A tailor, sir. A stone-cutter or a painter could not have made him so ill, though they had been but two years o' th' trade.   50

CORNWALL.   Speak yet, how grew your quarrel?

OSWALD.   This ancient ruffian, sir, whose life I have spar'd at suit of his grey beard, —

KENT.   Thou whoreson zed! thou unnecessary letter! My lord, if you will give me leave, I will tread this unbolted villain into mortar, and daub the wall of a jakes with him. Spare my grey beard, you wagtail?   56

CORNWALL.   Peace, sirrah!
You beastly knave, know you no reverence?

KENT.   Yes, sir; but anger hath a privilege.

CORNWALL.   Why art thou angry?   60

KENT.   That such a slave as this should wear a sword,
Who wears no honesty. Such smiling rogues as these,
Like rats, oft bite the holy cords a-twain
Which are too intrinse t' unloose; smooth every passion
That in the natures of their lords rebel;   65
[Bring] oil to fire, snow to their colder moods;
[Renege,] affirm, and turn their halcyon beaks
With every gale and vary of their masters,
Knowing nought, like dogs, but following.
A plague upon your epileptic visage!   70
Smile you my speeches, as I were a fool?
Goose, if I had you upon Sarum Plain,
I'd drive ye cackling home to Camelot.

CORNWALL.   What, art thou mad, old fellow?

GLOUCESTER.   How fell you out? Say that.   75

KENT.   No contraries hold more antipathy
Than I and such a knave.

CORNWALL.   Why dost thou call him knave? What is his fault?

KENT.   His countenance likes me not.

CORNWALL.   No more, perchance, does mine, nor his, nor hers.   80

KENT.   Sir, 'tis my occupation to be plain;

47. **disclaims in:** renounces.   54. **zed:** Z, often omitted in old dictionaries. 55. **unbolted:** coarse.   56. **jakes:** privy.   63. **holy cords:** *i.e.*, of natural affection. 64. **intrinse:** intricate.   **smooth:** humor.   66. [Bring] Q. *Being* F.   67. [Renege] F₂: deny. *Revenge* F₁. **halcyon:** kingfisher, which, if hung up, was believed always to turn with its bill to the wind.   72. **Sarum:** Salisbury.   73. **Camelot:** Winchester.   79. **likes:** pleases.

I have seen better faces in my time
Than stands on any shoulder that I see
Before me at this instant.
    CORNWALL.   This is some fellow
Who, having been prais'd for bluntness, doth affect   85
A saucy roughness, and constrains the garb
Quite from his nature. He cannot flatter, he;
An honest mind and plain, he must speak truth!
An they will take it, so; if not, he's plain.
These kind of knaves I know, which in this plainness   90
Harbour more craft and more corrupter ends
Than twenty silly ducking observants
That stretch their duties nicely.
    KENT.   Sir, in good sooth, in sincere verity,
Under the allowance of your great aspect,   95
Whose influence, like the wreath of radiant fire
On [flickering] Phœbus' front, —
    CORNWALL.   What mean'st by this?
    KENT.   To go out of my dialect, which you discommend so much. I know, sir, I am no flatterer. He that beguil'd you in a plain accent was a plain knave; which for my part I will not be, though I should win your displeasure to entreat me to't.   101
    CORNWALL.   What was th' offence you gave him?
    OSWALD.   I never gave him any.
It pleas'd the King his master very late
To strike at me, upon his misconstruction;   105
When he, compact, and flattering his displeasure,
Tripp'd me behind; being down, insulted, rail'd,
And put upon him such a deal of man
[That 't] worthied him, got praises of the King
For him attempting who was self-subdued;   110
And, in the fleshment of this [dread] exploit,
Drew on me here again.
    KENT.   None of these rogues and cowards
But Ajax is their fool.
    CORNWALL.   Fetch forth the stocks!
You stubborn ancient knave, you reverend braggart,
We'll teach you —
    KENT.   Sir, I am too old to learn.   115
Call not your stocks for me; I serve the King,
On whose employment I was sent to you.

86. **constrains the garb:** forces the manner. 92. **observants:** obsequious attendants. 93. **nicely:** punctiliously. 97. **[flickering]** Q. *flicking* F. 106. **compact:** taking his side. 108. **put . . . man:** took such a heroic attitude. 109. **[That 't]** (Anon.) *That* F. *That* Q. 110. **attempting:** attacking. 111. **fleshment:** excitement from first success. **[dread]** Q. *dead* F. 113. **But . . . fool:** but pick on a plain blunt fellow like Ajax (?).

You shall do small respects, show too bold malice
Against the grace and person of my master,
Stocking his messenger.   120
    CORNWALL.   Fetch forth the stocks! As I have life and honour,
There shall he sit till noon.
    REGAN.   Till noon! Till night, my lord; and all night too.
    KENT.   Why, madam, if I were your father's dog,
You should not use me so.
    REGAN.   Sir, being his knave, I will.   125

    [Stocks brought out.

    CORNWALL.   This is a fellow of the self-same colour
Our sister speaks of. Come, bring away the stocks!
    GLOUCESTER.   Let me beseech your Grace not to do so.
[His fault is much, and the good King his master
Will check him for't. Your purpos'd low correction   130
Is such as basest and contemned'st wretches
For pilferings and most common trespasses
Are punish'd with.] The King must take it ill
That he, so slightly valued in his messenger,
Should have him thus restrain'd.
    CORNWALL.   I'll answer that.   135
    REGAN.   My sister may receive it much more worse
To have her gentleman abus'd, assaulted,
[For following her affairs. Put in his legs.]

    [KENT is put in the stocks.]

[Come, my good] lord, away.

    [Exeunt [all but GLOUCESTER and KENT].

    GLOUCESTER.   I am sorry for thee, friend; 'tis the Duke's pleasure,   140
Whose disposition, all the world well knows,
Will not be rubb'd nor stopp'd. I'll entreat for thee.
    KENT.   Pray, do not, sir. I have watch'd and travell'd hard;
Some time I shall sleep out, the rest I'll whistle.
A good man's fortune may grow out at heels.   145
Give you good morrow!
    GLOUCESTER.   The Duke's to blame in this; 'twill be ill taken. *[Exit.*
    KENT.   Good King, that must approve the common saw,

129–133. [His . . . with.] Q. Om. F.   131. contemned'st (Capell). *temnest* or
contened Q.   133. King Q. *King his master needs* F.   138. [For . . . legs.] Q.
Om. F.   139. [Come, my good] Q. *Cornwall. Come my* F.   143. watch'd: been
awake long. Cf. 1. 158.   148. approve . . . saw: prove the proverb true.

Thou out of heaven's benediction com'st
To the warm sun!   150
Approach, thou beacon to this under globe,
That by thy comfortable beams I may
Peruse this letter! Nothing almost sees miracles
But misery. I know 'tis from Cordelia,
Who hath most fortunately been inform'd   155
Of my obscured course; [reads] "— and shall find time
From this enormous state — seeking to give
Losses their remedies." — All weary and o'er-watch'd,
Take vantage, heavy eyes, not to behold
This shameful lodging.   160
Fortune, good-night! Smile once more; turn thy wheel! [Sleeps.]

[SCENE 3. The same.]

Enter EDGAR.

EDGAR.   I heard myself proclaim'd;
And by the happy hollow of a tree
Escap'd the hunt. No port is free; no place
That guard and most unusual vigilance
Does not attend my taking. Whiles I may scape   5
I will preserve myself, and am bethought
To take the basest and most poorest shape
That every penury, in contempt of man,
Brought near to beast. My face I'll grime with filth,
Blanket my loins, elf all my hairs in knots,   10
And with presented nakedness out-face
The winds and persecutions of thy sky.
The country gives me proof and precedent
Of Bedlam beggars, who, with roaring voices,
Strike in their numb'd and mortified arms   15
Pins, wooden pricks, nails, sprigs of rosemary;
And with this horrible object, from low farms,
Poor pelting villages, sheep-cotes, and mills,
Sometimes with lunatic bans, sometimes with prayers,
Enforce their charity. Poor Turlygod! poor Tom!   20
That's something yet. Edgar I nothing am. [Exit.

149–150. out . . . sun: from better to worse.   161. Smile . . . wheel! Q attaches
once more to *turn* rather than *smile.*

Scene iii, 5. attend my taking: wait to capture me.   10. elf: tangle as in
elf-locks.   11. presented: exposed.   17. object: aspect.   18. pelting: petty.
19. bans: curses.   21. Edgar . . . am: of Edgar nothing will remain.

[SCENE 4. *The same.*]

Enter LEAR, FOOL, *and* GENTLEMAN. [KENT *in the stocks.*]

LEAR.   'Tis strange that they should so depart from home,
And not send back my messengers.

GENTLEMAN.   As I learn'd,
The night before there was no purpose in them
Of this remove.

KENT.   Hail to thee, noble master!

LEAR.   Ha!   5
Mak'st thou this shame thy pastime?

KENT.   No, my lord.

FOOL.   Ha, ha! he wears cruel garters. Horses are tied by the heads,
dogs and bears by th' neck, monkeys by th' loins, and men by th' legs.
When a man's over-lusty at legs, then he wears wooden nether-stocks.

LEAR.   What's he that hath so much thy place mistook   10
To set thee here?

KENT.   It is both he and she;
Your son and daughter.

LEAR.   No.

KENT.   Yes.

LEAR.   No, I say.   15

KENT.   I say, yea.

[LEAR.   No, no, they would not.

KENT.   Yes, they have.]

LEAR.   By Jupiter, I swear, no.

KENT.   By Juno, I swear, ay.

LEAR.   They durst not do't;   20
They could not, would not do't. 'Tis worse than murder
To do upon respect such violent outrage.
Resolve me with all modest haste which way
Thou mightst deserve, or they impose, this usage,
Coming from us.

KENT.   My lord, when at their home   25
I did commend your Highness' letters to them,
Ere I was risen from the place that show'd
My duty kneeling, came there a reeking post,
Stew'd in his haste, half breathless, panting forth
From Goneril his mistress salutations;   30
Deliver'd letters, spite of intermission,
Which presently they read. On those contents,
They summon'd up their meiny, straight took horse;

Scene iv, 9. **nether-stocks:** stockings.   17–18. [LEAR. . . . have.] Q. Om. F.
22. **upon respect:** deliberately.   23. **Resolve:** inform.   31. **spite of intermission:**
careless of interrupting.   33. **meiny:** retinue.

Commanded me to follow, and attend
The leisure of their answer; gave me cold looks: 35
And meeting here the other messenger,
Whose welcome, I perceiv'd, had poison'd mine, —
Being the very fellow which of late
Display'd so saucily against your Highness, —
Having more man than wit about me, drew.   40
He rais'd the house with loud and coward cries.
Your son and daughter found this trespass worth
The shame which here it suffers.

    FOOL.   Winter's not gone yet, if the wild geese fly that way.

> "Fathers that wear rags   45
>   Do make their children blind;
> But fathers that bear bags
>   Shall see their children kind.
> Fortune, that arrant whore,
>   Ne'er turns the key to th' poor."   50

But, for all this, thou shalt have as many dolours for thy daughters as
thou canst tell in a year.

    LEAR.   O, how this mother swells up toward my heart!
Hysterica passio, down, thou climbing sorrow,
Thy element's below! — Where is this daughter?   55

    KENT.   With the Earl, sir, here within.

    LEAR.   Follow me not;
Stay here. [*Exit.*

    GENTLEMAN.   Made you no more offence but what you speak of?

    KENT.   None.

How chance the King comes with so small a number?   60

    FOOL.   An thou hadst been set i' th' stocks for that question, thou'dst
well deserv'd it.

    KENT.   Why, Fool?   63

    FOOL.   We'll set thee to school to an ant, to teach thee there's no
labouring i' th' winter. All that follow their noses are led by their eyes
but blind men; and there's not a nose among twenty but can smell him
that's stinking. Let go thy hold when a great wheel runs down a hill, lest
it break thy neck with following; but the great one that goes upward, let
him draw thee after. When a wise man gives thee better counsel, give me
mine again; I would have none but knaves follow it, since a fool gives it.

> "That sir which serves and seeks for gain,   71
>   And follows but for form,
> Will pack when it begins to rain,
>   And leave thee in the storm.

---

39. **Display'd:** showed himself.   51. **dolours:** with a pun on *dollars.*   52. **tell:**
count.   53. **mother:** hysteria.

But I will tarry; the Fool will stay,   75
   And let the wise man fly.
The knave turns fool that runs away;
   The Fool no knave, perdy."

Re-enter LEAR *and* GLOUCESTER.

KENT.   Where learn'd you this, Fool?
FOOL.   Not i' th' stocks, fool.
LEAR.   Deny to speak with me? They are sick? They are weary?   80
They have travell'd all the night? Mere fetches;
The images of revolt and flying off.
Fetch me a better answer.
   GLOUCESTER.   My dear lord,
You know the fiery quality of the Duke;   85
How unremovable and fix'd he is
In his own course.
   LEAR.   Vengeance! plague! death! confusion!
"Fiery"? What "quality"? Why, Gloucester, Gloucester,
I'd speak with the Duke of Cornwall and his wife.   90
   GLOUCESTER.   Well, my good lord, I have inform'd them so.
   LEAR.   "Inform'd" them! Dost thou understand me, man?
   GLOUCESTER.   Ay, my good lord.
   LEAR.   The King would speak with Cornwall; the dear father
Would with his daughter speak, commands [her] service.   95
Are they "inform'd" of this? My breath and blood!
"Fiery"? The fiery duke? Tell the hot duke that —
No, but not yet; may be he is not well.
Infirmity doth still neglect all office
Whereto our health is bound; we are not ourselves   100
When nature, being oppress'd, commands the mind
To suffer with the body. I'll forbear;
And am fallen out with my more headier will,
To take the indispos'd and sickly fit   104
For the sound man. — Death on my state! wherefore [*looking on* KENT]
Should he sit here? This act persuades me
That this remotion of the Duke and her
Is practice only. Give me my servant forth.
Go tell the Duke and 's wife I'd speak with them,   109
Now, presently. Bid them come forth and hear me,
Or at their chamber-door I'll beat the drum
Till it cry sleep to death.
   GLOUCESTER.   I would have all well betwixt you. [*Exit.*
   LEAR.   O me, my heart, my rising heart! But, down!   114

82. **fetches:** tricks.   83. **images:** signs.   **flying off:** deserting.   95. **[her]** Q. *tends*
F.   99. **office:** duty.   103. **headier:** impetuous.   107. **remotion:** removal.
108. **practice:** trickery.   112. **cry . . . to death:** murder.

FOOL.   Cry to it, nuncle, as the cockney did to the eels when she put
'em i' th' paste alive; she knapp'd 'em o' th' coxcombs with a stick, and
cried, "Down, wantons, down!" 'Twas her brother that, in pure kindness
to his horse, buttered his hay.

Enter CORNWALL, REGAN, GLOUCESTER, *and* Servants.

LEAR.   Good morrow to you both.
CORNWALL.   Hail to your Grace!

[KENT *is set at liberty.*

REGAN.   I am glad to see your Highness.   120
LEAR.   Regan, I think you are; I know what reason
I have to think so. If thou shouldst not be glad,
I would divorce me from thy mother's tomb,
Sepulchring an adulteress. [*To* KENT.] O, are you free?
Some other time for that. Beloved Regan,   125
Thy sister's naught. O Regan, she hath tied
Sharp-tooth'd unkindness, like a vulture, here. [*Points to his heart.*]
I can scarce speak to thee; thou'lt not believe
With how deprav'd a quality — O Regan!
REGAN.   I pray you, sir, take patience. I have hope   130
You less know how to value her desert
Than she to scant her duty.
LEAR.   Say, how is that?
REGAN.   I cannot think my sister in the least
Would fail her obligation. If, sir, perchance
She have restrain'd the riots of your followers,   135
'Tis on such ground and to such wholesome end
As clears her from all blame.
LEAR.   My curses on her!
REGAN.   O, sir, you are old;
Nature in you stands on the very verge
Of her confine. You should be rul'd and led
By some discretion that discerns your state   140
Better than you yourself. Therefore, I pray you,
That to our sister you do make return;
Say you have wrong'd her, sir.
LEAR.   Ask her forgiveness?
Do you but mark how this becomes the house: 145
"Dear daughter, I confess that I am old; [*kneeling*]
Age is unnecessary. On my knees I beg
That you'll vouchsafe me raiment, bed, and food."

126. **naught:** wicked.   129. **quality:** manner.   145. **house:** royal family.   147.
Age is unnecessary: old people are useless.

REGAN.   Good sir, no more; these are unsightly tricks.
Return you to my sister.
  LEAR [rising].   Never, Regan: 150
She hath abated me of half my train;
Look'd black upon me; struck me with her tongue,
Most serpent-like, upon the very heart.
All the stor'd vengeances of heaven fall
On her ingrateful top! Strike her young bones,   155
You taking airs, with lameness!
  CORNWALL.   Fie, sir, fie!
  LEAR.   You nimble lightnings, dart your blinding flames
Into her scornful eyes! Infect her beauty,
You fen-suck'd fogs, drawn by the powerful sun,
To fall and [blast her pride!]   160
  REGAN.   O the blest gods! so will you wish on me,
When the rash mood is on.
  LEAR.   No, Regan, thou shalt never have my curse.
Thy tender-hefted nature shall not give
Thee o'er to harshness. Her eyes are fierce; but thine   165
Do comfort and not burn. 'Tis not in thee
To grudge my pleasures, to cut off my train,
To bandy hasty words, to scant my sizes,
And in conclusion to oppose the bolt
Against my coming in. Thou better know'st   170
The offices of nature, bond of childhood,
Effects of courtesy, dues of gratitude.
Thy half o' th' kingdom hast thou not forgot,
Wherein I thee endow'd.
  REGAN.   Good sir, to th' purpose.

[Tucket within.

  LEAR.   Who put my man i' th' stocks?

Enter steward [OSWALD.]

  CORNWALL.   What trumpet 's that?   175
  REGAN.   I know 't; my sister's. This approves her letter,
That she would soon be here. [To OSWALD.] Is your lady come?
  LEAR.   This is a slave whose easy-borrowed pride
Dwells in the [fickle] grace of her he follows.
Out, varlet, from my sight!

155. **top:** head. **young bones:** bones of her unborn child. 156. **taking:** infec-
tious. 160. **fall:** humble. [**blast her pride**] Q. *blister* F. 164. **tender-hefted:**
gentle. 168. **sizes:** allowances. 172. **Effects:** manifestations. 178. **easy-borrowed:** not justified by his own qualities, but on the reflection of his mistress's
position. 179. [**fickle**] Q. *sickly* F.

CORNWALL.   What means your Grace?   180

Enter GONERIL.

LEAR. Who stock'd my servant? Regan, I have good hope
Thou didst not know on't. — Who comes here? O heavens,
If you do love old men, if your sweet sway
Allow obedience, if you yourselves are old,
Make it your cause; send down, and take my part!   185
[*To* GONERIL.] Art not asham'd to look upon this beard?
O Regan, will you take her by the hand?
GONERIL. Why not by th' hand, sir? How have I offended?
All's not offence that indiscretion finds
And dotage terms so.
LEAR.   O sides, you are too tough;   190
Will you yet hold? How came my man i' th' stocks?
CORNWALL. I set him there, sir; but his own disorders
Deserv'd much less advancement.
LEAR.   You! did you?
REGAN. I pray you, father, being weak, seem so.
If, till the expiration of your month,   195
You will return and sojourn with my sister,
Dismissing half your train, come then to me.
I am now from home, and out of that provision
Which shall be needful for your entertainment.
LEAR. Return to her, and fifty men dismiss'd!   200
No, rather I abjure all roofs, and choose
To wage against the enmity o' th' air;
To be a comrade with the wolf and owl, —
Necessity's sharp pinch. Return with her?
Why, the hot-blooded France, that dowerless took   205
Our youngest born, I could as well be brought
To knee his throne, and, squire-like, pension beg
To keep base life afoot. Return with her?
Persuade me rather to be slave and sumpter
To this detested groom. [*Pointing at* OSWALD.]
GONERIL.   At your choice, sir.   210
LEAR. I prithee, daughter, do not make me mad;
I will not trouble thee, my child; farewell!
We'll no more meet, no more see one another.
But yet thou art my flesh, my blood, my daughter;
Or rather a disease that's in my flesh,   215
Which I must needs call mine; thou art a boil,
A plague-sore, an embossed carbuncle,

184. **Allow:** approve. 202. **wage:** contend. 209. **sumpter:** pack-horse. 217.
embossed: swollen.

In my corrupted blood. But I'll not chide thee;
Let shame come when it will, I do not call it.
I do not bid the thunder-bearer shoot,　　　　　　　　　220
Nor tell tales of thee to high-judging Jove.
Mend when thou canst; be better at thy leisure.
I can be patient; I can stay with Regan,
I and my hundred knights.

REGAN.　　　　　　　　　　　　Not altogether so;
I look'd not for you yet, nor am provided　　　　　225
For your fit welcome. Give ear, sir, to my sister;
For those that mingle reason with your passion
Must be content to think you old, and so —
But she knows what she does.

LEAR.　　　　　　　　　　Is this well spoken?

REGAN.　　I dare avouch it, sir. What, fifty followers!　　230
Is it not well? What should you need of more?
Yea, or so many, sith that both charge and danger
Speak 'gainst so great a number? How, in one house,
Should many people under two commands
Hold amity? 'Tis hard; almost impossible.　　　　235

GONERIL.　　Why might not you, my lord, receive attendance
From those that she calls servants or from mine?

REGAN.　　Why not, my lord? If then they chanc'd to slack ye,
We could control them. If you will come to me, —
For now I spy a danger — I entreat you　　　　　240
To bring but five and twenty; to no more
Will I give place or notice.

LEAR.　　I gave you all.

REGAN.　　　　　　　　　　And in good time you gave it.

LEAR.　　Made you my guardians, my depositaries,
But kept a reservation to be followed　　　　　245
With such a number. What, must I come to you
With five and twenty, Regan? Said you so?

REGAN.　　And speak 't again, my lord; no more with me.

LEAR.　　Those wicked creatures yet do look well-favour'd
When others are more wicked; not being the worst　　250
Stands in some rank of praise. [To GONERIL.] I'll go with thee.
Thy fifty yet doth double five and twenty,
And thou art twice her love.

GONERIL.　　　　　　　　　Hear me, my lord:
What need you five and twenty, ten, or five,
To follow in a house where twice so many　　　　255
Have a command to tend you?

REGAN.　　　　　　　　　　What need one?

232. **charge:** expense.　　238. **slack:** be lacking in their services.

LEAR.   O, reason not the need! Our basest beggars
Are in the poorest thing superfluous.
Allow not nature more than nature needs,
Man's life is cheap as beast's. Thou art a lady;   260
If only to go warm were gorgeous,
Why, nature needs not what thou gorgeous wear'st,
Which scarcely keeps thee warm. But, for true need, —
You heavens, give me that patience, patience I need!
You see me here, you gods, a poor old man,   265
As full of grief as age; wretched in both!
If it be you that stirs these daughters' hearts
Against their father, fool me not so much
To bear it tamely; touch me with noble anger,
And let not women's weapons, water-drops,   270
Stain my man's cheeks! No, you unnatural hags,
I will have such revenges on you both
That all the world shall — I will do such things, —
What they are, yet I know not; but they shall be
The terrors of the earth. You think I'll weep: 275
No, I'll not weep.
I have full cause of weeping; but this heart

(Storm and tempest.)

Shall break into a hundred thousand flaws,
Or ere I'll weep. O, Fool! I shall go mad!

[Exeunt LEAR, GLOUCESTER, KENT, and FOOL.

CORNWALL.   Let us withdraw; 'twill be a storm.   280
REGAN.   This house is little; the old man and 's people
Cannot be well bestow'd.
GONERIL.   'Tis his own blame; hath put himself from rest,
And must needs taste his folly.
REGAN.   For his particular, I'll receive him gladly,   285
But not one follower.
GONERIL.   So am I purpos'd.
Where is my Lord of Gloucester?

Re-enter GLOUCESTER.

CORNWALL.   Follow'd the old man forth. He is return'd.
GLOUCESTER.   The King is in high rage.

---

258. Are . . . superfluous: have at the worst more than bare necessities.
278. flaws: fragments.   285. For his particular: as far as he himself is concerned.

CORNWALL.   Whither is he going?
GLOUCESTER.   He calls to horse; but will I know not whither.   290
CORNWALL.   'Tis best to give him way; he leads himself.
GONERIL.   My lord, entreat him by no means to stay.
GLOUCESTER.   Alack, the night comes on, and the high winds
Do sorely ruffle; for many miles about
There 's scarce a bush.
REGAN.   O, sir, to wilful men,   295
The injuries that they themselves procure
Must be their schoolmasters. Shut up your doors.
He is attended with a desperate train,
And what they may incense him to, being apt
To have his ear abus'd, wisdom bids fear.   300
CORNWALL.   Shut up your doors, my lord; 'tis a wild night:
My Regan counsels well. Come out o' th' storm.

[*Exeunt.*

ACT THREE

SCENE 1.   [*The open country near Gloucester's castle.*]

Storm still. Enter KENT *and a* GENTLEMAN, *severally.*

KENT.   Who's there, besides foul weather?
GENTLEMAN.   One minded like the weather, most unquietly.
KENT.   I know you. Where's the King?
GENTLEMAN.   Contending with the fretful elements;
Bids the wind blow the earth into the sea,   5
Or swell the curled waters 'bove the main,
That things might change or cease; [tears his white hair,
Which the impetuous blasts with eyeless rage
Catch in their fury, and make nothing of;
Strives in his little world of man to out-scorn   10
The to-and-fro-conflicting wind and rain.
This night, wherein the cub-drawn bear would couch,
The lion and the belly-pinched wolf
Keep their fur dry, unbonneted he runs,
And bids what will take all.]
KENT.   But who is with him?   15
GENTLEMAN.   None but the Fool, who labours to out-jest
His heart-struck injuries.

---

294. ruffle: bluster.   300. abus'd: misled.

Act III, Scene i, 6. main: mainland.   7-15. [tears . . . all.] Q. Om. F.
12. cub-drawn: sucked dry.

KENT.   Sir, I do know you,
And dare upon the warrant of my note
Commend a dear thing to you. There is division,
Although as yet the face of it is cover'd   20
With mutual cunning, 'twixt Albany and Cornwall;
Who have — as who have not, that their great stars
Thron'd and set high? — servants, who seem no less,
Which are to France the spies and speculations
Intelligent of our state. What hath been seen,   25
Either in snuffs and packings of the Dukes,
Or the hard rein which both of them have borne
Against the old kind king, or something deeper,
Whereof perchance these are but furnishings —
[But, true it is, from France there comes a power   30
Into this scattered kingdom; who already,
Wise in our negligence, have secret feet
In some of our best ports, and are at point
To show their open banner. Now to you:
If on my credit you dare build so far   35
To make your speed to Dover, you shall find
Some that will thank you, making just report
Of how unnatural and bemadding sorrow
The King hath cause to plain.
I am a gentleman of blood and breeding;   40
And, from some knowledge and assurance, offer
This office to you.]
    GENTLEMAN. I will talk further with you.
    KENT.   No, do not.
For confirmation that I am much more
Than my out-wall, open this purse and take   45
What it contains. If you shall see Cordelia, —
As fear not but you shall, — show her this ring,
And she will tell you who that fellow is
That yet you do not know. Fie on this storm!
I will go seek the King.   50
    GENTLEMAN. Give me your hand. Have you no more to say?
    KENT. Few words, but, to effect, more than all yet;
That, when we have found the King, — in which your pain
That way, I'll this, — he that first lights on him
Holla the other.   55

    [*Exeunt [severally]*.

18. **note**: knowledge (of you). 19. **dear**: important. 24. **speculations**: ob-
servers. 25. **Intelligent**: giving information. 26. **snuffs**: resentments. **packings**:
plots. 30–42. [**But . . . you**] Q. Om. F. 30. **power**: armed force. 31. **scattered**: divided. 33. **at point**: ready. 39. **plain**: complain. 45. **out-wall**:
exterior. 52. **to effect**: in effect, in importance.

SCENE 2. [*The same.*] *Storm still.*

Enter LEAR *and* FOOL.

LEAR.   Blow, winds, and crack your cheeks! Rage! Blow!
You cataracts and hurricanoes, spout
Till you have drench'd our steeples, drown'd the cocks!
You sulph'rous and thought-executing fires,
Vaunt-couriers of oak-cleaving thunderbolts,   5
Singe my white head! And thou, all-shaking thunder,
Strike flat the thick rotundity o' th' world!
Crack nature's moulds, all germens spill at once
That makes ingrateful man!   9
  FOOL.   O nuncle, court holy-water in a dry house is better than this
rain water out o' door. Good nuncle, in; ask thy daughters' blessing.
Here's a night pities neither wise men nor fools.
  LEAR.   Rumble thy bellyful! Spit, fire! Spout, rain!
Nor rain, wind, thunder, fire are my daughters.
I tax not you, you elements, with unkindness;   15
I never gave you kingdom, call'd you children;
You owe me no subscription. Then let fall
Your horrible pleasure. Here I stand your slave,
A poor, infirm, weak, and despis'd old man;
But yet I call you servile ministers,   20
That will with two pernicious daughters join
Your high-engender'd battles 'gainst a head
So old and white as this. Oh! Oh! 'tis foul!
  FOOL.   He that has a house to put 's head in has a good head-piece.

> "The cod-piece that will house   25
>   Before the head has any,
> The head and he shall louse;
>   So beggars marry many.
> The man that makes his toe
>   What he his heart should make   30
> Shall of a corn cry woe,
>   And turn his sleep to wake."

For there was never yet fair woman but she made mouths in a glass.

Enter KENT.

  LEAR.   No, I will be the pattern of all patience; I will say nothing.
  KENT.   Who's there?   35

Scene   ii, 3.   cocks: weathercocks.   5.   Vaunt-couriers: forerunners.   8.
germens: germs, seeds.   10.   court holy-water: flattery.   17.   subscription: allegiance.   22.   high-engender'd: produced in the heavens.

FOOL.   Marry, here's grace and a cod-piece; that's a wise man and a fool.

KENT.   Alas, sir, are you here? Things that love night
Love not such nights as these; the wrathful skies
Gallow the very wanderers of the dark,   40
And make them keep their caves. Since I was man,
Such sheets of fire, such bursts of horrid thunder,
Such groans of roaring wind and rain, I never
Remember to have heard. Man's nature cannot carry
Th' affliction nor the fear.

LEAR.   Let the great gods,   45
That keep this dreadful pudder o'er our heads,
Find out their enemies now. Tremble, thou wretch
That has within thee undivulged crimes,
Unwhipp'd of justice! Hide thee, thou bloody hand;
Thou perjur'd, and thou simular of virtue   50
That are incestuous! Caitiff, to pieces shake,
That under covert and convenient seeming
Has practis'd on man's life! Close pent-up guilts,
Rive your concealing continents, and cry
These dreadful summoners grace. I am a man   55
More sinn'd against than sinning.

KENT.   Alack, bare-headed!
Gracious my lord, hard by here is a hovel;
Some friendship will it lend you 'gainst the tempest.
Repose you there, while I to this hard house —
More harder than the stones whereof 'tis rais'd,   60
Which even but now, demanding after you,
Deni'd me to come in — return, and force
Their scanted courtesy.

LEAR.   My wits begin to turn.
Come on, my boy. How dost, my boy? Art cold?
I am cold myself. Where is this straw, my fellow?   65
The art of our necessities is strange
And can make vile things precious. Come, your hovel.
Poor Fool and knave, I have one part in my heart
That's sorry yet for thee.

FOOL [singing].   "He that has and a little tiny wit, —   70
                      With heigh-ho, the wind and the rain, —
                    Must make content with his fortunes fit,
                      For the rain it raineth every day."

LEAR.   True, boy. Come, bring us to this hovel.

[Exeunt LEAR and KENT].

40. Gallow: frighten. 46. pudder: turmoil. 50. simular of: pretender to.
54. continents: disguises. 54–55. cry . . . grace: ask mercy. 62. Deni'd . . .
in: refused to admit me. 66. art of: skill created by.

FOOL.   This is a brave night to cool a courtezan.   I'll speak a prophecy
ere I go: 76

>   When priests are more in word than matter;
>   When brewers mar their malt with water;
>   When nobles are their tailors' tutors;
>   No heretics burn'd, but wenches' suitors;   80
>   When every case in law is right;
>   No squire in debt, nor no poor knight;
>   When slanders do not live in tongues;
>   Nor cutpurses come not to throngs;
>   When usurers tell their gold i' th' field;   85
>   And bawds and whores do churches build;
>   Then shall the realm of Albion
>   Come to great confusion.
>   Then comes the time, who lives to see 't,
>   That going shall be us'd with feet.   90

This prophecy Merlin shall make; for I live before his time. [*Exit.*

SCENE 3.   [*Gloucester's castle.*]

Enter GLOUCESTER *and* EDMUND.

GLOUCESTER.   Alack, alack, Edmund, I like not this unnatural dealing.
When I desired their leave that I might pity him, they took from me the
use of mine own house; charg'd me on pain of perpetual displeasure
neither to speak of him, entreat for him, or any way sustain him.

EDMUND.   Most savage and unnatural!   5

GLOUCESTER.   Go to; say you nothing.   There is division between the
Dukes, and a worse matter than that.   I have received a letter this night;
'tis dangerous to be spoken; I have lock'd the letter in my closet.   These
injuries the King now bears will be revenged home; there is part of a
power already footed.   We must incline to the King.   I will look him and
privily relieve him.   Go you and maintain talk with the Duke that my
charity be not of him perceived.   If he ask for me, I am ill and gone to
bed.   If I die for it, as no less is threat'ned me, the King my old master
must be relieved.   There is strange things toward, Edmund; pray you, be
careful. [*Exit.*   15

EDMUND.   This courtesy, forbid thee, shall the Duke
Instantly know; and of that letter too.
This seems a fair deserving, and must draw me
That which my father loses; no less than all.
The younger rises when the old doth fall. [*Exit.*   20

77–90. **When . . . feet.** This prophecy is influenced by a so-called "Chaucer's
Prophecy," and is probably not by Shakespeare.

Scene iii, 10. **footed:** landed.   16. **forbid thee:** which you are forbidden to
render.   18. **deserving:** action by which I shall acquire merit.

SCENE 4.   [*The open country. Before a hovel.*]

Enter LEAR, KENT, *and* FOOL.

KENT.   Here is the place, my lord; good my lord, enter.
The tyranny of the open night 's too rough
For nature to endure.

[*Storm still.*

LEAR.   Let me alone.
KENT.   Good my lord, enter here.
LEAR.   Wilt break my heart?
KENT.   I had rather break mine own. Good my lord, enter.   5
LEAR.   Thou think'st 'tis much that this contentious storm
Invades us to the skin; so 'tis to thee;
But where the greater malady is fix'd,
The lesser is scarce felt. Thou'dst shun a bear;
But if thy flight lay toward the roaring sea,   10
Thou'dst meet the bear i' th' mouth. When the mind 's free,
The body 's delicate; the tempest in my mind
Doth from my senses take all feeling else
Save what beats there. Filial ingratitude!
Is it not as this mouth should tear this hand   15
For lifting food to't? But I will punish home.
No, I will weep no more. In such a night
To shut me out! Pour on! I will endure.
In such a night as this! O Regan, Goneril!
Your old kind father, whose frank heart gave all, ——   20
O, that way madness lies; let me shun that;
No more of that.
KENT.   Good my lord, enter here.
LEAR.   Prithee, go in thyself; seek thine own ease.
This tempest will not give me leave to ponder
On things would hurt me more. But I'll go in.   25
[*To the* FOOL.] In, boy; go first. You houseless poverty, ——
Nay, get thee in. I'll pray, and then I'll sleep.

[*Exit* [FOOL].

Poor naked wretches, wheresoe'er you are,
That bide the pelting of this pitiless storm,
How shall your houseless heads and unfed sides,   30
Your loop'd and window'd raggedness, defend you
From seasons such as these? O, I have ta'en

Scene iv, 12. **delicate:** sensitive.   31. **loop'd and window'd:** full of holes.

Too little care of this! Take physic, pomp;
Expose thyself to feel what wretches feel,
That thou mayst shake the superflux to them,   35
And show the heavens more just.

    EDGAR [*within*]. Fathom and half, fathom and half! Poor Tom!

[*The* FOOL *runs out from the hovel.*]

    FOOL.   Come not in here, nuncle, here's a spirit. Help me, help me!
    KENT.   Give me thy hand. Who's there?
    FOOL.   A spirit, a spirit! He says his name's poor Tom.   40
    KENT.   What are thou that dost grumble there i' th' straw? Come
forth.

[*Enter* EDGAR, *disguised as a madman.*]

    EDGAR.   Away! the foul fiend follows me!

        "Through the sharp hawthorn blow the winds."

Hum! go to thy bed, and warm thee.   45
    LEAR.   Did'st thou give all to thy daughters, and art thou come to this?
    EDGAR.   Who gives anything to poor Tom? whom the foul fiend hath
led through fire and through flame, and through [ford] and whirlpool,
o'er bog and quagmire; that hath laid knives under his pillow, and halters
in his pew; set ratsbane by his porridge; made him proud of heart, to ride
on a bay trotting-horse over four-inch'd bridges, to course his own shadow
for a traitor. Bless thy five wits! Tom's a-cold, — O, do de, do de, do de.
Bless thee from whirlwinds, star-blasting, and taking! Do poor Tom some
charity, whom the foul fiend vexes. There could I have him now, — and
there, — and there again, and there.   55

[*Storm still.*

    LEAR.   Has his daughters brought him to this pass?
Couldst thou save nothing? Wouldst thou give 'em all?
    FOOL.   Nay, he reserv'd a blanket, else we had been all sham'd.
    LEAR.   Now, all the plagues that in the pendulous air
Hang fated o'er men's faults light on thy daughters!   60
    KENT.   He hath no daughters, sir.
    LEAR.   Death, traitor! nothing could have subdu'd nature
To such a lowness but his unkind daughters.
Is it the fashion, that discarded fathers
Should have thus little mercy on their flesh?   65

48. [**ford**] foord Q. *Sword* F. 51. **course:** chase. 53. **taking:** infection.
59. **pendulous:** suspended.

Judicious punishment! 'Twas this flesh begot
Those pelican daughters.

EDGAR.   "Pillicock sat on Pillicock-hill."

Alow, alow, loo, loo!

FOOL.   This cold night will turn us all to fools and madmen.   70

EDGAR.   Take heed o' th' foul fiend. Obey thy parents; keep thy [word justly]; swear not; commit not with man's sworn spouse; set not thy sweet heart on proud array. Tom 's a-cold.

LEAR.   What hast thou been?   74

EDGAR.   A scrving-man, proud in heart and mind; that curl'd my hair; wore gloves in my cap; serv'd the lust of my mistress' heart and did the act of darkness with her; swore as many oaths as I spake words, and broke them in the sweet face of heaven: one that slept in the contriving of lust, and wak'd to do it. Wine lov'd I dearly, dice dearly; and in woman outparamour'd the Turk: false of heart, light of ear, bloody of hand; hog in sloth, fox in stealth, wolf in greediness, dog in madness, lion in prey. Let not the creaking of shoes nor the rustling of silks betray thy poor heart to woman. Keep thy foot out of brothels, thy hand out of plackets, thy pen from lenders' books, and defy the foul fiend.

"Still through the hawthorn blows the cold wind."   85

Says suum, mun, nonny. Dolphin my boy, boy, sessa! let him trot by.

[Storm still.

LEAR.   Thou wert better in a grave than to answer with thy uncover'd body this extremity of the skies. Is man no more than this? Consider him well. Thou ow'st the worm no silk, the beast no hide, the sheep no wool, the cat no perfume. Ha! here 's three on 's are sophisticated! Thou art the thing itself; unaccommodated man is no more but such a poor, bare, forked animal as thou art. Off, off, you lendings! come, unbutton here. *[Tearing off his clothes.]*   93

Enter GLOUCESTER, *with a torch.*

FOOL.   Prithee, nuncle, be contented; 'tis a naughty night to swim in. Now a little fire in a wild field were like an old lecher's heart; a small spark, all the rest on 's body cold. Look, here comes a walking fire.   96

EDGAR.   This is the foul [fiend] Flibbertigibbet; he begins at curfew,

---

67. **pelican.** Young pelicans were believed to feed on their mother's blood. 71–72. **[word justly]** (Pope). *words justice* F. *words justly* Q.   76. **gloves:** (as his mistress's favors).   80. **Turk:** Sultan. **light of ear:** credulous.   83. **placket:** opening in a petticoat.   90. **cat:** civet cat.   91. **unaccommodated:** naked. 92. **lendings:** things not really belonging to one, clothes.   97. **[fiend]** Q. Om. F.

and walks [till the] first cock; he gives the web and the pin, squints the
eye, and makes the hare-lip; mildews the white wheat, and hurts the poor
creature of earth.   100

        "St. Withold footed thrice the 'old;
          He met the night-mare and her ninefold;
            Bid her alight,
             And her troth plight,
        And, aroint thee, witch, aroint thee!"   105

KENT.   How fares your Grace?

LEAR.   What's he?

KENT.   Who's there? What is't you seek?

GLOUCESTER.   What are you there? Your names?   109

EDGAR.   Poor Tom, that eats the swimming frog, the toad, the tadpole,
the wall-newt, and the water; that in the fury of his heart, when the foul
fiend rages, eats cow-dung for salads; swallows the old rat and the ditch-
dog; drinks the green mantle of the standing pool; who is whipp'd from
tithing to tithing, and stock'd, punish'd, and imprison'd; who hath three
suits to his back, six shirts to his body.   115

        Horse to ride, and weapon to wear;
         But mice and rats, and such small deer,
        Have been Tom's food for seven long year.

Beware my follower. Peace, Smulkin; peace, thou fiend!

GLOUCESTER.   What, hath your Grace no better company?   120

EDGAR.   The prince of darkness is a gentleman.
Modo he's call'd, and Mahu.

GLOUCESTER.   Our flesh and blood, my lord, is grown so vile
That it doth hate what gets it.

EDGAR.   Poor Tom 's a-cold.   125

GLOUCESTER.   Go in with me; my duty cannot suffer
To obey in all your daughters' hard commands.
Though their injunction be to bar my doors
And let this tyrannous night take hold upon you,
Yet have I ventur'd to come seek you out,   130
And bring you where both fire and food is ready.

LEAR.   First let me talk with this philosopher.
What is the cause of thunder?

KENT.   Good my lord, take his offer; go into th' house.

LEAR.   I'll talk a word with this same learned Theban.   135
What is your study?

EDGAR.   How to prevent the fiend, and to kill vermin.

LEAR.   Let me ask you one word in private.

98. [till the] Q. *at* F. **web . . . pin**: cataract. 101. **St. Withold** (Theobald)
is supposed to be St. Vitalis. *Swithold* F. **'old**: wold. 102. **ninefold**: nine
foals(?), imps(?). 105. **aroint thee**: begone. 111. **water**: water-newt, a lizard.
114. **tithing**: district. 124. **gets**: begets. 137. **prevent**: anticipate.

KENT.   Importune him once more to go, my lord;
His wits begin t' unsettle.
     GLOUCESTER.   Canst thou blame him?   140

[*Storm still.*

His daughters seek his death. Ah, that good Kent!
He said it would be thus, poor banish'd man!
Thou say'st the King grows mad; I'll tell thee, friend,
I am almost mad myself. I had a son,
Now outlaw'd from my blood; he sought my life,   145
But lately, very late. I lov'd him, friend,
No father his son dearer; true to tell thee,
The grief hath craz'd my wits. What a night 's this!
I do beseech your Grace, —
     LEAR.   O, cry you mercy, sir.
Noble philosopher, your company.   150
     EDGAR.   Tom 's a-cold.
     GLOUCESTER.   In, fellow, there, into th' hovel; keep thee warm.
     LEAR.   Come, let's in all.
     KENT.   This way, my lord.
     LEAR.   With him;
I will keep still with my philosopher.
     KENT.   Good my lord, soothe him; let him take the fellow.   155
     GLOUCESTER.   Take him you on.
     KENT.   Sirrah, come on; go along with us.
     LEAR.   Come, good Athenian.
     GLOUCESTER.   No words, no words: hush.

     EDGAR.   "Child Rowland to the dark tower came;   160
               His word was still, 'Fie, foh, and fum,
               I smell the blood of a British man.' "

[*Exeunt.*

SCENE 5.   [*Gloucester's castle.*]

Enter CORNWALL *and* EDMUND.

     CORNWALL.   I will have my revenge ere I depart his house.
     EDMUND.   How, my lord, I may be censured that nature thus gives
way to loyalty, something fears me to think of.
     CORNWALL.   I now perceive, it was not altogether your brother's evil
disposition made him seek his death; but a provoking merit, set a-work
by a reproveable badness in himself.   6

Scene v, 2. **censured:** judged.   5. **his:** Gloucester's.   **provoking merit:** a good
quality that incited him.

> Mastiff, greyhound, mongrel grim,
> Hound or spaniel, brach or [lym],
> Or bobtail [tike] or trundle-tail,
> Tom will make him weep and wail;   65
> For, with throwing thus my head,
> Dogs leapt the hatch, and all are fled.

Do de, de, de. Sessa! Come, march to wakes and fairs and market-towns.
Poor Tom, thy horn is dry.   69

LEAR.   Then let them anatomize Regan; see what breeds about her
heart. Is there any cause in nature that make these hard hearts? [To
EDGAR.] You, sir, I entertain for one of my hundred; only I do not like the
fashion of your garments. You will say they are Persian, but let them be
chang'd.   74

Re-enter GLOUCESTER.

KENT.   Now, good my lord, lie here and rest a while.
LEAR.   Make no noise, make no noise; draw the curtains; so, so, so.
We'll go to supper i' th' morning.
FOOL.   And I'll go to bed at noon.
GLOUCESTER.   Come hither, friend; where is the King my master?
KENT.   Here, sir; but trouble him not, his wits are gone.   80
GLOUCESTER.   Good friend, I prithee, take him in thy arms;
I have o'erheard a plot of death upon him.
There is a litter ready; lay him in't,
And drive toward Dover, friend, where thou shalt meet
Both welcome and protection. Take up thy master.   85
If thou shouldst dally half an hour, his life,
With thine and all that offer to defend him
Stand in assured loss. Take up, take up;
And follow me, that will to some provision
Give thee quick conduct.
KENT.   [Oppressed nature sleeps.   90
This rest might yet have balm'd thy broken sinews,
Which, if convenience will not allow,
Stand in hard cure. (*To the* FOOL.) Come, help to bear thy master;
Thou must not stay behind.]
GLOUCESTER.   Come, come, away.

[*Exeunt* [*all but* EDGAR].

[EDGAR.   When we our betters see bearing our woes,   95
We scarcely think our miseries our foes.

---

63. [lym] (Hanmer): bloodhound. *Hym* F.   64. [tike] Q: cur. *tight* F. trundle-
tail: curled tail.   67. hatch: lower half of a divided door.   72. entertain:
engage.   90–94. [Oppressed . . . behind.] Q. Om. F.   91. sinews: nerves.
95–108. [EDGAR. . . . lurk.] Q. Om. F.

Who alone suffers, suffers most i' th' mind,
Leaving free things and happy shows behind;
But then the mind much sufferance doth o'erskip,
When grief hath mates, and bearing fellowship.   100
How light and portable my pain seems now,
When that which makes me bend makes the King bow,
He childed as I fathered! Tom, away!
Mark the high noises; and thyself bewray
When false opinion, whose wrong thoughts defile thee,   105
In thy just proof repeals and reconciles thee.
What will hap more to-night, safe scape the King!
Lurk, lurk.] [*Exit.*]

SCENE 7.   [*Gloucester's castle.*]

Enter CORNWALL, REGAN, GONERIL, *Bastard* [EDMUND], *and Servants.*

CORNWALL [*to* GONERIL].   Post speedily to my lord your husband; show
him this letter. The army of France is landed. — Seek out the traitor
Gloucester.

[*Exeunt some of the* Servants.]

REGAN.   Hang him instantly.
GONERIL.   Pluck out his eyes.   5
CORNWALL.   Leave him to my displeasure. — Edmund, keep you our
sister company; the revenges we are bound to take upon your traitorous
father are not fit for your beholding. Advise the Duke, where you are
going, to a most festinate preparation; we are bound to the like. Our posts
shall be swift and intelligent betwixt us. Farewell, dear sister; farewell,
my Lord of Gloucester.   11

Enter steward [OSWALD].

How now! where's the King?
OSWALD.   My Lord of Gloucester hath convey'd him hence.
Some five or six and thirty of his knights,
Hot questrists after him, met him at gate,   15
Who, with some other of the lord's dependants,
Are gone with him toward Dover, where they boast
To have well-armed friends.
CORNWALL.   Get horses for your mistress.

100. **bearing:** suffering.   101. **portable:** bearable.   104. **bewray:** disclose.   106.
repeals: recalls.   107. **What:** whatever.
Scene vii, 9. festinate: speedy.   15. **questrists:** searchers.

GONERIL.   Farewell, sweet lord, and sister.
CORNWALL.   Edmund, farewell.

[Exeunt [GONERIL, EDMUND, *and* OSWALD].

                             Go seek the traitor Gloucester,   20
Pinion him like a thief, bring him before us.

[Exeunt other Servants.]

Though well we may not pass upon his life
Without the form of justice, yet our power
Shall do a court'sy to our wrath, which men
May blame, but not control.

Enter GLOUCESTER *and* Servants.

                         Who's there? The traitor?   25
REGAN.   Ingrateful fox! 'tis he.
CORNWALL.   Bind fast his corky arms.
GLOUCESTER.   What means your Graces? Good my friends, consider
You are my guests. Do me no foul play, friends.
CORNWALL.   Bind him, I say.

[Servants *bind him.*]

REGAN.   Hard, hard. O filthy traitor!   30
GLOUCESTER.   Unmerciful lady as you are, I'm none.
CORNWALL.   To this chair bind him. Villain, thou shalt find —

[REGAN *plucks his beard.*]

GLOUCESTER.   By the kind gods, 'tis most ignobly done
To pluck me by the beard.
REGAN.   So white, and such a traitor!
GLOUCESTER.   Naughty lady,   35
These hairs, which thou dost ravish from my chin,
Will quicken, and accuse thee. I am your host:
With robber's hands my hospitable favours
You should not ruffle thus. What will you do?
CORNWALL.   Come, sir, what letters had you late from France?   40
REGAN.   Be simple-answer'd, for we know the truth.
CORNWALL.   And what confederacy have you with the traitors
Late footed in the kingdom?

---

27. **corky:** withered. 37. **quicken:** become alive. 38. **favours:** features. 39.
ruffle: outrage.

REGAN.   To whose hands you have sent the lunatic king,
Speak.

GLOUCESTER.   I have a letter guessingly set down,   45
Which came from one that's of a neutral heart,
And not from one oppos'd.

CORNWALL.   Cunning.

REGAN.   And false.

CORNWALL.   Where hast thou sent the King?

GLOUCESTER.   To Dover.

REGAN.   Wherefore to Dover? Wast thou not charg'd at peril —   50

CORNWALL.   Wherefore to Dover? Let him answer that.

GLOUCESTER.   I am tied to th' stake, and I must stand the course.

REGAN.   Wherefore to Dover?

GLOUCESTER.   Because I would not see thy cruel nails
Pluck out his poor old eyes; nor thy fierce sister   55
In his anointed flesh stick boarish fangs.
The sea, with such a storm as his bare head
In hell-black night endur'd, would have buoy'd up
And quench'd the stelled fires;
Yet, poor old heart, he holp the heavens to rain.   60
If wolves had at thy gate howl'd that stern time,
Thou shouldst have said, "Good porter, turn the key."
All cruels else subscribe; but I shall see
The winged vengeance overtake such children.

CORNWALL.   See 't shalt thou never. Fellows, hold the chair.   65
Upon these eyes of thine I'll set my foot.

GLOUCESTER.   He that will think to live till he be old,
Give me some help! — O cruel! O you gods!

REGAN.   One side will mock another; th' other too.

CORNWALL.   If you see vengeance, —

[FIRST] SERVANT.   Hold your hand, my lord!   70
I have serv'd you ever since I was a child;
But better service have I never done you
Than now to bid you hold.

REGAN.   How now, you dog!

[FIRST] SERVANT.   If you did wear a beard upon your chin,
I'd shake it on this quarrel. What do you mean?   75

CORNWALL.   My villain!

[*They draw and fight.*]

[FIRST] SERVANT.   Nay, then, come on, and take the chance of anger.

REGAN.   Give me thy sword. A peasant stand up thus? [*Takes a sword,
and runs at him behind.*

52. **course:** attack of the dogs (bear-baiting). 59. **stelled fires:** stars. 63. **All
. . . subscribe:** not satisfactorily explained. All other cruelties yield to this(?).
75. **What . . . mean?** Probably this should be given to Cornwall or Regan.

[FIRST] SERVANT.   Oh, I am slain! My lord, you have one eye left
To see some mischief on him. Oh! [*Dies.*]   80
  CORNWALL.   Lest it see more, prevent it. Out, vile jelly!
Where is thy lustre now?
  GLOUCESTER.   All dark and comfortless. Where's my son Edmund?
Edmund, enkindle all the sparks of nature,
To quit this horrid act.
  REGAN.   Out, treacherous villain!   85
Thou call'st on him that hates thee. It was he
That made the overture of thy treasons to us,
Who is too good to pity thee.
  GLOUCESTER.   O my follies! then Edgar was abus'd.
Kind gods, forgive me that, and prosper him!   90
  REGAN.   Go thrust him out at gates, and let him smell
His way to Dover.

            (*Exit* [*one*] *with* GLOUCESTER.)

                    How is't, my lord? How look you?
  CORNWALL.   I have received a hurt; follow me, lady.
Turn out that eyeless villain; throw this slave
Upon the dunghill. Regan, I bleed apace;   95
Untimely comes this hurt. Give me your arm.

            [*Exit* CORNWALL, *led by* REGAN.]

  [SECOND SERVANT.   I'll never care what wickedness I do,
If this man come to good.
  THIRD SERVANT.   If she live long,
And in the end meet the old course of death,
Women will all turn monsters.   100
  SECOND SERVANT.   Let's follow the old earl, and get the Bedlam
To lead him where he would: his roguish madness
Allows itself to anything.
  THIRD SERVANT.   Go thou: I'll fetch some flax and whites of eggs
To apply to his bleeding face. Now, Heaven help him!]   105

      Exeunt [*severally*].

───────────────────────────

87. **made the overture:** disclosed.   89. **abus'd:** wronged.   97–105. [SECOND
SERVANT.... him!] Q. Om. F.   99. **old:** usual.

ACT FOUR

Scene 1.   [*The open country near Gloucester's castle.*]

Enter EDGAR.

EDGAR.   Yet better thus, and known to be contemn'd,
Than, still contemn'd and flatter'd, to be worst.
The lowest and most dejected thing of fortune
Stands still in esperance, lives not in fear.
The lamentable change is from the best;   5
The worst returns to laughter. Welcome, then,
Thou unsubstantial air that I embrace!
The wretch that thou hast blown unto the worst
Owes nothing to thy blasts.

Enter GLOUCESTER, *led by an* OLD MAN.

                                But who comes here?
My father, poorly led? World, world, O world!   10
But that thy strange mutations make us hate thee,
Life would not yield to age.
    OLD MAN.   O, my good lord, I have been your tenant, and your father's
tenant, these fourscore years.
    GLOUCESTER.   Away, get thee away! Good friend, be gone;   15
Thy comforts can do me no good at all;
Thee they may hurt.
    OLD MAN.   You cannot see your way.
    GLOUCESTER.   I have no way, and therefore want no eyes;
I stumbled when I saw. Full oft 'tis seen,
Our means secure us, and our mere defects   20
Prove our commodities. O dear son Edgar,
The food of thy abused father's wrath!
Might I but live to see thee in my touch
I'd say I had eyes again!
    OLD MAN.   How now! Who's there?
    EDGAR [*aside*].   O gods! Who is't can say, "I am at the worst"?   25
I am worse than e'er I was.
    OLD MAN.   'Tis poor mad Tom.
    EDGAR [*aside*].   And worse I may be yet; the worst is not
So long as we can say, "This is the worst."
    OLD MAN.   Fellow, where goest?

Act IV, Scene i, 1. contemn'd: despised.   **4. esperance**: hope.   **6. The
worst . . . laughter**: any change from the worst must be for the better.   **9. Owes
nothing**: cannot be called on to pay anything more.   **12. Life . . . age**: we should
never live to be old.   **20. secure**: make careless.   **21. commodities**: advantages.
22. food: object. **abused**: deceived.

GLOUCESTER.   Is it a beggar-man?

OLD MAN.   Madman and beggar too.   30

GLOUCESTER.   He has some reason, else he could not beg.
I' th' last night's storm I such a fellow saw,
Which made me think a man a worm. My son
Came then into my mind, and yet my mind
Was then scarce friends with him. I have heard more since.   35
As flies to wanton boys, are we to th' gods,
They kill us for their sport.

EDGAR [aside].   How should this be?
Bad is the trade that must play fool to sorrow,
Ang'ring itself and others. — Bless thee, master!

GLOUCESTER.   Is that the naked fellow?

OLD MAN.   Ay, my lord.   40

GLOUCESTER.   [Then, prithee,] get thee away. If, for my sake,
Thou wilt o'ertake us hence a mile or twain
I' th' way toward Dover, do it for ancient love;
And bring some covering for this naked soul,
Which I'll entreat to lead me.

OLD MAN.   Alack, sir, he is mad.   45

GLOUCESTER.   'Tis the time's plague, when madmen lead the blind.
Do as I bid thee, or rather do thy pleasure;
Above the rest, be gone.

OLD MAN.   I'll bring him the best 'parel that I have,
Come on't what will. [Exit.   50

GLOUCESTER.   Sirrah, naked fellow, —

EDGAR.   Poor Tom 's a-cold. [Aside.] I cannot daub it further.

GLOUCESTER.   Come hither, fellow.

EDGAR [aside].   And yet I must. — Bless thy sweet eyes, they bleed.

GLOUCESTER.   Know'st thou the way to Dover?   55

EDGAR.   Both stile and gate, horse-way and foot-path. Poor Tom hath
been scar'd out of his good wits. Bless thee, good man's son, from the
foul fiend! [Five fiends have been in poor Tom at once; of lust, as Obidi-
cut; Hobbididence, prince of dumbness; Mahu, of stealing; Modo, of
murder; Flibbertigibbet, of mopping and mowing, who since possesses
chambermaids and waiting-women. So, bless thee, master!]   61

GLOUCESTER.   Here, take this purse, thou whom the heavens' plagues
Have humbled to all strokes. That I am wretched
Makes thee the happier; heavens, deal so still!
Let the superfluous and lust-dieted man,   65
That slaves your ordinance, that will not see
Because he does not feel, feel your power quickly.
So distribution should undo excess,

41. [Then, prithee,] Q. Om. F.   52. daub: dissemble.   58–61. [Five . . .
master!] Q. Om. F.   60. mopping and mowing: making faces.   65. superfluous: having too much.   66. slaves your ordinance: makes your laws sub-
ordinate to his desires.

And each man have enough. Dost thou know Dover?
    EDGAR. Ay, master.   70
    GLOUCESTER. There is a cliff, whose high and bending head
Looks fearfully in the confined deep.
Bring me but to the very brim of it,
And I'll repair the misery thou dost bear
With something rich about me. From that place   75
I shall no leading need.
    EDGAR.   Give me thy arm;
Poor Tom shall lead thee.

    [*Exeunt.*

        SCENE 2. [*Before the Duke of Albany's palace.*]

Enter GONERIL, *Bastard* [EDMUND], *and steward* [OSWALD].

    GONERIL. Welcome, my lord! I marvel our mild husband
Not met us on the way. — Now, where's your master?
    OSWALD. Madam, within; but never man so chang'd.
I told him of the army that was landed;
He smil'd at it. I told him you were coming;   5
His answer was, "The worse." Of Gloucester's treachery,
And of the loyal service of his son,
When I inform'd him, then he call'd me sot,
And told me I had turn'd the wrong side out.
What most he should dislike seems pleasant to him;   10
What like, offensive.
    GONERIL [*to* EDMUND]. Then shall you go no further.
It is the cowish terror of his spirit,
That dares not undertake; he'll not feel wrongs
Which tie him to an answer. Our wishes on the way
May prove effects. Back, Edmund, to my brother;   15
Hasten his musters and conduct his powers.
I must change [arms] at home, and give the distaff
Into my husband's hands. This trusty servant
Shall pass between us. Ere long you are like to hear,
If you dare venture in your own behalf,   20
A mistress's command. Wear this; spare speech;
Decline your head. This kiss, if it durst speak,
Would stretch thy spirits up into the air.
Conceive, and fare thee well.
    EDMUND. Yours in the ranks of death. [*Exit.*
    GONERIL.   My most dear Gloucester!   25
O, the difference of man and man!

71. **bending:** overhanging.
    Scene ii, 8. sot: fool. 12. **cowish:** cowardly. 15. **prove effects:** be realized.
17. **[arms]** Q. *names* F. Goneril will take the sword.

To thee a woman's services are due;
My Fool usurps my body.

OSWALD.   Madam, here comes my lord. [Exit.

Enter the DUKE OF ALBANY.

GONERIL.   I have been worth the whistle.
ALBANY.   O Goneril!
You are not worth the dust which the rude wind   30
Blows in your face. [I fear your disposition.
That nature which contemns its origin
Cannot be bordered certain in itself.
She that herself will sliver and disbranch
From her material sap, perforce must wither   35
And come to deadly use.
GONERIL.   No more; the text is foolish.
ALBANY.   Wisdom and goodness to the vile seem vile;
Filths savour but themselves. What have you done?
Tigers, not daughters, what have you perform'd?   40
A father, and a gracious aged man,
Whose reverence even the head-lugg'd bear would lick,
Most barbarous, most degenerate! have you madded.
Could my good brother suffer you to do it?
A man, a prince, by him so benefited!   45
If that the heavens do not their visible spirits
Send quickly down to tame these vile offences,
It will come,
Humanity must perforce prey on itself,
Like monsters of the deep.]
GONERIL.   Milk-liver'd man!   50
That bear'st a cheek for blows, a head for wrongs,
Who hast not in thy brows an eye discerning
Thine honour from thy suffering, [that not know'st
Fools do those villains pity who are punish'd
Ere they have done their mischief, where's thy drum?   55
France spreads his banners in our noiseless land,
With plumed helm thy state begins to threat;
Whiles thou, a moral fool, sits still, and criest,
"Alack, why does he so?"]
ALBANY.   See thyself, devil!
Proper deformity seems not in the fiend   60
So horrid as in woman.
GONERIL.   O vain fool!

31–50. [I fear . . . deep.] Q. Om. F.   33. bordered certain: kept within bounds.
35. material: essential to life.   53–59. [that . . . so?"] Q. Om. F.   56. noiseless: peaceful.   60. Proper: that belongs to him.

[ALBANY.   Thou changed and self-cover'd thing, for shame!
Be-monster not thy feature. Were't my fitness
To let these hands obey my blood,
They are apt enough to dislocate and tear   65
Thy flesh and bones. Howe'er thou art a fiend,
A woman's shape doth shield thee.
   GONERIL.   Marry, your manhood — Mew!

Enter a MESSENGER.

   ALBANY.   What news?]
   MESSENGER.   O, my good lord, the Duke of Cornwall 's dead;   70
Slain by his servant, going to put out
The other eye of Gloucester.
   ALBANY.   Gloucester's eyes!
   MESSENGER.   A servant that he bred, thrill'd with remorse,
Oppos'd against the act, bending his sword
To his great master; who, thereat enrag'd,   75
Flew on him, and amongst them fell'd him dead;
But not without that harmful stroke which since
Hath pluck'd him after.
   ALBANY.   This shows you are above,
You [justicers,] that these our nether crimes
So speedily can venge! But, O poor Gloucester!   80
Lost he his other eye?
   MESSENGER.   Both, both, my lord.
This letter, madam, craves a speedy answer.
'Tis from your sister.
   GONERIL [*aside*].   One way I like this well;
But being widow, and my Gloucester with her,   85
May all the building in my fancy pluck
Upon my hateful life. Another way,
The news is not so tart. — I'll read, and answer. [*Exit.*
   ALBANY.   Where was his son when they did take his eyes?
   MESSENGER.   Come with my lady hither.
   ALBANY.   He is not here.   90
   MESSENGER.   No, my good lord; I met him back again.
   ALBANY.   Knows he the wickedness?
   MESSENGER.   Ay, my good lord; 'twas he inform'd against him;
And quit the house on purpose that their punishment
Might have the freer course.
   ALBANY.   Gloucester, I live   95
To thank thee for the love thou show'dst the King,

62–69. [ALBANY. . . . news?] Q. Om. F.   62. self-cover'd: whose real self is
hidden.   63. Were't my fitness: were it suitable for me.   64. blood: impulse.
73. remorse: pity.   79. [justicers] Q. *justices* F. nether: committed here below.
86. pluck: pull down.

And to revenge thine eyes. Come hither, friend;
Tell me what more thou know'st.

[*Exeunt.*

[Scene 3.   *The French camp near Dover.*

Enter KENT *and a* GENTLEMAN.

KENT.   Why the King of France is so suddenly gone back, know you
no reason?

GENTLEMAN.   Something he left imperfect in the state, which since
his coming forth is thought of; which imports to the kingdom so much
fear and danger that his personal return was most required and necessary.

KENT.   Who hath he left behind him General?   6

GENTLEMAN.   The Marshal of France, Monsieur La Far.

KENT.   Did your letters pierce the Queen to any demonstration of grief?

GENTLEMAN.   [Ay, sir]; she took them, read them in my presence;
And now and then an ample tear trill'd down   10
Her delicate cheek. It seem'd she was a queen
Over her passion, who, most rebel-like,
Sought to be king o'er her.

KENT.   O, then it mov'd her.

GENTLEMAN.   Not to a rage; patience and sorrow [strove]
Who should express her goodliest. You have seen   15
Sunshine and rain at once: her smiles and tears
Were like a better way; those happy smilets
That play'd on her ripe lip seem'd not to know
What guests were in her eyes, which, parted thence,
As pearls from diamonds dropp'd. In brief,   20
Sorrow would be a rarity most beloved,
If all could so become it.

KENT.   Made she no verbal question?

GENTLEMAN.   Faith, once or twice she heav'd the name of "father"
Pantingly forth, as if it press'd her heart;
Cried, "Sisters! sisters! Shame of ladies! sisters!   25
Kent! father! sisters! What, i' th' storm? i' th' night?
Let pity not be believ'd!" There she shook
The holy water from her heavenly eyes;
And clamour moistened; then away she started
To deal with grief alone.

KENT.   It is the stars,   30
The stars above us, govern our conditions;

Scene iii, Q. Om. F.   9. [Ay, sir] (Johnson). *I say* Q.   14. [strove] (Pope).
streme Q.   17. like a better way: more beautiful than "sunshine and rain at once."
21. rarity: something precious.   29. clamour moistened: Q. adds *her.* The
passage is probably corrupt. Tears followed her outcry(?).

Else one self mate and make could not beget
Such different issues. You spoke not with her since?
    GENTLEMAN.   No.
    KENT.   Was this before the King return'd?
    GENTLEMAN.   No, since.   35
    KENT.   Well, sir, the poor distressed Lear 's i' th' town;
Who sometime, in his better tune, remembers
What we are come about, and by no means
Will yield to see his daughter.
    GENTLEMAN.   Why, good sir?
    KENT.   A sovereign shame so elbows him. His own unkindness,   40
That stripp'd her from his benediction, turn'd her
To foreign casualties, gave her dear rights
To his dog-hearted daughters, — these things sting
His mind so venomously, that burning shame
Detains him from Cordelia.
    GENTLEMAN.   Alack, poor gentleman.   45
    KENT.   Of Albany's and Cornwall's powers you heard not?
    GENTLEMAN.   'Tis so, they are afoot.
    KENT.   Well, sir, I'll bring you to our master Lear,
And leave you to attend him. Some dear cause
Will in concealment wrap me up a while;   50
When I am known aright, you shall not grieve
Lending me this acquaintance. I pray you, go
Along with me.]

    [*Exeunt.*

SCENE 4.   [*The same. A tent.*]

Enter, with drum and colours, CORDELIA, [DOCTOR], *and Soldiers.*

    CORDELIA.   Alack, 'tis he! Why, he was met even now
As mad as the vex'd sea, singing aloud,
Crown'd with rank fumiter and furrow-weeds,
With hardocks, hemlock, nettles, cuckoo-flowers,
Darnel, and all the idle weeds that grow   5
In our sustaining corn. A century send forth;

32. **self mate and make:** same husband and wife. 39. **yield:** consent. 40. **sovereign:** over-mastering. **elbows:** holds him aloof(?). 42. **casualties:** risks. 49. **dear:** important.
    Scene iv, S.D. [DOCTOR] Q. *Gentlemen* F. 3. **fumiter:** fumitory. 4. **hardocks:** perhaps for *burdocks* or *harlock,* wild mustard. 5. **Darnel:** a general term for weed; sometimes specifically rye-grass. 6. **century:** body of a hundred men. *Centery* F. *centurie* Q.

Search every acre in the high-grown field,
And bring him to our eye.

[*Exit an Officer.*]

What can man's wisdom
In the restoring his bereaved sense?
He that helps him take all my outward worth.   10
[DOCTOR.]   There is means, madam.
Our foster-nurse of nature is repose,
The which he lacks; that to provoke in him,
Are many simples operative, whose power
Will close the eye of anguish.
    CORDELIA.   All blest secrets,   15
All you unpublish'd virtues of the earth,
Spring with my tears! be aidant and remediate
In the good man's [distress]! Seek, seek for him,
Lest his ungovern'd rage dissolve the life
That wants the means to lead it.

Enter a MESSENGER.

    MESSENGER.   News, madam!   20
The British powers are marching hitherward.
    CORDELIA.   'Tis known before; our preparation stands
In expectation of them. O dear father,
It is thy business that I go about;
Therefore great France   25
My mourning and importun'd tears hath pitied.
No blown ambition doth our arms incite,
But love, dear love, and our ag'd father's right.
Soon may I hear and see him!

[*Exeunt.*

SCENE [5. *Gloucester's castle.*]

Enter REGAN *and steward* [OSWALD].

    REGAN.   But are my brother's powers set forth?
    OSWALD.   Ay, madam.
    REGAN.   Himself in person there?

11. [DOCTOR.] Q. *Gentleman* F. 14. **simples:** medicinal herbs. 17. **aidant:**
helpful. **remediate:** healing. 18. [distress] Q. *desires* F. 26. **importun'd:**
importunate, urgent. *important* Q. 27. **blown:** puffed up.

OSWALD.   Madam, with much ado.
Your sister is the better soldier.
    REGAN.   Lord Edmund spake not with your lord at home?
    OSWALD.   No, madam.   5
    REGAN.   What might import my sister's letter to him?
    OSWALD.   I know not, lady.
    REGAN.   Faith, he is posted hence on serious matter.
It was great ignorance, Gloucester's eyes being out,
To let him live; where he arrives he moves   10
All hearts against us. Edmund, I think, is gone,
In pity of his misery, to dispatch
His nighted life; moreover, to descry
The strength o' th' enemy.
    OSWALD.   I must needs after him, madam, with my letter.   15
    REGAN.   Our troops set forth to-morrow, stay with us;
The ways are dangerous.
    OSWALD.   I may not, madam;
My lady charg'd my duty in this business.
    REGAN.   Why should she write to Edmund? Might not you
Transport her purposes by word? Belike   20
Some things — I know not what. I'll love thee much —
Let me unseal the letter.
    OSWALD.   Madam, I had rather —
    REGAN.   I know your lady does not love her husband;
I am sure of that; and at her late being here
She gave strange œillades and most speaking looks   25
To noble Edmund. I know you are of her bosom.
    OSWALD.   I, madam?
    REGAN.   I speak in understanding; y' are, I know 't.
Therefore I do advise you, take this note:
My lord is dead; Edmund and I have talk'd;   30
And more convenient is he for my hand
Than for your lady's. You may gather more.
If you do find him, pray you, give him this;
And when your mistress hears thus much from you,
I pray, desire her call her wisdom to her.   35
So, fare you well.
If you do chance to hear of that blind traitor,
Preferment falls on him that cuts him off.
    OSWALD.   Would I could meet him, madam! I should show
What party I do follow.
    REGAN.   Fare thee well.   40
    [*Exeunt.*

    Scene v, 2. **with much ado:** persuaded with difficulty.   13. **nighted:** blinded.
25. **œillades:** amorous glances.   26. **of her bosom:** in her confidence.   29. **take
this note:** note this.

SCENE [6. *Fields near Dover.*]

Enter GLOUCESTER *and* EDGAR [*dressed like a peasant*].

GLOUCESTER.   When shall I come to th' top of that same hill?
EDGAR.   You do climb up it now; look, how we labour.
GLOUCESTER.   Methinks the ground is even.
EDGAR.   Horrible steep.
Hark, do you hear the sea?
GLOUCESTER.   No, truly.
EDGAR.   Why, then, your other senses grow imperfect   5
By your eyes' anguish.
GLOUCESTER.   So may it be, indeed.
Methinks thy voice is alter'd, and thou speak'st
In better phrase and matter than thou didst.
EDGAR.   You're much deceiv'd. In nothing am I chang'd
But in my garments.
GLOUCESTER.   Methinks you're better spoken.   10
EDGAR.   Come on, sir, here's the place; stand still. How fearful
And dizzy 'tis, to cast one's eyes so low!
The crows and choughs that wing the midway air
Show scarce so gross as beetles. Half way down
Hangs one that gathers samphire, dreadful trade!   15
Methinks he seems no bigger than his head.
The fishermen, that walk upon the beach,
Appear like mice; and yond tall anchoring bark,
Diminish'd to her cock; her cock, a buoy
Almost too small for sight. The murmuring surge,   20
That on th' unnumb'red idle pebbles chafes,
Cannot be heard so high. I'll look no more,
Lest my brain turn, and the deficient sight
Topple down headlong.
GLOUCESTER.   Set me where you stand.
EDGAR.   Give me your hand; you are now within a foot   25
Of th' extreme verge. For all beneath the moon
Would I not leap upright.
GLOUCESTER.   Let go my hand.
Here, friend, 's another purse; in it a jewel
Well worth a poor man's taking. Fairies and gods
Prosper it with thee! Go thou further off;   30
Bid me farewell, and let me hear thee going.
EDGAR.   Now fare ye well, good sir.
GLOUCESTER.   With all my heart.
EDGAR.   Why I do trifle thus with his despair
Is done to cure it.

Scene vi, 13. **choughs:** jackdaws. 14. **gross:** big. 15. **samphire:** sea-fennel,
used for pickling. 19. **cock:** cock-boat.

GLOUCESTER [*kneeling*].   O you mighty gods!
This world I do renounce, and in your sights   35
Shake patiently my great affliction off.
If I could bear it longer, and not fall
To quarrel with your great opposeless wills,
My snuff and loathed part of nature should
Burn itself out. If Edgar live, O bless him!   40
Now, fellow, fare thee well. [*He falls.*
  EDGAR.   Gone, sir; farewell!
— And yet I know not how conceit may rob
The treasury of life, when life itself
Yields to the theft. Had he been where he thought,
By this had thought been past. Alive or dead? —   45
Ho, you sir! friend! Hear you, sir! speak! —
Thus might he pass indeed; yet he revives. —
What are you, sir?
  GLOUCESTER.   Away, and let me die.
  EDGAR.   Hadst thou been aught but gossamer, feathers, air,
So many fathom down precipitating,   50
Thou 'dst shiver'd like an egg: but thou dost breathe;
Hast heavy substance; bleed'st not; speak'st; art sound.
Ten masts at each make not the altitude
Which thou hast perpendicularly fell.
Thy life's a miracle. Speak yet again.   55
  GLOUCESTER.   But have I fall'n, or no?
  EDGAR.   From the dread summit of this chalky bourn.
Look up a-height; the shrill-gorg'd lark so far
Cannot be seen or heard. Do but look up.
  GLOUCESTER.   Alack, I have no eyes.   60
Is wretchedness depriv'd that benefit,
To end itself by death? 'Twas yet some comfort,
When misery could beguile the tyrant's rage,
And frustrate his proud will.
  EDGAR.   Give me your arm.
Up: so. How is't? Feel you your legs? You stand.   65
  GLOUCESTER.   Too well, too well.
  EDGAR.   This is above all strangeness.
Upon the crown o' th' cliff, what thing was that
Which parted from you?
  GLOUCESTER.   A poor unfortunate beggar.
  EDGAR.   As I stood here below, methought his eyes
Were two full moons; he had a thousand noses,   70
Horns whelk'd and waved like the [enridged] sea.
It was some fiend; therefore, thou happy father,

---

39. **snuff**: burnt wick, useless remnant.   42. **conceit**: imagination.   47. **pass**: die.
53. **at each**: end to end.   57. **bourn**: boundary.   58. **a-height**: on high.
71. **whelk'd**: twisted.   [enridged] Q.   *enraged* F.

Think that the clearest gods, who make them honours
Of men's impossibilities, have preserv'd thee.

 GLOUCESTER. I do remember now. Henceforth I'll bear 75
Affliction till it do cry out itself
"Enough, enough," and die. That thing you speak of,
I took it for a man; often 't would say,
"The fiend, the fiend!" He led me to that place.

 EDGAR. Bear free and patient thoughts.

Enter LEAR [*fantastically dressed with wild flowers*].

           But who comes here? 80
The safer sense will ne'er accommodate
His master thus.

 LEAR. No, they cannot touch me for [coining];
I am the King himself.

 EDGAR. O thou side-piercing sight! 85

 LEAR. Nature's above art in that respect. There's your press-money.
That fellow handles his bow like a crow-keeper; draw me a clothier's yard.
Look, look, a mouse! Peace, peace; this piece of toasted cheese will do't.
There's my gauntlet; I'll prove it on a giant. Bring up the brown bills. O,
well flown, bird! I' th' clout, i' th' clout! Hewgh! Give the word.

 EDGAR. Sweet marjoram.

 LEAR. Pass. 92

 GLOUCESTER. I know that voice.

 LEAR. Ha! Goneril, with a white beard! They flatter'd me like a
dog, and told me I had the white hairs in my beard ere the black ones
were there. To say "ay" and "no" to everything that I said! "Ay" and
"no" too was no good divinity. When the rain came to wet me once,
and the wind to make me chatter; when the thunder would not peace
at my bidding; there I found 'em, there I smelt 'em out. Go to, they are
not men o' their words: they told me I was everything; 'tis a lie, I am not
ague-proof. 101

 GLOUCESTER. The trick of that voice I do well remember.
Is't not the King?

 LEAR.   Ay, every inch a king!
When I do stare, see how the subject quakes.
I pardon that man's life. What was thy cause? 105
Adultery?
Thou shalt not die. Die for adultery! No:
The wren goes to't, and the small gilded fly
Does lecher in my sight.

73. **clearest:** most pure. 80. **free:** fearless. 81. **The safer sense:** a sane mind.
accommodate: dress up. 83. **[coining]** Q. *crying* F. 86. **press-money:** money
given to a conscript. 87. **clothier's yard:** an arrow a cloth-yard long. 89. **brown
bills:** men carrying pikes stained brown. 90. **clout:** center of the target.
105. **cause:** accusation.

Let copulation thrive; for Gloucester's bastard son   110
Was kinder to his father than my daughters
Got 'tween the lawful sheets.
To't, luxury, pell-mell! for I lack soldiers.
Behold yond simp'ring dame,
Whose face between her forks presages snow,   115
That minces virtue, and does shake the head
To hear of pleasure's name, —
The fitchew nor the soiled horse goes to't
With a more riotous appetite.
Down from the waist they are Centaurs,   120
Though women all above;
But to the girdle do the gods inherit,
Beneath is all the fiends';
There's hell, there's darkness, there's the sulphurous pit,   124
Burning, scalding, stench, consumption; fie, fie, fie! pah, pah! Give me an
ounce of civet; good apothecary, sweeten my imagination. There's money
for thee.

GLOUCESTER.   O, let me kiss that hand!

LEAR.   Let me wipe it first; it smells of mortality.

GLOUCESTER.   O ruin'd piece of nature! This great world   130
Shall so wear out to nought. Dost thou know me?

LEAR.   I remember thine eyes well enough. Dost thou squiny at me?
No, do thy worst, blind Cupid; I'll not love. Read thou this challenge;
mark but the penning of it.

GLOUCESTER.   Were all thy letters suns, I could not see.   135

EDGAR [aside].   I would not take this from report. It is;
And my heart breaks at it.

LEAR.   Read.

GLOUCESTER.   What, with the case of eyes?   139

LEAR.   O, ho, are you there with me? No eyes in your head, nor no
money in your purse? Your eyes are in a heavy case, your purse in a light;
yet you see how this world goes.

GLOUCESTER.   I see it feelingly.   143

LEAR.   What, art mad? A man may see how this world goes with no
eyes. Look with thine ears; see how yond justice rails upon yond simple
thief. Hark, in thine ear: change places, and, handy-dandy, which is the
justice, which is the thief? Thou hast seen a farmer's dog bark at a
beggar?

GLOUCESTER.   Ay, sir.   149

LEAR.   And the creature run from the cur? There thou mightst behold
the great image of authority: a dog's obey'd in office.
Thou rascal beadle, hold thy bloody hand!
Why dost thou lash that whore? Strip thy own back;

---

113. **luxury:** lust.   115. **forks:** part of the head-dress. **snow:** coldness, chastity.
116. **minces:** affects coyly.   118. **fitchew:** pole-cat. **soiled:** richly fed.   122. **inherit:** possess.   132. **squiny:** squint.   139. **case:** sockets.

Thou hotly lusts to use her in that kind
For which thou whip'st her. The usurer hangs the cozener.   155
Through tatter'd clothes great vices do appear;
Robes and furr'd gowns hide all. [Plate] sins with gold,
And the strong lance of justice hurtless breaks;
Arm it in rags, a pigmy's straw does pierce it.
None does offend, none, I say, none; I'll able 'em.   160
Take that of me, my friend, who gave the power
To seal th' accuser's lips. Get thee glass eyes,
And, like a scurvy politician, seem
To see the things thou dost not. Now, now, now, now.
Pull off my boots; harder, harder: so.   165
   EDGAR.   O, matter and impertinency mix'd!
Reason in madness!
   LEAR.   If thou wilt weep my fortunes, take my eyes.
I know thee well enough; thy name is Gloucester.
Thou must be patient; we came crying hither.   170
Thou know'st, the first time that we smell the air,
We wawl and cry. I will preach to thee; mark.
   GLOUCESTER.   Alack, alack the day!
   LEAR.   When we are born, we cry that we are come
To this great stage of fools. — This' a good block.   175
It were a delicate stratagem, to shoe
A troop of horse with felt. I'll put 't in proof;
And when I have stol'n upon these son-in-laws,
Then, kill, kill, kill, kill, kill, kill!

Enter a GENTLEMAN [*with* Attendants].

   GENTLEMAN.   O, here he is! Lay hand upon him. Sir,   180
Your most dear daughter —
   LEAR.   No rescue? What, a prisoner? I am even
The natural fool of fortune. Use me well;
You shall have ransom. Let me have surgeons;
I am cut to th' brains.
   GENTLEMAN.   You shall have anything.   185
   LEAR.   No seconds? All myself?
Why, this would make a man a man of salt,
To use his eyes for garden water-pots,
[Ay, and laying autumn's dust.
   GENTLEMAN.   Good sir, —]

---

155. **cozener:** petty cheat.   157. **[Plate]** (Theobald). *Place* F. The reference is
to plate armor.   160. **able:** warrant.   166. **impertinency:** irrelevance.   175. **block:**
hat.   186. **seconds:** supporters.   187. **salt:** tears.   189. **[Ay . . . sir, —]** Q.
Om. F.

LEAR.   I will die bravely, like a smug bridegroom. What!   190
I will be jovial. Come, come; I am a king,
My masters, know you that?
    GENTLEMAN.   You are a royal one, and we obey you.
    LEAR.   Then there's life in't. Come, an you get it, you shall get it by
running. Sa, sa, sa, sa.   195

[Exit [running; Attendants follow].

    GENTLEMAN.   A sight most pitiful in the meanest wretch,
Past speaking of in a king! Thou hast [one] daughter
Who redeems Nature from the general curse
Which twain have brought her to.
    EDGAR.   Hail, gentle sir.
    GENTLEMAN.   Sir, speed you: what's your will?   200
    EDGAR.   Do you hear aught, sir, of a battle toward?
    GENTLEMAN.   Most sure and vulgar; every one hears that,
Which can distinguish sound.
    EDGAR.   But, by your favour,
How near's the other army?
    GENTLEMAN.   Near and on speedy foot; the main descry   205
Stands on the hourly thought.
    EDGAR.   I thank you, sir; that's all.
    GENTLEMAN.   Though that the Queen on special cause is here,
Her army is mov'd on. [Exit.
    EDGAR.   I thank you, sir.
    GLOUCESTER.   You ever-gentle gods, take my breath from me;
Let not my worser spirit tempt me again   210
To die before you please!
    EDGAR.   Well pray you, father.
    GLOUCESTER.   Now, good sir, what are you?
    EDGAR.   A most poor man, made tame to fortune's blows;
Who by the art of known and feeling sorrows,
Am pregnant to good pity. Give me your hand,   215
I'll lead you to some biding.
    GLOUCESTER.   Hearty thanks;
The bounty and the benison of Heaven
To boot, and boot!

Enter steward [OSWALD].

    OSWALD.   A proclaim'd prize! Most happy!
That eyeless head of thine was first fram'd flesh
To raise my fortunes. Thou old unhappy traitor,   220

197. [one] Q. a F. 201. **toward:** imminent. 202. **vulgar:** of common knowledge. 205–206. **the main . . . thought:** every hour we expect to catch sight of the
main body. 214. **art:** experience. 215. **pregnant:** ready. 216. **biding:** dwelling.

Briefly thyself remember; the sword is out
That must destroy thee.
    GLOUCESTER.   Now let thy friendly hand
Put strength enough to't.

[EDGAR *interposes*.]

    OSWALD.   Wherefore, bold peasant,
Dar'st thou support a publish'd traitor? Hence;
Lest that the infection of his fortune take   225
Like hold on thee. Let go his arm.
    EDGAR.   'Chill not let go, zir, without vurther 'casion.
    OSWALD.   Let go, slave, or thou diest!   228
    EDGAR.   Good gentleman, go your gait, and let poor volk pass. An
'chud ha' bin zwagger'd out of my life, 'twould not ha' bin zo long as 'tis
by a vortnight. Nay, come not near th' old man; keep out, 'che vor ye, or
Ise try whether your costard or my ballow be the harder. 'Chill be plain
with you.
    OSWALD.   Out, dunghill!   234
    EDGAR.   'Chill pick your teeth, zir. Come, no matter vor your foins.

[*They fight, and* EDGAR *knocks him down*.]

    OSWALD.   Slave, thou hast slain me. Villain, take my purse.
If ever thou wilt thrive, bury my body;
And give the letters which thou find'st about me
To Edmund Earl of Gloucester; seek him out
Upon the English party. O, untimely death!   240
Death! [*Dies.*
    EDGAR.   I know thee well; a serviceable villain,
As duteous to the vices of thy mistress
As badness would desire.
    GLOUCESTER.   What, is he dead?
    EDGAR.   Sit you down, father; rest you.
Let's see these pockets; the letters that he speaks of   245
May be my friends. He's dead; I am only sorry
He had no other death's-man. Let us see.
Leave, gentle wax; and, manners, blame us not.
To know our enemies' minds, we rip their hearts;
Their papers, is more lawful.   250
    (*Reads the letter.*) "Let our reciprocal vows be rememb'red. You have
many opportunities to cut him off; if your will want not, time and place
will be fruitfully offer'd. There is nothing done, if he return the con-

---

221. **thyself remember:** think on your soul's welfare.   227. **'Chill:** I will. Edgar
takes the part of a peasant and uses Southern dialect.   229–230. **An 'chud:** if I
could.   231. **'che vor:** I warn.   232. **Ise:** I shall. **costard:** head. **ballow:** cudgel.
235. **foins:** thrusts.   248. **Leave:** by your leave.

queror; then am I the prisoner, and his bed my gaol; from the loathed
warmth whereof deliver me, and supply the place for your labour.   255
                    "Your — wife, so I would say —
                              "Affectionate servant,
                                        "GONERIL."

O indistinguish'd space of woman's will!
A plot upon her virtuous husband's life;   260
And the exchange my brother! Here, in the sands,
Thee I'll rake up, the post unsanctified
Of murderous lechers; and in the mature time
With this ungracious paper strike the sight
Of the death-practis'd duke. For him 'tis well   265
That of thy death and business I can tell.
    GLOUCESTER.   The King is mad; how stiff is my vile sense
That I stand up and have ingenious feeling
Of my huge sorrows! Better I were distract;
So should my thoughts be sever'd from my griefs,   270

[*Drum afar off.*

And woes by wrong imaginations lose
The knowledge of themselves.
    EDGAR.   Give me your hand.
Far off, methinks, I hear the beaten drum.
Come, father, I'll bestow you with a friend.

[*Exeunt.*

SCENE 7.   [*A tent in the French camp.*]

Enter CORDELIA, KENT, *and* [DOCTOR].

    CORDELIA.   O thou good Kent, how shall I live and work
To match thy goodness? My life will be too short,
And every measure fail me.
    KENT.   To be acknowledg'd, madam, is o'erpaid.
All my reports go with the modest truth;   5
Nor more nor clipp'd, but so.
    CORDELIA.   Be better suited;
These weeds are memories of those worser hours.
I prithee, put them off.
    KENT.   Pardon, dear madam;
Yet to be known shortens my made intent.

257. **servant**: lover.   259. **indistinguish'd space**: unlimited range.   **will**: lust.
262. **rake**: cover.   265. **death-practis'd**: whose death is plotted.   268. **ingenious**:
conscious.   274. **bestow**: lodge.

    Scene vii, S.D. [DOCTOR] Q. *Gentlemen* F.   9. **shortens**: interferes with.
made: prearranged.

My boon I make it, that you know me not   10
Till time and I think meet.
 CORDELIA. Then be't so, my good lord. [*To the* DOCTOR.] How does
  the King?
 [DOCTOR]. Madam, sleeps still.
 CORDELIA. O you kind gods,
Cure this great breach in his abused nature!   15
Th' untun'd and jarring senses, O, wind up
Of this child-changed father!
 [DOCTOR].   So please your Majesty
That we may wake the King? He hath slept long.
 CORDELIA. Be govern'd by your knowledge, and proceed
I' th' sway of your own will.

   Enter LEAR *in a chair carried by* Servants. [GENTLEMAN *in attendance.*]

             Is he array'd?   20
 GENTLEMAN. Ay, madam; in the heaviness of sleep
We put fresh garments on him.
 [DOCTOR]. Be by, good madam, when we do awake him;
I doubt [not] of his temperance.
 [CORDELIA.   Very well.
 DOCTOR. Please you, draw near. — Louder the music there!]   25
 CORDELIA. O my dear father! Restoration hang
Thy medicine on my lips; and let this kiss
Repair those violent harms that my two sisters
Have in thy reverence made!
 KENT.   Kind and dear princess!
 CORDELIA. Had you not been their father, these white flakes   30
Did challenge pity of them. Was this a face
To be oppos'd against the [warring] winds?
[To stand against the deep dread-bolted thunder?
In the most terrible and nimble stroke
Of quick, cross lightning? to watch — poor perdu! —   35
With this thin helm?] Mine enemy's dog,
Though he had bit me, should have stood that night
Against my fire; and wast thou fain, poor father,
To hovel thee with swine and rogues forlorn
In short and musty straw? Alack, alack!   40
'Tis wonder that thy life and wits at once
Had not concluded all. He wakes; speak to him.

13, 17, 23. [DOCTOR]. Q. *Gentleman* F.   16. **wind up.** The figure is of a stringed
instrument.   17. **child-changed:** changed by his children's conduct.   24. [**not**]
Q. Om. F. **temperance:** sanity.   24–25. [**CORDELIA. . . . there!**] Q. Om. F.
32. [**warring**] Q. *iarring* F.   33–36. [**To . . . helm?**] Q. Om. F.   35. **cross:** zig-
zag. **perdu:** a sentinel placed in a dangerous station.   36. **helm:** covering (of
hair).   42. **all:** altogether.

DOCTOR.   Madam, do you; 'tis fittest.
CORDELIA.   How does my royal lord? How fares your Majesty?
LEAR.   You do me wrong to take me out o' th' grave.   45
Thou art a soul in bliss; but I am bound
Upon a wheel of fire, that mine own tears
Do scald like molten lead.
CORDELIA.   Sir, do you know me?
LEAR.   You are a spirit, I know; where did you die?
CORDELIA.   Still, still, far wide!   50
DOCTOR.   He's scarce awake; let him alone a while.
LEAR.   Where have I been? Where am I? Fair daylight?
I am mightily abus'd. I should ev'n die with pity,
To see another thus. I know not what to say.
I will not swear these are my hands. Let's see;   55
I feel this pin prick. Would I were assur'd
Of my condition!
CORDELIA.   O, look upon me, sir,
And hold your hand in benediction o'er me.
[No, sir,] you must not kneel.
LEAR.   Pray, do not mock me.
I am a very foolish fond old man,   60
Fourscore and upward, not an hour more nor less;
And, to deal plainly,
I fear I am not in my perfect mind.
Methinks I should know you, and know this man;
Yet I am doubtful; for I am mainly ignorant   65
What place this is, and all the skill I have
Remembers not these garments; nor I know not
Where I did lodge last night. Do not laugh at me;
For, as I am a man, I think this lady
To be my child Cordelia.
CORDELIA.   And so I am, I am.   70
LEAR.   Be your tears wet? Yes, faith. I pray, weep not.
If you have poison for me, I will drink it.
I know you do not love me; for your sisters
Have, as I do remember, done me wrong:
You have some cause, they have not.
CORDELIA.   No cause, no cause.   75
LEAR.   Am I in France?
KENT.   In your own kingdom, sir.
LEAR.   Do not abuse me.
DOCTOR.   Be comforted, good madam; the great rage,
You see, is kill'd in him: [and yet it is danger
To make him even o'er the time he has lost.]   80

---

50. **wide:** astray.   59. [**No, sir,**] Q. Om. F.   65. **mainly:** completely.   79–80.
[**and . . . lost.**] Q. Om. F.

Desire him to go in; trouble him no more
Till further settling.
    CORDELIA.   Will't please your Highness walk?
    LEAR.   You must bear with me.
Pray you now, forget and forgive; I am old and foolish.   84

[*Exeunt [all but* KENT *and* GENTLEMAN].

[GENTLEMAN.   Holds it true, sir, that the Duke of Cornwall was so
slain?
    KENT.   Most certain, sir.
    GENTLEMAN.   Who is conductor of his people?
    KENT.   As 'tis said, the bastard son of Gloucester.   89
    GENTLEMAN.   They say Edgar, his banish'd son, is with the Earl of
Kent in Germany.
    KENT.   Report is changeable. 'Tis time to look about; the powers of
the kingdom approach apace.
    GENTLEMAN.   The arbitrement is like to be bloody. Fare you well,
sir. [*Exit.*]   95
    KENT.   My point and period will be throughly wrought,
Or well or ill, as this day's battle's fought.] [*Exit.*

ACT FIVE

SCENE 1.   [*The British camp, near Dover.*]

Enter, with drum and colours, EDMUND, REGAN, *Gentlemen, and*
Soldiers.

    EDMUND.   Know of the Duke if his last purpose hold,
Or whether since he is advis'd by aught
To change the course. He's full of alteration
And self-reproving; bring his constant pleasure. [*To a Gentleman, who
        goes out.*]
    REGAN.   Our sister's man is certainly miscarried.   5
    EDMUND.   'Tis to be doubted, madam.
    REGAN.   Now, sweet lord,
You know the goodness I intend upon you.
Tell me — but truly — but then speak the truth,
Do you not love my sister?
    EDMUND.   In honour'd love.

85–97. [GENTLEMAN. . . . fought.] Q. Om. F.   96. **My . . . period:** the question
of my end.
    Act V, Scene i, 4. constant pleasure: fixed decision.   5. **is . . . miscarried:**
has met disaster.   6. **doubted:** feared. Cf. 1. 12, *doubtful.*

REGAN.   But have you never found my brother's way   10
To the forfended place?
  [EDMUND.   That thought abuses you.
  REGAN.   I am doubtful that you have been conjunct
And bosom'd with her, — as far as we call hers.]
  EDMUND.   No, by mine honour, madam.
  REGAN.   I never shall endure her. Dear my lord,   15
Be not familiar with her.
  EDMUND.   Fear me not.
She and the Duke her husband!

  Enter, with drum and colours, ALBANY, GONERIL, *and* Soldiers.

  [GONERIL [*aside*].   I had rather lose the battle than that sister
Should loosen him and me.]
  ALBANY.   Our very loving sister, well be-met.   20
Sir, this I heard: the King is come to his daughter,
With others whom the rigour of our state
Forc'd to cry out. [Where I could not be honest,
I never yet was valiant. For this business,
It toucheth us, as France invades our land,   25
Not bolds the King, with others, whom, I fear,
Most just and heavy causes make oppose.
  EDMUND.   Sir, you speak nobly.]
  REGAN.   Why is this reason'd?
  GONERIL.   Combine together 'gainst the enemy;
For these domestic and particular broils   30
Are not the question here.
  ALBANY.   Let's then determine
With the ancient of war on our proceeding.
  [EDMUND.   I shall attend you presently at your tent.]
  REGAN.   Sister, you'll go with us?
  GONERIL.   No.   35
  REGAN.   'Tis most convenient; pray you, go with us.
  GONERIL [*aside*].   O, ho, I know the riddle. — I will go.

  [*Exeunt both the armies.* [*As they are going out,*] *enter* EDGAR [*disguised.* ALBANY *remains*].

  EDGAR.   If e'er your Grace had speech with man so poor,
Hear me one word.
  ALBANY.   I'll overtake you. — Speak.

11. **forfended:** forbidden. **abuses:** deceives.   11–13. [EDMUND. . . . hers.] Q. Om. F.   13. **bosom'd:** intimate.   **as . . . hers:** to the utmost limit.   18–19. [GONERIL . . . me.] Q. Om. F.   23–28. [Where . . . nobly.] Q. Om. F.   26. **Not bolds:** not as it encourages.   28. **reason'd:** discussed.   32. **ancient:** veterans.   33. [EDMUND. . . . tent.] Q. Om. F.   36. **convenient:** suitable.

EDGAR.   Before you fight the battle, ope this letter.   40
If you have victory, let the trumpet sound
For him that brought it. Wretched though I seem,
I can produce a champion that will prove
What is avouched there. If you miscarry,
Your business of the world hath so an end,   45
And machination ceases. Fortune love you!
      ALBANY.   Stay till I have read the letter.
      EDGAR.   I was forbid it.
When time shall serve, let but the herald cry,
And I'll appear again. [Exit.
      ALBANY.   Why, fare thee well; I will o'erlook thy paper.   50

Re-enter EDMUND.

      EDMUND.   The enemy's in view; draw up your powers.
Here is the guess of their true strength and forces
By diligent discovery; but your haste
Is now urg'd on you.
      ALBANY.   We will greet the time. [Exit.
      EDMUND.   To both these sisters have I sworn my love;   55
Each jealous of the other as the stung
Are of the adder. Which of them shall I take?
Both? one? or neither? Neither can be enjoy'd,
If both remain alive. To take the widow
Exasperates, makes mad her sister Goneril;   60
And hardly shall I carry out my side,
Her husband being alive. Now then we'll use
His countenance for the battle; which being done,
Let her who would be rid of him devise
His speedy taking off. As for the mercy   65
Which he intends to Lear and to Cordelia,
The battle done, and they within our power,
Shall never see his pardon; for my state
Stands on me to defend, not to debate. [Exit.

SCENE 2.   [A field between the two camps.]

Alarum within. Enter, with drum and colours, LEAR, CORDELIA, and
Soldiers, over the stage; and exeunt. Enter EDGAR and GLOUCESTER.

      EDGAR.   Here, father, take the shadow of this tree
For your good host; pray that the right may thrive.

53. discovery: scouting.   54. greet the time: meet the occasion.   69. Stands on:
requires.

Scene ii, 2. host: shelterer.

If ever I return to you again,
I'll bring you comfort.
    GLOUCESTER.   Grace go with you, sir!

    [*Exit* [EDGAR]. *Alarum and retreat within. Re-enter* EDGAR.

    EDGAR.   Away, old man; give me thy hand; away!   5
King Lear hath lost, he and his daughter ta'en.
Give me thy hand; come on.
    GLOUCESTER.   No further, sir; a man may rot even here.
    EDGAR.   What, in ill thoughts again? Men must endure
Their going hence even as their coming hither;   10
Ripeness is all. Come on.
    GLOUCESTER.   And that's true too.

    [*Exeunt.*

SCENE 3. [*The British camp near Dover.*]

Enter, in conquest, with drum and colours, EDMUND; LEAR *and* CORDELIA
as prisoners: CAPTAIN, Soldiers, *etc.*

    EDMUND.   Some officers take them away. Good guard,
Until their greater pleasures first be known
That are to censure them.
    CORDELIA.   We are not the first
Who with best meaning have incurr'd the worst.
For thee, oppressed king, I am cast down;   5
Myself could else out-frown false Fortune's frown.
Shall we not see these daughters and these sisters?
    LEAR.   No, no, no, no! Come, let's away to prison;
We two alone will sing like birds i' th' cage.
When thou dost ask me blessing, I'll kneel down   10
And ask of thee forgiveness. So we'll live,
And pray, and sing, and tell old tales, and laugh
At gilded butterflies, and hear poor rogues
Talk of court news; and we'll talk with them too,
Who loses and who wins; who's in, who's out;   15
And take upon 's the mystery of things
As if we were God's spies; and we'll wear out,
In a wall'd prison, packs and sects of great ones,
That ebb and flow by th' moon.
    EDMUND.   Take them away.

    Scene iii, 2. their greater pleasures: the desires of those greater persons.
3. **censure:** judge.   17. **God's spies:** spies on God's ways.

LEAR. Upon such sacrifices, my Cordelia, 20
The gods themselves throw incense. Have I caught thee?
He that parts us shall bring a brand from heaven,
And fire us hence like foxes. Wipe thine eyes;
The good-years shall devour them, flesh and fell,
Ere they shall make us weep. We'll see 'em starv'd first. 25
Come.

[*Exeunt* [LEAR *and* CORDELIA, *guarded*].

EDMUND. Come hither, captain; hark.
Take thou this note [*giving a paper*]; go follow them to prison.
One step I have advanc'd thee; if thou dost
As this instructs thee, thou dost make thy way
To noble fortunes. Know thou this, that men 30
Are as the time is; to be tender-minded
Does not become a sword. Thy great employment
Will not bear question; either say thou'lt do't,
Or thrive by other means.
    CAPTAIN. I'll do't, my lord.
    EDMUND. About it; and write happy when thou'st done. 35
Mark, I say instantly; and carry it so
As I have set it down.
    [CAPTAIN. I cannot draw a cart, nor eat dried oats;
If it be man's work, I'll do't.] [*Exit.*

Flourish. Enter ALBANY, GONERIL, REGAN, [*another* CAPTAIN] *and*
Soldiers.

ALBANY. Sir, you have show'd to-day your valiant strain, 40
And fortune led you well. You have the captives
Who were the opposites of this day's strife;
I do require them of you, so to use them
As we shall find their merits and our safety
May equally determine.
    EDMUND.   Sir, I thought it fit 45
To send the old and miserable king
To some retention [and appointed guard];
Whose age had charms in it, whose title more,
To pluck the common bosom on his side,
And turn our impress'd lances in our eyes 50

23. **foxes.** Foxes were driven from their holes by fire and smoke.   24. **good-years:**
an expression for some vague evil influence. **fell:** skin.   32. **sword:** soldier.
35. **write happy:** call yourself lucky.   38–39. [CAPTAIN. . . . do't.] Q. Om. F.
47. [and . . . guard] Q. Om. F.   49. **common bosom:** affection of the multitude.
50. **impress'd lances:** weapons of our soldiers who have been pressed into our
army.

Which do command them. With him I sent the Queen,
My reason all the same; and they are ready
To-morrow, or at further space, t' appear
Where you shall hold your session. [At this time
We sweat and bleed: the friend hath lost his friend;   55
And the best quarrels, in the heat, are curs'd
By those that feel their sharpness:
The question of Cordelia and her father
Requires a fitter place.]
   ALBANY.   Sir, by your patience,
I hold you but a subject of this war,   60
Not as a brother.
   REGAN.   That's as we list to grace him.
Methinks our pleasure might have been demanded,
Ere you had spoke so far. He led our powers,
Bore the commission of my place and person;
The which immediacy may well stand up,   65
And call itself your brother.
   GONERIL.   Not so hot.
In his own grace he doth exalt himself,
More than in your addition.
   REGAN.   In my rights,
By me invested, he compeers the best.
   ALBANY.   That were the most, if he should husband you.   70
   REGAN.   Jesters do oft prove prophets.
   GONERIL.   Holla, holla!
That eye that told you so look'd but a-squint.
   REGAN.   Lady, I am not well; else I should answer
From a full-flowing stomach. General,
Take thou my soldiers, prisoners, patrimony;   75
Dispose of them, of me; the walls are thine.
Witness the world, that I create thee here
My lord and master.
   GONERIL.   Mean you to enjoy him?
   ALBANY.   The let-alone lies not in your good will.
   EDMUND.   Nor in thine, lord.
   ALBANY.   Half-blooded fellow, yes.   80
   REGAN [to EDMUND].   Let the drum strike, and prove my title thine.
   ALBANY.   Stay yet; hear reason. Edmund, I arrest thee
On capital treason; and, in thy arrest,
This gilded serpent. [Pointing to GONERIL.] For your claim, fair sister,
I bar it in the interest of my wife.   85
'Tis she is sub-contracted to this lord,

54–59. [At . . . place.] Q. Om. F.   65. immediacy: close connection.   68. your
addition: what you call him.   69. compeers: equals.   74. stomach: anger.
76. the walls. Theobald proposed to read they all.   79. let-alone: power of pre-
venting it.

And I, her husband, contradict your bans.
If you will marry, make your loves to me,
My lady is bespoke.
    GONERIL.   An interlude!
    ALBANY.   Thou art arm'd, Gloucester; let the trumpet sound.   90
If none appear to prove upon thy person
Thy heinous, manifest, and many treasons,
There is my pledge [*throwing down a glove*]. I'll [prove] it on thy heart,
Ere I taste bread, thou art in nothing less
Than I have here proclaim'd thee.
    REGAN.   Sick, O, sick!   95
    GONERIL [*aside*].   If not, I'll ne'er trust medicine.
    EDMUND.   There's my exchange [*throwing down a glove*]. What in
        the world he is
That names me traitor, villain-like he lies.
Call by the trumpet; — he that dares approach,
On him, on you, who not? I will maintain   100
My truth and honour firmly.
    ALBANY.   A herald, ho!
    [EDMUND.   A herald, ho, a herald!]
    ALBANY.   Trust to thy single virtue; for thy soldiers,
All levied in my name, have in my name
Took their discharge.
    REGAN.   My sickness grows upon me.   105
    ALBANY.   She is not well; convey her to my tent.

[*Exit* REGAN, *led*.] *Enter a* HERALD.

Come hither, herald, — Let the trumpet sound —
And read out this.
    [CAPTAIN.   Sound, trumpet!]   109

[*A trumpet sounds.*

HERALD (*reads*).   "If any man of quality or degree within the lists of
the army will maintain upon Edmund, supposed Earl of Gloucester, that
he is a manifold traitor, let him appear by the third sound of the trumpet.
He is bold in his defence."
    [EDMUND.   Sound!]

[*First trumpet.*

HERALD.   Again!   115

89. **interlude:** comedy.   93. [**prove**] Q. *make* F.   102. [**EDMUND. . . . herald!**]
Q. Om. F.   103. **virtue:** strength.   109. [**CAPTAIN. . . . trumpet!**] Q. Om. F.
111. **supposed:** pretended.   114. [**EDMUND. Sound!**] Q. Om. F.

[*Second trumpet.*

HERALD.   Again!

[*Third trumpet.* [*Trumpet answers within. Enter* EDGAR, *at the third sound, armed, with a trumpet before him.*

ALBANY.   Ask him his purposes, why he appears
Upon this call o' th' trumpet.
HERALD.   What are you?
Your name, your quality? and why you answer
This present summons?
EDGAR.   Know, my name is lost,   120
By treason's tooth bare-gnawn and canker-bit,
Yet am I noble as the adversary
I come to cope.
ALBANY.   Which is the adversary?
EDGAR.   What's he that speaks for Edmund Earl of Gloucester?
EDMUND.   Himself; what say'st thou to him?
EDGAR.   Draw thy sword.   125
That, if my speech offend a noble heart,
Thy arm may do thee justice; here is mine.
Behold, it is the privilege of mine honours,
My oath, and my profession. I protest,
Maugre thy strength, place, youth, and eminence,   130
Despite thy victor-sword and fire-new fortune,
Thy valour, and thy heart, thou art a traitor;
False to thy gods, thy brother, and thy father;
Conspirant 'gainst this high illustrious prince;
And, from th' extremest upward of thy head   135
To the descent and dust below thy foot,
A most toad-spotted traitor. Say thou "No,"
This sword, this arm, and my best spirits are bent
To prove upon thy heart, whereto I speak,
Thou liest.
EDMUND.   In wisdom I should ask thy name;   140
But, since thy outside looks so fair and warlike,
And that thy tongue some 'say of breeding breathes,
What safe and nicely I might well delay
By rule of knighthood, I disdain and spurn.
Back do I toss these treasons to thy head;   145
With the hell-hated lie o'erwhelm thy heart;
Which, for they yet glance by and scarcely bruise,

121. canker-bit: worm-eaten. 128. the privilege (Pope). *my privilege, The* F. honours: rank. 130. Maugre: in spite of. 131. fire-new: brand-new. 136. descent: lowest part. 142. 'say: trace. 143. safe and nicely: safely and with technical correctness.

This sword of mine shall give them instant way
Where they shall rest for ever. Trumpets, speak!

[*Alarums. They fight.* [EDMUND *falls.*]

ALBANY.   Save him, save him!
GONERIL.   This is [mere] practice, Gloucester.   150
By th' law of war thou wast not bound to answer
An unknown opposite. Thou art not vanquish'd,
But cozen'd and beguil'd.
ALBANY.   Shut your mouth, dame,
Or with this paper shall I stop it. Hold, sir. —
Thou worse than any name, read thine own evil.   155
No tearing, lady; I perceive you know it.
GONERIL.   Say, if I do, the laws are mine, not thine.
Who can arraign me for't? [*Exit.*]
ALBANY.   Most monstrous! oh! —
Know'st thou this paper?
EDMUND.   Ask me not what I know.
ALBANY.   Go after her; she's desperate; govern her.   160
EDMUND.   What you have charg'd me with, that have I done;
And more, much more; the time will bring it out.
'Tis past, and so am I. But what are thou
That hast this fortune on me? If thou'rt noble,
I do forgive thee.
EDGAR.   Let's exchange charity.   165
I am no less in blood than thou art, Edmund;
If more, the more thou'st wrong'd me.
My name is Edgar, and thy father's son.
The gods are just, and of our pleasant vices,
Make instruments to plague us.   170
The dark and vicious place where thee he got
Cost him his eyes.
EDMUND.   Thou'st spoken right, 'tis true.
The wheel is come full circle; I am here.
ALBANY.   Methought thy very gait did prophesy
A royal nobleness. I must embrace thee.   175
Let sorrow split my heart, if ever I
Did hate thee or thy father!
EDGAR.   Worthy prince, I know't.
ALBANY.   Where have you hid yourself?
How have you known the miseries of your father?
EDGAR.   By nursing them, my lord. List a brief tale;   180
And when 'tis told, oh, that my heart would burst!
The bloody proclamation to escape,

150. [mere] Q. Om. F.   160. **govern**: restrain.

That follow'd me so near, — oh, our lives' sweetness!
That we the pain of death would hourly die
Rather than die at once! — taught me to shift   185
Into a madman's rags, t' assume a semblance
That very dogs disdain'd; and in this habit
Met I my father with his bleeding rings,
Their precious stones new lost; became his guide,
Led him, begg'd for him, sav'd him from despair;   190
Never, — O fault! — reveal'd myself unto him,
Until some half-hour past, when I was arm'd.
Not sure, though hoping, of this good success,
I ask'd his blessing, and from first to last
Told him our pilgrimage; but his flaw'd heart,   195
Alack, too weak the conflict to support!
'Twixt two extremes of passion, joy and grief,
Burst smilingly.
    EDMUND.   This speech of yours hath mov'd me,
And shall perchance do good. But speak you on;
You look as you had something more to say.   200
    ALBANY.   If there be more, more woeful, hold it in;
For I am almost ready to dissolve,
Hearing of this.
    [EDGAR.   This would have seem'd a period
To such as love not sorrow; but another,
To amplify too much, would make much more,   205
And top extremity.
Whilst I was big in clamour came there in a man,
Who, having seen me in my worst estate,
Shunn'd my abhorr'd society; but then, finding
Who 'twas that so endur'd, with his strong arms   210
He fastened on my neck, and bellowed out
As he'd burst heaven; threw him on my father;
Told the most piteous tale of Lear and him
That ever ear receiv'd; which in recounting,
His grief grew puissant, and the strings of life   215
Began to crack. Twice then the trumpets sounded,
And there I left him tranc'd.
    ALBANY.   But who was this?
    EDGAR.   Kent, sir, the banish'd Kent; who in disguise
Follow'd his enemy king, and did him service
Improper for a slave.]   220

    Enter a GENTLEMAN *with a bloody knife.*

195. **flaw'd:** cracked.   203–220. [EDGAR. . . . **slave.**] Q. Om. F.   204–206. **but
. . . extremity:** one more such circumstance, amplifying what is already too
much, would increase it and pass all limits.   207. **big in clamour:** loud in grief.
212. **him** (Theobald). *me* Q.   217. **tranc'd:** unconscious.

GENTLEMAN.   Help, help, O, help!

EDGAR.   What kind of help?

ALBANY.   Speak, man.

EDGAR.   What means this bloody knife?

GENTLEMAN.   'Tis hot, it smokes;
It came even from the heart of — O, she's dead!

ALBANY.   Who dead? Speak, man.

GENTLEMAN.   Your lady, sir, your lady; and her sister   225
By her is poison'd; she confesses it.

EDMUND.   I was contracted to them both. All three
Now marry in an instant.

EDGAR.   Here comes Kent.

Enter KENT.

ALBANY.   Produce the bodies, be they alive or dead.
This judgement of the heavens, that makes us tremble,   230
Touches us not with pity.

[*Exit* GENTLEMAN.]

                              — O, is this he?
The time will not allow the compliment
Which very manners urges.

KENT.   I am come
To bid my king and master aye good-night.
Is he not here?

ALBANY.   Great thing of us forgot!   235
Speak, Edmund, where's the King? and where's Cordelia?

[*The bodies of* GONERIL *and* REGAN *are brought in.*]

See'st thou this object, Kent?

KENT.   Alack, why thus?

EDMUND.   Yet Edmund was belov'd!
The one the other poison'd for my sake,
And after slew herself.   240

ALBANY.   Even so. Cover their faces.

EDMUND.   I pant for life. Some good I mean to do,
Despite of mine own nature. Quickly send,
Be brief in it, to th' castle; for my writ
Is on the life of Lear and on Cordelia.   245
Nay, send in time.

ALBANY.   Run, run, O, run!

EDGAR.   To who, my lord? Who has the office? Send
Thy token of reprieve.

EDMUND.   Well thought on. Take my sword,
Give it the captain.
   EDGAR.   Haste thee, for thy life.   250

[*Exit* GENTLEMAN.]

   EDMUND.   He hath commission from thy wife and me
To hang Cordelia in the prison, and
To lay the blame upon her own despair,
That she fordid herself.
   ALBANY.   The gods defend her! Bear him hence a while.   255

[EDMUND *is borne off.*] *Re-enter* LEAR *with* CORDELIA *in his* arms
[GENTLEMAN *following*].

   LEAR.   Howl, howl, howl! O, you are men of stones!
Had I your tongues and eyes, I'd use them so
That heaven's vault should crack. She's gone for ever!
I know when one is dead, and when one lives;
She's dead as earth. Lend me a looking-glass;   260
If that her breath will mist or stain the stone,
Why, then she lives.
   KENT.   Is this the promis'd end?
   EDGAR.   Or image of that horror?
   ALBANY.   Fall, and cease!
   LEAR.   This feather stirs; she lives! If it be so,
It is a chance which does redeem all sorrows   265
That ever I have felt.
   KENT [*kneeling*].   O my good master!
   LEAR.   Prithee, away.
   EDGAR.   'Tis noble Kent, your friend.
   LEAR.   A plague upon you, murderers, traitors all!
I might have sav'd her; now she's gone for ever!
Cordelia, Cordelia! stay a little. Ha!   270
What is't thou say'st? Her voice was ever soft,
Gentle, and low; an excellent thing in woman.
I kill'd the slave that was a-hanging thee.
   GENTLEMAN.   'Tis true, my lords, he did.
   LEAR.   Did I not, fellow?
I have seen the day, with my good biting falchion   275
I would have made him skip. I am old now,
And these same crosses spoil me. Who are you?
Mine eyes are not o' th' best. I'll tell you straight.

---

254. **fordid:** destroyed.   261. **stone:** polished crystal, mirror.   262. **promis'd end:** Last Judgment.   277. **crosses:** sufferings.

KENT.   If Fortune brag of two she lov'd and hated,
One of them we behold.   280
   LEAR.   This is a dull sight. Are you not Kent?
   KENT.   The same,
Your servant Kent. Where is your servant Caius?
   LEAR.   He's a good fellow, I can tell you that;
He'll strike, and quickly too. He's dead and rotten.
   KENT.   No, my good lord; I am the very man, —   285
   LEAR.   I'll see that straight.
   KENT.   — That, from your first of difference and decay,
Have follow'd your sad steps —
   LEAR.   You are welcome hither.
   KENT.   Nor no man else; all's cheerless, dark, and deadly.
Your eldest daughters have fordone themselves,   290
And desperately are dead.
   LEAR.   Ay, so I think.
   ALBANY.   He knows not what he says; and vain is it
That we present us to him.

Enter a MESSENGER.

   EDGAR.   Very bootless.
   MESSENGER.   Edmund is dead, my lord.
   ALBANY.   That's but a trifle here. —
You lords and noble friends, know our intent.   295
What comfort to this great decay may come
Shall be appli'd. For us, we will resign,
During the life of this old majesty,
To him our absolute power; [*to* EDGAR *and* KENT] you, to your rights,
With boot, and such addition as your honours   300
Have more than merited. All friends shall taste
The wages of their virtue, and all foes
The cup of their deservings. O, see, see!
   LEAR.   And my poor fool is hang'd! No, no, no life!
Why should a dog, a horse, a rat, have life,   305
And thou no breath at all? Thou'lt come no more,
Never, never, never, never, never!
Pray you, undo this button. Thank you, sir.
Do you see this? Look on her, look, her lips,
Look there, look there! [*Dies.*
   EDGAR.   He faints! My lord, my lord!   310
   KENT.   Break, heart; I prithee, break!
   EDGAR.   Look up, my lord.

_____

287. **first . . . decay:** beginning of the change and decay of your fortunes.
304. **poor fool:** Cordelia.

KENT.   Vex not his ghost; O, let him pass! He hates him
That would upon the rack of this tough world
Stretch him out longer.

EDGAR.   He is gone, indeed.

KENT.   The wonder is he hath endur'd so long;   315
He but usurp'd his life.

ALBANY.   Bear them from hence. Our present business
Is general woe. [*To* KENT *and* EDGAR.] Friends of my soul, you twain
Rule in this realm, and the gor'd state sustain.

KENT.   I have a journey, sir, shortly to go.   320
My master calls me; I must not say no.

EDGAR.   The weight of this sad time we must obey;
Speak what we feel, not what we ought to say.
The oldest hath borne most; we that are young
Shall never see so much, nor live so long.   325

[*Exeunt, with a dead march.*

Curtain

319. gor'd: wounded.   322. EDGAR F. *Duke* Q.

Jean Racine (1639–1699) cannot be accused of base motives in re-writing Euripides' classic tragedy, *Hippolytus* (428 B.C.). He was follow-ing a trend which began to emerge after the suppression of religious drama in 1548. As the critic Sainte-Beuve noted, French drama shifted its attention from Christian mystery plays to ancient tragedies without any intermediate steps. Translations of the Greek tragic and comic poets became popular, followed, in 1552, by the first French neoclassical tragedy. Naturally, the French tragedies which sought to imitate the antique drama did not recreate quite the quality or the effect.

Because of the rigid academic interpretation of *The Poetics* of Aris-totle, Racine and his colleague Pierre Corneille (1606–1684) found themselves forced to work within fairly narrow limits of what was then thought to be appropriate to be said and shown. The famous three unities were invoked: time, place, and action. A five-act structure was deemed proper, and the poetic pattern was the Alexandrine, rhyming couplets in iambic hexameter. The scene, as in *Phaedra* (1678), was usually not described beyond locating it by name — in a city, before a palace, or in a chamber. The strong, visual, physical action which adds interest to much of the Elizabethan tragedy is missing, as it often is in Greek tragedy. Scenes of horror take place offstage. But little "rules" like this were followed slavishly, with no particular reason behind them. In the classic period, there were customarily only two or three actors to play all the roles, so battles and deaths could not practically take place on stage. There were, of course, no such practical physical limi-tations in seventeenth-century France. In short, a rarified form of drama emerged that owed much to a misreading of the classic critics and dramas and to lack of knowledge about the actual circumstances of production in the fifth century B.C.

Given artificial limitations, however, both Racine and Corneille were able to create remarkable characters, provoke honest emotional conflicts, and successfully mold the French language to serve their poetic insights. In *Phaedra*, for example, the poetry is unexcelled, the tragedy undeniable, and the character of Phaedra so vibrant and arresting that it is still one of the most popular tragic roles. In Euripides' version, the role is strong and fascinating, but the title character, Hippolytus, is pivotal. The tragic downfall of greatest interest is his, and it is caused by his lack of moder-ation, his relentless pursuit of the hunt, and his shunning of women. Phaedra and Theseus also make tragic decisions, but theirs are inter-twined with the agonies of Hippolytus, not actions of a subplot or plots. Racine's contribution to the legend, aside from the beauties of his poetry, lies mainly in focusing more on Phaedra than on her stepson.

Racine had been educated and strongly influenced by the Jansenist sect of Catholicism at Port-Royal, a school of thought which denied free will. No doubt Phaedra's uncontrollable passion appealed to the philoso-pher and playwright in Racine. Phaedra burns with an accursed love which should never have been spoken or consummated. Only when she believes Theseus dead does she dare to speak of it, and Hippolytus, clean-cut fellow that he is, tries valiantly to mistake her meaning. Spurned, she is willing to exist on almost any terms just to be near Hippolytus. When Theseus does return, it is not Phaedra but the nurse who tells him, falsely, that the queen has been approached by Hippolytus. This sets in motion a train of events which culminates in Hippolytus' death and Phaedra's subsequent anguished confession and suicide by poison.

This structuring and elaboration of detail changes Euripides' original considerably. In *Hippolytus*, Phaedra's love is revealed to him not by her but by the nurse, giving her at first more restraint of character than Racine allows. Her vengeance, though, is more terrible, for she unjustly contrives Hippolytus's destruction by leaving behind an incriminating note. In effect, Euripides' Phaedra is able to revenge herself beyond the grave. Obviously, what Racine intended was not what Euripides had in mind. Each poet chose different focal points and somewhat different ways to tell an interesting story of human passion and fatal misunderstanding.

That cannot be too much stressed, for there is a tendency to accept the first literary version of a well-known myth as the "right" one, praising those that follow more in terms of the accuracy of the reproduction of the plot details of the original than in valuing them as independent works of art. Naturally, not every play based on *Hippolytus* — or even *Amphitryon*, which now has at least thirty-eight versions, if Giraudoux's count in *Amphitryon 38* is to be trusted — has been or will be worthy to be called art. In fact, a slavish retelling of the tale, without Euripides' talent for structure, his feeling for character, or his sense of language, is apt to be nothing more than boring hack work, hardly worth reading or staging.

Racine's inspiration, then, was not purely that of a revival or a new translation into French of an ancient drama. It was the result of studying the old fable and finding in it elements which could be rearranged to discover new truths about human emotions, pushed to their outer limits. That he succeeded is really quite remarkable, considering the stylistic limitations. Both he and Corneille were not always so skillful, however, and that is why *Phaedra* is included in this anthology rather than some of the other neoclassical tragedies they wrote.

G.L.

JEAN RACINE

Phaedra

TRANSLATED BY WESLEY GODDARD

Characters

THESEUS, king of Athens, son of Aegeus
PHAEDRA, wife of Theseus, daughter of Minos and of
    Pasiphae
HIPPOLYTUS, son of Theseus and of Antiope, queen of
    the Amazons
ARICIA, a princess of the royal house of Athens
OENONE, nurse and confidant of Phaedra
THERAMENES, tutor and friend of Theseus
ISMENE, confidant of Aricia
PANOPE, a lady in the court of Phaedra
GUARDS

The scene is at Troezen, a city in the Peloponnesus.

ACT ONE

(HIPPOLYTUS and THERAMENES enter.)

HIPPOLYTUS.   My mind is made up. I am leaving, Theramenes,
And ending my stay in gracious Troezen,
For, shaken as I am by dreadful doubts,
I begin to feel shame at my idleness.
Six months and more my father has been away,
And yet I do not know the fate of one so dear to me;
I do not even know what regions may be hiding him.

THERAMENES.   And in what regions, my lord, would you then search?
Already, in answer to your just fears,
I have sailed the two seas* that surround Corinth;
I have asked for Theseus of the people on those shores

---

* An asterisk in the text indicates an explanatory note at the bottom of the
page.
the two seas: The Ionian and the Aegean Seas.

Where one sees Acheron* lose itself among the dead;
I have visited Elis* and, leaving Taenarus,*
Have gone on to the sea where Icarus* fell.
With what new hope, in what happy place,
Do you expect to find the trace of his steps?
   Who knows, indeed, if the King your father
Wants the secret of his absence learned?
While we, along with you, fear for his life,
He may be quietly hiding his newest loves,*
Waiting, that some deluded loving girl . . .
   HIPPOLYTUS.   Theramenes, stop, and show respect for Theseus.
Long since recovered from his youthful ways,
He is now held back by no unworthy obstacle;
And with his inconstancy ended by his own vows,
Phaedra for long has feared no rivals.
   In short, by searching for him, I will follow duty,
And I will flee this place which I dare see no more.
   THERAMENES.   Since when, my lord, do you fear the sight
Of this peaceful place, so dear to your childhood,
And which I have seen that you prefer
To the pompous tumult of Athens and the court?
What danger, or rather what pain, sends you away?
   HIPPOLYTUS.   Those happy times are gone. All has changed
Since the gods have sent here to these shores
The daughter of Minos and Pasiphae.*
   THERAMENES.   I understand. I know the cause of your suffering.
Phaedra here distresses you and hurts your sight:
A dangerous stepmother, who showed her true self
By sending you to exile when first she saw you.
But her hate, which once enveloped you,
Either has vanished or is now much weakened.
   Besides, what risks can you be made to face
By a dying woman, by one who wants to die?
Phaedra, struck by an ill of which she will not speak,
Weary of herself and of the very day,
Can she form plots against you?

   Acheron: a river flowing from Epirus, a country of northwestern Greece, into Hades.
   Elis: a country of ancient Greece, on the western shore of the Peloponnesus.
   Taenarus: southernmost tip of the Peloponnesus.
   Icarus: the son of Daedalus; he fell into the Aegean, having escaped from the labyrinth of Crete by the use of wings insecurely fastened on with wax, which melted in the sun.
   his newest loves: Theseus had already seduced Antiope, Ariadne, Phaedra, Helen, and Peribea.
   daughter of Minos and Pasiphae: this early mention of Pasiphae, famous because of her unnatural love for a bull, establishes the hereditary taint in Phaedra's character.

HIPPOLYTUS.   Her empty hate is not what I fear.
Hippolytus, in leaving, flees another enemy.
I flee, I will admit it, that young Aricia,
Descendant of a fatal line conspiring against us.

THERAMENES.   What! Do you yourself, my lord, persecute her?
Did ever this sweet sister of the cruel Pallantides*
Have a hand in the schemes of her treacherous brothers?
Must you now hate her innocent charms?

HIPPOLYTUS.   If I hated her, I would not flee.

THERAMENES (after a pause).   My lord, may I be allowed to interpret
     your flight?
Could it be you are no more that proud Hippolytus,
Implacable enemy of the laws of love
And of the yoke that Theseus has so often worn?
Is Venus, so long disdained by your pride,
Trying in this to justify Theseus,
And by putting you on a level with other men
Has she forced you to burn incense on her altars?
    Would you be in love, my lord?

HIPPOLYTUS.   Friend, what are you saying?
You who have known my thoughts since I first took breath,
Can you ask me to disavow in shame
The feelings of a heart so proud, so disdainful?
Small wonder that an Amazon mother* should give
With her milk this pride which seems to astound you.
Indeed, with years and growing knowledge of myself,
I came to approve of what I saw in me.
    Attached to me by a sincere devotion,
You would tell me then the story of my father.
You know how my heart, attentive to your voice,
Warmed to hear the tale of his noble exploits,
When you painted for me this fearless hero
Consoling the mortals upon the absence of Alcides —*
The monsters destroyed and the brigands punished,
Procrustes,* Cercyon, and Sciron, and Sinis,
And the scattered bones of the giant of Epidaurus,*

Pallantides: the fifty brothers of Aricia (reduced to six by Racine) who were killed by their cousin Theseus, with whom they were rivals for the throne of Athens.

Amazon mother: Antiope, Hippolytus' mother by an earlier marriage of Theseus, had been queen of the Amazons, a warlike nation of women.

Alcides: another name for Hercules.

Procrustes, etc.: all Greek brigands, famous for their methods of torture, who were killed by Theseus.

Epidaurus: a town on the Aegean coast, the home of another of Theseus' victims.

And Crete smoking with the blood of the Minotaur.*
  But then you told of less glorious deeds:
His faith offered everywhere and everywhere received,
Helen* stolen from her parents in Sparta,
Salamis a witness to the tears of Peribea;*
So many more, whose names have escaped him,
Too credulous hearts that his love has deceived:
Ariadne* telling the rocks of her abandonment,
Phaedra, too, abducted, but to a happier end.*
  You know how, regretting to hear this talk,
I often pressed you to shorten your account;
Happy, had I been able to erase from memory
This shameful half of so fine a tale!
  Would I, in my turn, see myself bound by love?
And would the gods have so degraded me?
Unmanly sighs are all the more contemptible
Without the great deeds which can excuse the King;
For no monsters subdued by me as yet
Have given me the right to be as frail as he.
  Yet even had my resistance been softened,
Would I have chosen Aricia to be my conqueror?
Would not my wandering senses remember
The eternal obstacle which lies between us?
My father rejects her, and by severest laws
He forbids any heirs be given to her brothers,
For he fears an offspring of this guilty stock.
With their sister he wants to bury their name,
And never for her will wedding fires be lit
While yet she lives and still is in his care.
Should I espouse her rights against an angry father?
Shall I make a show of such temerity
And like a fool embark upon an insane love . . .
  THERAMENES.   My lord, though one's final hour be known above,
Still heaven ignores the reasons that guide our acts.
Theseus opens your eyes while wishing to close them,
And his hate, fanning in you a rebellious love,
Lends to his enemy one grace she did not have.

Minotaur: a monster — half man, half bull — shut up in the labyrinth of Crete, living off human sacrifices until killed by Theseus. The Minotaur was born of the union between Pasiphae and a bull and was thus the half-brother of Phaedra.

Helen: abducted by Theseus, later the wife of Menelaus, and eventually the cause of the Trojan War.

Peribea: abandoned by Theseus and later married to the king of Salamis.

Ariadne: Phaedra's sister, abandoned by Theseus on the Island of Naxos.

happier end: because Phaedra, at least, was legitimately married to Theseus.

So why be afraid of a love that is pure?
If its promise is sweet, do you not dare to taste it,
Or will you always maintain such a timorous scruple?
Do you fear being lost in the path of Hercules?*
What hearts has Venus not been known to master?
And where would you be, you who are fighting the goddess,
If Antiope,* like you, opposed to her laws,
Had not burned with a chaste love for Theseus?
    But what do you gain by affecting this proud talk?
Admit it; you are changed. And for some days
One sees you less often, arrogant and alone,
Now making a chariot fly along the shore,
Now, wise in the art invented by Neptune,*
Making docile a courser till then unbroken.
Today the forests echo less often to your cries.
Charged with an inner fire, your eyes are heavy.
There can be no doubt: you are in love, you burn;
You are dying from an ill which you would hide.
Has Aricia cast a spell and been able to please you?
    HIPPOLYTUS.   Theramenes, I am leaving and will search for my father.
    THERAMENES.   Will you see Phaedra before you go, my lord?
    HIPPOLYTUS.   Such is my plan. You may tell her of it.

(*Exit* THERAMENES.)

Let us see her, since thus my duty orders.

(*He sees* OENONE *entering.*)

    But what new distress troubles her dear Oenone?
    OENONE.   Alas, my lord, what trouble can equal mine?
The Queen has nearly reached her fated end,
And though I watch both night and day,
She dies in my arms of an ill that she conceals.
Some eternal disorder reigns within her soul.
Her uneasy grief takes her from her bed;
She wants to see the day; yet her deep sadness
Commands me ever to let her be alone . . .
    She comes.
    HIPPOLYTUS.   It is enough. I will leave her here
And will not show to her a hateful face.

(*Exit* HIPPOLYTUS *as* PHAEDRA *enters.*)

Hercules: Hercules was also noted as a woman-chaser.
Antiope: the mother of Hippolytus.
Neptune: though god of the sea, he also was responsible for introducing the
horse and horsemanship to the Greeks.

PHAEDRA.   Let us go no farther. Let us stop, dear Oenone.
I can hold up no more. My strength abandons me.
My eyes are blinded by the light I see again,
And my trembling knees give way beneath me. (*She sits.*)*
Alas!

OENONE.   Almighty gods, may our tears appease you!

PHAEDRA.   How these vain jewels, how these veils weigh upon me!
What meddling hand, in making all these knots,
Has thus arranged my hair upon my brow?
Everything overwhelms me and hurts me and conspires to hurt me.

OENONE.   Thus one sees how her wishes overrule one another!
You yourself, condemning your unjust resolve,
Urged on our hands to adorn you;
You yourself, remembering your earlier strength,
Wanted to show yourself and to see again the light.
You see it, Madam; and, ready now to hide,
You hate the day that you came out to find.

PHAEDRA (*looking toward the sun*).   Noble and brilliant father of a
          woeful family,
You whose daughter my mother was proud to be,
Who blush in shame at the trouble you see me in,
Sun,* I come to look on you for one last time.

OENONE.   What! You will not give up this cruel desire?
Shall I always see you, renouncing life,
Make dismal preparations for your death?

PHAEDRA.   Oh, gods! That I might be seated in the forest shade,
That I might, through a cloud of noble dust,
Follow with my eye a chariot coursing down the field!

OENONE.   What, Madam?

PHAEDRA.   I am mad. Where am I, and what have I said?
Where have I let wander my wishes — and my mind?
I have lost it; the gods have robbed me of its use.
Oenone, the blush of shame covers my face;
I let you see too well my miseries,
And my eyes, despite me, fill with tears.

OENONE.   Ah, if you must blush, blush for the silence
Which but aggravates the violence of your hurt.
Refusing all our aid, deaf to all our words,
Do you, without pity, want to end your days?
What madness cuts them short in the middle of their run?
What spell or what poison has dried up their source?
   Three times have the shadows darkened the heavens
Since sleep last entered upon your eyes;
And three times the day has chased away dark night

(**She sits**): the only stage direction given by Racine in the entire play.
Sun: Phaedra's mother, Pasiphae, was the daughter of Apollo, the sun god.

Since your body has languished without food.
By what frightful purpose are you tempted?
By what right do you lay hands upon yourself?
You offend the gods, the authors of your life;
You betray the husband to whom your promise binds you;
You betray, in the end, your own unhappy children,
Whom you thrust beneath a yoke of iron.
Consider that the same day will rob them of their mother
And give hope to the foreign woman's son,
To that implacable enemy of you and of your blood,
The son whom an Amazon has borne,
That Hippolytus . . .

    PHAEDRA.   Oh, gods!

    OENONE.   This reproach touches you.

    PHAEDRA.   Wretch, what name did your mouth utter?

    OENONE.   Well, your anger burst forth with good reason.
I like to see you tremble at this baleful name.
Live then. May love and duty bring you back to life.
Live. Do not let the son of a Scythian,*
Crushing your children beneath a hateful power,
Command the finest blood of Greece and of the gods.*
But do not delay. Each moment brings you nearer death.
Build up at once your weakened strength,
While still the torch of life endures
And, though nearly out, can yet be lit again.

    PHAEDRA.   I have made it burn too long, in guilt.

    OENONE.   What, do you feel torn by some remorse?
What crime has brought about such torment?
Can your hands be stained by innocent blood?

    PHAEDRA.   Thanks be to heaven, my hands bear no guilt.
If only my heart were as innocent as they!

    OENONE.   What awful project, then, have you begotten
That your heart should still be struck with terror?

    PHAEDRA.   I have said enough. Spare me the rest.
I die, to save myself so painful a confession.

    OENONE.   Die, then, and keep your inhuman silence;
But seek another hand to close your eyes.
Though you have but a spark of life within you,
My soul will be the first to go among the dead.
A thousand open roads lead always down,
And my just bitterness will find the shortest way.
    Cruel one, when has my devotion proved untrue?
Do you recall that my arms held you at your birth?

    Scythian: *i.e.*, an Amazon, Scythia being an area north of the Caspian Sea inhabited by the Amazons.
    of Greece and of the gods: Phaedra's sons have Theseus as a father and both Apollo and Jupiter as ultimate ancestors.

For you I left all — my native land, my children.
Is this the way to repay my loyalty?
   PHAEDRA.   What fruit do you want from so much argument?
You would tremble with horror should I break my silence.
   OENONE.   And what could you tell me that would equal
The horror of seeing you expire before my eyes?
   PHAEDRA.   When you know my crime and the fate which crushes me,
I shall die none the less, but I shall die more guilty yet.
   OENONE (*kneeling*).   Madam, in the name of the tears I have shed
      for you,
By your knees which I clasp to my heart,
Free my mind of this dreadful doubt.
   PHAEDRA.   You wish it. Rise.
   OENONE.   Speak. I listen to your words.
   PHAEDRA.   Heaven, what shall I say, and where do I begin?
   OENONE.   Offend me no more with these vain fears.
   PHAEDRA.   This is the fatal anger of Venus, and her hate!
To what madness my mother was driven by love!*
   OENONE.   Forget the past, Madam, and may to all posterity
An eternal silence hide this memory.
   PHAEDRA.   Ariadne, my sister, wounded too by such love,
You died on the shores where you were abandoned.
   OENONE.   What are you doing, Madam? And what torment
Stirs you against all your family today?
   PHAEDRA.   Since Venus wishes it, of this piteous line
I perish the last, the most wretched of all.
   OENONE.   Are you in love?
   PHAEDRA.   I know love in all its fury.
   OENONE.   For whom?
   PHAEDRA.   You are about to hear the ultimate horror.
I love . . . At this fatal name I tremble, I quake.
I love . . .
   OENONE.   Whom?
   PHAEDRA.   You know the son of the Amazon,
That prince whom so long I myself have oppressed?
   OENONE.   Hippolytus! Great gods!
   PHAEDRA.   It is you who have named him.
   OENONE.   Merciful heaven! My blood freezes in my veins.
The despair and crime that befall a cursed race!
That fated voyage* that led to this unhappy strand!
Did you need to come here to this dangerous shore?
   PHAEDRA.   My ill comes from further back. No sooner
Was I engaged by law to the son of Aegeus,
Than my repose, my happiness, seemed assured.

driven by love: Venus was responsible for Pasiphae's love of the bull.
fated voyage: the trip of Phaedra and Oenone to Troezen.

Then Athens showed me my proud enemy;
I saw him, I blushed, I paled at his sight.
A new emotion troubled my lost soul.
My eyes no longer saw; I could not speak;
I felt my whole body both burning and benumbed.
   In all this I saw Venus and her fearful fires,
Inevitable torments of the family she pursues — *
Torments I thought I could avoid by vows:
I built a temple to her and adorned it with care;
I surrounded myself with victims of sacrifice
And sought in their entrails my wandering mind.
   Powerless remedies for an incurable love!
In vain on the altars my hand burned the incense.
While to the name of the goddess my lips formed prayers,
I adored Hippolytus. And seeing him always,
Even at the foot of the altars that I caused to smoke,
I offered all to this god I dared not name.
   I avoided him everywhere; then, height of misery!
I found him again in the face of his father.
Against myself at last I dared revolt:
I inflamed my heart that I might persecute him.
To banish the enemy whom I worshiped
I assumed the ill-will of an unjust stepmother;
I urged his exile, and by my constant cries
Tore him from his father's arms and heart.
   I breathed at last, Oenone, and since his going,
My calmer days have flowed in innocence.
Submissive to my husband, and hiding my torment,
I nursed the fruit of this ill-fated marriage.*
   Vain precautions against a cruel destiny!
Brought to Troezen by my husband himself,
I saw again the enemy I had banished.
My wound, still too fresh, bled again.
It is no longer an ardor hidden in my veins;
It is Venus clutching tight her prey.
   I have conceived a just terror of my crime
And held my life in hate, my love in horror.
I wanted in death to preserve my honor
And to rob the day of so criminal a love.
   I could not withstand your tears and your arguments;
I have confessed all to you, nor do I repent it,
If only, respecting the nearness of my death,

---

   the family she pursues: Venus continues to punish Phaedra's family because it was Apollo who had revealed the secret of the love between the goddess and Mars.

   fruit of this ill-fated marriage: *i.e.,* her two sons by Theseus.

You no longer afflict me with unjust reproaches
And if you cease to preserve to no avail
The last bit of warmth on the point of vanishing.

(*Enter* PANOPE.)

PANOPE.   I wish that I could hide this tragic news,
Madam, but to you I must reveal it.
Death has robbed you of your invincible husband,
And this calamity is known to all but you.
    OENONE.   Panope, what did you say?
    PANOPE.   That the Queen, deluded,
In vain prays heaven for Theseus' return,
And that from the ships just arrived in port
Hippolytus, his son, has learned of his death.
    PHAEDRA.   Heaven!
    PANOPE.   For the choice of a master, Athens is divided.
Some give their vote to your son, Madam;
Others, forgetting the law of the state,
Dare give their voice to the son of the foreigner.
It is even said that one insolent group
Wants to put Aricia on the throne.
    I felt that I should warn you of this peril.
Hippolytus is about to leave, and it is feared
That if he should go to Athens in this unforeseen storm
He might carry with him a whole inconstant people.
    OENONE.   Panope, that is enough. The Queen, who hears you,
Will not neglect this important news.

(*Exit* PANOPE.)

    Madam, I had ceased urging you to live;
Already I expected to follow you to the tomb
And had no voice left to change your mind,
But this new misfortune prescribes new obligations.
Your situation changes and takes another face.
The King is no more, Madam. You must take his place.
His death leaves you a son to whom you owe yourself:
A slave if he loses you, a king if you live.
On whom, in his grief, do you want him to lean?
His tears will have no hand to wipe them away;
And his innocent cries, rising to the gods,
Will turn his ancestors against his mother.
    Live. You need reproach yourself no more.
Your love has become an ordinary love.
Theseus in dying has just undone the knots

Which made all the crime and horror of your passion.
Hippolytus becomes for you less dangerous,
And you can see him now with no trace of guilt.
    Perhaps, convinced of your aversion,
He plans to serve as leader to sedition.
Correct his error. Change his heart and mind.
As king of these happy shores, Troezen is his portion,
But he knows that the laws give to your son
The proud ramparts which Minerva built.*
You have, both of you, a legitimate enemy:
Unite, both of you, to fight Aricia.

    PHAEDRA.   Very well, by your counsel I will let myself be led.
Let us live, if I can be brought to life,
And if the love of a son at this dismal time
Can awaken my feeble spirits once again.

ACT TWO

(*Enter* ARICIA *and* ISMENE.)

    ARICIA.   Hippolytus asks to see me in this place?
Hippolytus seeks me and wants to say farewell?
Ismene, is this true? You are not mistaken?

    ISMENE.   This is the first effect of Theseus' death.
Prepare yourself, Madam, to see on every side
Men turn to you who were held off by Theseus.
Aricia at last is mistress of her days.
And soon at her feet she will see all Greece.

    ARICIA.   This is not, Ismene, an unfounded tale?
I am no more a slave and have no enemies?

    ISMENE.   No, Madam, the gods no longer are opposed to you,
And Theseus has joined the ghosts of your brothers.

    ARICIA.   Do they say what accident has ended his days?

    ISMENE.   Unbelievable stories are told of his death.
They say that as the ravisher of his newest love,
This faithless husband was swallowed by the seas.
They say too — and this account is widely spread —
That with Pirithous* he descended into hell,
Where he saw the Cocytus* and its shadowy banks
And showed himself alive among the infernal shades,
But that he could not return from those gloomy parts
And recross the border that can be crossed but once.

    ramparts which Minerva built: *i.e.,* Athens.
    Pirithous: king of the Lapithae, who was thought to have gone to Hades with his friend Theseus to abduct Persephone.
    Cocytus: a river of Hades.

ARICIA.   Shall I believe that a mortal, before his final hour,
Can descend early to the abode of the dead?
What spell drew him to those fearful shores?

ISMENE.   Theseus is dead, Madam, and you alone still doubt.
Athens already mourns, Troezen has heard the news
And recognizes Hippolytus for king.
Phaedra in this palace, fearful for her son,
Asks counsel of her troubled friends.

ARICIA.   And you think that Hippolytus, more human than his father,
Will lighten the burden of my chains,
That he will have pity on my misfortune?

ISMENE.   Madam, I do believe it.

ARICIA.   Do you really know the insensitive Hippolytus?
By what foolish hope do you believe he pities me
And respects in me alone a sex which he disdains?
You can see for how long he has avoided our path
And has sought only those places where we cannot be found.

ISMENE.   I know all that has been said of his coldness.
But I have seen this proud Hippolytus beside you,
And even as I looked, the fame of his aloofness
Redoubled my curiosity. And yet his aspect
Agreed in no way with the stories that they tell.
At your first glance upon him, I saw he was troubled.
His eyes, already languishing, tried to avoid you,
But in vain; they could not turn away.
The name of lover perhaps wounds his pride;
But he has a lover's eyes, though he lack the words.

ARICIA.   How my heart, dear Ismene, listens eagerly
To a tale that may have little base!
You who know me, can you believe
That this sad plaything of a pitiless fate,
This heart ever nourished on bitterness and tears,
Should know love and all its foolish pain?
Descendant of a king, noble son of the Earth,*
I alone escaped from the fury of war.
I lost, in the flower of their youth, six brothers —
They were the hope of an illustrious house.
The sword reaped all, and the dampened ground
Drank with regret* the blood of Erechtheus' heirs.
You know, since their death, by what stern laws
All Greeks are forbidden to show pity for me.
It is feared that the sister's rash flame of love
May bring to life the ashes of her brothers.
But you know too with what disdainful eye

son of the Earth: Aricia is a descendant in a direct line from the Earth, through
his son Erechtheus.
Drank with regret: because the Pallantides were descended from the Earth.

I looked on the concern of the distrustful King.
You know that, always contemptuous of love,
I often forgave the unjust Theseus,
Whose harshness seconded my scorn.
   At that time my eyes had not yet seen his son.
Not that by my eyes alone, shamefully bewitched,
Do I love his beauty and his much-praised grace,
Gifts that nature has freely accorded him,
Which he scorns and of which he seems unaware.
I love, I prize in him, more noble wealth:
The virtues of his father, but not the weaknesses.
I love, I will confess, that splendid pride
Which never has submitted to the yoke of love.
   Phaedra thinks herself honored by the sighs of Theseus.
As for me, I am more proud and flee the easy glory
Of winning an homage offered to a thousand more
And of entering a heart open on every side.
But to sway a will till then inflexible,
To bring pain to an insensitive soul,
To enchain a captive, amazed to be in irons,
Revolting in vain against a pleasing yoke:
That is what I want; that is what excites me.
   Hercules was easier to disarm than Hippolytus
And, vanquished more often* and sooner overcome,
Brought less renown to those who subdued him.
   But, dear Ismene, alas, what rash hope is mine!
I can meet with nothing but his too great resistance.
You may someday hear me, humble in my pain,
Bemoaning the same pride which I admire today.
Can Hippolytus love? By what good fortune
Could I have swayed . . .
   ISMENE.   You will hear him speak himself.
He comes to you.

   (*Enter* HIPPOLYTUS.)

HIPPOLYTUS.   Madam, before I leave,
I felt that I should speak of what awaits you.
My father no longer lives. My well-founded fears
Foretold the reason for his too-long absence:
Death alone, putting an end to his brilliant deeds,
Could hide him from the universe so long.
At last the gods surrender to the deadly Fates*
The friend, the companion, the successor to Alcides.

   vanquished more often: *i.e.*, by love.
   Fates: the three goddesses of destiny and death.

(Surely even your hate, admitting his virtues,
Listens without distaste to these names that are his due.)
  One hope lightens my deathly grief:
I can free you from a strict surveillance;
I revoke the laws whose harshness I deplored;
You are mistress of yourself and of your heart.
And in this Troezen, which now belongs to me,
Once the heritage of my forefather Pittheus,*
And which, without debate, has named me king,
I leave you free, and more free than I.
  ARICIA.   Restrain your goodness, whose excess confounds me.
To honor my misfortune with such generous care
Is to place me, my lord, more than you think,
Under as severe laws as those from which you free me.
  HIPPOLYTUS.   In the choice of a successor, uncertain Athens
Speaks of you, of me, of the son of the Queen.
  ARICIA.   Of me, my lord?
  HIPPOLYTUS.   I know, without wishing to deceive myself,
That an insolent law appears to reject me:
Greece reproaches me my foreign mother.
But if as a rival I had only my brother,
I could well save from capricious laws
Certain genuine rights that I have over him.
  A more legitimate brake puts a stop to my daring:
I cede to you, or rather I return, a place
And sceptre received of old by your forebears
From that famous mortal* conceived by the Earth.
Adoption put them in Aegeus' hands.*
Later Athens, enhanced and protected by my father,
Recognized with joy so noble a king
And left your unhappy brothers to forgetfulness.
  Now Athens calls you back within her walls.
She has suffered enough from a lengthy quarrel,
And long enough has the blood of your family
Made the fields smoke from which they came.
  Troezen obeys me. The countryside of Crete
Offers a rich retreat to the son of Phaedra.
Attica is yours. I go and will unite for you
All the voices now divided between us.
  ARICIA.   Of all that I hear, astonished and confused,
I almost fear, I do fear a dream deceives me.

Pittheus: the maternal grandfather of Theseus, founder of Troezen.
famous mortal: Erechtheus.
Adoption put them in Aegeus' hands: Aegeus, the father of Theseus, and
Pallas, the father of Aricia, were both sons of Pandion, king of Athens. But
Aegeus was only an adopted son, whereas Pallas was legitimate. Thus Aricia's
claim to the throne of Athens is valid.

Am I awake? Can I believe that such a plan is true?
What god, my lord, has put it in your heart?
How right that your fame is spread afar,
And yet the truth surpasses reputation!
  In my favor do you really give over your claim?
Was it not enough that you should not hate me
And that for so long you could preserve your soul
From that enmity . . .
  HIPPOLYTUS.   I hate you, Madam?
In whatever light my pride may have been painted,
Can one believe a monster gave me birth?
What savage ways, what hardened hate
Could not be softened merely by seeing you?
Could I resist the delusive charm . . .
  ARICIA.   What, my lord?
  HIPPOLYTUS.   I have gone too far.
I see that reason yields to the violence of love.
  But since I have now begun to break my silence,
Madam, I must go on. I must inform you
Of a secret my heart no longer can contain.
  You see before you a pitiful prince,
An enduring example of a presumptuous pride.
I have been haughtily rebellious against love,
Have long jeered at the irons of her captives,
And, deploring the shipwreck of weaker men,
Hoped always to watch the storms from shore.
  But now, enslaved by the common law,
By what passion I see myself carried away!
One moment has vanquished my rash audacity;
My arrogant soul is at last dependent.
For nearly six months, ashamed and in despair,
Bearing everywhere the arrow by which I am torn,
I have contended in vain against you, against myself.
With you present, I flee; absent, I find you.
In the depths of the forest your image follows me.
The light of the day, the shades of the night,
Everything retraces for my eyes the charms that I avoid.
Everything vies to deliver the rebel Hippolytus to you.
And as the only fruit of all my useless efforts,
I search now for myself but can no longer find me.
My bow, my javelins, my chariot, all annoy me;
I no longer remember the lessons of Neptune;*
Only my groans reecho in the woods,
And my idle coursers have forgotten my voice.
  Perhaps the tale of a love so unrestrained

lessons of Neptune: *i.e.*, horsemanship.

Makes you blush in shame at the work you have done.
And what uncouth speech to offer you a heart!
What a strange captive for so fair a bond!
Yet the offer, to your eyes, should be the more precious.
Remember that I speak a language strange to me;
So do not reject these vows, badly expressed,
Which Hippolytus without you would never have made.

(*Enter* THERAMENES.)

THERAMENES.   My lord, the Queen comes, and I have come ahead.
She seeks you.
    HIPPOLYTUS.   Me?
    THERAMENES.   I do not know her thought,
But you are being asked for in her behalf.
Phaedra wants to speak to you before your leaving.
    HIPPOLYTUS.   Phaedra? What can I say to her? And what can she
        expect?
    ARICIA.   My lord, you cannot refuse to hear her.
Though you are too convinced of her ill-feeling,
You owe to her tears some shadow of pity.
    HIPPOLYTUS (*to* ARICIA).   Meanwhile you go. And I am leaving. And
        I do not know
If I offend the charms which I adore!
I do not know if the heart I leave in your hands . . .
    ARICIA.   Go, Prince, and follow your generous designs.
Make Athens submissive to my power.
I accept all the gifts that you offer me.
But this empire, after all so great, so glorious,
Is not of your gifts the dearest to my eyes.

(*Exeunt* ARICIA *and* ISMENE.)

HIPPOLYTUS.   Friend, are you ready? But the Queen comes near.
Go, that all for our departure be prepared in haste.
Have the signal given, run, order, and return
To deliver me soon from this unwelcome talk.

(*Exit* THERAMENES *as* PHAEDRA *and* OENONE *enter.*)

PHAEDRA.   Here he is. All my blood flows back to my heart.
I forget, in seeing him, what I came to say.
    OENONE.   Remember a son who has hope but in you.
    PHAEDRA (*to* HIPPOLYTUS).   They say a quick departure takes you
        from us,
My lord. To your grief I come to join my tears.

And I come to expose my fears for a son.
My son has now no father, and the day is not far
That will make him witness to my death besides.
Already a thousand enemies attack him in his youth.
You alone can take up his defense against them.
But a secret remorse troubles my spirit.
I fear I have closed your ear to his cries.
I tremble lest your rightful anger
Against his hateful mother should fall on him.

HIPPOLYTUS.   Madam, I have no thoughts so base as that.

PHAEDRA.   If you should hate me, I would not complain,
My lord. You have seen me striving to hurt you,
And could not read in the depths of my heart.
I have taken pains to expose myself to your enmity.
I could not permit you on the shores where I lived.
Declaring myself against you in public and alone,
I tried to put the seas between us.
I even forbade, by a special law,
That anyone utter your name before me.
If, however, the pain be measured by the offense,
If only hate can bring about your hate,
Then never was woman more deserving of pity,
And less deserving, my lord, of your enmity.

HIPPOLYTUS.   For the rights of her children a jealous mother
Rarely forgives the son of another wife.
Madam, I know this. Harassing suspicions
Are the most common fruits of a second marriage.
Anyone else would have taken the same offense.
And I might have suffered more outrages yet.

PHAEDRA.   Ah, my lord, here I dare attest that heaven
Has excepted me from that common law,
That a very different care troubles and consumes me!

HIPPOLYTUS.   Madam, this is not the time still to torment yourself.
Perhaps your husband yet sees the light of day.
Heaven may answer our tears and accord his return.
Neptune protects him, and this guardian god
Will not be implored in vain by my father.

PHAEDRA.   No one sees twice the shores of the dead,
My lord. Since Theseus has seen that sombre place,
You hope in vain a god will send him back to you.
And the miserly Acheron does not loose its prey.
    What am I saying? He is not dead, for he breathes in you.
Still before my eyes I think I see my husband.
I see him, I speak to him, and my heart . . . I wander.
My lord, my insane passion declares itself despite me.

HIPPOLYTUS.   I see the marvelous effect of your love.

Dead though he is, Theseus is present to your eyes;
Your soul is still afire with love of him.

  PHAEDRA.   Yes, Prince, I languish, I burn for Theseus.
I love him, but not as he is seen in hell —
Inconstant lover of a thousand women,
Gone to dishonor the couch of the god of the dead — *
But faithful, but proud, and even a little shy,
Charming, young, trailing all hearts behind him,
Such as our gods are painted — or such as I see you.
He had your bearing, your eyes, your speech;
The same noble modesty colored his face
When he crossed the waters of our Crete,
Well deserving the love of the daughters of Minos.*
    What were you doing then? Why, without Hippolytus,
Did he assemble the elite of the heroes of Greece?
Why could you not then, though still too young,
Board the ship which put him on our shores?
Through you, the monster of Crete* would have perished,
Despite all the turnings of his endless lair.
To lead you in safety through the bewildering maze
My sister would have armed you with the fateful thread.*
    But no, I would have acted before her in this plan;
Love would first have given the thought to me.
It is I, Prince, it is I whose useful aid
Would have taught you the turnings of the Labyrinth.
What care that charming head would then have cost me!
A thread would not have made your lover sure enough.
Companion in the peril which you had to seek,
I myself before you would have wished to walk;
And Phaedra, gone down with you into the Labyrinth,
With you would have been saved or lost.

  HIPPOLYTUS.   Gods! What do I hear? Madam, do you forget
That Theseus is my father, and that he is your husband?

  PHAEDRA.   And what makes you think that I have lost this memory,
Prince? Have I abandoned all concern for my name?

  HIPPOLYTUS.   Madam, pardon me, I admit, blushing,
That I misunderstood an innocent speech.
My shame forbids me to look upon you;
And I go . . .

  PHAEDRA.   Oh, cruel one, you understood me too well.

  god of the dead: Theseus was said to have gone to Hades with Pirithous to
abduct Persephone, wife of Pluto.
    daughters of Minos: Ariadne and Phaedra.
    monster of Crete: the Minotaur.
    fateful thread: Ariadne had given Theseus a thread to enable him to find his
way out of the labyrinth after killing the Minotaur.

I have told you enough for you to see the truth.
So now you know Phaedra and all of her passion.
I love. Think not that at the moment when I love you,
I approve of myself, innocent in my own eyes,
Nor that an easy complaisance has strengthened the poison
Of the mad love that troubles my reason.
The ill-fated object of a heavenly vengeance,
I abhor myself more even than you detest me.
The gods are my witness, those gods who in my breast
Kindled the fatal fire of all my line,
Those gods who have taken a cruel pride
In leading astray the heart of a feeble woman.
    You, in your own mind, recall the past.
To shun you was not enough; I drove you away.
I wanted to seem odious to you, inhuman;
The better to resist you, I sought your hate.
But how did my vain efforts bring me any gain?
You hated me more; I loved you no less.
Your misfortunes but lent you more and newer charms.
I languished and was consumed, by flames and by tears.
You need only your eyes to be convinced,
If for a moment your eyes could look at me.
    What am I saying? This avowal I have made,
This so shameful avowal, do you think that I willed it?
Trembling for a son whom I dared not fail,
I came to beg you not to hate him.
Futile hope of a heart too full of what it loves!
Alas, I could speak to you only of yourself.
    Avenge yourself, punish me for an odious love.
Worthy son of the hero who gave you life,
Deliver the universe from a monster that offends you.
The widow of Theseus dares to love his son!
    Believe me, this awful monster must not escape you.
Here is my heart. Here your hand must strike.
Impatient already to expiate its offense,
I feel it advance as if to meet your arm.
Strike! Or if you think it unworthy of your blows,
If your hate refuse me so mild a punishment,
Or if your hand would be dipped in blood too vile,
Stay your arm, but lend me your sword.
Give me it! (*She pulls his sword from its scabbard.*)
    OENONE (*rushing to* PHAEDRA *and seizing the sword*).   What are you
        doing, Madam? Merciful gods!
But someone comes. Avoid a hateful witness.
Come, go in, flee certain shame.

(*Exeunt* PHAEDRA *and* OENONE *as* THERAMENES *enters.*)

THERAMENES.   Is that Phaedra who flees, or rather is dragged away?
Why, my lord, why these marks of grief?
I see you without your sword, abashed and pale.
    HIPPOLYTUS.   Theramenes, let us escape. My surprise has overwhelmed
    me.
I cannot without horror look upon myself.
Phaedra . . . But no, may this horrible secret
Lie buried forever in deep forgetfulness.
    THERAMENES.   If you wish to leave, the ship is set to sail.
But Athens, my lord, has already declared itself.
Its chiefs have heard the votes of all its tribes.
Your brother has won, and Phaedra has the upper hand.
    HIPPOLYTUS.   Phaedra?
    THERAMENES.   A herald, charged with the will of Athens,
Has just put in her hands the reins of the State.
Her son is king, my lord.
    HIPPOLYTUS.   Gods, you who know her,
Is it then her virtue you are rewarding?
    THERAMENES.   However, a secret rumor says the King still lives.
They claim that Theseus has appeared in Epirus.
But I, who searched for him, my lord, I know too well . . .
    HIPPOLYTUS.   No matter, let us hear all and neglect nothing.
Let us examine this rumor; let us go to the source.
If it does not deserve to delay my going,
Then let us leave and at whatever price
Place the sceptre in hands that are worthy of holding it.*

ACT THREE

(*Enter* PHAEDRA *and* OENONE.)

    PHAEDRA.   Oh, take away these honors* that are sent me!
How can you hope that I should show myself?
Why do you try to calm my tormented mind?
Hide me well, instead, for I have spoken but too much.
The transports of my madness have been spread abroad;
I have said what one should never hear.
Heaven, how he listened to me! And by what detours
He tried, unfeeling, to elude my words!
How he hoped for nothing but a quick escape,
And how his shame did but increase my own!
Why did you turn me from my fatal plan?
Alas, when I held his sword against my breast,

---

hands that are worthy of holding it: *i.e.*, in the hands of Aricia.
take away these honors: sent by Athens to the mother of the new king.

Did he pale for me? Did he snatch it away?
It was enough that I should touch it once
To make it horrible to his inhuman eyes;
That steel thereafter would profane his hands.

    OENONE.   Thus in your misery, thinking only of your woes,
You nourish a flame that you had best put out.
Is it not better, worthy daughter of Minos,
To seek your repose in more noble concerns
And, in place of the ingrate who resorts to flight,
To reign and to direct the affairs of state?

    PHAEDRA.   I, reign! I, bring a state under my law,
When my feeble reason rules me no more!
When I have abandoned control of my senses!
When under a yoke of shame I barely breathe!
When I am dying!

    OENONE.   Then flee!

    PHAEDRA.   I cannot leave him.

    OENONE.   You dared to banish him, yet dare not go away!

    PHAEDRA.   It is too late. He knows of my mad love.
The limits of strict modesty are passed;
I have revealed my shame to the eyes of my conqueror,
And hope, despite me, has crept into my heart.
You yourself, calling back my waning strength
And my breath, already hovering on my lips,
By your deceiving counsel made me live again.
You made me glimpse the truth that I could love him.

    OENONE.   Alas, whether innocent or guilty of your misfortune,
What would I not have done to save you?
But if ever an offense angered your spirit,
Can you forget the scorn of an arrogant man?
With what cruel eyes his stubborn indifference
Left you nearly prostrate at his feet.
How odious he was in his savage pride!
Why, at that moment, could Phaedra not have my eyes?

    PHAEDRA.   Oenone, he may abandon this pride that hurts you.
He was reared in the forests, and so he is uncouth,
And, hardened by savage ways, Hippolytus
Hears talk of love for the first time.
Perhaps his silence was due to his surprise,
And perhaps our complaints have been too severe.

    OENONE.   Remember that a barbarian formed him in her womb.

    PHAEDRA.   Though a barbarian and a Scythian, still she loved.

    OENONE.   He has for all the sex a hate that is his destiny.

    PHAEDRA.   I shall then see no rival preferred to me.
So all of your counsels are now out of place.
Serve my madness, Oenone, and not my reason.
    Since to love he shows an inaccessible heart,

Let us hunt a more sensitive spot to attack.
The charms of an empire seemed to affect him.
Athens attracted him; he could not hide the fact.
Already his ships had turned their prows that way,
And the sails floated free in the wind.

  Go find for me this young ambitious man,
Oenone; make the crown shine before his eyes.
On his brow must be placed the sacred diadem;
I want only the honor of fixing it there myself.
Let us give him this power that I can hold no more.
He will instruct my son in the art of command
And may perhaps be willing to play a father's role.
In his power I place both son and mother.

  Try any means, indeed, to sway him.
Your words will be received more readily than mine.
Press him, weep, wail; bemoan a dying Phaedra.
Do not be ashamed to take a pleading voice.
I will approve all you do; in you lies my only hope.
Go. I await your return, that I may live or die.

    (*Exit* OENONE.)

  Oh you, who see the shame to which I have come,
Implacable Venus, am I humbled enough?
You cannot further push your cruelty.
Your triumph is complete; your every shaft has carried.
  Cruel goddess, if you wish more glory yet,
Attack an enemy who is more rebellious to you.
Hippolytus flees from you, and, braving your wrath,
Never has bent his knee before your altars.
Your name seems to offend his proud ears.
Goddess, avenge yourself. Our cause is the same.
May he love . . .

    (*Enter* OENONE.)

  But already you return, Oenone?
He hates me; he will not listen.
  OENONE.   You must give up all thought of this fruitless love,
Madam. Remember your past virtue.
The King, thought dead, will appear before your eyes.
Theseus has arrived. Theseus is in this place.
To see him, the people rush headlong.
I was going, at your command, to seek Hippolytus,
When a thousand cries burst forth toward heaven . . .
  PHAEDRA.   My husband lives, Oenone; that is enough.
I have confessed in shame a love that wrongs him.
He lives. I want to know no more.

OENONE.   What?

PHAEDRA.   I had foretold it; but you would not believe.
Your tears prevailed over my rightful remorse.
I might have died this morning, worthy to be mourned.
I followed your counsel; and I die dishonored.

OENONE.   You die?

PHAEDRA.   Just heaven! What have I done today?
My husband will appear, and with him his son.
I will see the witness of my adulterous love
Watch in what fashion I dare approach his father,
My heart full of sighs which he would not hear,
My eyes wet with tears which he cruelly rebuffed.
Do you think, sensitive as he is to the honor of Theseus,
That he will hide from him the love which enflames me?
Will he let his father be betrayed, and his king?
Can he restrain the horror he feels for me?
Even his silence would be in vain. I know my guilt,
Oenone, and am not of those brazen women
Who, enjoying calm peace even in their crime,
Can prepare a brow which never shows a blush.
I know my passions; I recall them, every one.
Even now I feel these walls and these arches
Are about to speak and, ready to accuse me,
Wait only for my husband, that they may tell him all.
Let me die, that death deliver me from so much horror.
Is the end of life so great a calamity?
Death holds no terror for those who are wretched.
I fear only the name that I shall leave behind —
What a frightful heritage for my unhappy sons!
The blood of Jupiter* must strengthen their hearts;
But whatever just pride this lineage inspires,
The crime of a mother is a heavy load.
I tremble lest talk, alas too true,
May someday reproach them for a guilty mother.
I tremble lest, weighted down by this hateful burden,
Neither will dare to raise his eyes again.

OENONE.   You must not doubt that I pity them both;
And never was fear better founded than yours.
But why must you expose them to such affronts?
Why must you stand as witness against yourself?
If you do this, they will say that the guilty Phaedra
Flees the fearful sight of a husband she has wronged.
Hippolytus is happy that, at the cost of your life,
You support, by dying, the charges that he makes.
What then could I answer to him who accuses you?

Jupiter: through Minos, her two sons are descended from Jupiter.

Too easily before him would I be rendered silent.
In his awful triumph I can see him rejoice
And tell of your shame to whoever wants to hear.
Ah, may rather the fire of heaven consume me!
    But do not deceive me. Is he still dear to you?
With what eye do you look upon that audacious prince?
    PHAEDRA.   I see him as a monster, frightful to my eyes.
    OENONE.   Why then concede to him a full victory?
You fear him. Dare to accuse him first
Of the crime with which he may charge you today.
What will belie you? Everything speaks against him:
His sword, happily left in your own hands,
Your present agitation, your anger in the past,
His father warned against him by your cries,
And his exile, which you yourself obtained.
    PHAEDRA.   Am I then to crush and blacken innocence?
    OENONE.   My zeal needs nothing but your silence,
Though, trembling like you, I too feel some remorse.
You would see me meet more readily a thousand deaths.
But since I would lose you, without this painful cure,
Everything yields before the value of your life.
I will speak.
    Theseus, embittered by what I tell him,
Will limit his vengeance to the exile of his son.
A punishing father, Madam, is still a father;
A light penalty is all his wrath demands.
But even should innocent blood be spilled,
What is too much when your honor is at stake?
It is too dear a treasure to risk a compromise.
Whatever law it imposes, you must submit,
Madam, and to save your embattled honor,
You must sacrifice all, even virtue itself.
    Someone comes. I see Theseus.
    PHAEDRA.   Ah, I see Hippolytus.
In his insolent eyes, I can see my ruin written.
(*To* OENONE.) Do what you wish; I surrender to your will.
In my present turmoil, I can do nothing for myself.

(*Enter* THESEUS *and* HIPPOLYTUS, *separately.*)

    THESEUS.   Fortune no longer runs counter to my hopes,
Madam, and puts within your arms . . .
    PHAEDRA.   Stop, Theseus,
And do not profane such pleasing raptures,
For I deserve no more this tender show of feeling.
You have been wronged. In your absence
Jealous fortune has not spared your wife.

Unworthy to please you or even to come near,
I must henceforth think only of hiding myself. (*Exit.*)

THESEUS. What is this strange welcome given to your father,
My son?

HIPPOLYTUS. Phaedra alone can explain this mystery.
But if my earnest wishes can move you,
Allow me, my lord, to see her no more.
Permit this shaken Hippolytus forever
To quit those regions where Phaedra lives.

THESEUS. You will leave me, my son?

HIPPOLYTUS. I did not seek her out;
It is you who led her to these shores.
It was your wish, my lord, in the land of Troezen
To leave in trust Aricia and the Queen,
And I was given the duty of guarding them.
But what duty now can hold me here?

Long enough in the forests has my idle youth
Shown its skill against lowly enemies.
May I not flee this unworthy repose
And color my lance in more noble blood?
You had not yet reached my present age
When your arm had already felt the weight
Of more than one tyrant, one ferocious beast.
Already the favored persecutor of oppression,
You had made safe the shores of the two seas;*
The free voyager feared no further outrage.
Already Hercules, hearing the fame of your blows,
Could rest from his labors and put his faith in you.
And I, the unknown son of a glorious father,
I am still far from even my mother's steps.
Allow my courage at last to find a goal,
And if ever some monster was able to escape you,
Let me lay at your feet his worthy hide.
Or let the lasting memory of a beautiful death,
Immortalizing my days so nobly ended,
Prove to the universe that I was your son.

THESEUS. What do I see? What horror, spread about this place,
Makes my distracted family flee before my eyes?
If I return so feared, so little wanted,
Why, heaven, did you free me from my prison?
I had but one friend.* His unwise passion
Ravished the wife of the tyrant of Epirus.*

two seas: the Ionian and the Aegean Seas.
I had but one friend: Pirithous.
tyrant of Epirus: As Racine points out in his preface, Theseus accompanied
Pirithous to Epirus, not to Hades.

To my sorrow I served his amorous designs;
But angered fate blinded the two of us.
The tyrant surprised me without defense, without arms;
I saw Pirithoüs, unhappy object of my tears,
Thrown by the barbarian to cruel monsters
Which feed on the blood of unlucky mortals.
As for me, he shut me in sombre caves,
Deep regions near the kingdom of the dead.
The gods, six months after, at last remembered me,
And I deceived the eyes by which I was guarded.
I purged nature of a perfidious enemy;
To his own monsters he served as fodder.
　　And when with joy I think I am returning
To what the gods have left that was dearest to me —
When my soul, delivered to itself again,
Comes to feast upon so dear a sight,
I meet only trembling by way of welcome.
All flee; all refuse my embrace.
And I myself, feeling the terror I inspire,
Could wish to be again in the prisons of Epirus.
　　Speak. Phaedra complains that I am wronged.
Who has betrayed me? Why am I not avenged?
Has Greece, to whom my arm has so often been of aid,
Accorded some asylum to the criminal?
You do not answer me. My son, my own son,
Is he in collusion with my enemies?
　　I will go in. It is clinging to a doubt that crushes me.
I will learn at one time both the crime and the guilty one;
Let Phaedra explain at last the distress I see in her. (*Exit.*)
　　hippolytus.　What did those words mean,* which chilled me with
　　　　fear?
Does Phaedra, still a prey to her wild madness,
Want to accuse herself and bring herself to ruin?
Gods, what will the King say? What mortal poison
Love has spread throughout his house!
　　Myself, full of a fire which he condemns —
How he looked upon me once, and how he finds me now!
　　Black forebodings come to frighten me.
But innocence, after all, has nothing to fear.
Come, let us seek elsewhere by what happy means
I can move my father to tenderness
And tell him of a love he may wish to change
But which he, with all his power, can never shake.

what did those words mean: *i.e.,* Phaedra's last speech.

ACT FOUR

(*Enter* THESEUS *and* OENONE.)

THESEUS.   Ah, what is this I hear? A brazen traitor
Planned this outrage against the honor of his father?
With what harshness you pursue me, destiny!
I know not where I am going, I know not where I am.
Oh, tenderness and goodness too ill rewarded!
Audacious scheme! Detestable thought!
    To achieve the goal of his black love
The shameless wretch made use of force.
I recognized the sword, the weapon of his fury,
That steel with which I armed him for a nobler cause.
Could no ties of blood hold him in check?
And did Phaedra defer his punishment?
Did Phaedra's silence spare the guilty one?
    OENONE.   Phaedra spared instead a pitiful father.
Shamed by the scheme of a lover lost to passion
And by the criminal fire that burned within him,
Phaedra was about to die, and her murderous hand
Would have extinguished the innocent light in her eyes.
I saw her lifted arm. I ran to save her.
I alone preserved her for your love,
And bemoaning at once her trouble and your alarm,
I came, despite me, to interpret her tears.
    THESEUS.   False-hearted son! He could not keep from paling.
I saw him shudder from fear at meeting me
And was amazed to see his lack of joy;
His cold embrace froze my tenderness.
    But this guilty love by which he is devoured,
Had it already been declared in Athens?
    OENONE.   My lord, remember the complaint of the Queen.
A criminal love was cause of all her hate.
    THESEUS.   And this passion then began anew in Troezen?
    OENONE.   I have told you, my lord, all that has occurred.
But the Queen is left too long in her mortal grief;
Allow me to leave you, to be nearer to her. (*Exit.*)
    THESEUS (*alone, seeing* HIPPOLYTUS *approach*).   Ah, here he is. Great
        gods, at this noble bearing,
What eye would not have been deceived like mine?
Must it be that the sacred mark of virtue
Can shine on the brow of a profane adulterer?
Should one not be able, by positive signs,
To recognize the heart of perfidious mortals?

(*Enter* HIPPOLYTUS.)

HIPPOLYTUS. May I ask what gloomy cloud, my lord,
Has come to trouble your august brow?
Dare you not confide in me the secret?
　　THESEUS. Traitor! Can you really show yourself before me?
Monster, whom the thunder-bolts too long have spared,
Foul remnant of the brigands of whom I purged the earth!
After the transports of horror-tainted love
Have brought their madness to your father's bed,
You dare to show your hateful self to me;
You appear in a place you have filled with infamy,
And you do not seek, under an unknown sky,
Some land where my name has not yet reached!
　　Fly, traitor. Do not come here to defy my hate
And tempt a wrath that I can scarcely hold.
It is enough for me to earn the eternal disgrace
Of having given life to so treacherous a son,
Without having your death, shameful blot on my name,
Defile the glory of my noble deeds.
　　Fly; and if you do not wish a sudden punishment
To add your name to those my hand has scourged,
Take care that the sun which gives us light
May never see you set your rash foot here.
Fly, I say, with speed and no return.
Let none of my States see your countenance again.
　　And Neptune, remember — when through my courage
Your shores were cleansed of foul assassins —
Remember that to reward my successful efforts
You promised to grant the first of my wishes.
Through all the long hardship of a cruel prison
I did not ask aid of your immortal power.
Miserly of the help that I await from you,
I have saved my wishes for some greater need.
I implore you today. Avenge an unhappy father.
Now I abandon this traitor to your wrath.
Smother in his blood his shameless desires.
By your fury will Theseus know your goodness.
　　HIPPOLYTUS. Phaedra accuses me of a criminal love!
Such an excess of horror strikes my soul dumb;
So many unforeseen blows crush me at one time
That they steal my speech and choke my voice.
　　THESEUS. Traitor, you assumed that in cowardly silence
Phaedra would bury your brutal insolence,
But in fleeing, you should not have abandoned
The sword that in her hands helps to condemn you.
Or rather, at one blow, adding to your treachery,
You should have robbed her of both speech and life.

HIPPOLYTUS.   Justly angered by so black a lie,
I should here let truth speak out, my lord,
But I suppress a secret touching you.
Be pleased with the respect which seals my lips,
And without seeking to add to your own grief,
Examine my life, and think of what I am.
Crimes must always come before great crimes.
Whoever has crossed the borders fixed by law
May in the end violate the most sacred rights.
But like virtue itself, crime has its degrees,
And never has timid innocence been seen
To pass abruptly to the extremes of license.
A single day does not turn a virtuous mortal
Into a false-hearted murderer, an incestuous coward.
Reared at the bosom of a virtuous woman,
I have not been untrue to her divine origin;*
And Pittheus,* considered a sage among all men,
Deigned to instruct me when I left her care.
I do not wish to paint myself with vanity;
But if some virtue has fallen to my share,
I believe I have above all displayed
The hate of those crimes imputed to me.
It is thus that I am known in Greece.
I have pushed virtue to the point of bluntness.
You know the inflexible rigor of my mind,
Nor is the day more pure than the depths of my heart.
And yet they claim Hippolytus, lost in a profane love . . .
THESEUS.   Yes, it is this same pride, wretch, that condemns you.
I see the hateful nature of your coldness:
Phaedra alone has charmed your shameless eyes,
And for all other women your indifferent soul
Has disdained to burn with an innocent flame.
HIPPOLYTUS.   No, I cannot hide from you that my heart
Has not disdained to burn with a chaste love.
At your feet I confess my true offense:
I love. I love, it is true, despite your prohibition,
For Aricia holds my hopes in slavery to her law.
The daughter of Pallas has conquered your son.
I adore her, and my soul, rebellious to your command,
Can neither sigh nor burn but for her alone.
THESEUS.   You love her? Heaven! But no, the stratagem is gross.
You pretend to be a criminal, to justify yourself.
HIPPOLYTUS.   My lord, six months I have shunned her, and I love.
Tremblingly I came to tell you this yourself.

her divine origin: his mother Antiope was the daughter of Mars.
Pittheus: king of Troezen, who brought up both his grandson Theseus and his
great-grandson Hippolytus.

And now, can nothing show you your mistake?
By what awful oath can you be reassured?
May the earth, may heaven, may all nature . . .
    THESEUS.   Villains must always have recourse to perjury.
Cease, cease, and spare me an unwelcome speech,
If your false virtue can do nothing else.
    HIPPOLYTUS.   To you it seems false and full of artifice.
Phaedra, in her heart, does me greater justice.
    THESEUS.   Oh, how your impudence arouses my wrath!
    HIPPOLYTUS (after a pause).   What time do you prescribe for my exile,
        and what place?
    THESEUS.   If you were beyond the columns of Alcides,*
I would still think myself too near a traitor.
    HIPPOLYTUS.   What friends will pity when you abandon me
And charge me with this awful crime which you suspect?
    THESEUS.   Go seek some friends whose perverse esteem
Honors adultery and applauds incest —
Traitors, wretches without honor and without law,
Worthy of protecting an evil one like you.
    HIPPOLYTUS.   You speak to me still of adultery and incest?
I say no more. Yet Phaedra had a mother,
Phaedra is of a blood, as you well know,
More tainted with these horrors than is mine.
    THESEUS.   What! Your madness now loses all restraint.
For the last time, take yourself from my sight.
Leave, traitor. Do not wait for a furious father
To have you dragged from here in disgrace.

        (Exit HIPPOLYTUS.)

    Wretch, you go to your certain death.
Neptune, by the river terrible to the gods themselves,*
Gave me his word and now will execute it.
A vengeful god follows you; you cannot avoid him.
    I loved you; and I feel, despite your offense,
My heart already troubled at your fate.
But you have obliged me to condemn you.
Has ever a father, indeed, been more wronged?
Just gods, who see the grief that overwhelms me,
How could I have bred so guilty a son?

        (Enter PHAEDRA.)

    columns of Alcides: the Straits of Gibraltar, the furthest limit of Hercules'
voyages.
    river terrible to the gods themselves: the Styx, by which the gods swore irre-
vocable oaths.

PHAEDRA.   My lord, I come to you, filled with a just fear,
For your redoubtable voice reached to where I stood.
I am afraid a prompt result may have followed your threat,
But if there still is time, then spare your son.
Respect your own blood, I come to beg of you.
Save me from the horror of hearing it cry out;
Do not prepare for me the eternal grief
Of letting it be shed by a father's hand.
    THESEUS.   No, Madam, my hand has not dipped into my blood,
But none the less, the wretch has not escaped me.
An immortal hand is charged with his destruction;
Neptune owes me this, and you will be avenged.
    PHAEDRA.   Neptune owes it to you! So then your angry prayers . . .
    THESEUS.   What! Do you already fear they may be heard?
Rather, join me in my lawful prayers.
Retrace his crimes for me in all their blackness;
Arouse my anger, still too slow, too restrained.
    All of his crimes are still unknown to you.
His fury against you pours out in abuse:
Your mouth, he says, is full of deception.
He claims that Aricia has his heart and pledge,
That he loves her.
    PHAEDRA.   What, my lord?
    THESEUS.   He said it before me.
But I know how to pass off an empty artifice.
Let us hope for prompt justice from Neptune;
I myself go again to the foot of his altars
To press him to fulfill his immortal oath.   (Exit.)
    PHAEDRA.   He leaves. What is this news that has struck my ear?
What fire, scarcely out, awakens in my heart?
What bolt of thunder, oh heaven, what fatal tidings!
    I flew with all speed to the aid of his son,
And, tearing myself from the arms of Oenone,
I gave in to the remorse which tortured me.
Who knows where this repentance might have led?
Perhaps I would have ended by accusing myself.
Perhaps, if my voice had not been stopped,
The awful truth would have escaped me.
    Hippolytus feels, yet feels nothing for me!
Aricia has his heart! Aricia has his pledge!
Oh gods! When at my pleas the unrelenting ingrate
Showed so proud an eye, so austere a brow,
I thought his heart, still shut against love,
Was armed against all my sex alike.
Another, however, has broken his indifference;
Before his cruel eyes, another has found compassion.
Perhaps he has a heart easy to be moved,

And I am the only one he cannot endure.
Should I then undertake to defend him?

(*Enter* OENONE.)

Dear Oenone, do you know what I have learned?
   OENONE.   No, but in truth I come to you in trembling,
Pale at the intention which made you leave;
I feared a frenzy that might be fatal to you.
   PHAEDRA.   Oenone, who would believe it? I had a rival.
   OENONE.   What?
   PHAEDRA.   Hippolytus loves, and I cannot doubt it.
This proud enemy whom none could subdue,
Whom respect offended, whom pleas importuned,
This tiger, whom I could never meet without fear,
Submissive, tamed, admits a conqueror:
Aricia has found the way into his heart.
   OENONE.   Aricia?
   PHAEDRA.   Oh, pain never before felt!
For what new torment have I saved myself?
All that I have suffered — my fears, my transports,
The fury of my fires, the horror of my remorse,
And the unbearable hurt of a cruel refusal —
Was but a pale foretaste of my torment now.
They love. By what spell did they deceive my eyes?
How have they seen each other? Since when? And where?
   (*To* OENONE.) You knew. Why did you leave me in ignorance?
Could you not tell me of their furtive love?
Have they been often seen speaking, searching for one another?
In the depths of the forest did they go to hide?
   Alas, they saw each other with full liberty.
As heaven approved the innocence of their sighs,
They followed without remorse their lovers' inclination.
For them the days dawned serene and clear,
And I, sad reject of all nature,
I hid from the day; I fled the light.
   Death was the only god I dared to implore,
And I awaited the moment when I should expire.
Nourished with gall and with my tears,
Still too closely observed in my misfortune,
I dared not drown myself in weeping.
Trembling, I tasted this deathly pleasure,
And, disguising my sorrow behind a serene brow,
I had often to deny myself my tears.
   OENONE.   What fruit will they receive from their vain love?
They will not meet again.
   PHAEDRA.   They will always love.
At the moment that I speak — oh, awful thought —

They defy the fury of my insane passion.
Despite the very exile which is to separate them,
They take a thousand oaths never to be parted.
No, I cannot bear a happiness that so offends me,
Oenone. Have pity of my jealous rage.
　　Aricia must die. Against a hateful line
I must arouse the anger of my husband.
Let him not be content to punish lightly,
For the crime of the sister surpasses that of her brothers.
In my jealous transport, I want to beg this of him.
　　What am I doing? Where does my reason wander?
I, jealous? And is Theseus the one whom I implore?
My husband lives, and I still burn with love.
For whom? To whose heart does my love aspire?
　　Each word I utter stands my hair upright.
My crimes now have overflowed the measure;
I exhale a scent of incest and deception;
My murderous hands, ready for revenge,
Burn to plunge themselves in innocent blood.
　　And yet I live, and I can stand the sight
Of that sacred sun from whom I am descended?
My ancestor is the father and master of the gods;*
The heavens, the whole universe, are full of my forebears.
Where can I hide? Let me fly into the infernal night.
But what do I say? My father Minos holds the fatal urn;
Destiny, they say, placed it in his stern hands,
And there in hell he judges all the pallid mortals.
Ah, how his shade, appalled, will tremble
When he sees his daughter before his eyes,
Obliged to admit so many varied crimes,
And crimes perhaps as yet unknown in hell!
　　What will you say, my father, at this fearful sight?
I think I see the urn fall from your hand;
I think I see you, seeking some new torture,
Become the tormentor of your own blood.
Pardon! A cruel goddess* has destroyed your family;
See her vengeance in the madness of your daughter.
Alas, of the awful crime whose shame follows me,
My unhappy heart has never reaped the fruit.
Pursued by misfortune unto my last breath,
I end in torment a life of pain.
　　OENONE.　　Thrust aside, Madam, a terror that has no base,
And look with another eye upon an excusable mistake.

　My ancestor is the father and master of the gods: on her father's side, Phaedra
is descended from Jupiter.
　A cruel goddess: Venus.

You love. One cannot vanquish his destiny;
You were carried along by a spell of fate.
Is this, then, an unheard-of marvel among us?
Has love triumphed over none but you?
Weakness is but too natural to human beings;
Mortal, you must suffer the fate of a mortal.
You complain of a yoke imposed long ago.
The very gods, the gods who live on Olympus,
Those who strike terror into criminals,
Have themselves sometimes burned with illicit fire.

PHAEDRA.   What do I hear? What counsel dare you give?
So till the end you wish to poison me,
Wretch? That is how you have ruined me.
You gave me back the light that I tried to flee;
Your prayers made me forget my duty;
I was avoiding Hippolytus, and you made me see him.
How was this your affair? Why has your blasphemous mouth,
By accusing him, dared to blacken his life?
He now may die, and the sacrilegious prayer
Of a maddened father will be fulfilled.
   I listen to you no more. Go, hateful beast!
Go. Leave to me the care of my pitiful fate.
May a just heaven repay you worthily,
And may your punishment forever frighten
All those who, like you, by cowardly guile,
Nourish the weakness of the unhappy great,
Push them to the brink toward which their heart inclines,
And smooth for them the road to crime —
Detestable flatterers, the most deadly gift
That heavenly anger can make to those who rule! (*Exit.*)

OENONE (*alone*).   Oh, gods! To serve her I have done all, left all;
And I am thus repaid. (*Long pause.*) I have well deserved it.

ACT FIVE

(*Enter* ARICIA, HIPPOLYTUS, *and* ISMENE.)

ARICIA.   What, you can keep silent in this extreme peril
And leave in error a father who loves you?
Cruel one, if, disdaining the power of my tears,
You consent so easily to see me no more,
Then go. Leave behind a sad Aricia.
But at least in leaving, safeguard your life,
Defend your honor from a shameful reproach,
And force your father to revoke his prayers.

There still is time. Why, by what caprice,
Do you leave the field free to your accuser?
Enlighten Theseus.

    HIPPOLYTUS.   Ah, what have I not said?
Should I have brought to light his bed's disgrace?
Should I, in telling too truthful a story,
Have made my father blush with unworthy shame?
You alone have pierced this hateful mystery;
To pour out my heart, I have but you and the gods.
I could not hide from you — judge whether I love —
All that I wanted to hide from myself.

   But remember that I revealed it under seal of secrecy.
Forget, if you can, that I have spoken to you,
Madam, and never may so pure a mouth
Open to tell of this horrible adventure.
Let us place our trust in the fairness of the gods,
For they have every reason to vindicate me,
And Phaedra, soon or late punished for her crime,
Will not avoid her merited disgrace.
This is as much as I require of you;
All the rest I leave to my free wrath.

   Quit the slavery to which you are reduced;
Dare to follow me; dare to join me in flight;
Tear yourself from a baleful and ungodly place,
Where virtue breathes a poisoned air.
To hide your quick departure, take advantage
Of the confusion that my disgrace creates.
I can assure you of the means of flight,
For as yet you have no guards but mine.
Powerful defenders will take up our quarrel;
Argos extends its arms, and Sparta calls to us.
To our common friends let us carry our just complaints.
Let us not allow Phaedra, profiting by our disgrace,
To drive the two of us from my father's throne
And promise to her son both my heritage and yours.
   The opportunity is good; we must embrace it.
What fear withholds you? You balance undecided?
It is your interest alone that inspires my daring.
When I am all fire, whence comes your ice?
Are you afraid to follow in the steps of an exile?

    ARICIA.   Alas, how such banishment would be dear to me!
In what joyful transports, tied to your fate,
Would I live forgotten by all other mortals,
But not being united by so sweet a bond,
Can I with honor flee with you?
I know, without wounding the most exacting honor,
I can deliver myself from the hands of your father;

I am not tearing myself from my parents' bosom,
And flight is allowed him who flees his tyrants.
But you love me, my lord, and my threatened name . . .
  HIPPOLYTUS.   No, no, I have too much regard for your reputation.
A nobler plan brings me before you:
Flee from your enemies, and follow your husband.
Free in our misfortune, since so heaven decrees,
The pledging of our faith depends on no one else.
Not always must a wedding be lit by torches.
At the gates of Troezen, and among the tombs,
Ancient sepulchre of the princes of my people,
Is a sacred temple, fearful to perjurers.
It is there that mortals dare not swear in vain.
The perfidious receive a sudden punishment,
And no greater barrier to a lie exists
Than fear of finding inevitable death.
There, if you believe me, with an eternal love,
We will go to confirm our solemn troth.
We will take as witness the god we worship there,
And we both will pray him to serve as father to us.
I will call upon the most sacred of our gods.
Both chaste Diana and august Juno
And all gods, indeed, in witness to my love,
Will guarantee the worth of my holy promises.
  ARICIA.   The King comes. Flee, Prince, and leave at once.
To hide my departure, I will stay a while.
Go. And leave me some faithful guide
To lead my timid steps toward you.

  (*Exit* HIPPOLYTUS *as* THESEUS *enters.*)

  THESEUS.   Gods, shed light on my trouble, and deign
To show me the truth I come here to seek.
  ARICIA (*to* ISMENE).   Think of everything, dear Ismene, and be ready
    for flight.

  (*Exit* ISMENE.)

  THESEUS.   You change color and seem abashed, Madam.
What was Hippolytus doing in this place?
  ARICIA.   My lord, he was bidding me an eternal farewell.
  THESEUS.   Your eyes were able to subdue that rebellious heart,
And his first sighs are your triumphant work.
  ARICIA.   My lord, I cannot deny the truth to you.
He has not inherited your unjust hate;
He did not treat me as a criminal.

THESEUS. I understand. He swore eternal love to you.
But do not feel assured of that inconstant heart,
For he has sworn as much to others.

ARICIA. He, my lord?

THESEUS. You should have rendered him less flighty.
How could you bear this horrible sharing?

ARICIA. And how can you bear that this horrible slander
Should blacken the course of so fine a life?
Have you so little knowledge of his heart?
Do you so ill distinguish crime from innocence?
Must it be that to your eyes alone a hateful cloud
Conceals his virtue that shines to other eyes?
Oh, this is giving him up to perfidious tongues.
Stop. Repent of your murderous prayers.
Fear, my lord, fear lest a stern heaven
Should hate you enough to fulfill your wish.
Often in its anger it accepts our sacrifice;
Its gifts are often the punishment of our crimes.

THESEUS. No, you wish in vain to excuse his outrage;
Your love blinds you in favor of the wretch.
But I believe positive, irreproachable witnesses.
I have seen tears, I have seen true tears flow.

ARICIA. Take care, my lord. Your invincible hands
Have freed men from monsters without number,
But all are not destroyed, and you let one
Still live . . . Your son, my lord, forbids me to go on.
Aware of the respect for you he wishes to preserve,
I would afflict him too much if I dared to finish.
I imitate his reserve and flee from your presence
That I may not be forced to break my silence. (*Exit*.)

THESEUS (*alone*). What is her thought? What do her words hide,
Begun so many times, and always interrupted?
Do they seek to disturb me through a vain pretense?
Are the two of them agreed to put me to the torture?
And as for me, despite my harsh severity,
What plaintive voice cries in the depths of my heart?
A secret pity afflicts and moves me.
A second time I will question Oenone.
I wish to be better informed of all the crime.
Guards, have Oenone come out and approach alone.

(*Enter* PANOPE.)

PANOPE. I do not know the project that the Queen debates,
My lord, but from the emotion that stirs her I fear the worst.
A mortal despair is painted on her face,
And the pallor of death already is upon her.

Already, sent away in shame from her presence,
Oenone has thrown herself into the sea.
No one knows from whence came this mad intent,
And the waves evermore will hide her from our view.

THESEUS.   What do I hear?

PANOPE.   Her death has not relieved the Queen;
The trouble seems to grow in her uncertain soul.
Sometimes, to soften her secret pain,
She takes her children and bathes them in tears,
And suddenly, renouncing maternal love,
Her hand with horror pushes them away.
Her irresolute steps lead her at random;
Her distracted eye no longer recognizes us.
Three times she has written, and, changing her mind,
Three times she has torn the letter she had begun.
Deign to see her, my lord; deign to give her aid.

THESEUS.   Oh, heaven, Oenone is dead, and Phaedra wants to die?
Have my son recalled; let him come to his defense!
Let him come to speak to me. I am ready to listen.
Do not hasten, Neptune, your deadly godsend,
For I prefer my wishes never to be granted.
I perhaps believed too soon unfaithful witnesses,
And too soon I lifted my cruel hands to you.
Ah, what anguish may follow that prayer!

(*Enter* THERAMENES.)

Theramenes, is that you? What have you done with my son?
I entrusted him to you from the tenderest age.
But whence come these tears I see you shed?
What is my son doing?

THERAMENES.   Oh, tardy and superfluous care!
Futile tenderness! Hippolytus is no more.

THESEUS.   Gods!

THERAMENES.   I have seen perish the most gracious of mortals,
And, I dare to say again, my lord, the least guilty.

THESEUS.   My son is no more? When I hold out to him my arms
The impatient gods have hastened his end?
What blow stole him from me? What sudden thunderbolt?

THERAMENES.   Scarcely had we left the gates of Troezen,
Than he was in his chariot. His grieving guards,
Ranged all about him, were silent as he.
Pensively he followed the road to Mycenae,
Letting the reins float free above his horses.
His proud coursers, which one used to see,
Full of noble zeal, obedient to his voice,

Now with saddened eye and lowered head
Seemed to conform to his sad thoughts.
　　A terrible cry, come from the depths of the sea,
At that moment troubled the quiet of the air;
And from the bosom of the earth a formidable voice
Answered with a moan this dreadful sound.
In our very hearts our blood was frozen,
And on the alerted horses the mane stood up.
　　Meanwhile on the face of the liquid plain
There rises, boiling, a watery mountain.
The wave comes near, breaks, and vomits before our eyes,
Amid a flood of foam, a furious monster.
His wide brow is armed with menacing horns,
His whole body covered with yellowing scales;
Untamable bull, hot-headed dragon —
His crupper curls in tortuous folds.
His long bellowing makes the shore tremble.
With horror heaven looks on this savage shape.
The earth is aroused, the air infected;
The sea, which brought him, withdraws in terror.
All flee. Without making show of fruitless courage,
In the nearby temple they seek safety.
　　Hippolytus alone, worthy son of a hero,
Stops his coursers, seizes his javelins,
Rushes upon the beast, and with well-thrown spear
Makes a great wound in his side.
In rage and in pain the leaping monster
Falls moaning at the feet of the horses,
Rolls and turns on them a flaming mouth,
Which covers them with smoke, with blood and fire.
Fear carries them off, and deaf this one time,
They no longer know either rein or voice.
In useless effort their master exhausts himself.
They redden the bit with a bloody foam.
It is said that in this awful confusion there was even seen
A god who pressed their dusty flanks with goads.
Across the rocks, fright rushes them.
The axle cries and breaks. The intrepid Hippolytus
Sees his shattered chariot fly in splinters;
He himself falls, entangled in the reins.
　　Excuse my grief. This cruel scene
Will be for me an eternal source of tears.
I saw, my lord, I saw your unhappy son
Dragged by the horses whom his hand had fed.
He wants to call them back, and his voice frightens them.
They run. His whole body is soon but one wound.
The plain reechoes to our grievous cries.

At last their impetuous dash is slowed;
They stop, not far from those ancient tombs*
Where lie the cold remains of the kings his ancestors.
I run, panting, and his guard follows me.
The trail of his noble blood shows us the way;
The rocks are stained; the dripping brambles
Carry the bloody strands of his hair.
I arrive; I call him. Then, giving me his hand,
He opens his dying eyes, and closes them at once.
"Heaven," he says, "takes an innocent life.
After my death, care well for sad Aricia.
Dear friend, if my father, one day disabused,
Regrets the misfortune of a son falsely blamed,
To appease my blood and my plaintive shade,
Tell him to treat his captive with gentleness,
To give her back . . . " At this word, the hero, dead,
Left in my arms but his disfigured body,
A sad thing, in which triumphed the anger of the gods,
And which the eye of his very father would not know.

      THESEUS.   Oh, my son! Dear hope of which I have robbed myself!
Inexorable gods who have served me too well!
To what mortal regrets my life is now given over!

      THERAMENES.   Timid Aricia then arrived.
She was coming, my lord, flying from your wrath,
To take him as husband before the gods.
She approaches. She sees the grass, red and smoking;
She sees (what a sight for the eyes of a lover!)
Hippolytus outstretched, without form, without color.
She tries for a time to doubt her misfortune,
And, no longer knowing this hero she adores,
She sees Hippolytus and yet asks for him.
But too sure at last that he is before her eyes,
By a sorrowing look she accuses the gods;
And cold, moaning, and almost inanimate,
She falls in a swoon at the feet of her lover.
Ismene is beside her; Ismene, all in tears,
Calls her back to life, or rather back to grief.
    And as for me, I have come, cursing life,
To tell you the last wish of a hero
And to fulfill, my lord, the unhappy duty
Which his dying heart placed upon me.
But I see his mortal enemy approach.

     (*Enter* PHAEDRA.)

---

those ancient tombs: where Aricia was to meet Hippolytus.

THESEUS (*to* PHAEDRA).   Well, you triumph, and my son is without
  life.
Ah, what I have cause to fear, and what cruel suspicion,
Excusing him in my heart, alarms me with reason!
But, Madam, he is dead. Take your victim.
Enjoy his death, unjust or legitimate.
I consent that my eyes may always be deluded.
I believe him a criminal, since you accuse him.
His death offers reason enough for my tears
Without my going to seek hateful enlightenment,
Which, unable to return him to my just grief,
Might only serve to increase my misery.
    Let me, far from you and far from these shores,
Flee the bloody image of my torn son.
Bewildered, pursued by this memory of death,
I would banish myself from the entire universe.
    Everything seems to rise against my injustice.
The glory of my name even increases my torture;
Less known to mortals, I could hide myself the better.
I hate the very care with which the gods honor me,
And I leave to bewail their murdering favors,
Without bothering them more with futile prayers.
Whatever they do for me, their deadly goodness
Can never repay me for what they have taken.
    PHAEDRA.   No, Theseus, I must break an unjust silence.
I must give back his innocence to your son.
He was not guilty.
    THESEUS.   Ah, unhappy father!
And it was on your word that I condemned him!
Cruel one, do you believe yourself sufficiently excused . . .
    PHAEDRA.   Moments are dear to me. Listen to me, Theseus.
It is I who on this chaste and respectful son
Dared to cast an impure and incestuous eye.
Heaven* placed in my breast a deadly flame;
The detestable Oenone did all the rest.
She feared that Hippolytus, learning of my madness,
Might reveal the love that horrified him;
So the treacherous woman, imposing on my weakness,
Hastened to accuse him first before you.
She has punished herself and, fleeing my wrath,
Has sought in the waves too easy a penalty.
The sword would already have cut short my destiny,
But I allowed Virtue, compromised, to moan.
Exposing my remorse before you, I wanted
To go down among the dead by a slower route.

  Heaven: more specifically, Venus.

I have poured into my burning veins
A poison which Medea* brought to Athens.
Already the venom, having reached my dying heart,
Casts upon it a cold it has never known.
Already I see but through a cloud
Both the sky and the husband that my presence offends;
And death, hiding from my eyes the light,
Gives back to the day, which they defiled, all its purity.

    PANOPE.   She dies, my lord!

    THESEUS.   Of so black an act
Would that the memory might die with her.
Let us go, too well aware, alas, of my error,
To mix our tears with the blood of my unhappy son.
Let us go to embrace what remains of him,
To expiate the madness of a prayer I curse.
Let us render him the honors he has well deserved,
And the better to appease his angered shade,
Despite the plotting of an unjust family,*
Let his loved one be for me a daughter, from today.

Curtain

Medea: wife of Jason, famous for her magic philters.
an unjust family: the Pallantides.

Or, The World Well Lost (1678) is the balance of the title John Dryden (1631–1700) chose for his neoclassicizing of Shakespeare's *Antony and Cleopatra* (1606–1607). Dryden properly admired the greatness of Shakespeare's work, but his classical education and passion for order could not but consider the structural looseness of the Elizabethan dramatists a fault. He applied the unities of time, place, and action to heighten the effect of the tragedy. And naturally, he did not come up with an improvement over Shakespeare. The problem on one level is poetic talent. Shakespeare's conception of the story, his vision of the major characters, and his command of diction and imagery form the more impressive achievement. Shakespeare's very freedom in letting his story move around in space and develop in time was an advantage; rules and limitations tend to hamper initial inspiration and curb composition.

Dryden's feelings about tragic heroes were tempered by his time. The Restoration was a period of moral, ethical, and social change. The old value of individualism, so palpable in the Renaissance and so ably used by Shakespeare, was being leveled by democraticization. And Dryden's heroes, particularly Antony and Cleopatra, partly reflect this. Their problem, and the central conflict of the play, is that their passions and philosophies — their identities — are outmoded, and they are having to face it.

Consequently, locale in *All for Love* is unimportant. Dryden's characters, thanks to their out-of-time, out-of-place natures and concerns, are isolated from their social, political, and physical settings. The very thing that illuminates the struggle of Shakespeare's *Antony and Cleopatra* with so much depth and richness — the physical shifts between the cold rationality of Rome and the exotic, decadent emotionalism of Egypt — is lacking in *All for Love*.

Instead, Dryden emphasizes internal dilemmas and conflicts. Each character represents a different pull on Antony. To Octavia he has freely given and should continue to give the noble love of a husband. To Cleopatra he has freely given and should continue to give the sexual passion of his whole life. He owes Ventidius authority and Dolabella friendship. Having been regarded by each of these people as superhuman, he now must prove it. And of course he cannot. What weakens him, compared to Shakespeare's Antony, is that the bind he is caught in seems not of his own making but initiated by the other characters. All of them have a clear idea of Antony, but the whole man is the sum of these parts. His identity is being challenged not by himself but by the people he is related to.

By concentrating on the very strength of the characters and their separate but equal pulls on Antony, Dryden perhaps makes the conflict more immediate and more impressive than in Shakespeare's version, whose richness of detail tends to dissipate its effect. Octavia's noble and unselfish love calling him back to matrimonial duty, Ventidius' veneration calling him back to responsibility as a captain and ruler of the Roman Empire, and Dolabella's friendship calling him back to peace of mind are all equally attractive to Antony. Even Cleopatra's passion — though he knows it saps his power and resolve and erodes his vitality and virility — is genuine, not malicious, and so its pull is as worthy to him as the others.

All for Love is an affecting heroic tragedy, in which Dryden has successfully avoided the horrors and excesses of Jacobean *grand guignol*. The strong element of noble love makes it an exercise in the romantic, but it is never sentimental or mawkish. The tightness of its structure — a potential hazard — Dryden turns into a virtue. The crisis is over when the play begins, and what we see on the stage is the dénouement of two lives coming inevitably to their end. The bare bones of the plot may not seem very dramatic, but the way Antony and Cleopatra meet their fate captures the attention. Just as Antony prepares decisive actions which will free him to return to his responsibilities as a captain and ruler of the Roman Empire, Cleopatra or one of her servants devises some trap to work on his love — or his sense of guilt — and prevent him from going. That she does it from love and from terror of losing love is made quite clear; she is not motivated by the malice of the melodramatic villain.

Though Dryden's poetry is not as powerful as Shakespeare's, it does sustain action, character, and thought. Were Dryden's drama the only play in verse on this theme, it might be much easier to see the real beauties of the language. Dryden does deal with noble sentiments nobly — without making them seem elegantly artificial or impossibly embarrassing. When Octavia, potentially the most mawkish of the characters, offers Antony his freedom, her expression is little short of exalted. And yet Dryden was himself very modest about his reworking of Shakespeare. He said: "If Shakespeare were stripped of all the bombasts in his passions, and dressed in the most vulgar words, we should find the beauties of his thoughts remaining; if his embroideries were burnt down, there would still be silver at the bottom of the melting pot; but I fear (at least I fear it for myself) that we, who ape his sounding words, have nothing of his thought . . . there is not so much as a dwarf within our giant's clothes."[1]

C.L.

[1] Barrett H. Clark, *European Theories of the Drama* (New York: Crown, 1965), p. 155.

JOHN DRYDEN

All for Love[1]

Characters

MARK ANTONY
VENTIDIUS, *his General*
DOLABELLA, *his Friend*
ALEXAS, *the Queen's Eunuch*
SERAPION, *Priest of Isis*
MYRIS, *another Priest*
SERVANTS *to Antony*
CLEOPATRA, *Queen of Egypt*
OCTAVIA, *Antony's Wife*
CHARMION ⎱ *Cleopatra's Maids*
IRAS   ⎰
Antony's two little DAUGHTERS
PRIESTS, LICTORS, COMMANDERS, ATTENDANTS,
    EGYPTIANS, ROMANS

PROLOGUE

What flocks of critics hover here today,
As vultures wait on armies for their prey,
All gaping for the carcass of a play!
With croaking notes they bode some dire event,
And follow dying poets by the scent.
Ours gives himself for gone; y'have watched your time!
He fights this day unarmed (without his rhyme)
And brings a tale which often has been told,
As sad as Dido's and almost as old.
His hero, whom you wits his bully call,
Bates of his mettle and scarce rants at all.
He's somewhat lewd but a well-meaning mind;
Weeps much, fights little, but is wond'rous kind;
In short, a pattern and companion fit
For all the keeping tonies of the pit.

---

[1] This version of *All for Love* follows the 1678 quarto, but modernizes spellings, typography, and punctuation throughout. A number of valuable suggestions for emendation have been drawn from J. H. Wilson's text.

I could name more: a wife, and mistress too,
Both (to be plain) too good for most of you;
The wife well-natured, and the mistress true.
    Now, poets, if your fame has been his care,
Allow him all the candor you can spare.
A brave man scorns to quarrel once a day,
Like Hectors, in at every petty fray.
Let those find fault whose wit's so very small,
They've need to show that they can think at all.
Errors, like straws, upon the surface flow;
He who would search for pearls must dive below.
Fops may have leave to level all they can,
As pigmies would be glad to lop a man.
Half-wits are fleas, so little and so light,
We scarce could know they live but that they bite.
But as the rich, when tired with daily feasts,
For change become their next poor tenant's guests,
Drink hearty draughts of ale from plain brown bowls,
And snatch the homely rasher from the coals,
So you, retiring from much better cheer,
For once may venture to do penance here.
And since that plenteous autumn now is past,
Whose grapes and peaches have indulged your taste,
Take in good part, from our poor poet's board,
Such rivelled fruits as winter can afford.

ACT ONE

(*The Temple of Isis. Enter* SERAPION, MYRIS, PRIESTS *of Isis.*)

SERAPION.   Portents and prodigies are grown so frequent
That they have lost their name. Our fruitful Nile
Flowed ere the wonted season with a torrent
So unexpected and so wondrous fierce
That the wild deluge overtook the haste
Even of the hinds that watched it. Men and beasts
Were borne above the tops of trees that grew
On th' utmost margin of the water-mark.
Then, with so swift an ebb the flood drove backward,
It slipt from underneath the scaly herd:
Here monstrous phocae panted on the shore;
Forsaken dolphins there with their broad tails
Lay lashing the departing waves; hard by 'em,
Sea-horses, floundering in the slimy mud,
Tossed up their heads, and dashed the ooze about them.

(*Enter* ALEXAS *behind them.*)

MYRIS.   Avert these omens, Heaven!

SERAPION.   Last night, between the hours of twelve and one,
In a lone aisle of the temple while I walked,
A whirlwind rose that with a violent blast
Shook all the dome; the doors around me clapped;
The iron wicket that defends the vault
Where the long race of Ptolemies is laid
Burst open and disclosed the mighty dead.
From out each monument, in order placed,
An armèd ghost starts up: the boy-king last
Reared his inglorious head. A peal of groans
Then followed, and a lamentable voice
Cried, "Egypt is no more!" My blood ran back,
My shaking knees against each other knocked;
On the cold pavement down I fell entranced,
And so unfinished left the horrid scene.

ALEXAS (showing himself).   And dreamed you this? or did invent the
        story
To frighten our Egyptian boys withal,
And train them up betimes in fear of priesthood?

SERAPION.   My lord, I saw you not,
Nor meant my words should reach your ears; but what
I uttered was most true.

ALEXAS.   A foolish dream,
Bred from the fumes of indigested feasts
And holy luxury.

SERAPION.   I know my duty;
This goes no farther.

ALEXAS.   'Tis not fit it should,
Nor would the times now bear it, were it true.
All southern, from yon hills, the Roman camp
Hangs o'er us black and threating like a storm
Just breaking on our heads.

SERAPION.   Our faint Egyptians pray for Antony;
But in their servile hearts they own Octavius.

MYRIS.   Why then does Antony dream out his hours,
And tempts not fortune for a noble day
Which might redeem what Actium lost?

ALEXAS.   He thinks 'tis past recovery.

SERAPION.   Yet the foe
Seems not to press the siege.

ALEXAS.   Oh, there's the wonder.
Maecenas and Agrippa, who can most
With Caesar, are his foes. His wife Octavia,
Driven from his house, solicits her revenge;
And Dolabella, who was once his friend,

Upon some private grudge now seeks his ruin;
Yet still war seems on either side to sleep.

SERAPION. 'Tis strange that Antony, for some days past,
Has not beheld the face of Cleopatra,
But here in Isis' temple lives retired,
And makes his heart a prey to black despair.

ALEXAS. 'Tis true; and we much fear he hopes by absence
To cure his mind of love.

SERAPION.   If he be vanquished
Or make his peace, Egypt is doomed to be
A Roman province, and our plenteous harvests
Must then redeem the scarceness of their soil.
While Antony stood firm, our Alexandria
Rivaled proud Rome (dominion's other seat),
And Fortune, striding like a vast Colossus,
Could fix an equal foot of empire here.

ALEXAS. Had I my wish, these tyrants of all nature
Who lord it o'er mankind, should perish — perish
Each by the other's sword; but, since our will
Is lamely followed by our power, we must
Depend on one, with him to rise or fall.

SERAPION. How stands the queen affected?

ALEXAS.   Oh, she dotes,
She dotes, Serapion, on this vanquished man,
And winds herself about his mighty ruins;
Whom would she yet forsake, yet yield him up,
This hunted prey, to his pursuer's hands,
She might preserve us all; but 'tis in vain —
This changes my designs, this blasts my counsels,
And makes me use all means to keep him here,
Whom I could wish divided from her arms
Far as the earth's deep center. Well, you know
The state of things; no more of your ill omens
And black prognostics; labor to confirm
The people's hearts.

(*Enter* VENTIDIUS, *talking aside with a* GENTLEMAN *of Antony's.*)

SERAPION. These Romans will o'erhear us.
But who's that stranger? By his warlike port,
His fierce demeanor, and erected look,
He's of no vulgar note.

ALEXAS.   Oh, 'tis Ventidius,
Our emperor's great lieutenant in the East,
Who first showed Rome that Parthia could be conquered.

When Antony returned from Syria last,
He left this man to guard the Roman frontiers.
   SERAPION.   You seem to know him well.
   ALEXAS.   Too well. I saw him in Cilicia first,
When Cleopatra there met Antony.
A mortal foe he was to us and Egypt.
But — let me witness to the worth I hate —
A braver Roman never drew a sword;
Firm to his prince, but as a friend, not slave.
He ne'er was of his pleasures; but presides
O'er all his cooler hours and morning counsels;
In short, the plainness, fierceness, rugged virtue
Of an old true-stamped Roman lives in him.
His coming bodes I know not what of ill
To our affairs. Withdraw, to mark him better;
And I'll acquaint you why I sought you here,
And what's our present work.

   (*They withdraw to a corner of the stage; and* VENTIDIUS, *with the other,
comes forward to the front.*)

   VENTIDIUS.   Not see him, say you?
I say I must and will.
   GENTLEMAN.   He has commanded,
On pain of death, none should approach his presence.
   VENTIDIUS.   I bring him news will raise his drooping spirits,
Give him new life.
   GENTLEMAN.   He sees not Cleopatra.
   VENTIDIUS.   Would he had never seen her!
   GENTLEMAN.   He eats not, drinks not, sleeps not, has no use
Of anything but thought; or, if he talks,
'Tis to himself, and then, 'tis perfect raving.
Then he defies the world, and bids it pass;
Sometimes he gnaws his lip and curses loud
The boy Octavius; then he draws his mouth
Into a scornful smile and cries, "Take all,
The world's not worth my care."
   VENTIDIUS.   Just, just his nature.
Virtue's his path; but sometimes 'tis too narrow
For his vast soul; and then he starts out wide,
And bounds into a vice that bears him far
From his first course and plunges him in ills;
But when his danger makes him find his fault,
Quick to observe, and full of sharp remorse,
He censures eagerly his own misdeeds,
Judging himself with malice to himself,
And not forgiving what as man he did,

Because his other parts are more than man.
He must not thus be lost.

(ALEXAS *and the* PRIESTS *come forward.*)

ALEXAS.   You have your full instructions, now advance;
Proclaim your orders loudly.
SERAPION.   Romans, Egyptians, hear the queen's command!
Thus Cleopatra bids: Let labor cease;
To pomp and triumphs give this happy day
That gave the world a lord: 'tis Antony's.
Live, Antony; and Cleopatra, live!
Be this the general voice sent up to heaven,
And every public place repeat this echo.
VENTIDIUS (*aside*).   Fine pageantry!
SERAPION.   Set out before your doors
The images of all your sleeping fathers,
With laurels crowned; with laurels wreathe your posts
And strew with flowers the pavement; let the priests
Do present sacrifice; pour out the wine
And call the gods to join with you in gladness.
VENTIDIUS.   Curse on the tongue that bids this general joy!
Can they be friends of Antony, who revel
When Antony's in danger? Hide, for shame,
You Romans, your great grandsires' images,
For fear their souls should animate their marbles,
To blush at their degenerate progeny.
ALEXAS.   A love which knows no bounds to Antony
Would mark the day with honors when all heaven
Labored for him, when each propitious star
Stood wakeful in his orb to watch that hour
And shed his better influence. Her own birthday
Our queen neglected like a vulgar fate
That passed obscurely by.
VENTIDIUS.   Would it had slept,
Divided far from his, till some remote
And future age had called it out, to ruin
Some other prince, not him!
ALEXAS.   Your emperor,
Though grown unkind, would be more gentle than
T' upbraid my queen for loving him too well.
VENTIDIUS.   Does the mute sacrifice upbraid the priest?
He knows him not his executioner.
Oh, she has decked his ruin with her love,
Led him in golden bands to gaudy slaughter,
And made perdition pleasing. She has left him
The blank of what he was.

I tell thee, eunuch, she has quite unmanned him.
Can any Roman see and know him now,
Thus altered from the lord of half mankind,
Unbent, unsinewed, made a woman's toy,
Shrunk from the vast extent of all his honors,
And cramped within a corner of the world?
O Antony!
Thou bravest soldier and thou best of friends!
Bounteous as nature; next to nature's God!
Couldst thou but make new worlds, so wouldst thou give 'em,
As bounty were thy being; rough in battle
As the first Romans when they went to war;
Yet, after victory, more pitiful
Than all their praying virgins left at home!
    ALEXAS.   Would you could add to those more shining virtues,
His truth to her who loves him.
    VENTIDIUS.   Would I could not!
But wherefore waste I precious hours with thee?
Thou art her darling mischief, her chief engine,
Antony's other fate. Go, tell thy queen
Ventidius is arrived to end her charms.
Let your Egyptian timbrels play alone,
Nor mix effeminate sounds with Roman trumpets.
You dare not fight for Antony; go pray,
And keep your coward's holiday in temples.

    (*Exeunt* ALEXAS, SERAPION. *Re-enter the* GENTLEMEN *of* Mark
Antony.)

    SECOND GENTLEMAN.   The emperor approaches and commands
On pain of death that none presume to stay.
    FIRST GENTLEMAN.   I dare not disobey him. (*Going out with the
    other.*)
    VENTIDIUS.   Well, I dare.
But I'll observe him first unseen, and find
Which way his humor drives. The rest I'll venture. (*Withdraws.*)

    (*Enter* ANTONY, *walking with a disturbed motion before he speaks.*)

    ANTONY.   They tell me 'tis my birthday, and I'll keep it
With double pomp of sadness.
'Tis what the day deserves which gave me breath.
Why was I raised the meteor of the world,
Hung in the skies and blazing as I traveled,
Till all my fires were spent, and then cast downward
To be trod out by Caesar?

VENTIDIUS (*aside*).   On my soul,
'Tis mournful, wondrous mournful!
    ANTONY.   Count thy gains.
Now, Antony, wouldst thou be born for this?
Glutton of fortune, thy devouring youth
Has starved thy wanting age.
    VENTIDIUS (*aside*).   How sorrow shakes him!
So now the tempest tears him up by the roots,
And on the ground extends the noble ruin.
    ANTONY (*having thrown himself down*).   Lie there, thou shadow of
      an emperor;
The place thou pressest on thy mother earth
Is all thy empire now; now it contains thee;
Some few days hence, and then 'twill be too large,
When thou'rt contracted in thy narrow urn,
Shrunk to a few cold ashes. Then Octavia
(For Cleopatra will not live to see it),
Octavia then will have thee all her own,
And bear thee in her widowed hand to Caesar;
Caesar will weep, the crocodile will weep,
To see his rival of the universe
Lie still and peaceful there. I'll think no more on 't.
    Give me some music; look that it be sad.
I'll soothe my melancholy till I swell
And burst myself with sighing. —

    (*Soft music.*)

'Tis somewhat to my humor. Stay, I fancy
I'm now turned wild, a commoner of nature;
Of all forsaken and forsaking all,
Live in a shady forest's sylvan scene,
Stretched at my length beneath some blasted oak,
I lean my head upon the mossy bark
And look just of a piece as I grew from it;
My uncombed locks, matted like mistletoe,
Hang o'er my hoary face; a murm'ring brook
Runs at my foot.
    VENTIDIUS (*aside*).   Methinks I fancy
Myself there, too.
    ANTONY.   The herd come jumping by me,
And, fearless, quench their thirst while I look on,
And take me for their fellow-citizen.
More of this image, more it lulls my thoughts.

    (*Soft music again.*)

VENTIDIUS.   I must disturb him; I can hold no longer.   (*Stands before him.*)

ANTONY (*starting up*).   Art thou Ventidius?

VENTIDIUS.   Are you Antony?
I'm liker what I was than you to him
I left you last.

ANTONY.   I'm angry.

VENTIDIUS.   So am I.

ANTONY.   I would be private.   Leave me.

VENTIDIUS.   Sir, I love you,
And therefore will not leave you.

ANTONY.   Will not leave me!
Where have you learned that answer?   Who am I?

VENTIDIUS.   My emperor; the man I love next Heaven;
If I said more, I think 'twere scarce a sin —
You're all that's good and god-like.

ANTONY.   All that's wretched.
You will not leave me then?

VENTIDIUS.   'Twas too presuming
To say I would not; but I dare not leave you,
And 'tis unkind in you to chide me hence
So soon, when I so far have come to see you.

ANTONY.   Now thou hast seen me, art thou satisfied?
For, if a friend, thou hast beheld enough;
And, if a foe, too much.

VENTIDIUS (*weeping*).   Look, emperor, this is no common dew.
I have not wept this forty years; but now
My mother comes afresh into my eyes;
I cannot help her softness.

ANTONY.   By heaven, he weeps! poor, good old man, he weeps!
The big round drops course one another down
The furrows of his cheeks. — Stop 'em, Ventidius,
Or I shall blush to death; they set my shame,
That caused 'em, full before me.

VENTIDIUS.   I'll do my best.

ANTONY.   Sure, there's contagion in the tears of friends —
See, I have caught it, too.   Believe me, 'tis not
For my own griefs, but thine. — Nay, father!

VENTIDIUS.   Emperor!

ANTONY.   Emperor!   Why, that's the style of victory;
The conqu'ring soldier, red with unfelt wounds,
Salutes his general so; but never more
Shall that sound reach my ears.

VENTIDIUS.   I warrant you.

ANTONY.   Actium, Actium!   Oh! —

VENTIDIUS.   It sits too near you.

ANTONY.   Here, here it lies, a lump by day,

And, in my short, distracted, nightly slumbers,
The hag that rides my dreams.
    VENTIDIUS.   Out with it; give it vent.
    ANTONY.   Urge not my shame.
I lost a battle.
    VENTIDIUS.   So has Julius done.
    ANTONY.   Thou favor'st me, and speak'st not half thou think'st;
For Julius fought it out, and lost it fairly,
But Antony —
    VENTIDIUS.   Nay, stop not.
    ANTONY.   Antony,
(Well, thou wilt have it), like a coward fled,
Fled while his soldiers fought; fled first, Ventidius.
Thou long'st to curse me, and I give thee leave.
I know thou cam'st prepared to rail.
    VENTIDIUS.   I did.
    ANTONY.   I'll help thee. — I have been a man, Ventidius.
    VENTIDIUS.   Yes, and a brave one; but —
    ANTONY.   I know thy meaning.
But I have lost my reason, have disgraced
The name of soldier with inglorious ease.
In the full vintage of my flowing honors,
Sat still, and saw it pressed by other hands.
Fortune came smiling to my youth, and wooed it,
And purple greatness met my ripened years.
When first I came to empire, I was borne
On tides of people crowding to my triumphs —
The wish of nations! and the willing world
Received me as its pledge of future peace.
I was so great, so happy, so beloved,
Fate could not ruin me, till I took pains,
And worked against my fortune, chid her from me,
And turned her loose; yet she came again.
My careless days and my luxurious nights
At length have wearied her, and now she's gone,
Gone, gone, divorced for ever. Help me, soldier,
To curse this madman, this industrious fool,
Who labored to be wretched. Pr'ythee, curse me.
    VENTIDIUS.   No.
    ANTONY.   Why?
    VENTIDIUS.   You are too sensible already
Of what you've done, too conscious of your failings;
And, like a scorpion, whipped by others first
To fury, sting yourself in mad revenge.
I would bring balm and pour it in your wounds,
Cure your distempered mind and heal your fortunes.
    ANTONY.   I know thou would'st.

VENTIDIUS. I will.

ANTONY. Ha, ha, ha, ha!

VENTIDIUS. You laugh.

ANTONY. I do, to see officious love
Give cordials to the dead.

VENTIDIUS. You would be lost, then?

ANTONY. I am.

VENTIDIUS. I say you are not. Try your fortune,

ANTONY. I have, to th' utmost. Dost thou think me desperate
Without just cause? No, when I found all lost
Beyond repair, I hid me from the world,
And learned to scorn it here; which now I do
So heartily, I think it is not worth
The cost of keeping.

VENTIDIUS. Caesar thinks not so.
He'll thank you for the gift he could not take.
You would be killed like Tully, would you? Do,
Hold out your throat to Caesar, and die tamely.

ANTONY. No, I can kill myself; and so resolve.

VENTIDIUS. I can die with you, too, when time shall serve,
But fortune calls upon us now to live,
To fight, to conquer.

ANTONY. Sure, thou dream'st, Ventidius.

VENTIDIUS. No; 'tis you dream. You sleep away your hours
In desperate sloth, miscalled philosophy.
Up, up, for honor's sake! Twelve legions wait you
And long to call you chief. By painful journeys
I led them, patient both of heat and hunger,
Down from the Parthian marches to the Nile.
'Twill do you good to see their sunburnt faces,
Their scarred cheeks, and chopped hands.
There's virtue in 'em.
They'll sell those mangled limbs at dearer rates
Than yon trim band can buy.

ANTONY. Where left you them?

VENTIDIUS. I said in Lower Syria.

ANTONY. Bring them hither;
There may be life in these.

VENTIDIUS. They will not come.

ANTONY. Why didst thou mock my hopes with promised aids,
To double my despair? They're mutinous.

VENTIDIUS. Most firm and loyal.

ANTONY. Yet they will not march
To succor me. O trifler!

VENTIDIUS. They petition
You would make haste to head them.

ANTONY. I'm besieged.

VENTIDIUS.   There's but one way shut up.
How came I hither?
    ANTONY.   I will not stir.
    VENTIDIUS.   They would perhaps desire
A better reason.
    ANTONY.   I have never used
My soldiers to demand a reason of
My actions. Why did they refuse to march?
    VENTIDIUS.   They said they would not fight for Cleopatra.
    ANTONY.   What was 't they said?
    VENTIDIUS.   They said they would not fight for Cleopatra.
Why should they fight, indeed, to make her conquer,
And make you more a slave? to gain you kingdoms
Which, for a kiss at your next midnight feast,
You'll sell to her? Then she new-names her jewels
And calls this diamond such or such a tax;
Each pendant in her ear shall be a province.
    ANTONY.   Ventidius, I allow your tongue free license
On all my other faults; but, on your life,
No word of Cleopatra. She deserves
More worlds than I can lose.
    VENTIDIUS.   Behold, you powers,
To whom you have intrusted humankind!
See Europe, Afric, Asia, put in balance,
And all weighed down by one light, worthless woman!
I think the gods are Antonies and give,
Like prodigals, this nether world away
To none but wasteful hands.
    ANTONY.   You grow presumptuous.
    VENTIDIUS.   I take the privilege of plain love to speak.
    ANTONY.   Plain love! Plain arrogance, plain insolence!
Thy men are cowards, thou, an envious traitor,
Who, under seeming honesty, hast vented
The burden of thy rank, o'erflowing gall.
O that thou wert my equal, great in arms
As the first Caesar was, that I might kill thee
Without a stain to honor!
    VENTIDIUS.   You may kill me;
You have done more already, — called me traitor.
    ANTONY.   Art thou not one?
    VENTIDIUS.   For showing you yourself,
Which none else durst have done? But had I been
That name which I disdain to speak again,
I needed not have sought your abject fortunes,
Come to partake your fate, to die with you.
What hindered me t' have led my conquering eagles
To fill Octavius' bands? I could have been

A traitor then, a glorious, happy traitor,
And not have been so called.

ANTONY.   Forgive me, soldier;
I've been too passionate.

VENTIDIUS.   You thought me false;
Thought my old age betrayed you. Kill me, sir,
Pray, kill me. Yet you need not; your unkindness
Has left your sword no work.

ANTONY.   I did not think so.
I said it in my rage. Pr'ythee, forgive me.
Why didst thou tempt my anger by discovery
Of what I would not hear?

VENTIDIUS.   No prince but you
Could merit that sincerity I used,
Nor durst another man have ventured it;
But you, ere love misled your wandering eyes,
Were sure the chief and best of human race,
Framed in the very pride and boast of nature;
So perfect that the gods who formed you wondered
At their own skill, and cried, "A lucky hit
Has mended our design." Their envy hindered,
Else you had been immortal, and a pattern,
When Heaven would work for ostentation's sake
To copy out again.

ANTONY.   But Cleopatra —
Go on, for I can bear it now.

VENTIDIUS.   No more.

ANTONY.   Thou dar'st not trust my passion, but thou may'st;
Thou only lov'st, the rest have flattered me.

VENTIDIUS.   Heaven's blessing on your heart for that kind word!
May I believe you love me? Speak again.

ANTONY.   Indeed I do. Speak this, and this, and this. (*Hugging him.*)
Thy praises were unjust, but I'll deserve them,
And yet mend all. Do with me what thou wilt;
Lead me to victory! Thou know'st the way.

VENTIDIUS.   And will you leave this —

ANTONY.   Pr'ythee, do not curse her,
And I will leave her; though Heaven knows I love
Beyond life, conquest, empire, all but honor;
But I will leave her.

VENTIDIUS.   That's my royal master;
And shall we fight?

ANTONY.   I warrant thee, old soldier.
Thou shalt behold me once again in iron;
And at the head of our old troops that beat
The Parthians, cry aloud, "Come, follow me!"

VENTIDIUS.   Oh, now I hear my emperor! In that word

Octavius fell. Gods, let me see that day,
And, if I have ten years behind, take all;
I'll thank you for th' exchange.
  ANTONY.   O Cleopatra!
  VENTIDIUS. Again?
  ANTONY.   I've done. In that last sigh, she went.
Caesar shall know what 'tis to force a lover
From all he holds most dear.
  VENTIDIUS.   Methinks you breathe
Another soul. Your looks are more divine;
You speak a hero, and you move a god.
  ANTONY. Oh, thou hast fired me! My soul's up in arms,
And mans each part about me. Once again
That noble eagerness of fight has seized me,
That eagerness with which I darted upward
To Cassius' camp. In vain the steepy hill
Opposed my way; in vain a war of spears
Sung round my head and planted all my shield;
I won the trenches while my foremost men
Lagged on the plain below.
  VENTIDIUS.   Ye gods, ye gods,
For such another hour!
  ANTONY.   Come on, my soldier!
Our hearts and arms are still the same. I long
Once more to meet our foes, that thou and I,
Like time and death, marching before our troops,
May taste fate to them, mow them out a passage,
And, entering where the foremost squadrons yield,
Begin the noble harvest of the field.

 (*Exeunt.*)

ACT TWO

(*Enter* CLEOPATRA, IRAS, *and* ALEXAS.)

 CLEOPATRA. What shall I do or whither shall I turn?
Ventidius has o'ercome, and he will go.
 ALEXAS. He goes to fight for you.
 CLEOPATRA. Then he would see me ere he went to fight.
Flatter me not. If once he goes, he's lost,
And all my hopes destroyed.
 ALEXAS.   Does this weak passion
Become a mighty queen?
 CLEOPATRA.   I am no queen.
Is this to be a queen, to be besieged

By yon insulting Roman, and to wait
Each hour the victor's chain? These ills are small;
For Antony is lost, and I can mourn
For nothing else but him. Now come, Octavius,
I have no more to lose! Prepare thy bands;
I'm fit to be a captive; Antony
Has taught my mind the fortune of a slave.

    IRAS.   Call reason to assist you.

    CLEOPATRA.   I have none,
And none would have. My love's a noble madness,
Which shows the cause deserved it. Moderate sorrow
Fits vulgar love, and for a vulgar man,
But I have loved with such transcendent passion,
I soared, at first, quite out of reason's view,
And now am lost above it. No, I'm proud
'Tis thus. Would Antony could see me now!
Think you he would not sigh? Though he must leave me,
Sure, he would sigh, for he is noble-natured,
And bears a tender heart. I know him well.
Ah, no, I know him not; I knew him once,
But now 'tis past.

    IRAS.   Let it be past with you.
Forget him, madam.

    CLEOPATRA.   Never, never, Iras.
He once was mine; and once, though now 'tis gone,
Leaves a faint image of possession still.

    ALEXAS.   Think him unconstant, cruel, and ungrateful.

    CLEOPATRA.   I cannot. If I could, those thoughts were vain.
Faithless, ungrateful, cruel though he be,
I still must love him.

    (*Enter* CHARMION.)

                Now, what news, my Charmion?
Will he be kind? And will he not forsake me?
Am I to live, or die? — nay, do I live?
Or am I dead? For when he gave his answer,
Fate took the word, and then I lived or died.

    CHARMION.   I found him, madam —

    CLEOPATRA.   A long speech preparing?
If thou bring'st comfort, haste, and give it me,
For never was more need.

    IRAS.   I know he loves you.

    CLEOPATRA.   Had he been kind, her eyes had told me so
Before her tongue could speak it. Now she studies
To soften what he said; but give me death

Just as he sent it, Charmion, undisguised,
And in the words he spoke.

    CHARMION.   I found him, then,
Encompassed round, I think, with iron statues;
So mute, so motionless his soldiers stood,
While awfully he cast his eyes about
And every leader's hopes or fears surveyed.
Methought he looked resolved, and yet not pleased.
When he beheld me struggling in the crowd,
He blushed, and bade make way.

    ALEXAS.   There's comfort yet.

    CHARMION.   Ventidius fixed his eyes upon my passage
Severely, as he meant to frown me back,
And sullenly gave place. I told my message,
Just as you gave it, broken and disordered;
I numbered in it all your sighs and tears,
And while I moved your pitiful request,
That you but only begged a last farewell,
He fetched an inward groan; and every time
I named you, sighed as if his heart were breaking,
But shunned my eyes and guiltily looked down.
He seemed not now that awful Antony
Who shook an armed assembly with his nod;
But, making show as he would rub his eyes,
Disguised and blotted out a falling tear.

    CLEOPATRA.   Did he then weep? And was I worth a tear?
If what thou hast to say be not as pleasing,
Tell me no more, but let me die contented.

    CHARMION.   He bid me say, he knew himself so well,
He could deny you nothing if he saw you;
And therefore —

    CLEOPATRA.   Thou wouldst say, he would not see me?

    CHARMION.   And therefore begged you not to use a power
Which he could ill resist; yet he should ever
Respect you as he ought.

    CLEOPATRA.   Is that a word
For Antony to use to Cleopatra?
O that faint word, *respect!* how I disdain it!
Disdain myself for loving, after it!
He should have kept that word for cold Octavia.
Respect is for a wife. Am I that thing,
That dull, insipid lump, without desires,
And without power to give them?

    ALEXAS.   You misjudge;
You see through love, and that deludes your sight,
As what is straight seems crooked through the water.

But I, who bear my reason undisturbed,
Can see this Antony, this dreaded man,
A fearful slave who fain would run away,
And shuns his master's eyes. If you pursue him,
My life on 't, he still drags a chain along
That needs must clog his flight.
   CLEOPATRA.   Could I believe thee! —
   ALEXAS.   By every circumstance I know he loves,
True, he's hard pressed by int'rest and by honor;
Yet he but doubts and parleys and casts out
Many a long look for succor.
   CLEOPATRA.   He sends word
He fears to see my face.
   ALEXAS.   And would you more?
He shows his weakness who declines the combat,
And you must urge your fortune. Could he speak
More plainly? To my ears the message sounds —
"Come to my rescue, Cleopatra, come;
Come, free me from Ventidius — from my tyrant;
See me and give me a pretense to leave him!"
I hear his trumpets. This way he must pass.
Please you, retire a while; I'll work him first,
That he may bend more easy.
   CLEOPATRA.   You shall rule me;
But all, I fear, in vain. (*Exit with* CHARMION *and* IRAS.)
   ALEXAS.   I fear so, too,
Though I concealed my thoughts, to make her bold,
But 'tis our utmost means, and fate befriend it! (*Withdraws.*)

   (*Enter* LICTORS *with fasces, one bearing the eagle; then enter* ANTONY
with VENTIDIUS, *followed by other* COMMANDERS.)

   ANTONY.   Octavius is the minion of blind chance
But holds from virtue nothing.
   VENTIDIUS.   Has he courage?
   ANTONY.   But just enough to season him from coward.
Oh, 'tis the coldest youth upon a charge,
The most deliberate fighter! If he ventures
(As in Illyria once, they said, he did,
To storm a town), 'tis when he cannot choose;
When all the world have fixed their eyes upon him,
And then he lives on that for seven years after;
But at a close revenge he never fails.
   VENTIDIUS.   I heard you challenged him.
   ANTONY.   I did, Ventidius.
What think'st thou was his answer? 'Twas so tame! —
He said he had more ways than one to die;
I had not.

VENTIDIUS. Poor!

ANTONY.   He has more ways than one,
But he would choose them all before that one.

VENTIDIUS. He first would choose an ague or a fever.

ANTONY. No; it must be an ague, not a fever;
He has not warmth enough to die by that.

VENTIDIUS. Or old age and a bed.

ANTONY.   Ay, there's his choice,
He would live like a lamp to the last wink,
And crawl upon the utmost verge of life.
O Hercules! Why should a man like this,
Who dares not trust his fate for one great action,
Be all the care of Heaven? Why should he lord it
O'er fourscore thousand men, of whom each one
Is braver than himself?

VENTIDIUS.   You conquered for him
Philippi knows it; there you shared with him
That empire which your sword made all your own.

ANTONY. Fool that I was, upon my eagle's wings
I bore this wren till I was tired with soaring,
And now he mounts above me.
Good heavens, is this — is this the man who braves me?
Who bids my age make way? Drives me before him
To the world's ridge and sweeps me off like rubbish?

VENTIDIUS. Sir, we lose time; the troops are mounted all.

ANTONY. Then give the word to march.
I long to leave this prison of a town,
To join thy legions, and in open field
Once more to show my face. Lead, my deliverer.

(*Enter* ALEXAS.)

ALEXAS.   Great emperor,
In mighty arms renowned above mankind,
But in soft pity to th' oppressed, a god,
This message sends the mournful Cleopatra
To her departing lord.

VENTIDIUS.   Smooth sycophant!

ALEXAS. A thousand wishes and ten thousand prayers,
Millions of blessings wait you to the wars;
Millions of sighs and tears she sends you, too,
And would have sent
As many dear embraces to your arms,
As many parting kisses to your lips,
But those, she fears, have wearied you already.

VENTIDIUS (*aside*). False crocodile!

ALEXAS. And yet she begs not now you would not leave her;
That were a wish too mighty for her hopes,

Too presuming
For her low fortune and your ebbing love;
That were a wish for her more prosperous days,
Her blooming beauty and your growing kindness.

    ANTONY (aside).   Well, I must man it out. — What would the queen?

    ALEXAS.   First, to these noble warriors who attend
Your daring courage in the chase of fame, —
Too daring and too dangerous for her quiet, —
She humbly recommends all she holds dear,
All her own cares and fears, — the care of you.

    VENTIDIUS.   Yes, witness Actium.

    ANTONY.   Let him speak, Ventidius.

    ALEXAS.   You, when his matchless valor bears him forward
With ardor too heroic, on his foes,
Fall down, as she would do, before his feet;
Lie in his way and stop the paths of death.
Tell him this god is not invulnerable,
That absent Cleopatra bleeds in him,
And, that you may remember her petition,
She begs you wear these trifles as a pawn
Which, at your wished return, she will redeem (*gives jewels to the* COM-
    MANDERS)
With all the wealth of Egypt.
This to the great Ventidius she presents,
Whom she can never count her enemy,
Because he loves her lord.

    VENTIDIUS.   Tell her, I'll none on 't;
I'm not ashamed of honest poverty;
Not all the diamonds of the east can bribe
Ventidius from his faith. I hope to see
These and the rest of all her sparkling store
Where they shall more deservingly be placed.

    ANTONY.   And who must wear 'em then?

    VENTIDIUS.   The wronged Octavia.

    ANTONY.   You might have spared that word.

    VENTIDIUS.   And he, that bribe.

    ANTONY.   But have I no remembrance?

    ALEXAS.   Yes, a dear one;
Your slave the queen —

    ANTONY.   My mistress.

    ALEXAS.   Then your mistress;
Your mistress would, she says, have sent her soul,
But that you had long since; she humbly begs
This ruby bracelet, set with bleeding hearts,
The emblems of her own, may bind your arm. (*Presenting a bracelet.*)

    VENTIDIUS.   Now, my best lord, in honor's name, I ask you,
For manhood's sake and for your own dear safety,

Touch not these poisoned gifts,
Infected by the sender; touch 'em not;
Myriads of bluest plagues lie underneath them,
And more than aconite has dipped the silk.

 ANTONY. Nay, now you grow too cynical, Ventidius;
A lady's favors may be worn with honor.
What, to refuse her bracelet! On my soul,
When I lie pensive in my tent alone,
'Twill pass the wakeful hours of winter nights.
To tell these pretty beads upon my arm,
To count for every one a soft embrace,
A melting kiss at such and such a time,
And now and then the fury of her love
When — And what harm's in this?

 ALEXAS.   None, none, my lord,
But what's to her, that now 'tis past forever.

 ANTONY (*going to tie it*). We soldiers are so awkward — help me tie it.

 ALEXAS. In faith, my lord, we courtiers, too, are awkward
In these affairs; so are all men indeed,
Even I, who am not one. But shall I speak?

 ANTONY. Yes, freely.

 ALEXAS.   Then, my lord, fair hands alone
Are fit to tie it; she who sent it can.

 VENTIDIUS. Hell! death! this eunuch pander ruins you.
You will not see her?

 (ALEXAS *whispers to an* ATTENDANT, *who goes out.*)

 ANTONY.   But to take my leave.

 VENTIDIUS. Then I have washed an Aethiop. You're undone;
You're in the toils; you're taken; you're destroyed;
Her eyes do Caesar's work.

 ANTONY.   You fear too soon.
I'm constant to myself; I know my strength;
And yet she shall not think me barbarous neither,
Born in the depths of Afric. I'm a Roman,
Bred to the rules of soft humanity.
A guest, and kindly used, should bid farewell.

 VENTIDIUS. You do not know
How weak you are to her, how much an infant;
You are not proof against a smile or glance;
A sigh will quite disarm you.

 ANTONY.   See, she comes!
Now you shall find your error. — Gods, I thank you.
I formed the danger greater than it was,
And now 'tis near, 'tis lessened.

 VENTIDIUS.   Mark the end yet.

 (*Enter* CLEOPATRA, CHARMION, *and* IRAS.)

ANTONY. Well, madam, we are met.

CLEOPATRA. Is this a meeting?
Then, we must part?

ANTONY. We must.

CLEOPATRA. Who says we must?

ANTONY. Our own hard fates.

CLEOPATRA. We make those fates ourselves.

ANTONY. Yes, we have made them; we have loved each other
Into our mutual ruin.

CLEOPATRA. The gods have seen my joys with envious eyes;
I have no friends in heaven, and all the world,
As 'twere the business of mankind to part us,
Is armed against my love. Even you yourself
Join with the rest; you, you are armed against me.

ANTONY. I will be justified in all I do
To late posterity, and therefore hear me.
If I mix a lie
With any truth, reproach me freely with it;
Else, favor me with silence.

CLEOPATRA. You command me,
And I am dumb.

VENTIDIUS (aside). I like this well; he shows authority.

ANTONY. That I derive my ruin
From you alone —

CLEOPATRA. O heavens! I ruin you!

ANTONY. You promised me your silence, and you break it
Ere I have scarce begun.

CLEOPATRA. Well, I obey you.

ANTONY. When I beheld you first, it was in Egypt,
Ere Caesar saw your eyes, you gave me love,
And were too young to know it; that I settled
Your father in his throne was for your sake;
I left th' acknowledgment for time to ripen.
Caesar stepped in and with a greedy hand
Plucked the green fruit ere the first blush of red,
Yet cleaving to the bough. He was my lord,
And was, beside, too great for me to rival.
But I deserved you first, though he enjoyed you.
When, after, I beheld you in Cilicia,
An enemy to Rome, I pardoned you.

CLEOPATRA. I cleared myself —

ANTONY. Again you break your promise.
I loved you still and took your weak excuses,
Took you into my bosom, stained by Caesar,
And not half mine. I went to Egypt with you,
And hid me from the business of the world,

Shut out inquiring nations from my sight
To give whole years to you.
    VENTIDIUS (*aside*).   Yes, to your shame be 't spoken.
    ANTONY.   How I loved,
Witness, ye days and nights and all your hours
That danced away with down upon your feet,
As all your business were to count my passion!
One day passed by and nothing saw but love;
Another came and still 'twas only love.
The suns were wearied out with looking on,
And I untired with loving.
I saw you every day, and all the day;
And every day was still but as the first,
So eager was I still to see you more.
    VENTIDIUS.   'Tis all too true.
    ANTONY.   Fulvia, my wife, grew jealous,
As she indeed had reason; raised a war
In Italy to call me back.
    VENTIDIUS.   But yet
You went not.
    ANTONY.   While within your arms I lay,
The world fell moldering from my hands each hour,
And left me scarce a grasp — I thank your love for 't.
    VENTIDIUS.   Well pushed: that last was home.
    CLEOPATRA.   Yet may I speak?
    ANTONY.   If I have urged a falsehood, yes; else, not.
Your silence says I have not. Fulvia died
(Pardon, you gods, with my unkindness died);
To set the world at peace I took Octavia,
This Caesar's sister; in her pride of youth
And flower of beauty did I wed that lady,
Whom, blushing, I must praise, because I left her.
You called; my love obeyed the fatal summons.
This raised the Roman arms; the cause was yours,
I would have fought by land where I was stronger;
You hindered it; yet, when I fought at sea,
Forsook me fighting; and (O stain to honor!
O lasting shame!) I knew not that I fled,
But fled to follow you.
    VENTIDIUS.   What haste she made to hoist her purple sails!
And, to appear magnificent in flight,
Drew half our strength away.
    ANTONY.   All this you caused.
And would you multiply more ruins on me?
This honest man, my best, my only friend,
Has gathered up the shipwreck of my fortunes;

Twelve legions I have left, my last recruits,
And you have watched the news, and bring your eyes
To seize them, too. If you have aught to answer,
Now speak, you have free leave.

ALEXAS (aside). She stands confounded.
Despair is in her eyes.

VENTIDIUS. Now lay a sigh i' th' way to stop his passage;
Prepare a tear and bid it for his legions;
'Tis like they shall be sold.

CLEOPATRA. How shall I plead my cause when you, my judge,
Already have condemned me? Shall I bring
The love you bore me for my advocate?
That now is turned against me, that destroys me;
For love, once past, is, at the best, forgotten,
But oft'ner sours to hate. 'Twill please my lord
To ruin me, and therefore I'll be guilty.
But could I once have thought it would have pleased you,
That you would pry, with narrow searching eyes,
Into my faults, severe to my destruction,
And watching all advantages with care
That serve to make me wretched? Speak, my lord,
For I end here. Though I deserve this usage,
Was it like you to give it?

ANTONY. Oh, you wrong me
To think I sought this parting or desired
To accuse you more than what will clear myself
And justify this breach.

CLEOPATRA. Thus low I thank you,
And, since my innocence will not offend,
I shall not blush to own it.

VENTIDIUS (aside). After this,
I think she'll blush at nothing.

CLEOPATRA. You seem grieved
(And therein you are kind) that Caesar first
Enjoyed my love, though you deserved it better.
I grieve for that, my lord, much more than you;
For, had I first been yours, it would have saved
My second choice: I never had been his,
And ne'er had been but yours. But Caesar first,
You say, possessed my love. Not so, my lord.
He first possessed my person: you, my love.
Caesar loved me, but I loved Antony.
If I endured him after, 'twas because
I judged it due to the first name of men,
And, half constrained, I gave as to a tyrant
What he would take by force.

VENTIDIUS.   O Siren! Siren!
Yet grant that all the love she boasts were true,
Has she not ruined you? I still urge that,
The fatal consequence.

     CLEOPATRA.   The consequence, indeed,
For I dare challenge him, my greatest foe,
To say it was designed. 'Tis true I loved you,
And kept you far from an uneasy wife, —
Such Fulvia was.
Yes, but he'll say you left Octavia for me; —
And can you blame me to receive that love
Which quitted such desert for worthless me?
How often have I wished some other Caesar,
Great as the first, and as the second, young,
Would court my love to be refused for you!

     VENTIDIUS.   Words, words; but Actium, sir; remember Actium.

     CLEOPATRA.   Even there I dare his malice. True, I counseled
To fight at sea, but I betrayed you not.
I fled, but not to the enemy. 'Twas fear.
Would I had been a man, not to have feared!
For none would then have envied me your friendship,
Who envy me your love.

     ANTONY.   We're both unhappy.
If nothing else, yet our ill fortune parts us.
Speak; would you have me perish by my stay?

     CLEOPATRA.   If, as a friend, you ask my judgment, go;
If as a lover, stay. If you must perish —
'Tis a hard word — but stay.

     VENTIDIUS.   See now th' effects of her so boasted love!
She strives to drag you down to ruin with her;
But could she 'scape without you, oh, how soon
Would she let go her hold and haste to shore
And never look behind!

     CLEOPATRA.   Then judge my love by this. (*Giving* ANTONY *a
writing.*)
Could I have borne
A life or death, a happiness or woe
From yours divided, this had given me means.

     ANTONY.   By Hercules, the writing of Octavius!
I know it well; 'tis that proscribing hand,
Young as it was, that led the way to mine
And left me but the second place in murder. —
See, see, Ventidius! here he offers Egypt,
And joins all Syria to it as a present,
So, in requital, she forsake my fortunes
And join her arms with his.

CLEOPATRA.   And yet you leave me!
You leave me, Antony; and yet I love you,
Indeed I do. I have refused a kingdom;
That's a trifle;
For I could part with life, with anything,
But only you. Oh, let me die but with you!
Is that a hard request?

ANTONY.   Next living with you,
'Tis all that Heaven can give.

ALEXAS (aside).   He melts; we conquer.

CLEOPATRA.   No; you shall go. Your interest calls you hence;
Yes, your dear interest pulls too strong for these
Weak arms to hold you here. (Takes his hand.)
Go; leave me, soldier
(For you're no more a lover), leave me dying;
Push me, all pale and panting, from your bosom,
And, when your march begins, let one run after,
Breathless almost for joy, and cry, "She's dead."
The soldiers shout; you then perhaps may sigh
And muster all your Roman gravity.
Ventidius chides; and straight your brow clears up,
As I had never been.

ANTONY.   Gods, 'tis too much —
Too much for man to bear.

CLEOPATRA.   What is 't for me, then,
A weak, forsaken woman and a lover? —
Here let me breathe my last. Envy me not
This minute in your arms. I'll die apace,
As fast as e'er I can, and end your trouble.

ANTONY.   Die! Rather let me perish; loosened nature
Leap from its hinges! Sink the props of heaven,
And fall the skies to crush the nether world!
My eyes, my soul, my all! (Embraces her.)

VENTIDIUS.   And what's this toy
In balance with your fortune, honor, fame?

ANTONY.   What is 't, Ventidius? It outweighs 'em all;
Why, we have more than conquered Caesar now.
My queen's not only innocent, but loves me.
This, this is she who drags me down to ruin!
"But could she 'scape without me, with what haste
Would she let slip her hold and make to shore
And never look behind!"
Down on thy knees, blasphemer as thou art,
And ask forgiveness of wronged innocence.

VENTIDIUS.   I'll rather die than take it. Will you go?

ANTONY.   Go! Whither? Go from all that's excellent!
Faith, honor, virtue, all good things forbid

That I should go from her who sets my love
Above the price of kingdoms Give, you gods,
Give to your boy, your Caesar,
This rattle of a globe to play withal,
This gewgaw world, and put him cheaply off.
I'll not be pleased with less than Cleopatra.

    CLEOPATRA.   She's wholly yours My heart's so full of joy
That I shall do some wild extravagance
Of love in public, and the foolish world.
Which knows not tenderness, will think me mad.

    VENTIDIUS.   O women! women! women! all the gods
Have not such power of doing good to man
As you of doing harm (*Exit.*)

    ANTONY   Our men are armed.
Unbar the gate that looks to Caesar's camp.
I would revenge the treachery he meant me;
And long security makes conquest easy.
I'm eager to return before I go,
For all the pleasures I have known beat thick
On my remembrance. — How I long for night!
That both the sweets of mutual love may try,
And once triumph o'er Caesar ere we die.

    (*Exeunt.*)

ACT THREE

(*At one door enter* CLEOPATRA, CHARMION, IRAS, *and* ALEXAS, *a train of* EGYPTIANS; *at the other,* ANTONY *and* ROMANS. *The entrance on both sides is prepared by music; the trumpets first sounding on* ANTONY'S *part, then answered by timbrels, and such, on* CLEOPATRA'S. CHARMION *and* IRAS *hold a laurel wreath betwixt them. A dance of* EGYPTIANS. *After the ceremony* CLEOPATRA *crowns* ANTONY.)

    ANTONY.   I thought how those white arms would fold me in,
And strain me close and melt me into love;
So pleased with that sweet image, I sprung forwards,
And added all my strength to every blow.

    CLEOPATRA.   Come to me, come, my soldier, to my arms!
You've been too long away from my embraces,
But, when I have you fast and all my own,
With broken murmurs and with amorous sighs.
I'll say you were unkind, and punish you,
And mark you red with many an eager kiss.

    ANTONY.   My brighter Venus!

    CLEOPATRA.   O my greater Mars!

ANTONY.   Thou join'st us well, my love!
Suppose me come from the Phlegraean plains
Where gasping giants lay, cleft by my sword,
And mountain-tops pared off each other blow
To bury those I slew. Receive me, goddess!
Let Caesar spread his subtle nets, like Vulcan;
In thy embraces I would be beheld
By heaven and earth at once;
And make their envy what they meant their sport.
Let those who took us blush; I would love on
With awful state, regardless of their frowns,
As their superior god.
There's no satiety of love in thee:
Enjoyed, thou still art new; perpetual spring
Is in thy arms; the ripened fruit but falls,
And blossoms rise to fill its empty place,
And I grow rich by giving.

(*Enter* VENTIDIUS, *and stands apart.*)

ALEXAS.   Oh, now the danger's past, your general comes!
He joins not in your joys, nor minds your triumphs;
But with contracted brows looks frowning on,
As envying your success.
ANTONY.   Now, on my soul, he loves me; truly loves me;
He never flattered me in any vice,
But awes me with his virtue. Even this minute
Methinks, he has a right of chiding me. —
Lead to the temple — I'll avoid his presence;
It checks too strong upon me.

(*Exeunt the rest. As* ANTONY *is going,* VENTIDIUS *pulls him by the robe.*)

VENTIDIUS.   Emperor!
ANTONY (*looking back*).   'Tis the old argument. I pr'ythee, spare me.
VENTIDIUS.   But this one hearing, emperor.
ANTONY.   Let go
My robe; or, by my father Hercules —
VENTIDIUS.   By Hercules his father, that's yet greater,
I bring you somewhat you would wish to know.
ANTONY.   Thou seest we are observed; attend me here,
And I'll return. (*Exit.*)
VENTIDIUS.   I'm waning in his favor, yet I love him;
I love this man who runs to meet his ruin;
And sure the gods, like me, are fond of him.
His virtues lie so mingled with his crimes,

As would confound their choice to punish one
And not reward the other.

(*Enter* ANTONY.)

ANTONY.   We can conquer,
You see, without your aid.
We have dislodged their troops;
They look on us at distance and, like curs
'Scaped from the lion's paw, they bay far off,
And lick their wounds and faintly threaten war.
Five thousand Romans with their faces upward
Lie breathless on the plain.
    VENTIDIUS.   'Tis well; and he
Who lost them could have spared ten thousand more.
Yet if, by this advantage, you could gain
An easier peace while Caesar doubts the chance
Of arms —
    ANTONY.   Oh, think not on 't, Ventidius!
The boy pursues my ruin, he'll no peace;
His malice is considerate in advantage.
Oh, he's the coolest murderer! so staunch,
He kills, and keeps his temper.
    VENTIDIUS.   Have you no friend
In all his army who has power to move him?
Maecenas, or Agrippa, might do much.
    ANTONY.   They're both too deep in Caesar's interests.
We'll work it out by dint of sword, or perish.
    VENTIDIUS.   Fain I would find some other.
    ANTONY.   Thank thy love.
Some four or five such victories as this
Will save thy further pains.
    VENTIDIUS.   Expect no more — Caesar is on his guard.
I know, sir, you have conquered against odds,
But still you draw supplies from one poor town,
And of Egyptians. He has all the world,
And at his back nations come pouring in
To fill the gaps you make. Pray, think again,
    ANTONY.   Why does thou drive me from myself, to search
For foreign aids? — to hunt my memory,
And range all o'er a waste and barren place
To find a friend? The wretched have no friends. —
Yet I had one, the bravest youth of Rome,
Whom Caesar loves beyond the love of women;
He could resolve his mind as fire does wax,
From that hard, rugged image melt him down,
And mold him in what softer form he pleased.

VENTIDIUS.   Him would I see — that man of all the world;
Just such a one we want.
    ANTONY.   He loved me, too;
I was his soul; he lived not but in me.
We were so closed within each other's breasts,
The rivets were not found that joined us first.
That does not reach us yet; we were so mixed
As meeting streams, both to ourselves were lost;
We were one mass; we could not give or take
But from the same, for he was I, I he.
    VENTIDIUS (aside).   He moves as I would wish him.
    ANTONY.   After this
I need not tell his name. — 'Twas Dolabella.
    VENTIDIUS.   He's now in Caesar's camp.
    ANTONY.   No matter where.
Since he's no longer mine. He took unkindly
That I forbade him Cleopatra's sight,
Because I feared he loved her. He confessed
He had a warmth which, for my sake, he stifled,
For 'twere impossible that two, so one,
Should not have loved the same. When he departed,
He took no leave, and that confirmed my thoughts.
    VENTIDIUS.   It argues that he loved you more than her,
Else he had stayed. But he perceived you jealous,
And would not grieve his friend. I know he loves you.
    ANTONY.   I should have seen him, then, ere now.
    VENTIDIUS.   Perhaps
He has thus long been laboring for your peace.
    ANTONY.   Would he were here!
    VENTIDIUS.   Would you believe he loved you?
I read your answer in your eyes — you would.
Not to conceal it longer, he has sent
A messenger from Caesar's camp with letters.
    ANTONY.   Let him appear.
    VENTIDIUS.   I'll bring him instantly.

(Exit VENTIDIUS, re-enters immediately with DOLABELLA.)

    ANTONY.   'Tis he himself! himself, by holy friendship! (Runs to embrace him.)
Art thou returned at last, my better half?
Come, give me all myself! Let me not live,
If the young bridegroom, longing for his night,
Was ever half so fond!
    DOLABELLA.   I must be silent, for my soul is busy
About a nobler work; she's new come home,

Like a long-absent man, and wanders o'er
Each room, a stranger to her own, to look
If all be safe.
  ANTONY.   Thou hast what's left of me;
For I am now so sunk from what I was,
Thou find'st me at my lowest water-mark.
The rivers that ran in and raised my fortunes
Are all dried up, or take another course;
What I have left is from my native spring.
I've still a heart that swells in scorn of fate
And lifts me to my banks.
  DOLABELLA.   Still you are lord of all the world to me.
  ANTONY.   Why, then I yet am so; for thou art all.
If I had any joy when thou wert absent,
I grudged it to myself; methought I robbed
Thee of thy part. But, O my Dolabella!
Thou hast beheld me other than I am.
Hast thou not seen my morning chambers filled
With sceptred slaves who waited to salute me?
With eastern monarchs who forgot the sun
To worship my uprising? — menial kings
Ran coursing up and down my palace-yard,
Stood silent in my presence, watched my eyes,
And at my least command all started out
Like racers to the goal.
  DOLABELLA.   Slaves to your fortune.
  ANTONY.   Fortune is Caesar's now; and what am I?
  VENTIDIUS.   What you have made yourself; I will not flatter.
  ANTONY.   Is this friendly done?
  DOLABELLA.   Yes; when his end is so, I must join with him;
Indeed, I must; and yet you must not chide;
Why am I else your friend?
  ANTONY.   Take heed, young man,
How thou upbraid'st my love. The queen has eyes,
And thou, too, hast a soul. Canst thou remember
When, swelled with hatred, thou beheld'st her first,
As accessory to thy brother's death?
  DOLABELLA.   Spare my remembrance; 'twas a guilty day
And still the blush hangs here.
  ANTONY.   To clear herself
For sending him no aid, she came from Egypt.
Her galley down the silver Cydnos rowed,
The tackling silk, the streamers waved with gold;
The gentle winds were lodged in purple sails;
Her nymphs, like Nereids, round her couch were placed,
Where she, another sea-born Venus, lay.

DOLABELLA.   No more; I would not hear it.
ANTONY.   Oh, you must!
She lay, and leant her cheek upon her hand,
And cast a look so languishingly sweet
As if, secure of all beholders' hearts,
Neglecting, she could take them. Boys like Cupids
Stood fanning with their painted wings the winds
That played about her face; but if she smiled,
A darting glory seemed to blaze abroad,
That men's desiring eyes were never wearied,
But hung upon the object. To soft flutes
The silver oars kept time; and while they played,
The hearing gave new pleasure to the sight,
And both, to thought. 'Twas heaven or somewhat more;
For she so charmed all hearts, that gazing crowds
Stood panting on the shore, and wanted breath
To give their welcome voice.
Then, Dolabella, where was then thy soul?
Was not thy fury quite disarmed with wonder?
Didst thou not shrink behind me from those eyes
And whisper in my ear, "Oh, tell her not
That I accused her of my brother's death"?
    DOLABELLA.   And should my weakness be a plea for yours?
Mine was an age when love might be excused,
When kindly warmth, and when my springing youth,
Made it a debt to nature. Yours —
    VENTIDIUS.   Speak boldly.
Yours, he would say, in your declining age,
When no more heat was left but what you forced,
When all the sap was needful for the trunk,
When it went down, then you constrained the course,
And robbed from nature to supply desire;
In you (I would not use so harsh a word)
'Tis but plain dotage.
    ANTONY.   Ha!
    DOLABELLA.   'Twas urged too home. —
But yet the loss was private that I made;
'Twas but myself I lost. I lost no legions;
I had no world to lose, no people's love.
    ANTONY.   This from a friend?
    DOLABELLA.   Yes, Antony, a true one;
A friend so tender that each word I speak
Stabs my own heart before it reach your ear.
Oh, judge me not less kind because I chide!
To Caesar I excuse you.
    ANTONY.   O ye gods!
Have I then lived to be excused to Caesar?

DOLABELLA. As to your equal.

ANTONY.   Well, he's but my equal;
While I wear this, he never shall be more.

DOLABELLA.   I bring conditions from him.

ANTONY.   Are they noble?
Methinks thou shouldst not bring them else; yet he
Is full of deep dissembling; knows no honor
Divided from his interest. Fate mistook him,
For nature meant him for an usurer;
He's fit indeed to buy, not conquer, kingdoms.

VENTIDIUS.   Then, granting this,
What power was theirs who wrought so hard a temper
To honorable terms?

ANTONY.   It was my Dolabella, or some god.

DOLABELLA.   Nor I, nor yet Maecenas, nor Agrippa;
They were your enemies, and I, a friend,
Too weak alone; yet 'twas a Roman's deed.

ANTONY.   'Twas like a Roman done; show me that man
Who has preserved my life, my love, my honor;
Let me but see his face.

VENTIDIUS.   That task is mine,
And, Heaven, thou know'st how pleasing. (*Exit.*)

DOLABELLA.   You'll remember
To whom you stand obliged?

ANTONY.   When I forget it,
Be thou unkind, and that's my greatest curse.
My queen shall thank him, too.

DOLABELLA.   I fear she will not.

ANTONY.   But she shall do 't — the queen, my Dolabella!
Hast thou not still some grudgings of thy fever?

DOLABELLA.   I would not see her lost.

ANTONY.   When I forsake her,
Leave me, my better stars! for she has truth
Beyond her beauty. Caesar tempted her,
At no less price than kingdoms, to betray me,
But she resisted all; and yet thou chid'st me
For loving her too well. Could I do so?

(*Re-enter* VENTIDIUS *with* OCTAVIA, *leading* ANTONY's *two little* DAUGHTERS.)

DOLABELLA.   Yes; there's my reason.

ANTONY.   Where? — Octavia there! (*Starting back.*)

VENTIDIUS.   What — is she poison to you? — a disease?
Look on her, view her well, and those she brings.
Are they all strangers to your eyes? has nature
No secret call, no whisper they are yours?

DOLABELLA.   For shame, my lord, if not for love, receive them
With kinder eyes. If you confess a man,
Meet them, embrace them, bid them welcome to you.
Your arms should open, even without your knowledge,
To clasp them in; your feet should turn to wings,
To bear you to them; and your eyes dart out
And aim a kiss ere you could reach the lips.

    ANTONY.   I stood amazed to think how they came hither.

    VENTIDIUS.   I sent for 'em; I brought 'em in, unknown
To Cleopatra's guards.

    DOLABELLA.   Yet are you cold?

    OCTAVIA.   Thus long I have attended for my welcome,
Which, as a stranger, sure I might expect.
Who am I?

    ANTONY.   Caesar's sister.

    OCTAVIA.   That's unkind.
Had I been nothing more than Caesar's sister,
Know, I had still remained in Caesar's camp.
But your Octavia, your much injured wife,
Though banished from your bed, driven from your house,
In spite of Caesar's sister, still is yours.
'Tis true, I have a heart disdains your coldness,
And prompts me not to seek what you should offer;
But a wife's virtue still surmounts that pride.
I come to claim you as my own; to show
My duty first; to ask, nay beg, your kindness.
Your hand, my lord; 'tis mine, and I will have it.   (*Taking his hand.*)

    VENTIDIUS.   Do, take it; thou deserv'st it.

    DOLABELLA.   On my soul,
And so she does; she's neither too submissive,
Nor yet too haughty; but so just a mean
Shows, as it ought, a wife and Roman too.

    ANTONY.   I fear, Octavia, you have begged my life.

    OCTAVIA.   Begged it, my lord?

    ANTONY.   Yes, begged it, my ambassadress;
Poorly and basely begged it of your brother.

    OCTAVIA.   Poorly and basely I could never beg.
Nor could my brother grant.

    ANTONY.   Shall I, who, to my kneeling slave, could say,
"Rise up and be a king," shall I fall down
And cry, "Forgive me, Caesar?" Shall I set
A man, my equal, in the place of Jove,
As he could give me being? No — that word
"Forgive" would choke me up
And die upon my tongue.

    DOLABELLA.   You shall not need it.

ANTONY.　I will not need it. Come, you've all betrayed me —
My friend too! — to receive some vile conditions.
My wife has bought me with her prayers and tears,
And now I must become her branded slave.
In every peevish mood she will upbraid
The life she gave; if I but look awry,
She cries, "I'll tell my brother."

OCTAVIA.　　　　　　　　My hard fortune
Subjects me still to your unkind mistakes.
But the conditions I have brought are such
You need not blush to take; I love your honor,
Because 'tis mine. It never shall be said
Octavia's husband was her brother's slave.
Sir, you are free — free, even from her you loathe;
For, though my brother bargains for your love,
Makes me the price and cément of your peace,
I have a soul like yours; I cannot take
Your love as alms, nor beg what I deserve.
I'll tell my brother we are reconciled;
He shall draw back his troops, and you shall march
To rule the East. I may be dropped at Athens —
No matter where. I never will complain,
But only keep the barren name of wife,
And rid you of the trouble.

VENTIDIUS.　Was ever such a strife of sullen honor!
Both scorn to be obliged.

DOLABELLA.　Oh, she has touched him in the tenderest part;
See how he reddens with despite and shame,
To be outdone in generosity!

VENTIDIUS.　See how he winks! how he dries up a tear,
That fain would fall!

ANTONY.　Octavia, I have heard you, and must praise
The greatness of your soul;
But cannot yield to what you have proposed,
For I can ne'er be conquered but by love,
And you do all for duty. You would free me,
And would be dropped at Athens; was 't not so?

OCTAVIA.　It was, my lord.

ANTONY.　　　　　　　Then I must be obliged
To one who loves me not; who, to herself,
May call me thankless and ungrateful man. —
I'll not endure it — no.

VENTIDIUS (*aside*).　I am glad it pinches there.

OCTAVIA.　Would you triumph o'er poor Octavia's virtue?
That pride was all I had to bear me up;
That you might think you owed me for your life,

And owed it to my duty, not my love.
I have been injured, and my haughty soul
Could brook but ill the man who slights my bed.

    ANTONY.   Therefore you love me not.

    OCTAVIA.   Therefore, my lord,
I should not love you.

    ANTONY.   Therefore you would leave me?

    OCTAVIA.   And therefore I should leave you — if I could.

    DOLABELLA.   Her soul's too great, after such injuries,
To say she loves; and yet she lets you see it.
Her modesty and silence plead her cause.

    ANTONY.   O Dolabella, which way shall I turn?
I find a secret yielding in my soul;
But Cleopatra, who would die with me,
Must she be left? Pity pleads for Octavia,
But does it not plead more for Cleopatra?

    VENTIDIUS.   Justice and pity both plead for Octavia;
For Cleopatra, neither.
One would be ruined with you, but she first
Had ruined you; the other, you have ruined,
And yet she would preserve you.
In everything their merits are unequal.

    ANTONY.   O my distracted soul!

    OCTAVIA.   Sweet Heaven, compose it! —
Come, come, my lord, if I can pardon you,
Methinks you should accept it. Look on these —
Are they not yours? or stand they thus neglected
As they are mine? Go to him, children, go;
Kneel to him, take him by the hand, speak to him,
For you may speak and he may own you, too,
Without a blush — and so he cannot all
His children. Go, I say, and pull him to me,
And pull him to yourselves from that bad woman.
You, Agrippina, hang upon his arms,
And you, Antonia, clasp about his waist.
If he will shake you off, if he will dash you
Against the pavement, you must bear it, children,
For you are mine, and I was born to suffer.

    (Here the CHILDREN go to him, et cetera.)

    VENTIDIUS.   Was ever sight so moving? — Emperor!

    DOLABELLA.   Friend!

    OCTAVIA.   Husband!

    BOTH CHILDREN.   Father!

    ANTONY.   I am vanquished. Take me,
Octavia — take me, children — share me all. (Embracing them.)

I've been a thriftless debtor to your loves,
And run out much, in riot, from your stock,
But all shall be amended.

OCTAVIA.   O blest hour!

DOLABELLA.   O happy change!

VENTIDIUS.   My joy stops at my tongue,
But it has found two channels here for one,
And bubbles out above.

ANTONY (*to* OCTAVIA).   This is thy triumph. Lead me where thou wilt,
Even to thy brother's camp.

OCTAVIA.   All there are yours,

(*Enter* ALEXAS *hastily.*)

ALEXAS.   The queen, my mistress, sir, and yours —

ANTONY.   'Tis past. —
Octavia, you shall stay this night. Tomorrow
Caesar and we are one.

(*Exit, leading* OCTAVIA; DOLABELLA *and the* CHILDREN *follow.*)

VENTIDIUS.   There's news for you! Run, my officious eunuch,
Be sure to be the first — haste forward!
Haste, my dear eunuch, haste! (*Exit.*)

ALEXAS.   This downright fighting fool, this thick-skulled hero,
This blunt, unthinking instrument of death,
With plain, dull virtue has outgone my wit.
Pleasure forsook my earliest infancy;
The luxury of others robbed my cradle,
And ravished thence the promise of a man.
Cast out from nature, disinherited
Of what her meanest children claim by kind,
Yet greatness kept me from contempt. That's gone.
Had Cleopatra followed my advice,
Then he had been betrayed who now forsakes.
She dies for love, but she has known its joys.
Gods, is this just that I, who know no joys,
Must die because she loves?

(*Enter* CLEOPATRA, CHARMION, IRAS, *train.*)

O madam, I have seen what blasts my eyes!
Octavia's here.

CLEOPATRA.   Peace with that raven's note.
I know it, too, and now am in
The pangs of death.

ALEXAS.   You are no more a queen —
Egypt is lost.

CLEOPATRA.   What tell'st thou me of Egypt?
My life, my soul is lost! Octavia has him! —
O fatal name to Cleopatra's love!
My kisses, my embraces now are hers,
While I — But thou hast seen my rival. Speak —
Does she deserve this blessing? Is she fair?
Bright as a goddess? and is all perfection
Confined to her? — It is. Poor I was made
Of that coarse matter which, when she was finished,
The gods threw by for rubbish.
    ALEXAS.   She's indeed a very miracle.
    CLEOPATRA.   Death to my hopes, a miracle!
    ALEXAS (bowing).   A miracle —
I mean, of goodness; for in beauty, madam,
You make all wonders cease.
    CLEOPATRA.   I was too rash.
Take this in part of recompense. But, oh! (giving a ring)
I fear thou flatter'st me.
    CHARMION.   She comes! She's here!
    IRAS.   Fly, madam, Caesar's sister!
    CLEOPATRA.   Were she the sister of the thunderer Jove,
And bore her brother's lightning in her eye,
Thus would I face my rival.

(Meets OCTAVIA with VENTIDIUS. OCTAVIA bears up to her. Their trains
come up on either side.)

    OCTAVIA.   I need not ask if you are Cleopatra,
Your haughty carriage —
    CLEOPATRA.   Shows I am a queen.
Nor need I ask who you are.
    OCTAVIA.   A Roman;
A name that makes and can unmake a queen.
    CLEOPATRA.   Your lord, the man who serves me, is a Roman.
    OCTAVIA.   He was a Roman, till he lost that name
To be a slave in Egypt; but I come
To free him thence.
    CLEOPATRA.   Peace, peace, my lover's Juno.
When he grew weary of that household clog,
He chose my easier bonds.
    OCTAVIA.   I wonder not
Your bonds are easy. You have long been practiced
In that lascivious art. He's not the first
For whom you spread your snares: let Caesar witness.
    CLEOPATRA.   I loved not Caesar; 'twas but gratitude
I paid his love. The worst your malice can
Is but to say the greatest of mankind

Has been my slave. The next, but far above him
In my esteem, is he whom law calls yours,
But whom his love made mine.

    OCTAVIA (*coming up closer to her*). I would view nearer
That face which has so long usurped my right,
To find the inevitable charms that catch
Mankind so sure, that ruined my dear lord.

    CLEOPATRA. Oh, you do well to search, for had you known
But half these charms, you had not lost his heart.

    OCTAVIA. Far be their knowledge from a Roman lady —
Far from a modest wife! Shame of our sex,
Dost thou not blush to own those black endearments
That make sin pleasing?

    CLEOPATRA.   You may blush, who want them.
If bounteous nature, if indulgent heaven
Have given me charms to please the bravest man,
Should I not thank them? Should I be ashamed,
And not be proud? I am, that he has loved me.
And when I love not him, heaven change this face
For one like that.

    OCTAVIA. Thou lov'st him not so well.

    CLEOPATRA. I love him better, and deserve him more.

    OCTAVIA. You do not — cannot. You have been his ruin.
Who made him cheap at Rome but Cleopatra?
Who made him scorned abroad but Cleopatra?
At Actium, who betrayed him? Cleopatra!
Who made his children orphans, and poor me
A wretched widow? Only Cleopatra.

    CLEOPATRA. Yet she who loves him best is Cleopatra.
If you have suffered, I have suffered more.
You bear the specious title of a wife
To gild your cause and draw the pitying world
To favor it. The world contemns poor me,
For I have lost my honor, lost my fame,
And stained the glory of my royal house,
And all to bear the branded name of mistress.
There wants but life, and that, too, I would lose
For him I love.

    OCTAVIA. Be 't so, then; take thy wish. (*Exit followed by her train.*)

    CLEOPATRA. And 'tis my wish,
Now he is lost for whom alone I lived.
My sight grows dim, and every object dances
And swims before me in the maze of death.
My spirits, while they were opposed, kept up;
They could not sink beneath a rival's scorn,
But now she's gone, they faint.

ALEXAS.   Mine have had leisure
To recollect their strength and furnish counsel
To ruin her, who else must ruin you.

CLEOPATRA.   Vain promiser!
Lead me, my Charmion; nay, your hand, too, Iras.
My grief has weight enough to sink you both.
Conduct me to some solitary chamber,
And draw the curtains round;
Then leave me to myself, to take alone
My fill of grief.
There I till death will his unkindness weep,
As harmless infants moan themselves asleep.

(*Exeunt.*)

ACT FOUR

(ANTONY, DOLABELLA.)

DOLABELLA.   Why would you shift it from yourself on me?
Can you not tell her you must part?

ANTONY.   I cannot.
I could pull out an eye and bid it go,
And t' other should not weep. O Dolabella,
How many deaths are in this word, *Depart!*
I dare not trust my tongue to tell her so —
One look of hers would thaw me into tears,
And I should melt till I were lost again.

DOLABELLA.   Then let Ventidius —
He's rough by nature.

ANTONY.   Oh, he'll speak too harshly;
He'll kill her with the news. Thou, only thou!

DOLABELLA.   Nature has cast me in so soft a mould
That but to hear a story feigned for pleasure,
Of some sad lover's death moistens my eyes,
And robs me of my manhood. I should speak
So faintly, with such fear to grieve her heart,
She'd not believe it earnest.

ANTONY.   Therefore — therefore
Thou, only thou art fit. Think thyself me,
And when thou speak'st (but let it first be long),
Take off the edge from every sharper sound,
And let our parting be as gently made
As other loves begin. Wilt thou do this?

DOLABELLA.   What you have said so sinks into my soul
That, if I must speak, I shall speak just so.

ANTONY.   I leave you then to your sad task.
Farewell!
I sent her word to meet you. (*Goes to the door and comes back.*) I forgot.
Let her be told I'll make her peace with mine.
Her crown and dignity shall be preserved,
If I have power with Caesar. — Oh, be sure
To think on that!
    DOLABELLA.   Fear not, I will remember.

(ANTONY *goes again to the door and comes back.*)

ANTONY.   And tell her, too, how much I was constrained;
I did not this but with extremest force.
Desire her not to hate my memory,
For I still cherish hers; — insist on that.
    DOLABELLA.   Trust me, I'll not forget it.
    ANTONY.   Then that's all. (*Goes out and
        returns again.*)
Wilt thou forgive my fondness this once more?
Tell her, though we shall never meet again,
If I should hear she took another love,
The news would break my heart. — Now I must go,
For every time I have returned, I feel
My soul more tender, and my next command
Would be to bid her stay, and ruin both. (*Exit.*)
    DOLABELLA.   Men are but children of a larger growth;
Our appetites as apt to change as theirs,
And full as craving, too, and full as vain;
And yet the soul, shut up in her dark room,
Viewing so clear abroad, at home sees nothing;
But like a mole in earth, busy and blind,
Works all her folly up and casts it outward
To the world's open view. Thus I discovered,
And blamed, the love of ruined Antony,
Yet wish that I were he, to be so ruined.

(*Enter* VENTIDIUS *above.*)

VENTIDIUS.   Alone, and talking to himself? concerned, too?
Perhaps my guess is right; he loved her once,
And may pursue it still.
    DOLABELLA.   O friendship! friendship!
Ill canst thou answer this; and reason, worse.
Unfaithful in the attempt; hopeless to win;
And, if I win, undone; mere madness all.
And yet the occasion's fair. What injury
To him, to wear the robe which he throws by?

VENTIDIUS.   None, none at all. This happens as I wish,
To ruin her yet more with Antony.

(*Enter* CLEOPATRA, *talking with* ALEXAS; CHARMION, IRAS *on the other side.*)

DOLABELLA.   She comes! What charms have sorrow on that face!
Sorrow seems pleased to dwell with so much sweetness;
Yet, now and then, a melancholy smile
Breaks loose like lightning in a winter's night,
And shows a moment's day.
    VENTIDIUS.   If she should love him, too — her eunuch there!
That porc'pisce bodes ill weather. Draw, draw nearer,
Sweet devil, that I may hear.
    ALEXAS.   Believe me; try

(DOLABELLA *goes over to* CHARMION *and* IRAS; *seems to talk with them.*)

To make him jealous; jealousy is like
A polished glass held to the lips when life's in doubt;
If there be breath; 'twill catch the damp, and show it.
    CLEOPATRA.   I grant you, jealousy's a proof of love,
But 'tis a weak and unavailing medicine;
It puts out the disease, and makes it show,
But has no power to cure.
    ALEXAS.   'Tis your last remedy, and strongest, too.
And then this Dolabella — who so fit
To practice on? He's handsome, valiant, young,
And looks as he were laid for nature's bait
To catch weak women's eyes.
He stands already more than half suspected
Of loving you. The least kind word or glance
You give this youth will kindle him with love;
Then, like a burning vessel set adrift,
You'll send him down amain before the wind
To fire the heart of jealous Antony.
    CLEOPATRA.   Can I do this? Ah, no. My love's so true
That I can neither hide it where it is,
Nor show it where it is not. Nature meant me
A wife — a silly, harmless, household dove,
Fond without art, and kind without deceit;
But Fortune, that has made a mistress of me,
Has thrust me out to the wide world, unfurnished
Of falsehood to be happy.
    ALEXAS.   Force yourself.
The event will be, your lover will return

Doubly desirous to possess the good
Which once he feared to lose.

CLEOPATRA.   I must attempt it,

(Exit ALEXAS.)

But oh, with what regret! (She comes up to DOLABELLA.)

VENTIDIUS.   So, now the scene draws near; they're in my reach.

CLEOPATRA (to DOLABELLA).   Discoursing with my women! Might not I
Share in your entertainment?

CHARMION.   You have been
The subject of it, madam.

CLEOPATRA.   How! and how?

IRAS.   Such praises of your beauty!

CLEOPATRA.   Mere poetry.
Your Roman wits, your Gallus and Tibullus,
Have taught you this from Cytheris and Delia.

DOLABELLA.   Those Roman wits have never been in Egypt;
Cytheris and Delia else had been unsung.
I, who have seen — had I been born a poet,
Should choose a nobler name.

CLEOPATRA.   You flatter me.
But 'tis your nation's vice. All of your country
Are flatterers, and all false. Your friend's like you.
I'm sure he sent you not to speak these words.

DOLABELLA.   No, madam, yet he sent me —

CLEOPATRA.   Well, he sent you —

DOLABELLA.   Of a less pleasing errand.

CLEOPATRA.   How less pleasing?
Less to yourself, or me?

DOLABELLA.   Madam, to both.
For you must mourn, and I must grieve to cause it.

CLEOPATRA.   You, Charmion, and your fellow, stand at distance —
(Aside.) Hold up, my spirits. — Well, now your mournful matter,
For I'm prepared — perhaps can guess it, too.

DOLABELLA.   I wish you would, for 'tis a thankless office
To tell ill news; and I, of all your sex,
Most fear displeasing you.

CLEOPATRA.   Of all your sex
I soonest could forgive you if you should.

VENTIDIUS.   Most delicate advances! — Woman! woman!
Dear, damned, inconstant sex!

CLEOPATRA.   In the first place,
I am to be forsaken. Is 't not so?

DOLABELLA.   I wish I could not answer to that question.

CLEOPATRA.   Then pass it o'er, because it troubles you;
I should have been more grieved another time.
Next, I'm to lose my kingdom — Farewell, Egypt!
Yet, is there any more?

DOLABELLA.   Madam, I fear
Your too deep sense of grief has turned your reason.

CLEOPATRA.   No, no, I'm not run mad; I can bear fortune,
And love may be expelled by other love,
As poisons are by poisons.

DOLABELLA   You o'erjoy me, madam,
To find your griefs so moderately borne.
You've heard the worst; all are not false like him.

CLEOPATRA.   No. Heaven forbid they should.

DOLABELLA.   Some men are constant.

CLEOPATRA.   And constancy deserves reward, that's certain.

DOLABELLA.   Deserves it not, but give it leave to hope.

VENTIDIUS.   I'll swear thou hast my leave. I have enough. —
But how to manage this! Well, I'll consider. (Exit.)

DOLABELLA.   I came prepared
To tell you heavy news — news which, I thought,
Would fright the blood from your pale cheeks to hear,
But you have met it with a cheerfulness
That makes my task more easy; and my tongue,
Which on another's message was employed,
Would gladly speak its own.

CLEOPATRA.   Hold, Dolabella.
First tell me, were you chosen by my lord?
Or sought you this employment?

DOLABELLA.   He picked me out; and, as his bosom friend,
He charged me with his words.

CLEOPATRA.   The message then
I know was tender, and each accent smooth,
To mollify that rugged word, Depart.

DOLABELLA.   Oh, you mistake. He chose the harshest words;
With fiery eyes and with contracted brows
He coined his face in the severest stamp;
And fury shook his fabric like an earthquake;
He heaved for vent, and burst like bellowing Aetna.
In sounds scarce human — "Hence, away, for ever,
Let her begone, the blot of my renown,
And bane of all my hopes!

(All the time of this speech CLEOPATRA seems more and more concerned till she sinks quite down.)

Let her be driven as far as man can think
From man's commèrce! she'll poison to the center."

CLEOPATRA.   Oh, I can bear no more!

DOLABELLA.   Help, help! — O wretch! O cursèd, cursèd wretch!
What have I done!

CHARMION.   Help, chafe her temples, Iras.

IRAS.   Bend, bend her forward quickly.

CHARMION.   Heaven be praised,
She comes again.

CLEOPATRA.   Oh, let him not approach me.
Why have you brought me back to this loathed being,
The abode of falsehood, violated vows,
And injured love? For pity, let me go;
For, if there be a place of long repose,
I'm sure I want it. My disdainful lord
Can never break that quiet, nor awake
The sleeping soul with hollowing in my tomb
Such words as fright her hence. — Unkind, unkind!

DOLABELLA (kneeling).   Believe me, 'tis against myself I speak.
That sure deserves belief — I injured him:
My friend ne'er spoke those words. Oh, had you seen
How often he came back, and every time
With something more obliging and more kind
To add to what he said; what dear farewells;
How almost vanquished by his love he parted,
And leaned to what unwillingly he left!
I, traitor as I was, for love of you
(But what can you not do, who made me false?)
I forged that lie; for whose forgiveness kneels
This self-accused, self-punished criminal.

CLEOPATRA.   With how much ease believe we what we wish!
Rise, Dolabella; if you have been guilty,
I have contributed, and too much love
Has made me guilty too.
The advance of kindness which I made was feigned
To call back fleeting love by jealousy,
But 'twould not last. Oh, rather let me lose
Than so ignobly trifle with his heart!

DOLABELLA.   I find your breast fenced round from human reach,
Transparent as a rock of solid crystal,
Seen through, but never pierced. My friend, my friend!
What endless treasure hast thou thrown away,
And scattered, like an infant, in the ocean,
Vain sums of wealth, which none can gather thence!

CLEOPATRA.   Could you not beg
An hour's admittance to his private ear?
Like one who wanders through long barren wilds,
And yet foreknows no hospitable inn
Is near to succor hunger, eats his fill

Before his painful march,
So would I feed a while my famished eyes
Before we part, for I have far to go,
If death be far, and never must return.

(*Enter* VENTIDIUS *with* OCTAVIA, *behind.*)

VENTIDIUS.   From hence you may discover — Oh, sweet, sweet!
Would you, indeed? The pretty hand in earnest?
    DOLABELLA.   I will, for this reward. (*Takes her hand.*) Draw it not
    back,
'Tis all I e'er will beg.
    VENTIDIUS.   They turn upon us.
    OCTAVIA.   What quick eyes has guilt!
    VENTIDIUS.   Seem not to have observed them, and go on.

(*They enter.*)

    DOLABELLA.   Saw you the emperor, Ventidius?
    VENTIDIUS.   No.
I sought him, but I heard that he was private,
None with him but Hipparchus, his freedman.
    DOLABELLA.   Know you his business?
    VENTIDIUS.   Giving him instructions
And letters to his brother Caesar.
    DOLABELLA.   Well,
He must be found.

(*Exeunt* DOLABELLA *and* CLEOPATRA.)

    OCTAVIA.   Most glorious impudence!
    VENTIDIUS.   She looked, methought,
As she would say, "Take your old man, Octavia,
Thank you, I'm better here." Well, but what use
Make we of this discovery?
    OCTAVIA.   Let it die.
    VENTIDIUS.   I pity Dolabella. But she's dangerous;
Her eyes have power beyond Thessalian charms
To draw the moon from heaven; for eloquence,
The sea-green Syrens taught her voice their flatt'ry;
And while she speaks, night steals upon the day,
Unmarked of those that hear. Then she's so charming
Age buds at sight of her, and swells to youth;
The holy priests gaze on her when she smiles,
And with heaved hands, forgetting gravity,
They bless her wanton eyes. Even I, who hate her,
With a malignant joy behold such beauty,

And while I curse, desire it. Antony
Must needs have some remains of passion still,
Which may ferment into a worse relapse
If now not fully cured. I know, this minute,
With Caesar he's endeavoring her peace.

OCTAVIA.   You have prevailed: — But for a further purpose (*walks off*)
I'll prove how he will relish this discovery.
What, make a strumpet's peace! it swells my heart;
It must not, shall not be.

VENTIDIUS.   His guards appear.
Let me begin, and you shall second me.

(*Enter* ANTONY.)

ANTONY.   Octavia, I was looking you, my love.
What, are your letters ready? I have given
My last instructions.

OCTAVIA.   Mine, my lord, are written.

ANTONY.   Ventidius. (*Drawing him aside.*)

VENTIDIUS.   My lord?

ANTONY.   A word in private. —
When saw you Dolabella?

VENTIDIUS.   Now, my lord,
He parted hence; and Cleopatra with him.

ANTONY.   Speak softly. — 'Twas by my command he went
To bear my last farewell.

VENTIDIUS (*aloud*).   It looked indeed
Like your farewell.

ANTONY.   More softly. — My farewell?
What secret meaning have you in those words
Of "my farewell"? He did it by my order.

VENTIDIUS (*aloud*).   Then he obeyed your order. I suppose
You bid him do it with all gentleness,
All kindness, and all — love.

ANTONY.   How she mourned,
The poor forsaken creature!

VENTIDIUS.   She took it as she ought; she bore your parting
As she did Caesar's, as she would another's.
Were a new love to come.

ANTONY (*aloud*).   Thou dost belie her;
Most basely and maliciously belie her.

VENTIDIUS.   I thought not to displease you; I have done.

OCTAVIA (*coming up*).   You seem disturbed, my lord.

ANTONY.   A very trifle.
Retire, my love.

VENTIDIUS.   It was indeed a trifle.
He sent —

ANTONY (angrily).   No more. Look how thou disobey'st me;
Thy life shall answer it.

OCTAVIA.   Then 'tis no trifle.

VENTIDIUS (to OCTAVIA).   'Tis less — a very nothing. You too saw it,
As well as I, and therefore 'tis no secret.

ANTONY.   She saw it!

VENTIDIUS.   Yes. She saw young Dolabella —

ANTONY.   Young Dolabella!

VENTIDIUS.   Young, I think him young,
And handsome too, and so do others think him.
But what of that? He went by your command,
Indeed, 'tis probable, with some kind message,
For she received it graciously; she smiled;
And then he grew familiar with her hand,
Squeezed it, and worried it with ravenous kisses;
She blushed, and sighed, and smiled, and blushed again;
At last she took occasion to talk softly,
And brought her cheek up close, and leaned on his;
At which, he whispered kisses back on hers;
And then she cried aloud that constancy
Should be rewarded. —

OCTAVIA.   This I saw and heard.

ANTONY.   What woman was it whom you heard and saw
So playful with my friend? Not Cleopatra?

VENTIDIUS.   Even she, my lord,

ANTONY.   My Cleopatra?

VENTIDIUS.   Your Cleopatra;
Dolabella's Cleopatra;
Every man's Cleopatra.

ANTONY.   Thou liest.

VENTIDIUS.   I do not lie, my lord.
Is this so strange? Should mistresses be left,
And not provide against a time of change?
You know she's not much used to lonely nights.

ANTONY.   I'll think no more on 't.
I know 'tis false, and see the plot betwixt you. —
You needed not have gone this way, Octavia.
What harms it you that Cleopatra's just?
She's mine no more. I see, and I forgive.
Urge it no further, love.

OCTAVIA.   Are you concerned
That she's found false?

ANTONY.   I should be, were it so,
For though 'tis past, I would not that the world
Should tax my former choice, that I loved one
Of so light note, but I forgive you both.

VENTIDIUS.   What has my age deserved that you should think
I would abuse your ears with perjury?
If Heaven be true, she's false.
ANTONY.   Though heaven and earth
Should witness it, I'll not believe her tainted.
VENTIDIUS.   I'll bring you, then, a witness
From hell to prove her so. — Nay, go not back (*seeing* ALEXAS *just enter-
ing, and starting back*),
For stay you must and shall.
ALEXAS.   What means my lord?
VENTIDIUS.   To make you do what most you hate, — speak truth.
You are of Cleopatra's private counsel,
Of her bed-counsel, her lascivious hours;
Are conscious of each nightly change she makes,
And watch her, as Chaldaeans do the moon,
Can tell what signs she passes through, what day.
ALEXAS.   My noble lord!
VENTIDIUS.   My most illustrious pander,
No fine set speech, no cadence, no turned periods,
But a plain homespun truth is what I ask:
I did myself o'erhear your queen make love
To Dolabella. Speak. For I will know
By your confession what more passed betwixt them;
How near the business draws to your employment;
And when the happy hour.
ANTONY.   Speak truth, Alexas; whether it offend
Or please Ventidius, care not. Justify
Thy injured queen from malice. Dare his worst.
OCTAVIA (*aside*).   See how he gives him courage! how he fears
To find her false! and shuts his eyes to truth,
Willing to be misled!
ALEXAS.   As far as love may plead for woman's frailty,
Urged by desert and greatness of the lover,
So far, divine Octavia, may my queen
Stand even excused to you for loving him
Who is your lord; so far, from brave Ventidius,
May her past actions hope a fair report.
ANTONY.   'Tis well, and truly spoken. Mark, Ventidius.
ALEXAS.   To you, most noble emperor, her strong passion
Stands not excused, but wholly justified.
Her beauty's charms alone, without her crown,
From Ind and Meroë drew the distant vows
Of sighing kings; and at her feet were laid
The sceptres of the earth exposed on heaps,
To choose where she would reign.
She thought a Roman only could deserve her,

And of all Romans only Antony;
And, to be less than wife to you, disdained
Their lawful passion.

    ANTONY.   'Tis but truth.

    ALEXAS.   And yet, though love and your unmatched desert
Have drawn her from the due regard of honor,
At last Heaven opened her unwilling eyes
To see the wrongs she offered fair Octavia,
Whose holy bed she lawlessly usurped.
The sad effects of this improsperous war
Confirmed those pious thoughts.

    VENTIDIUS (aside).   Oh, wheel you there?
Observe him now; the man begins to mend,
And talk substantial reason. — Fear not, eunuch,
The emperor has given thee leave to speak.

    ALEXAS.   Else had I never dared to offend his ears
With what the last necessity has urged
On my forsaken mistress; yet I must not
Presume to say her heart is wholly altered.

    ANTONY.   No, dare not for thy life, I charge thee dare not
Pronounce that fatal word!

    OCTAVIA (aside).   Must I bear this? Good Heaven, afford me patience!

    VENTIDIUS.   On, sweet eunuch; my dear half-man, proceed.

    ALEXAS.   Yet Dolabella
Has loved her long. He, next my god-like lord,
Deserves her best; and should she meet his passion,
Rejected as she is by him she loved —

    ANTONY.   Hence from my sight! for I can bear no more.
Let furies drag thee quick to hell; let all
The longer damned have rest; each torturing hand
Do thou employ till Cleopatra comes;
Then join thou too, and help to torture her!

    (Exit ALEXAS, thrust out by ANTONY.)

    OCTAVIA.   'Tis not well,
Indeed, my lord, 'tis much unkind to me,
To show this passion, this extreme concernment
For an abandoned, faithless prostitute.

    ANTONY.   Octavia, leave me. I am much disordered.
Leave me, I say.

    OCTAVIA.   My lord!

    ANTONY.   I bid you leave me.

    VENTIDIUS.   Obey him, madam. Best withdraw a while,
And see how this will work.

    OCTAVIA.   Wherein have I offended you, my lord,
That I am bid to leave you? Am I false

Or infamous? Am I a Cleopatra?
Were I she,
Base as she is, you would not bid me leave you,
But hang upon my neck, take slight excuses,
And fawn upon my falsehood.
   ANTONY.   'Tis too much,
Too much, Octavia. I am pressed with sorrows
Too heavy to be borne, and you add more.
I would retire and recollect what's left
Of man within, to aid me.
   OCTAVIA.   You would mourn
In private for your love, who has betrayed you.
You did but half return to me; your kindness
Lingered behind with her. I hear, my lord,
You make conditions for her,
And would include her treaty. Wondrous proofs
Of love to me!
   ANTONY.   Are you my friend, Ventidius?
Or are you turned a Dolabella too,
And let this Fury loose?
   VENTIDIUS.   Oh, be advised,
Sweet madam, and retire.
   OCTAVIA.   Yes, I will go, but never to return.
You shall no more be haunted with this Fury.
My lord, my lord, love will not always last
When urged with long unkindness and disdain.
Take her again whom you prefer to me;
She stays but to be called. Poor cozened man!
Let a feigned parting give her back your heart,
Which a feigned love first got; for injured me,
Though my just sense of wrongs forbid my stay,
My duty shall be yours.
To the dear pledges of our former love
My tenderness and care shall be transferred,
And they shall cheer, by turns, my widowed nights.
So, take my last farewell, for I despair
To have you whole, and scorn to take you half.

(*Exit* OCTAVIA.)

   VENTIDIUS.   I combat Heaven, which blasts my best designs;
My last attempt must be to win her back;
But oh! I fear in vain. (*Exit.*)
   ANTONY.   Why was I framed with this plain, honest heart,
Which knows not to disguise its griefs and weakness,
But bears its workings outward to the world?
I should have kept the mighty anguish in,

And forced a smile at Cleopatra's falsehood.
Octavia had believed it, and had stayed.
But I am made a shallow-forded stream,
Seen to the bottom; all my clearness scorned,
And all my faults exposed. — See where he comes

(*Enter* DOLABELLA.)

Who has profaned the sacred name of friend,
And worn it into vileness!
With how secure a brow, and specious form,
He gilds the secret villain! Sure that face
Was meant for honesty, but Heaven mismatched it,
And furnished treason out with nature's pomp
To make its work more easy.
    DOLABELLA.   O my friend!
    ANTONY.   Well, Dolabella, you performed my message!
    DOLABELLA.   I did, unwillingly.
    ANTONY.   Unwillingly?
Was it so hard for you to bear our parting?
You should have wished it.
    DOLABELLA.   Why?
    ANTONY.   Because you love me.
And she received my message with as true,
With as unfeigned a sorrow as you brought it?
    DOLABELLA.   She loves you, even to madness.
    ANTONY.   Oh, I know it.
You, Dolabella, do not better know
How much she loves me. And should I
Forsake this beauty? This all-perfect creature?
    DOLABELLA.   I could not, were she mine.
    ANTONY.   And yet you first
Persuaded me. How come you altered since?
    DOLABELLA.   I said at first I was not fit to go;
I could not hear her sighs and see her tears,
But pity must prevail. And so perhaps
It may again with you, for I have promised
That she should take her last farewell. And see,
She comes to claim my word.

(*Enter* CLEOPATRA.)

    ANTONY.   False Dolabella!
    DOLABELLA.   What's false, my lord?
    ANTONY.   Why, Dolabella's false,
And Cleopatra's false — both false and faithless.
Draw near, you well-joined wickedness, you serpents

Whom I have in my kindly bosom warmed,
Till I am stung to death.
    DOLABELLA.   My lord, have I
Deserved to be thus used?
    CLEOPATRA.   Can Heaven prepare
A newer torment? Can it find a curse
Beyond our separation?
    ANTONY.   Yes, if fate
Be just, much greater. Heaven should be ingenious
In punishing such crimes. The rolling stone
And gnawing vulture were slight pains, invented
When Jove was young, and no examples known
Of mighty ills. But you have ripened sin
To such a monstrous growth 'twill pose the gods
To find an equal torture. Two, two such! —
Oh, there's no farther name, — two such! to me,
To me, who locked my soul within your breasts,
Had no desires, no joys, no life, but you.
When half the globe was mine, I gave it you
In dowry with my heart; I had no use,
No fruit of all, but you. A friend and mistress
Was what the world could give. O Cleopatra!
O Dolabella! how could you betray
This tender heart which with an infant fondness
Lay lulled betwixt your bosoms and there slept,
Secure of injured faith?
    DOLABELLA.   If she has wronged you,
Heaven, hell, and you, revenge it.
    ANTONY.   If she wronged me!
Thou wouldst evade thy part of guilt. But swear
Thou lov'st not her.
    DOLABELLA.   Not so as I love you.
    ANTONY.   Not so? Swear, swear, I say, thou dost not love her.
    DOLABELLA.   No more than friendship will allow.
    ANTONY.   No more?
Friendship allows thee nothing. Thou art perjured —
And yet thou didst not swear thou lov'd'st her not,
But not so much, no more. O trifling hypocrite,
Who dar'st not own to her, thou dost not love,
Nor own to me, thou dost. Ventidius heard it;
Octavia saw it.
    CLEOPATRA.   They are enemies.
    ANTONY.   Alexas is not so. He, he confessed it;
He, who, next hell, best knew it, he avowed it.
Why do I seek a proof beyond yourself?
(To DOLABELLA.) You, whom I sent to bear my last farewell,
Returned to plead her stay.

DOLABELLA.   What shall I answer?
If to have loved be guilt, then I have sinned;
But if to have repented of that love
Can wash away my crime, I have repented.
Yet, if I have offended past forgiveness,
Let not her suffer. She is innocent.
    CLEOPATRA.   Ah, what will not a woman do who loves?
What means will she refuse to keep that heart
Where all her joys are placed? 'Twas I encouraged,
'Twas I blew up the fire that scorched his soul,
To make you jealous, and by that regain you.
But all in vain. I could not counterfeit;
In spite of all the dams, my love broke o'er,
And drowned my heart again; fate took the occasion,
And thus one minute's feigning has destroyed
My whole life's truth.
    ANTONY.   Thin cobweb arts of falsehood,
Seen, and broke through at first.
    DOLABELLA.   Forgive your mistress.
    CLEOPATRA.   Forgive your friend.
    ANTONY.   You have convinced yourselves.
You plead each other's cause. What witness have you
That you but meant to raise my jealousy?
    CLEOPATRA.   Ourselves, and Heaven.
    ANTONY.   Guilt witnesses for guilt. Hence, love and friendship!
You have no longer place in human breasts;
These two have driven you out. Avoid my sight!
I would not kill the man whom I have loved,
And cannot hurt the woman. But avoid me,
I do not know how long I can be tame,
For, if I stay one minute more, to think
How I am wronged, my justice and revenge
Will cry so loud within me that my pity
Will not be heard for either.
    DOLABELLA.   Heaven has but
Our sorrow for our sins, and then delights
To pardon erring man. Sweet mercy seems
Its darling attribute, which limits justice
As if there were degrees in infinite,
And infinite would rather want perfection
Than punish to extent.
    ANTONY.   I can forgive
A foe, but not a mistress and a friend.
Treason is there in its most horrid shape
Where trust is greatest, and the soul, resigned,
Is stabbed by its own guards. I'll hear no more. —
Hence from my sight forever!

CLEOPATRA.   How? Forever?
I cannot go one moment from your sight,
And must I go forever?
My joys, my only joys, are centered here.
What place have I to go to? My own kingdom?
That I have lost for you. Or to the Romans?
They hate me for your sake. Or must I wander
The wide world o'er, a helpless, banished woman,
Banished for love of you — banished from you?
Aye, there's the banishment! Oh, hear me, hear me
With strictest justice, for I beg no favor,
And if I have offended you, then kill me, ·
But do not banish me.
    ANTONY.   I must not hear you.
I have a fool within me takes your part,
But honor stops my ears.
    CLEOPATRA.   For pity hear me!
Would you cast off a slave who followed you?
Who crouched beneath your spurn? — He has no pity!
See if he gives one tear to my departure,
One look, one kind farewell. O iron heart!
Let all the gods look down and judge betwixt us,
If he did ever love!
    ANTONY.   No more. — Alexas!
    DOLABELLA.   A perjured villain!
    ANTONY (*to* CLEOPATRA).   Your Alexas, yours.
    CLEOPATRA.   Oh, 'twas his plot, his ruinous design,
T'engage you in my love by jealousy.
Hear him. Confront him with me. Let him speak.
    ANTONY.   I have, I have.
    CLEOPATRA.   And if he clear me not —
    ANTONY.   Your creature! one who hangs upon your smiles!
Watches your eye to say or to unsay
Whate'er you please! I am not to be moved.
    CLEOPATRA.   Then must we part? Farewell, my cruel lord!
Th' appearance is against me, and I go,
Unjustified, forever from your sight.
How I have loved, you know; how yet I love,
My only comfort is, I know myself.
I love you more, even now you are unkind,
Than when you loved me most; so well, so truly
I'll never strive against it but die pleased
To think you once were mine.
    ANTONY.   Good heaven, they weep at parting!
Must I weep too? That calls them innocent.
I must not weep. And yet I must, to think
That I must not forgive. —

Live, but live wretched; 'tis but just you should,
Who made me so. Live from each other's sight.
Let me not hear, you meet. Set all the earth
And all the seas betwixt your sundered loves;
View nothing common but the sun and skies.
Now, all take several ways;
And each your own sad fate, with mine, deplore;
That you were false, and I could trust no more.

(*Exeunt severally.*)

ACT FIVE

(CLEOPATRA, CHARMION, IRAS.)

CHARMION.   Be juster, Heaven; such virtue punished thus
Will make us think that chance rules all above,
And shuffles with a random hand the lots
Which man is forced to draw.
     CLEOPATRA.   I could tear out these eyes that gained his heart,
And had not power to keep it. O the curse
Of doting on, even when I find it dotage!
Bear witness, gods, you heard him bid me go;
You whom he mocked with imprecating vows
Of promised faith! — I'll die! I will not bear it.
You may hold me — (*she pulls out her dagger, and they hold her*)
But I can keep my breath; I can die inward,
And choke this love.

(*Enter* ALEXAS.)

IRAS.   Help, O Alexas, help!
The queen grows desperate; her soul struggles in her
With all the agonies of love and rage,
And strives to force its passage.
     CLEOPATRA.   Let me go.
Art thou there, traitor! — Oh,
Oh, for a little breath, to vent my rage!
Give, give me way, and let me loose upon him.
     ALEXAS.   Yes, I deserve it for my ill-timed truth.
Was it for me to prop
The ruins of a falling majesty?
To place myself beneath the mighty flaw,
Thus to be crushed and pounded into atoms
By its o'erwhelming weight? 'Tis too presuming

For subjects to preserve that wilful power
Which courts its own destruction.

    CLEOPATRA.   I would reason
More calmly with you. Did not you o'errule
And force my plain, direct, and open love
Into these crooked paths of jealousy?
Now, what's the event? Octavia is removed,
But Cleopatra's banished. Thou, thou villain,
Hast pushed my boat to open sea, to prove
At my sad cost, if thou canst steer it back.
It cannot be; I'm lost too far; I'm ruined! —
Hence, thou imposter, traitor, monster, devil! —
I can no more. Thou, and my griefs, have sunk
Me down so low that I want voice to curse thee.

    ALEXAS.   Suppose some shipwrecked seaman near the shore,
Dropping and faint with climbing up the cliff;
If, from above, some charitable hand
Pull him to safety, hazarding himself
To draw the other's weight, would he look back
And curse him for his pains? The case is yours;
But one step more, and you have gained the height.

    CLEOPATRA.   Sunk, never more to rise.

    ALEXAS.   Octavia's gone, and Dolabella banished.
Believe me, madam, Antony is yours.
His heart was never lost, but started off
To jealousy, love's last retreat and covert,
Where it lies hid in shades, watchful in silence,
And listening for the sound that calls it back.
Some other, any man ('tis so advanced)
May perfect this unfinished work, which I
(Unhappy only to myself) have left
So easy to his hand.

    CLEOPATRA.   Look well thou do 't; else —

    ALEXAS.   Else what your silence threatens. — Antony
Is mounted up the Pharos, from whose turret
He stands surveying our Egyptian galleys
Engaged with Caesar's fleet. Now death or conquest!
If the first happen, fate acquits my promise;
If we o'ercome, the conqueror is yours.

(*A distant shout within.*)

    CHARMION.   Have comfort, madam. Did you mark that shout?

(*Second shout nearer.*)

    IRAS.   Hark! they redouble it.

ALEXAS.   'Tis from the port.
The loudness shows it near. Good news, kind heavens!
    CLEOPATRA.   Osiris make it so!

(*Enter* SERAPION.)

    SERAPION.   Where, where's the queen?
    ALEXAS.   How frightfully the holy coward stares
As if not yet recovered of the assault,
When all his gods and, what's more dear to him,
His offerings were at stake!
    SERAPION.   O horror, horror!
Egypt has been; our latest hour is come;
The queen of nations from her ancient seat
Is sunk forever in the dark abyss;
Time has unrolled her glories to the last,
And now closed up the volume.
    CLEOPATRA.   Be more plain.
Say whence thou comest, though fate is in thy face,
Which from thy haggard eyes looks wildly out,
And threatens ere thou speakest.
    SERAPION.   I came from Pharos —
From viewing (spare me, and imagine it)
Our land's last hope, your navy —
    CLEOPATRA.   Vanquished?
    SERAPION.   No.
They fought not.
    CLEOPATRA.   Then they fled!
    SERAPION.   Nor that. I saw,
With Antony, your well-appointed fleet
Row out; and thrice he waved his hand on high,
And thrice with cheerful cries they shouted back.
'Twas then false Fortune like a fawning strumpet
About to leave the bankrupt prodigal,
With a dissembled smile would kiss at parting,
And flatter to the last; the well-timed oars
Now dipt from every bank, now smoothly run
To meet the foe; and soon indeed they met,
But not as foes. In few, we saw their caps
On either side thrown up. The Egyptian galleys,
Received like friends, passed through and fell behind
The Roman rear. And now they all come forward,
And ride within the port.
    CLEOPATRA.   Enough, Serapion.
I've heard my doom. — This needed not, you gods:
When I lost Anthony, your work was done.

'Tis but superfluous malice. — Where's my lord?
How bears he this last blow?

SERAPION.   His fury cannot be expressed by words.
Thrice he attempted headlong to have fallen
Full on his foes, and aimed at Caesar's galley;
Withheld, he raves on you; cries he's betrayed.
Should he now find you —

ALEXAS.   Shun him. Seek your safety
Till you can clear your innocence.

CLEOPATRA.   I'll stay.

ALEXAS.   You must not. Haste you to your monument,
While I make speed to Caesar.

CLEOPATRA.   Caesar! No,
I have no business with him.

ALEXAS.   I can work him
To spare your life, and let this madman perish.

CLEOPATRA.   Base, fawning wretch! wouldst thou betray him too?
Hence from my sight! I will not hear a traitor.
'Twas thy design brought all this ruin on us. —
Serapion, thou art honest. Counsel me —
But haste, each moment's precious.

SERAPION.   Retire. You must not yet see Antony.
He who began this mischief,
'Tis just he tempt the danger. Let him clear you;
And, since he offered you his servile tongue,
To gain a poor precarious life from Caesar
Let him expose that fawning eloquence,
And speak to Antony.

ALEXAS.   O heaven! I dare not;
I meet my certain death.

CLEOPATRA.   Slave, thou deservest it. —
Not that I fear my lord, will I avoid him;
I know him noble. When he banished me,
And thought me false, he scorned to take my life;
But I'll be justified, and then die with him.

ALEXAS.   O pity me, and let me follow you!

CLEOPATRA.   To death, if thou stir hence. Speak if thou canst
Now for thy life which basely thou wouldst save,
While mine I prize at — this. Come, good Serapion.

(*Exeunt* CLEOPATRA, SERAPION, CHARMION, *and* IRAS.)

ALEXAS.   O that I less could fear to lose this being,
Which, like a snowball in my coward hand,
The more 'tis grasped, the faster melts away.
Poor reason! what a wretched aid art thou!

For still, in spite of thee,
These two long lovers, soul and body, dread
Their final separation. Let me think;
What can I say to save myself from death,
No matter what becomes of Cleopatra?

ANTONY (*within*). Which way? where?

VENTIDIUS (*within*). This leads to the monument.

ALEXAS. Ah me! I hear him; yet I'm unprepared,
My gift of lying's gone;
And this court-devil, which I so oft have raised,
Forsakes me at my need. I dare not stay,
Yet cannot far go hence. (*Exit.*)

(*Enter* ANTONY *and* VENTIDIUS.)

ANTONY. O happy Caesar! thou hast men to lead!
Think not 'tis thou hast conquered Antony,
But Rome has conquered Egypt. I'm betrayed.

VENTIDIUS. Curse on this treacherous train!
Their soil and heaven infect them all with baseness,
And their young souls come tainted to the world
With the first breath they draw.

ANTONY. The original villain sure no god created;
He was a bastard of the sun by Nile,
Aped into man; with all his mother's mud
Crusted about his soul.

VENTIDIUS. The nation is
One universal traitor, and their queen
The very spirit and extract of them all.

ANTONY. Is there yet left
A possibility of aid from valor?
Is there one god unsworn to my destruction?
The least unmortgaged hope? for, if there be,
Methinks I cannot fall beneath the fate
Of such a boy as Caesar.
The world's one half is yet in Antony,
And from each limb of it that's hewed away,
The soul comes back to me.

VENTIDIUS. There yet remain
Three legions in the town. The last assault
Lopt off the rest. If death be your design —
As I must wish it now — these are sufficient
To make a heap about us of dead foes,
An honest pile for burial.

ANTONY. They're enough.
We'll not divide our stars, but, side by side,
Fight emulous, and with malicious eyes

Survey each other's acts, so every death
Thou giv'st, I'll take on me as a just debt,
And pay thee back a soul.
    VENTIDIUS.   Now you shall see I love you. Not a word
Of chiding more. By my few hours of life,
I am so pleased with this brave Roman fate
That I would not be Caesar to outlive you.
When we put off this flesh and mount together,
I shall be shown to all the ethereal crowd, —
"Lo, this is he who died with Antony!"
    ANTONY.   Who knows but we may pierce through all their troops,
And reach my veterans yet? 'tis worth the 'tempting
To o'erleap this gulf of fate,
And leave our wondering destinies behind.

    (*Enter* ALEXAS, *trembling.*)

    VENTIDIUS.   See, see, that villain!
See Cleopatra stamped upon that face
With all her cunning, all her arts of falsehood!
How she looks out through those dissembling eyes!
How he has set his count'nance for deceit,
And promises a lie before he speaks!
(*Drawing.*) Let me dispatch him first.
    ALEXAS.   O spare me, spare me!
    ANTONY.   Hold! He's not worth your killing. — On thy life,
Which thou may'st keep because I scorn to take it,
No syllable to justify thy queen.
Save thy base tongue its office.
    ALEXAS.   Sir, she's gone
Where she shall never be molested more
By love, or you.
    ANTONY.   Fled to her Dolabella!
Die, traitor! I revoke my promise! die! (*Going to kill him.*)
    ALEXAS.   O hold! she is not fled.
    ANTONY.   She is. My eyes
Are open to her falsehood; my whole life
Has been a golden dream of love and friendship;
But, now I wake, I'm like a merchant roused
From soft repose to see his vessel sinking,
And all his wealth cast o'er. Ingrateful woman!
Who followed me but as the swallow summer,
Hatching her young ones in my kindly beams,
Singing her flatteries to my morning wake;
But now my winter comes, she spreads her wings,
And seeks the spring of Caesar.

ALEXAS.   Think not so:
Her fortunes have in all things mixed with yours.
Had she betrayed her naval force to Rome,
How easily might she have gone to Caesar,
Secure by such a bribe.

VENTIDIUS.   She sent it first,
To be more welcome after.

ANTONY.   'Tis too plain,
Else would she have appeared to clear herself.

ALEXAS.   Too fatally she has. She could not bear
To be accused by you, but shut herself
Within her monument, looked down and sighed,
While from her unchanged face the silent tears
Dropped, as they had not leave, but stole their parting.
Some undistinguished words she inly murmured;
At last she raised her eyes, and, with such looks
As dying Lucrece cast —

ANTONY.   My heart forebodes —

VENTIDIUS.   All for the best; — go on.

ALEXAS.   She snatched her poniard,
And, ere we could prevent the fatal blow,
Plunged it within her breast, then turned to me:
"Go, bear my lord," said she, "my last farewell,
And ask him if he yet suspect my faith."
More she was saying, but death rushed betwixt.
She half pronounced your name with her last breath,
And buried half within her.

VENTIDIUS.   Heaven be praised!

ANTONY.   Then art thou innocent, my poor dear love?
And art thou dead?
O those two words! their sound should be divided;
Hadst thou been false, and died; or hadst thou lived,
And hadst been true — But innocence and death!
This shows not well above. Then what am I,
The murderer of this truth, this innocence!
Thoughts cannot form themselves in words so horrid
As can express my guilt!

VENTIDIUS.   Is 't come to this? The gods have been too gracious,
And thus you thank 'em for 't!

ANTONY (to ALEXAS).   Why stayest thou here?
Is it for thee to spy upon my soul
And see its inward mourning? Get thee hence.
Thou art not worthy to behold what now
Becomes a Roman emperor to perform.

ALEXAS (aside).   He loves her still:
His grief betrays it. Good! the joy to find

She's yet alive completes the reconcilement.
I've saved myself and her. But, oh! the Romans!
Fate comes too fast upon my wit,
Hunts me too hard, and meets me at each double. (*Exit.*)

VENTIDIUS.   Would she had died a little sooner, though,
Before Octavia went; you might have treated;
Now 'twill look tame, and would not be received.
Come, rouse yourself, and let's die warm together.

ANTONY.   I will not fight: there's no more work for war.
The business of my angry hours is done.

VENTIDIUS.   Caesar is at your gates.

ANTONY.   Why, let him enter;
He's welcome now.

VENTIDIUS.   What lethargy has crept into your soul?

ANTONY.   'Tis but a scorn of life, and just desire
To free myself from bondage.

VENTIDIUS.   Do it bravely.

ANTONY.   I will; but not by fighting. O Ventidius!
What should I fight for now? — my queen is dead.
I was but great for her; my power, my empire,
Were but my merchandise to buy her love,
And conquered kings, my factors. Now she's dead,
Let Caesar take the world, —
An empty circle since the jewel's gone
Which made it worth my strife; my being's nauseous;
For all the bribes of life are gone away.

VENTIDIUS.   Would you be taken?

ANTONY.   Yes, I would be taken,
But as a Roman ought, — dead, my Ventidius.
For I'll convey my soul from Caesar's reach,
And lay down life myself. 'Tis time the world
Should have a lord, and know whom to obey.
We two have kept its homage in suspense,
And bent the globe, on whose each side we trod,
Till it was dinted inwards. Let him walk
Alone upon 't; I'm weary of my part.
My torch is out; and the world stands before me
Like a black desert at th' approach of night.
I'll lay me down and stray no farther on.

VENTIDIUS.   I could be grieved,
But that I'll not outlive you. Choose your death,
For I have seen him in such various shapes,
I care not which I take — I'm only troubled,
The life I bear is worn to such a rag,
'Tis scarce worth giving. I could wish, indeed,
We threw it from us with a better grace;

That, like two lions taken in the toils,
We might at least thrust out our paws and wound
The hunters that inclose us.

ANTONY.   I have thought on it.
Ventidius, you must live.

VENTIDIUS.   I must not, sir.

ANTONY.   Wilt thou not live to speak some good of me?
To stand by my fair fame and guard the approaches
From the ill tongues of men?

VENTIDIUS.   Who shall guard mine
For living after you?

ANTONY.   Say I command it.

VENTIDIUS.   If we die well, our deaths will speak themselves,
And need no living witness.

ANTONY.   Thou hast loved me,
And fain I would reward thee. I must die.
Kill me, and take the merit of my death
To make thee friends with Caesar.

VENTIDIUS.   Thank your kindness.
You said I loved you; and in recompense
You bid me turn a traitor. — Did I think
You would have used me thus? — that I should die
With a hard thought of you?

ANTONY.   Forgive me, Roman.
Since I have heard of Cleopatra's death,
My reason bears no rule upon my tongue,
But lets my thought break all at random out.
I've thought better; do not deny me twice.

VENTIDIUS. By Heaven, I will not.
Let it not be to outlive you.

ANTONY.   Kill me first,
And then die thou; for 'tis but just thou serve
Thy friend before thyself.

VENTIDIUS.   Give me your hand.
We soon shall meet again. Now farewell, emperor! — (*Embrace.*)
Methinks that word's too cold to be my last:
Since death sweeps all distinctions, farewell, friend!
That's all —
I will not make a business of a trifle;
And yet I cannot look on you and kill you;
Pray turn your face.

ANTONY.   I do. Strike home, be sure.

VENTIDIUS. Home as my sword will reach. (*Kills himself.*)

ANTONY.   Oh, thou mistak'st;
That wound was none of thine; give it me back;
Thou robb'st me of my death.

VENTIDIUS.   I do, indeed;
But think 'tis the first time I e'er deceived you,
If that may plead my pardon. — And you, gods,
Forgive me if you will; for I die perjured
Rather than kill my friend. (*Dies.*)

ANTONY.   Farewell! Ever my leader, even in death!
My queen and thou have got the start of me,
And I'm the lag of honor. — Gone so soon?
Is death no more? he used him carelessly,
With a familiar kindness; ere he knocked,
Ran to the door and took him in his arms,
As who should say, "You're welcome at all hours,
A friend need give no warning." Books had spoiled him,
For all the learn'd are cowards by profession.
'Tis not worth
My farther thought; for death, for aught I know,
Is but to think no more. Here's to be satisfied. (*Falls on his sword.*)
I've missed my heart. O unperforming hand!
Thou never couldst have erred in a worse time.
My fortune jades me to the last; and death,
Like a great man, takes state, and makes me wait
For my admittance. —

(*Trampling within.*)

                    Some, perhaps, from Caesar.
If he should find me living, and suspect
That I played booty with my life! I'll mend
My work ere they can reach me. (*Rises upon his knees.*)

(*Enter* CLEOPATRA, CHARMION, IRAS.)

CLEOPATRA.   Where is my lord? where is he?
CHARMION.   There he lies,
And dead Ventidius by him.
CLEOPATRA.   My fears were prophets; I am come too late. (*Runs to
            him.*)
O that accursed Alexas!
ANTONY.   Art thou living?
Or am I dead before I knew, and thou
The first kind ghost that meets me?
CLEOPATRA.   Help me seat him.
Send quickly, send for help!

(*They place him in a chair.*)

ANTONY.   I am answered.
We live both. Sit thee down, my Cleopatra;
I'll make the most I can of life, to stay
A moment more with thee.

CLEOPATRA.   How is it with you?

ANTONY.   'Tis as with a man
Removing in a hurry; all packed up,
But one dear jewel that his haste forgot;
And he, for that, returns upon the spur;
So I come back for thee.

CLEOPATRA.   Too long, you heavens, you have been cruel to me;
Now show your mended faith, and give me back
His fleeting life!

ANTONY.   It will not be, my love;
I keep my soul by force.
Say but, thou are not false.

CLEOPATRA.   'Tis now too late
To say I'm true: I'll prove it, and die with you.
Unknown to me, Alexas feigned my death,
Which, when I knew, I hastened to prevent
This fatal consequence. My fleet betrayed
Both you and me.

ANTONY.   And Dolabella —

CLEOPATRA.   Scarce
Esteemed before he loved; but hated now.

ANTONY.   Enough. My life's not long enough for more.
Thou say'st thou wilt come after: I believe thee,
For I can now believe whate'er thou sayest,
That we may part more kindly.

CLEOPATRA.   I will come.
Doubt not, my life, I'll come, and quickly too;
Caesar shall triumph o'er no part of thee.

ANTONY.   But grieve not, while thou stay'st,
My last disastrous times.
Think we have had a clear and glorious day,
And Heaven did kindly to delay the storm
Just till our close of evening. Ten years' love,
And not a moment lost, but all improved
To the utmost joys, — what ages have we lived!
And now to die each other's; and, so dying,
While hand in hand, we walk in groves below,
Whole troops of lovers' ghosts shall flock about us,
And all the train be ours.

CLEOPATRA.   Your words are like the notes of dying swans,
Too sweet to last. Were there so many hours
For your unkindness, and not one for love?

ANTONY.   No, not a minute. — This one kiss — more worth
Than all I leave to Caesar. (*Dies.*)
    CLEOPATRA.   O tell me so again,
And take ten thousand kisses for that word.
My lord, my lord! Speak, if you yet have being;
Sign to me, if you cannot speak; or cast
One look! Do anything that shows you live.
    IRAS.   He's gone too far to hear you,
And this you see, a lump of senseless clay,
The leavings of a soul.
    CHARMION.   Remember, madam,
He charged you not to grieve.
    CLEOPATRA.   And I'll obey him.
I have not loved a Roman not to know
What should become his wife — his wife, my Charmion!
For 'tis to that high title I aspire,
And now I'll not die less. Let dull Octavia
Survive to mourn him, dead. My nobler fate
Shall knit our spousals with a tie too strong
For Roman laws to break.
    IRAS.   Will you then die?
    CLEOPATRA.   Why shouldst thou make that question?
    IRAS.   Caesar is merciful.
    CLEOPATRA.   Let him be so
To those that want his mercy. My poor lord
Made no such covenant with him to spare me
When he was dead. Yield me to Caesar's pride?
What! to be led in triumph through the streets,
A spectacle to base plebeian eyes,
While some dejected friend of Antony's
Close in a corner, shakes his head, and mutters
A secret curse on her who ruined him?
I'll none of that.
    CHARMION.   Whatever you resolve,
I'll follow, even to death.
    IRAS.   I only feared
For you, but more should fear to live without you.
    CLEOPATRA.   Why, now, 'tis as it should be. Quick, my friends,
Dispatch. Ere this, the town's in Caesar's hands.
My lord looks down concerned, and fears my stay,
Lest I should be surprised.
Keep him not waiting for his love too long.
You, Charmion, bring my crown and richest jewels;
With them, the wreath of victory I made
(Vain augury!) for him who now lies dead.
You, Iras, bring the cure of all our ills.

IRAS.   The aspics, madam?

CLEOPATRA.   Must I bid you twice?

(*Exeunt* CHARMION *and* IRAS.)

'Tis sweet to die when they would force life on me,
To rush into the dark abode of death,
And seize him first. If he be like my love,
He is not frightful, sure.
We're now alone in secrecy and silence;
And is not this like lovers? I may kiss
These pale, cold lips; Octavia does not see me.
And oh! 'tis better far to have him thus
Than see him in her arms. — Oh, welcome, welcome!

(*Enter* CHARMION *and* IRAS.)

CHARMION.   What must be done?

CLEOPATRA.   Short ceremony, friends,
But yet it must be decent. First, this laurel
Shall crown my hero's head; he fell not basely,
Nor left his shield behind him. — Only thou
Couldst triumph o'er thyself; and thou alone
Wert worthy so to triumph.

CHARMION.   To what end
These ensigns of your pomp and royalty?

CLEOPATRA.   Dull that thou art! why, 'tis to meet my love
As when I saw him first on Cydnos' bank,
All sparkling, like a goddess; so adorned,
I'll find him once again. My second spousals
Shall match my first in glory. Haste, haste, both,
And dress the bride of Antony.

CHARMION.   — 'Tis done.

CLEOPATRA.   Now seat me by my lord. I claim this place,
For I must conquer Caesar, too, like him,
And win my share o' th' world. — Hail, you dear relics
Of my immortal love!
O let no impious hand remove you hence,
But rest forever here! Let Egypt give
His death that peace which it denied his life. —
Reach me the casket.

IRAS.   Underneath the fruit
The aspic lies.

CLEOPATRA.   Well, thou kind deceiver! (*Putting aside the leaves.*)
Thou best of thieves, who, with an easy key,
Dost open life and, unperceived by us,
Even steal us from ourselves, discharging so
Death's dreadful office better than himself,

Touching our limbs so gently into slumber
That Death stands by, deceived by his own image,
And thinks himself but sleep.
    SERAPION (*within*).   The queen, where is she?
The town is yielded, Caesar's at the gates.
    CLEOPATRA.   He comes too late to invade the rights of death.
Haste, bare my arm, and rouse the serpent's fury. (*Holds out her arm,
    and draws it back.*)
Coward flesh,
Wouldst thou conspire with Caesar to betray me
As thou wert none of mine? I'll force thee to 't,
And not be sent by him,
But bring, myself, my soul to Antony. (*Turns aside, and then shows her
    arm bloody.*)
Take hence. The work is done.
    SERAPION (*within*).   Break ope the door
And guard the traitor well.
    CHARMION.   The next is ours.
    IRAS.   Now, Charmion, to be worthy
Of our great queen and mistress.

    (*They apply the aspics.*)

    CLEOPATRA.   Already, death, I feel thee in my veins.
I go with such a will to find my lord
That we shall quickly meet.
A heavy numbness creeps through every limb,
And now 'tis at my head. My eyelids fall,
And my dear love is vanished in a mist. —
Where shall I find him — where? O turn me to him,
And lay me on his breast! — Caesar, thy worst.
Now part us, if thou canst. (*Dies.*)

    (IRAS *sinks down at her feet, and dies;* CHARMION *stands behind her
chair, as dressing her head. Enter* SERAPION, *two* PRIESTS, ALEXAS, *bound,
and* EGYPTIANS.)

    PRIEST.   Behold, Serapion,
What havoc death has made!
    SERAPION.   'Twas what I feared. —
Charmion, is this well done?
    CHARMION.   Yes, 'tis well done, and like a queen, the last
Of her great race. I follow her. (*Sinks down; dies.*)
    ALEXAS.   'Tis true,
She has done well. Much better thus to die
Than live to make a holiday in Rome.
    SERAPION.   See, see how the lovers sit in state together,
As they were giving laws to half mankind!

Th' impression of a smile, left in her face,
Shows she died pleased with him for whom she lived,
And went to charm him in another world.
Caesar's just entering; grief has now no leisure.
Secure that villain as our pledge of safety
To grace the imperial triumph. — Sleep, blest pair,
Secure from human chance, long ages out,
While all the storms of fate fly o'er your tomb;
And fame to late posterity shall tell,
No lovers lived so great or died so well.

(*Exeunt.*)

EPILOGUE

Poets, like disputants when reasons fail,
Have one sure refuge left — and that's to rail.
Fop, coxcomb, fool, are thundered through the pit;
And this is all their equipage of wit.
We wonder how the devil this difference grows
Betwixt our fools in verse, and yours in prose;
For, 'faith, the quarrel rightly understood,
'Tis civil war with their own flesh and blood.
The threadbare author hates the gaudy coat;
And swears at the gilt coach, but swears afoot;
For 'tis observed of every scribbling man,
He grows a fop as fast as e'er he can;
Prunes up, and asks his oracle, the glass,
If pink or purple best become his face.
For our poor wretch, he neither rails nor prays;
Nor likes your wit just as you like his plays;
He has not yet so much of Mr. Bayes.
He does his best; and if he cannot please,
Would quickly sue out his writ of ease.
Yet, if he might his own grand jury call,
By the fair sex he begs to stand or fall.
Let Caesar's power the men's ambition move,
But grace you him who lost the world for love!
Yet if some antiquated lady say,
The last age is not copied in his play;
Heaven help the man who for that face must drudge,
Which only has the wrinkles of a judge.
Let not the young and beauteous join with those;
For should you raise such numerous hosts of foes,
Young wits and sparks he to his aid must call;
'Tis more than one man's work to please you all.

Curtain

Art, it is often said, imitates life. In the work of August Strindberg (1894–1912), the question is more one of the kind of life being imitated — and how. Strindberg closely documented in his writings his own intense struggles for emotional mastery, his bouts of insanity, and his extreme difficulties in personal relationships, particularly with women. His insights proved profitable not only to himself but to his dramas.

Miss Julie (1888) belongs to the Naturalistic period in Strindberg's work, and it deals partly with a favorite Naturalistic theme, class struggle. But by paralleling the class-struggle theme with a battle-of-the-sexes theme, based on his own painful experiences which had reached a climax three years before with the end of his destructive marriage to Siri von Essen, he gave the plot and characters a new kind of life which had previously not distinguished the plays of Emile Zola or the novels of the brothers Goncourt. The Naturalists put great emphasis on the environment and the early training of men, especially in the lower levels of society, as determinant forces in molding them into adults. They customarily suggested that the degradation of the lower classes was all society's fault — the individual could hardly be blamed for being lamed — and that society should be reformed so that such men could take their rightful place in it. It was inconceivable that the dregs of society had, in fact, already found their place.

Strindberg's Naturalism was hardly of this stamp. John Gassner has pointed out the parallels between the sex war and the class war in *Miss Julie*. But Strindberg's dramatic concern with the artificially based but nonetheless real stratification of classes in the Sweden of his time was probably less motivated by an overwhelming desire for the benefits of egalitarian democracy than it was by the artistic instinct for forceful, understandable images or symbols which could more powerfully underscore the external power of the woman — her position — and the internal power of the man — his masculinity.

The drama of class distinctions in *Miss Julie* is undeniable. Miss Julie and Jean quite simply come from such different classes that their training and resultant attitudes toward life and themselves doom the match as totally unsuitable: Miss Julie is accustomed to command, not to work; Jean is accustomed to obey and to work. As it is devised, however, the drama is not a social tract for marriage counseling. It is concerned with uncontrolled emotions breaking loose in spite of class distinctions and the demands of convention. What Miss Julie has done — or has allowed to happen — is wrong for the time, the place, and her position. She has obeyed no rule; emotion has been her only advisor and she has followed it without thought of the consequences. Jean, on the other hand, is more of a pragmatist. He is able to take anything that comes his way, use it, and discard it when it proves no longer useful or convenient. When Miss Julie gives way to her emotions, she loses her superiority;

362

Jean not only maintains his but increases it. Yet, for all that, he cannot be his own master in this social system.

It is both interesting and important to note how a very small detail, a simple action, a tiny object forgotten or neglected, can precipitate a disaster which has been brewing in a tragic protagonist. In *Miss Julie*, it is a simple if startling action: Jean's brutal killing of the canary. It brings down Miss Julie's romantic house of cards and provokes an impassioned speech revealing in brilliant detail her final awareness of who she is and what her future life would have been, had she gone through with the plan to run away with Jean.

Even though Strindberg's work, including *Miss Julie*, was largely autobiographical, his personal experiences were transmuted, as John Gassner notes, crystallized into something finer — the sick oyster producing the beautiful pearl. As Gassner says, "It is gratifying to observe his artistic victories over disease and exhilarating to find him transforming common enough morbidity into uncommonly absorbing drama."[1] What made Strindberg different from other mental patients also helped make him the father of the modern psychological drama. While Strindberg had *illness* in common with them, stresses Gassner, they did not have *genius* in common with him.

Strindberg's plays distill the essence of his struggles into a deeper and more realized experience. Locales and situations are not actual; they are synthesized. No character is Strindberg himself or any other single person. Indeed, as Maurice Valency insists, Strindberg's characters "are composites assembled in accordance with the author's theoretical preconceptions, formulated, as if by a chemist, out of pre-established elements in carefully calculated proportions. They represent, if we may believe his words, something between a compound and a *collage*."[2] They belong, Valency believes, "to a world that is as unreal, and as sensational, as the world of Van Gogh; and they therefore live with a life that is so intense that it can be expressed only through hyperbole."[3]

G.L.

---

[1] John Gassner, "Strindberg: Pearl and Oyster," *Dramatic Soundings* (New York: Crown, 1968), p. 63.

[2] Maurice Valency, *The Flower and the Castle* (New York: Macmillan, 1963), p. 388.

[3] *Ibid.*, p. 387.

AUGUST STRINDBERG

Miss Julie

TRANSLATED BY EVERT SPRINCHORN

Characters

MISS JULIE, twenty-five years old
JEAN, valet, thirty years old
CHRISTINE, the cook, thirty-five years old

(SCENE: The action of the play takes place in the
kitchen of the Count's manor house on Midsummer Eve
in Sweden in the 1880's.)

(The scene is a large kitchen. The walls and ceiling are covered with
draperies and hangings. The rear wall runs obliquely upstage from the
left. On this wall to the left are two shelves with pots and pans of copper,
iron, and pewter. The shelves are decorated with goffered paper. A little
to the right can be seen three-fourths of a deep arched doorway with two
glass doors, and through them can be seen a fountain with a statue of
Cupid, lilac bushes in bloom, and the tops of some Lombardy poplars.
From the left of the stage the corner of a large, Dutch-tile kitchen stove
protrudes with part of the hood showing. Projecting from the right side
of the stage is one end of the servants' dining table of white pine, with a
few chairs around it. The stove is decorated with branches of birch leaves;
the floor is strewn with juniper twigs. On the end of the table is a large
Japanese spice jar filled with lilacs. An icebox, a sink, a wash basin. Over
the door a big, old-fashioned bell; and to the left of the door the gaping
mouth of a speaking tube.

CHRISTINE is standing at the stove, frying something. She is wearing a
light-colored cotton dress and an apron. JEAN enters, dressed in livery and
carrying a pair of high-top boots with spurs. He sets them where they are
clearly visible.)

JEAN. Tonight she's wild again. Miss Julie's absolutely wild!
CHRISTINE. You took your time getting back!
JEAN. I took the Count down to the station, and on my way back as
I passed the barn I went in for a dance. And there was Miss Julie leading
the dance with the game warden. But then she noticed me. And she
ran right into my arms and chose me for the ladies' waltz. And she's been
dancing ever since like — like I don't know what. She's absolutely wild!

CHRISTINE. That's nothing new. But she's been worse than ever during the last two weeks, ever since her engagement was broken off.

JEAN. Yes, I never did hear all there was to that. He was a good man, too, even if he wasn't rich. Well, that's a woman for you. (*He sits down at the end of the table.*) But, tell me, isn't it strange that a young girl like her — all right, young woman — prefers to stay home with the servants rather than go with her father to visit her relatives?

CHRISTINE. I suppose she's ashamed to face them after the fiasco with her young man.

JEAN. No doubt. He wouldn't take any nonsense from her. Do you know what happened, Christine? I do. I saw the whole thing, even though I didn't let on.

CHRISTINE. Don't tell me you were there?

JEAN. Well, I was. They were in the barnyard one evening — and she was training him, as she called it. Do you know what she was doing? She was making him jump over her riding whip — training him like a dog. He jumped over twice, and she whipped him both times. But the third time, he grabbed the whip from her, broke it in a thousand pieces — and walked off.

CHRISTINE. So that's what happened. Well, what do you know.

JEAN. Yes, that put an end to that affair. — What have you got for me that's really good, Christine?

CHRISTINE (*serving him from the frying pan*). Just a little bit of kidney. I cut it especially for you.

JEAN. (*smelling it*). Wonderful! My special délice! (*Feeling the plate.*) Hey, you didn't warm the plate!

CHRISTINE. You're more fussy than the Count himself when you set your mind to it. (*She rumples his hair gently.*)

JEAN (*irritated*). Cut it out! Don't muss up my hair. You know I don't like that!

CHRISTINE. Oh, now don't get mad. Can I help it if I like you?

(JEAN *eats.* CHRISTINE *gets out a bottle of beer.*)

JEAN. Beer on Midsummer Eve! No thank you! I've got something much better than that. (*He opens a drawer in the table and takes out a bottle of red wine with a gold seal.*) Do you see that? Gold Seal. Now give me a glass. — No, a wine glass of course. I'm drinking it straight.

CHRISTINE (*goes back to the stove and puts on a small saucepan*). Lord help the woman who gets you for a husband. You're an old fussbudget!

JEAN. Talk, talk! You'd consider yourself lucky if you got yourself a man as good as me. It hasn't done you any harm to have people think I'm your fiancé. (*He tastes the wine.*) Very good. Excellent. But warmed just a little too little. (*Warming the glass in his hands.*) We bought this in Dijon. Four francs a liter, unbottled — and the tax on top of that. . . . What on earth are you cooking? It smells awful!

CHRISTINE. Some damn mess that Miss Julie wants for her dog.

JEAN. You should watch your language, Christine. . . . Why do you have to stand in front of the stove on a holiday, cooking for that mutt? Is it sick?

CHRISTINE. Oh, she's sick, all right! She sneaked out to the gate-keeper's mongrel and — got herself in a fix. And Miss· Julie, you know, can't stand anything like that.

JEAN. She's too stuck-up in some ways and not proud enough in others. Just like her mother. The countess felt right at home in the kitchen or down in the barn with the cows, but when she went driving, one horse wasn't enough for her; she had to have a pair. Her sleeves were always dirty, but her buttons had the royal crown on them. As for Miss Julie, she doesn't seem to care how she looks and acts. I mean, she's not really refined, not really. Just now, down at the barn, she grabbed the game warden right from under Anna's eyes and asked him to dance. You wouldn't see anybody in our class doing a thing like that. But that's what happens when the gentry try to act like the common people — they become common! . . . But she is beautiful! Statuesque! Ah, those shoulders — and those — so forth, and so forth!

CHRISTINE. Oh, don't exaggerate. Clara tells me all about her, and Clara dresses her.

JEAN. Clara, pooh! You women are always jealous of each other. I've been out riding with her. . . . And how she can dance . . . !

CHRISTINE. Listen, Jean, you are going to dance with me, aren't you, when I am finished here?

JEAN. Certainly! Of course I am.

CHRISTINE. Promise?

JEAN. Promise! Listen, if I say I'm going to do a thing, I do it. . . . Christine, I thank you for a delicious meal. (*He shoves the cork back into the bottle.*)

(MISS JULIE *appears in the doorway, talking to someone outside.*)

MISS JULIE. I'll be right back. Don't wait for me.

(JEAN *slips the bottle into the table drawer quickly and rises respectfully.* MISS JULIE *comes in and crosses over to* CHRISTINE, *who is at the stove.*)

Did you get it ready?

(CHRISTINE *signals that* JEAN *is present.*)

JEAN (*polite and charming*). Are you ladies sharing secrets?

MISS JULIE (*flipping her handkerchief in his face*). Don't be nosey!

JEAN. Oh, that smells good! Violets.

MISS JULIE (*flirting with him*). Don't be impudent! And don't tell

me you're an expert on perfumes, too. I know you're an expert dancer. —
No, don't look! Go away!

JEAN (*inquisitive, but deferential*). What are you cooking? A witch's
brew for Midsummer Eve? Something that reveals what the stars have
in store for you, so you can see the face of your future husband?

MISS JULIE (*curtly*). You'd have to have good eyes to see that. (*To*
CHRISTINE.) Pour it into a small bottle, and seal it tight. . . . Jean, come
and dance a schottische with me.

JEAN (*hesitating*). I hope you don't think I'm being rude, but I've
already promised this dance to Christine.

MISS JULIE. She can always find someone else. Isn't that so, Christine? You don't mind if I borrow Jean for a minute, do you?

CHRISTINE. It isn't up to me. If Miss Julie is gracious enough to invite you, it isn't right for you to say no, Jean. You go on, and thank her
for the honor.

JEAN. Frankly, Miss Julie, I don't want to hurt your feelings, but I
wonder if it is wise — I mean for you to dance twice in a row with the
same partner. Especially since the people around here are so quick to
spread gossip.

MISS JULIE (*bridling*). What do you mean? What kind of gossip?
What are you trying to say?

JEAN (*retreating*). If you insist on misunderstanding me, I'll have to
speak more plainly. It just doesn't look right for you to prefer one of
your servants to the others who are hoping for the same unusual honor.

MISS JULIE. Prefer! What an idea! I'm really surprised. I, the
mistress of the house, am good enough to come to their dance, and when
I feel like dancing, I want to dance with someone who knows how to lead.
After all I don't want to look ridiculous.

JEAN. As you wish. I am at your orders.

MISS JULIE (*gently*). Don't take it as an order. Tonight we're all
just happy people at a party. There's no question of rank. Now give me
your arm. — Don't worry, Christine. I won't run off with your boy
friend.

(JEAN *gives her his arm and leads her out.*

PANTOMIME SCENE. *This should be played as if the actress were actually alone. She turns her back on the audience when she feels like it; she
does not look out into the auditorium; she does not hurry as if she were
afraid the audience would grow impatient.*

CHRISTINE *alone. In the distance the sound of the violins playing the
schottische.* CHRISTINE, *humming in time with the music, cleans up after*
JEAN, *washes the dishes, dries them, and puts them away in a cupboard.
Then she takes off her apron, takes a little mirror from one of the table
drawers, and leans it against the jar of lilacs on the table. She lights a
tallow candle, heats a curling iron, and curls the bangs on her forehead.
Then she goes to the doorway and stands listening to the music. She
comes back to the table and finds the handkerchief that* MISS JULIE *left*

behind. She smells it, spreads it out, and then, as if lost in thought, stretches it, smooths it out, and folds it in four.

JEAN *enters alone.*)

JEAN. I told you she was wild! You should have seen the way she was dancing. Everyone was peeking at her from behind the doors and laughing at her. Can you figure her out, Christine?

CHRISTINE. You might know it's her monthlies, Jean. She always acts peculiar then. . . . Well, are you going to dance with me?

JEAN. You're not mad at me because I broke my promise?

CHRISTINE. Of course not. Not for a little thing like that, you know that. And I know my place.

JEAN (*grabs her around the waist*). You're a sensible girl, Christine. You're going to make somebody a good wife —

(MISS JULIE, *coming in, sees them together. She is unpleasantly surprised.*)

MISS JULIE (*with forced gaiety*). Well, aren't you the gallant beau — running away from your partner!

JEAN. On the contrary, Miss Julie. As you can see, I've hurried back to the partner I deserted.

MISS JULIE (*changing tack*). You know, you're the best dancer I've met. — But why are you wearing livery on a holiday? Take it off at once.

JEAN. I'd have to ask you to leave for a minute. My black coat is hanging right here — (*he moves to the right and points*).

MISS JULIE. You're not embarrassed because I'm here, are you? Just to change your coat? Go in your room and come right back again. Or else you can stay here and I'll turn my back.

JEAN. If you'll excuse me, Miss Julie. (*He goes off to the right. His arm can be seen as he changes his coat.*)

MISS JULIE (*to* CHRISTINE). Tell me something, Christine. Is Jean your fiancé? He seems so intimate with you.

CHRISTINE. Fiancé? I suppose so. At least that's what we say.

MISS JULIE. What do you mean?

CHRISTINE. Well, Miss Julie, you have had fiancés yourself, and you know —

MISS JULIE. But we were properly engaged — !

CHRISTINE. I know, but did anything come of it?

(JEAN *comes back, wearing a cutaway coat and derby.*)

MISS JULIE. Très gentil, monsieur Jean! Très gentil!

JEAN. Vous voulez plaisanter, madame.

MISS JULIE. Et vous voulez parler français! Where did you learn to speak French?

JEAN. In Switzerland. I was *sommelier* in one of the biggest hotels in Lucerne.

MISS JULIE. But you look quite the gentleman in that coat! *Charmant!* (*She sits down at the table.*)

JEAN. Flatterer!

MISS JULIE (*stiffening*). Who said I was flattering you?

JEAN. My natural modesty would not allow me to presume that you were paying sincere compliments to someone like me, and therefore I assumed that you were exaggerating, or, in other words, flattering me.

MISS JULIE. Where on earth did you learn to talk like that? Do you go to the theatre often?

JEAN. And other places. You don't think I stayed inside the house for six years when I was a valet in Stockholm, do you?

MISS JULIE. But weren't you born in this district?

JEAN. My father worked as a farmhand on the county attorney's estate, next door to yours. I used to see you when you were little. But of course you didn't notice me.

MISS JULIE. Did you really?

JEAN. Yes. I remember one time in particular. — But I can't tell you about that!

MISS JULIE. Of course you can. Oh, come on, tell me. Just this once — for me.

JEAN. No. No, I really couldn't. Not now. Some other time maybe.

MISS JULIE. Some other time? That means never. What's the harm in telling me now?

JEAN. There's no harm. I just don't feel like it. — Look at her.

(*He nods at* CHRISTINE, *who has fallen asleep in a chair by the stove.*)

MISS JULIE. Won't she make somebody a pretty wife! I'll bet she snores, too.

JEAN. No, she doesn't. But she talks in her sleep.

MISS JULIE (*cynically*). Now how would you know she talks in her sleep?

JEAN (*coolly*). I've heard her. . . . (*Pause. They look at each other.*)

MISS JULIE. Why don't you sit down?

JEAN. I wouldn't take the liberty in your presence.

MISS JULIE. But if I were to order you — ?

JEAN. I'd obey.

MISS JULIE. Well then, sit down. — Wait a minute. Could you get me something to drink first?

JEAN. I don't know what there is in the icebox. Only beer, I suppose.

MISS JULIE. *Only* beer?! I have simple tastes. I prefer beer to wine.

(JEAN *takes a bottle of beer from the icebox and opens it. He looks in the cupboard for a glass and a saucer, and serves her.*)

JEAN.   At your service.

MISS JULIE.   Thank you. Don't you want to drink, too?

JEAN.   I'm not much of a beer-drinker, but if it's your wish —

MISS JULIE.   My wish! I should think a gentleman would want to keep his lady company.

JEAN.   That's a point well taken! (*He opens another bottle and takes a glass.*)

MISS JULIE.   Now drink a toast to me!

(JEAN *hesitates.*)

You're not shy, are you? A big, strong man like you?

(*Playfully,* JEAN *kneels and raises his glass in mock gallantry.*)

JEAN.   To my lady's health!

MISS JULIE.   Bravo! Now if you would kiss my shoe, you will have hit it off perfectly.

(JEAN *hesitates, then boldly grasps her foot and touches it lightly with his lips.*)

Superb! You should have been an actor.

JEAN (*rising*).   This has got to stop, Miss Julie! Someone might come and see us.

MISS JULIE.   What difference would that make?

JEAN.   People would talk, that's what! If you knew how their tongues were wagging out there just a few minutes ago, you wouldn't —

MISS JULIE.   What sort of things did they say? Tell me. Sit down and tell me.

JEAN.   I don't want to hurt your feelings, but they used expressions that — that hinted at certain — you know what I mean. After all, you're not a child. And when they see a woman drinking, alone with a man — and a servant at that — in the middle of the night — well . . .

MISS JULIE.   Well what?! Besides, we're not alone. Christine is here.

JEAN.   Sleeping!

MISS JULIE.   I'll wake her up then. (*She goes over to* CHRISTINE). Christine! Are you asleep?

(CHRISTINE *babbles in her sleep.*)

Christine! — how soundly she sleeps!

CHRISTINE (*talking in her sleep*).   Count's boots are brushed . . . put on the coffee . . . right away, right away, right . . . mm — mm . . . poofff . . .

(MISS JULIE *grabs* CHRISTINE's *nose.*)

MISS JULIE. Wake up, will you!

JEAN (*sternly*). Let her alone!

MISS JULIE (*sharply*). What!

JEAN. She's been standing over the stove all day. She's worn out when evening comes. Anyone asleep is entitled to some respect.

MISS JULIE (*changing tack*). That's a very kind thought. It does you credit. Thank you. (*She offers* JEAN *her hand.*) Now come on out and pick some lilacs for me.

(*During the following,* CHRISTINE *wakes up and, drunk with sleep, shuffles off to the right to go to bed. A polka can be heard in the distance.*)

JEAN. With you, Miss Julie?

MISS JULIE. Yes, with me.

JEAN. That's no good. Absolutely not.

MISS JULIE. I don't know what you're thinking. Maybe you're letting your imagination run away with you.

JEAN. I'm not. The other people are.

MISS JULIE. In what way? Imagining that I'm — *verliebt* in a servant?

JEAN. I'm not conceited, but it's been known to happen. And to these people nothing's sacred.

MISS JULIE. Why, I believe you're an aristocrat!

JEAN. Yes, I am.

MISS JULIE. I'm climbing down —

JEAN. Don't climb down, Miss Julie! Take my advice. No one will ever believe that you climbed down deliberately. They'll say that you fell.

MISS JULIE. I think more highly of these people than you do. Let's see who's right! Come on! (*She looks him over, challenging him.*)

JEAN. You know, you're very strange.

MISS JULIE. Perhaps. But then so are you. . . . Besides, everything is strange. Life, people, everything. It's all scum, drifting and drifting on the water until it sinks — sinks. There's a dream I have every now and then. It's coming back to me now. I'm sitting on top of a pillar that I've climbed up somehow and I don't know how to get back down. When I look down I get dizzy. I have to get down but I don't have the courage to jump. I can't hold on much longer and I want to fall; but I don't fall. I know I won't have any peace until I get down; no rest until I get down, down on the ground. And if I ever got down on the ground, I'd want to go farther down, right down into the earth. . . . Have you ever felt anything like that?

JEAN. Never! I used to dream that I'm lying under a tall tree in a dark woods. I want to get up, up to the very top, to look out over the bright landscape with the sun shining on it, to rob the bird's nest up there with the golden eggs in it. I climb and I climb, but the trunk is so thick, and so smooth, and it's such a long way to that first branch. But I know that if I could just reach that first branch, I'd go right to the top as if on a ladder. I've never reached it yet, but some day I will — even if only in my dreams.

MISS JULIE. Here I am talking about dreams with you. Come out with me. Only into the park a way. (*She offers him her arm, and they start to go.*)

JEAN. Let's sleep on nine midsummer flowers, Miss Julie, and then our dreams will come true!

(MISS JULIE *and* JEAN *suddenly turn around in the doorway.* JEAN *is holding his hand over one eye.*)

MISS JULIE. You've caught something in your eye. Let me see.

JEAN. It's nothing. Just a bit of dust. It'll go away.

MISS JULIE. The sleeve of my dress must have grazed your eye. Sit down and I'll help you. (*She takes him by the arm and sits him down. She takes his head and leans it back. With the corner of her handkerchief she tries to get out the bit of dust.*) Now sit still, absolutely still. (*She slaps his hand.*) Do as you're told. Why, I believe you're trembling — a big, strong man like you. (*She feels his biceps.*) With such big arms!

JEAN (*warningly*). Miss Julie!

MISS JULIE. Yes, Monsieur Jean?

JEAN. *Attention! Je ne suis qu'un homme!*

MISS JULIE. Sit still, I tell you! . . . There now! It's out. Kiss my hand and thank me!

JEAN (*rising to his feet*). Listen to me, Miss Julie! — Christine has gone to bed! — Listen to me, I tell you!

MISS JULIE. Kiss my hand first!

JEAN. Listen to me!

MISS JULIE. Kiss my hand first!

JEAN. All right. But you'll have no one to blame but yourself.

MISS JULIE. For what?

JEAN. For what! Are you twenty-five years old and still a child? Don't you know it's dangerous to play with fire?

MISS JULIE. Not for me. I'm insured!

JEAN (*boldly*). Oh, no, you're not! And even if you are, there's inflammable stuff next door.

MISS JULIE. Meaning you?

JEAN. Yes. Not just because it's me, but because I'm a young man —

MISS JULIE. And irresistibly handsome? What incredible conceit! A Don Juan, maybe! Or a Joseph! Yes, bless my soul, that's it: you're a Joseph!

JEAN. You think so?!

MISS JULIE. I'm almost afraid so!

(JEAN *boldly steps up to her, grabs her around the waist, kisses her. She slaps his face.*)

None of that!

JEAN.   Are you still playing games or are you serious?

MISS JULIE.   I'm serious.

JEAN.   Then you must have been serious just a moment ago, too! You take your games too seriously and that's dangerous. Well, I'm tired of your games, and if you'll excuse me, I'll return to my work. (*Takes up the boots and starts to brush them.*) The Count will be wanting his boots on time, and it's long past midnight.

MISS JULIE.   Put those boots down.

JEAN.   No! This is my job. It's what I'm here for. But I never undertook to be a playmate for you. That's something I could never be. I consider myself too good for that.

MISS JULIE.   You are proud.

JEAN.   In some ways. Not in others.

MISS JULIE.   Have you ever been in love?

JEAN.   We don't use that word around here. But I've been — interested in a lot of girls, if that's what you mean. . . . I even got sick once because I couldn't have the one I wanted — really sick, like the princes in the Arabian Nights — who couldn't eat or drink for love.

MISS JULIE.   Who was the girl?

(JEAN *does not reply.*)

Who was she?

JEAN.   You can't make me tell you that.

MISS JULIE.   Even if I ask you as an equal — ask you — as a friend? . . . Who was she?

JEAN.   You.

MISS JULIE (*sitting down*).   How — amusing. . . .

JEAN.   Yes, maybe so. Ridiculous. . . . That's why I didn't want to tell you about it before. But now I'll tell you the whole story. . . . Have you any idea what the world looks like from below? Of course you haven't. No more than a hawk or eagle has. You hardly ever see their backs because they're always soaring above us. I lived with seven brothers and sisters — and a pig — out on the waste land where there wasn't even a tree growing. But from my window I could see the wall of the Count's garden with the apple trees sticking up over it. That was the Garden of Eden for me, and there were many angry angels with flaming swords standing guard over it. But in spite of them, I and the other boys found a way to the Tree of Life. . . . I'll bet you despise me.

MISS JULIE.   All boys steal apples.

JEAN.   That's what you say now. But you still despise me. Never mind. One day I went with my mother into this paradise to weed the onion beds. Next to the vegetable garden stood a Turkish pavilion, shaded by jasmine and hung all over with honeysuckle. I couldn't imagine what it was used for. I only knew I had never seen such a beautiful building. People went in, and came out again. And one day the door was left open. I sneaked in. The walls were covered with portraits of kings and emperors, and the windows had red curtains with tassels on them. — You do know what kind of place I'm talking about, don't you? . . . I — (*He breaks off a lilac and holds it under Miss Julie's nose.*) I had never been inside a castle, never seen anything besides the church. But this was more beautiful. And no matter what I tried to think about, my thoughts always came back — to that little pavilion. And little by little there arose in me a desire to experience just for once the whole pleasure of. . . . *Enfin*, I sneaked in, looked about, and marveled. Then I heard someone coming! There was only one way out — for the upper-class people. But for me there was one more — a lower one. And I had no other choice but to take it.

(MISS JULIE, *who has taken the lilac from* JEAN, *lets it fall to the table.*)

Then I began to run like mad, plunging through the raspberry bushes, ploughing through the strawberry patches, and came up on the rose terrace. And there I caught sight of a pink dress and a pair of white stockings. That was you. I crawled under a pile of weeds, under — well, you can imagine what it was like — under thistles that pricked me and wet dirt that stank to high heaven. And all the while I could see you walking among the roses. I said to myself, "If it's true that a thief can enter heaven and be with the angels, isn't it strange that a poor man's child here on God's green earth can't enter the Count's park and play with the Count's daughter."

MISS JULIE (*sentimentally*). Do you think all poor children have felt that way?

JEAN (*hesitatingly at first, then with mounting conviction*). If all poor ch — ? Yes — yes, naturally. Of course!

MISS JULIE. It must be terrible to be poor.

JEAN (*with exaggerated pain and poignancy*). Oh, Miss Julie! You don't know! A dog can lie on the sofa with its mistress; a horse can have its nose stroked by the hand of a countess; but a servant — ! (*Changing his tone.*) Of course, now and then you meet somebody with guts enough to work his way up in the world, but how often? — Anyway, you know what I did afterwards? I threw myself into the millstream with all my clothes on. Got fished out and spanked. But the following Sunday, when Pa and everybody else in the house went to visit Grandma, I arranged things so I'd be left behind. Then I washed myself all over with soap and warm water, put on my best clothes, and went off to church — just to see you there once more. I saw you, and then I went home determined to die. But I wanted to die beautifully and comfortably, without pain. I remembered that it was fatal to sleep under an alder bush. And we had a big one that had just blossomed out. I stripped it of every leaf and blossom it had and made a bed of them in a bin of oats. Have you ever noticed how smooth oats are? As smooth as the touch of human skin. . . . So I pulled the lid of the bin shut and closed my eyes — fell asleep. And when they woke me I was really very sick. But I didn't die, as you can see.

— What was I trying to prove? I don't know. There was no hope of winning you. But you were a symbol of the absolute hopelessness of my ever getting out of the circle I was born in.

MISS JULIE. You know, you have a real gift for telling stories. Did you go to school?

JEAN. A little. But I've read a lot of novels and gone to the theatre. And I've also listened to educated people talk. That's how I've learned the most.

MISS JULIE. You mean to tell me you stand around listening to what we're saying!

JEAN. Certainly! And I've heard an awful lot, I can tell you — sitting on the coachman's seat or rowing the boat. One time I heard you and a girl friend talking —

MISS JULIE. Really? . . . And just what did you hear?

JEAN. Well, now, I don't know if I could repeat it. I can tell you I was a little amazed. I couldn't imagine where you had learned such words. Maybe at bottom there isn't such a big difference as you might think, between people and people.

MISS JULIE. How vulgar! At least people in my class don't behave like you when we're engaged.

JEAN (looking her in the eye). Are you sure? — Come on now, it's no use playing the innocent with me.

MISS JULIE. He was a beast. The man I offered my love to was a beast.

JEAN. That's what you all say — afterwards.

MISS JULIE. All?

JEAN. I'd say so, since I've heard the same expression used several times before in similar circumstances.

MISS JULIE. What kind of circumstances?

JEAN. The kind we're talking about. I remember the last time I —

MISS JULIE (rising). That's enough! I don't want to hear any more.

JEAN. How strange! Neither did she! . . . Well, now if you'll excuse me, I'll go to bed.

MISS JULIE (softly). Go to bed on Midsummer Eve?

JEAN. That's right. Dancing with that crowd up there really doesn't amuse me.

MISS JULIE. Jean, get the key to the boathouse and row me out on the lake. I want to see the sun come up.

JEAN. Do you think that's wise?

MISS JULIE. You sound as if you were worried about your reputation.

JEAN. Why not? I don't particularly care to be made ridiculous, or to be kicked out without a recommendation just when I'm trying to establish myself. Besides, I have a certain obligation to Christine.

MISS JULIE. Oh, I see. It's Christine now.

JEAN. Yes, but I'm thinking of you, too. Take my advice, Miss Julie, and go up to your room.

MISS JULIE.   When did you start giving me orders?

JEAN.   Just this once. For your own sake! Please! It's very late. You're so tired, you're drunk. You don't know what you're doing. Go to bed, Miss Julie. — Besides, if my ears aren't deceiving me, they're coming this way, looking for me. If they find us here together, you're done for!

THE CHORUS (*is heard coming nearer singing*).

> Two ladies came from out the clover,
> Tri-di-ri-di-ralla, tri-di-ri-di-ra.
> And one of them was green all over,
> Tri-di-ri-di-ralla-la.
> They told us they had gold aplenty,
> Tri-di-ri-di-ralla, tri-di-ri-di-ra.
> But neither of them owned a penny,
> Tri-di-ri-di-ralla-la.
> This wreath for you I may be plaiting,
> Tri-di-ri-di-ralla, tri-di-ri-di-ra.
> But it's for another I am waiting,
> Tri-di-ri-ralla-la!

MISS JULIE.   I know these people. I love them just as they love me. Let them come. You'll find out.

JEAN.   No, Miss Julie, they don't love you! They take the food you give them, but they spit on it as soon as your back is turned. Believe me! Just listen to them. Listen to what they're singing. — No, you'd better not listen.

MISS JULIE (*listening*).   What are they singing?

JEAN.   A dirty song — about you and me!

MISS JULIE.   How disgusting! Oh, what cowardly, sneaking —

JEAN.   That's what the mob always is — cowards! You can't fight them; you can only run away.

MISS JULIE.   Run away? Where? There's no way out of here. And we can't go in to Christine.

JEAN.   What about my room? What do you say? The rules don't count in a situation like this. You can trust me. I'm your friend, remember? Your true, devoted, and respectful friend.

MISS JULIE.   But suppose — suppose they looked for you there?

JEAN.   I'll bolt the door. If they try to break it down, I'll shoot. Come, Miss Julie! (*On his knees.*) Please, Miss Julie!

MISS JULIE (*meaningfully*).   You promise me that you — ?

JEAN.   I swear to you!

(MISS JULIE *goes out quickly to the right.* JEAN *follows her impetuously.*)

THE BALLET. *The country people enter in festive costumes, with flowers in their hats. The fiddler is in the lead. A keg of small beer and a little keg of liquor, decorated with greenery, are set up on the table. Glasses are brought out. They all drink and start to sing the song. Then they form a circle and sing and dance the round dance, "Two ladies came from out the clover." At the end of the dance they all leave singing.*

MISS JULIE comes in alone; looks at the devastated kitchen; clasps her hands together; then takes out a powder puff and powders her face. JEAN enters. He is in high spirits.)

JEAN. You see! You heard them, didn't you? You've got to admit it's impossible to stay here.

MISS JULIE. No, I don't. But even if I did, what could we do?

JEAN. Go away, travel, get away from here!

MISS JULIE. Travel? Yes — but where?

JEAN. Switzerland, the Italian lakes. You've never been there?

MISS JULIE. No. Is it beautiful?

JEAN. Eternal summer, oranges, laurel trees, ah . . . !

MISS JULIE. But what are we going to do there?

JEAN. I'll set up a hotel — a first-class hotel with a first-class clientele.

MISS JULIE. Hotel?

JEAN. I tell you that's the life! Always new faces, new languages. Not a minute to think about yourself or worry about your nerves. No looking for something to do. The work keeps you busy. Day and night the bells ring, the trains whistle, the busses come and go. And all the while the money comes rolling in. I tell you it's the life!

MISS JULIE. Yes, that's the life. But what about me?

JEAN. The mistress of the whole place, the star of the establishment! With your looks — and your personality — it can't fail. It's perfect! You'll sit in the office like a queen, setting your slaves in motion by pressing an electric button. The guests will file before your throne and timidly lay their treasures on your table. You can't imagine how people tremble when you shove a bill in their face! I'll salt the bills and you'll sugar them with your prettiest smile. Come on, let's get away from here — (*he takes a timetable from his pocket*) — right away — the next train! We'll be in Malmo at 6:30; Hamburg 8:40 in the morning; Frankfurt to Basle in one day; and to Como by way of the Gotthard tunnel in — let me see — three days! Three days!

MISS JULIE. You make it sound so wonderful. But, Jean, you have to give me strength. Tell me you love me. Come and put your arms around me.

JEAN (*hesitates*). I want to . . . but I don't dare. Not any more, not in this house. I do love you — without a shadow of a doubt. How can you doubt that, Miss Julie?

MISS JULIE (*shyly, very becomingly*). You don't have to be formal with me, Jean. You can call me Julie. There aren't any barriers between us now. Call me Julie.

JEAN (*agonized*). I can't! There are still barriers between us, Miss Julie, as long as we stay in this house! There's the past, there's the Count. I've never met anyone I feel so much respect for. I've only got to see his gloves lying on a table and I shrivel up. I only have to hear that bell ring and I shy like a frightened horse. I only have to look at his boots standing there so stiff and proud and I feel my spine bending. (*He kicks the boots.*) Superstitions, prejudices that they've drilled into us since we were children! But they can be forgotten just as easily! Just we get to another country where they have a republic! They'll crawl on their hands and knees when they see my uniform. On their hands and knees, I tell you! But not me! Oh, no. I'm not made for crawling. I've got guts, backbone. And once I grab that first branch, you just watch me climb. I may be a valet now, but next year I'll be owning property; in ten years, I'll be living off my investments. Then I'll go to Rumania, get myself some decorations, and maybe — notice I only say maybe — end up as a count!

MISS JULIE. How wonderful, wonderful.

JEAN. Listen, in Rumania you can buy titles. You'll be a countess after all. My countess.

MISS JULIE. But I'm not interested in that. I'm leaving all that behind. Tell me you love me, Jean, or else — or else what difference does it make what I am?

JEAN. I'll tell you a thousand times — but later! Not now. And not here. Above all, let's keep our feelings out of this or we'll make a mess of everything. We have to look at this thing calmly and coolly, like sensible people. (*He takes out a cigar, clips the end, and lights it.*) Now you sit there and I'll sit here, and we'll talk as if nothing had happened.

MISS JULIE (*in anguish*). My God, what are you? Don't you have any feelings?

JEAN. Feelings? Nobody's got more feelings than I have. But I've learned how to control them.

MISS JULIE. A few minutes ago you were kissing my shoe — and now — !

JEAN (*harshly*). That was a few minutes ago. We've got other things to think about now!

MISS JULIE. Don't speak to me like that, Jean!

JEAN. I'm just trying to be sensible. We've been stupid once; let's not be stupid again. Your father might be back at any moment, and we've got to decide our future before then. — Now what do you think about my plans? Do you approve or don't you?

MISS JULIE. I don't see anything wrong with them. Except one thing. For a big undertaking like that, you'd need a lot of capital. Have you got it?

JEAN (*chewing on his cigar*). Have I got it? Of course I have. I've got my knowledge of the business, my vast experience, my familiarity with languages. That's capital that counts for something, let me tell you.

MISS JULIE. You can't even buy the railway tickets with it.

JEAN. That's true. That's why I need a backer — someone to put up the money.

MISS JULIE. Where can you find him on a moment's notice?

JEAN. You'll find him — if you want to be my partner.

MISS JULIE. I can't. And I don't have a penny to my name.

(*Pause.*)

JEAN. Then you can forget the whole thing.

MISS JULIE. Forget — ?

JEAN. And things will stay just the way they are.

MISS JULIE. Do you think I'm going to live under the same roof with you as your mistress? Do you think I'm going to have people sneering at me behind my back? How do you think I'll ever be able to look my father in the face after this? No, no! Take me away from here, Jean — the shame, the humiliation. . . . What have I done? Oh, my God, my God! What have I done? (*She bursts into tears.*)

JEAN. Now don't start singing that tune. It won't work. What have you done that's so awful? You're not the first.

MISS JULIE (*crying hysterically*). Now you despise me! — I'm falling, I'm falling!

JEAN. Fall down to me, and I'll lift you up again!

MISS JULIE. What awful hold did you have over me? What drove me to you? The weak to the strong? The falling to the rising! Or maybe it was love? Love? This? You don't know what love is!

JEAN. Want to bet? Did you think I was a virgin?

MISS JULIE. You're vulgar! The things you say, the things you think!

JEAN. That's the way I was brought up and that's the way I am! Now don't get hysterical. And don't play the fine lady with me. We're eating off the same platter now. . . . That's better. Come over here and be a good girl and I'll treat you to something special. (*He opens the table drawer and takes out the wine bottle. He pours the wine into two used glasses.*)

MISS JULIE. Where did you get that wine?

JEAN. From the wine cellar.

MISS JULIE. My father's burgundy!

JEAN. Should be good enough for his son-in-law.

MISS JULIE. I was drinking beer and you — !

JEAN. That shows that I have better taste than you.

MISS JULIE. Thief!

JEAN. You going to squeal on me?

MISS JULIE. Oh, God! Partner in crime with a petty house thief! I must have been drunk; I must have been walking in my sleep. Midsummer Night! Night of innocent games —

JEAN. Yes, very innocent!

MISS JULIE (*pacing up and down*). Is there anyone here on earth as miserable as I am?

JEAN. Why be miserable? After such a conquest! Think of poor Christine in there. Don't you think she's got any feelings?

MISS JULIE. I thought so a while ago, but I don't now. A servant's a servant —

JEAN. And a whore's a whore!

MISS JULIE (*falls to her knees and clasps her hands together*). Oh, God in heaven, put an end to my worthless life! Lift me out of this awful filth I'm sinking in! Save me! Save me!

JEAN. I feel sorry for you, I have to admit it. When I was lying in the onion beds, looking up at you on the rose terrace, I — I'm telling you the truth now — I had the same dirty thoughts that all boys have.

MISS JULIE. And you said you wanted to die for me!

JEAN. In the oat bin? That was only a story.

MISS JULIE. A lie, you mean.

JEAN (*beginning to get sleepy*). Practically. I think I read it in the paper about a chimney sweep who curled up in a woodbin with some lilacs because they were going to arrest him for nonsupport of his child.

MISS JULIE. Now I see you for what you are.

JEAN. What did you expect me to do? It's always the fancy talk that gets the women.

MISS JULIE. You dog!

JEAN. You bitch!

MISS JULIE. Well, now you've seen the eagle's back —

JEAN. Wasn't exactly its back — !

MISS JULIE. I was going to be your first branch — !

JEAN. A rotten branch —

MISS JULIE. I was going to be the window dressing for your hotel — !

JEAN. And I the hotel — !

MISS JULIE. Sitting at the desk, attracting your customers, padding your bills — !

JEAN. I could manage that myself — !

MISS JULIE. How can a human soul be so dirty and filthy?

JEAN. Then why don't you clean it up?

MISS JULIE. You lackey! You shoeshine boy! Stand up when I talk to you!

JEAN. You lackey lover! You bootblack's tramp! Shut your mouth and get out of here! Who do you think you are telling me I'm coarse? I've never seen anybody in my class behave as crudely as you did tonight. Have you ever seen any of the girls around here grab at a man like you did? Do you think any of the girls of my class would throw themselves at a man like that? I've never seen the like of it except in animals and prostitutes!

MISS JULIE (*crushed*). That's right! Hit me! Walk all over me! It's all I deserve. I'm rotten. But help me! Help me to get out of this — if there is any way out for me!

JEAN (*less harsh*). I'd be doing myself an injustice if I didn't admit that part of the credit for this seduction belongs to me. But do you think a person in my position would have dared to look twice at you if you hadn't asked for it? I'm still amazed —

MISS JULIE. And still proud.

JEAN. Why not? But I've got to confess the victory was a little too easy to give me any real thrill.

MISS JULIE. Go on, hit me more!

JEAN (*standing up*). No. . . . I'm sorry for what I said. I never hit a person who's down, especially a woman. I can't deny that, in one way, it was good to find out that what I saw glittering up above was only fool's gold, to have seen that the eagle's back was as gray as its belly, that the smooth cheek was just powder, and that there could be dirt under the manicured nails, that the handkerchief was soiled even though it smelled of perfume. But in another way, it hurt me to find that everything I was striving for wasn't very high above me after all, wasn't even real. It hurts me to see you sink far lower than your own cook. Hurts, like seeing the last flowers cut to pieces by the autumn rains and turned to muck.

MISS JULIE. You talk as if you already stood high above me.

JEAN. Well, don't I? Don't forget I could make you a countess but you can never make me a count.

MISS JULIE. But I have a father for a count. You can never have that!

JEAN. True. But I might father my own counts — that is, if —

MISS JULIE. You're a thief! I'm not!

JEAN. There are worse things than being a thief. A lot worse. And besides, when I take a position in a house, I consider myself a member of the family — in a way, like a child in the house. It's no crime for a child to steal a few ripe cherries when they're falling off the trees, is it? (*He begins to feel passionate again.*) Miss Julie, you're a beautiful woman, much too good for the likes of me. You got carried away by your emotions and now you want to cover up your mistake by telling yourself that you love me. You don't love me. You might possibly have been attracted by my looks — in which case your kind of love is no better than mine. But I could never be satisfied to be just an animal for you, and I could never make you love me.

MISS JULIE. Are you so sure of that?

JEAN. You mean there's a chance? I could love you, there's no doubt about that. You're beautiful, you're refined — (*he goes up to her and takes her hand*) — educated, lovable when you want to be, and once you set a man's heart on fire, I'll bet it burns forever. (*He puts his arm around her waist.*) You're like hot wine with strong spices. One of your kisses is enough to —

(*He attempts to lead her out, but she rather reluctantly breaks away from him.*)

MISS JULIE. Let me go. You don't get me that way.

JEAN. Then how? Not by petting you and not with pretty words, not by planning for the future, not by saving you from humiliation! Then how, tell me how?

MISS JULIE. How? How? I don't know how! I don't know at all! —
I hate you like I hate rats, but I can't get away from you.

JEAN. Then come away with me!

MISS JULIE (*pulling herself together*). Away? Yes, we'll go away! —
But I'm so tired. Pour me a glass of wine, will you?

(JEAN *pours the wine.* MISS JULIE *looks at her watch.*)

Let's talk first. We still have a little time. (*She empties the glass of wine
and holds it out for more.*)

JEAN. Don't overdo it. You'll get drunk.

MISS JULIE. What difference does it make?

JEAN. What difference? It looks cheap. — What did you want to
say to me?

MISS JULIE. We're going to run away together, right? But we'll talk
first — that is, I'll talk. So far you've done all the talking. You've told
me your life, now I'll tell you mine. That way we'll know each other
through and through before we become traveling companions.

JEAN. Wait a minute. Excuse me, but are you sure you won't regret
this afterwards, when you've surrendered your secrets?

MISS JULIE. I thought you were my friend.

JEAN. I am — sometimes. But don't count on me.

MISS JULIE. You don't mean that. Anyway, everybody knows my
secrets. — My mother's parents were very ordinary people, just com-
moners. She was brought up, according to the theories of her time, to
believe in equality, the independence of women, and all that. And she
had a strong aversion to marriage. When my father proposed to her, she
swore she would never become his wife, but that she might consent to
become his mistress. He told her that he had no desire to see the woman
he loved enjoy less respect than he did. But she said she didn't care what
the world thought, and, thinking he couldn't live without her, he accepted her conditions. But from then on he was cut off from his old circle
of friends, and left without anything to do in the house, which couldn't
keep him occupied anyway. I was born — against my mother's wishes, as
far as I can make out. My mother decided to bring me up as a nature
child. And on top of that I had to learn everything a boy learns, so I
could be living proof that women were just as good as men. I had to wear
boy's clothes, learn to handle horses — but not to milk the cows. I was
made to groom the horses and train them, and learn farming and go hunting — I even had to learn to slaughter the animals — it was disgusting!
And on the estate all the men were set to doing the work of women, and
the women to doing men's work — with the result that the whole place
threatened to fall to pieces, and we became the local laughing-stock.
Finally my father must have come out of his trance. He rebelled, and
everything was changed according to his wishes. Then my mother got
sick. I don't know what kind of sickness it was, but she often had con-

vulsions, and she would hide herself in the attic or in the garden, and
sometimes she would stay out all night. Then there occurred that big fire
you've heard about. The house, the stables, the cowsheds, all burned
down — and under very peculiar circumstances that led one to suspect
arson. You see, the accident occurred the day after the insurance expired,
and the premiums on the new policy, which my father had sent in, were
delayed through the messenger's carelessness, and didn't arrive on time.
(*She refills her glass and drinks.*)

JEAN. You've had enough.

MISS JULIE. Who cares! — We were left without a penny to our
name. We had to sleep in the carriages. My father didn't know where to
turn for money to rebuild the house. Then Mother suggested to him that
he might try to borrow money from an old friend of hers, who owned a
brick factory not far from here. Father takes out a loan, but there's no
interest charged, which surprises him. So the place was rebuilt. (*She
drinks some more.*) Do you know who set fire to the place?

JEAN. Your honorable mother!

MISS JULIE. Do you know who the brick manufacturer was?

JEAN. Your mother's lover?

MISS JULIE. Do you know whose money it was?

JEAN. Let me think a minute. . . . No, I give up.

MISS JULIE. It was my mother's!

JEAN. The Count's, you mean. Or was there a marriage settlement?

MISS JULIE. There wasn't a settlement. My mother had a little
money of her own which she didn't want under my father's control, so
she invested it with her — friend.

JEAN. Who grabbed it!

MISS JULIE. Precisely. He appropriated it. Well, my father finds out
what happened. But he can't go to court, can't pay his wife's lover, can't
prove that it's his wife's money. That was how my mother got her revenge because he had taken control of the house. He was on the verge of
shooting himself. There was even a rumor that he tried and failed. But
he took a new lease on life and he forced my mother to pay for her mistakes. Can you imagine what those five years were like for me? I loved
my father, but I took my mother's side because I didn't know the whole
story. She had taught me to hate all men — you've heard how she hated
men — and I swore to her that I'd never be slave to any man.

JEAN. But you got engaged to the attorney.

MISS JULIE. Only to make him slave to me.

JEAN. But he didn't want any of that?

MISS JULIE. Oh, he wanted to well enough, but I didn't give him the
chance. I got bored with him.

JEAN. Yes, so I noticed — in the barnyard.

MISS JULIE. What did you notice?

JEAN. I saw what I saw. He broke off the engagement.

MISS JULIE. That's a lie! It was I who broke it off. Did he tell you
that? He's beneath contempt!

JEAN.   Come on now, he isn't as bad as that. So you hate men, Miss Julie?

MISS JULIE.   Yes, I do. . . . Most of the time. But sometimes, when I can't help myself — oh . . . (*she shudders in disgust*).

JEAN.   Then you hate me, too?

MISS JULIE.   You have no idea how much! I'd like to see you killed like an animal —

JEAN.   Like when you're caught in the act with an animal: you get two years at hard labor and the animal is killed. Right?

MISS JULIE.   Right!

JEAN.   But there's no one to catch us — and no animal! What are we going to do?

MISS JULIE.   Go away from here.

JEAN.   To torture ourselves to death?

MISS JULIE.   No. To enjoy ourselves for a day or two, or a week, for as long as we can — and then — to die —

JEAN.   Die? How stupid! I've got a better idea: start a hotel!

MISS JULIE (*continuing without hearing* JEAN).   — on the shores of Lake Como, where the sun is always shining, where the laurels bloom at Christmas, and the golden oranges glow on the trees.

JEAN.   Lake Como is a stinking wet hole, and the only oranges I saw there were on the fruit stands. But it's a good tourist spot with a lot of villas and cottages that are rented out to lovers. Now there's a profitable business. You know why? They rent the villa for the whole season, but they leave after three weeks.

MISS JULIE (*innocently*).   Why after only three weeks?

JEAN.   Because they can't stand each other any longer. Why else? But they still have to pay the rent. Then you rent it out again to another couple, and so on. There's no shortage of love — even if it doesn't last very long.

MISS JULIE.   Then you don't want to die with me?

JEAN.   I don't want to die at all! I enjoy life too much. And moreover, I consider taking your own life a sin against the Providence that gave us life.

MISS JULIE.   You believe in God? You?

JEAN.   Yes, certainly I do! I go to church every other Sunday. — Honestly, I've had enough of this talk. I'm going to bed.

MISS JULIE.   Really? You think you're going to get off that easy? Don't you know that a man owes something to the woman he's dishonored?

JEAN (*takes out his purse and throws a silver coin on the table*).   There you are. I don't want to owe anybody anything.

MISS JULIE (*ignoring the insult*).   Do you know what the law says — ?

JEAN.   Aren't you lucky the law says nothing about the women who seduce men!

MISS JULIE (*still not hearing him*).   What else can we do but go away from here, get married, and get divorced?

JEAN. Suppose I refuse to enter into this mésalliance?

MISS JULIE. Mésalliance?

JEAN. For me! I've got better ancestors than you. I don't have any female arsonist in my family.

MISS JULIE. How can you know?

JEAN. You can't prove the opposite because we don't have any family records — except in the police courts. But I've read the whole history of your family in that book on the drawing-room table. Do you know who the founder of your family line was? A miller — who let his wife sleep with the king one night during the Danish war. I don't have any ancestors like that. I don't have any ancestors at all! But I can become an ancestor myself.

MISS JULIE. This is what I get for baring my heart and soul to someone too low to understand, for sacrificing the honor of my family —

JEAN. Dishonor! — I warned you, remember? Drinking makes one talk, and talking's bad.

MISS JULIE. Oh, how sorry I am! . . . If only it had never happened! . . . If only you at least loved me!

JEAN. For the last time — what do you expect of me? Do you want me to cry? Jump over your whip? Kiss you? Do you want me to lure you to Lake Como for three weeks and then — ? What am I supposed to do? What do you want? I've had more than I can take. This is what I get for involving myself with women. . . . Miss Julie, I can see that you're unhappy; I know that you're suffering; but I simply cannot understand you. My people don't behave like this. We don't hate each other. We make love for the fun of it, when we can get any time off from our work. But we don't have time for it all day and all night like you do. If you ask me, you're sick, Miss Julie. . . . You know your mother's mind was affected. We've got whole counties affected with pietism. Your mother's trouble was a kind of pietism. Everybody's catching it.

MISS JULIE. You can be understanding, Jean. You're talking to me like a human being now.

JEAN. Well, be human yourself. You spit on me but you don't let me wipe it off — on you!

MISS JULIE. Help me, Jean. Help me. Tell me what I should do, that's all — which way to go.

JEAN. For Christ's sake, if only I knew myself!

MISS JULIE. I've been crazy — I've been out of my mind — but does that mean there's no way out for me?

JEAN. Stay here as if nothing had happened. Nobody knows anything.

MISS JULIE. Impossible! Everybody who works here knows. Christine knows.

JEAN. They don't know a thing. And anyhow they'd never believe it.

MISS JULIE (slowly, significantly). But . . . it might happen again.

JEAN. That's true!

MISS JULIE. And there might be consequences.

JEAN (stunned). Consequences!! What on earth have I been thinking of! You're right. There's only one thing to do: get away from here!

Immediately! I can't go with you — that would give the whole game away. You'll have to go by yourself. Somewhere — I don't care where!

MISS JULIE. By myself? Where? — Oh, no, Jean, I can't. I can't!

JEAN. You've got to! Before the Count comes back. You know as well as I do what will happen if you stay here. After one mistake, you figure you might as well go on, since the damage is already done. Then you get more and more careless until — finally you're exposed. I tell you, you've got to get out of the country. Afterwards you can write to the Count and tell him everything — leaving me out, of course. He'd never be able to guess it was me. Anyway, I don't think he'd exactly like to find that out.

MISS JULIE. I'll go — if you'll come with me!

JEAN. Lady, are you out of your mind!? "Miss Julie elopes with her footman." The day after tomorrow it would be in all the papers. The Count would never live it down.

MISS JULIE. I can't go away. I can't stay. Help me. I'm so tired, so awfully tired. . . . Tell me what to do. Order me. Start me going. I can't think any more, can't move any more. . . .

JEAN. Now do you realize how weak you all are? What gives you the right to go strutting around with your noses in the air as if you owned the world? All right, I'll give you your orders. Go up and get dressed. Get some traveling money. And come back down here.

MISS JULIE (*almost in a whisper*). Come up with me!

JEAN. To your room? . . . You're going crazy again! (*He hesitates a moment.*) No! No! Go! Right now! (*He takes her hand and leads her out.*)

MISS JULIE (*as she is leaving*). Don't be so harsh, Jean.

JEAN. Orders always sound harsh. You've never had to take them.

(JEAN, *left alone, heaves a sigh of relief and sits down at the table. He takes out a notebook and a pencil and begins to calculate, counting aloud now and then. The pantomime continues until* CHRISTINE *enters, dressed for church, and carrying* JEAN's *white tie and shirt front in her hand.*)

CHRISTINE. Lord in Heaven, what a mess! What on earth have you been doing?

JEAN. It was Miss Julie. She dragged the whole crowd in here. You must have been sleeping awfully sound if you didn't hear anything.

CHRISTINE. I slept like a log.

JEAN. You already dressed for church?

CHRISTINE. Yes, indeed. Don't you remember you promised to go to Communion with me today?

JEAN. Oh, yes, of course. I remember. I see you've brought my things. All right. Come on, put it on me.

(*He sits down, and* CHRISTINE *starts to put the white tie and shirt front on him. Pause.* JEAN *yawns.*)

What's the lesson for today?

CHRISTINE.   The beheading of John the Baptist, I suppose.

JEAN.   My God, that will go on forever. — Hey, you're choking me! . . . Oh, I'm so sleepy, so sleepy.

CHRISTINE.   What were you doing up all night? You look green in the face.

JEAN.   I've been sitting here talking with Miss Julie.

CHRISTINE.   That girl! She doesn't know how to behave herself!

(*Pause.*)

JEAN.   Tell me something, Christine. . . .

CHRISTINE.   Well, what?

JEAN.   Isn't it strange when you think about it? Her, I mean.

CHRISTINE.   What's so strange?

JEAN.   Everything!

(*Pause.* CHRISTINE *looks at the half-empty glasses on the table.*)

CHRISTINE.   Have you been drinking with her?

JEAN.   Yes!

CHRISTINE.   Shame on you! — Look me in the eyes! You haven't . . . ?

JEAN.   Yes!

CHRISTINE.   Is it possible? Is it really possible?

JEAN (*after a moment's consideration*).   Yes. It is.

CHRISTINE.   Oh, how disgusting! I could never have believed anything like this would happen! No. No. This is too much!

JEAN.   Don't tell me you're jealous of her?

CHRISTINE.   No, not of her. If it had been Clara — or Sophie — I would have scratched your eyes out! But her — ? That's different. I don't know why. . . . But it's still disgusting!

JEAN.   Then you're mad at her?

CHRISTINE.   No. Mad at you. You were mean and cruel to do a thing like that, very mean. The poor girl! . . . But let me tell you, I'm not going to stay in this house a moment longer, not when I can't have any respect for my employers.

JEAN.   Why do you want to respect them?

CHRISTINE.   Don't try to be smart. You don't want to work for people who behave immorally, do you? Well, do you? If you ask me, you'd be lowering yourself by doing that.

JEAN.   Oh, I don't know. I think it's rather comforting to find out that they're not one bit better than we are.

CHRISTINE.   Well, I don't. If they're not any better, there's no point in us trying to be like them. — And think of the Count. Think of all the sorrows he's been through in his time. No, sir, I won't stay in this house any longer. . . . Imagine! You, of all people! If it had been the attorney fellow; if it had been somebody respectable —

JEAN.   Now just a minute — !

CHRISTINE.   Oh, you're all right in your own way. But there's a big difference between one class and another. You can't deny that. — No, this is something I can never get over. She was so proud, and so sarcastic about men, you'd never believe she'd go and throw herself at one. And at someone like you! And *she* was going to have Diana shot, because the poor thing ran after the gatekeeper's mongrel! — Well, I tell you, I've had enough! I'm not going to stay here any longer. On the twenty-fourth of October, I'm leaving.

JEAN.   Then what'll you do?

CHRISTINE.   Well, since you brought it up, it's about time that you got yourself a decent place, if we're going to get married.

JEAN.   Why should I go looking for another place? I could never get a place like this if I'm married.

CHRISTINE.   Well, of course not! But you could get a job as a door-keeper, or maybe try to get a government job as a caretaker somewhere. The government don't pay much, but they pay regular. And there's a pension for the wife and children.

JEAN (wryly).   Fine, fine! But I'm not the kind of fellow who thinks about dying for his wife and children this early in the game. I hate to say it, but I've got slightly bigger plans than that.

CHRISTINE.   Plans! Hah! What about your obligations? You'd better start giving them a little thought!

JEAN.   Don't start nagging me about obligations! I know what I have to do without you telling me. (*He hears a sound upstairs.*) Anyhow, we'll have plenty of chance to talk about this later. You just go and get yourself ready, and we'll be off to church.

CHRISTINE.   Who is that walking around up there?

JEAN.   I don't know. Clara, I suppose. Who else?

CHRISTINE (*starting to leave*).   It can't be the Count, can it? Could he have come back without anybody hearing him?

JEAN (*frightened*).   The Count? No, it can't be. He would have rung.

CHRISTINE (*leaving*).   God help us! I've never heard of the like of this.

(*The sun has now risen and strikes the tops of the trees in the park. The light shifts gradually until it is shining very obliquely through the windows.* JEAN *goes to the door and signals.* MISS JULIE *enters, dressed for travel, and carrying a small bird cage, covered with a towel. She sets the cage down on a chair.*)

MISS JULIE.   I'm ready now.

JEAN.   Shh! Christine's awake.

MISS JULIE (*she is extremely tense and nervous during the following*). Did she suspect anything?

JEAN.   She doesn't know a thing. — My God, what happened to you?

MISS JULIE. What do you mean? Do I look so strange?

JEAN. You're white as a ghost, and you've — excuse me — but you've got dirt on your face.

MISS JULIE. Let me wash it off. (*She goes over to the wash basin and washes her face and hands.*) There! Do you have a towel? . . . Oh, look the sun's coming up!

JEAN. That breaks the magic spell!

MISS JULIE. Yes, we were spellbound last night, weren't we? Midsummer madness . . . Jean, listen to me! Come with me. I've got the money!

JEAN. Enough?

MISS JULIE. Enough for a start. Come with me, Jean. I can't travel alone today. Midsummer Day on a stifling hot train, packed in with crowds of people, all staring at me — stopping at every station when I want to be flying. I can't, Jean, I can't! . . . And everything will remind me of the past. Midsummer Day when I was a child and the church was decorated with leaves . . . birch leaves and lilacs . . . the table spread for dinner with friends and relatives . . . and after dinner, dancing in the park, with flowers and games. Oh, no matter how far you travel, the memories tag right along in the baggage car . . . and the regrets, and the remorse.

JEAN. All right, I'll go with you! But it's got to be now — before it's too late! This very instant!

MISS JULIE. Hurry and get dressed! (*She picks up the bird cage.*)

JEAN. But no baggage! It would give us away.

MISS JULIE. Nothing. Only what we can take to our seats.

JEAN (*as he gets his hat*). What in the devil have you got there? What is that?

MISS JULIE. It's only my canary. I can't leave it behind.

JEAN. A canary! My God, do you expect us to carry a bird cage around with us? You're crazy. Put that cage down!

MISS JULIE. It's the only thing I'm taking with me from my home — the only living thing who loves me since Diana was unfaithful to me! Don't be cruel, Jean. Let me take it with me.

JEAN. I told you to put that cage down! — And don't talk so loud. Christine can hear us.

MISS JULIE. No, I won't leave it with a stranger. I won't. I'd rather have you kill it.

JEAN. Let me have the little pest, and I'll wring its neck.

MISS JULIE. Yes, but don't hurt it. Don't — No, I can't do it!

JEAN. Don't worry, I can. Give it here.

(MISS JULIE *takes the bird out of the cage and kisses it.*)

MISS JULIE. Oh, my little Serena, must you die and leave your mistress?

JEAN. You don't have to make a scene of it. It's a question of your whole life and future. You're wasting time!

(JEAN grabs the canary from her, carries it to the chopping block and picks up a meat cleaver. MISS JULIE turns away).

You should have learned how to kill chickens instead of shooting revolvers — (he brings the cleaver down) — then a drop of blood wouldn't make you faint.

MISS JULIE (screaming). Kill me too! Kill me! You can kill an innocent creature without turning a hair — then kill me. Oh, how I hate you! I loathe you! There's blood between us. I curse the moment I first laid eyes on you! I curse the moment I was conceived in my mother's womb. (She approaches the chopping block as if drawn to it against her will.) No, I don't want to go yet. I can't. — I have to see. — Shh! I hear a carriage coming! (She listens but keeps her eyes fastened on the chopping block and cleaver.) You don't think I can stand the sight of blood, do you? You think I'm so weak! Oh, I'd love to see your blood and your brains on that chopping block. I'd love to see the whole of your sex swimming in a sea of blood just like that. I think I could drink out of your skull. I'd like to bathe my feet in your ribs! I could eat your heart roasted whole! — You think I'm weak! You think I loved you because my womb hungered for your seed. You think I want to carry your brood under my heart and nourish it with my blood! Bear your child and take your name! Come to think of it, what is your name anyway? I've never heard your last name. You probably don't even have one. I'd be Mrs. Doorkeeper or Madame Floorsweeper. You dog with my name on your collar — you lackey with my initials on your buttons! Do you think I'm going to share you with my cook and fight over you with my maid?! Ohhh! — You think I'm a coward who's going to run away. No, I'm going to stay. Come hell or high water, I don't care! My father will come home — find his bureau broken into — his money gone. Then he rings — on that bell — two rings for the valet. And then he sends for the sheriff — and I tell him everything. Everything! Oh, it'll be wonderful to have it all over . . . if only it will be over. . . . He'll have a stroke and die. Then there'll be an end to all of us. There'll be peace . . . and quiet . . . forever. . . . His coat of arms will be broken on the coffin; the Count's line dies out. But the valet's line will continue in an orphanage, win triumphs in the gutter, and end in jail!

(CHRISTINE enters, dressed for church and with a hymn-book in her hand. MISS JULIE rushes over to her and throws herself into her arms as if seeking protection.)

Help me, Christine! Help me against this man!

CHRISTINE (cold and unmoved). This is a fine way to behave on a holy day! (*She sees the chopping block.*) Just look at the mess you've made there! How do you explain that? And what's all this shouting and screaming about?

MISS JULIE.   Christine, you're a woman, you're my friend! I warn you, watch out for this — this monster!

JEAN (*ill at ease and a little embarrassed*).   If you ladies are going to talk, I think I'll go and shave. (*He slips out to the right.*)

MISS JULIE.   You've got to understand, Christine! You've got to listen to me!

CHRISTINE.   No, I don't. I don't understand this kind of shenanigans at all. Where do you think you're going dressed like that? And Jean with his hat on? — Well? — Well?

MISS JULIE.   Listen to me, Christine! If you'll just listen to me, I'll tell you everything.

CHRISTINE.   I don't want to know anything.

MISS JULIE.   You've got to listen to me — !

CHRISTINE.   What about? About your stupid behavior with Jean? I tell you that doesn't bother me at all, because it's none of my business. But if you have any silly idea about talking him into skipping out with you, I'll soon put a stop to that.

MISS JULIE (*extremely tense*).   Christine, please don't get upset. Listen to me. I can't stay here, and Jean can't stay here. So you see, we have to go away.

CHRISTINE.   Hm, hm, hm.

MISS JULIE (*suddenly brightening up*).   Wait! I've got an idea! Why couldn't all three of us go away together? — out of the country — to Switzerland — and start a hotel. I've got the money, you see. Jean and I would be responsible for the whole affair — and Christine, you could run the kitchen, I thought. Doesn't that sound wonderful! Say yes! Say you'll come, Christine, then everything will be settled. Say you will! Please! (*She throws her arms around* CHRISTINE *and pats her.*)

CHRISTINE (*remaining aloof and unmoved*).   Hm. Hm.

MISS JULIE (*presto tempo*).   You've never been traveling, Christine. You have to get out and see the world. You can't imagine how wonderful it is to travel by train — constantly new faces — new countries. We'll go to Hamburg, and stop over to look at the zoo — you'll love that. And we'll go to the theatre and the opera. And then when we get to Munich, we'll go to the museums, Christine. They have Rubenses and Raphaels there — those great painters, you know. Of course you've heard about Munich where King Ludwig lived — you know, the king who went mad. And then we can go and see his castles — they're built just like the ones you read about in fairy tales. And from there it's just a short trip to Switzerland — with the Alps. Think of the Alps, Christine, covered with snow in the middle of the summer. And oranges grow there, and laurel trees that are green the whole year round.

(JEAN *can be seen in the wings at the right, sharpening his straight razor on a strap held between his teeth and his left hand. He listens to*

MISS JULIE *with a satisfied expression on his face, now and then nodding approvingly.* MISS JULIE *continues tempo prestissimo.*)

— And that's where we'll get a hotel. I'll sit at the desk while Jean stands at the door and receives the guests, goes out shopping, writes the letters. What a life that will be! The train whistle blowing, then the bus arriving, then a bell ringing upstairs, then the bell in the restaurant rings — and I'll be making out the bills — and I know just how much to salt them — you can't imagine how timid tourists are when you shove a bill in their face! — And you, Christine, you'll run the whole kitchen — there'll be no standing at the stove for you — of course not. If you're going to talk to the people, you'll have to dress neatly and elegantly. And with your looks — I'm not trying to flatter you, Christine — you'll run off with some man one fine day — a rich Englishman, that's who it'll be, they're so easy to — (*slowing down*) — to catch. — Then we'll all be rich. — We'll build a villa on Lake Como. — Maybe it does rain there sometimes, but — (*more and more lifelessly*) — the sun has to shine sometimes, too — even if it looks cloudy. — And — then . . . Or else we can always travel some more — and come back . . . (*pause*) — here . . . or somewhere else . . .

CHRISTINE. Do you really believe a word of that yourself, Miss Julie?

MISS JULIE (*completely beaten*). Do I believe a word of it myself?

CHRISTINE. Do you?

MISS JULIE (*exhausted*). I don't know. I don't believe anything any more. (*She sinks down on the bench and lays her head between her arms on the table.*) Nothing. Nothing at all.

CHRISTINE (*turns to the right and faces* JEAN). So! You were planning to run away, were you?

JEAN (*nonplused, lays his razor down on the table*). We weren't exactly going to run away! Don't exaggerate. You heard Miss Julie's plans. Even if she's tired now after being up all night, her plans are perfectly feasible.

CHRISTINE. Well, just listen to you! Did you really think you could get me to cook for that little —

JEAN (*sharply*). You keep a respectful tongue in your mouth when you talk to your mistress! Understand?

CHRISTINE. Mistress!

JEAN. Yes, mistress!

CHRISTINE. Well, of all the — ! I don't have to listen —

JEAN. Yes, you do! You need to listen more and talk less. Miss Julie is your mistress. Don't forget that! And if you're going to despise her for what she did, you ought to despise yourself for the same reason.

CHRISTINE. I've always held myself high enough to —

JEAN. High enough to make you look down on others!

CHRISTINE. — enough to keep from lowering myself beneath my position. No one can say that the Count's cook has ever had anything to do with the stable groom or the swineherd. No one can say that!

JEAN. Yes, aren't you lucky you got involved with a decent man!

CHRISTINE. What kind of a decent man is it who sells the oats from the Count's stables?

JEAN. Listen to who's talking! You get a commission on the groceries and take bribes from the butcher!

CHRISTINE. How can you say a thing like that!

JEAN. And you tell me you can't respect your employers any more! You! You!

CHRISTINE. Are you going to church or aren't you? I should think you'd need a good sermon after your exploits.

JEAN. No, I'm not going to church! You can go alone and confess your own sins.

CHRISTINE. Yes, I'll do just that. And I'll come back with enough forgiveness to cover yours, too. Our Redeemer suffered and died on the cross for all our sins, and if we come to Him in faith and with a penitent heart, He will take all our sins upon Himself.

JEAN. Grocery sins included?

MISS JULIE. Do you really believe that, Christine?

CHRISTINE. With all my heart, as sure as I'm standing here. It was the faith I was born into, and I've held on to it since I was a little girl, Miss Julie. Where sin aboundeth, there grace aboundeth also.

MISS JULIE. If I had your faith, Christine, if only ——

CHRISTINE. But you see, that's something you can't have without God's special grace. And it is not granted to everyone to receive it.

MISS JULIE. Then who receives it?

CHRISTINE. That's the secret of the workings of grace, Miss Julie, and God is no respecter of persons. With him the last shall be the first ——

MISS JULIE. In that case, he does have respect for the last, doesn't he?

CHRISTINE (continuing). —— and it is easier for a camel to go through the eye of a needle than for a rich man to enter the kingdom of God. That's how things are, Miss Julie. I'm going to leave now — alone. And on my way out I'm going to tell the stable boy not to let any horses out, in case anyone has any ideas about leaving before the Count comes home. Goodbye. (She leaves.)

JEAN. She's a devil in skirts! — And all because of a canary!

MISS JULIE (listlessly). Never mind the canary. . . . Do you see any way out of this, any end to it?

JEAN (after thinking for a moment). No.

MISS JULIE. What would you do if you were in my place?

JEAN. In your place? Let me think. . . . An aristocrat, a woman, and fallen. . . . I don't know. — Or maybe I do.

MISS JULIE (picks up the razor and makes a gesture with it). Like this?

JEAN. Yes. But I wouldn't do it, you understand. That's the difference between us.

MISS JULIE. Because you're a man and I'm a woman? What difference does that make?

JEAN. Just the difference that there is — between a man and a woman.

MISS JULIE. I want to! But I can't do it. My father couldn't do it either, that time he should have done it.

JEAN. No, he was right not to do it. He had to get his revenge first.

MISS JULIE. And now my mother is getting her revenge again through me.

JEAN. Haven't you ever loved your father, Miss Julie?

MISS JULIE. Yes, enormously. But I must have hated him too. I must have hated him without knowing it. It was he who brought me up to despise my own sex, to be half woman and half man. Who's to blame for what has happened? My father, my mother, myself? Myself? I don't have a self that's my own. I don't have a single thought I didn't get from my father, not an emotion I didn't get from my mother. And that last idea — about all people being equal — I got that from him, my betrothed. That's why I say he's beneath contempt. How can it be my own fault? Put the blame on Jesus, like Christine does? I'm too proud to do that — and too intelligent, thanks to what my father taught me. . . . A rich man can't get into heaven? That's a lie. But at least Christine, who's got money in the savings bank, won't get in. . . . Who's to blame? What difference does it make who's to blame? I'm still the one who has to bear the guilt, suffer the consequences —

JEAN. Yes, but —

(*The bell rings sharply twice.* MISS JULIE *jumps up.* JEAN *changes his coat.*)

The Count's back! What if Christine — ? (*He goes to the speaking tube, taps on it, and listens.*)

MISS JULIE. Has he looked in his bureau yet?

JEAN. This is Jean, sir! (*Listens. The audience cannot hear what the Count says.*) Yes, sir! (*Listens.*) Yes, sir! Yes, as soon as I can. (*Listens.*) Yes, at once, sir! (*Listens.*) Very good, sir! In half an hour.

MISS JULIE (*trembling with anxiety*). What did he say? For God's sake, what did he say?

JEAN. He ordered his boots and his coffee in half an hour.

MISS JULIE. Half an hour then! . . . Oh, I'm so tired. I can't bring myself to do anything. Can't repent, can't run away, can't stay, can't live . . . can't die. Help me, Jean. Command me, and I'll obey like a dog. Do me this last favor. Save my honor, save his name. You know what I ought to do but can't force myself to do. Let me use your will power. You command me and I'll obey.

JEAN. I don't know — I can't either, not now. I don't know why. It's as if this coat made me — . I can't give you orders in this. And now, after the Count has spoken to me, I — I can't really explain it — but — I've got the backbone of a damned lackey! If the Count came down here now and ordered me to cut my throat, I'd do it on the spot.

MISS JULIE. Pretend that you're him, and that I'm you. You were such a good actor just a while ago, when you were kneeling before me.

You were the aristocrat then. Or else — have you ever been to the theatre and seen a hypnotist?

(JEAN *nods.*)

He says to his subject, "Take this broom!" and he takes it. He says, "Now sweep!" and he sweeps.

JEAN. But the person has to be asleep!

MISS JULIE. I'm already asleep. The whole room has turned to smoke. You seem like an iron stove, a stove that looks like a man in black with a high hat. Your eyes are glowing like coals when the fire dies out. Your face is a white smudge, like the ashes.

(*The sun is shining in on the floor and falls on* JEAN.)

It's so good and warm — (*she rubs her hands together as if warming them at a fire*) — and so bright — and so peaceful.

JEAN (*takes the razor and puts it in her hand*). There's the broom. Go now, when the sun is up — out into the barn — and — (*he whispers in her ear*).

MISS JULIE (*waking up*). Thanks! I'm going to get my rest. But tell me one thing. Tell me that the first can also receive the gift of grace. Tell me that, even if you don't believe it.

JEAN. The first? I can't tell you that. — But wait a moment, Miss Julie. I know what I can tell you. You're no longer among the first. You're among — the last.

MISS JULIE. That's true! I'm among the very last. I am the last! — Oh! — Now I can't go! Tell me just once more, tell me to go!

JEAN. Now I can't either. I can't!

MISS JULIE. And the first shall be the last. . . .

JEAN. Don't think — don't think! You're taking all my strength away. You're making me a coward. . . . What! I thought I saw the bell move. No. . . . Let me stuff some paper in it. — Afraid of a bell! But it isn't just a bell. There's somebody behind it. A hand that makes it move. And there's something that makes the hand move. — Stop your ears, that's it, stop your ears! But it only rings louder. Rings louder and louder until you answer it. And then it's too late. Then the sheriff comes — and then —

(*There are two sharp rings on the bell.* JEAN *gives a start, then straightens himself up.*)

It's horrible! But there's no other way for it to end. — Go!

(MISS JULIE *walks resolutely out through the door.*)

Curtain

There is a tendency, when comparing the two major nineteenth-century Scandinavian dramatists, to label the Norwegian, Henrik Ibsen (1828–1906), as the plodding author of social problem plays carpentered with almost mechanical skill, and the Swede, August Strindberg, as the versatile writer of history plays, Naturalistic dramas, and Expressionistic and even Surrealistic works. That judgment is unfair to Ibsen for a number of reasons. First, Ibsen, like Strindberg, wrote in a variety of dramatic genres. Both Strindberg and Ibsen were attracted by historical themes. Ibsen was fascinated by certain religious concepts, to wit, his early dramas *Brand* (1866) and *Emperor and Galilean* (1873). *Peer Gynt* (1867) is a lyrical fantasy, cast in the images and locales of Norwegian folklore and the wider world, of a man's Faustian longing for knowledge and mastery. These works bear little resemblance to *A Doll's House* (1879) or *Hedda Gabler* (1890), plain-spoken tracts about the condition of nineteenth-century women which shocked polite society when they first appeared.

In *The Master Builder* (1892), Ibsen again moves away from the social realism of his best-known works. The play is, despite the fussy realism of much of its dialogue, mystical and poetic in its vision. It foreshadows a deeper mystique in late works like *When We Dead Awaken* (1900), in which the peculiar and frightening kernel of wisdom is: When we dead awaken, we find that we have not *lived*. Surely something of this pathetic knowledge is moving in Master Solness, not to mention Ibsen.

Perhaps it will prejudice a reading of *The Master Builder* to say that the dialogue is fussily realistic. Ibsen wrote in the language of his time, with a real ear for the way people actually talked, and vanquished the prevailing stagey or romantic clichés of the drama. Unfortunately, however, English translations made in his own time — notably William Archer's — which still hold the stage since no royalties have to be paid on them, now sound dated and awkward.

At the same time, Ibsen was intent on providing adequate exposition and keeping his plot moving along toward its climax. His admiration of the well-made plays of Eugène Scribe led him to set the scene, introduce the characters, and plan the dramatic action very carefully so that all incidents would be thoroughly, believably prepared for. Neither Sigmund Freud nor Eugene O'Neill were household names when Ibsen wrote his major works, so all this meticulous planning and explaining was essential. Enough misunderstandings were provoked in critics and audiences when he was painfully clear.

Several themes in *The Master Builder* are of special interest to modern readers. The conflict between successful but threatened maturity and struggling but powerful youth is interestingly portrayed in the struggle between Solness and Ragnar Brovik, with Master Solness seeking to prevent Brovik from winning the acclaim he deserves, but at the same time keeping Brovik's talents and services under his own control. The fear of eclipse that urges this dishonesty motivates other compulsive activities of the Master as well: hypnotizing Katya; cruelty to old Brovik; climbing the tower; perpetuating his guilt feelings for Aline.

The conflict manifests itself in a different way between Solness and Hilde Wangel. Solness has always had an eye for attractive women and has fed on their admiration and affection. Now, however, he is growing older; age and guilt are stifling him; he fails in his relationship with Hilde. Riesmanian alienation was never more alive than in his own alienation from his wife, from his profession, and from his god. The themes of ambition thwarted by guilt and individuality thwarted by duty and convention are eloquently expounded by Ibsen some fifty years before the Existentialists and seventy-five years before the Hippies.

Solness feels he has prospered in the construction business at the expense of Aline: the fire gave him the impetus he needed to succeed, while it took away from Aline the babies, any chance of having more, and therefore her purpose in life. Solness feels guilty of ruining her life himself, and his guilt prompts him to turn away from god — he stops building churches. Instead, he tries to expiate his sin against Aline by building what he has robbed her of — homes for mothers and fathers and children. Solness' last great building project — a house that he foolishly hopes will be a real home for Aline and himself — ironically proves his undoing.

The tower Solness has built for his house, the church steeples he built in the past, the many references to mountains and mountain climbing and castles-in-the-air should be images readily explicable to all students of Freud. Their implications, including Solness' fatal plunge from the scaffolding, not only carry sexual connotations but also symbolize Solness' ambition and Hilde's spirit. The church steeples and the tower on his house are obviously phallic symbols of an aging man's frustrated wish to erect *something*. Mountains and climbing is another continuous thread. No matter how much we box ourselves up in houses, civilizations, and conventions, Nature surrounds us and intrudes on us all to remind us of our true place in the natural world. In *The Master Builder*, the mountains symbolize our struggle to climb up out of our lowness and smallness; Hilde herself, who climbs mountains, personifies the symbol for Solness. Solness, in one sense, may be seen as an aging priest-king, trying to hold on to power, mastery, even love. That is in the play, certainly, but it is not to be read solely on that level. It is not just a combat between age and youth, with youth automatically the winner. It is also a parable of man's striving to exceed the limits of his own physical nature, to attain something beyond, something he does not understand.

G.L.

HENRIK IBSEN

The Master Builder

TRANSLATED BY KJELL AMBLE

Characters

KNUT BROVIK
RAGNAR BROVIK, *his son*
KAIA FOSSLI, *Ragnar's fiancée and Solness' secretary*
HALVARD SOLNESS, *the master builder*
MRS. SOLNESS, *his wife*
DR. HERDAL, *Mrs. Solness' doctor*
HILDE WANGEL, *a young woman*
GROUP OF LADIES, CROWD OF PEOPLE

ACT ONE

(*A plainly furnished room in the house of Master Builder* SOLNESS. *On the left, double doors lead to the hall. On the right, another door leads to the inner rooms. In the back wall, an open door leads to the drafts-men's office. In front, on the left, a desk with books, papers, and writing materials. Above the door, a fireplace. In the right-hand corner, a sofa with a table and a couple of chairs. On the table, a water pitcher and glasses. In the foreground, to the right, the Master Builder's desk with chairs behind and in front of it. Lighted desk lamps on the table in the draftsmen's office, on the table in the corner, and on the desk to the left.*

KNUT BROVIK *and his son* RAGNAR *sit in the draftsmen's office working on blueprints and calculations.* KAIA FOSSLI *sits at the desk in the front room writing in the main ledger.* KNUT BROVIK *is a thin old man with white hair and beard. He wears a somewhat threadbare but neatly pre-served black coat, glasses, and a slightly discolored white scarf.* RAGNAR BROVIK *is in his thirties, a well-dressed, blond man who stoops a little.* KAIA FOSSLI *is a frail young girl in her early twenties, neatly dressed but of sickly appearance. She wears glasses. For a while, all three work in silence.*)

KNUT BROVIK (*rises suddenly, as if in distress. Breathing heavily and with difficulty, he comes forward and appears in the doorway*). I'm not sure I can stand this much longer!

KAIA (*goes over to him*). It's really bad tonight, isn't it, Uncle?

397

BROVIK.   I'm afraid it is. Gets worse every day.

RAGNAR (*has got up and now comes over to them*).   Why don't you go home, Dad. You could use a little sleep, you know.

BROVIK (*impatiently*).   Go to bed, eh? Just lie down and take it, is that what you mean?

KAIA.   Well, take a little walk, anyway.

RAGNAR.   Yes, why don't you! I'll go with you.

BROVIK (*vehemently*).   I'm not leaving! Not until he gets here! I'm going to have a talk with him tonight — (*intensely bitter*) with him — the Big One.

KAIA.   Oh, no, Uncle, please don't!

RAGNAR.   No, Dad, you'd better let that wait for a while.

BROVIK (*breathes with difficulty*).   Oh no! No more waiting! I haven't much time for that now.

KAIA (*listening*).   Sh! He's back!

(*All three resume their work. Brief silence. Master Builder* HALVARD SOLNESS *enters from the hall. He is a middle-aged man, strong and healthy, with close-cropped curly hair, a dark moustache, and thick dark eyebrows. He wears a greyish-green, buttoned-up coat of a slightly old-fashioned cut with the collar turned up. On his head he wears a soft grey felt hat, and he carries a couple of portfolios under his arm.*)

SOLNESS (*by the door, pointing to the draftsmen's office, in a whisper*).   Have they gone?

KAIA (*in a low voice, shaking her head*).   No. (*She removes her glasses.*)

(SOLNESS *comes forward, throws his hat on a chair, puts the portfolios on the table by the sofa, and comes back toward the desk.* KAIA *keeps writing in the ledger but seems nervous and fidgety.*)

SOLNESS (*aloud*).   What are you doing, Miss Fossli?

KAIA (*with a start*).   Oh, the same old thing — today's entries —

SOLNESS.   Let's have a look. (*Leaning over her, he pretends to be checking the ledger while whispering.*)   Kaia?

KAIA (*keeps working, in a low voice*).   Yes?

SOLNESS.   Why do you always take off your glasses when I come in?

KAIA (*as before*).   Because they make me look so ugly.

SOLNESS (*with a smile*).   And you don't want to look ugly, do you, Kaia?

KAIA (*with a quick side-glance at him*).   I should say not! Especially when you're here.

SOLNESS (*strokes her hair gently*).   Kaia, my child —

KAIA (*pulling her head away a little*).   Sh! They can hear you!

SOLNESS (*strolls across the room, stops and turns by the door to the draftsmen's office*).   Did anyone stop by to see me while I was out?

RAGNAR (*rises*).   Yes, the young couple who want to build at Løvstrand.

SOLNESS (*growls*). They've been here again, eh? Well, they'll have to wait, that's all. I haven't quite made up my mind about the design yet.

RAGNAR (*comes closer, with some hesitation*). They could hardly wait to see the drawings, sir.

SOLNESS (*growls again*). Oh, I'm sure of it! There's nothing new about that!

BROVIK (*looks up*). They'd love to move into a place of their own, you see.

SOLNESS. Sure, sure! Nothing new about that either! They'll settle for anything. I know! Just a place to stay in will do, but not a home to live in. No, thank you! If that's all they want, they'd better get someone else. Tell them that the next time.

BROVIK (*puzzled, pushing his glasses up to his forehead*). Someone else? Are you willing to let the contract go?

SOLNESS (*impatiently*). Yes, damn it, yes! And why not? I'd rather do that than build a lot of junk. (*Vehemently.*) I don't even know those people!

BROVIK. They're well off, if that's what you mean. Ragnar knows them. He's a friend of the family. They're well off, all right.

SOLNESS. Well off, well off! I don't mean that. For heaven's sake, can't I make myself understood any more? (*Angrily.*) It just so happens that I don't like to get involved with people I don't know! I don't care who they get, but it won't be me.

BROVIK (*rises*). You really mean that?

SOLNESS (*sullenly*). I do — for once. (*He walks about the room.*)

(BROVIK *exchanges a look with* RAGNAR, *who makes a warning gesture, then exits to the draftsmen's office.*)

BROVIK. If I may, I'd like to have a few words with you.

SOLNESS. Well?

BROVIK (*to* KAIA). Why don't you go in there for a while, Kaia?

KAIA (*uneasily*). But, Uncle —

BROVIK. Please, my child! And close the door.

(KAIA *goes reluctantly into the draftsmen's office, glances anxiously and pleadingly at* SOLNESS, *then shuts the door.*)

(*Lowers his voice.*) I didn't want them to find out what condition I'm in.

SOLNESS. Yes, come to think of it, you haven't looked well lately.

BROVIK. I'm near the end. I get weaker day by day.

SOLNESS. Why don't you sit down?

BROVIK. Thank you.

SOLNESS (*moves the chair before his desk closer*). How's that?

BROVIK (*has seated himself with difficulty*). I think you know that my main worry is Ragnar and his future?

SOLNESS. Ragnar? Why, he'll stay here with me, of course.

BROVIK. He doesn't want that — the way things are now.

SOLNESS. He's well taken care of here, isn't he? Still, if it's a matter of more money, I'm sure we can —

BROVIK. No, no, you don't understand. (*Impatiently.*) Can't you see it's time he should be given a chance to work on his own?

SOLNESS (*without looking at him*). Are you sure Ragnar is sufficiently qualified for that?

BROVIK. I'm not — and that's the thing that bothers me more than anything else. I'm beginning to have my doubts about the boy. It would have been a different matter if you'd given him a word of encouragement now and then. But you haven't done that. And yet I can't help thinking that he is qualified. He has to be!

SOLNESS. But what does he know about it? I mean, really know? Except how to draw, of course.

BROVIK (*looks at him with suppressed hatred and says in a hoarse voice*). Know! And what did you know about it when you were working for me? That didn't stop you from (*breathes with difficulty*) — from pushing your way up, leaving me behind — and a lot of other people, too.

SOLNESS. Well, you see — things worked out for me.

BROVIK. You're right there. Everything worked out for you. That's why I was hoping you would be kind enough to give him a chance to show what he can do — before I die. I'd like to see them get married, too.

SOLNESS (*sharply*). Does she want that?

BROVIK. Not Kaia so much. But Ragnar talks about it all the time. (*Pleadingly.*) Can't you see how important it is that you give him a chance to prove his worth? I have to see my boy do something on his own, do you hear?

SOLNESS (*cross*). But what the hell have I got to do with it? I'm not a client!

BROVIK. He has a client. An important one.

SOLNESS (*uneasy, puzzled*). Has he?

BROVIK. Yes, if it is all right with you.

SOLNESS. Who is this client?

BROVIK (*hesitates*). It's the young couple who want to build that house at Løvstrand.

SOLNESS. Just a minute now! That's the one I'm going to build.

BROVIK. But you didn't seem to be interested in it.

SOLNESS (*flares up*). Not interested! What gave you that idea?

BROVIK. You did. You said so a moment ago.

SOLNESS. Well, now, I wouldn't attach too much significance to remarks like that. So, they'd let Ragnar build their house, eh?

BROVIK. Yes. He's a friend of the family, you see. He's made a few drawings, too — well, just for fun, you understand — a few estimates and things —

SOLNESS. And the people who're going to live there, are they pleased with those drawings?

BROVIK.   Yes. So if you'd just take a look at them and approve them —

SOLNESS.   Then they would let Ragnar build their house.

BROVIK.   They seemed quite impressed with his approach, called it "new," "original," and all that.

SOLNESS.   Oho! New, eh? Not like the old-fashioned junk I put up, I suppose!

BROVIK.   They thought it was different, that's all.

SOLNESS (*with suppressed anger*).   So it was Ragnar they came to see — while I was out.

BROVIK.   They came to see you — to find out whether you would be willing to step aside —

SOLNESS (*flares up*).   I — step aside!

BROVIK.   That is, in case you were to approve his drawings.

SOLNESS.   I — step aside for your son!

BROVIK.   Well, withdraw from the contract.

SOLNESS.   What's the difference? (*Laughs angrily.*) So that's it! Halvard Solness is to withdraw now. Make room for younger men — for a bright, new generation! Just like that! Room! Room!

BROVIK.   God knows there is room enough for more than one man.

SOLNESS.   Not really. But what's that got to do with it? The point is I'll never withdraw. I'll never step aside for anyone! Never of my own free will, at any rate. Never!

BROVIK (*rises with difficulty*).   Am I to face death, then, without peace or joy, without faith in Ragnar, without the satisfaction of having seen him do one single work on his own? Is that what you want?

SOLNESS (*turns away and mutters*).   Don't ask any more now.

BROVIK.   No, answer me! Am I to leave this life in such misery?

SOLNESS (*after a short struggle with himself, in a low but firm voice*). You'll have to leave it as best you can.

BROVIK.   I see. (*Walks away.*)

SOLNESS (*follows him, half in desperation*).   I've no choice in the matter! Can't you understand that? I am what I am! I can't change my nature!

BROVIK.   No — I guess not. (*He reels and stops by the table in front of the sofa.*)   May I have a glass of water?

SOLNESS.   Of course. (*Fills a glass and hands it to him.*)

BROVIK.   Thank you. (*He drinks and puts the glass down.*)

SOLNESS (*goes over to the door of the draftsmen's office and opens it*). Ragnar — you'd better take your father home now.

(RAGNAR *rises quickly. He and* KAIA *come into the front room.*)

RAGNAR.   What's the matter, Dad?

BROVIK.   Give me your arm, Son. Let's go.

RAGNAR.   All right. Come along, Kaia.

SOLNESS.   Miss Fossli will have to stay. I have a letter to write.

BROVIK (*looks at* SOLNESS). Good night. Sleep well — if you can.

SOLNESS. Good night.

(BROVIK *and* RAGNAR *leave by the hall door.* KAIA *goes to her desk.* SOLNESS, *his head bent, stands by his desk chair.*)

KAIA (*uncertainly*). You want me to take a letter?

SOLNESS (*snaps*). Of course not! (*Gives her a withering look.*) Kaia!

KAIA (*anxiously, in a low voice*). Yes?

SOLNESS (*points dramatically to a spot on the floor*). Come here! Now!

KAIA (*hesitantly*). Yes.

SOLNESS (*as before*). Closer!

KAIA (*obeying him*). What do you want?

SOLNESS (*looks at her for a while*). Are you the one who's behind all this?

KAIA. Oh no! You mustn't think that!

SOLNESS. But what about this idea of getting married?

KAIA (*in a low voice*). Well, Ragnar and I have been engaged for some time now — and so —

SOLNESS. And so you think it's time to get it over with, is that it?

KAIA. That's what Ragnar and Uncle say. And so I have to give in, I suppose.

SOLNESS (*more gently*). Kaia, are you quite sure you don't care a little for Ragnar, too?

KAIA. I cared a great deal for Ragnar once — before I came here to you.

SOLNESS. But not any more? Not at all?

KAIA (*passionately, reaching out toward him*). Oh, you know very well who I care for now! There's no one else and never will be!

SOLNESS. That's what you say. And still you plan to leave me, letting me stay here all by myself.

KAIA. But couldn't I stay here with you even if Ragnar — ?

SOLNESS (*rejects her*). No! That's out of the question. If Ragnar goes off to work for himself, then *he*'ll need you.

KAIA (*wringing her hands*). Oh, I don't see how I can leave you! You've no idea how much I —

SOLNESS. Then get these stupid notions out of his head! Marry him if you like — (*checks himself*). What I mean is — he has a good position here, so make him stay. Then I can keep you, too, you see — my dear Kaia.

KAIA. Yes, how wonderful that would be. If only things would work out like that!

SOLNESS (*takes her head in his hands and whispers*). I can't do without you, you see — have to have you here with me every day.

KAIA (*enraptured, nervously*). Oh, my god! My god!

SOLNESS (*kisses her hair*). Kaia — Kaia!

KAIA (*sinks down at his feet*). Oh, you're so good to me! So good!

SOLNESS (*angrily*). Get up! Get up, damn it! Someone's coming!

(*He helps her up. She staggers over to the desk.* MRS. SOLNESS *appears in the door on the right. She is a thin, blond, haggard woman who shows traces of former beauty. She is elegantly dressed in black, speaks rather slowly and in a plaintive voice.*)

MRS. SOLNESS (*in the doorway*). Halvard!

SOLNESS (*turns*). Yes, dear?

MRS. SOLNESS (*with a glance at* KAIA). I've come at an inopportune moment, I see.

SOLNESS. Not at all. Miss Fossli is just taking a letter for me.

MRS. SOLNESS. Yes — so I see.

SOLNESS. What do you want, Aline?

MRS. SOLNESS. I just want to tell you that Dr. Herdal stopped by. Would you like to join us, Halvard?

SOLNESS (*looks at her suspiciously*). Hm — what does he want?

MRS. SOLNESS. Nothing in particular. He came to call on me and would like to see you, too, I guess.

SOLNESS (*laughs quietly*). Yes, I suppose he would. Well, better ask him to wait then.

MRS. SOLNESS. You'll be in shortly, won't you?

SOLNESS. Maybe. Later, my dear — later. In a while.

MRS. SOLNESS (*with another look at* KAIA). Well, don't forget now, Halvard. (*She leaves, closing the door behind her.*)

KAIA (*in a low voice*). Oh, my god! I'm afraid she misunderstood —

SOLNESS. I don't think so. Don't worry about it. Still, you'd better go now, Kaia.

KAIA. Yes, yes, I will.

SOLNESS (*sternly*). And make sure you get this other matter taken care of, all right?

KAIA. Oh, yes! If I have anything to say about it!

SOLNESS. I want it settled, once and for all! Do you hear?

KAIA (*anxiously*). If there's no other way, I'll gladly break up with him.

SOLNESS (*flares up*). Break up? Are you mad! What would that accomplish!

KAIA (*in despair*). I'd rather do that than leave you. I have to stay here with you, don't you see? I have to!

SOLNESS (*bursts out*). But — damn it — what about Ragnar? It's he I'd like to —

KAIA (*horrified*). So it's mostly for his sake you'd like me to —

SOLNESS (*checks himself*). Of course not! You don't understand. (*Gently, quietly.*) It's you I want, Kaia, more than anything else. But if Ragnar doesn't stay, I can't expect to keep you here, can I? There, there, run along now.

KAIA. Yes. Well — good night.

SOLNESS. Good night. (*As she is about to leave.*) Oh, by the way — are Ragnar's drawings in there?

KAIA. I think so.

SOLNESS. See if you can find them, will you? I might have a look at them, after all.

KAIA (*happily*). Oh, would you?

SOLNESS. For your sake, dear Kaia. All right, go on, now!

KAIA (*hurries into the draftsmen's office, searches anxiously in a drawer, finds the drawings and brings them*). Here they are.

SOLNESS. Good. Put them on that table over there.

KAIA (*puts them down*). Well, good night. (*Pleadingly.*) And you're not angry with me?

SOLNESS. Of course I'm not angry with you. Good night, dear Kaia. (*Glances in the direction of the door on the right.*) Well, don't just stand there! Go home!

(MRS. SOLNESS *and* DR. HERDAL *enter by the door on the right. He is a stout, elderly man with a round, genial face and sparse, blond hair, who wears glasses.*)

MRS. SOLNESS (*as she enters*). I couldn't keep the doctor waiting any longer, Halvard.

SOLNESS. Well, come in, then.

MRS. SOLNESS (*to* KAIA, *who is just turning off the desk lamp*). All finished with your letter, Miss Fossli?

KAIA (*confused*). Letter?

SOLNESS. Yes, it was just a short one.

MRS. SOLNESS. Oh, I'm sure it was.

SOLNESS. You may go now, Miss Fossli. And make sure you're here on time in the morning.

KAIA. I will. Good night, Mrs. Solness. (*She leaves by the door to the hall.*)

MRS. SOLNESS. You're quite pleased with that girl, aren't you, Halvard?

SOLNESS. I certainly am. She's useful in a lot of ways.

MRS. SOLNESS. So it seems.

HERDAL. Is she good at bookkeeping, too?

SOLNESS. Well — I'm sure she's learned something about it these last two years. She's willing, too — no matter what you ask her to do.

MRS. SOLNESS. That's nice.

SOLNESS. Oh, it is! Especially for a man who's not exactly used to a thing like that.

MRS. SOLNESS (*gently reproachful*). Do you really mean that, Halvard?

SOLNESS. No, of course not, my dear. I'm sorry.

MRS. SOLNESS. All right. Well, Dr. Herdal, can I count on you to come back later and have tea with us?

HERDAL. One more patient to see and I'll be back!

MRS. SOLNESS. Good. (*She goes out by the door to the right.*)

SOLNESS. Are you in a hurry, Doctor?

HERDAL. No, not at all.

SOLNESS. May I have a word with you?

HERDAL. By all means.

SOLNESS. Let's sit down, then. (*Sitting down at his desk, he motions the doctor to take the chair in front of it and looks at him searchingly.*) Tell me — did you notice anything about Aline?

HERDAL. Just now, you mean?

SOLNESS. Yes. In her attitude toward me. Did you notice anything?

HERDAL (*smiles*). Well, damn it — I could hardly help noticing that your wife —

SOLNESS. Well?

HERDAL. That she isn't particularly fond of Miss Fossli.

SOLNESS. Is that all? Yes, I've noticed that myself.

HERDAL. You can hardly blame her, you know.

SOLNESS. For what?

HERDAL. For not cherishing the thought of your having another woman around you all the time.

SOLNESS. No, I guess you're right. I can see her point. Still, there's nothing I can do about it.

HERDAL. Can't you get a man to handle her job?

SOLNESS. No, I can't. It's not that simple.

HERDAL. I'm thinking of your wife's health. We both know how weak she is, and if this kind of arrangement is too much of a strain on her —

SOLNESS. So what? I don't mean it like that, of course, but I have to keep Kaia Fossli. Can't use anyone else.

HERDAL. No one at all?

SOLNESS (*snaps*). No one.

HERDAL (*pushes his chair closer*). Mr. Solness, do you mind if I ask you a rather personal question?

SOLNESS. Go ahead.

HERDAL. Women, you know — Well, a funny thing about them is that they have such a damned fine intuition — about certain things. Wouldn't you say so?

SOLNESS. Oh, absolutely. I quite agree.

HERDAL. Now, listen. Since your wife can't stand the sight of that woman —

SOLNESS. Well, what about it?

HERDAL. Isn't it possible that she may have the slightest bit of reason to feel like that?

SOLNESS (*looks at him and gets up*). Oho!

HERDAL.   I don't want to offend you, but isn't it?

SOLNESS (*firmly*).   No.

HERDAL.   Not the tiniest reason, eh?

SOLNESS.   It's all in her mind.

HERDAL.   I'm aware that you've known quite a few women over the years.

SOLNESS.   I don't deny it.

HERDAL.   And that you got involved with some of them.

SOLNESS.   I don't deny that either.

HERDAL.   But when it comes to Miss Fossli, it's a different matter.

SOLNESS.   It certainly is. At least as far as I'm concerned.

HERDAL.   Yes, but what about her?

SOLNESS.   I don't think you have the right to ask that, Doctor.

HERDAL.   Nonsense! It's your wife's intuition we're concerned with now.

SOLNESS.   So we are. Well, come to think of it — (*lowers his voice*) in a way Aline's intuition, as you call it, has already proven itself.

HERDAL.   What did I tell you?

SOLNESS (*sits down*).   Dr. Herdal, let me tell you a strange story. That is, if you don't mind listening.

HERDAL.   Oh, I like listening to strange stories.

SOLNESS.   Good! Perhaps you remember that I let Knut Brovik and his son come to work for me — at the time when everything collapsed around the old man?

HERDAL.   Vaguely, yes.

SOLNESS.   They are really quite talented, you see, each in his own field. But then the son got himself engaged. And next thing you know he wants to get married and start to build on his own! They're all alike, these young people —

HERDAL (*laughs*).   Yes, they do have this nasty habit of wanting to get married.

SOLNESS.   Well, anyway — that wasn't the way I had planned it. I could use Ragnar myself. The old man, too. He's damned good at calculating stresses and cubic content and all that kind of stuff, you see.

HERDAL.   That's part of the job, I guess.

SOLNESS.   Yes, it is. But Ragnar had only one thing on his mind: he simply had to get out and start working for himself. That's all there was to it.

HERDAL.   But he's still with you, isn't he?

SOLNESS.   That's just the point. You see, one day Kaia Fossli dropped in to see them about something or other. She'd never been here before, and when I saw how infatuated they were with each other, it suddenly occurred to me that if I could get her to work for me, maybe Ragnar would change his mind about leaving.

HERDAL.   That wasn't such a bad idea.

SOLNESS.   No, but of course I didn't breathe a word about it then. I just stood there looking at her — and wished with all my might that I had her here. Except for a few words about this and that, I didn't speak to her at all. And then she left.

HERDAL. Well?

SOLNESS. But late the next day, after old Brovik and Ragnar had gone home, she came back. And from the way she behaved, it seemed as though we'd come to some kind of agreement.

HERDAL. Agreement? What about?

SOLNESS. The very thing I had wished for so intensely. But never said a word about.

HERDAL. That's strange.

SOLNESS. Yes, wasn't it? And then she wanted to know what kind of job it was and if she could start the next day. Things like that.

HERDAL. Don't you think she did it in order to be near her boyfriend?

SOLNESS. Yes, I thought of that. But that wasn't it. Once she was here with me, she more or less drifted away from him.

HERDAL. Drifted over to you, I suppose.

SOLNESS. Yes, body and soul. I can't even look at her when her back is turned. She knows. And whenever I'm near her, she starts to tremble and shiver. What do you make of that?

HERDAL. That's rather obvious, isn't it?

SOLNESS. Maybe. But what about that other thing? The fact that she thought I'd told her out loud what I had only willed and wished for — silently, inwardly, to myself. How do you explain a thing like that, Dr. Herdal?

HERDAL. I don't. I won't go into that.

SOLNESS. That's what I thought. And that's why I never mentioned it before. — What a damn nuisance it is, having to go through this daily pretense of — And it's not fair to her either, poor girl. (*Vehemently.*) But I can't do anything else! If she runs out on me, Ragnar is bound to follow.

HERDAL. And what does your wife know about all this?

SOLNESS. Nothing.

HERDAL. Why on earth don't you tell her?

SOLNESS (*looks at him intently and says in a low voice*). Because somehow I enjoy torturing myself by letting Aline suspect me unjustly.

HERDAL (*shakes his head*). I'm afraid I haven't the faintest idea what you're talking about.

SOLNESS. Don't you see? It's like making a small payment on a huge, staggering debt —

HERDAL. To your wife?

SOLNESS. Yes, to my wife. It perks me up a little. Gives me the right to breathe more freely for a while.

HERDAL. I don't understand a word of this.

SOLNESS (*interrupts him; gets up*). All right, then — let's not talk about it. (*He saunters across the room, comes back and stops beside the desk, and looks at the doctor with a sly smile.*) You think you've done a good job of getting me started now, eh, Doctor?

HERDAL (*a little irritated*). Getting you started? Now, what's that supposed to mean?

SOLNESS. Oh, come now! Or don't you think I've noticed?

HERDAL. Noticed what?

SOLNESS (*slowly, in a low voice*). That you're here to keep an eye on me.

HERDAL. Keep an eye on you? Why the devil should I want to do that?

SOLNESS. Because you think I'm — (*flares up*). Hell! You think the same thing about me that Aline does.

HERDAL. And what's that?

SOLNESS (*in control of himself again*). That I'm a little — well, ill.

HERDAL. You ill? She never mentioned that to me. But my dear friend, what could be the matter with you?

SOLNESS (*leans over the back of the chair and whispers*). Aline thinks I'm mad. That's what's the matter.

HERDAL (*gets up*). For heaven's sake, Mr. Solness —

SOLNESS. No, seriously — she does! What's more, she's made you believe it, too! Don't you think I've noticed that from the way you behave? But you haven't fooled me for a minute, Doctor, I can assure you!

HERDAL (*looks at him in amazement*). I've never tried to do anything of the kind. Believe me, I haven't.

SOLNESS (*with an incredulous smile*). You haven't, eh?

HERDAL. Never! And I'm sure I can speak for your wife, too.

SOLNESS. Better leave her out of it, Doctor. Who knows? She may be right in a way.

HERDAL. Now, really! What sort of nonsense —

SOLNESS (*interrupts him, with a sweeping gesture*). Never mind! Let's not pursue this matter any further. It's better left as it is. (*Changes to a mood of restrained merriment.*) No, tell me this, Doctor — ahh —

HERDAL. Yes?

SOLNESS. Since you don't think that I'm ill — or crazy — or mad or anything like that —

HERDAL. Well?

SOLNESS. Then I suppose you consider me a very happy man?

HERDAL. Why not?

SOLNESS (*laughs*). Why not? Yes, yes — why not! God forbid! What a privilege it is to be Halvard Solness, the master builder! *The* master builder, in fact. Oh yes, that's a privilege, all right!

HERDAL. Well, to me it seems that fortune has been bending over backwards trying to please you.

SOLNESS (*represses a gloomy smile*). That's true. Can't complain about that.

HERDAL. Remember that creaky old barn that burned down? What a lucky break that was!

SOLNESS (*seriously*). It was Aline's family home. Remember that, too.

HERDAL. Oh, I realize it must have been a terrible blow to *her* —

SOLNESS. That was twelve or thirteen years ago — and she still hasn't gotten over it.

HERDAL. Isn't that because of what happened afterwards?

SOLNESS. Yes, among other things.

HERDAL. But you yourself — you built your own future on those ruins. You started out as a poor country boy, and here you are, the leading man of your profession. My friend, if you haven't had good fortune on your side I don't know who has!

SOLNESS (*looks cautiously at him*). I know. That's what worries me more than anything else.

HERDAL. Worries you? That fortune has favored you?

SOLNESS. Yes, I worry about it. Day and night I worry about it. Because some day the tide will turn, you see.

HERDAL. Nonsense! Why should that happen?

SOLNESS (*firmly, with conviction*). Because of the younger generation.

HERDAL. The younger generation? Oh, come now! You're not an old man yet by a long shot. No, don't you worry, the foundations you're building on today are more solid than they ever were.

SOLNESS. The tide will turn. I know it will. I can feel it coming — the day when one of those youngsters will stand up and demand: "Step aside!" And then the whole gang of them will jump to their feet and join in a chorus of threats and cries: "Make room — make room — make room!" You'll see, Doctor — one of these days the younger generation will come knocking at my door —

HERDAL (*laughs*). All right, let it!

SOLNESS. Yes, let it! And that will be the end of the master builder.

(*There is a knock at the door on the left.*)

(*Starts.*) What was that? Did you hear something?

HERDAL. Someone's at the door.

SOLNESS (*in a loud voice*). Come in!

(HILDE WANGEL *enters through the hall door. She is of medium height and has a fine, supple build. Her face is suntanned. She is dressed for hiking, wears a comfortable skirt, a scarf around her head, carries a knapsack on her back, a sleeping bag, and a stick whittled from the branch of a tree.*)

HILDE (*goes over to* SOLNESS, *her eyes sparkling with cheerfulness*). Good evening!

SOLNESS (*looks at her with uncertainty*). Good evening —

HILDE (*laughs*). Don't tell me you don't recognize me!

SOLNESS. I'm afraid I don't.

HERDAL (*comes over to them*). But I do, young lady.

HILDE (*pleased*). Hello there! What a pleasant surprise!

HERDAL. It certainly is! For me, at least. (*To* SOLNESS.) You see, this young lady and I got acquainted at one of the mountain resorts this summer. (*To* HILDE.) What happened to the rest of the ladies up there?

HILDE.   Oh, they didn't stay long! They left in a hurry!

HERDAL.   They didn't care for all the fun we had in the evenings, eh?

HILDE.   I don't think they did!

HERDAL (*shakes a finger at her*).   I can't say I blame them. After all, you did flirt with us, you know.

HILDE.   Of course I did! I had to have some fun after all that knitting with a bunch of musty old maids.

HERDAL (*laughs*).   I couldn't agree with you more!

SOLNESS.   Have you been in town for some time?

HILDE.   I just got here.

HERDAL.   Are you all alone, Miss Wangel?

HILDE.   Of course!

SOLNESS.   Wangel? Is your name Wangel?

HILDE (*looks at him in merry surprise*).   It certainly is.

SOLNESS.   Are you by any chance related to Dr. Wangel at Lysanger?

HILDE (*as before*).   Related? I'm his daughter!

SOLNESS.   Well, then we have met before. I once spent a summer up there building a tower on the old church.

HILDE (*more serious now*).   Yes, you did.

SOLNESS.   But that was a long time ago.

HILDE (*stares fixedly at him*).   Ten years ago — to be exact.

SOLNESS.   And then you were just a child, I suppose?

HILDE (*casually*).   About twelve or thirteen, anyway.

HERDAL.   Is this your first trip to town, Miss Wangel?

HILDE.   Yes, it is.

SOLNESS.   Then you can't know many people here.

HILDE.   No. No one except you. And then your wife, of course.

SOLNESS.   You know her, too?

HILDE.   Just slightly. We spent a few days together, at the sanatorium.

SOLNESS.   I see.

HILDE.   She'd be glad to see me, she said, if I ever came to town. (*Smiles.*) Not that I needed an invitation, of course.

SOLNESS.   Funny she never mentioned a word about it —

(HILDE *puts the stick on the table by the sofa. She takes off her knapsack and lays it and the sleeping bag on the sofa.* DR. HERDAL *offers to help her.* SOLNESS *stands watching her.*)

HILDE (*comes back to him*).   Well, is it all right with you if I stay overnight?

SOLNESS.   I can't see why not.

HILDE.   I've nothing to wear except this, you see. This and another set of underwear that I've stashed away in my knapsack. But it's got to be washed first. It's absolutely filthy.

SOLNESS.   Well, we'll see what we can do. I'd better tell my wife —

HERDAL.   Then I'll be off to see my patient.

SOLNESS.   All right. But you'll be back later, won't you?

HERDAL (*merrily, with a glance at* HILDE). Oh, I will! You can be damn sure of that! (*Laughs.*) So you were right after all, Mr. Solness!

SOLNESS.   What do you mean?

HERDAL.   The younger generation did come knocking at your door!

SOLNESS (*cheerfully*). Oh, I see! But this is different, isn't it?

HERDAL.   Oh yes! Quite, quite different! (*He leaves by the hall door.*)

SOLNESS (*opens the door, right, and calls in*). Aline! Will you come in here, please? There's a Miss Wangel here whom I believe you know.

MRS. SOLNESS (*appears in the doorway*). Who, did you say? (*Sees* HILDE.) Oh, hello, Miss Wangel! (*Goes over to her and shakes hands.*) So you did come to town after all.

SOLNESS.   Miss Wangel just arrived. She'd like to stay here overnight.

MRS. SOLNESS.   Would she? Well, I'd like that very much.

SOLNESS.   She needs to fix her clothes and that sort of thing.

MRS. SOLNESS.   I'll help you in any way I can. That's my duty, isn't it? Where's your luggage?

HILDE.   I don't have any.

MRS. SOLNESS.   Oh, I see. Well, then maybe you'd like to stay here and talk to my husband while I get a room ready for you?

SOLNESS.   What about one of the nurseries? They're all ready as it is.

MRS. SOLNESS.   Yes, we've plenty of room there. (*To* HILDE.) Now, please sit down and rest, won't you? (*She leaves by the door on the right.*)

(HILDE, *her hands clasped behind her back, wanders about the room looking at various things.* SOLNESS, *also with his hands clasped behind his back, stands beside his desk watching her.*)

HILDE (*stops and looks at him*). Do you have a lot of nurseries here?

SOLNESS.   We have three of them.

HILDE.   That *is* a lot. Then I suppose you have an awful lot of children, too?

SOLNESS.   No, we have no children. But now you can be the child here for a while.

HILDE.   Yes — for tonight. I won't cry, though. Tonight, you see, I'd like to sleep like a log.

SOLNESS.   You must be very tired.

HILDE.   Not a bit! But it's so terribly exciting just to lie in bed and dream.

SOLNESS.   Do you often dream at night?

HILDE.   Oh, I do! Nearly every night.

SOLNESS.   What do you dream about?

HILDE.   I'm not going to tell you. Not tonight. Some other time, maybe. (*She wanders around the room again, stops by Kaia's desk and rummages a little among the books and papers.*)

SOLNESS (*goes over to her*). Are you looking for something?

HILDE. No, just looking. (*Turns.*) Do you mind?

SOLNESS. Go right ahead.

HILDE. What's that monster of a book for?

SOLNESS. My secretary uses it. She keeps track of income and expenses — things of that sort.

HILDE. A female?

SOLNESS (*smiles*). Yes.

HILDE. And she works here with you?

SOLNESS. Yes.

HILDE. Is she married?

SOLNESS. No, she's single.

HILDE. Well!

SOLNESS. But I think she'll get married soon now.

HILDE. Good for her.

SOLNESS. But not for me. Then I'll be without a secretary.

HILDE. Can't you find someone else who's just as good?

SOLNESS. Perhaps you would like to try it? Keep track of things in that monster of a book?

HILDE (*looks at him disdainfully*). Is that a joke? Or don't you think I have better things to do? No, thank you! (*She wanders around the room again and sits in Solness' chair.*)

(SOLNESS *goes over to her and stands beside the desk.*)

(*In the same vein.*) I'm sure there are better things for me to do around here. (*Looks at him and smiles.*) Don't you think so, too?

SOLNESS. Oh, I'm sure of it. And first of all I suppose you plan to go shopping and get some nice clothes to wear?

HILDE (*gaily*). No, I don't think I'll bother with that.

SOLNESS. Oh?

HILDE. I've squandered my money, you see.

SOLNESS (*laughs*). No luggage, and no money!

HILDE. That's right! Oh heck, what would I do with it, anyway!

SOLNESS. You know — I really like you for that!

HILDE. Just for that?

SOLNESS. Among other things. (*Sits on the edge of the desk.*) Is your father still alive?

HILDE. Oh, yes.

SOLNESS. Maybe you're thinking of going to school here?

HILDE. No, that never occurred to me.

SOLNESS. But you're going to stay for a while, aren't you?

HILDE. That depends. (*She sits for a while and looks at him, half seriously, half with a suppressed smile. Then she takes off her scarf and puts it on the desk.*) Master Builder!

SOLNESS. Yes.

HILDE. Are you a very forgetful person?

SOLNESS. Forgetful? Not as far as I know.

HILDE. Then why aren't you willing to talk to me about what happened up there?

SOLNESS (*startled for a moment*).   At Lysanger? (*Indifferently.*) What's there to talk about?

HILDE (*looks at him reproachfully*).   How can you say that!

SOLNESS.   All right, suppose you talk about it, then.

HILDE.   When the tower was finished, the whole town was ready to celebrate —

SOLNESS.   Oh, yes! Now, there's one thing I won't forget.

HILDE (*smiles*).   Really? That's very kind of you!

SOLNESS.   Kind?

HILDE.   The band was playing, and there were lots and lots of people. My friends and I were dressed in white, and we all had flags —

SOLNESS.   Ah yes! Those flags! That's another thing I haven't forgotten!

HILDE.   And then you climbed up the scaffolding — right to the top! You had a huge wreath in your hand, and you hung it up high on the weather vane.

SOLNESS (*curtly interrupting*).   I used to do that in those days. It's an old tradition, you see.

HILDE.   How wonderful it was, how perfectly thrilling to see you way up there. What if he were to slip and fall — he, the master builder himself!

SOLNESS (*as if wanting to change the subject*).   Oh yes, that could easily have happened, too. You see, one of those damn little devils in white was making such a fuss down there, screaming up at me all the time —

HILDE (*sparkling with delight*).   "Hurray for Master Builder Solness!" Yes!

SOLNESS.   And she was waving her flag so furiously at me that I began to feel dizzy.

HILDE (*seriously now, in a low voice*).   That damn little devil was me.

SOLNESS (*stares fixedly at her*).   I can see that now. It must have been you.

HILDE (*sparkles again*).   How wonderful it was, how terribly exciting! I never dreamed there was a master builder in the entire world who could ever build such a tremendously high tower. And then to see you — the master builder himself — standing at the very top of it! And not the least bit dizzy! That's what made *me* feel — well, dizzy just thinking about it.

SOLNESS.   What made you so sure I wasn't — ?

HILDE (*refusing to listen*).   That's enough! Shame on you! I knew it was so because I felt it — in here. Besides, how else could you stand up there and sing?

SOLNESS (*stares at her in amazement*).   Sing! Did I sing up there?

HILDE.   You certainly did.

SOLNESS (*shakes his head*).   I've never sung a note in my life.

HILDE.   Well — you sang then! It sounded like harps in the air.

SOLNESS (*thoughtfully*).   This is all very strange.

HILDE (*is silent for a while, then looks at him and says in a low voice*). What really mattered, you know — came afterwards.

SOLNESS.   What really mattered?

HILDE (*sparkling with vivacity*).   You're not going to tell me that I have to remind you of *that*!

SOLNESS.   Yes, better remind me a little of that, too.

HILDE.   Don't you remember the big banquet they gave for you at the club?

SOLNESS.   Yes. That must have been the same afternoon. I left the next morning.

HILDE.   And after the banquet, you were invited to our house —

SOLNESS.   You're quite right, Miss Wangel. It's amazing how well you remember every trifle.

HILDE.   Trifle! Well! And the fact that I was all alone in the living room when you came in — perhaps that was a trifle, too?

SOLNESS.   You were all alone?

HILDE (*ignoring him*).   You didn't call me a damn little devil then.

SOLNESS.   No, I don't suppose I did.

HILDE.   As a matter of fact, you said I looked irresistible in my white dress — like a little princess.

SOLNESS.   I'm sure you did, Miss Wangel. Besides, I was in a particularly good mood that day —

HILDE.   And then you said that when I grew up, I was going to be your princess.

SOLNESS (*chuckles*).   I said that, too, eh?

HILDE.   Yes, you did. And when I asked you how long I'd have to wait, you said you'd come back for me in ten years — like a troll — and carry me off. To Spain, or some place like that. And you promised to buy me a kingdom there.

SOLNESS (*as before*).   Well, after a good dinner you're bound to feel a little generous, I suppose. But did I really say all that?

HILDE (*laughs softly*).   Yes! You even told me what you'd like to call it.

SOLNESS.   Call what?

HILDE.   My kingdom! You'd call it the Kingdom of Orangia, you said.

SOLNESS.   Well, that's a tasty name.

HILDE.   I didn't like it at all. It sounded as though you were making fun of me.

SOLNESS.   Now, why should I do that?

HILDE.   That's what I'd like to know — considering what you did next.

SOLNESS.   And what on earth did I do next?

HILDE.   Don't tell me you've forgotten that, too! There's a limit, you know.

SOLNESS.   I know, but — Well, give me a hint, anyway.

HILDE (*looks at him intently*).   You kissed me, Master Builder.

SOLNESS (*gets up, openmouthed*). I did!

HILDE. Yes, you did. You took me in your arms and bent me over backwards and kissed me. Many times.

SOLNESS. Now, my dear Miss Wangel — !

HILDE (*gets up*). You're not going to deny it, are you?

SOLNESS. I most certainly am!

HILDE (*looks at him scornfully*). Well! (*She turns and walks slowly over to the fireplace where she stops and stands motionless with her back to him and with her hands clasped behind her back. A short pause.*)

SOLNESS (*goes cautiously over to her and stands behind her*). Miss Wangel — ?

(HILDE *is silent and does not move.*)

Now, don't stand there like a statue. You must have dreamed these things. (*He puts his hand on her arm.*) Listen —

(HILDE *makes an impatient movement with her arm.*)

(*A thought strikes him.*) Or else — wait a minute! Perhaps there's more to it than that!

(HILDE *does not move.*)

(*In a low voice, but with emphasis.*) I must have thought about all this. I must have willed it, wanted it, desired it. So that — Wouldn't that explain it?

(HILDE *is still silent.*)

(*Impatiently.*) All right, then, damn it! Let's say I did it, too!

HILDE (*turns her head a little but does not look at him*). Then you do admit it?

SOLNESS. Yes. Anything you like.

HILDE. That you put your arms around me?

SOLNESS. Oh yes!

HILDE. And bent me over backwards?

SOLNESS. Way over backwards.

HILDE. And kissed me?

SOLNESS. That, too.

HILDE. Many times?

SOLNESS. As many as you like.

HILDE (*turns quickly around, her eyes once more sparkling with delight*). You see! I finally managed to worm it out of you!

SOLNESS (*cannot help smiling*). Can you imagine — forgetting a thing like that!

HILDE (*sulks again; walks away from him*). Oh, I can imagine, all right. You've probably kissed all kinds of women since then.

SOLNESS. I hope you don't believe that.

(HILDE *sits down in front of his desk.* SOLNESS *stands leaning against it.*)

(*Watching her closely.*) Miss Wangel?

HILDE. Yes?

SOLNESS. Let's see, now — what else happened between us?

HILDE. Why, nothing! You know that. Then all the others came in, and — ugh!

SOLNESS. Of course! How could I forget that!

HILDE. You haven't forgotten a thing. You're a little ashamed of yourself, that's all. Nobody forgets a thing like that.

SOLNESS. No, I wouldn't think so.

HILDE (*sparkling again; looks at him*). You're not going to tell me you don't even remember what day it was?

SOLNESS. Well, now that you mention it —

HILDE. I'm speaking of the day you hung the wreath on the tower! When was it? Come on, tell me!

SOLNESS. Hm — I'm not sure I remember the exact date, but I do know it was ten years ago — some time in the fall.

HILDE (*nods her head slowly and repeatedly*). So it was — ten years ago. On the nineteenth of September.

SOLNESS. Yes, something like that. Well, you've got a remarkable memory, I must say! (*Stops and thinks.*) Now, just a minute — ! That's today, isn't it? Yes, today is the nineteenth of September!

HILDE. Yes, it is. And the ten years are up. And you didn't come — as you promised you would.

SOLNESS. Promised? Threatened I would, I suppose you mean?

HILDE. It didn't sound like a threat to me.

SOLNESS. I must have been joking, then.

HILDE. Was that all you wanted to do? Joke with me?

SOLNESS. Well, maybe I was teasing you in one way or another. I'll be damned if I know. But it must have been something like that. You were only a child then.

HILDE. Oh, perhaps I wasn't such a child either. Not the kind of brat you have in mind, anyway.

SOLNESS (*looks searchingly at her*). Are you trying to tell me that all this time you seriously thought I'd come back some day?

HILDE (*suppresses a half-roguish smile*). Of course! I expected that of you.

SOLNESS. That I'd come to your home and take you with me?

HILDE. Just like a troll — yes!

SOLNESS. And make you a princess?

HILDE. That's what you promised.

SOLNESS. And give you a kingdom, too?

HILDE (*gazing at the ceiling*). Why not? After all, it didn't have to be a kingdom in the ordinary sense of the word.

SOLNESS. But something else just as nice?

HILDE. Oh, at least as nice. (*Looks at him now and then.*) If you could build the highest church tower in the world, why not take on a kingdom of some kind as well? Or so I thought.

SOLNESS (*shakes his head*). You're a difficult person to figure out, Miss Wangel.

HILDE. I can't see why. It's really quite simple.

SOLNESS. What I can't make out is whether you really mean what you say or whether you're just having a little fun —

HILDE (*smiles*). Whether I'm joking, you mean? The way you were?

SOLNESS. Yes, joking! Only this time the joke is on both of us. (*Looks at her.*) How long have you known that I was married?

HILDE. All along. Why do you ask that?

SOLNESS (*casually*). Oh, just wondered, I guess. (*Looks solemnly at her and says in a low voice.*) Why have you come?

HILDE. I want my kingdom. The time is up, you know.

SOLNESS (*cannot help laughing*). Still at it, eh?

HILDE (*gaily*). You bet I am! Let's have that kingdom, Master Builder. (*Raps the table.*) My kingdom on the table!

SOLNESS (*sits down at his desk*). Seriously now, why have you come? What do you want here?

HILDE. Well, first of all I'd like to go around and see everything you've built.

SOLNESS. That'll keep you busy for a while!

HILDE. You've built an awful lot, I understand.

SOLNESS. Yes, I have. Particularly during the last few years.

HILDE. Church towers, too? Immensely high ones?

SOLNESS. No, I don't build church towers any more. Nor churches either.

HILDE. Then what do you build now?

SOLNESS. Homes for people to live in.

HILDE (*thoughtfully*). Can't you put little towers on them, too?

SOLNESS (*startled*). What do you mean?

HILDE. I mean — something which soars bravely upwards — with the weather vane up so high it makes you dizzy to look at it.

SOLNESS (*ponders for a while*). It's strange you should say that. There's nothing else I'd rather do.

HILDE (*impatiently*). Then why don't you do it?

SOLNESS (*shakes his head*). No, people don't want that.

HILDE. They don't? Well!

SOLNESS (*in a lighter vein*). But I'm building a new home for myself now. Right next to this one.

HILDE. For yourself?

SOLNESS. Yes. It's almost finished, too. And there's a tower on that.

HILDE.   A high tower?

SOLNESS.   Yes.

HILDE.   Immensely high?

SOLNESS.   I'm sure people will say it's too high — for a home.

HILDE.   I want to take a look at that tower, the first thing in the morning.

SOLNESS (*sits resting his cheek on his hand and stares at her*).   Tell me, Miss Wangel — what is your name? Your first name, I mean.

HILDE.   You know! It's Hilde.

SOLNESS (*as before*).   Hilde —

HILDE.   Don't you remember? You said it a lot that day you didn't — behave yourself.

SOLNESS.   I did that, too?

HILDE.   But then you said "Hilde, my child." And I didn't care for that.

SOLNESS.   So you didn't care for that, Miss Hilde?

HILDE.   No, not on that occasion. But I'm sure I won't object to "Princess Hilde."

SOLNESS.   I see. Princess Hilde of — of — Now, what was the name of that kingdom?

HILDE.   To heck with that stupid kingdom! What I have in mind is quite a different one!

SOLNESS (*still gazing at her, he has now leaned back in his chair*).   How strange! The more I think about it, the more I'm convinced that what I've been tormenting myself with all these years —

HILDE.   Well?

SOLNESS.   — is a memory of something forgotten — an experience I once had but couldn't quite remember.

HILDE.   I thought that secretary of yours was keeping track of things for you.

SOLNESS.   Ah, yes! But things like that I've had to keep track of myself.

HILDE.   Then all the trolls in this world have done a very good job of confusing you, Master Builder.

SOLNESS.   So they have. (*Gets up slowly.*) I'm very glad you came to me just now.

HILDE.   Are you?

SOLNESS.   Yes. I've been sitting here by myself, so helpless, just watching it all. (*Lowers his voice.*) The fact is I've become afraid — so terribly afraid of the younger generation.

HILDE (*with a snort of contempt*).   Pooh! That's nothing to be afraid of!

SOLNESS.   Oh yes, it is! And that's why I've barricaded myself here. (*Secretively.*) Yes, the younger generation will come one day and bang on my door! It'll break in on me!

HILDE.   If that's the case, why don't you let it in, then?

SOLNESS.   Let it in?

HILDE.   Yes. Give it a chance to make friends with you.

SOLNESS.   No, no! Why, the younger generation — that's retribution, don't you see? It heralds the turn of the tide and carries a new banner.

HILDE (*stands up, looks at him and says, as a quiver passes over her lips*). Can I be of use to you, Master Builder?

SOLNESS.   Yes, I've no doubt about that now! Because you, too, carry a new banner. And then it's youth against youth!

HERDAL (*comes in through the hall door*).   Ah, you're still here!

SOLNESS.   Yes, we had quite a few things to talk about.

HILDE.   Some more than others, actually.

HERDAL.   Oh?

HILDE.   It's been lots of fun! And why not, considering the master builder's fantastic memory? You don't have to remind him of anything, not even the slightest trifle!

MRS. SOLNESS (*comes in by the door right*).   Well, Miss Wangel, your room's ready now.

HILDE.   Oh, you're so kind to me.

SOLNESS (*to his wife*).   The nursery?

MRS. SOLNESS.   Yes. The middle one. But it's time for dinner now, isn't it?

SOLNESS (*nodding to* HILDE).   Hilde sleeps in the nursery, yes.

MRS. SOLNESS (*looks at him*).   Hilde?

SOLNESS.   Yes, her name is Hilde. I knew her when she was a child.

MRS. SOLNESS.   Did you, Halvard? Well, let's have dinner. The table is set.

(*She takes* DR. HERDAL's *arm and goes out with him to the right. Meanwhile* HILDE *has been picking up her things.*)

HILDE (*quickly, lowering her voice*).   Did you mean what you said just now? I can be of use to you?

SOLNESS (*takes her things from her*).   You're the one I've always needed.

HILDE (*looks at him with happy eyes full of wonder and clasps her hands*).   Oh, wonderful, wonderful Master Builder. Then you do keep promises, after all.

SOLNESS.   Promises?

HILDE.   Yes! Then I have my kingdom, don't you see?

SOLNESS (*involuntarily*).   Hilde!

HILDE (*again a quiver passes over her lips*).   Or a part of it — anyway.

(*She goes out to the right.* SOLNESS *follows her.*)

ACT TWO

(*An attractively furnished small living room in* SOLNESS' *house. A glass door leading out to the veranda and garden in the back wall. The right-hand corner is broken by a bay in which there are flower stands and a large* window. A similar bay in the left-hand corner contains a small door papered like the wall. In each of the side walls, an ordinary door. In the right foreground, a console table with a large mirror. An abundance of flowers and plants. In the left foreground, a sofa with a table and chairs. Further back, a bookcase. Out in the room in front of the bay window, a small table and a couple of chairs. It is early in the day.

Master Builder SOLNESS sits by the small table with Ragnar Brovik's portfolio open in front of him. He leafs through the drawings, taking a closer look at some of them. MRS. SOLNESS goes silently about with a little watering can, tending her flowers. She is dressed in black, as before. Her hat, overcoat, and umbrella lie on a chair by the mirror. Now and then, without her noticing, SOLNESS watches her closely. Neither of them speaks.

KAIA FOSSLI comes quietly in through the door on the left.)

SOLNESS (turns his head and says, rather casually). Oh, hello there.

KAIA. I just wanted to let you know that I'm here.

SOLNESS. Yes — well, good. And Ragnar?

KAIA. No, not yet. He had to wait for the doctor. But he'll be here soon to talk to you about the —

SOLNESS. How's the old man doing?

KAIA. Not very well. He's so sorry he has to stay in bed today.

SOLNESS. That's perfectly all right. Well, go back to work now.

KAIA. Yes. (Stops at the door.) Would you like to see Ragnar when he gets here?

SOLNESS. No — not particularly.

(KAIA goes out to the left. SOLNESS continues to look through the drawings.)

MRS. SOLNESS (over by the plants). I suppose he'll die, too.

SOLNESS (looks at her). He too? What do you mean?

MRS. SOLNESS (not answering). Oh yes. Old Brovik — he'll die now, too. You'll see, Halvard.

SOLNESS. Aline dear, shouldn't you take your walk now?

MRS. SOLNESS. Yes, I should, shouldn't I? (She goes on tending her flowers.)

SOLNESS (bent over the drawings). Is she still asleep?

MRS. SOLNESS (looks at him). Is it Miss Wangel you're sitting there thinking about?

SOLNESS (casually). Just happened to remember her.

MRS. SOLNESS. Miss Wangel got up a long time ago.

SOLNESS. Did she?

MRS. SOLNESS. When I looked in she was fixing her clothes. (She stands in front of the mirror, slowly putting on her hat.)

SOLNESS (after a brief pause). Then we did get to use one of the nurseries after all, Aline.

MRS. SOLNESS. Yes, we did.

SOLNESS.　That's better than having them all empty, don't you think?

MRS. SOLNESS.　You're right there. This emptiness is really quite unbearable.

SOLNESS (*closes the portfolio, gets up and goes over to her*).　Aline, I'm sure things'll be different from now on — more pleasant, easier to live with. Especially for you.

MRS. SOLNESS (*looks at him*).　From now on?

SOLNESS.　Yes, you'll see, Aline —

MRS. SOLNESS.　You mean — because she's here?

SOLNESS (*restrains himself*).　What I mean is — after we've moved into the new house.

MRS. SOLNESS (*picks up her overcoat*).　Do you really think so, Halvard? That that will change anything?

SOLNESS.　What else am I to believe? You believe so, too, don't you?

MRS. SOLNESS.　I put very little faith in the new house.

SOLNESS (*dejected*).　I'm very sorry to hear that. It's mostly for your sake that I built it. (*He wants to help her on with the coat.*)

MRS. SOLNESS (*moving away*).　You're doing far too much for my sake.

SOLNESS (*with a certain vehemence*).　Don't say that, Aline! I can't stand that kind of talk from you.

MRS. SOLNESS.　All right, Halvard — then I won't say it.

SOLNESS.　Anyway, I still think I'm right. Things'll be much better for you over there. You'll see.

MRS. SOLNESS.　Oh, my god — better for me!

SOLNESS (*eagerly*).　Yes, they will! Believe me, they will! You see — there'll be so much over there to remind you of your own home —

MRS. SOLNESS.　Of what belonged to my father and mother. And was ravaged by the fire — all of it.

SOLNESS (*in a subdued voice*).　Poor Aline. That was a terrible blow for you.

MRS. SOLNESS (*breaking out in lamentation*).　You can build as much as you like, Halvard — but you'll never manage to build a real home for me again!

SOLNESS (*walks away*).　Then let's not talk about it any more, for god's sake!

MRS. SOLNESS.　We never do, anyway. You always seem to avoid it.

SOLNESS (*stops abruptly and looks at her*).　I do? Why? Why should I avoid it?

MRS. SOLNESS.　Oh, I understand you so well, Halvard. I know you want to spare me — find excuses for me, too. You'll do anything you can for me.

SOLNESS (*looks at her in astonishment*).　For you! Is that what you think, Aline?

MRS. SOLNESS.　Yes, of course it is.

SOLNESS (*involuntarily, to himself*).　That, too!

MRS. SOLNESS.　But that's the way it was meant to be, I suppose — about the old house. Heaven knows that accidents will occur —

solness. You're right. That sort of thing is beyond our control — they say.

mrs. solness. It's the terrible thing the fire brought with it I can't — I just can't!

solness (*vehemently*). Don't think about it, Aline!

mrs. solness. I have to think about it. Have to talk about it for once, too. Because I don't think I can bear it any longer — not having the right to forgive myself for any of it.

solness (*bursts out*). Forgive yourself — !

mrs. solness. Yes, I had a duty to all of you — both to you and to the little ones. I should have hardened myself. I shouldn't have let the horror of it all overwhelm me — or the grief for my home that burned down. (*Wringing her hands.*) Oh, Halvard, if I'd only been strong enough!

solness (*in a low voice, deeply moved, comes closer*). Aline — I want you to promise me never again to let such thoughts bother you. Now, promise!

mrs. solness. Good heavens — promise! Promise! It's easy enough to promise —

solness (*clenching his fists, he crosses the room*). What a mess! Not the faintest ray of hope to cheer up the gloomy atmosphere of this home!

mrs. solness. But this is no home, Halvard.

solness. No, I guess you're right. (*Darkly.*) And god knows you may be right about the new house, too.

mrs. solness. Oh, yes! It'll be just as cold and empty over there as it is here.

solness (*vehemently*). Then why on earth did we build it? Can you tell me that?

mrs. solness. That's a question only you can answer, Halvard.

solness (*glancing at her suspiciously*). What do you mean by that, Aline?

mrs. solness. What do I mean?

solness. Yes, damn it! You said it in a strange way, as though you meant something else.

mrs. solness. I didn't, I assure you —

solness (*comes closer*). Come on, now — I know what I know. I've got eyes and ears too, Aline. Don't you forget that!

mrs. solness. I don't know what you're talking about. I really don't.

solness (*places himself in front of her*). Isn't it true that you manage to find a hidden meaning in the most innocent thing I say?

mrs. solness. I? Do I do that?

solness (*laughs*). Not that I blame you, Aline. After all, you've got a sick man to worry about.

mrs. solness (*anxiously*). Sick! Are you ill, Halvard?

solness (*bursts out*). Half mad, then! Crazy! Call me what you like.

mrs. solness (*gropes for the back of the chair and sits down*). Halvard — for god's sake — !

solness. But you're both wrong — you and your doctor. I'm nothing of the kind.

(*He paces the floor.* mrs solness *watches him anxiously. He comes back to her and speaks calmly.*)

When you come right down to it, there's nothing the matter with me at all.

mrs. solness. Yes, don't you think so too, Halvard? But — what's worrying you, then?

solness. It's this terrible burden of debt that keeps weighing me down —

mrs. solness. Debt! But you're not in debt to anyone, Halvard!

solness (*moved, in a low voice*). I owe a staggering debt to you, Aline — to you — you.

mrs. solness (*rises slowly*). What's behind all this? You might as well tell me right away.

solness. There's nothing to tell! I've never done you any harm — not knowingly, at any rate. And yet, there's this nagging guilt feeling at my throat — stifling me.

mrs. solness. Guilt feeling? Toward me?

solness. Toward you most of all.

mrs. solness. Then you really are — ill, Halvard.

solness (*darkly*). Must be, I suppose. Or something like that. (*Looks toward the door on the right which is being opened.*) Ah, here's one who'll cheer us up!

hilde wangel (*enters. She has made some alteration in her dress, which looks neater*). Good morning, Master Builder!

solness (*nods*). Did you sleep well?

hilde. Fantastically! Like a child in a cradle. I lay there and stretched myself like a — well, princess!

solness (*smiles a little*). Quite comfortable, then?

hilde. I'll say.

solness. Been dreaming, too?

hilde. Oh yes. But that was awful.

solness. Oh?

hilde. Yes. You see, I dreamed I fell off a terribly high and steep cliff. Don't you ever dream about things like that?

solness. Oh yes — now and then —

hilde. Terribly exciting, isn't it — as you sort of — keep falling?

solness. It's more like a chill up your spine, I think.

hilde. Do you pull your legs up under you while it goes on?

solness. Yes, as high as I can.

hilde. So do I.

mrs. solness (*takes her umbrella*). Well, Halvard, I'd better go shopping now. (*To* hilde.) And I'll see if I can pick up a few things for you, Miss Wangel.

HILDE (*about to throw her arms around* MRS. SOLNESS' *neck*). Oh, dear, wonderful Mrs. Solness! How very nice of you! You're so terribly kind —

MRS. SOLNESS (*checking her, she frees herself*). Not at all. It's only my duty. And that's why I'm happy to do it.

HILDE (*pouts, piqued*). Oh, well, then, why not let me do it? It's all right for me to go out the way I look now. Or don't you think so?

MRS. SOLNESS. To be quite frank with you, I think people might stare at you a little.

HILDE (*contemptuously*). Pooh! Is that all? But that's fun.

SOLNESS (*with suppressed bad temper*). Yes, but people might think you're mad, too, you see.

HILDE. Mad? Are there so many mad people here in town?

SOLNESS (*points at his forehead*). Here's one, anyway.

HILDE. You, Master Builder!

MRS. SOLNESS. Now really, Halvard!

SOLNESS. Haven't you noticed that yet?

HILDE. No, I certainly haven't. (*Thinks, then chuckles.*) Well, maybe I have, in a way — now that I think of it.

SOLNESS. You hear that, Aline?

MRS. SOLNESS. In what way, Miss Wangel?

HILDE. I'm not going to tell you.

SOLNESS. Please — do!

HILDE. No, thank you — I'm not that mad.

MRS. SOLNESS. When you and Miss Wangel are alone I'm sure she'll tell you, Halvard.

SOLNESS. Oh, you think so?

MRS. SOLNESS. I'm sure of it. After all, you've known her for quite some time — ever since she was a child, in fact. (*She goes out by the door on the left.*)

HILDE (*after a short pause*). I don't think your wife could ever get to like me, even if she tried to.

SOLNESS. Is that the impression she's made on you?

HILDE. Haven't you noticed that yourself?

SOLNESS (*evasively*). Aline's become quite shy lately.

HILDE. Has she really?

SOLNESS. Oh, I'm sure you'll see what a kind, gentle, and really fine person she is, once you know her a little better.

HILDE. If that's the case, then why did she have to say this thing about duty?

SOLNESS. Duty?

HILDE. Yes, didn't you hear her say that she wanted to get me a few things? It was her duty, she said. I can't stand that ugly, nasty word.

SOLNESS. Why not?

HILDE. Because it sounds so cold and sharp and stingy. Duty, duty, duty! Don't you think so too, that it sort of stings you?

SOLNESS. Hm — haven't given it much thought.

HILDE. It does! And if she's as kind as you say she is, why would she put it like that?

SOLNESS. What on earth did you want her to say?

HILDE. Oh, she could have said that she wanted to do it because she likes me an awful lot. Something like that. Something that was really warm and cordial, don't you see?

SOLNESS (*looks at her*). Is that the way you want it?

HILDE. Exactly. (*She walks about, stops in front of the bookcase and looks at the books.*) You've got an awful lot of books, haven't you?

SOLNESS. Oh, I've collected a few.

HILDE. Do you read them all?

SOLNESS. I tried to in the old days. Do you read much?

HILDE. Oh no! Not any more. I don't get what they're trying to say.

SOLNESS. That's just the way I feel.

HILDE (*strolls about again, stops by the little table, opens the portfolio and leafs through the drawings*). Did you make all these drawings?

SOLNESS. No, they were done by a young man who's helping me out.

HILDE. Someone you've been training?

SOLNESS. Well, I suppose he's learned something from me, too.

HILDE (*sits*). He must be very smart, then? (*Looks at a drawing.*) Isn't he?

SOLNESS. He's not too bad. Not for my use, anyway.

HILDE. Oh yes! I'm sure he must be terribly smart.

SOLNESS. Can you tell that from his drawings?

HILDE. Ffft! These scribbles! No, but if he's been trained by you —

SOLNESS. Oh, I've trained quite a few people around here. Even so, they're just as bad as they ever were.

HILDE (*looks at him and shakes her head*). Even if my life depended upon it, I'd never be able to figure out how you can be so stupid.

SOLNESS. Stupid? You really think I am stupid, eh?

HILDE. I certainly do — wasting your time on training all those people.

SOLNESS (*starts*). Well? Why not?

HILDE (*gets up, half in earnest, half laughing*). Gosh, no, Master Builder. What good'll that do! No one else but you should have the right to build. You should do all of it yourself — you alone. Now you know.

SOLNESS (*involuntarily*). Hilde — !

HILDE. Yes?

SOLNESS. What on earth gave you that idea?

HILDE. You think it's wrong of me to think like that?

SOLNESS. No, I don't mean that. But let me tell you something.

HILDE. All right?

SOLNESS. You see — that's the very idea I've been tossing around in my mind for quite some time.

HILDE. Of course. I don't blame you.

SOLNESS (*looks searchingly at her*). And I suppose you've noticed that.

HILDE. No, I can't say I have.

SOLNESS. But a moment ago — when you said I was a little mad — in a certain way — ?

HILDE. Oh, I had something else in mind then.

SOLNESS. But what?

HILDE. Never mind, Master Builder.

SOLNESS (*walks across the room*). All right, as you wish. (*Stops by the bay window.*) Come here, and I'll show you something.

HILDE (*comes closer*). What is it?

SOLNESS. Look — over there in the garden.

HILDE. Well?

SOLNESS (*points*). Right above the big quarry —

HILDE. Is that the new house?

SOLNESS. The one I'm building now, yes. It's almost finished.

HILDE. It's got a very high tower, hasn't it?

SOLNESS. The scaffolding is still up.

HILDE. So that's your new house.

SOLNESS. Yes.

HILDE. The one you'll be moving into soon?

SOLNESS. Yes.

HILDE (*looks at him*). Are there nurseries in that house, too?

SOLNESS. Three, same as here.

HILDE. But no children.

SOLNESS. There won't be any either.

HILDE (*with a half-smile*). That's what I said — isn't it?

SOLNESS. What did you say?

HILDE. That you're — sort of — mad in a way, after all.

SOLNESS. So that's what you had in mind?

HILDE. Yes, all the empty nurseries, like the one I slept in.

SOLNESS (*lowers his voice*). We've had children — Aline and I.

HILDE (*looks at him tensely*). You have — !

SOLNESS. Two little boys. Both the same age.

HILDE. Twins?

SOLNESS. Yes. Eleven or twelve years ago.

HILDE (*gently*). Then both must be — ? You don't have those twins any more, do you?

SOLNESS (*quietly, moved*). We only had them for about three weeks, not even that long. (*Bursts out.*) Oh Hilde, I can't tell you how much I appreciate your being here! At last I have someone I can talk to!

HILDE. Weren't you able to do that — with her?

SOLNESS. Not about this. Not the way I want to, and have to. (*Darkly.*) Not about so many other things either, for that matter.

HILDE (*in a low voice*). Was that all you meant when you said you needed me?

SOLNESS. Yes, I suppose it was. Yesterday, anyway. But today I'm not so sure any more — (*breaking off*). Let's sit down, Hilde. Why don't you sit in that sofa there? Then you can see the garden.

(HILDE *sits in the corner of the sofa.* SOLNESS *pulls up a chair.*)

Would you like to hear about it?

HILDE. Yes. I'd love to sit here and listen to you.

SOLNESS (*sits down*). Then I'll tell you all about it.

HILDE. I've got a clear view of both you and the garden now, Master Builder. So tell me! Now!

SOLNESS (*points through the bay window*). On that hill over there, where the new house is being built —

HILDE. Yes?

SOLNESS. That's where Aline and I were living during the first years of our marriage. That's the site of the old house that belonged to her mother. We took it over after her. And all of this huge garden came with it.

HILDE. Did that house have a tower too?

SOLNESS. Oh no. It was a big and ugly crate to look at. But inside it was warm and cozy.

HILDE. Then what did you do with that old junk — tear it down?

SOLNESS. No. It burned down.

HILDE. The whole thing?

SOLNESS. Yes.

HILDE. Was that a tremendous blow to you, or what?

SOLNESS. That depends on how you look at it. That fire meant a start for me as a builder.

HILDE. All right, then — ?

SOLNESS. But we had just had our two little boys then —

HILDE. Yes, those poor little twins.

SOLNESS. They were so strong and healthy when they were born. And they grew so fast that you could tell the difference every day.

HILDE. Babies grow an awful lot at first, don't they?

SOLNESS. The most beautiful thing I ever saw was Aline lying there with the two of them. — But then came the night of the fire —

HILDE (*excitedly*). What happened? Tell me! Was anyone trapped by the fire?

SOLNESS. No, everyone got out of the house safely.

HILDE. Then what?

SOLNESS. But Aline was terribly shaken up by it all — the noise and commotion — the frenzied evacuation of the house — and then the freezing cold of the night. — They had to be carried out, you see, the way I'd seen them lying there — both she and the little ones.

HILDE. And they couldn't take that?

SOLNESS. Yes, they could take it all right. But then Aline came down with a fever that affected her milk. She still insisted on nursing them herself. It was her duty, she said. And so both our little boys — (*wringing his hands*). Oh!

HILDE.   They didn't pull through?

SOLNESS.   No, they didn't. And that's how we lost them.

HILDE.   It must have been terribly hard for you.

SOLNESS.   Hard for me? Yes, but ten times harder for Aline. (*Clenching his fists in suppressed fury.*) Why are things like that allowed to happen in this world! (*Shortly and firmly.*) From that day on I'd rather not build churches any more.

HILDE.   Not even the church tower at Lysanger?

SOLNESS.   Not even that. I remember how happy and relieved I was when that tower was finally finished.

HILDE.   So do I.

SOLNESS.   And now I don't build things like that any more. Not at all! Neither churches nor church towers.

HILDE (*nods slowly*).   Only houses for people to live in.

SOLNESS.   Homes for human beings, Hilde.

HILDE.   But homes with high towers and spires on them.

SOLNESS.   Yes, if I can. (*In a lighter vein.*) Anyway — as I told you — that fire gave me a start. As a builder, I mean.

HILDE.   Why don't you call yourself an architect like the others?

SOLNESS.   Oh, I haven't studied enough for that. Most of what I know I've found out for myself.

HILDE.   But you still got ahead, didn't you, Master Builder?

SOLNESS.   Yes, because of that fire. I subdivided nearly all this land into lots, and on those lots I built according to my own ideas. After that I had no trouble at all.

HILDE (*looks searchingly at him*).   I'm sure you must be a very happy man, the way things are going for you.

SOLNESS (*dejected*).   Happy? You think so, too, same as everybody else?

HILDE.   Yes, why not? If only you could stop thinking about those two little boys —

SOLNESS (*slowly*).   Those two little boys — they're not easily forgotten, Hilde.

HILDE (*a little uncertain*).   Are they still in your way, after all these years?

SOLNESS (*looks directly at her without replying*).   A happy man, you said —

HILDE.   Yes. You are, aren't you? I mean, apart from that?

SOLNESS (*still looking at her*).   When I told you this thing about the fire — hm —

HILDE.   Yes?

SOLNESS.   Weren't you struck by one thing in particular?

HILDE (*tries in vain to remember*).   No. Did I miss something?

SOLNESS (*with subtle emphasis*).   If it weren't for that fire, I wouldn't have been able to build homes for human beings — cozy, warm, cheerful homes where parents and their children could live in comfort and joy, realizing what a wonderful thing it is to be alive. And, above all, what a wonderful thing it is to belong wholeheartedly to each other.

HILDE (*eagerly*). Yes, but aren't you happy to know that you can build such wonderful homes for them?

SOLNESS. I had to pay a terrible price for that opportunity, Hilde.

HILDE. But are you sure you'll never get over that?

SOLNESS. Yes. In order to build homes for others I had to give up every hope of ever getting a home of my own. I mean, a real home with parents and children.

HILDE (*cautiously*). Why was that? Why every hope?

SOLNESS (*nods slowly*). That was the price I had to pay for the good fortune people talk so much about. (*Breathing heavily.*) That good fortune — if you can call it that — wasn't bought cheaply, Hilde.

HILDE (*as before*). Don't you think things will turn out for the better?

SOLNESS. Oh no, never. That's another result of the fire and of Aline's illness afterwards.

HILDE (*looks at him with an enigmatic expression*). And yet you build all these nurseries!

SOLNESS (*seriously*). Haven't you ever noticed, Hilde, that the impossible — that it sort of calls and beckons you?

HILDE (*reflects*). The impossible? (*Vivaciously.*) Oh yes! Do you feel that too?

SOLNESS. Yes, I do.

HILDE. Then you, too, must have some kind of troll in you.

SOLNESS. Why troll?

HILDE. Well, what else can you call it?

SOLNESS (*gets up*). I guess you're right. (*Vehemently.*) But how can I help feeling like a troll — the way things are falling into line for me! Always!

HILDE. What do you mean?

SOLNESS (*in a low voice, moved*). Now listen to this, Hilde. Everything I've done, built, created in terms of beauty, comfort, warmth — magnificence, too — (*clenching his fists*) oh, what a terrible thing to think of — !

HILDE. What's so terrible about it?

SOLNESS. All of that I've had to make up for, pay for — not with money, but with human happiness, my own and others'! So you see, Hilde, that's the price I — and other people too — have had to pay for my position as an artist. And every day I have to witness that price being paid for me again. Again, again, and again!

HILDE (*gets up, looks intently at him*). Now you're thinking of — of her.

SOLNESS. Yes, of Aline. You see, Aline, too, had her calling in life, the way I had mine. (*His voice quivers.*) But hers had to be bungled and crushed and smashed to pieces so that mine could freely force its way towards some kind of triumph and victory. Yes, Aline too had a talent for building, you see.

HILDE. She did? For building?

SOLNESS (*shaking his head*). I don't mean houses and towers and spires — not the kind of things I'm putting up.

HILDE. What, then?

SOLNESS (*softly, moved*). She had a gift for building up the souls of little children, Hilde — building them up so that they could rise in harmony and in noble, beautiful forms; so that these souls could later grow and reach the lofty heights of responsible adults. That was Aline's particular talent. And now all of it is lying there, unused and unusable, to no purpose at all — just like the ruins after a fire.

HILDE. Yes, but even if this were true — ?

SOLNESS. It is true! It is! I know it is.

HILDE. All right, but at least you're not to blame for it.

SOLNESS (*lets his eyes dwell on her and nods slowly*). That's just what I don't know — the ugly doubt that gnaws at me day and night.

HILDE. What do you mean?

SOLNESS. Suppose I was to blame — in a way.

HILDE. For the fire you mean?

SOLNESS. For everything — the whole business. And on the other hand, I may have had nothing at all to do with it.

HILDE (*looks at him worriedly*). Oh, Master Builder — if you can say a thing like that, then you must be — well, ill.

SOLNESS. Hm — always will be, too, I'm afraid, on that score.

(RAGNAR BROVIK *cautiously opens the little door in the left corner.* HILDE *steps forward.*)

RAGNAR (*noticing* HILDE). Oh — excuse me, Mr. Solness — (*he turns as if to leave*).

SOLNESS. No, come on in. Let's get this matter settled.

RAGNAR. Yes — I wish we could.

SOLNESS. I hear your father is not doing too well.

RAGNAR. No, the end is near now. And that's why I'm begging you to write a few kind words on one of those drawings. Anything that he'd be proud to read before he —

SOLNESS (*vehemently*). Don't talk to me any more about these drawings of yours!

RAGNAR. Have you looked at them?

SOLNESS. Yes, I have.

RAGNAR. And they're no good? And I suppose I'm no good either?

SOLNESS (*evasively*). Stay on here with me, Ragnar. Then you'll have everything your own way. Then you can marry Kaia and have no worries any more. You might even be happy. Just don't think about building on your own.

RAGNAR. All right. Then I'd better go home and tell him that. I promised him I would. — That's really all I can tell him, then — before he dies?

SOLNESS (*groans*). Tell him — tell him anything you like. I don't know! (*In an outburst.*) I can't handle this matter in any other way, Ragnar!

RAGNAR. Then I suppose you don't need the drawings any more?

SOLNESS. No, take them! They're over there on the table.

RAGNAR (*goes to the table*). Thank you.

HILDE (*puts her hand on the portfolio*). No, leave them.

SOLNESS. Why?

HILDE. Because I'd like to take a look at them.

SOLNESS. But didn't you look them over — (*To* RAGNAR.) Well — leave them, then.

RAGNAR. All right.

SOLNESS. And now you'd better get home to your father.

RAGNAR. Yes, I suppose so.

SOLNESS (*as if in despair*). Ragnar — you musn't ask of me what I cannot do! Do you hear, Ragnar! You mustn't do that!

RAGNAR. I'm sorry. Well, if you'll excuse me — (*he bows and leaves by the door in the corner*).

HILDE (*goes over to the chair by the mirror, sits down, and looks angrily at* SOLNESS). What an awful thing to do.

SOLNESS. Do you think so, too?

HILDE. Yes, awful, awful! Hard and vicious and cruel.

SOLNESS. Oh, you don't understand my side of it.

HILDE. What's that got to do with it? You shouldn't be like that.

SOLNESS. But you just said yourself that no one but me should be allowed to build.

HILDE. I can say that. But you shouldn't.

SOLNESS. Who has a better right, considering the price I paid for my position in life?

HILDE. Sure — the price of domestic bliss and all that. I know.

SOLNESS. You can throw in my peace of mind, too.

HILDE (*gets up*). Peace of mind! (*Intensely.*) Yes, you're right there! Poor Master Builder — you imagine that —

SOLNESS (*with a quiet, chuckling laugh*). Sit down again, Hilde, and I'll tell you something funny.

HILDE (*sits down, excitedly*). All right.

SOLNESS. It sounds like such a stupid little thing. You see, what the whole mess is about is no more than a crack in a chimney.

HILDE. Is that all?

SOLNESS. Well, to begin with, anyway. (*He moves a chair closer to* HILDE *and sits.*)

HILDE (*impatiently, tapping her knee*). All right, then — that crack in the chimney!

SOLNESS. I'd noticed a crack in the flue a long time before the fire, and every time I was up in the attic I checked to see if it was still there.

HILDE. And it was?

SOLNESS. Yes. Because nobody else knew about it.

HILDE. Didn't you tell anybody?

SOLNESS. No, I didn't.

HILDE. Didn't you think of fixing that crack, either?

SOLNESS. I thought about it all right, but I never got around to it. each time I decided to do something about it, it was just as if a hand was holding me back. Not today, I'd think. Tomorrow. And so nothing came of it.

HILDE. But why did you fool around like that?

SOLNESS. Because I was thinking things over. (*Slowly and in a low voice.*) Through that tiny black crack in the chimney I might perhaps force my way out into the open — as a builder.

HILDE (*looks straight in front of her*). It must have been exciting.

SOLNESS. Irresistible. Quite irresistible. And at that time everything seemed so simple and straightforward. I wanted it to be some time during winter. Shortly before dinner. I would be out driving with Aline. In the meantime the people at home would get a blazing fire going in the fireplace —

HILDE. It was supposed to be very cold that day, wasn't it?

SOLNESS. Oh, terribly cold. And of course they wanted Aline to find the place warm and cozy when she got back.

HILDE. She gets cold very easily, doesn't she?

SOLNESS. She does. And then, on our way home, we were supposed to see the smoke.

HILDE. Just the smoke?

SOLNESS. First the smoke. But as we approached the gate, the whole crate would be ablaze. — That's the way I wanted it.

HILDE. My god, if it only had happened like that!

SOLNESS. You can say that again, Hilde.

HILDE. You're quite sure that the cause of the fire was that little crack in the chimney?

SOLNESS. No, on the contrary. I'm quite sure the crack in the chimney had nothing at all to do with the fire.

HILDE. What!

SOLNESS. It's been clearly established that the fire started in a closet on the other side of the house.

HILDE. Then why do you sit here making such a fuss about that stupid crack in the chimney?

SOLNESS. Do you mind if I go on, Hilde?

HILDE. No, not as long as you promise to make sense.

SOLNESS. I'll try. (*Moves his chair closer.*)

HILDE. Then on with it, Master Builder.

SOLNESS (*confidentially*). Hilde, don't you believe that there are a few chosen individuals who've been graced with the power to wish for something, desire something, will something — so persistently and so — mercilessly — that they'll get it in the end? Don't you believe that?

HILDE (*with an enigmatic expression in her eyes*). If that is true, we'll soon see if I'm one of them.

SOLNESS. Now, you can't do these things all on your own. Oh no, if you want to get anywhere, the helpers and the servers will have to be in on it. But since they never come by themselves, you have to call on them — persistently. What I mean, of course, is inwardly.

HILDE. Who are these helpers and servers?

SOLNESS. Well, let's talk about that some other time. Right now we'd better stick to this business of the fire.

HILDE. Don't you think the fire would have come anyway — even if you hadn't wished for it?

SOLNESS. If old Brovik had been the owner of that house, it would never have burned down so conveniently for him — I can tell you that. He doesn't understand how to call on those helpers, you see, or on the servers. (*Gets up restlessly.*) So you see, Hilde — then I *am* to blame for the death of the two little boys. And I can't see how I can free myself of guilt for the fact that Aline never got to do what she should and could do. And what she wanted to do more than anything else.

HILDE. But you just said yourself that these helpers and servers —

SOLNESS. Who called on them? I did! And then they came and bowed to my will. (*In rising agitation.*) That's what people around here call having good fortune on your side. But I'll tell you what that kind of fortune feels like! It feels like a big, open wound here on my chest. And then the helpers and servers go around flaying pieces of skin off other people in order to patch my wound. But my wound hasn't healed yet and never will — never! Oh, if you knew how it throbs and burns sometimes.

HILDE (*looks attentively at him*). You are ill, Master Builder. Very ill, I'm afraid.

SOLNESS. Why don't you say mad? That's what you mean, isn't it?

HILDE. No, I don't think there's anything wrong with your mind.

SOLNESS. Then what is it? Tell me.

HILDE. I wonder if you weren't born with a frail conscience.

SOLNESS. Frail conscience? What the devil is that?

HILDE. I mean that your conscience is rather sensitive, sort of delicate. It can't take on the big hauls — can't lift and carry any load to speak of.

SOLNESS (*growls*). Hm! What sort of conscience would you like me to have?

HILDE. In your case I'd like it to be kind of — well, robust.

SOLNESS. Oh? Robust, eh? Perhaps you have a robust conscience?

HILDE. Yes, I think so. I've never noticed it wasn't.

SOLNESS. But then you haven't had much of a chance to test it either, have you?

HILDE (*a quiver passes over her lips*). Oh, it wasn't too easy to leave my dad. I'm terribly fond of him.

SOLNESS. Oh well, for a month or two —

HILDE.   I don't think I'll ever go back.

SOLNESS.   You don't? But why did you leave him?

HILDE (*half seriously, half teasingly*).   The ten years are up, remember?

SOLNESS.   Nonsense. Was anything wrong at home?

HILDE (*seriously now*).   It was this thing within me that urged and drove me here. It lured and tempted me, too.

SOLNESS (*eagerly*).   That's it! That's it, Hilde! There's a troll in you too — same as in me. And, you see, the troll in you — that's the thing that calls on the powers out there. And then you have to give in whether you want to or not.

HILDE.   I'm beginning to think you're right, Master Builder.

SOLNESS (*walks about the room*).   And then all the devils in this world, Hilde — the ones you can't even see!

HILDE.   Are there devils, too?

SOLNESS (*stops*).   Oh yes, good devils and bad devils. Blond devils and black-haired ones. If you could tell what kind it is — the light ones or the dark ones — when they grab hold of you. (*Walks about.*) Oho! It would be simple enough then.

HILDE (*follows him with her eyes*).   Or if you had that kind of obnoxiously healthy conscience so that you wouldn't hesitate to do anything you really wanted to.

SOLNESS (*stops by the console table*).   I'm sure most people are the same cowards as I am in that respect.

HILDE.   Maybe you're right.

SOLNESS (*leans on the table*).   In the sagas — have you read any of the old sagas?

HILDE.   Oh yes! In the days when I used to read books —

SOLNESS.   In the sagas you can read about Vikings who sailed to foreign countries and plundered and burned and slayed the men —

HILDE.   And captured women —

SOLNESS.   And carried them off —

HILDE.   Took them home in their ships —

SOLNESS.   And carried on with them like — like the worst of trolls.

HILDE (*looks in front of her with a half-veiled expression in her eyes*). I think that must have been exciting.

SOLNESS (*with a short, growling laughter*).   To capture women? Sure.

HILDE.   No, to be captured.

SOLNESS (*looks at her a moment*).   I see.

HILDE (*as if changing the subject*).   But what are you getting at with all these Vikings, Master Builder?

SOLNESS.   Well, what robust consciences those characters must have had! When they came home, they sat down to eat and drink heartily. They were happy like children. And what about the women! They often refused to be separated from them. Can you understand a thing like that, Hilde?

HILDE.   I can understand those women very well.

SOLNESS.   Oho! Maybe you'd feel the same way?

HILDE.   Why not?

SOLNESS.   Living — of your own free will — with a barbarian like that?

HILDE.   If I'd fallen in love with that barbarian, why not?

SOLNESS.   But how could you fall in love with someone like that?

HILDE.   For heaven's sake, you don't decide for yourself whom you're going to love, do you?

SOLNESS (*looks meditatively at her*).   No — I guess the troll in us sees to that.

HILDE (*half laughing*).   Yes, and all the cute little devils you know so well. The blond and the black-haired both.

SOLNESS (*warmly, quietly*).   In that case I hope the devils will choose kindly for you, Hilde.

HILDE.   They already have. Once and for all.

SOLNESS (*looks deep into her eyes*).   Hilde, you are like a wild bird of the woods, you know that?

HILDE.   I'm nothing of the kind. I don't hide away under the bushes.

SOLNESS.   All right, then. Maybe you're more like a bird of prey.

HILDE.   That's more like it — in a way. (*With sudden vehemence.*) And why not a bird of prey? Why shouldn't I go hunting as well? And catch the prey I've set my eyes on? If only I can get my claws into it and bring it down.

SOLNESS.   Hilde — do you know what you are?

HILDE.   I suppose you'll call me a falcon next.

SOLNESS.   No, you're like a dawning day. When I look at you — it's as if I'm looking into the sunrise.

HILDE.   Tell me, Master Builder — are you quite sure you've never called on me? Inwardly, I mean?

SOLNESS (*slowly and in a low voice*).   I'm ready to believe I must have.

HILDE.   What did you want with me?

SOLNESS.   You are youth, Hilde.

HILDE (*smiles*).   The youth you're so afraid of?

SOLNESS (*nods slowly*).   And that I'm yearning for in my heart.

HILDE (*gets up, walks over to the little table, and picks up Ragnar Brovik's portfolio, which she holds out to* SOLNESS).   Suppose we get on with these drawings —

SOLNESS (*abruptly, dismissing it*).   Put them away! I've seen enough of them.

HILDE.   But you were going to comment on them, weren't you?

SOLNESS.   Comment on them! Not on your life!

HILDE.   But the old man is dying! Can't you give him and his son a moment's happiness before they part? Then he might get a chance to build, too.

SOLNESS.   You bet he will. He's made sure of that — that fellow.

HILDE.   Well, for heaven's sake, if that's the case, it can't do any harm to lie a little!

SOLNESS. Lie? (*Furiously.*) Hilde — get those damn drawings out of my sight!

HILDE (*pulls the portfolio back a little*). All right, all right — don't bite me. — You're a fine one to talk about trolls. You act like one yourself. (*Looks around.*) Where can I find a pen?

SOLNESS. I don't know.

HILDE (*walks toward the door*). I'm sure your secretary knows —

SOLNESS. Stay where you are, Hilde! — What harm is there in lying, you said. Well, I suppose I could do that for his old father's sake. He's a prey I once caught and brought down.

HILDE. He is?

SOLNESS. I needed room for myself. But that Ragnar must never be allowed to get ahead.

HILDE. Poor boy, how can he, if he's no good —

SOLNESS (*comes closer, looks at her and whispers*). If Ragnar Brovik gets ahead, he'll knock me to the ground. He'll catch me the way I caught his father and bring me down.

HILDE. Bring you down? Is he good enough for that?

SOLNESS. You bet he is! He's the youth who's ready to knock at my door and make an end of Master Builder Solness.

HILDE (*looks at him with silent reproach*). And yet you wanted to lock him out. Shame on you, Master Builder!

SOLNESS. Why shouldn't I? *I* never won a battle without a fight — Besides, I'm afraid the helpers and servers won't obey me any more.

HILDE. Then you'll have to get along without them, that's all there is to it.

SOLNESS. It's hopeless, Hilde. The tide will turn — maybe sooner, maybe later. But retribution will come.

HILDE (*frightened, putting her hands over her ears*). Don't talk like that! Do you want to kill me? Do you want to rob me of what means more to me than life itself?

SOLNESS. And what's that?

HILDE. To see you great. To see you with a wreath in your hand, way up there on a church tower. (*Calm again.*) All right, give me a pencil then. You do have a pencil, don't you?

SOLNESS (*takes one from his pocket*). Here's one.

HILDE (*puts the portfolio on the table by the sofa*). Good. And now we'll sit down over here, Master Builder.

(SOLNESS *seats himself by the table.* HILDE *stands behind him, leaning over the back of the chair.*)

And then we'll write on these drawings. Something really, really nice and cordial is what we'll write on them. For this stupid Roar, or whatever his name is.

SOLNESS (*writes a few lines, turns his head and looks up at her*). Tell me something, Hilde.

HILDE. Yes?

SOLNESS. Since you've been waiting for me all these years —

HILDE. Ten years — yes.

SOLNESS. Why didn't you write to me? Then I could have answered you.

HILDE (*quickly*). No, no, no! That's just what I didn't want.

SOLNESS. Why not?

HILDE. I was afraid that might ruin everything. — But we were going to write something on those drawings, Master Builder.

SOLNESS. So we were.

HILDE (*leaning over him, she watches while he writes*). Let's make it kind and really cordial now. Oh, how I hate — how I hate this Roald —

SOLNESS (*as he writes*). Have you never really loved anyone, Hilde?

HILDE (*in a hard voice*). What did you say?

SOLNESS. Have you never loved anyone?

HILDE. Anyone else, I suppose you mean.

SOLNESS (*looks up at her*). Anyone else — of course. You never have? In all these ten years? Never?

HILDE. Oh well, once in a while, when I was furious with you for not coming back.

SOLNESS. Then you have cared for others too?

HILDE. A little bit. For a week or so. For heaven's sake, Master Builder, you know how it is!

SOLNESS. Hilde — what have you come for?

HILDE. Let's not waste any more time. That poor old man may die on us.

SOLNESS. Answer me, Hilde. What is it you want from me?

HILDE. I want my kingdom.

SOLNESS. Hm — (*he glances quickly toward the door on the left, then goes on writing on the drawings*).

MRS. SOLNESS (*enters at that moment. She carries a few packages*). I've brought a few things for you, Miss Wangel. The big parcels will be sent out later.

HILDE. Oh, how very kind of you!

MRS. SOLNESS. Only my duty, that's all.

SOLNESS (*reading through what he has written*). Aline.

MRS. SOLNESS. Yes.

SOLNESS. Did you notice if she — if my secretary was out there?

MRS. SOLNESS. Of course she was.

SOLNESS (*putting the drawings into the portfolio*). Hm —

MRS. SOLNESS. She was sitting at her desk as usual — when I go through the room.

SOLNESS (*gets up*). Then I'll give these things to her and tell her that —

HILDE (*takes the portfolio from him*). Please, let me have that pleasure! (*She goes toward the door but stops and turns.*) What's her name?

solness. Miss Fossli.

hilde. Ugh, how formal! Her first name, I mean.

solness. Kaia — I think.

hilde (opens the door and calls). Kaia, come in here! Hurry up! The Master Builder wants to talk to you.

kaia (enters and stands inside the door. She casts a frightened look at him). What is it?

hilde (handing her the portfolio). There you are, Kaia! The Master Builder has okayed them now.

kaia. Oh — at last!

solness. Give them to the old man as soon as you can.

kaia. I'll take them home right away.

solness. Yes, do that. And then Ragnar will get his chance to build on his own.

kaia. Oh — is it all right if he stops by later to thank you for everything — ?

solness (in a hard voice). I want no thanks! Tell him that from me.

kaia. Yes, I'll —

solness. And tell him, too, that from now on I won't need him any more. The same goes for you.

kaia (a low voice). You won't need me either?

solness. You'll have other things to think about now — and live for. And that's as it should be. Better get home with those drawings now, Miss Fossli. At once, do you hear!

kaia (as before). Yes, Mr. Solness. (Goes out.)

mrs. solness. My, what deceitful eyes she has.

solness. She! That poor little fool?

mrs. solness. Oh — I can see for myself, Halvard — Do you really mean to let them go?

solness. Yes.

mrs. solness. Her too?

solness. Isn't that the way you wanted it?

mrs. solness. But how can you be without her? But then I'm sure you have a replacement on hand — don't you, Halvard?

hilde (merrily). I'm no good at sitting behind a desk, anyway.

solness. All right, all right — we'll manage, Aline. All I want you to worry about now is moving into the new home — as soon as you can. This evening we'll hang the wreath (turns to hilde) — at the very top of the spire. What do you say to that, Hilde?

hilde (looks at him with sparkling eyes). It'll be just wonderful to see you way up there again.

solness. Me?

mrs. solness. My god, Miss Wangel, what are you thinking of! My husband — who gets so dizzy!

hilde. Dizzy! No, he doesn't!

mrs. solness. He certainly does.

HILDE. But I've seen him myself — way up on a high church tower.

MRS. SOLNESS. Yes, I've heard people talk about that. But that's impossible!

SOLNESS (*vehemently*). Impossible — yes, impossible! But there I was, all the same.

MRS. SOLNESS. How can you say that, Halvard? You can't even stand going out on the balcony on the second floor. You've always been like that.

SOLNESS. Then you might be in for a surprise this evening.

MRS. SOLNESS (*anxiously*). No, no, no! I hope to god I won't! I'll call the doctor right away. I'm sure he can talk you out of it.

SOLNESS. Aline, please — !

MRS. SOLNESS. You must be ill, you see! That's what it is. You're ill, Halvard! Oh, my god — my god! (*She hurries out to the right.*)

HILDE (*looks at him, tensely*). Is it true or isn't it?

SOLNESS. That I get dizzy?

HILDE. That my master builder dare not — cannot climb as high as he builds?

SOLNESS. So that's how you look at it.

HILDE. Yes.

SOLNESS. Is there no part of me that's safe from you, Hilde?

HILDE (*looks toward the bay window*). Up there, then. Way up there —

SOLNESS (*goes closer*). There's a room up there, Hilde — And there you could live like a princess.

HILDE (*indefinably; half seriously, half jesting*). That's what you promised, isn't it?

SOLNESS. Did I really?

HILDE. Shame on you, Master Builder! You said you'd make me a princess and give me a kingdom. And then you bent me over backwards and — well!

SOLNESS (*cautiously*). Are you quite sure it isn't all a dream — a memory of something you once imagined?

HILDE (*sharply*). Meaning you didn't do it, maybe?

SOLNESS. I hardly know myself — (*lowering his voice*). But there's one thing I am sure of now —

HILDE. What's that? Tell me!

SOLNESS. That I should have done it.

HILDE (*buoyantly*). You dizzy? Not on your life!

SOLNESS. Let's hang the wreath this evening, then — Princess Hilde.

HILDE (*with an air of bitterness*). Yes — over your new home!

SOLNESS. Over the new house — that'll never be a home for me. (*He goes out through the garden door.*)

HILDE (*looks in front of her with a veiled expression and whispers. The only words heard are*):   — terribly exciting —

ACT THREE

(*A large, broad veranda of Master Builder* SOLNESS' *house. Part of the house, with a door leading out to the veranda, is seen on the left. A railing along the veranda on the right. At the back, from the end of the veranda, steps lead down to the garden below. Large, old trees in the garden spread their branches over the veranda and toward the house. Through the trees, at the far right, a glimpse is caught of the lower part of the new villa with scaffolding around the tower section. In the background the garden is bounded by an old wooden fence. Beyond the fence, a street with low, dilapidated little houses. Evening sky with sunlit clouds. On the veranda a garden bench stands along the wall of the house, and in front of it a long table. On the other side of the table, an armchair and some stools. All the furniture is wickerwork.*

MRS. SOLNESS, *wrapped in a large, white crepe shawl, sits resting in the armchair and gazing off to the right. In a little while* HILDE WANGEL *comes up the steps from the garden. She is dressed as before and has her scarf around her head. She has pinned a little bouquet of small common flowers on her blouse.*)

MRS. SOLNESS (*turns her head a little*). You've been out for a walk in the garden, Miss Wangel?

HILDE. Yes, I've been having a look around.

MRS. SOLNESS. You've found some flowers too, I see.

HILDE. Oh yes! There's lots of them there — among the bushes.

MRS. SOLNESS. Really? At this time of the year? I hardly ever get down there, you see.

HILDE (*comes closer*). What? You mean to tell me you don't run down there every morning?

MRS. SOLNESS (*with a faint smile*). I don't "run" any place, I'm afraid. Not any more.

HILDE. But don't you even go down once in a while to say hello to all the beautiful things there?

MRS. SOLNESS. It's all so strange to me now. I'm almost afraid to look at it again.

HILDE. Your own garden!

MRS. SOLNESS. I don't feel it's mine any more.

HILDE. But how can you possibly —

MRS. SOLNESS. No, no, it isn't. It's not the way it was when my father and mother were alive. They've chopped off a huge chunk of the garden, Miss Wangel, split it up into small lots and built homes for strangers on them — people I don't know, people who sit in their windows and stare at me.

HILDE (*brightly*). Mrs. Solness?

MRS. SOLNESS. Yes?

HILDE. Do you mind if I stay here with you for a while?

MRS. SOLNESS. Why, of course not — if you want to.

HILDE (*moves a stool over to the armchair and sits down*). Ah, this is just the spot where I can sit basking in the sun, like a cat.

MRS. SOLNESS (*puts her hand gently on* HILDE's *neck*). It's kind of you to talk to me. I thought you were going inside to my husband.

HILDE. What would I want with him?

MRS. SOLNESS. Maybe you'd want to help him.

HILDE. No, thank you. Anyway — he's not in. He's over there with the men. But he seemed to be in such a bad mood that I didn't dare to talk to him.

MRS. SOLNESS. Oh, he's kind and gentle really.

HILDE. He is?

MRS. SOLNESS. I don't believe you know him well enough yet, Miss Wangel.

HILDE (*looks at her warmly*). Are you happy now that you're moving into the new house?

MRS. SOLNESS. I should be, I know. It's what Halvard wants —

HILDE. Oh, not only that —

MRS. SOLNESS. Oh, no, Miss Wangel. It's my duty to accept what he wants. But it isn't always easy to force your mind to obedience.

HILDE. No, I don't suppose it is.

MRS. SOLNESS. Believe me, it isn't. Not when you have as many faults as I have.

HILDE. Or when you've suffered as much as you have.

MRS. SOLNESS. How do you know that?

HILDE. Your husband told me.

MRS. SOLNESS. With me he hardly ever mentions those things — Yes, I've had more than my share of suffering in life, Miss Wangel.

HILDE (*looks sympathetically at her and nods slowly*). Poor Mrs. Solness. First you had the fire —

MRS. SOLNESS (*with a sigh*). Yes, all I could call my own was lost.

HILDE. And then came what was worse.

MRS. SOLNESS (*looks questioningly at her*). Worse?

HILDE. Yes, worst of all.

MRS. SOLNESS. What do you mean?

HILDE (*in a low voice*). That you lost your two little boys.

MRS. SOLNESS. Oh, them. Well, that's a different matter. That was an act of Providence — the sort of thing we'd better accept as it is and try to be thankful for.

HILDE. Are you able to do that?

MRS. SOLNESS. Not always, I'm afraid. I know very well it's my duty. But I can't.

HILDE. Well, who can blame you?

MRS. SOLNESS. And time and again I have to remind myself that I was justly punished —

HILDE. What for?

MRS. SOLNESS. For not being firm enough in the face of misfortune.

HILDE. But what's that got to do with —

MRS. SOLNESS. No, no, Miss Wangel — don't talk to me any more about the two little boys. We can only be happy for them. They're much, much better off now. No, it's the loss of the little things in life that breaks your heart — all those little things that people hardly know about.

HILDE (*puts her arms on* MRS. SOLNESS' *knee and looks up at her warmly*). Dear Mrs. Solness — what kind of things? Please, tell me!

MRS. SOLNESS. As I say — just little things. All the old portraits on the walls were burned. So were all the old silk dresses that had belonged to my family for so long. And my mother's and grandmother's lace — and their precious jewels — all of that burned too. (*Darkly.*) And then the dolls!

HILDE. The dolls?

MRS. SOLNESS (*on the verge of tears*). I had nine lovely dolls.

HILDE. And they were burned too?

MRS. SOLNESS. Yes, all of them. Oh, it was so hard — so hard for me.

HILDE. Had you kept those dolls ever since you were a little girl?

MRS. SOLNESS. I didn't just keep them. The dolls and I went on living together.

HILDE. After you'd grown up?

MRS. SOLNESS. Yes, long after that.

HILDE. After you were married too?

MRS. SOLNESS. Oh yes. As long as he didn't see them. And then they were trapped by the fire, poor things. Nobody thought of saving them. Oh, it makes me so sad to think of it. Please don't laugh at me, Miss Wangel.

HILDE. I'm not laughing.

MRS. SOLNESS. In a way they were alive too. I carried them under my heart — just like unborn little children.

HERDAL (*hat in hand, comes out through the door and sees* MRS. SOLNESS *and* HILDE). Well, so you're out here catching yourself a cold, Mrs. Solness.

MRS. SOLNESS. But it's so nice and warm today.

HERDAL. Yes, it is, isn't it? Well, what did you want to see me about? I got your message.

MRS. SOLNESS (*gets up*). Yes, I'd like to have a word with you.

HERDAL. Good. Then I suppose we'd better go inside. (*To* HILDE.) Still dressed for mountain climbing, Miss Wangel?

HILDE (*gaily, gets up*). Oh yes — with all the trimmings! But I don't intend to go breaking my neck today, Doctor. Today you and I will stay quietly below and watch.

HERDAL. Watch what?

MRS. SOLNESS (*to* HILDE *in a low, frightened voice*). Sh, sh — for god's sake! He's coming! Make sure you get that notion out of his head. And do let's be friends, Miss Wangel. Can't we?

HILDE (*throwing her arms impetuously around* MRS. SOLNESS' *neck*). Oh, if we only could.

MRS. SOLNESS (*gently freeing herself*). All right, all right! There he is, Doctor. Let me talk to you.

HERDAL. About him?

MRS. SOLNESS. Yes, about him. Come in, please.

(MRS. SOLNESS *and* DR. HERDAL *go into the house. In a moment Master Builder* SOLNESS *comes up the steps from the garden. A serious expression comes over* HILDE'S *face.*)

SOLNESS (*with a glance at the door that is closed cautiously from within*). Hilde, have you noticed that as soon as I come, she leaves?

HILDE. I've noticed that as soon as you come, you make her leave.

SOLNESS. Maybe so, but I can't help that. (*Looks closely at her.*) Are you cold, Hilde? You look as if you were.

HILDE. I've just come out of a tomb.

SOLNESS. What do you mean?

HILDE. That I've been chilled to the bone, Master Builder.

SOLNESS (*slowly*). I think I understand —

HILDE. Why did you come up here?

SOLNESS. I happened to see you from over there.

HILDE. Then you must have seen her too?

SOLNESS. I knew she'd leave as soon as I came.

HILDE. Are you hurt by the fact that she seems to avoid you?

SOLNESS. It's a kind of relief, too.

HILDE. That she's not under your eyes all the time?

SOLNESS. Yes.

HILDE. So that you don't always have to see how much she suffers because of the little boys?

SOLNESS. Yes. Mostly that.

(HILDE *wanders along the veranda with her hands behind her back, stops by the railing and looks out over the garden.*)

(*After a short pause.*) Did you have a long talk with her?

(HILDE *stands motionless and does not answer.*)

I'm asking you if you had a long talk with her.

(HILDE *is silent, as before.*)

What did she talk about, Hilde?

(HILDE *remains silent.*)

About the little boys? Poor Aline!

(HILDE *shudders nervously, then nods rapidly a couple of times.*)

She'll never get over it. Never! (*Goes closer.*) Now you're standing there like a statue again — same as last night.

HILDE (*turns and looks at him with wide, serious eyes*). I want to leave.

SOLNESS (*sharply*). Leave!

HILDE. Yes.

SOLNESS. I won't let you!

HILDE. But what'll I do here now?

SOLNESS. Just be here, Hilde!

HILDE (*looks him up and down*). No, thank you. You know it wouldn't stop there.

SOLNESS (*recklessly*). So much the better!

HILDE (*vehemently*). I just can't hurt somebody I know! Can't take what belongs to her.

SOLNESS. Who says you should?

HILDE (*as before*). A stranger, yes! That's a different story — a person I never laid eyes on. But somebody I've learned to know — ! No! No! Ugh!

SOLNESS. But what have I said to suggest anything like that?

HILDE. Oh, Master Builder, you know very well what would happen, and that's why I'm leaving.

SOLNESS. And what'll become of me when you're gone? What'll I have to live for then? Afterwards?

HILDE (*with an enigmatic expression in her eyes*). I can't see what you've got to worry about. You have your duties to her. Better live for those duties.

SOLNESS. Too late. All these powers, these — these —

HILDE. Devils.

SOLNESS. Yes, devils! And the troll in me too. They've sapped her of the strength to live. (*Laughs in despair.*) They did it for the sake of my own happiness! That's what they did! (*Darkly.*) And now she's dead — because of me. And I'm chained alive to the dead. (*In anguish.*) I — I who can't live without joy in life!

HILDE (*goes around the table and sits on the bench with her elbows on the table and her head in her hands. She sits looking at him for a while*). What will you build next?

SOLNESS (*shaking his head*). Don't think I'll build much more now.

HILDE. No more of those warm, happy homes for mom and dad and all the kids?

SOLNESS. I'm not sure they'll be much in demand from now on.

HILDE. Poor Master Builder — you who've spent ten years of your life building a future on nothing else!

SOLNESS. You can say that again, Hilde.

HILDE (*in an outburst*). Oh, how silly it is — the whole thing!

SOLNESS. What thing?

HILDE. This business of being afraid to reach out for your own happiness. For your own life! Just because somebody you know is in your way.

SOLNESS.   Someone you've no right to push aside.

HILDE.   Who knows if we really don't have a right. And then again — Oh, I wish I could sleep and forget the whole mess! (*She puts her arms flat on the table, rests her left cheek on her hands, and closes her eyes.*)

SOLNESS (*turns the armchair around and sits down by the table*).   Your father's place at Lysanger — was that a warm and happy home for you, Hilde?

HILDE (*motionless, as if half asleep*).   A cage is all I had.

SOLNESS.   And you don't want to go back in there?

HILDE (*as before*).   Birds of the forest never like cages.

SOLNESS.   They'd rather go hunting in the open air —

HILDE (*still as before*).   Birds of prey would rather go hunting —

SOLNESS (*lets his eyes dwell on her*).   If we only had a little more of the Viking spirit, Hilde —

HILDE (*in her usual voice, opens her eyes but does not move*).   And the other thing? Say it!

SOLNESS.   A robust conscience.

HILDE (*sits up vivaciously, her eyes once more happy and sparkling. She nods at him*).   Now I know what you're going to build next!

SOLNESS.   Then you know more than I do, Hilde.

HILDE.   Sure I do! Master builders are so stupid, you know.

SOLNESS.   And what's it going to be?

HILDE (*nods again*).   The castle.

SOLNESS.   What castle?

HILDE.   My castle, of course.

SOLNESS.   So you want a castle now.

HILDE.   You owe me a kingdom, don't you?

SOLNESS.   That's what you keep telling me.

HILDE.   Yes, you owe me a kingdom, all right. And did you ever hear of a kingdom without a castle?

SOLNESS (*more and more animated*).   No, I don't believe I did.

HILDE.   Good! Then build it for me! Now!

SOLNESS (*laughs*).   You want it right away, eh?

HILDE.   Of course! The ten years are up now. And I'm not going to wait any more. So — let's have that castle, Master Builder!

SOLNESS.   It's no joke to owe you anything, Hilde.

HILDE.   You should have thought of that before. It's too late now. All right, then — (*raps the table*) my castle on the table! It's my castle, and I want it now!

SOLNESS (*more serious, leaning toward her with his arms on the table*). What sort of castle did you have in mind, Hilde?

HILDE (*her expression grows increasingly veiled as she goes on. She seems to be peering into her own mind. Slowly*).   My castle is going to stand high up. Way up high is where it's going to stand — with a clear view on all sides so that I can see for miles and miles around.

SOLNESS.   And I suppose you'd want a high tower to go with it?

HILDE.   Oh, a tremendously high tower. And on the very top of that tower there's going to be a balcony. And out on that balcony is where I'll stand —

SOLNESS (*instinctively clenching his forehead*).   How can you want to stand at such a dizzy height —

HILDE.   Oh yes! At that dizzy height is where I'll stand watching the others — the ones who build churches. And homes for mom and dad and the kids. And that's where you'll be watching it with me.

SOLNESS (*in a low voice*).   Will the master builder be allowed to come up to the princess?

HILDE.   If the master builder wants to.

SOLNESS (*lower still*).   Then I think the master builder will come.

HILDE (*nods*).   The master builder — will come.

SOLNESS.   But he'll never build again — that poor master builder.

HILDE (*vivaciously*).   Oh yes, he will! We'll do it together. And then we'll build the most wonderful, wonderful thing in all the world.

SOLNESS (*tensely*).   Hilde — tell me what that is!

HILDE (*looks at him with a smile, shakes her head a little, purses her lips and speaks to him as though he were a child*).   Oh, these master builders! They're such very — very stupid people.

SOLNESS.   They certainly are. Now, tell me what it is — the most wonderful thing in the world that we're going to build together?

HILDE (*is silent for a moment, then says, with an enigmatic expression in her eyes*).   Castles in the air.

SOLNESS.   Castles in the air?

HILDE (*nods*).   Yes, castles in the air! Do you know what a castle in the air is?

SOLNESS.   It's the most wonderful thing in the world, you say.

HILDE (*jumps to her feet and makes a deprecating gesture with her hand*).   I see! These castles in the air — they're easy to resort to when you're in a bind, aren't they? And they're easy to build, too — (*gives him a scornful look*) especially when you're a builder who's got a — a dizzy conscience.

SOLNESS (*gets up*).   From this day on you and I will build together, Hilde.

HILDE (*with a half-doubting smile*).   You mean — some kind of real castle in the air?

SOLNESS.   Yes. One with a solid foundation.

(*RAGNAR BROVIK comes out of the house carrying a large, green wreath with flowers and silk ribbons.*)

HILDE (*joyfully*).   The wreath! Oh, it's going to be absolutely marvelous!

SOLNESS (*puzzled*).   Are you bringing the wreath, Ragnar?

RAGNAR.   I promised the foreman I would.

SOLNESS (*relieved*).   Well, then, I suppose your father is better?

RAGNAR.   No.

SOLNESS.   Wasn't he cheered up by what I wrote?

RAGNAR.   It came too late.

SOLNESS.   Too late!

RAGNAR.   When she came with it, he was unconscious. He'd had a stroke.

SOLNESS.   Then why don't you go home! You've got to look after your father.

RAGNAR.   He doesn't need me any more.

SOLNESS.   But you ought to be with him.

RAGNAR.   She's with him now.

SOLNESS (*somewhat uncertain*).   Kaia?

RAGNAR (*gives him a dark look*).   Yes — Kaia.

SOLNESS.   Go home, Ragnar — to both of them. Let me have the wreath.

RAGNAR (*suppressing a mocking smile*).   You don't mean you're going to —

SOLNESS.   I'll take it down there myself. (*Takes the wreath from him.*) Go home, now. We won't need you today.

RAGNAR.   I know you won't be needing me from now on. But today I'm staying.

SOLNESS.   Then stay — if that's what you want.

HILDE (*by the railing*).   Master Builder — this is where I'll stand watching you.

SOLNESS.   Me!

HILDE.   It'll be terribly exciting.

SOLNESS (*in a low voice*).   We'll talk about that later, Hilde. (*He takes the wreath and goes down the steps into the garden.*)

HILDE (*watches him go, then turns to* RAGNAR).   You might at least have thanked him.

RAGNAR.   Thanked him? For what?

HILDE.   For what, my foot!

RAGNAR.   It's probably you I ought to thank, if anyone.

HILDE.   How can you say that?

RAGNAR (*without answering her*).   But you'd better watch out, miss! You don't really know him yet.

HILDE (*fiery*).   Nobody knows him as I do!

RAGNAR (*with an embittered laugh*).   Thank him, who's held me down year after year! He, who's made my own father doubt me — who's made me doubt myself. And all that because he — !

HILDE (*her suspicions aroused*).   Because what — ? Tell me!

RAGNAR.   Because he wanted to keep her with him.

HILDE (*with a start toward him*).   The girl at the desk!

RAGNAR.   Yes.

HILDE (*threateningly, with clenched fists*).   That's not true! You're lying!

RAGNAR.   I didn't want to believe it either — until today, when she said it herself.

HILDE (*as if beside herself*).   What did she say? I want to know! Now! Now!

RAGNAR.   She said that he's taken complete possession of her mind — that he's made her think of no one but himself. She said that she can never let him go, that she wants to stay here with him —

HILDE (*with flashing eyes*).   She won't be allowed to!

RAGNAR (*as if testing her*).   Who won't allow her?

HILDE (*quickly*).   He won't, either!

RAGNAR.   Sure. I understand everything now. She'd only be in the way from now on, wouldn't she?

HILDE.   You don't understand a thing! I'll tell you why he hung on to her.

RAGNAR.   Why don't you?

HILDE.   So he could keep you.

RAGNAR.   Did he tell you that?

HILDE.   No, but that's how it is! It must be! (*Wildly.*) I will — I will have it that way!

RAGNAR.   And the moment you came — he let her go.

HILDE.   It was you he let go! Why should he care about any old office girl like her?

RAGNAR (*thinks it over*).   Can it be that he's been afraid of me all this time?

HILDE.   He afraid! I wouldn't be so cocky if I were you.

RAGNAR.   Oh, I'm sure he must have realized a long time ago that I've got something in me, too. Besides — afraid — that's exactly what he is, you see.

HILDE.   Now, who's going to believe that about him!

RAGNAR.   Yes, the great master builder is afraid in a way. Not of robbing people of their happiness in life, the way he did with my father and me — oh no. But when it comes to climbing up a measly bit of scaffolding — then see if he doesn't pray to god for help and protection!

HILDE.   If you'd only seen him way up there — at the same dizzy height that I once saw him!

RAGNAR.   Did you see him then?

HILDE.   I certainly did. How proud and free he was as he stood there tying the wreath to the weather vane!

RAGNAR.   I know he had the courage to do it once in his life. Just once. The young people around here have been talking about it quite often. But no power on earth can get him to do it again.

HILDE.   He'll do it again today!

RAGNAR (*scornfully*).   That's what you think!

HILDE.   We'll see it, I tell you!

RAGNAR.   And I tell you we won't.

HILDE (*violently, uncontrollably*).   I will see it! I will and I must see it!

RAGNAR.   But he won't do it. He simply doesn't dare. It's a frailty he's got — he, the great master builder.

MRS. SOLNESS (*comes out of the house on to the veranda and looks about*).   Isn't he here? Where did he go?

RAGNAR.   Mr. Solness is over there with the men.

HILDE.   He took the wreath.

MRS. SOLNESS (*terrified*).   He took the wreath! Oh, my god — my god! Brovik — go down to him! Make sure you get him up here!

RAGNAR.   Shall I tell him you want to see him?

MRS. SOLNESS.   Oh yes, do — No, no — don't tell him I want to see him! Better tell him someone else is here and that he should come at once.

RAGNAR.   Good. I'll do that, Mrs. Solness. (*He goes down the steps and out through the garden.*)

MRS. SOLNESS.   Oh, Miss Wangel, you can't imagine how much I worry about him.

HILDE.   What's there to worry about?

MRS. SOLNESS.   Oh, I'm sure you understand that. Suppose he's serious about climbing that scaffolding!

HILDE (*tensely*).   Do you think he will?

MRS. SOLNESS.   I never know what he'll do. He might do anything!

HILDE.   Ah, maybe you, too, think that he's — kind of — ?

MRS. SOLNESS.   I don't know what to think any more. The doctor has told me so many things about him, and when I relate them to what I've heard him say now and then —

HERDAL (*looks out through the door*).   Isn't he here yet?

MRS. SOLNESS.   I'm afraid not. But I've sent for him, anyway.

HERDAL (*comes closer*).   Then I think you'd better go inside, Mrs. Solness.

MRS. SOLNESS.   No, no. I want to stay here and wait for Halvard.

HERDAL.   But there are some ladies here to see you —

MRS. SOLNESS.   Oh, my god — not now!

HERDAL.   They said something about wanting to watch the proceedings.

MRS. SOLNESS.   Well, then, I suppose I'd better go in. After all, it is my duty.

HILDE.   Can't you ask those ladies to go away?

MRS. SOLNESS.   No, I can't very well do that. Now they're here it's my duty to see them. But you'd better stay here and talk to him when he comes.

HERDAL.   And make sure you keep him here as long as you can.

MRS. SOLNESS.   Yes, please do, my dear Miss Wangel — as long as you possibly can.

HILDE.   Wouldn't it be better if you did that?

MRS. SOLNESS.   Oh lord, I know it's my duty. But when you have so many duties —

HERDAL (*looks toward the garden*).   There he is!

MRS. SOLNESS.   Oh, dear — And I have to go in!

HERDAL (*to* HILDE). Don't tell him that I'm here.

HILDE. Don't worry. I'm sure I'll find something else to talk to him about.

MRS. SOLNESS. And make sure you keep him here. I think you can do that better than anyone else.

(MRS. SOLNESS *and* DR. HERDAL *go into the house.* HILDE *remains standing on the veranda.*)

SOLNESS (*comes up the steps from the garden*). I hear someone wants to see me.

HILDE. That's right. I'm the one, Master Builder.

SOLNESS. Oh, I see. I was afraid it might be Aline and the doctor.

HILDE. You seem to be afraid of so many things.

SOLNESS. Do you think so?

HILDE. Well, people say you're afraid of crawling around on top of scaffoldings — for one thing.

SOLNESS. That's a different matter.

HILDE. Then you are afraid of it?

SOLNESS. Yes, I am.

HILDE. Afraid you might fall down and kill yourself?

SOLNESS. No, not that.

HILDE. What, then?

SOLNESS. I'm afraid of retribution, Hilde.

HILDE. Of retribution? (*Shaking her head.*) I don't understand.

SOLNESS. Sit down, and I'll tell you something.

HILDE. Go right ahead! Now! (*She sits on the stool by the railing and looks expectantly at him.*)

SOLNESS (*throws his hat on the table*). As you know, I started out building churches.

HILDE (*nods*). Yes, I know that.

SOLNESS. You see, when I was a boy I grew up in a pious home out in the country. That's why I thought of this business of building churches as the noblest thing I could do.

HILDE. All right.

SOLNESS. And I think I can say that I built those tiny, simple churches with such honesty, fervor, and devotion that —

HILDE. That — what?

SOLNESS. Well, that I think he should have been pleased with me.

HILDE. He? Who's "he"?

SOLNESS. He who was going to have those churches, of course! He whose honor and glory they were meant to serve.

HILDE. Oh, I see! But are you sure he wasn't — kind of — pleased with you?

SOLNESS (*scornfully*). He pleased with me! How can you talk like that, Hilde? He, who let the troll in me stomp around the way it saw fit. He, who made all these — these — well, who made them serve me on a stand-by basis twenty-four hours a day.

HILDE. The devils?

SOLNESS. Yes — both kinds! Oh no, I had a pretty good idea that he wasn't pleased with me. (*Secretively.*) And that's why he let the old house burn down.

HILDE. Was that why?

SOLNESS. Yes, don't you see? He wanted me to have a chance to become a true master in my field, so that I could build churches more worthy of him. At first I didn't understand what he was up to, but then, all of a sudden, it dawned on me.

HILDE. When was that?

SOLNESS. When I was building the church tower at Lysanger.

HILDE. That's what I thought.

SOLNESS. I didn't know anyone up there and had plenty of time for brooding and meditation. And then I saw clearly why he had taken my little children from me. He didn't want me to be tied down by anything else. Nothing like love and happiness for me, you see. I was to be a master builder only, and nothing else. And for the rest of my life I was to go on building for him. (*Laughs.*) But I soon had my say on that score!

HILDE. What did you do?

SOLNESS. First I searched and tested my own will —

HILDE. And then?

SOLNESS. Then I did the impossible — I no less than he.

HILDE. The impossible?

SOLNESS. I'd never been able to climb up to and stand at a great height. But that day I did it.

HILDE (*jumps to her feet*). Yes, yes, you did!

SOLNESS. And as I stood there on top of that tower hanging the wreath, I said to him: Now listen to me, you mighty one! From this day on I want to be a master builder who's as free in his field as you are in yours. I won't build churches for you any more, only homes for people to live in.

HILDE (*her eyes wide and sparkling*). That was the song I heard in the air!

SOLNESS. But he got back at me later on.

HILDE. What do you mean by that?

SOLNESS (*looks dejectedly at her*). Building homes for people isn't worth a damn, Hilde.

HILDE. Is that how you feel now?

SOLNESS. Yes, because now I realize that people have no use for the homes they live in. Not in order to be happy, anyway. And I wouldn't have had much use for a home like that either, if I'd had one. (*With a quiet, embittered laugh.*) So that's what it all amounts to, now that I look back on it — nothing built, really, and nothing sacrificed for the sake of building, either. Nothing, nothing — it all comes to nothing.

HILDE. And now you'll never build again.

SOLNESS (*animated*). Oh yes! I'm just about to begin!

HILDE. What's that? What? Tell me now!

SOLNESS. The only place where I may be able to make room for human happiness — that's what I'm going to build next.

HILDE (*looks firmly at him*). Master Builder — now you're thinking of our castles in the air.

SOLNESS. Yes — castles in the air.

HILDE. I'm afraid you'd get dizzy before we got halfway up.

SOLNESS. Not if you're with me, Hilde.

HILDE (*with an air of suppressed indignation*). Only me? Won't there be others?

SOLNESS. Who else?

HILDE. Oh — that poor little Kaia at the desk. Aren't you going to take her along, too?

SOLNESS. Oho! So that's what Aline was talking to you about.

HILDE. Are you or aren't you?

SOLNESS (*vehemently*). I won't answer that! You'll have to believe in me all the way!

HILDE. For ten years I've believed in you — all the way.

SOLNESS. You'll have to go on believing in me!

HILDE. Then let me see you way up there, high and free!

SOLNESS (*darkly*). Oh, Hilde — I was in a holiday mood then.

HILDE (*passionately*). I want it! I want it! (*Imploringly.*) Just once more, Master Builder! Do the impossible again!

SOLNESS (*stands looking deeply into her eyes*). If I try, Hilde, I'll stand up there and talk to him the way I did before.

HILDE (*in mounting tension*). What will you say to him?

SOLNESS. I'll say to him: Listen to me, almighty lord — judge me as you will, but from now on I'll build only the most wonderful thing in the world —

HILDE (*carried away*). Yes — yes — yes!

SOLNESS. I'll build it with a princess I love —

HILDE. Yes, tell him that! Tell him!

SOLNESS. Yes. And then I'll say to him: I'm going to go down now and take her in my arms and kiss her.

HILDE. Many times! Tell him that!

SOLNESS. Many, many times, I'll say.

HILDE. And then — ?

SOLNESS. Then I'll wave my hat — and come down to earth again — and do what I told him.

HILDE (*with outstretched arms*). Now I see you the way you were when there was a song in the air!

SOLNESS (*looks at her, his head lowered*). How have you become what you are, Hilde?

HILDE. How have you made me what I am?

SOLNESS (*abruptly, firmly*). The princess is going to have her castle.

HILDE (*jubilantly, clapping her hands*). Oh, Master Builder — ! My wonderful, wonderful castle. Our castle in the air!

solness.   On a solid foundation —

(*Barely glimpsed through the trees is a crowd of people that has gathered in the street. The distant music of a brass band is heard from behind the new house.* mrs. solness, *with a fur piece around her neck,* dr. herdal, *with her white shawl on his arm, and a few ladies, come out on the veranda. At the same time* ragnar brovik *comes up from the garden.*)

mrs. solness (*to* ragnar).   Are we going to have music, too?

ragnar.   Oh yes! (*To* solness.) The foreman wanted me to tell you that he's ready to go up with the wreath.

solness (*taking his hat*).   Good, I'll go down there myself.

mrs. solness (*anxiously*).   Why are you going, Halvard?

solness (*snaps*).   I've got to be down below with the men.

mrs. solness.   Oh, down below. But please stay down below, won't you?

solness.   I always do, don't I — on a weekday? (*He goes down the steps and out through the garden.*)

mrs. solness (*calls after him from the railing*).   And make sure you ask the foreman to be careful! Promise me that, Halvard!

herdal (*to* mrs. solness).   I was right! He's forgotten all about that crazy notion of his.

mrs. solness.   Oh, what a relief! Two of our men have already fallen down, and both were killed on the spot. (*Turns to* hilde.) Thank you for prevailing upon him, Miss Wangel. I don't think I would have been able to do it.

herdal (*gaily*).   Yes, Miss Wangel, I'm sure you're good at prevailing upon people when you put your mind to it!

(mrs. solness *and* dr. herdal *join the ladies who are over by the steps where they stand looking out through the garden.* hilde *remains standing by the railing in the foreground.* ragnar *goes over to her.*)

ragnar (*with suppressed laughter, lowers his voice*).   Miss Wangel — do you see all those young people over there?

hilde.   Yes.

ragnar.   They're my friends. They're here to watch the master.

hilde.   Why?

ragnar.   They want to see him afraid of climbing up on his own house.

hilde.   So, that's what the little boys want!

ragnar (*with wrath and scorn*).   He's held us down long enough. Now it's our turn to see him stay down below with the rest of us.

hilde.   You won't. Not this time.

ragnar (*smiles*).   Oh? Where else?

hilde.   Way — way up on top is where you'll see him!

ragnar (*laughs*).   Is that right!

hilde.   On the top is where he wants to be. And that's where you'll see him too.

ragnar.   Of course he wants to! But he can't. His head would swim before he got half way up. And then he'd have to crawl down again on his hands and knees!

HERDAL (*pointing*).   Look! There goes the foreman up the ladder.

MRS. SOLNESS.   He's got the wreath. I hope he's careful!

RAGNAR (*stares in disbelief, then shouts*).   But it's —

HILDE (*jubilantly*).   It's the master builder himself!

MRS. SOLNESS (*screams in terror*).   Yes, it's Halvard! Oh, my god — ! Halvard! Halvard!

HERDAL.   Sh. Don't shout at him!

MRS. SOLNESS (*beside herself*).   I must go to him! Get him down again!

HERDAL (*restraining her*).   Don't move — all of you. Not a sound!

HILDE (*motionless, following* SOLNESS *with her eyes*).   He's climbing, climbing. Higher — always higher! Look! Just look!

RAGNAR (*breathlessly*).   He's got to turn back now. What else can he do!

HILDE.   He's climbing — climbing. He's almost there.

MRS. SOLNESS.   Oh, I can't stand it any more. I can't bear to look at him!

HERDAL.   Don't look at him, then.

HILDE.   There he is, on top of the scaffolding! All the way up!

HERDAL.   Don't move, anyone! Do you hear!

HILDE (*jubilantly, with quiet intensity*).   At last! At last! Now I see him great and free again!

RAGNAR (*almost speechless*).   But this is —

HILDE.   That's how I've seen him all these ten years. See how confidently he stands up there! Terribly exciting, after all. Look! He's hanging the wreath on the spire!

RAGNAR.   It's impossible! I can't believe my own eyes.

HILDE.   Yes, it *is* the impossible he's doing now! (*With an enigmatic expression in her eyes.*) Can you see anyone else up there with him?

RAGNAR.   There's no one else.

HILDE.   Yes, there's someone he's quarreling with.

RAGNAR.   You're wrong.

HILDE.   Don't you hear a song in the air either?

RAGNAR.   It must be the wind in the treetops.

HILDE.   I hear a song. A mighty song! (*Shouts in wild ecstasy.*) Look, look! He's waving his hat! And now he's waving at us down here. Wave back to him! Because now — now it is finished! (*Snatches the white shawl from the doctor, waves it, and shouts up to* SOLNESS.) Hurray for Master Builder Solness!

HERDAL.   Stop it! Stop it, for god's sake!

(*The* LADIES *on the veranda wave their handkerchiefs, and shouts of* "Hurray!" *come from the street below. Suddenly there is a silence, then the crowd bursts into cries of horror. A human body, along with some*

*planks and pieces of splintered wood, is indistinctly glimpsed plunging
down between the trees.)*

MRS. SOLNESS *and the* LADIES (*simultaneously*). He's falling! He's
falling!

(MRS. SOLNESS *sways, falls back in a faint, and is caught by the ladies
amid cries and confusion. The crowd in the street breaks through the
fence and storms into the garden.* DR. HERDAL *rushes down there too.
A short pause.*)

HILDE (*stares fixedly upward and says as if petrified*). My master
builder.

RAGNAR (*leans, trembling, against the railing*). He must have been
killed on the spot.

ONE OF THE LADIES (*as* MRS. SOLNESS *is carried into the house*). Run
for the doctor —

RAGNAR. I can't move —

ANOTHER LADY. Then call down to him!

RAGNAR (*tries to shout*). How is he? Is he alive?

A VOICE (*from down in the garden*). The master builder is dead!

OTHER VOICES (*closer*). His head's been crushed. He fell into the
quarry.

HILDE (*turns to* RAGNAR *and says quietly*). I can't see him up there
now.

RAGNAR. What a terrible thing to happen. He couldn't do it — after
all.

HILDE (*as if in a quiet, dazed triumph*). But he did get to the top.
And I heard harps in the air. (*Waves the shawl upwards and cries with
wild intensity.*) My — my master builder!

Curtain

Probably no other woman except Eve and the Virgin Mary has excited more interest in novelists, poets, and playwrights than Saint Joan. The bibliography of essays, articles, investigations, critiques, novels, poems, pageants, plays, and films on this enigmatic young woman is staggering. Among the playwrights who have been fascinated by her character are Schiller, Claudel, Anouilh, Brecht — and George Bernard Shaw (1856–1950). Too often, the odor of self-righteousness smothers the scent of common humanity in heroic figures from the past who have been given the peculiar honor of canonization. Around the actual historical person grows up a romantic thicket of miraculous stories, moral fables, and fantastic traditions, a tangle almost impossible to cut away. Joan has her share, and Shaw does not scorn to include some in *Saint Joan* (1923) — the changing of the wind and the unburnable heart, for example.

But what makes Shaw's Joan such a novelty, even today, is the fresh, astringent way he portrayed her. His Joan is "a genius and a saint," combining girlish innocence and faith with an almost masculine capacity for organization and strength of character: she is both a visionary and "a born boss." Shaw would scoff at the notion that determination, steadfastness, or inner strength are more masculine than feminine, yet Joan's unselfconscious power, aggressiveness, and self-knowledge have as little to do with the typical feminine virtues and behavior of his time as Joan's. She was ignorant and presumptuous, but she was neither mad nor suicidal. Shaw explains her triumphs in battle as the result of good military strategy, not luck; her voices as the product of her intense imagination working on her eminent common sense, not magic; her leap from the prison tower as the frantic effort to save the battle of Compiègne, not an attempt to kill herself.

> Everything she did was thoroughly calculated; and though the process was so rapid that she was hardly conscious of it, and ascribed it all to her voices, she was a woman of policy and not of blind impulse.[1]
>
> • • • • •
>
> This combination of inept youth and academic ignorance with great natural capacity, push, courage, devotion, originality and oddity, fully accounts for all the facts in Joan's career, and makes her a credible historical and human phenomenon . . .[2]

Shaw's play successfully strips Joan of legend and romanticism. But Shaw had a larger purpose than dispelling fictions. He shows that Joan's condemnation and death were in a very real, classically tragic sense her

---

[1] G. B. Shaw, "Preface to *Saint Joan*," *The Theatre of Bernard Shaw*, ed. Alan S. Downer (New York: Dodd, Mead & Company, 1961), Vol. II, p. 661.
[2] *Ibid.*, p. 663.

own doing. Like Antigone, Joan declared a law higher than man's law, followed it, and fulfilled it. Antigone, of course, operated on a much more rational level. That is, even though her actions were dangerous to her physical safety, they were the product of her reason and will. Joan, on the other hand, received her instructions from her voices, *i.e.*, imagination and emotion. It remains for the reader and viewer to decide whether either woman's presumption in going against the laws and orders of her time and place was a heroic downfall through the tragic flaw of *hubris* — thinking, in one's pride, that one knows better than the rest of society — or whether it was an heroic apotheosis — knowing that one is right to act despite the threatened terrors of anathema and death.

Shaw has been careful not to confront Joan with villains. Each man who opposes her has his reasons. Warwick sees all too clearly that her passion for France's freedom threatens the survival of the feudal landlords with a new nationalism. The Church authorities realize that her dependence on her voices heralds a new heresy: protestantism, the worship of God without ecclesiastical intercession. The sincere guardians of the *status quo* naturally do not want to see it change. Significantly, though, the churchmen (save De Stogumber, but in the context of the play, he is stronger as an Englishman than a Catholic) do not intrigue for Joan's death. Instead, they strive to save both her soul and her body, with more vigor than our modern courts would perhaps have shown. Within the framework of the beliefs and theology of their age, so succinctly revealed in the trial scene, they have every reason to think they are right and Joan is wrong.

Because Shaw leavens *Saint Joan* with a generous share of lively comedy and boisterous good humor, of which Joan herself is often the perpetrator, unwary readers may tend to forget that this is a tragedy beyond Joan's pathetic recantation, sentence, and execution. But the elation of laughter is part of Shaw's plan: it heightens the contrast between Joan's innocent and noble nature and the narrow sophistication of those who use and reject her.

Shaw makes it quite clear that although there are fools and villains in the world, most men are just trying to get along without making too many waves. Personalities like Joan are too powerful to be ignored, too demanding to be endured. They exalt the imagination at the same time they intimidate the will. What they ask — the challenge they set — is too much for mere mortals. Even now the world is not ready for its saints.

G.L.

BERNARD SHAW

Saint Joan*

Characters

Captain Robert de Baudricourt
Steward
Joan
Bertrand de Poulengey
Archbishop of Rheims
Duke de la Trémouille
Bluebeard (Gilles de Rais)
Captain La Hire
Charles VII, *Dauphin, then King of France*
Duchess de la Trémouille
Duke of Vendôme
Dunois, *"Bastard of Orleans"*
Master John de Stogumber, *an English chaplain*
Richard de Beauchamp, Earl of Warwick
Peter Cauchon, *Right Reverend Bishop of Beauvais*
Brother John Lemaître, O.S.D., *Inquisitor*
John d'Estivet, *Canon of Bayeux*
de Courcelles, *Canon of Paris*
Brother Martin Ladvenu, O.S.D.
Executioner
Soldier
Gentleman
Courtiers, Knights, Ladies-in-Waiting, Canons, Doctors
of Laws and Theology, Dominican Monks, Scribes,
English and French Soldiers, Assistants to the Ex-
ecutioner, Sentry, Four Pages

---

* This edition retains Shaw's idiosyncrasies in spelling — *shew* for *show*, *Shakespear* for *Shakespeare*, etc. — and punctuation: "The apostrophes in ain't, don't, haven't, etc., look so ugly that the most careful printing cannot make a page of colloquial dialogue as handsome as a page of classical dialogue. Besides, shan't should be sha' 'n't, if the wretched pedantry of indicating the elision is to be carried out. I have written aint, dont, havnt, shant, shouldnt and wont for twenty years with perfect impunity, using the apostrophe only where its omission would suggest another word: for example, hell for he'll. There is not the faintest reason for persisting in the ugly and silly trick of peppering pages with these uncouth bacilli. I also write thats, whats, lets, for the colloquial forms of that is, what is, let us; and I have not yet been prosecuted."

458

Scene 1

(*A fine spring morning on the river Meuse, between Lorraine and Champagne, in the year 1429 A.D., in the castle of Vaucouleurs.*

CAPTAIN ROBERT DE BAUDRICOURT, *a military squire, handsome and physically energetic, but with no will of his own, is disguising that defect in his usual fashion by storming terribly at his* STEWARD, *a trodden worm, scanty of flesh, scanty of hair, who might be any age from 18 to 55, being the sort of man whom age cannot wither because he has never bloomed.*

The two are in a sunny stone chamber on the first floor of the castle. At a plain strong oak table, seated in chair to match, the captain presents his left profile. The steward stands facing him at the other side of the table, if so deprecatory a stance as his can be called standing. The mullioned thirteenth-century window is open behind him. Near it in the corner is a turret with a narrow arched doorway leading to a winding stair which descends to the courtyard. There is a stout fourlegged stool under the table, and a wooden chest under the window.)

ROBERT. No eggs! No eggs!! Thousand thunders, man, what do you mean by no eggs?

STEWARD. Sir: it is not my fault. It is the act of God.

ROBERT. Blasphemy. You tell me there are no eggs; and you blame your Maker for it.

STEWARD. Sir: what can I do? I cannot lay eggs.

ROBERT (*sarcastic*). Ha! You jest about it.

STEWARD. No, sir, God knows. We all have to go without eggs just as you have, sir. The hens will not lay.

ROBERT. Indeed! (*Rising.*) Now listen to me, you.

STEWARD (*humbly*). Yes, sir.

ROBERT. What am I?

STEWARD. What are you, sir?

ROBERT (*coming at him*). Yes: what am I? Am I Robert, squire of Baudricourt and captain of this castle of Vaucouleurs; or am I a cowboy?

STEWARD. Oh, sir, you know you are a greater man here than the king himself.

ROBERT. Precisely. And now, do you know what you are?

STEWARD. I am nobody, sir, except that I have the honor to be your steward.

ROBERT (*driving him to the wall, adjective by adjective*). You have not only the honor of being my steward, but the privilege of being the worst, most incompetent, drivelling snivelling jibbering jabbering idiot of a steward in France. (*He strides back to the table.*)

STEWARD (*cowering on the chest*). Yes, sir: to a great man like you I must seem like that.

ROBERT (*turning*). My fault, I suppose. Eh?

STEWARD (*coming to him deprecatingly*). Oh, sir: you always give
my most innocent words such a turn!

ROBERT.   I will give your neck a turn if you dare tell me, when I ask
you how many eggs there are, that you cannot lay any.

STEWARD (*protesting*).   Oh sir, oh sir —

ROBERT.   No: not oh sir, oh sir, but no sir, no sir. My three Barbary
hens and the black are the best layers in Champagne. And you come
and tell me that there are no eggs! Who stole them? Tell me that, before I kick you out through the castle gate for a liar and a seller of my
goods to thieves. The milk was short yesterday, too: do not forget that.

STEWARD (*desperate*).   I know, sir. I know only too well. There is
no milk: there are no eggs: tomorrow there will be nothing.

ROBERT.   Nothing! You will steal the lot: eh?

STEWARD.   No, sir: nobody will steal anything. But there is a spell
on us: we are bewitched.

ROBERT.   That story is not good enough for me. Robert de Baudricourt burns witches and hangs thieves. Go. Bring me four dozen eggs
and two gallons of milk here in this room before noon, or Heaven have
mercy on your bones! I will teach you to make a fool of me. (*He resumes
his seat with an air of finality.*)

STEWARD.   Sir: I tell you there are no eggs. There will be none — not
if you were to kill me for it — as long as The Maid is at the door.

ROBERT.   The Maid! What maid? What are you talking about?

STEWARD.   The girl from Lorraine, sir. From Domrémy.

ROBERT (*rising in fearful wrath*).   Thirty thousand thunders! Fifty
thousand devils! Do you mean to say that that girl, who had the impudence to ask to see me two days ago, and whom I told you to send back to
her father with my orders that he was to give her a good hiding, is here
still?

STEWARD.   I have told her to go, sir. She wont.

ROBERT.   I did not tell you to tell her to go: I told you to throw her
out. You have fifty men-at-arms and a dozen lumps of ablebodied servants to carry out my orders. Are they afraid of her?

STEWARD.   She is so positive, sir.

ROBERT (*seizing him by the scruff of the neck*).   Positive! Now see
here. I am going to throw you downstairs.

STEWARD.   No, sir. Please.

ROBERT.   Well, stop me by being positive. It's quite easy: any slut of
a girl can do it.

STEWARD (*hanging limp in his hands*).   Sir, sir: you cannot get rid
of her by throwing me out.

(ROBERT *has to let him drop. He squats on his knees on the floor,
contemplating his master resignedly.*)

You see, sir, you are much more positive than I am. But so is she.

ROBERT. I am stronger than you are, you fool.

STEWARD. No, sir: it isnt that: it's your strong character, sir. She is weaker than we are: she is only a slip of a girl; but we cannot make her go.

ROBERT. You parcel of curs: you are afraid of her.

STEWARD (*rising cautiously*). No, sir: we are afraid of you; but she puts courage into us. She really doesnt seem to be afraid of anything. Perhaps you could frighten her, sir.

ROBERT (*grimly*). Perhaps. Where is she now?

STEWARD. Down in the courtyard, sir, talking to the soldiers as usual. She is always talking to the soldiers except when she is praying.

ROBERT. Praying! Ha! You believe she prays, you idiot. I know the sort of girl that is always talking to soldiers. She shall talk to me a bit. (*He goes to the window and shouts fiercely through it.*) Hallo, you there!

A GIRL'S VOICE (*bright, strong and rough*). Is it me, sir?

ROBERT. Yes, you.

THE VOICE. Be you captain?

ROBERT. Yes, damn your impudence, I be captain. Come up here. (*To the soldiers in the yard.*) Shew her the way, you. And shove her along quick. (*He leaves the window, and returns to his place at the table, where he sits magisterially.*)

STEWARD (*whispering*). She wants to go and be a soldier herself. She wants you to give her soldier's clothes. Armor, sir! And a sword! Actually! (*He steals behind* ROBERT.)

(JOAN *appears in the turret doorway. She is an ablebodied country girl of 17 or 18, respectably dressed in red, with an uncommon face: eyes very wide apart and bulging as they often do in very imaginative people, a long well-shaped nose with wide nostrils, a short upper lip, resolute but full-lipped mouth, and handsome fighting chin. She comes eagerly to the table, delighted at having penetrated to* BAUDRICOURT'S *presence at last, and full of hope as to the result. His scowl does not check or frighten her in the least. Her voice is normally a hearty coaxing voice, very confident, very appealing, very hard to resist.*)

JOAN (*bobbing a curtsey*). Good morning, captain squire. Captain: you are to give me a horse and armor and some soldiers, and send me to the Dauphin. Those are your orders from my Lord.

ROBERT (*outraged*). Orders from your lord! And who the devil may your lord be? Go back to him, and tell him that I am neither duke nor peer at his orders: I am squire of Baudricourt; and I take no orders except from the king.

JOAN (*reassuringly*). Yes, squire: that is all right. My Lord is the King of Heaven.

ROBERT. Why, the girl's mad. (*To the* STEWARD.) Why didnt you tell me so, you blockhead?

STEWARD.   Sir: do not anger her: give her what she wants.

JOAN (*impatient, but friendly*).   They all say I am mad until I talk to them, squire. But you see that it is the will of God that you are to do what He has put into my mind.

ROBERT.   It is the will of God that I will send you back to your father with orders to put you under lock and key and thrash the madness out of you. What have you to say to that?

JOAN.   You think you will, squire; but you will find it all coming quite different. You said you would not see me; but here I am.

STEWARD (*appealing*).   Yes, sir. You see, sir.

ROBERT.   Hold your tongue, you.

STEWARD (*abjectly*).   Yes, sir.

ROBERT (*to* JOAN, *with a sour loss of confidence*).   So you are presuming on my seeing you, are you?

JOAN (*sweetly*).   Yes, squire.

ROBERT (*feeling that he has lost ground, brings down his two fists squarely on the table, and inflates his chest imposingly to cure the unwelcome and only too familiar sensation*).   Now listen to me. I am going to assert myself.

JOAN (*busily*).   Please do, squire. The horse will cost sixteen francs. It is a good deal of money; but I can save it on the armor. I can find a soldier's armor that will fit me well enough: I am very hardy; and I do not need beautiful armor made to my measure like you wear. I shall not want many soldiers: the Dauphin will give me all I need to raise the siege of Orleans.

ROBERT (*flabbergasted*).   To raise the siege of Orleans!

JOAN (*simply*).   Yes, squire: that is what God is sending me to do. Three men will be enough for you to send with me if they are good men and gentle to me. They have promised to come with me. Polly and Jack and —

ROBERT.   Polly!! You impudent baggage, do you dare call squire Bertrand de Poulengey Polly to my face?

JOAN.   His friends call him so, squire: I did not know he had any other name. Jack —

ROBERT.   That is Monsieur John of Metz, I suppose?

JOAN.   Yes, squire. Jack will come willingly: he is a very kind gentleman, and gives me money to give to the poor. I think John Godsave will come, and Dick the Archer, and their servants John of Honecourt and Julian. There will be no trouble for you, squire: I have arranged it all: you have only to give the order.

ROBERT (*contemplating her in a stupor of amazement*).   Well, I am damned!

JOAN (*with unruffled sweetness*).   No, squire: God is very merciful; and the blessed saints Catherine and Margaret, who speak to me every day (*he gapes*), will intercede for you. You will go to paradise; and your name will be remembered for ever as my first helper.

ROBERT (*to the* STEWARD, *still much bothered, but changing his tone as he pursues a new clue*). Is this true about Monsieur de Poulengey?

STEWARD (*eagerly*). Yes, sir, and about Monsieur de Metz too. They both want to go with her.

ROBERT (*thoughtful*). Mf! (*He goes to the window, and shouts into the courtyard.*) Hallo! You there: send Monsieur de Poulengey to me, will you? (*He turns to* JOAN.) Get out; and wait in the yard.

JOAN (*smiling brightly at him*). Right, squire. (*She goes out.*)

ROBERT (*to the* STEWARD). Go with her, you, you dithering imbecile. Stay within call; and keep your eye on her. I shall have her up here again.

STEWARD. Do so in God's name, sir. Think of those hens, the best layers in Champagne; and —

ROBERT. Think of my boot; and take your backside out of reach of it.

(*The* STEWARD *retreats hastily and finds himself confronted in the doorway by* BERTRAND DE POULENGEY, *a lymphatic French gentleman-at-arms, aged 36 or thereabout, employed in the department of the provost-marshal, dreamily absent-minded, seldom speaking unless spoken to, and then slow and obstinate in reply: altogether in contrast to the self-assertive, loud-mouthed, superficially energetic, fundamentally will-less* ROBERT. *The steward makes way for him, and vanishes.*

POULENGEY *salutes, and stands awaiting orders.*)

(*Genially.*) It isnt service, Polly. A friendly talk. Sit down. (*He hooks the stool from under the table with his instep.*)

(POULENGEY *relaxing, comes into the room; places the stool between the table and the window; and sits down ruminatively.* ROBERT, *half sitting on the end of the table, begins the friendly talk.*)

Now listen to me, Polly. I must talk to you like a father.

(POULENGEY *looks up at him gravely for a moment, but says nothing.*)

It's about this girl you are interested in. Now, I have seen her. I have talked to her. First, she's mad. That doesnt matter. Second, she's not a farm wench. She's a bourgeoise. That matters a good deal. I know her class exactly. Her father came here last year to represent his village in a lawsuit: he is one of their notables. A farmer. Not a gentleman farmer: he makes money by it, and lives by it. Still, not a laborer. Not a mechanic. He might have a cousin a lawyer, or in the Church. People of this sort may be of no account socially; but they can give a lot of bother to the authorities. That is to say, to me. Now no doubt it seems to you a very simple thing to take this girl away, humbugging her into the belief that you are taking her to the Dauphin. But if you get her into trouble, you may get me into no end of a mess, as I am her father's lord, and responsible for her protection. So friends or no friends, Polly, hands off her.

POULENGEY (*with deliberate impressiveness*). I should as soon think of the Blessed Virgin herself in that way, as of this girl.

ROBERT (*coming off the table*). But she says you and Jack and Dick have offered to go with her. What for? You are not going to tell me that you take her crazy notion of going to the Dauphin seriously, are you?

POULENGEY (*slowly*). There is something about her. They are pretty foulmouthed and foulminded down there in the guardroom, some of them. But there hasnt been a word that has anything to do with her being a woman. They have stopped swearing before her. There is something. Something. It may be worth trying.

ROBERT. Oh, come, Polly! pull yourself together. Commonsense was never your strong point; but this is a little too much. (*He retreats disgustedly.*)

POULENGEY (*unmoved*). What is the good of commonsense? If we had any commonsense we should join the Duke of Burgundy and the English king. They hold half the country, right down to the Loire. They have Paris. They have this castle: you know very well that we had to surrender it to the Duke of Bedford, and that you are only holding it on parole. The Dauphin is in Chinon, like a rat in a corner, except that he wont fight. We dont even know that he *is* the Dauphin: his mother says he isnt; and she ought to know. Think of that! the queen denying the legitimacy of her own son!

ROBERT. Well, she married her daughter to the English king. Can you blame the woman?

POULENGEY. I blame nobody. But thanks to her, the Dauphin is down and out; and we may as well face it. The English will take Orleans: the Bastard will not be able to stop them.

ROBERT. He beat the English the year before last at Montargis. I was with him.

POULENGEY. No matter: his men are cowed now; and he cant work miracles. And I tell you that nothing can save our side now but a miracle.

ROBERT. Miracles are all right, Polly. The only difficulty about them is that they dont happen nowadays.

POULENGEY. I used to think so. I am not so sure now. (*Rising, and moving ruminatively towards the window.*) At all events this is not a time to leave any stone unturned. There is something about the girl.

ROBERT. Oh! You think the girl can work miracles, do you?

POULENGEY. I think the girl herself is a bit of a miracle. Anyhow, she is the last card left in our hand. Better play her than throw up the game. (*He wanders to the turret.*)

ROBERT (*wavering*). You really think that?

POULENGEY (*turning*). Is there anything else left for us to think?

ROBERT (*going to him*). Look here, Polly. If you were in my place would you let a girl like that do you out of sixteen francs for a horse?

POULENGEY. I will pay for the horse.

ROBERT. You will!

POULENGEY. Yes: I will back my opinion.

ROBERT. You will really gamble on a forlorn hope to the tune of sixteen francs?

POULENGEY. It is not a gamble.

ROBERT. What else is it?

POULENGEY. It is a certainty. Her words and her ardent faith in God have put fire into me.

ROBERT (*giving him up*). Whew! You are as mad as she is.

POULENGEY (*obstinately*). We want a few mad people now. See where the sane ones have landed us!

ROBERT (*his irresoluteness now openly swamping his affected decisiveness*). I shall feel like a precious fool. Still, if you feel sure — ?

POULENGEY. I feel sure enough to take her to Chinon — unless you stop me.

ROBERT. This is not fair. You are putting the responsibility on me.

POULENGEY. It is on you whichever way you decide.

ROBERT. Yes: thats just it. Which way am I to decide? You dont see how awkward this is for me. (*Snatching at a dilatory step with an unconscious hope that* JOAN *will make up his mind for him.*) Do you think I ought to have another talk to her?

POULENGEY (*rising*). Yes. (*He goes to the window and calls.*) Joan!

JOAN'S VOICE. Will he let us go, Polly?

POULENGEY. Come up. Come in. (*Turning to* ROBERT.) Shall I leave you with her?

ROBERT. No: stay here; and back me up.

(POULENGEY *sits down on the chest.* ROBERT *goes back to his magisterial chair, but remains standing to inflate himself more imposingly.* JOAN *comes in, full of good news.*)

JOAN. Jack will go halves for the horse.

ROBERT. Well!! (*He sits, deflated.*)

POULENGEY (*gravely*). Sit down, Joan.

JOAN (*checked a little, and looking to* ROBERT). May I?

ROBERT. Do what you are told.

(JOAN *curtsies and sits down on the stool between them.* ROBERT *outfaces his perplexity with his most peremptory air.*)

What is your name?

JOAN (*chattily*). They always call me Jenny in Lorraine. Here in France I am Joan. The soldiers call me The Maid.

ROBERT. What is your surname?

JOAN. Surname? What is that? My father sometimes calls himself d'Arc; but I know nothing about it. You met my father. He —

ROBERT. Yes, yes: I remember. You come from Domrémy in Lorraine, I think.

JOAN. Yes; but what does it matter? we all speak French.

ROBERT. Dont ask questions: answer them. How old are you?

JOAN. Seventeen: so they tell me. It might be nineteen. I dont remember.

ROBERT. What did you mean when you said that St Catherine and St Margaret talked to you every day?

JOAN. They do.

ROBERT. What are they like?

JOAN (suddenly obstinate). I will tell you nothing about that: they have not given me leave.

ROBERT. But you actually see them; and they talk to you just as I am talking to you?

JOAN. No: it is quite different. I cannot tell you: you must not talk to me about my voices.

ROBERT. How do you mean? voices?

JOAN. I hear voices telling me what to do. They come from God.

ROBERT. They come from your imagination.

JOAN. Of course. That is how the messages of God come to us.

POULENGEY. Checkmate.

ROBERT. No fear! (To JOAN.) So God says you are to raise the siege of Orleans?

JOAN. And to crown the Dauphin in Rheims Cathedral.

ROBERT (gasping). Crown the D——! Gosh!

JOAN. And to make the English leave France.

ROBERT (sarcastic). Anything else?

JOAN (charming). Not just at present, thank you, squire.

ROBERT. I suppose you think raising a siege is as easy as chasing a cow out of a meadow. You think soldiering is anybody's job?

JOAN. I do not think it can be very difficult if God is on your side, and you are willing to put your life in His hand. But many soldiers are very simple.

ROBERT (grimly). Simple! Did you ever see English soldiers fighting?

JOAN. They are only men. God made them just like us; but He gave them their own country and their own language; and it is not His will that they should come into our country and try to speak our language.

ROBERT. Who has been putting such nonsense into your head? Dont you know that soldiers are subject to their feudal lord, and that it is nothing to them or to you whether he is the duke of Burgundy or the king of England or the king of France? What has their language to do with it?

JOAN. I do not understand that a bit. We are all subject to the King of Heaven; and He gave us our countries and our languages, and meant us to keep to them. If it were not so it would be murder to kill an Englishman in battle; and you, squire, would be in great danger of hell fire. You must not think about your duty to your feudal lord, but about your duty to God.

POULENGEY. It's no use, Robert: she can choke you like that every time.

ROBERT. Can she, by Saint Dennis! We shall see. (*To* JOAN.) We are not talking about God: we are talking about practical affairs. I ask you again, girl, have you ever seen English soldiers fighting? Have you ever seen them plundering, burning, turning the countryside into a desert? Have you heard no tales of their Black Prince who was blacker than the devil himself, or of the English king's father?

JOAN. You must not be afraid, Robert —

ROBERT. Damn you, I am not afraid. And who gave you leave to call me Robert?

JOAN. You were called so in church in the name of our Lord. All the other names are your father's or your brother's or anybody's.

ROBERT. Tcha!

JOAN. Listen to me, squire. At Domrémy we had to fly to the next village to escape from the English soldiers. Three of them were left behind, wounded. I came to know these three poor goddams quite well. They had not half my strength.

ROBERT. Do you know why they are called goddams?

JOAN. No. Everyone calls them goddams.

ROBERT. It is because they are always calling on their God to condemn their souls to perdition. That is what goddam means in their language. How do you like it?

JOAN. God will be merciful to them; and they will act like His good children when they go back to the country He made for them, and made them for. I have heard the tales of the Black Prince. The moment he touched the soil of our country the devil entered into him and made him a black fiend. But at home, in the place made for him by God, he was good. It is always so. If I went into England against the will of God to conquer England, and tried to live there and speak its language, the devil would enter into me; and when I was old I should shudder to remember the wickednesses I did.

ROBERT. Perhaps. But the more devil you were the better you might fight. That is why the goddams will take Orleans. And you cannot stop them, nor ten thousand like you.

JOAN. One thousand like me can stop them. Ten like me can stop them with God on our side. (*She rises impetuously, and goes at him, unable to sit quiet any longer.*) You do not understand, squire. Our soldiers are always beaten because they are fighting only to save their skins; and the shortest way to save your skin is to run away. Our knights are thinking only of the money they will make in ransoms: it is not kill or be killed with them, but pay or be paid. But I will teach them all to fight that the will of God may be done in France; and then they will drive the poor goddams before them like sheep. You and Polly will live to see the day when there will not be an English soldier on the soil of France; and there will be but one king there: not the feudal English king, but God's French one.

ROBERT (*to* POULENGEY). This may be all rot, Polly; but the troops might swallow it, though nothing that we can say seems able to put any fight into them. Even the Dauphin might swallow it. And if she can put fight into him, she can put it into anybody.

POULENGEY. I can see no harm in trying. Can you? And there is something about the girl —

ROBERT (*turning to* JOAN). Now listen you to me; and (*desperately*) dont cut in before I have time to think.

JOAN (*plumping down on the stool again, like an obedient schoolgirl*). Yes, squire.

ROBERT. Your orders are, that you are to go to Chinon under the escort of this gentleman and three of his friends.

JOAN (*radiant, clasping her hands*). Oh, squire! Your head is all circled with light, like a saint's.

POULENGEY. How is she to get into the royal presence?

ROBERT (*who has looked up for his halo rather apprehensively*). I dont know: how did she get into my presence? If the Dauphin can keep her out he is a better man than I take him for. (*Rising.*) I will send her to Chinon; and she can say I sent her. Then let come what may: I can do no more.

JOAN. And the dress? I may have a soldier's dress, maynt I, squire?

ROBERT. Have what you please. I wash my hands of it.

JOAN (*wildly excited by her success*). Come, Polly. (*She dashes out.*)

ROBERT (*shaking* POULENGEY's *hand*). Goodbye, old man, I am taking a big chance. Few other men would have done it. But as you say, there is something about her.

POULENGEY. Yes: there is something about her. Goodbye. (*He goes out.*)

(ROBERT, *still very doubtful whether he has not been made a fool of by a crazy female, and a social inferior to boot, scratches his head and slowly comes back from the door.*

The STEWARD *runs in with a basket.*)

STEWARD. Sir, sir —

ROBERT. What now?

STEWARD. The hens are laying like mad, sir. Five dozen eggs!

ROBERT (*stiffens convulsively; crosses himself; and forms with his pale lips the words*) Christ in heaven! (*Aloud but breathless.*) She did come from God.

Scene 2

(*Chinon, in Touraine. An end of the throne-room in the castle, curtained off to make an antechamber. The* ARCHBISHOP OF RHEIMS, *close on 50, a full-fed political prelate with nothing of the ecclesiastic about him except his imposing bearing, and the Lord Chamberlain,* MONSEIGNEUR DE LA TRÉMOUILLE, *a monstrous arrogant wineskin of a man, are waiting for the* DAUPHIN. *There is a door in the wall to the right of the two men. It is late in the afternoon on the 8th of March, 1429. The* ARCHBISHOP *stands with dignity whilst the* CHAMBERLAIN, *on his left, fumes about in the worst of tempers.*)

LA TRÉMOUILLE. What the devil does the Dauphin mean by keeping us waiting like this? I dont know how you have the patience to stand there like a stone idol.

THE ARCHBISHOP. You see, I am an archbishop; and an archbishop is a sort of idol. At any rate he has to learn to keep still and suffer fools patiently. Besides, my dear Lord Chamberlain, it is the Dauphin's royal privilege to keep you waiting, is it not?

LA TRÉMOUILLE. Dauphin be damned! saving your reverence. Do you know how much money he owes me?

THE ARCHBISHOP. Much more than he owes me, I have no doubt, because you are a much richer man. But I take it he owes you all you could afford to lend him. That is what he owes me.

LA TRÉMOUILLE. Twenty-seven thousand: that was his last haul. A cool twenty-seven thousand!

THE ARCHBISHOP. What becomes of it all? He never has a suit of clothes that I would throw to a curate.

LA TRÉMOUILLE. He dines on a chicken or a scrap of mutton. He borrows my last penny; and there is nothing to shew for it. (A PAGE *appears in the doorway.*) At last!

THE PAGE. No, my lord: it is not His Majesty. Monsieur de Rais is approaching.

LA TRÉMOUILLE. Young Bluebeard! Why announce *him?*

THE PAGE. Captain La Hire is with him. Something has happened, I think.

(GILLES DE RAIS, *a young man of 25, very smart and self-possessed, and sporting the extravagance of a little curled beard dyed blue at a clean-shaven court, comes in. He is determined to make himself agreeable, but lacks natural joyousness, and is not really pleasant. In fact when he defies the Church some eleven years later he is accused of trying to extract pleasure from horrible cruelties, and hanged. So far, however, there is no shadow of the gallows on him. He advances gaily to the* ARCHBISHOP. *The* PAGE *withdraws.*)

BLUEBEARD. Your faithful lamb, Archbishop. Good day, my lord. Do you know what has happened to La Hire?

LA TRÉMOUILLE. He has sworn himself into a fit, perhaps.

BLUEBEARD. No: just the opposite. Foul Mouthed Frank, the only man in Touraine who could beat him at swearing, was told by a soldier that he shouldnt use such language when he was at the point of death.

THE ARCHBISHOP. Nor at any other point. But was Foul Mouthed Frank on the point of death?

BLUEBEARD. Yes: he has just fallen into a well and been drowned. La Hire is frightened out of his wits.

(CAPTAIN LA HIRE comes in: a war dog with no court manners and pronounced camp ones.)

I have just been telling the Chamberlain and the Archbishop. The Archbishop says you are a lost man.

LA HIRE (striding past BLUEBEARD, and planting himself between the ARCHBISHOP and LA TRÉMOUILLE). This is nothing to joke about. It is worse than we thought. It was not a soldier, but an angel dressed as a soldier.

THE ARCHBISHOP
THE CHAMBERLAIN } (exclaiming all together). An angel!
BLUEBEARD

LA HIRE. Yes, an angel. She has made her way from Champagne with half a dozen men through the thick of everything: Burgundians, goddams, deserters, robbers, and Lord knows who; and they never met a soul except the country folk. I know one of them: de Poulengey. He says she's an angel. If ever I utter an oath again may my soul be blasted to eternal damnation!

THE ARCHBISHOP. A very pious beginning, Captain.

(BLUEBEARD and LA TRÉMOUILLE laugh at him. The PAGE returns.)

THE PAGE. His Majesty.

(They stand perfunctorily at court attention. The DAUPHIN, aged 26, really King Charles the Seventh since the death of his father, but as yet uncrowned, comes in through the curtains with a paper in his hands. He is a poor creature physically; and the current fashion of shaving closely, and hiding every scrap of hair under the head-covering or headdress, both by women and men, makes the worst of his appearance. He has little narrow eyes, near together, a long pendulous nose that droops over his thick short upper lip, and the expression of a young dog accustomed to be kicked, yet incorrigible and irrepressible. But he is neither vulgar nor stupid; and he has a cheeky humor which enables him to hold his own in conversation. Just at present he is excited, like a child with a new toy. He comes to the ARCHBISHOP's left hand. BLUEBEARD and LA HIRE retire towards the curtains.)

CHARLES. Oh, Archbishop, do you know what Robert de Baudricourt is sending me from Vaucouleurs?

THE ARCHBISHOP (contemptuously). I am not interested in the newest toys.

CHARLES (indignantly). It isnt a toy. (Sulkily.) However, I can get on very well without your interest.

THE ARCHBISHOP. Your Highness is taking offence very unnecessarily.

CHARLES. Thank you. You are always ready with a lecture, arnt you?

LA TRÉMOUILLE (*roughly*). Enough grumbling. What have you got there?

CHARLES. What is that to you?

LA TRÉMOUILLE. It is my business to know what is passing between you and the garrison at Vaucouleurs. (*He snatches the paper from the* DAUPHIN's *hand, and begins reading it with some difficulty, following the words with his finger and spelling them out syllable by syllable.*)

CHARLES (*mortified*). You all think you can treat me as you please because I owe you money, and because I am no good at fighting. But I have the blood royal in my veins.

THE ARCHBISHOP. Even that has been questioned, your Highness. One hardly recognizes in you the grandson of Charles the Wise.

CHARLES. I want to hear no more of my grandfather. He was so wise that he used up the whole family stock of wisdom for five generations, and left me the poor fool I am, bullied and insulted by all of you.

THE ARCHBISHOP. Control yourself, sir. These outbursts of petulance are not seemly.

CHARLES. Another lecture! Thank you. What a pity it is that though you are an archbishop saints and angels dont come to see you!

THE ARCHBISHOP. What do you mean?

CHARLES. Aha! Ask that bully there (*pointing to* LA TRÉMOUILLE).

LA TRÉMOUILLE (*furious*). Hold your tongue. Do you hear?

CHARLES. Oh, I hear. You neednt shout. The whole castle can hear. Why dont you go and shout at the English, and beat them for me?

LA TRÉMOUILLE (*raising his fist*). You young —

CHARLES (*running behind the* ARCHBISHOP). Dont you raise your hand to me. It's high treason.

LA HIRE. Steady, Duke! Steady!

THE ARCHBISHOP (*resolutely*). Come, come! this will not do. My lord Chamberlain: please! please! we must keep some sort of order. (*To the* DAUPHIN.) And you, sir: if you cannot rule your kingdom, at least try to rule yourself.

CHARLES. Another lecture! Thank you.

LA TRÉMOUILLE (*handing the paper to the* ARCHBISHOP). Here: read the accursed thing for me. He has sent the blood boiling into my head: I cant distinguish the letters.

CHARLES (*coming back and peering round* LA TRÉMOUILLE's *left shoulder*). I will read it for you if you like. I can read, you know.

LA TRÉMOUILLE (*with intense contempt, not at all stung by the taunt*). Yes: reading is about all you are fit for. Can you make it out, Archbishop?

THE ARCHBISHOP. I should have expected more commonsense from De Baudricourt. He is sending some cracked country lass here —

CHARLES (*interrupting*). No: he is sending a saint: an angel. And she is coming to me: to me, the king, and not to you, Archbishop, holy as you are. She knows the blood royal if you dont. (*He struts up to the curtains between* BLUEBEARD *and* LA HIRE.)

THE ARCHBISHOP. You cannot be allowed to see this crazy wench.

CHARLES (*turning*). But I am the king; and I will.

LA TRÉMOUILLE (*brutally*). Then she cannot be allowed to see you. Now!

CHARLES. I tell you I will. I am going to put my foot down —

BLUEBEARD (*laughing at him*). Naughty! What would your wise grandfather say?

CHARLES. That just shews your ignorance, Bluebeard. My grandfather had a saint who used to float in the air when she was praying, and told him everything he wanted to know. My poor father had two saints, Marie de Maillé and the Gasque of Avignon. It is in our family; and I dont care what you say: I will have my saint too.

THE ARCHBISHOP. This creature is not a saint. She is not even a respectable woman. She does not wear women's clothes. She is dressed like a soldier, and rides round the country with soldiers. Do you suppose such a person can be admitted to your Highness's court?

LA HIRE. Stop. (*Going to the* ARCHBISHOP.) Did you say a girl in armor, like a soldier?

THE ARCHBISHOP. So De Baudricourt describes her.

LA HIRE. But by all the devils in hell — Oh, God forgive me, what am I saying? — by Our Lady and all the saints, this must be the angel that struck Foul Mouthed Frank dead for swearing.

CHARLES (*triumphantly*). You see! A miracle!

LA HIRE. She may strike the lot of us dead if we cross her. For Heaven's sake, Archbishop, be careful what you are doing.

THE ARCHBISHOP (*severely*). Rubbish! Nobody has been struck dead. A drunken blackguard who has been rebuked a hundred times for swearing has fallen into a well, and been drowned. A mere coincidence.

LA HIRE. I do not know what a coincidence is. I do know that the man is dead, and that she told him he was going to die.

THE ARCHBISHOP. We are all going to die, Captain.

LA HIRE (*crossing himself*). I hope not. (*He backs out of the conversation.*)

BLUEBEARD. We can easily find out whether she is an angel or not. Let us arrange when she comes that I shall be the Dauphin, and see whether she will find me out.

CHARLES. Yes: I agree to that. If she cannot find the blood royal I will have nothing to do with her.

THE ARCHBISHOP. It is for The Church to make saints: let De Baudricourt mind his own business, and not dare usurp the function of his priest. I say the girl shall not be admitted.

BLUEBEARD. But, Archbishop —

THE ARCHBISHOP (*sternly*). I speak in The Church's name. (*To the* DAUPHIN.) Do you dare say she shall?

CHARLES (*intimidated but sulky*). Oh, if you make it an excommunication matter, I have nothing more to say, of course. But you havnt read the end of the letter. De Baudricourt says she will raise the siege of Orleans, and beat the English for us.

LA TRÉMOUILLE. Rot!

CHARLES. Well, will you save Orleans for us, with all your bullying?

LA TRÉMOUILLE (*savagely*). Do not throw that in my face again: do you hear? I have done more fighting than you ever did or ever will. But I cannot be everywhere.

CHARLES. Well, that's something.

BLUEBEARD (*coming between the* ARCHBISHOP *and* CHARLES). You have Jack Dunois at the head of your troops in Orleans: the brave Dunois, the handsome Dunois, the wonderful invincible Dunois, the darling of all the ladies, the beautiful bastard. Is it likely that the country lass can do what he cannot do?

CHARLES. Why doesnt he raise the siege, then?

LA HIRE. The wind is against him.

BLUEBEARD. How can the wind hurt him at Orleans? It is not on the Channel.

LA HIRE. It is on the river Loire; and the English hold the bridge-head. He must ship his men across the river and upstream, if he is to take them in the rear. Well, he cannot, because there is a devil of a wind blowing the other way. He is tired of paying the priests to pray for a west wind. What he needs is a miracle. You tell me that what the girl did to Foul Mouthed Frank was no miracle. No matter: it finished Frank. If she changes the wind for Dunois, that may not be a miracle either; but it may finish the English. What harm is there in trying?

THE ARCHBISHOP (*who has read the end of the letter and become more thoughtful*). It is true that De Baudricourt seems extraordinarily impressed.

LA HIRE. De Baudricourt is a blazing ass; but he is a soldier; and if he thinks she can beat the English, all the rest of the army will think so too.

LA TRÉMOUILLE (*to the* ARCHBISHOP, *who is hesitating*). Oh, let them have their way. Dunois' men will give up the town in spite of him if somebody does not put some fresh spunk into them.

THE ARCHBISHOP. The Church must examine the girl before anything decisive is done about her. However, since his Highness desires it, let her attend the Court.

LA HIRE. I will find her and tell her. (*He goes out.*)

CHARLES. Come with me, Bluebeard; and let us arrange so that she will not know who I am. You will pretend to be me. (*He goes out through the curtains.*)

BLUEBEARD. Pretend to be that thing! Holy Michael! (*He follows the* DAUPHIN.)

LA TRÉMOUILLE. I wonder will she pick him out!

THE ARCHBISHOP. Of course she will.

LA TRÉMOUILLE. Why? How is she to know?

THE ARCHBISHOP. She will know what everybody in Chinon knows: that the Dauphin is the meanest-looking and worst-dressed figure in the Court, and that the man with the blue beard is Gilles de Rais.

LA TRÉMOUILLE. I never thought of that.

THE ARCHBISHOP. You are not so accustomed to miracles as I am. It is part of my profession.

LA TRÉMOUILLE (*puzzled and a little scandalized*). But that would not be a miracle at all.

THE ARCHBISHOP (*calmly*). Why not?

LA TRÉMOUILLE. Well, come! what *is* a miracle?

THE ARCHBISHOP. A miracle, my friend, is an event which creates faith. That is the purpose and nature of miracles. They may seem very wonderful to the people who witness them, and very simple to those who perform them. That does not matter: if they confirm or create faith they are true miracles.

LA TRÉMOUILLE. Even when they are frauds, do you mean?

THE ARCHBISHOP. Frauds deceive. An event which creates faith does not deceive: therefore it is not a fraud, but a miracle.

LA TRÉMOUILLE (*scratching his neck in his perplexity*). Well, I suppose as you are an archbishop you must be right. It seems a bit fishy to me. But I am no churchman, and dont understand these matters.

THE ARCHBISHOP. You are not a churchman; but you are a diplomatist and a soldier. Could you make our citizens pay war taxes, or our soldiers sacrifice their lives, if they knew what is really happening instead of what seems to them to be happening?

LA TRÉMOUILLE. No, by Saint Dennis: the fat would be in the fire before sundown.

THE ARCHBISHOP. Would it not be quite easy to tell them the truth?

LA TRÉMOUILLE. Man alive, they wouldn't believe it.

THE ARCHBISHOP. Just so. Well, The Church has to rule men for the good of their souls as you have to rule them for the good of their bodies. To do that, The Church must do as you do: nourish their faith by poetry.

LA TRÉMOUILLE. Poetry! I should call it humbug.

THE ARCHBISHOP. You would be wrong, my friend. Parables are not lies because they describe events that have never happened. Miracles are not frauds because they are often — I do not say always — very simple and innocent contrivances by which the priest fortifies the faith of his flock. When this girl picks out the Dauphin among his courtiers, it will not be a miracle for me, because I shall know how it has been done, and my faith will not be increased. But as for the others, if they feel the thrill of the supernatural, and forget their sinful clay in a sudden sense of the glory of God, it will be a miracle and a blessed one. And you will find that the girl herself will be more affected than anyone else. She will forget how she really picked him out. So, perhaps, will you.

LA TRÉMOUILLE. Well, I wish I were clever enough to know how much of you is God's archbishop and how much the most artful fox in Touraine. Come on, or we shall be late for the fun; and I want to see it, miracle or no miracle.

THE ARCHBISHOP (*detaining him a moment*). Do not think that I am a lover of crooked ways. There is a new spirit rising in men: we are at the dawning of a wider epoch. If I were a simple monk, and had not to rule men, I should seek peace for my spirit with Aristotle and Pythagoras rather than with the saints and their miracles.

LA TRÉMOUILLE.   And who the deuce was Pythagoras?

THE ARCHBISHOP.   A sage who held that the earth is round, and that it moves round the sun.

LA TRÉMOUILLE.   What an utter fool! Couldnt he use his eyes?

(*They go out together through the curtains, which are presently withdrawn, revealing the full depth of the throne-room with the Court assembled. On the right are two Chairs of State on a dais.* BLUEBEARD *is standing theatrically on the dais, playing the king, and, like the courtiers, enjoying the joke rather obviously. There is a curtained arch in the wall behind the dais; but the main door, guarded by men-at-arms, is at the other side of the room; and a clear path across is kept and lined by the courtiers.* CHARLES *is in this path in the middle of the room.* LA HIRE *is on his right. The* ARCHBISHOP, *on his left, has taken his place by the dais:* LA TRÉMOUILLE *at the other side of it. The* DUCHESS DE LA TRÉMOUILLE, *pretending to be the Queen, sits in the Consort's chair, with a group of ladies in waiting close by, behind the* ARCHBISHOP.*

The chatter of the courtiers makes such a noise that nobody notices the appearance of the PAGE *at the door.*)

THE PAGE.   The Duke of —

(*Nobody listens.*)

The Duke of —

(*The chatter continues. Indignant at his failure to command a hearing, he snatches the halberd of the nearest man-at-arms, and thumps the floor with it. The chatter ceases; and everybody looks at him in silence.*)

Attention! (*He restores the halberd to the man-at-arms.*) The Duke of Vendôme presents Joan the Maid to his Majesty.

CHARLES (*putting his finger on his lip*).   Ssh! (*He hides behind the nearest courtier, peering out to see what happens.*)

BLUEBEARD (*majestically*).   Let her approach the throne.

(JOAN, *dressed as a soldier, with her hair bobbed and hanging thickly round her face, is led in by a bashful and speechless nobleman, from whom she detaches herself to stop and look round eagerly for the* DAUPHIN.)

THE DUCHESS (*to the nearest lady in waiting*).   My dear! Her hair!

(*All the ladies explode in uncontrollable laughter.*)

BLUEBEARD (*trying not to laugh, and waving his hand in deprecation of their merriment*).   Ssh — ssh! Ladies! Ladies!!

JOAN (*not at all embarrassed*). I wear it like this because I am a soldier. Where be Dauphin?

(*A titter runs through the Court as she walks to the dais.*)

BLUEBEARD (*condescendingly*). You are in the presence of the Dauphin.

(JOAN *looks at him sceptically for a moment, scanning him hard up and down to make sure. Dead silence, all watching her. Fun dawns in her face.*)

JOAN. Coom, Bluebeard! Thou canst not fool me. Where be Dauphin?

(*A roar of laughter breaks out as* GILLES, *with a gesture of surrender, joins in the laugh, and jumps down from the dais beside* LA TRÉMOUILLE. JOAN, *also on the broad grin, turns back, searching along the row of courtiers, and presently makes a dive, and drags out* CHARLES *by the arm.*)

(*Releasing him and bobbing him a little curtsey.*) Gentle little Dauphin, I am sent to you to drive the English away from Orleans and from France, and to crown you king in the cathedral at Rheims, where all true kings of France are crowned.

CHARLES (*triumphant, to the Court*). You see, all of you: she knew the blood royal. Who dare say now that I am not my father's son? (*To* JOAN.) But if you want me to be crowned at Rheims you must talk to the Archbishop, not to me. There he is (*he is standing behind her*)!

JOAN (*turning quickly, overwhelmed with emotion*). Oh, my lord! (*She falls on both knees before him, with bowed head, not daring to look up.*) My lord: I am only a poor country girl; and you are filled with the blessedness and glory of God Himself; but you will touch me with your hands, and give me your blessing, wont you?

BLUEBEARD (*whispering to* LA TRÉMOUILLE). The old fox blushes.

LA TRÉMOUILLE. Another miracle!

THE ARCHBISHOP (*touched, putting his hand on her head*). Child: you are in love with religion.

JOAN (*startled: looking up at him*). Am I? I never thought of that. Is there any harm in it?

THE ARCHBISHOP. There is no harm in it, my child. But there is danger.

JOAN (*rising, with a sunflush of reckless happiness irradiating her face*). There is always danger, except in heaven. Oh, my lord, you have given me such strength, such courage. It must be a most wonderful thing to be Archbishop.

(*The Court smiles broadly: even titters a little.*)

THE ARCHBISHOP (*drawing himself up sensitively*).   Gentlemen: your levity is rebuked by this maid's faith. I am, God help me, all unworthy; but your mirth is a deadly sin.

(*Their faces fall. Dead silence.*)

BLUEBEARD.   My lord: we were laughing at her, not at you.

THE ARCHBISHOP.   What? Not at my unworthiness but at her faith! Gilles de Rais: this maid prophesied that the blasphemer should be drowned in his sin —

JOAN (*distressed*).   No!

THE ARCHBISHOP (*silencing her by a gesture*).   I prophesy now that you will be hanged in yours if you do not learn when to laugh and when to pray.

BLUEBEARD.   My lord: I stand rebuked. I am sorry: I can say no more. But if you prophesy that I shall be hanged, I shall never be able to resist temptation, because I shall always be telling myself that I may as well be hanged for a sheep as a lamb.

(*The courtiers take heart at this. There is more tittering.*)

JOAN (*scandalized*).   You are an idle fellow, Bluebeard; and you have great impudence to answer the Archbishop.

LA HIRE (*with a huge chuckle*).   Well said, lass! Well said!

JOAN (*impatiently to the ARCHBISHOP*).   Oh, my lord, will you send all these silly folks away so that I may speak to the Dauphin alone?

LA HIRE (*goodhumoredly*).   I can take a hint. (*He salutes; turns on his heel; and goes out.*)

THE ARCHBISHOP.   Come, gentlemen. The Maid comes with God's blessing, and must be obeyed.

(*The courtiers withdraw, some through the arch, others at the opposite side. The ARCHBISHOP marches across to the door, followed by the DUCHESS and LA TRÉMOUILLE. As the ARCHBISHOP passes JOAN, she falls on her knees, and kisses the hem of his robe fervently. He shakes his head in instinctive remonstrance; gathers the robe from her; and goes out. She is left kneeling directly in the DUCHESS's way.*)

THE DUCHESS (*coldly*).   Will you allow me to pass, please?

JOAN (*hastily rising, and standing back*).   Beg pardon, maam, I am sure.

(*The DUCHESS passes on. JOAN stares after her; then whispers to the DAUPHIN.*)

Be that Queen?

CHARLES.   No. She thinks she is.

JOAN (*again staring after the* DUCHESS). Oo-oo-ooh! (*Her awestruck amazement at the figure cut by the magnificently dressed lady is not wholly complimentary.*)

LA TRÉMOUILLE (*very surly*). I'll trouble your Highness not to gibe at my wife. (*He goes out. The others have already gone.*)

JOAN (*to the* DAUPHIN). Who be old Gruff-and-Grum?

CHARLES. He is the Duke de la Trémouille.

JOAN. What be his job?

CHARLES. He pretends to command the army. And whenever I find a friend I can care for, he kills him.

JOAN. Who does let him?

CHARLES (*petulantly moving to the throne side of the room to escape from her magnetic field*). How can I prevent him? He bullies me. They all bully me.

JOAN. Art afraid?

CHARLES. Yes: I am afraid. It's no use preaching to me about it. It's all very well for these big men with their armor that is too heavy for me, and their swords that I can hardly lift, and their muscle and their shouting and their bad tempers. They like fighting: most of them are making fools of themselves all the time they are not fighting; but I am quiet and sensible; and I dont want to kill people: I only want to be left alone to enjoy myself in my own way. I never asked to be a king: it was pushed on me. So if you are going to say "Son of St Louis: gird on the sword of your ancestors, and lead us to victory" you may spare your breath to cool your porridge; for I cannot do it. I am not built that way; and there is an end of it.

JOAN (*trenchant and masterful*). Blethers! We are all like that to begin with. I shall put courage into thee.

CHARLES. But I dont want to have courage put into me. I want to sleep in a comfortable bed, and not live in continual terror of being killed or wounded. Put courage into the others, and let them have their bellyful of fighting; but let me alone.

JOAN. It's no use, Charlie: thou must face what God puts on thee. If thou fail to make thyself king, thoult be a beggar: what else art fit for? Come! Let me see thee sitting on the throne. I have looked forward to that.

CHARLES. What is the good of sitting on the throne when the other fellows give all the orders? However! (*he sits enthroned, a piteous figure*) here is the king for you! Look your fill at the poor devil.

JOAN. Thourt not king yet, lad; thourt but Dauphin. Be not led away by them around thee. Dressing up dont fill empty noddle. I know the people: the real people that make thy bread for thee; and I tell thee they count no man king of France until the holy oil has been poured on his hair, and himself consecrated and crowned in Rheims Cathedral. And thou needs new clothes, Charlie. Why does not Queen look after thee properly?

CHARLES. We're too poor. She wants all the money we can spare to put on her own back. Besides, I like to see her beautifully dressed; and I dont care what I wear myself: I should look ugly anyhow.

JOAN. There is some good in thee, Charlie; but it is not yet a king's good.

CHARLES. We shall see. I am not such a fool as I look. I have my eyes open; and I can tell you that one good treaty is worth ten good fights. These fighting fellows lose all on the treaties that they gain on the fights. If we can only have a treaty, the English are sure to have the worst of it, because they are better at fighting than at thinking.

JOAN. If the English win, it is they that will make the treaty; and then God help poor France! Thou must fight, Charlie, whether thou will or no. I will go first to hearten thee. We must take our courage in both hands: aye, and pray for it with both hands too.

CHARLES (*descending from his throne and again crossing the room to escape from her dominating urgency*). Oh do stop talking about God and praying. I cant bear people who are always praying. Isnt it bad enough to have to do it at the proper times?

JOAN (*pitying him*). Thou poor child, thou hast never prayed in thy life. I must teach thee from the beginning.

CHARLES. I am not a child: I am a grown man and a father; and I will not be taught any more.

JOAN. Aye, you have a little son. He that will be Louis the Eleventh when you die. Would you not fight for him?

CHARLES. No: a horrid boy. He hates me. He hates everybody, selfish little beast! I dont want to be bothered with children. I dont want to be a father; and I dont want to be a son: especially a son of St Louis. I dont want to be any of these fine things you all have your heads full of: I want to be just what I am. Why cant you mind your own business, and let me mind mine?

JOAN (*again contemptuous*). Minding your own business is like minding your own body: it's the shortest way to make yourself sick. What is my business? Helping mother at home. What is thine? Petting lapdogs and sucking sugarsticks. I call that muck. I tell thee it is God's business we are here to do: not our own. I have a message to thee from God; and thou must listen to it, though thy heart break with the terror of it.

CHARLES. I dont want a message; but can you tell me any secrets? Can you do any cures? Can you turn lead into gold, or anything of that sort?

JOAN. I can turn thee into a king, in Rheims Cathedral; and that is a miracle that will take some doing, it seems.

CHARLES. If we go to Rheims, and have a coronation, Anne will want new dresses. We cant afford them. I am all right as I am.

JOAN. As you are! And what is that? Less than my father's poorest shepherd. Thourt not lawful owner of thy own land of France till thou be consecrated.

CHARLES. But I shall not be lawful owner of my own land anyhow. Will the consecration pay off my mortgages? I have pledged my last acre to the Archbishop and that fat bully. I owe money even to Bluebeard.

JOAN (earnestly). Charlie: I come from the land, and have gotten my strength working on the land; and I tell thee that the land is thine to rule righteously and keep God's peace in, and not to pledge at the pawn-shop as a drunken woman pledges her children's clothes. And I come from God to tell thee to kneel in the cathedral and solemnly give thy kingdom to Him for ever and ever, and become the greatest king in the world as His steward and His bailiff, His soldier and His servant. The very clay of France will become holy: her soldiers will be the soldiers of God: the rebel dukes will be rebels against God: the English will fall on their knees and beg thee let them return to their lawful homes in peace. Wilt be a poor little Judas, and betray me and Him that sent me?

CHARLES (tempted at last). Oh, if I only dare!

JOAN. I shall dare, dare, and dare again, in God's name! Art for or against me?

CHARLES (excited). I'll risk it. I warn you I shant be able to keep it up; but I'll risk it. You shall see. (Running to the main door and shouting.) Hallo! Come back, everybody. (To JOAN, as he runs back to the arch opposite.) Mind you stand by and dont let me be bullied. (Through the arch.) Come along, will you: the whole Court. (He sits down in the royal chair as they all hurry in to their former places, chattering and wondering.) Now I'm in for it; but no matter: here goes! (To the PAGE.) Call for silence, you little beast, will you?

THE PAGE (snatching a halberd as before and thumping with it repeatedly). Silence for His Majesty the King. The King speaks. (Peremptorily.) Will you be silent there? (Silence.)

CHARLES (rising). I have given the command of the army to The Maid. The Maid is to do as she likes with it. (He descends from the dais.)

(General amazement. LA HIRE, delighted, slaps his steel thigh-piece with his gauntlet.)

LA TRÉMOUILLE (turning threateningly towards CHARLES). What is this? I command the army.

(JOAN quickly puts her hand on CHARLES's shoulder as he instinctively recoils. CHARLES, with a grotesque effort culminating in an extravagant gesture, snaps his fingers in the CHAMBERLAIN's face.)

JOAN. Thourt answered, old Gruff-and-Grum. (Suddenly flashing out her sword as she divines that her moment has come.) Who is for God and His Maid? Who is for Orleans with me?

LA HIRE (carried away, drawing also). For God and His Maid! To Orleans!

ALL THE KNIGHTS (*following his lead with enthusiasm*).   To Orleans!

(JOAN, *radiant, falls on her knees in thanksgiving to God. They all kneel, except the* ARCHBISHOP, *who gives his benediction with a sign, and* LA TRÉMOUILLE, *who collapses, cursing.*)

Scene 3

(*Orleans, May 29th, 1429.* DUNOIS, *aged 26, is pacing up and down a patch of ground on the south bank of the silver Loire, commanding a long view of the river in both directions. He has had his lance stuck up with a pennon, which streams in a strong east wind. His shield with its bend sinister lies beside it. He has his commander's baton in his hand. He is well built, carrying his armor easily. His broad brow and pointed chin give him an equilaterally triangular face, already marked by active service and responsibility, with the expression of a goodnatured and capable man who has no affectations and no foolish illusions. His* PAGE *is sitting on the ground, elbows on knees, cheeks on fists, idly watching the water. It is evening; and both man and boy are affected by the loveliness of the Loire.*)

DUNOIS (*halting for a moment to glance up at the streaming pennon and shake his head wearily before he resumes his pacing*).   West wind, west wind, west wind. Strumpet: steadfast when you should be wanton, wanton when you should be steadfast. West wind on the silver Loire: what rhymes to Loire? (*He looks again at the pennon, and shakes his fist at it.*) Change, curse you, change, English harlot of a wind, change. West, west, I tell you. (*With a growl he resumes his march in silence, but soon begins again.*) West wind, wanton wind, wilful wind, womanish wind, false wind from over the water, will you never blow again?

THE PAGE (*bounding to his feet*).   See! There! There she goes!

DUNOIS (*startled from his reverie: eagerly*).   Where? Who? The Maid?

THE PAGE.   No: the kingfisher. Like blue lightning. She went into that bush.

DUNOIS (*furiously disappointed*).   Is that all? You infernal young idiot: I have a mind to pitch you into the river.

THE PAGE (*not afraid, knowing his man*).   It looked frightfully jolly, that flash of blue. Look! There goes the other!

DUNOIS (*running eagerly to the river brim*).   Where? Where?

THE PAGE (*pointing*).   Passing the reeds.

DUNOIS (*delighted*).   I see.

(*They follow the flight till the bird takes cover.*)

THE PAGE.   You blew me up because you were not in time to see them yesterday.

DUNOIS.   You knew I was expecting The Maid when you set up your yelping. I will give you something to yelp for next time.

THE PAGE. Arnt they lovely? I wish I could catch them.

DUNOIS. Let me catch you trying to trap them, and I will put you in the iron cage for a month to teach you what a cage feels like. You are an abominable boy.

(THE PAGE *laughs, and squats down as before.*)

(*Pacing.*) Blue bird, blue bird, since I am friend to thee, change thou the wind for me. No: it does not rhyme. He who has sinned for thee: thats better. No sense in it, though. (*He finds himself close to the page.*) You abominable boy! (*He turns away from him.*) Mary in the blue snood, kingfisher color: will you grudge me a west wind?

A SENTRY'S VOICE WESTWARD. Halt! Who goes there?

JOAN'S VOICE. The Maid.

DUNOIS. Let her pass. Hither, Maid! To me!

(JOAN, *in splendid armor, rushes in in a blazing rage. The wind drops; and the pennon flaps idly down the lance; but* DUNOIS *is too much occupied with* JOAN *to notice it.*)

JOAN (*bluntly*). Be you Bastard of Orleans?

DUNOIS (*cool and stern, pointing to his shield*). You see the bend sinister. Are you Joan the Maid?

JOAN. Sure.

DUNOIS. Where are your troops?

JOAN. Miles behind. They have cheated me. They have brought me to the wrong side of the river.

DUNOIS. I told them to.

JOAN. Why did you? The English are on the other side!

DUNOIS. The English are on both sides.

JOAN. But Orleans is on the other side. We must fight the English there. How can we cross the river?

DUNOIS (*grimly*). There is a bridge.

JOAN. In God's name, then, let us cross the bridge, and fall on them.

DUNOIS. It seems simple; but it cannot be done.

JOAN. Who says so?

DUNOIS. I say so; and older and wiser heads than mine are of the same opinion.

JOAN (*roundly*). Then your older and wiser heads are fatheads: they have made a fool of you; and now they want to make a fool of me too, bringing me to the wrong side of the river. Do you not know that I bring you better help than ever came to any general or any town?

DUNOIS (*smiling patiently*). Your own?

JOAN. No: the help and counsel of the King of Heaven. Which is the way to the bridge?

DUNOIS. You are impatient, Maid.

JOAN. Is this a time for patience? Our enemy is at our gates; and here we stand doing nothing. Oh, why are you not fighting? Listen to me: I will deliver you from fear. I —

DUNOIS (*laughing heartily, and waving her off*). No, no, my girl: if you delivered me from fear I should be a good knight for a story book, but a very bad commander of the army. Come! let me begin to make a soldier of you. (*He takes her to the water's edge.*) Do you see those two forts at this end of the bridge? the big ones?

JOAN. Yes. Are they ours or the goddams'?

DUNOIS. Be quiet, and listen to me. If I were in either of those forts with only ten men I could hold it against an army. The English have more than ten times ten goddams in those forts to hold them against us.

JOAN. They cannot hold them against God. God did not give them the land under those forts: they stole it from Him. He gave it to us. I will take those forts.

DUNOIS. Single-handed?

JOAN. Our men will take them. I will lead them.

DUNOIS. Not a man will follow you.

JOAN. I will not look back to see whether anyone is following me.

DUNOIS (*recognizing her mettle, and clapping her heartily on the shoulder*). Good. You have the makings of a soldier in you. You are in love with war.

JOAN (*startled*). Oh! And the Archbishop said I was in love with religion.

DUNOIS. I, God forgive me, am a little in love with war myself, the ugly devil! I am like a man with two wives. Do you want to be like a woman with two husbands?

JOAN (*matter-of-fact*). I will never take a husband. A man in Toul took an action against me for breach of promise; but I never promised him. I am a soldier: I do not want to be thought of as a woman. I will not dress as a woman. I do not care for the things women care for. They dream of lovers, and of money. I dream of leading a charge, and of placing the big guns. You soldiers do not know how to use the big guns: you think you can win battles with a great noise and smoke.

DUNOIS (*with a shrug*). True. Half the time the artillery is more trouble than it is worth.

JOAN. Aye, lad; but you cannot fight stone walls with horses: you must have guns, and much bigger guns too.

DUNOIS (*grinning at her familiarity, and echoing it*). Aye, lass; but a good heart and a stout ladder will get over the stoniest wall.

JOAN. I will be first up the ladder when we reach the fort, Bastard. I dare you to follow me.

DUNOIS. You must not dare a staff officer, Joan: only company officers are allowed to indulge in displays of personal courage. Besides, you must know that I welcome you as a saint, not as a soldier. I have daredevils enough at my call, if they could help me.

JOAN. I am not a daredevil: I am a servant of God. My sword is sacred: I found it behind the altar in the church of St Catherine, where God hid it for me; and I may not strike a blow with it. My heart is full of courage, not of anger. I will lead; and your men will follow: that is all I can do. But I must do it: you shall not stop me.

DUNOIS. All in good time. Our men cannot take those forts by a sally across the bridge. They must come by water, and take the English in the rear on this side.

JOAN (her military sense asserting itself). Then make rafts and put big guns on them; and let your men cross to us.

DUNOIS. The rafts are ready; and the men are embarked. But they must wait for God.

JOAN. What do you mean? God is waiting for them.

DUNOIS. Let Him send us a wind then. My boats are downstream: they cannot come up against both wind and current. We must wait until God changes the wind. Come: let me take you to the church.

JOAN. No. I love church; but the English will not yield to prayers: they understand nothing but hard knocks and slashes. I will not go to church until we have beaten them.

DUNOIS. You must: I have business for you there.

JOAN. What business?

DUNOIS. To pray for a west wind. I have prayed; and I have given two silver candlesticks; but my prayers are not answered. Yours may be: you are young and innocent.

JOAN. Oh yes: you are right. I will pray: I will tell St Catherine: she will make God give me a west wind. Quick: shew me the way to the church.

THE PAGE (sneezes violently). At-cha!!!

JOAN. God bless you, child! Coom, Bastard.

(They go out. The PAGE rises to follow. He picks up the shield, and is taking the spear as well when he notices the pennon, which is now streaming eastward.)

THE PAGE (dropping the shield and calling excitedly after them). Seigneur! Seigneur! Mademoiselle!

DUNOIS (running back). What is it? The kingfisher? (He looks eagerly for it up the river.)

JOAN (joining them). Oh, a kingfisher! Where?

THE PAGE. No: the wind, the wind, the wind (pointing to the pennon): that is what made me sneeze.

DUNOIS (looking at the pennon). The wind has changed. (He crosses himself.) God has spoken. (Kneeling and handing his baton to JOAN.) You command the king's army. I am your soldier.

THE PAGE (looking down the river). The boats have put off. They are ripping upstream like anything.

people will sell her to the Burgundians; the Burgundians will sell her to us; and there will probably be three or four middlemen who will expect their little commissions.

THE CHAPLAIN. Monstrous. It is all those scoundrels of Jews: they get in every time money changes hands. I would not leave a Jew alive in Christendom if I had my way.

THE NOBLEMAN. Why not? The Jews generally give value. They make you pay; but they deliver the goods. In my experience the men who want something for nothing are invariably Christians.

(*A page appears.*)

THE PAGE. The Right Reverend the Bishop of Beauvais: Monseigneur Cauchon.

(CAUCHON, *aged about 60, comes in. The* PAGE *withdraws. The two Englishmen rise.*)

THE NOBLEMAN (*with effusive courtesy*). My dear Bishop, how good of you to come! Allow me to introduce myself: Richard de Beauchamp, Earl of Warwick, at your service.

CAUCHON. Your lordship's fame is well known to me.

WARWICK. This reverend cleric is Master John de Stogumber.

THE CHAPLAIN (*glibly*). John Bowyer Spenser Neville de Stogumber, at your service, my lord: Bachelor of Theology, and Keeper of the Private Seal to His Eminence the Cardinal of Winchester.

WARWICK (*to* CAUCHON). You call him the Cardinal of England, I believe. Our king's uncle.

CAUCHON. Messire John de Stogumber: I am always the very good friend of His Eminence. (*He extends his hand to the* CHAPLAIN, *who kisses his ring.*)

WARWICK. Do me the honor to be seated. (*He gives* CAUCHON *his chair, placing it at the head of the table.*)

(CAUCHON *accepts the place of honor with a grave inclination.* WARWICK *fetches the leather stool carelessly, and sits in his former place. The* CHAPLAIN *goes back to his chair.*

Though WARWICK *has taken second place in calculated deference to the* BISHOP, *he assumes the lead in opening the proceedings as a matter of course. He is still cordial and expansive; but there is a new note in his voice which means that he is coming to business.*)

Well, my Lord Bishop, you find us in one of our unlucky moments. Charles is to be crowned at Rheims, practically by the young woman from Lorraine; and — I must not deceive you, nor flatter your hopes — we cannot prevent it. I suppose it will make a great difference to Charles's position.

CAUCHON. Undoubtedly. It is a masterstroke of The Maid's.

THE CHAPLAIN (*again agitated*). We were not fairly beaten, my lord. No Englishman is ever fairly beaten.

(CAUCHON *raises his eyebrow slightly, then quickly composes his face.*)

WARWICK. Our friend here takes the view that the young woman is a sorceress. It would, I presume, be the duty of your reverend lordship to denounce her to the Inquisition, and have her burnt for that offence.

CAUCHON. If she were captured in my diocese: yes.

WARWICK (*feeling that they are getting on capitally*). Just so. Now I suppose there can be no reasonable doubt that she is a sorceress.

THE CHAPLAIN. Not the least. An arrant witch.

WARWICK (*gently reproving the interruption*). We are asking for the Bishop's opinion, Messire John.

CAUCHON. We shall have to consider not merely our own opinions here, but the opinions — the prejudices, if you like — of a French court.

WARWICK (*correcting*). A Catholic court, my lord.

CAUCHON. Catholic courts are composed of mortal men, like other courts, however sacred their function and inspiration may be. And if the men are Frenchmen, as the modern fashion calls them, I am afraid the bare fact that an English army has been defeated by a French one will not convince them that there is any sorcery in the matter.

THE CHAPLAIN. What! Not when the famous Sir John Talbot himself has been defeated and actually taken prisoner by a drab from the ditches of Lorraine!

CAUCHON. Sir John Talbot, we all know, is a fierce and formidable soldier, Messire; but I have yet to learn that he is an able general. And though it pleases you to say that he has been defeated by this girl, some of us may be disposed to give a little of the credit to Dunois.

THE CHAPLAIN (*contemptuously*). The Bastard of Orleans!

CAUCHON. Let me remind —

WARWICK (*interposing*). I know what you are going to say, my lord. Dunois defeated me at Montargis.

CAUCHON (*bowing*). I take that as evidence that the Seigneur Dunois is a very able commander indeed.

WARWICK. Your lordship is the flower of courtesy. I admit, on our side, that Talbot is a mere fighting animal, and that it probably served him right to be taken at Patay.

THE CHAPLAIN (*chafing*). My lord: at Orleans this woman had her throat pierced by an English arrow, and was seen to cry like a child from the pain of it. It was a death wound; yet she fought all day; and when our men had repulsed all her attacks like true Englishmen, she walked alone to the wall of our fort with a white banner in her hand; and our men were paralyzed, and could neither shoot nor strike whilst the French fell on them and drove them on to the bridge, which immediately burst into flames and crumbled under them, letting them down into the river, where they were drowned in heaps. Was this your bastard's generalship? or were those flames the flames of hell, conjured up by witchcraft?

WARWICK. You will forgive Messire John's vehemence, my lord; but he has put our case. Dunois is a great captain, we admit; but why could he do nothing until the witch came?

CAUCHON. I do not say that there were no supernatural powers on her side. But the names on that white banner were not the names of Satan and Beelzebub, but the blessed names of our Lord and His holy mother. And your commander who was drowned — Clahz-da I think you call him —

WARWICK. Glasdale. Sir William Glasdale.

CAUCHON. Glass-dell, thank you. He was no saint; and many of our people think that he was drowned for his blasphemies against The Maid.

WARWICK (*beginning to look very dubious*). Well, what are we to infer from all this, my lord? Has The Maid converted you?

CAUCHON. If she had, my lord, I should have known better than to have trusted myself here within your grasp.

WARWICK (*blandly deprecating*). Oh! oh! My lord!

CAUCHON. If the devil is making use of this girl — and I believe he is —

WARWICK (*reassured*). Ah! You hear, Messire John? I knew your lordship would not fail us. Pardon my interruption. Proceed.

CAUCHON. If it be so, the devil has longer views than you give him credit for.

WARWICK. Indeed? In what way? Listen to this, Messire John.

CAUCHON. If the devil wanted to damn a country girl, do you think so easy a task would cost him the winning of half a dozen battles? No, my lord: any trumpery imp could do that much if the girl could be damned at all. The Prince of Darkness does not condescend to such cheap drudgery. When he strikes, he strikes at the Catholic Church, whose realm is the whole spiritual world. When he damns, he damns the souls of the entire human race. Against that dreadful design The Church stands ever on guard. And it is as one of the instruments of that design that I see this girl. She is inspired, but diabolically inspired.

THE CHAPLAIN. I told you she was a witch.

CAUCHON (*fiercely*). She is not a witch. She is a heretic.

THE CHAPLAIN. What difference does that make?

CAUCHON. You, a priest, ask me that! You English are strangely blunt in the mind. All these things that you call witchcraft are capable of a natural explanation. The woman's miracles would not impose on a rabbit; she does not claim them as miracles herself. What do her victories prove but that she has a better head on her shoulders than your swearing Glass-dells and mad bull Talbots, and that the courage of faith, even though it be a false faith, will always outstay the courage of wrath?

THE CHAPLAIN (*hardly able to believe his ears*). Does your lordship compare Sir John Talbot, three times Governor of Ireland, to a mad bull?!!!

WARWICK. It would not be seemly for you to do so, Messire John, as you are still six removes from a barony. But as I am an earl, and Talbot is only a knight, I may make bold to accept the comparison. (*To the* BISHOP.) My lord: I wipe the slate as far as the witchcraft goes. None the less, we must burn the woman.

CAUCHON. I cannot burn her. The Church cannot take life. And my first duty is to seek this girl's salvation.

WARWICK. No doubt. But you do burn people occasionally.

CAUCHON. No. When The Church cuts off an obstinate heretic as a dead branch from the tree of life, the heretic is handed over to the secular arm. The Church has no part in what the secular arm may see fit to do.

WARWICK. Precisely. And I shall be the secular arm in this case. Well, my lord, hand over your dead branch; and I will see that the fire is ready for it. If you will answer for The Church's part, I will answer for the secular part.

CAUCHON (*with smouldering anger*). I can answer for nothing. You great lords are too prone to treat The Church as a mere political convenience.

WARWICK (*smiling and propitiatory*). Not in England, I assure you.

CAUCHON. In England more than anywhere else. No, my lord: the soul of this village girl is of equal value with yours or your king's before the throne of God; and my first duty is to save it. I will not suffer your lordship to smile at me as if I were repeating a meaningless form of words, and it were well understood between us that I should betray the girl to you. I am no mere political bishop: my faith is to me what your honor is to you; and if there be a loophole through which this baptized child of God can creep to her salvation, I shall guide her to it.

THE CHAPLAIN (*rising in a fury*). You are a traitor.

CAUCHON (*springing up*). You lie, priest. (*Trembling with rage.*) If you dare do what this woman has done — set your country above the holy Catholic Church — you shall go to the fire with her.

THE CHAPLAIN. My lord: I — I went too far. I — (*he sits down with a submissive gesture*).

WARWICK (*who has risen apprehensively*). My lord: I apologize to you for the word used by Messire John de Stogumber. It does not mean in England what it does in France. In your language traitor means betrayer: one who is perfidious, treacherous, unfaithful, disloyal. In our country it means simply one who is not wholly devoted to our English interests.

CAUCHON. I am sorry: I did not understand. (*He subsides into his chair with dignity.*)

WARWICK (*resuming his seat, much relieved*). I must apologize on my own account if I have seemed to take the burning of this poor girl too lightly. When one has seen whole countrysides burnt over and over again as mere items in military routine, one has to grow a very thick skin. Otherwise one might go mad: at all events, I should. May I venture to assume that your lordship also, having to see so many heretics burned from time to time, is compelled to take — shall I say a professional view of what would otherwise be a very horrible incident?

CAUCHON. Yes: it is a painful duty: even, as you say, a horrible one. But in comparison with the horror of heresy it is less than nothing. I am not thinking of this girl's body, which will suffer for a few moments only, and which must in any event die in some more or less painful manner, but of her soul, which may suffer to all eternity.

WARWICK. Just so; and God grant that her soul may be saved! But the practical problem would seem to be how to save her soul without saving her body. For we must face it, my lord: if this cult of The Maid goes on, our cause is lost.

THE CHAPLAIN (*his voice broken like that of a man who has been crying*). May I speak, my lord?

WARWICK. Really, Messire John, I had rather you did not, unless you can keep your temper.

THE CHAPLAIN. It is only this. I speak under correction; but The Maid is full of deceit: she pretends to be devout. Her prayers and confessions are endless. How can she be accused of heresy when she neglects no observance of a faithful daughter of The Church?

CAUCHON (*flaming up*). A faithful daughter of The Church! The Pope himself at his proudest dare not presume as this woman presumes. She acts as if she herself were The Church. She brings the message of God to Charles; and The Church must stand aside. She will crown him in the cathedral of Rheims: she, not The Church! She sends letters to the King of England giving him God's command through her to return to his island on pain of God's vengeance, which she will execute. Let me tell you that the writing of such letters was the practice of the accursed Mahomet, the anti-Christ. Has she ever in all her utterances said one word of The Church? Never. It is always God and herself.

WARWICK. What can you expect? A beggar on horseback! Her head is turned.

CAUCHON. Who has turned it? The devil. And for a mighty purpose. He is spreading this heresy everywhere. The man Hus, burnt only thirteen years ago at Constance, infected all Bohemia with it. A man named WcLeef, himself an anointed priest, spread the pestilence in England; and to your shame you let him die in his bed. We have such people here in France too: I know the breed. It is cancerous: if it be not cut out, stamped out, burnt out, it will not stop until it has brought the whole body of human society into sin and corruption, into waste and ruin. By it an Arab camel driver drove Christ and His Church out of Jerusalem, and ravaged his way west like a wild beast until at last there stood only the Pyrenees and God's mercy between France and damnation. Yet what did the camel driver do at the beginning more than this shepherd girl is doing? He had his voices from the angel Gabriel: she has her voices from St Catherine and St Margaret and the Blessed Michael. He declared himself the messenger of God, and wrote in God's name to the kings of the earth. Her letters to them are going forth daily. It is not the Mother of God now to whom we must look for intercession, but to Joan the Maid. What will the world be like when The Church's accumulated wisdom and knowledge and experience, its councils of learned, venerable pious men, are thrust into the kennel by every ignorant laborer or dairymaid whom the devil can puff up with the monstrous self-conceit of being directly inspired from heaven? It will be a world of blood, of fury, of devastation, of each man striving for his own hand: in the end of a world wrecked back into barbarism. For now you have only Mahomet and his dupes, and the Maid and her dupes; but what will it be when every girl thinks herself a Joan and every man a Mahomet? I shudder to the very marrow of my bones when I think of it. I have fought it all my life; and I will fight it to the end. Let all this woman's sins be forgiven her except only this sin; for it is the sin against the Holy Ghost; and if she does not recant in the dust before the world, and submit herself to the last inch of her soul to her Church, to the fire she shall go if she once falls into my hand.

WARWICK (unimpressed). You feel strongly about it, naturally.

CAUCHON. Do not you?

WARWICK. I am a soldier, not a churchman. As a pilgrim I saw something of the Mahometans. They were not so illbred as I had been led to believe. In some respects their conduct compared favorably with ours.

CAUCHON (displeased). I have noticed this before. Men go to the East to convert the infidels. And the infidels pervert them. The Crusader comes back more than half a Saracen. Not to mention that all Englishmen are born heretics.

THE CHAPLAIN. Englishmen heretics!!! (Appealing to WARWICK.) My lord: must we endure this? His lordship is beside himself. How can what an Englishman believes be heresy? It is a contradiction in terms.

CAUCHON. I absolve you, Messire de Stogumber, on the ground of invincible ignorance. The thick air of your country does not breed theologians.

WARWICK. You would not say so if you heard us quarreling about religion, my lord! I am sorry you think I must be either a heretic or a blockhead because, as a travelled man, I know that the followers of Mahomet profess great respect for our Lord, and are more ready to forgive St Peter for being a fisherman than your lordship is to forgive Mahomet for being a camel driver. But at least we can proceed in this matter without bigotry.

CAUCHON. When men call the zeal of the Christian Church bigotry I know what to think.

WARWICK. They are only east and west views of the same thing.

CAUCHON (bitterly ironical). Only east and west! Only!

WARWICK. Oh, my Lord Bishop, I am not gainsaying you. You will carry The Church with you; but you have to carry the nobles also. To my mind there is a stronger case against The Maid than the one you have so forcibly put. Frankly, I am not afraid of this girl becoming another Mahomet, and superseding The Church by a great heresy. I think you exaggerate that risk. But have you noticed that in these letters of hers, she proposes to all the kings of Europe, as she has already pressed on Charles, a transaction which would wreck the whole social structure of Christendom?

CAUCHON.   Wreck The Church. I tell you so.

WARWICK (*whose patience is wearing out*).   My lord: pray get The Church out of your head for a moment; and remember that there are temporal institutions in the world as well as spiritual ones. I and my peers represent the feudal aristocracy as you represent The Church. We are the temporal power. Well, do you not see how this girl's idea strikes at us?

CAUCHON.   How does her idea strike at you, except as it strikes at all of us, through The Church?

WARWICK.   Her idea is that the kings should give their realms to God, and then reign as God's bailiffs.

CAUCHON (*not interested*).   Quite sound theologically, my lord. But the king will hardly care, provided he reign. It is an abstract idea: a mere form of words.

WARWICK.   By no means. It is a cunning device to supersede the aristocracy, and make the king sole and absolute autocrat. Instead of the king being merely the first among his peers, he becomes their master. That we cannot suffer: we call no man master. Nominally we hold our lands and dignities from the king, because there must be a keystone to the arch of human society; but we hold our lands in our own hands, and defend them with our own swords and those of our own tenants. Now by The Maid's doctrine the king will take our lands — our lands! — and make them a present to God; and God will then vest them wholly in the king.

CAUCHON.   Need you fear that? You are the makers of kings after all. York or Lancaster in England, Lancaster or Valois in France: they reign according to your pleasure.

WARWICK.   Yes; but only as long as the people follow their feudal lords, and know the king only as a travelling show, owning nothing but the highway that belongs to everybody. If the people's thoughts and hearts were turned to the king, and their lords became only the king's servants in their eyes, the king could break us across his knee one by one; and then what should we be but liveried courtiers in his halls?

CAUCHON.   Still you need not fear, my lord. Some men are born kings; and some are born statesmen. The two are seldom the same. Where would the king find counsellors to plan and carry out such a policy for him?

WARWICK (*with a not too friendly smile*).   Perhaps in The Church, my lord.

(CAUCHON, *with an equally sour smile, shrugs his shoulders, and does not contradict him.*)

Strike down the barons; and the cardinals will have it all their own way.

CAUCHON (*conciliatory, dropping his polemical tone*).   My lord: we shall not defeat The Maid if we strive against one another. I know well that there is a Will to Power in the world. I know that while it lasts there will be a struggle between the Emperor and the Pope, between the dukes and the political cardinals, between the barons and the kings. The devil divides us and governs. I see you are no friend to The Church: you are an earl first and last, as I am a churchman first and last. But can we not sink our differences in the face of a common enemy? I see now that what is in your mind is not that this girl has never once mentioned The Church, and thinks only of God and herself, but that she has never once mentioned the peerage, and thinks only of the king and herself.

WARWICK. Quite so. These two ideas of hers are the same idea at bottom. It goes deep, my lord. It is the protest of the individual soul against the interference of priest or peer between the private man and his God. I should call it Protestantism if I had to find a name for it.

CAUCHON (*looking hard at him*). You understand it wonderfully well, my lord. Scratch an Englishman, and find a Protestant.

WARWICK (*playing the pink of courtesy*). I think you are not entirely void of sympathy with The Maid's secular heresy, my lord. I leave you to find a name for it.

CAUCHON. You mistake me, my lord. I have no sympathy with her political presumptions. But as a priest I have gained a knowledge of the minds of the common people; and there you will find yet another most dangerous idea. I can express it only by such phrases as France for the French, England for the English, Italy for the Italians, Spain for the Spanish, and so forth. It is sometimes so narrow and bitter in country folk that it surprises me that this country girl can rise above the idea of her village for its villagers. But she can. She does. When she threatens to drive the English from the soil of France she is undoubtedly thinking of the whole extent of country in which French is spoken. To her the French-speaking people are what the Holy Scriptures describe as a nation. Call this side of her heresy Nationalism if you will: I can find you no better name for it. I can only tell you that it is essentially anti-Catholic and anti-Christian; for the Catholic Church knows only one realm, and that is the realm of Christ's kingdom. Divide that kingdom into nations, and you dethrone Christ. Dethrone Christ, and who will stand between our throats and the sword? The world will perish in a welter of war.

WARWICK. Well, if you will burn the Protestant, I will burn the Nationalist, though perhaps I shall not carry Messire John with me there. England for the English will appeal to him.

THE CHAPLAIN. Certainly England for the English goes without saying: it is the simple law of nature. But this woman denies to England her legitimate conquests, given her by God because of her peculiar fitness to rule over less civilized races for their own good. I do not understand what your lordships mean by Protestant and Nationalist: you are too learned and subtle for a poor clerk like myself. But I know as a matter of plain commonsense that the woman is a rebel; and that is enough for me. She rebels against Nature by wearing man's clothes, and fighting. She rebels against The Church by usurping the divine authority of the Pope. She rebels against God by her damnable league with Satan and his evil spirits against our army. And all these rebellions are only excuses for her great rebellion against England. That is not to be endured. Let her perish. Let her burn. Let her not infect the whole flock. It is expedient that one woman die for the people.

WARWICK (*rising*). My lord: we seem to be agreed.

CAUCHON (*rising also, but in protest*). I will not imperil my soul. I will uphold the justice of The Church. I will strive to the utmost for this woman's salvation.

WARWICK. I am sorry for the poor girl. I hate these severities. I will spare her if I can.

THE CHAPLAIN (*implacably*). I would burn her with my own hands.

CAUCHON (*blessing him*). Sancta simplicitas!

Scene 5

(*The ambulatory in the cathedral of Rheims, near the door of the vestry. A pillar bears one of the stations of the cross. The organ is playing the people out of the nave after the coronation.* JOAN *is kneeling in prayer before the station. She is beautifully dressed, but still in male attire. The organ ceases as* DUNOIS, *also splendidly arrayed, comes into the ambulatory from the vestry.*)

DUNOIS. Come, Joan! you have had enough praying. After that fit of crying you will catch a chill if you stay here any longer. It is all over: the cathedral is empty; and the streets are full. They are calling for The Maid. We have told them you are staying here alone to pray; but they want to see you again.

JOAN. No: let the king have all the glory.

DUNOIS. He only spoils the show, poor devil. No, Joan: you have crowned him; and you must go through with it.

(JOAN *shakes her head reluctantly.*)

(*Raising her.*) Come come! it will be over in a couple of hours. It's better than the bridge at Orleans: eh?

JOAN. Oh, dear Dunois, how I wish it were the bridge at Orleans again! We lived at that bridge.

DUNOIS. Yes, faith, and died too: some of us.

JOAN. Isnt it strange, Jack? I am such a coward: I am frightened beyond words before a battle; but it is so dull afterwards when there is no danger: oh, so dull! dull! dull!

DUNOIS. You must learn to be abstemious in war, just as you are in your food and drink, my little saint.

JOAN. Dear Jack: I think you like me as a soldier likes his comrade.

DUNOIS. You need it, poor innocent child of God. You have not many friends at court.

JOAN. Why do all these courtiers and knights and churchmen hate me? What have I done to them? I have asked nothing for myself except that my village shall not be taxed; for we cannot afford war taxes. I have brought them luck and victory: I have set them right when they were doing all sorts of stupid things: I have crowned Charles and made him a real king; and all the honors he is handing out have gone to them. Then why do they not love me?

DUNOIS (*rallying her*). Sim-ple-ton! Do you expect stupid people to love you for shewing them up? Do blundering old military dug-outs love the successful young captains who supersede them? Do ambitious politicians love the climbers who take the front seats from them? Do archbishops enjoy being played off their own altars, even by saints? Why, I should be jealous of you myself if I were ambitious enough.

JOAN. You are the pick of the basket here, Jack: the only friend I have among all these nobles. I'll wager your mother was from the country. I will go back to the farm when I have taken Paris.

DUNOIS. I am not so sure that they will let you take Paris.

JOAN (*startled*). What!

DUNOIS. I should have taken it myself before this if they had all been sound about it. Some of them would rather Paris took you, I think. So take care.

JOAN. Jack: the world is too wicked for me. If the goddams and the Burgundians do not make an end of me, the French will. Only for my voices I should lose all heart. That is why I had to steal away to pray here alone after the coronation. I'll tell you something, Jack. It is in the bells I hear my voices. Not to-day, when they all rang: that was nothing but jangling. But here in this corner, where the bells come down from heaven, and the echoes linger, or in the fields, where they come from a distance through the quiet of the countryside, my voices are in them. (*The cathedral clock chimes the quarter.*) Hark! (*She becomes rapt.*) Do you hear? "Dear-child-of-God": just what you said. At the half-hour they will say "Be-brave-go-on." At the three-quarters they will say "I-am-thy-Help." But it is at the hour, when the great bell goes after "God-will-save-France": it is then that St Margaret and St Catherine and sometimes even the blessed Michael will say things that I cannot tell beforehand. Then, oh then —

DUNOIS (*interrupting her kindly but not sympathetically*). Then, Joan, we shall hear whatever we fancy in the booming of the bell. You make me uneasy when you talk about your voices: I should think you were a bit cracked if I hadnt noticed that you give me very sensible reasons for what you do, though I hear you telling others you are only obeying Madame Saint Catherine.

JOAN (*crossly*). Well, I have to find reasons for you, because you do not believe in my voices. But the voices come first; and I find the reasons after: whatever you may choose to believe.

DUNOIS.   Are you angry, Joan?

JOAN.   Yes. (*Smiling.*) No: not with you. I wish you were one of the village babies.

DUNOIS.   Why?

JOAN.   I could nurse you for awhile.

DUNOIS.   You are a bit of a woman after all.

JOAN.   No: not a bit: I am a soldier and nothing else. Soldiers always nurse children when they get a chance.

DUNOIS.   That is true. (*He laughs.*)

(KING CHARLES, *with* BLUEBEARD *on his left and* LA HIRE *on his right, comes from the vestry, where he has been disrobing.* JOAN *shrinks away behind the pillar.* DUNOIS *is left between* CHARLES *and* LA HIRE.)

Well, your Majesty is an anointed king at last. How do you like it?

CHARLES.   I would not go through it again to be emperor of the sun and moon. The weight of those robes! I thought I should have dropped when they loaded that crown on to me. And the famous holy oil they talked so much about was rancid: phew! The Archbishop must be nearly dead: his robes must have weighed a ton: they are stripping him still in the vestry.

DUNOIS (*drily*).   Your majesty should wear armor oftener. That would accustom you to heavy dressing.

CHARLES.   Yes: the old jibe! Well, I am not going to wear armor: fighting is not my job. Where is The Maid?

JOAN (*coming forward between* CHARLES *and* BLUEBEARD, *and falling on her knee*).   Sire: I have made you king: my work is done. I am going back to my father's farm.

CHARLES (*surprised, but relieved*).   Oh, are you? Well, that will be very nice.

(JOAN *rises, deeply discouraged.*)

(*Continuing heedlessly.*) A healthy life, you know.

DUNOIS.   But a dull one.

BLUEBEARD.   You will find the petticoats tripping you up after leaving them off for so long.

LA HIRE.   You will miss the fighting. It's a bad habit, but a grand one, and the hardest of all to break yourself of.

CHARLES (*anxiously*).   Still, we dont want you to stay if you would really rather go home.

JOAN (*bitterly*).   I know well that none of you will be sorry to see me go.

(*She turns her shoulder to* CHARLES *and walks past him to the more congenial neighborhood of* DUNOIS *and* LA HIRE.)

LA HIRE. Well, I shall be able to swear when I want to. But I shall miss you at times.

JOAN. La Hire: in spite of all your sins and swears we shall meet in heaven; for I love you as I love Pitou, my old sheep dog. Pitou could kill a wolf. You will kill the English wolves until they go back to their country and become good dogs of God, will you not?

LA HIRE. You and I together: yes.

JOAN. No: I shall last only a year from the beginning.

ALL THE OTHERS. What!

JOAN. I know it somehow.

DUNOIS. Nonsense!

JOAN. Jack: do you think you will be able to drive them out?

DUNOIS (with quiet conviction). Yes: I shall drive them out. They beat us because we thought battles were tournaments and ransom markets. We played the fool while the goddams took war seriously. But I have learnt my lesson, and taken their measure. They have no roots here. I have beaten them before; and I shall beat them again.

JOAN. You will not be cruel to them, Jack?

DUNOIS. The goddams will not yield to tender handling. We did not begin it.

JOAN (suddenly). Jack: before I go home, let us take Paris.

CHARLES (terrified). Oh no no. We shall lose everything we have gained. Oh dont let us have any more fighting. We can make a very good treaty with the Duke of Burgundy.

JOAN. Treaty! (She stamps with impatience.)

CHARLES. Well, why not, now that I am crowned and anointed? Oh, that oil!

(The ARCHBISHOP comes from the vestry, and joins the group between CHARLES and BLUEBEARD.)

Archbishop: The Maid wants to start fighting again.

THE ARCHBISHOP. Have we ceased fighting, then? Are we at peace?

CHARLES. No: I suppose not; but let us be content with what we have done. Let us make a treaty. Our luck is too good to last; and now is our chance to stop before it turns.

JOAN. Luck! God has fought for us; and you call it luck! And you would stop while there are still Englishmen on this holy earth of dear France!

THE ARCHBISHOP (sternly). Maid: the king addressed himself to me, not to you. You forget yourself. You very often forget yourself.

JOAN (unabashed, and rather roughly). Then speak, you; and tell him that it is not God's will that he should take his hand from the plough.

THE ARCHBISHOP. If I am not so glib with the name of God as you are, it is because I interpret His will with the authority of The Church and of my sacred office. When you first came you respected it, and would not have dared to speak as you are now speaking. You came clothed with the virtue of humility; and because God blessed your enterprises accordingly, you have stained yourself with the sin of pride. The old Greek tragedy is rising among us. It is the chastisement of hubris.

CHARLES. Yes: she thinks she knows better than everyone else.

JOAN (*distressed, but naïvely incapable of seeing the effect she is producing*). But I do know better than any of you seem to. And I am not proud: I never speak unless I know I am right.

BLUEBEARD ⎱ (*exclaiming together*). ⎰ Ha ha!
CHARLES ⎰   ⎱ Just so.

THE ARCHBISHOP. How do you know you are right?

JOAN. I always know. My voices —

CHARLES. Oh, your voices, your voices. Why dont the voices come to me? I am king, not you.

JOAN. They do come to you; but you do not hear them. You have not sat in the field in the evening listening for them. When the angelus rings you cross yourself and have done with it; but if you prayed from your heart, and listened to the thrilling of the bells in the air after they stop ringing, you would hear the voices as well as I do. (*Turning brusquely from him.*) But what voices do you need to tell you what the blacksmith can tell you: that you must strike while the iron is hot? I tell you we must make a dash at Compiègne and relieve it as we relieved Orleans. Then Paris will open its gates; or if not, we will break through them. What is your crown worth without your capital?

LA HIRE. That is what I say too. We shall go through them like a red hot shot through a pound of butter. What do you say, Bastard?

DUNOIS. If our cannon balls were all as hot as your head, and we had enough of them, we should conquer the earth, no doubt. Pluck and impetuosity are good servants in war, but bad masters: they have delivered us into the hands of the English every time we have trusted to them. We never know when we are beaten: that is our great fault.

JOAN. You never know when you are victorious: that is a worse fault. I shall have to make you carry looking-glasses in battle to convince you that the English have not cut off all your noses. You would have been besieged in Orleans still, you and your councils of war, if I had not made you attack. You should always attack; and if you only hold on long enough the enemy will stop first. You dont know how to begin a battle; and you dont know how to use your cannons. And I do. (*She squats down on the flags with crossed ankles, pouting.*)

DUNOIS. I know what you think of us, General Joan.

JOAN. Never mind that, Jack. Tell them what you think of me.

DUNOIS. I think that God was on your side; for I have not forgotten how the wind changed, and how our hearts changed when you came; and by my faith I shall never deny that it was in your sign that we conquered. But I tell you as a soldier that God is no man's daily drudge, and no maid's either. If you are worthy of it he will sometimes snatch you out of the jaws of death and set you on your feet again; but that is all: once on your feet you must fight with all your might and all your craft. For he

has to be fair to your enemy too: dont forget that. Well, he set us on
our feet through you at Orleans; and the glory of it has carried us through
a few good battles here to the coronation. But if we presume on it further,
and trust to God to do the work we should do ourselves, we shall be
defeated; and serve us right!

JOAN.   But —

DUNOIS.   Sh! I have not finished. Do not think, any of you, that these
victories of ours were won without generalship. King Charles: you have
said no word in your proclamations of my part in this campaign; and I
make no complaint of that; for the people will run after The Maid and
her miracles and not after the Bastard's hard work finding troops for her
and feeding them. But I know exactly how much God did for us through
The Maid, and how much He left me to do by my own wits; and I tell
you that your little hour of miracles is over, and that from this time on he
who plays the war game best will win — if the luck is on his side.

JOAN.   Ah! if, if, if, if! If ifs and ands were pots and pans there'd be no
need of tinkers. (Rising impetuously.) I tell you, Bastard, your art of war
is no use, because your knights are no good for real fighting. War is only
a game to them, like tennis and all their other games: they make rules as
to what is fair and what is not fair, and heap armor on themselves and on
their poor horses to keep out the arrows; and when they fall they cant
get up, and have to wait for their squires to come and lift them to arrange
about the ransom with the man that has poked them off their horse. Cant
you see that all the like of that is gone by and done with? What use is
armor against gunpowder? And if it was, do you think men that are
fighting for France and for God will stop to bargain about ransoms, as
half your knights live by doing? No: they will fight to win; and they will
give up their lives out of their own hand into the hand of God when they
go into battle, as I do. Common folks understand this. They cannot
afford armor and cannot pay ransoms; but they follow me half naked into
the moat and up the ladder and over the wall. With them it is my life
or thine, and God defend the right! You may shake your head, Jack; and
Bluebeard may twirl his billygoat's beard and cock his nose at me; but
remember the day your knights and captains refused to follow me to
attack the English at Orleans! You locked the gates to keep me in; and it
was the townsfolk and the common people that followed me, and forced
the gate, and shewed you the way to fight in earnest.

BLUEBEARD (offended).   Not content with being Pope Joan, you must
be Caesar and Alexander as well.

THE ARCHBISHOP.   Pride will have a fall, Joan.

JOAN.   Oh, never mind whether it is pride or not: is it true? is it commonsense?

LA HIRE.   It is true. Half of us are afraid of having our handsome
noses broken; and the other half are out for paying off their mortgages.
Let her have her way, Dunois: she does not know everything; but she has
got hold of the right end of the stick. Fighting is not what it was; and
those who know least about it often make the best job of it.

DUNOIS. I know all that. I do not fight in the old way: I have learnt the lesson of Agincourt, of Poitiers and Crecy. I know how many lives any move of mine will cost; and if the move is worth the cost I make it and pay the cost. But Joan never counts the cost at all: she goes ahead and trusts to God: she thinks she has God in her pocket. Up to now she has had the numbers on her side; and she has won. But I know Joan; and I see that some day she will go ahead when she has only ten men to do the work of a hundred. And then she will find that God is on the side of the big battalions. She will be taken by the enemy. And the lucky man that makes the capture will receive sixteen thousand pounds from the Earl of Ouareek.

JOAN (flattered). Sixteen thousand pounds! Eh, laddie, have they offered that for me? There cannot be so much money in the world.

DUNOIS. There is, in England. And now tell me, all of you, which of you will lift a finger to save Joan once the English have got her? I speak first, for the army. The day after she has been dragged from her horse by a goddam or a Burgundian, and he is not struck dead: the day after she is locked in a dungeon, and the bars and bolts do not fly open at the touch of St Peter's angel: the day when the enemy finds out that she is as vulnerable as I am and not a bit more invincible, she will not be worth the life of a single soldier to us; and I will not risk that life, much as I cherish her as a companion-in-arms.

JOAN. I dont blame you, Jack: you are right. I am not worth one soldier's life if God lets me be beaten; but France may think me worth my ransom after what God has done for her through me.

CHARLES. I tell you I have no money; and this coronation, which is all your fault, has cost me the last farthing I can borrow.

JOAN. The Church is richer than you. I put my trust in The Church.

THE ARCHBISHOP. Woman: they will drag you through the streets, and burn you as a witch.

JOAN (running to him). Oh, my lord, do not say that. It is impossible. I a witch!

THE ARCHBISHOP. Peter Cauchon knows his business. The University of Paris has burnt a woman for saying that what you have done was well done, and according to God.

JOAN (bewildered). But why? What sense is there in it? What I have done is according to God. They could not burn a woman for speaking the truth.

THE ARCHBISHOP. They did.

JOAN. But you know that she was speaking the truth. You would not let them burn me.

THE ARCHBISHOP. How could I prevent them?

JOAN. You would speak in the name of The Church. You are a great prince of The Church. I would go anywhere with your blessing to protect me.

THE ARCHBISHOP. I have no blessing for you while you are proud and disobedient.

JOAN. Oh, why will you go on saying things like that? I am not proud and disobedient. I am a poor girl, and so ignorant that I do not know A from B. How could I be proud? And how can you say that I am disobedient when I always obey my voices, because they come from God.

THE ARCHBISHOP. The voice of God on earth is the voice of the Church Militant; and all the voices that come to you are the echoes of your own wilfulness.

JOAN. It is not true.

THE ARCHBISHOP (flushing angrily). You tell the Archbishop in his cathedral that he lies; and yet you say you are not proud and disobedient.

JOAN. I never said you lied. It was you that as good as said my voices lied. When have they ever lied? If you will not believe in them: even if they are only the echoes of my own commonsense, are they not always right? and are not your earthly counsels always wrong?

THE ARCHBISHOP (indignantly). It is waste of time admonishing you.

CHARLES. It always comes back to the same thing. She is right; and everyone else is wrong.

THE ARCHBISHOP. Take this as your last warning. If you perish through setting your private judgment above the instructions of your spiritual directors, The Church disowns you, and leaves you to whatever fate your presumption may bring upon you. The Bastard has told you that if you persist in setting up your military conceit above the counsels of your commanders —

DUNOIS (interposing). To put it quite exactly, if you attempt to relieve the garrison in Compiègne without the same superiority in numbers you had at Orleans —

THE ARCHBISHOP. The army will disown you, and will not rescue you. And His Majesty the King has told you that the throne has not the means of ransoming you.

CHARLES. Not a penny.

THE ARCHBISHOP. You stand alone: absolutely alone, trusting to your own conceit, your own ignorance, your own headstrong presumption, your own impiety in hiding all these sins under the cloak of a trust in God. When you pass through these doors into the sunlight, the crowd will cheer you. They will bring you their little children and their invalids to heal: they will kiss your hands and feet, and do what they can, poor simple souls, to turn your head, and madden you with the self-confidence that is leading you to your destruction. But you will be none the less alone: they cannot save you. We and we only can stand between you and the stake at which our enemies have burnt that wretched woman in Paris.

JOAN (her eyes skyward). I have better friends and better counsel than yours.

THE ARCHBISHOP. I see that I am speaking in vain to a hardened heart. You reject our protection, and are determined to turn us all against you. In future, then, fend for yourself; and if you fail, God have mercy on your soul.

DUNOIS.   That is the truth, Joan. Heed it.

JOAN.   Where would you all have been now if I had heeded that sort of truth? There is no help, no counsel, in any of you. Yes: I am alone on earth: I have always been alone. My father told my brothers to drown me if I would not stay to mind his sheep while France was bleeding to death: France might perish if only our lambs were safe. I thought France would have friends at the court of the king of France; and I find only wolves fighting for pieces of her poor torn body. I thought God would have friends everywhere, because He is the friend of everyone; and in my innocence I believed that you who now cast me out would be like strong towers to keep harm from me. But I am wiser now; and nobody is any the worse for being wiser. Do not think you can frighten me by telling me that I am alone. France is alone; and God is alone; and what is my loneliness before the loneliness of my country and my God? I see now that the loneliness of God is His strength: what would He be if He listened to your jealous little counsels? Well, my loneliness shall be my strength too: it is better to be alone with God: His friendship will not fail me, nor His counsel, nor His love. In His strength I will dare, and dare, and dare, until I die. I will go out now to the common people, and let the love in their eyes comfort me for the hate in yours. You will all be glad to see me burnt; but if I go through the fire I shall go through it to their hearts for ever and ever. And so, God be with me!

(*She goes from them. They stare after her in glum silence for a moment. Then* GILLES DE RAIS *twirls his beard.*)

BLUEBEARD.   You know, the woman is quite impossible. I dont dislike her, really; but what are you to do with such a character?

DUNOIS.   As God is my judge, if she fell into the Loire I would jump in in full armor to fish her out. But if she plays the fool at Compiègne, and gets caught, I must leave her to her doom.

LA HIRE.   Then you had better chain me up; for I could follow her to hell when the spirit rises in her like that.

THE ARCHBISHOP.   She disturbs my judgment too: there is a dangerous power in her outbursts. But the pit is open at her feet; and for good or evil we cannot turn her from it.

CHARLES.   If only she would keep quiet, or go home!

(*They follow her dispiritedly.*)

Scene 6

(*Rouen, 30th May 1431. A great stone hall in the castle, arranged for a trial-at-law, but not a trial-by-jury, the court being the Bishop's court with the Inquisition participating: hence there are two raised chairs side by side for the Bishop and the Inquisitor as judges. Rows of chairs radiating from them at an obtuse angle are for the canons, the doctors of law* and theology, and the Dominican monks, who act as assessors. In the angle is a table for the scribes, with stools. There is also a heavy rough wooden stool for the prisoner. All these are at the inner end of the hall. The further end is open to the courtyard through a row of arches. The court is shielded from the weather by screens and curtains.

Looking down the great hall from the middle of the inner end, the judicial chairs and scribes' table are to the right. The prisoner's stool is to the left. There are arched doors right and left. It is a fine sunshiny May morning.

warwick comes in through the arched doorway on the judges' side, followed by his page.)

the page (pertly). I suppose your lordship is aware that we have no business here. This is an ecclesiastical court; and we are only the secular arm.

warwick. I am aware of that fact. Will it please your impudence to find the Bishop of Beauvais for me, and give him a hint that he can have a word with me here before the trial, if he wishes?

the page (going). Yes, my lord.

warwick. And mind you behave yourself. Do not address him as Pious Peter.

the page. No, my lord. I shall be kind to him, because, when The Maid is brought in, Pious Peter will have to pick a peck of pickled pepper.

(cauchon enters through the same door with a Dominican monk and a canon, the latter carrying a brief.)

The Right Reverend his lordship the Bishop of Beauvais. And two other reverend gentlemen.

warwick. Get out; and see that we are not interrupted.

the page. Right, my lord (he vanishes airily).

cauchon. I wish your lordship good-morrow.

warwick. Good-morrow to your lordship. Have I had the pleasure of meeting your friends before? I think not.

cauchon (introducing the monk, who is on his right). This, my lord, is Brother John Lemaître, of the order of St Dominic. He is acting as deputy for the Chief Inquisitor into the evil of heresy in France. Brother John: the Earl of Warwick.

warwick. Your Reverence is most welcome. We have no Inquisitor in England, unfortunately; though we miss him greatly, especially on occasions like the present.

(The inquisitor smiles patiently, and bows. He is a mild elderly gentleman, but has evident reserves of authority and firmness.)

cauchon (introducing the canon, who is on his left). This gentleman is Canon John D'Estivet, of the Chapter of Bayeux. He is acting as Promoter.

WARWICK. Promoter?

CAUCHON. Prosecutor, you would call him in civil law.

WARWICK. Ah! prosecutor. Quite, quite. I am very glad to make your acquaintance, Canon D'Estivet.

(D'ESTIVET *bows. He is on the young side of middle age, well mannered, but vulpine beneath his veneer.*)

May I ask what stage the proceedings have reached? It is now more than nine months since The Maid was captured at Compiègne by the Burgundians. It is fully four months since I bought her from the Burgundians for a very handsome sum, solely that she might be brought to justice. It is very nearly three months since I delivered her up to you, my Lord Bishop, as a person suspected of heresy. May I suggest that you are taking a rather unconscionable time to make up your minds about a very plain case? Is this trial never going to end?

THE INQUISITOR (*smiling*). It has not yet begun, my lord.

WARWICK. Not yet begun! Why, you have been at it eleven weeks!

CAUCHON. We have not been idle, my lord. We have held fifteen examinations of The Maid: six public and nine private.

THE INQUISITOR (*always patiently smiling*). You see, my lord, I have been present at only two of these examinations. They were proceedings of the Bishop's court solely, and not of the Holy Office. I have only just decided to associate myself — that is, to associate the Holy Inquisition — with the Bishop's court. I did not at first think that this was a case of heresy at all. I regarded it as a political case, and The Maid as a prisoner of war. But having now been present at two of the examinations, I must admit that this seems to be one of the gravest cases of heresy within my experience. Therefore everything is now in order; and we proceed to trial this morning. (*He moves towards the judicial chairs.*)

CAUCHON. This moment, if your lordship's convenience allows.

WARWICK (*graciously*). Well, that is good news, gentlemen. I will not attempt to conceal from you that our patience was becoming strained.

CAUCHON. So I gathered from the threats of your soldiers to drown those of our people who favor The Maid.

WARWICK. Dear me! At all events their intentions were friendly to you, my lord.

CAUCHON (*sternly*). I hope not. I am determined that the woman shall have a fair hearing. The justice of The Church is not a mockery, my lord.

THE INQUISITOR (*returning*). Never has there been a fairer examination within my experience, my lord. The Maid needs no lawyers to take her part: she will be tried by her most faithful friends, all ardently desirous to save her soul from perdition.

D'ESTIVET. Sir: I am the Promoter; and it has been my painful duty to present the case against the girl; but believe me, I would throw up my case today and hasten to her defence if I did not know that men far my superiors in learning and piety, in eloquence and persuasiveness, have been sent to reason with her, to explain to her the danger she is running, and the ease with which she may avoid it. (*Suddenly bursting into forensic eloquence, to the disgust of* CAUCHON *and the* INQUISITOR, *who have listened to him so far with patronizing approval.*) Men have dared to say that we are acting from hate; but God is our witness that they lie. Have we tortured her? No. Have we ceased to exhort her; to implore her to have pity on herself; to come to the bosom of her Church as an erring but beloved child? Have we —

CAUCHON (*interrupting drily*). Take care, Canon. All that you say is true; but if you make his lordship believe it I will not answer for your life, and hardly for my own.

WARWICK (*deprecating, but by no means denying*). Oh, my lord, you are very hard on us poor English. But we certainly do not share your pious desire to save The Maid: in fact I tell you now plainly that her death is a political necessity which I regret but cannot help. If The Church lets her go —

CAUCHON (*with fierce and menacing pride*). If The Church lets her go, woe to the man, were he the Emperor himself, who dares lay a finger on her! The Church is not subject to political necessity, my lord.

THE INQUISITOR (*interposing smoothly*). You need have no anxiety about the result, my lord. You have an invincible ally in the matter: one who is far more determined than you that she shall burn.

WARWICK. And who is this very convenient partisan, may I ask?

THE INQUISITOR. The Maid herself. Unless you put a gag in her mouth you cannot prevent her from convicting herself ten times over every time she opens it.

D'ESTIVET. That is perfectly true, my lord. My hair bristles on my head when I hear so young a creature utter such blasphemies.

WARWICK. Well, by all means do your best for her if you are quite sure it will be of no avail. (*Looking hard at* CAUCHON.) I should be sorry to have to act without the blessing of The Church.

CAUCHON (*with a mixture of cynical admiration and contempt*). And yet they say Englishmen are hypocrites! You play for your side, my lord, even at the peril of your soul. I cannot but admire such devotion; but I dare not go so far myself. I fear damnation.

WARWICK. If we feared anything we could never govern England, my lord. Shall I send your people in to you?

CAUCHON. Yes: it will be very good of your lordship to withdraw and allow the court to assemble.

(WARWICK *turns on his heel, and goes out through the courtyard.* CAUCHON *takes one of the judicial seats; and* D'ESTIVET *sits at the scribes' table, studying his brief.*)

(*Casually, as he makes himself comfortable.*) What scoundrels these English nobles are!

THE INQUISITOR (*taking the other judicial chair on* CAUCHON's *left*). All secular power makes men scoundrels. They are not trained for the work; and they have not the Apostolic Succession. Our own nobles are just as bad.

(*The* BISHOP's *assessors hurry into the hall, headed by* CHAPLAIN DE STOGUMBER *and* CANON DE COURCELLES, *a young priest of 30. The scribes sit at the table, leaving a chair vacant opposite* D'ESTIVET. *Some of the assessors take their seats: others stand chatting, waiting for the proceedings to begin formally.* DE STOGUMBER, *aggrieved and obstinate, will not take his seat: neither will the* CANON, *who stands on his right.*)

CAUCHON.   Good morning, Master de Stogumber. (*To the* INQUISITOR.) Chaplain to the Cardinal of England.

THE CHAPLAIN (*correcting him*).   Of Winchester, my lord. I have to make a protest, my lord.

CAUCHON.   You make a great many.

THE CHAPLAIN.   I am not without support, my lord. Here is Master de Courcelles, Canon of Paris, who associates himself with me in my protest.

CAUCHON.   Well, what is the matter?

THE CHAPLAIN (*sulkily*).   Speak you, Master de Courcelles, since I do not seem to enjoy his lordship's confidence. (*He sits down in dudgeon next to* CAUCHON, *on his right.*)

COURCELLES.   My lord: we have been at great pains to draw up an indictment of The Maid on sixtyfour counts. We are now told that they have been reduced, without consulting us.

THE INQUISITOR.   Master de Courcelles: I am the culprit. I am overwhelmed with admiration for the zeal displayed in your sixtyfour counts; but in accusing a heretic, as in other things, enough is enough. Also you must remember that all the members of the court are not so subtle and profound as you, and that some of your very great learning might appear to them to be very great nonsense. Therefore I have thought it well to have your sixtyfour articles cut down to twelve —

COURCELLES (*thunderstruck*).   Twelve!!!

THE INQUISITOR.   Twelve will, believe me, be quite enough for your purpose.

THE CHAPLAIN.   But some of the most important points have been reduced almost to nothing. For instance, The Maid has actually declared that the blessed saints Margaret and Catherine, and the holy Archangel Michael, spoke to her in French. That is a vital point.

THE INQUISITOR.   You think, doubtless, that they should have spoken in Latin?

CAUCHON.   No: he thinks they should have spoken in English.

THE CHAPLAIN.   Naturally, my lord.

THE INQUISITOR.   Well, as we are all here agreed, I think, that these voices of The Maid are the voices of evil spirits tempting her to her damnation, it would not be very courteous to you, Master de Stogumber, or to the King of England, to assume that English is the devil's native language. So let it pass. The matter is not wholly omitted from the twelve articles. Pray take your places, gentlemen; and let us proceed to business.

(*All who have not taken their seats, do so.*)

THE CHAPLAIN. Well, I protest. That is all.

COURCELLES. I think it hard that all our work should go for nothing. It is only another example of the diabolical influence which this woman exercises over the court. (*He takes his chair, which is on the* CHAPLAIN'S *right.*)

CAUCHON. Do you suggest that I am under diabolical influence?

COURCELLES. I suggest nothing, my lord. But it seems to me that there is a conspiracy here to hush up the fact that The Maid stole the Bishop of Senlis's horse.

CAUCHON (*keeping his temper with difficulty*). This is not a police court. Are we to waste our time on such rubbish?

COURCELLES (*rising, shocked*). My lord: do you call the Bishop's horse rubbish?

THE INQUISITOR (*blandly*). Master de Courcelles: The Maid alleges that she paid handsomely for the Bishop's horse, and that if he did not get the money the fault was not hers. As that may be true, the point is one on which The Maid may well be acquitted.

COURCELLES. Yes, if it were an ordinary horse. But the Bishop's horse! how can she be acquitted for that? (*He sits down again, bewildered and discouraged.*)

THE INQUISITOR. I submit to you, with great respect, that if we persist in trying The Maid on trumpery issues on which we may have to declare her innocent, she may escape us on the great main issue of heresy, on which she seems so far to insist on her own guilt. I will ask you, therefore, to say nothing, when The Maid is brought before us, of these stealings of horses, and dancings round fairy trees with the village children, and prayings at haunted wells, and a dozen other things which you were diligently inquiring into until my arrival. There is not a village girl in France against whom you could not prove such things: they all dance round haunted trees, and pray at magic wells. Some of them would steal the Pope's horse if they got the chance. Heresy, gentlemen, heresy is the charge we have to try. The detection and suppression of heresy is my peculiar business: I am here as an inquisitor, not as an ordinary magistrate. Stick to the heresy, gentlemen; and leave the other matters alone.

CAUCHON. I may say that we have sent to the girl's village to make inquiries about her; and there is practically nothing serious against her.

THE CHAPLAIN ⎱ (*rising and* ⎰ Nothing serious, my lord —
COURCELLES   ⎰ *clamoring* ⎱ What! The fairy tree not —
             together).

CAUCHON (*out of patience*). Be silent, gentlemen; or speak one at a time.

(COURCELLES *collapses into his chair, intimidated.*)

THE CHAPLAIN (*sulkily resuming his seat*). That is what The Maid said to us last Friday.

CAUCHON. I wish you had followed her counsel, sir. When I say nothing serious, I mean nothing that men of sufficiently large mind to conduct an inquiry like this would consider serious. I agree with my colleague the Inquisitor that it is on the count of heresy that we must proceed.

LADVENU (*a young but ascetically fine-drawn Dominican who is sitting next* COURCELLES, *on his right*). But is there any great harm in the girl's heresy? Is it not merely her simplicity? Many saints have said as much as Joan.

THE INQUISITOR (*dropping his blandness and speaking very gravely*). Brother Martin: if you had seen what I have seen of heresy, you would not think it a light thing even in its most apparently harmless and even lovable and pious origins. Heresy begins with people who are to all appearance better than their neighbours. A gentle and pious girl, or a young man who has obeyed the command of our Lord by giving all his riches to the poor, and putting on the garb of poverty, the life of austerity, and the rule of humility and charity, may be the founder of a heresy that will wreck both Church and Empire if not ruthlessly stamped out in time. The records of the holy Inquisition are full of histories we dare not give to the world, because they are beyond the belief of honest men and innocent women; yet they all began with saintly simpletons. I have seen this again and again. Mark what I say: the woman who quarrels with her clothes, and puts on the dress of a man, is like the man who throws off his fur gown and dresses like John the Baptist: they are followed, as surely as the night follows the day, by bands of wild women and men who refuse to wear any clothes at all. When maids will neither marry nor take regular vows, and men reject marriage and exalt their lusts into divine inspirations, then, as surely as the summer follows the spring, they begin with polygamy, and end by incest. Heresy at first seems innocent and even laudable; but it ends in such a monstrous horror of unnatural wickedness that the most tender-hearted among you, if you saw it at work as I have seen it, would clamor against the mercy of The Church in dealing with it. For two hundred years the Holy Office has striven with these diabolical madnesses; and it knows that they begin always by vain and ignorant persons setting up their own judgment against The Church, and taking it upon themselves to be the interpreters of God's will. You must not fall into the common error of mistaking these simpletons for liars and hypocrites. They believe honestly and sincerely that their diabolical inspiration is divine. Therefore you must be on your guard against your natural compassion. You are all, I hope, merciful men: how else could you have devoted your lives to the service of our gentle Savior? You are going to see before you a young girl, pious and chaste; for I must tell you, gentlemen, that the things said of her by our English friends are supported by no evidence, whilst there is abundant testimony that her excesses have been excesses of religion and charity and not of worldliness and wantonness. This girl is not one of those whose hard features are the sign of hard hearts, and whose brazen looks and lewd demeanor condemn them before they are accused. The devilish pride that has led her into her present peril has left no mark on her countenance. Strange as it may seem to you, it has even left no mark on her character outside those special matters in which she is proud; so that you will see a diabolical pride and a natural humility seated side by side in the selfsame soul. Therefore be on your guard. God forbid that I should tell you to harden your hearts; for her punishment if we condemn her will be so cruel that we should forfeit our own hope of divine mercy were there one grain of malice against her in our hearts. But if you hate cruelty — and if any man here does not hate it I command him on his soul's salvation to quit this holy court — I say, if you hate cruelty, remember that nothing is so cruel in its consequences as the toleration of heresy. Remember also that no court of law can be so cruel as the common people are to those whom they suspect of heresy. The heretic in the hands of the Holy Office is safe from violence, is assured of a fair trial, and cannot suffer death, even when guilty, if repentance follows sin. Innumerable lives of heretics have been saved because the Holy Office has taken them out of the hands of the people, and because the people have yielded them up, knowing that the Holy Office would deal with them. Before the Holy Inquisition existed, and even now when its officers are not within reach, the unfortunate wretch suspected of heresy, perhaps quite ignorantly and unjustly, is stoned, torn in pieces, drowned, burned in his house with all his innocent children, without a trial, unshriven, unburied save as a dog is buried; all of them deeds hateful to God and most cruel to man. Gentlemen: I am compassionate by nature as well as by my profession; and though the work I have to do may seem cruel to those who do not know how much more cruel it would be to leave it undone, I would go to the stake myself sooner than do it if I did not know its righteousness, its necessity, its essential mercy. I ask you to address yourself to their trial in that conviction. Anger is a bad counsellor: cast out anger. Pity is sometimes worse: cast out pity. But do not cast out mercy. Remember only that justice comes first. Have you anything to say, my lord, before we proceed to trial?

CAUCHON. You have spoken for me, and spoken better than I could. I do not see how any sane man could disagree with a word that has fallen from you. But this I will add. The crude heresies of which you have told us are horrible; but their horror is like that of the black death: they rage for a while and then die out, because sound and sensible men will not under any incitement be reconciled to nakedness and incest and polygamy and the like. But we are confronted today throughout Europe with a heresy that is spreading among men not weak in mind nor diseased in brain: nay, the stronger the mind, the more obstinate the heretic. It is neither discredited by fantastic extremes nor corrupted by the common lusts of the flesh; but it, too, sets up the private judgment of the single erring mortal against the considered wisdom and experience of The Church. The mighty structure of Catholic Christendom will never be shaken by naked madmen or by the sins of Moab and Ammon. But it may be betrayed from within, and brought to barbarous ruin and desolation, by this arch heresy which the English Commander calls Protestantism.

THE ASSESSORS (*whispering*). Protestantism! What was that? What does the Bishop mean? Is it a new heresy? The English Commander, he said. Did you ever hear of Protestantism? etc., etc.

CAUCHON (*continuing*). And that reminds me. What provision has the Earl of Warwick made for the defence of the secular arm should The Maid prove obdurate, and the people be moved to pity her?

THE CHAPLAIN. Have no fear on that score, my lord. The noble earl has eight hundred men-at-arms at the gates. She will not slip through our English fingers even if the whole city be on her side.

CAUCHON (*revolted*). Will you not add, God grant that she repent and purge her sin?

THE CHAPLAIN. That does not seem to me to be consistent; but of course I agree with your lordship.

CAUCHON (*giving him up with a shrug of contempt*). The court sits.

THE INQUISITOR. Let the accused be brought in.

LADVENU (*calling*). The accused. Let her be brought in.

(JOAN, *chained by the ankles, is brought in through the arched door behind the prisoner's stool by a guard of English* SOLDIERS. *With them is the* EXECUTIONER *and his* ASSISTANTS. *They lead her to the prisoner's stool, and place themselves behind it after taking off her chain. She wears a page's black suit. Her long imprisonment and the strain of the examinations which have preceded the trial have left their mark on her; but her vitality still holds: she confronts the court unabashed, without a trace of the awe which their formal solemnity seems to require for the complete success of its impressiveness.*)

THE INQUISITOR (*kindly*). Sit down, Joan. (*She sits on the prisoner's stool.*) You look very pale today. Are you not well?

JOAN. Thank you kindly: I am well enough. But the Bishop sent me some carp; and it made me ill.

CAUCHON. I am sorry. I told them to see that it was fresh.

JOAN. You meant to be good to me, I know; but it is a fish that does not agree with me. The English thought you were trying to poison me —

CAUCHON ⎱ (*together*). ⎰ What!
THE CHAPLAIN ⎰   ⎱ No, my lord.

JOAN (*continuing*). They are determined that I shall be burnt as a witch; and they sent their doctor to cure me; but he was forbidden to bleed me because the silly people believe that a witch's witchery leaves her if she is bled; so he only called me filthy names. Why do you leave me in the hands of the English? I should be in the hands of The Church. And why must I be chained by the feet to a log of wood? Are you afraid I will fly away?

D'ESTIVET (harshly). Woman: it is not for you to question the court: it is for us to question you.

COURCELLES. When you were left unchained, did you not try to escape by jumping from a tower sixty feet high? If you cannot fly like a witch, how is it that you are still alive?

JOAN. I suppose because the tower was not so high then. It has grown higher every day since you began asking me questions about it.

D'ESTIVET. Why did you jump from the tower?

JOAN. How do you know that I jumped?

D'ESTIVET. You were found lying in the moat. Why did you leave the tower?

JOAN. Why would anybody leave a prison if they could get out?

D'ESTIVET. You tried to escape?

JOAN. Of course I did; and not for the first time either. If you leave the door of the cage open the bird will fly out.

D'ESTIVET (rising). That is a confession of heresy. I call the attention of the court to it.

JOAN. Heresy, he calls it! Am I a heretic because I try to escape from prison?

D'ESTIVET. Assuredly, if you are in the hands of The Church, and you wilfully take yourself out of its hands, you are deserting The Church; and that is heresy.

JOAN. It is great nonsense. Nobody could be such a fool as to think that.

D'ESTIVET. You hear, my lord, how I am reviled in the execution of my duty by this woman. (He sits down indignantly.)

CAUCHON. I have warned you before, Joan, that you are doing yourself no good by these pert answers.

JOAN. But you will not talk sense to me. I am reasonable if you will be reasonable.

THE INQUISITOR (interposing). This is not yet in order. You forget, Master Promoter, that the proceedings have not been formally opened. The time for questions is after she has sworn on the Gospels to tell us the whole truth.

JOAN. You say this to me every time. I have said again and again that I will tell you all that concerns this trial. But I cannot tell you the whole truth: God does not allow the whole truth to be told. You do not understand it when I tell it. It is an old saying that he who tells too much truth is sure to be hanged. I am weary of this argument: we have been over it nine times already. I have sworn as much as I will swear; and I will swear no more.

COURCELLES. My lord: she should be put to the torture.

THE INQUISITOR. You hear, Joan? That is what happens to the obdurate. Think before you answer. Has she been shewn the instruments?

THE EXECUTIONER. They are ready, my lord. She has seen them.

JOAN. If you tear me limb from limb until you separate my soul from my body you will get nothing out of me beyond what I have told you. What more is there to tell that you could understand? Besides, I cannot bear to be hurt; and if you hurt me I will say anything you like to stop the pain. But I will take it all back afterwards; so what is the use of it?

LADVENU. There is much in that. We should proceed mercifully.

COURCELLES. But the torture is customary.

THE INQUISITOR. It must not be applied wantonly. If the accused will confess voluntarily, then its use cannot be justified.

COURCELLES. But this is unusual and irregular. She refuses to take the oath.

LADVENU (*disgusted*). Do you want to torture the girl for the mere pleasure of it?

COURCELLES (*bewildered*). But it is not a pleasure. It is the law. It is customary. It is always done.

THE INQUISITOR. That is not so, Master, except when the inquiries are carried on by people who do not know their legal business.

COURCELLES. But the woman is a heretic. I assure you it is always done.

CAUCHON (*decisively*). It will not be done today if it is not necessary. Let there be an end of this. I will not have it said that we proceeded on forced confessions. We have sent our best preachers and doctors to this woman to exhort and implore her to save her soul and body from the fire: we shall not now send the executioner to thrust her into it.

COURCELLES. Your lordship is merciful, of course. But it is a great responsibility to depart from the usual practice.

JOAN. Thou art a rare noodle, Master. Do what was done last time is thy rule, eh?

COURCELLES (*rising*). Thou wanton: dost thou dare call me noodle?

THE INQUISITOR. Patience, Master, patience: I fear you will soon be only too terribly avenged.

COURCELLES (*mutters*). Noodle indeed! (*He sits down, much discontented.*)

THE INQUISITOR. Meanwhile, let us not be moved by the rough side of a shepherd lass's tongue.

JOAN. Nay: I am no shepherd lass, though I have helped with the sheep like anyone else. I will do a lady's work in the house — spin or weave — against any woman in Rouen.

THE INQUISITOR. This is not a time for vanity, Joan. You stand in great peril.

JOAN. I know it: have I not been punished for my vanity? If I had not worn my cloth of gold surcoat in battle like a fool, that Burgundian soldier would never have pulled me backwards off my horse; and I should not have been here.

THE CHAPLAIN. If you are so clever at woman's work why do you not stay at home and do it?

JOAN. There are plenty of other women to do it; but there is nobody to do my work.

CAUCHON. Come! we are wasting time on trifles. Joan: I am going to put a most solemn question to you. Take care how you answer; for your life and salvation are at stake on it. Will you for all you have said and done, be it good or bad, accept the judgment of God's Church on earth? More especially as to the acts and words that are imputed to you in this trial by the Promoter here, will you submit your case to the inspired interpretation of the Church Militant?

JOAN. I am a faithful child of The Church. I will obey The Church —

CAUCHON (hopefully leaning forward). You will?

JOAN. — provided it does not command anything impossible.

(CAUCHON sinks back in his chair with a heavy sigh. The INQUISITOR purses his lips and frowns. LADVENU shakes his head pitifully.)

D'ESTIVET. She imputes to The Church the error and folly of commanding the impossible.

JOAN. If you command me to declare that all that I have done and said, and all the visions and revelations I have had, were not from God, then that is impossible: I will not declare it for anything in the world. What God made me do I will never go back on; and what He has commanded or shall command I will not fail to do in spite of any man alive. That is what I mean by impossible. And in case The Church should bid me do anything contrary to the command I have from God, I will not consent to it, no matter what it may be.

THE ASSESSORS (shocked and indignant). Oh! The Church contrary to God! What do you say now? Flat heresy. This is beyond everything, etc., etc.

D'ESTIVET (throwing down his brief). My lord: do you need anything more than this?

CAUCHON. Woman: you have said enough to burn ten heretics. Will you not be warned? Will you not understand?

THE INQUISITOR. If the Church Militant tells you that your revelations and visions are sent by the devil to tempt you to your damnation, will you not believe that The Church is wiser than you?

JOAN. I believe that God is wiser than I; and it is His commands that I will do. All the things that you call my crimes have come to me by the command of God. I say that I have done them by the order of God: it is impossible for me to say anything else. If any Churchman says the contrary I shall not mind him: I shall mind God alone, whose command I always follow.

LADVENU (*pleading with her urgently*). You do not know what you are saying, child. Do you want to kill yourself? Listen. Do you not believe that you are subject to the Church of God on earth?

JOAN. Yes. When have I ever denied it?

LADVENU. Good. That means, does it not, that you are subject to our Lord the Pope, to the cardinals, the archbishops, and the bishops for whom his lordship stands here today?

JOAN. God must be served first.

D'ESTIVET. Then your voices command you not to submit yourself to the Church Militant?

JOAN. My voices do not tell me to disobey The Church; but God must be served first.

CAUCHON. And you, and not The Church, are to be the judge?

JOAN. What other judgment can I judge by but my own?

THE ASSESSORS (*scandalized*). Oh! (*They cannot find words.*)

CAUCHON. Out of your own mouth you have condemned yourself. We have striven for your salvation to the verge of sinning ourselves: we have opened the door to you again and again; and you have shut it in our faces and in the face of God. Dare you pretend, after what you have said, that you are in a state of grace?

JOAN. If I am not, may God bring me to it: if I am, may God keep me in it!

LADVENU. That is a very good reply, my lord.

COURCELLES. Were you in a state of grace when you stole the Bishop's horse?

CAUCHON (*rising in a fury*). Oh, devil take the Bishop's horse and you too! We are here to try a case of heresy; and no sooner do we come to the root of the matter than we are thrown back by idiots who understand nothing but horses. (*Trembling with rage, he forces himself to sit down.*)

THE INQUISITOR. Gentlemen, gentlemen: in clinging to these small issues you are The Maid's best advocates. I am not surprised that his lordship has lost patience with you. What does the Promoter say? Does he press these trumpery matters?

D'ESTIVET. I am bound by my office to press everything; but when the woman confesses a heresy that must bring upon her the doom of excommunication, of what consequence is it that she has been guilty also of offences which expose her to minor penances? I share the impatience of his lordship as to these minor charges. Only, with great respect, I must emphasize the gravity of two very horrible and blasphemous crimes which she does not deny. First, she has intercourse with evil spirits, and is therefore a sorceress. Second, she wears men's clothes, which is indecent, unnatural, and abominable; and in spite of our most earnest remonstrances and entreaties, she will not change them even to receive the sacrament.

JOAN. Is the blessed St Catherine an evil spirit? Is St Margaret? Is Michael the Archangel?

COURCELLES. How do you know that the spirit which appears to you is an archangel? Does he not appear to you as a naked man?

JOAN. Do you think God cannot afford clothes for him?

(*The* ASSESSORS *cannot help smiling, especially as the joke is against* COURCELLES.)

LADVENU. Well answered, Joan.

THE INQUISITOR. It is, in effect, well answered. But no evil spirit would be so simple as to appear to a young girl in a guise that would scandalize her when he meant her to take him for a messenger from the Most High. Joan: The Church instructs you that these apparitions are demons seeking your soul's perdition. Do you accept the instruction of The Church?

JOAN. I accept the messenger of God. How could any faithful believer in The Church refuse him?

CAUCHON. Wretched woman: again I ask you, do you know what you are saying?

THE INQUISITOR. You wrestle in vain with the devil for her soul, my lord: she will not be saved. Now as to this matter of the man's dress. For the last time, will you put off that impudent attire, and dress as becomes your sex?

JOAN. I will not.

D'ESTIVET (*pouncing*). The sin of disobedience, my lord.

JOAN (*distressed*). But my voices tell me I must dress as a soldier.

LADVENU. Joan, Joan: does not that prove to you that the voices are the voices of evil spirits? Can you suggest to us one good reason why an angel of God should give you such shameless advice?

JOAN. Why, yes: what can be plainer commonsense? I was a soldier living among soldiers. I am a prisoner guarded by soldiers. If I were to dress as a woman they would think of me as a woman; and then what would become of me? If I dress as a soldier they think of me as a soldier, and I can live with them as I do at home with my brothers. That is why St Catherine tells me I must not dress as a woman until she gives me leave.

COURCELLES. When will she give you leave?

JOAN. When you take me out of the hands of the English soldiers. I have told you that I should be in the hands of The Church, and not left night and day with four soldiers of the Earl of Warwick. Do you want me to live with them in petticoats?

LADVENU. My lord: what she says is, God knows, very wrong and shocking; but there is a grain of worldly sense in it such as might impose on a simple village maiden.

JOAN. If we were as simple in the village as you are in your courts and palaces, there would soon be no wheat to make bread for you.

CAUCHON. That is the thanks you get for trying to save her, Brother Martin.

LADVENU. Joan: we are all trying to save you. His lordship is trying to save you. The Inquisitor could not be more just to you if you were his own daughter. But you are blinded by a terrible pride and self-sufficiency.

JOAN. Why do you say that? I have said nothing wrong. I cannot understand.

THE INQUISITOR. The blessed St Athanasius has laid it down in his creed that those who cannot understand are damned. It is not enough to be simple. It is not enough even to be what simple people call good. The simplicity of a darkened mind is no better than the simplicity of a beast.

JOAN. There is great wisdom in the simplicity of a beast, let me tell you; and sometimes great foolishness in the wisdom of scholars.

LADVENU. We know that, Joan: we are not so foolish as you think us. Try to resist the temptation to make pert replies to us. Do you see that man who stands behind you (*he indicates the* EXECUTIONER)?

JOAN (*turning and looking at the man*). Your torturer? But the Bishop said I was not to be tortured.

LADVENU. You are not to be tortured because you have confessed everything that is necessary to your condemnation. That man is not only the torturer: he is also the Executioner. Executioner: let The Maid hear your answers to my questions. Are you prepared for the burning of a heretic this day?

THE EXECUTIONER. Yes, Master.

LADVENU. Is the stake ready?

THE EXECUTIONER. It is. In the market-place. The English have built it too high for me to get near her and make the death easier. It will be a cruel death.

JOAN (*horrified*). But you are not going to burn me now?

THE INQUISITOR. You realize it at last.

LADVENU. There are eight hundred English soldiers waiting to take you to the market-place the moment the sentence of excommunication has passed the lips of your judges. You are within a few short moments of that doom.

JOAN (*looking round desperately for rescue*). Oh God!

LADVENU. Do not despair, Joan. The Church is merciful. You can save yourself.

JOAN (*hopefully*). Yes: my voices promised me I should not be burnt. St Catherine bade me be bold.

CAUCHON. Woman: are you quite mad? Do you not yet see that your voices have deceived you?

JOAN. Oh no: that is impossible.

CAUCHON. Impossible! They have led you straight to your excommunication, and to the stake which is there waiting for you.

LADVENU (*pressing the point hard*). Have they kept a single promise to you since you were taken at Compiègne? The devil has betrayed you. The Church holds out its arms to you.

JOAN (*despairing*). Oh, it is true: it is true: my voices have deceived me. I have been mocked by devils: my faith is broken. I have dared and dared; but only a fool will walk into a fire: God, who gave me my commonsense, cannot will me to do that.

LADVENU. Now God be praised that He has saved you at the eleventh hour! (*He hurries to the vacant seat at the scribes' table, and snatches a sheet of paper, on which he sets to work writing eagerly.*)

CAUCHON. Amen!

JOAN. What must I do?

CAUCHON. You must sign a solemn recantation of your heresy.

JOAN. Sign? That means to write my name. I cannot write.

CAUCHON. You have signed many letters before.

JOAN. Yes; but someone held my hand and guided the pen. I can make my mark.

THE CHAPLAIN (*who has been listening with growing alarm and indignation*). My lord: do you mean that you are going to allow this woman to escape us?

THE INQUISITOR. The law must take its course, Master de Stogumber. And you know the law.

THE CHAPLAIN (*rising, purple with fury*). I know that there is no faith in a Frenchman. (*Tumult, which he shouts down.*) I know what my lord the Cardinal of Winchester will say when he hears of this. I know what the Earl of Warwick will do when he learns that you intend to betray him. There are eight hundred men at the gate who will see that this abominable witch is burnt in spite of your teeth.

THE ASSESSORS (*meanwhile*). What is this? What did he say? He accuses us of treachery! This is past bearing. No faith in a Frenchman! Did you hear that? This is an intolerable fellow. Who is he? Is this what English Churchmen are like? he must be mad or drunk, etc., etc.

THE INQUISITOR (*rising*). Silence, pray! Gentlemen: pray, silence! Master Chaplain: bethink you a moment of your holy office: of what you are, and where you are. I direct you to sit down.

THE CHAPLAIN (*folding his arms doggedly, his face working convulsively*). I will NOT sit down.

CAUCHON. Master Inquisitor: this man has called me a traitor to my face before now.

THE CHAPLAIN. So you are a traitor. You are all traitors. You have been doing nothing but begging this damnable witch on your knees to recant all through this trial.

THE INQUISITOR (*placidly resuming his seat*). If you will not sit, you must stand: that is all.

THE CHAPLAIN. I will NOT stand (*he flings himself back into his chair*).

LADVENU (*rising with the paper in his hand*). My lord: here is the form of recantation for The Maid to sign.

CAUCHON. Read it to her.

JOAN. Do not trouble. I will sign it.

THE INQUISITOR. Woman: you must know what you are putting your hand to. Read it to her, Brother Martin. And let all be silent.

LADVENU (*reading quietly*). "I, Joan, commonly called The Maid, a miserable sinner, do confess that I have most grievously sinned in the following articles. I have pretended to have revelations from God and the angels and the blessed saints, and perversely rejected The Church's warnings that these were temptations by demons. I have blasphemed abominably by wearing an immodest dress, contrary to the Holy Scripture and the canons of The Church. Also I have clipped my hair in the style of a man, and, against all the duties which have made my sex specially acceptable in heaven, have taken up the sword, even to the shedding of human blood, inciting men to slay each other, invoking evil spirits to delude them, and stubbornly and most blasphemously imputing these sins to Almighty God. I confess to the sin of sedition, to the sin of idolatry, to the sin of disobedience, to the sin of pride, and to the sin of heresy. All of which sins I now renounce and abjure and depart from, humbly thanking you Doctors and Masters who have brought me back to the truth and into the grace of our Lord. And I will never return to my errors, but will remain in communion with our Holy Church and in obedience to our Holy Father the Pope of Rome. All this I swear by God Almighty and the Holy Gospels, in witness whereto I sign my name to this recantation."

THE INQUISITOR. You understand this, Joan?

JOAN (*listless*). It is plain enough, sir.

THE INQUISITOR. And it is true?

JOAN. It may be true. If it were not true, the fire would not be ready for me in the market-place.

LADVENU (*taking up his pen and a book, and going to her quickly lest she should compromise herself again*). Come, child: let me guide your hand. Take the pen.

(*She does so; and they begin to write, using the book as a desk.*)

J.E.H.A.N.E. So. Now make your mark by yourself.

JOAN (*makes her mark, and gives him back the pen, tormented by the rebellion of her soul against her mind and body*). There!

LADVENU (*replacing the pen on the table, and handing the recantation to CAUCHON with a reverence*). Praise be to God, my brothers, the lamb has returned to the flock; and the shepherd rejoices in her more than in ninety and nine just persons. (*He returns to his seat.*)

THE INQUISITOR (*taking the paper from CAUCHON*). We declare thee by this act set free from the danger of excommunication in which thou stoodest. (*He throws the paper down to the table.*)

JOAN. I thank you.

THE INQUISITOR. But because thou hast sinned most presumptuously against God and the Holy Church, and that thou mayst repent thy errors in solitary contemplation, and be shielded from all temptation to return to them, we, for the good of thy soul, and for a penance that may wipe out thy sins and bring thee finally unspotted to the throne of grace, do condemn thee to eat the bread of sorrow and drink the water of affliction to the end of thy earthly days in perpetual imprisonment.

JOAN (*rising in consternation and terrible anger*).   Perpetual imprisonment! Am I not then to be set free?

LADVENU (*mildly shocked*).   Set free, child, after such wickedness as yours! What are you dreaming of?

JOAN.   Give me that writing. (*She rushes to the table; snatches up the paper; and tears it into fragments.*)   Light your fire: do you think I dread it as much as the life of a rat in a hole? My voices were right.

LADVENU.   Joan! Joan!

JOAN.   Yes: they told me you were fools (*the word gives great offence*), and that I was not to listen to your fine words nor trust to your charity. You promised me my life; but you lied (*indignant exclamations*). You think that life is nothing but not being stone dead. It is not the bread and water I fear: I can live on bread: when have I asked for more? It is no hardship to drink water if the water be clean. Bread has no sorrow for me, and water no affliction. But to shut me from the light of the sky and the sight of the fields and flowers; to chain my feet so that I can never again ride with the soldiers nor climb the hills; to make me breathe foul damp darkness, and keep from me everything that brings me back to the love of God when your wickedness and foolishness tempt me to hate Him: all this is worse than the furnace in the Bible that was heated seven times. I could do without my warhorse; I could drag about in a skirt; I could let the banners and the trumpets and the knights and soldiers pass me and leave me behind as they leave the other women, if only I could still hear the wind in the trees, the larks in the sunshine, the young lambs crying through the healthy frost, and the blessed blessed church bells that send my angel voices floating to me on the wind. But without these things I cannot live; and by your wanting to take them away from me, or from any human creature, I know that your counsel is of the devil, and that mine is of God.

THE ASSESSORS (*in great commotion*).   Blasphemy! blasphemy! She is possessed. She said our counsel was of the devil. And hers of God. Monstrous! The devil is in our midst, etc., etc.

D'ESTIVET (*shouting above the din*).   She is a relapsed heretic, obstinate, incorrigible, and altogether unworthy of the mercy we have shewn her. I call for her excommunication.

THE CHAPLAIN (*to the* EXECUTIONER).   Light your fire, man. To the stake with her.

(*The* EXECUTIONER *and his* ASSISTANTS *hurry out through the court-yard.*)

LADVENU.   You wicked girl: if your counsel were of God would He not deliver you?

JOAN.   His ways are not your ways. He wills that I go through the fire to His bosom; for I am His child, and you are not fit that I should live among you. That is my last word to you.

(*The* soldiers *seize her.*)

cauchon (*rising*).   Not yet.

(*They wait. There is a dead silence.* cauchon *turns to the* inquisitor *with an inquiring look. The* inquisitor *nods affirmatively. They rise solemnly, and intone the sentence antiphonally.*)

We decree that thou art a relapsed heretic.
   the inquisitor.   Cast out from the unity of the Church.
   cauchon.   Sundered from her body.
   the inquisitor.   Infected with the leprosy of heresy.
   cauchon.   A member of Satan.
   the inquisitor.   We declare that thou must be excommunicate.
   cauchon.   And now we do cast thee out, segregate thee, and abandon thee to the secular power.
   the inquisitor.   Admonishing the same secular power that it moderate its judgment of thee in respect of death and division of the limbs. (*He resumes his seat.*)
   cauchon.   And if any true sign of penitence appear in thee, to permit our Brother Martin to administer to thee the sacrament of penance.
   the chaplain.   Into the fire with the witch (*he rushes at her, and helps the soldiers to push her out.*)

(joan *is taken away through the courtyard. The* assessors *rise in disorder, and follow the* soldiers, *except* ladvenu, *who has hidden his face in his hands.*)

cauchon (*rising again in the act of sitting down*).   No, no: this is irregular. The representative of the secular arm should be here to receive her from us.
   the inquisitor (*also on his feet again*).   That man is an incorrigible fool.
   cauchon.   Brother Martin: see that everything is done in order.
   ladvenu.   My place is at her side, my lord. You must exercise your own authority. (*He hurries out.*)
   cauchon.   These English are impossible: they will thrust her straight into the fire. Look!

(*He points to the courtyard, in which the glow and flicker of fire can now be seen reddening the May daylight. Only the* bishop *and the* inquisitor *are left in the court.*)

(*Turning to go.*) We must stop that.

THE INQUISITOR (*calmly*). Yes; but not too fast, my lord.

CAUCHON (*halting*). But there is not a moment to lose.

THE INQUISITOR. We have proceeded in perfect order. If the English choose to put themselves in the wrong, it is not our business to put them in the right. A flaw in the procedure may be useful later on: one never knows. And the sooner it is over, the better for that poor girl.

CAUCHON (*relaxing*). That is true. But I suppose we must see this dreadful thing through.

THE INQUISITOR. One gets used to it. Habit is everything. I am accustomed to the fire: it is soon over. But it is a terrible thing to see a young and innocent creature crushed between these mighty forces, The Church and the Law.

CAUCHON. You call her innocent!

THE INQUISITOR. Oh, quite innocent. What does she know of The Church and the Law? She did not understand a word we were saying. It is the ignorant who suffer. Come, or we shall be late for the end.

CAUCHON (*going with him*). I shall not be sorry if we are: I am not so accustomed as you.

(*They are going out when* WARWICK *comes in, meeting them.*)

WARWICK. Oh, I am intruding. I thought it was all over. (*He makes a feint of retiring.*)

CAUCHON. Do not go, my lord. It is all over.

THE INQUISITOR. The execution is not in our hands, my lord; but it is desirable that we should witness the end. So by your leave — (*he bows, and goes out through the courtyard*).

CAUCHON. There is some doubt whether your people have observed the forms of law, my lord.

WARWICK. I am told that there is some doubt whether your authority runs in this city, my lord. It is not in your diocese. However, if you will answer for that I will answer for the rest.

CAUCHON. It is to God that we both must answer. Good morning, my lord.

WARWICK. My lord: good morning.

(*They look at one another for a moment with unconcealed hostility. Then* CAUCHON *follows the* INQUISITOR *out.* WARWICK *looks round. Finding himself alone, he calls for attendance.*)

Hallo: some attendance here! (*Silence.*) Hallo, there! (*Silence.*) Hallo! Brian, you young blackguard, where are you? (*Silence.*) Guard! (*Silence.*) They have all gone to see the burning: even that child.

(*The silence is broken by someone frantically howling and sobbing.*)

What in the devil's name — ?

(*The* CHAPLAIN *staggers in from the courtyard like a demented creature, his face streaming with tears, making the piteous sounds that* WARWICK has heard. He stumbles to the prisoner's stool, and throws himself upon it with heartrending sobs.)

(Going to him and patting him on the shoulder.) What is it, Master John? What is the matter?

THE CHAPLAIN (clutching at his hands). My lord, my lord: for Christ's sake pray for my wretched guilty soul.

WARWICK (soothing him). Yes, yes: of course I will. Calmly, gently —

THE CHAPLAIN (blubbering miserably). I am not a bad man, my lord.

WARWICK. No, no: not at all.

THE CHAPLAIN. I meant no harm. I did not know what it would be like.

WARWICK (hardening). Oh! You saw it, then?

THE CHAPLAIN. I did not know what I was doing. I am a hotheaded fool; and I shall be damned to all eternity for it.

WARWICK. Nonsense! Very distressing, no doubt; but it was not your doing.

THE CHAPLAIN (lamentably). I let them do it. If I had known, I would have torn her from their hands. You dont know: you havnt seen: it is so easy to talk when you dont know. You madden yourself with words: you damn yourself because it feels grand to throw oil on the flaming hell of your own temper. But when it is brought home to you; when you see the thing you have done; when it is blinding your eyes, stifling your nostrils, tearing your heart, then — then — (Falling on his knees.) O God, take away this sight from me! O Christ, deliver me from this fire that is consuming me! She cried to Thee in the midst of it: Jesus! Jesus! Jesus! She is in Thy bosom; and I am in hell for evermore.

WARWICK (summarily hauling him to his feet). Come come, man! you must pull yourself together. We shall have the whole town talking of this. (He throws him not too gently into a chair at the table.) If you have not the nerve to see these things, why do you not do as I do, and stay away?

THE CHAPLAIN (bewildered and submissive). She asked for a cross. A soldier gave her two sticks tied together. Thank God he was an Englishman! I might have done it; but I did not: I am a coward, a mad dog, a fool. But he was an Englishman too.

WARWICK. The fool! they will burn him too if the priests get hold of him.

THE CHAPLAIN (shaken with a convulsion). Some of the people laughed at her. They would have laughed at Christ. They were French people, my lord: I know they were French.

WARWICK. Hush! someone is coming. Control yourself.

(LADVENU comes back through the courtyard to WARWICK's right hand, carrying a bishop's cross which he has taken from a church. He is very grave and composed.)

I am informed that it is all over, Brother Martin.

LADVENU (*enigmatically*). We do not know, my lord. It may have only just begun.

WARWICK. What does that mean, exactly?

LADVENU. I took this cross from the church for her that she might see it to the last: she had only two sticks that she put into her bosom. When the fire crept round us, and she saw that if I held the cross before her I should be burnt myself, she warned me to get down and save myself. My lord: a girl who could think of another's danger in such a moment was not inspired by the devil. When I had to snatch the cross from her sight, she looked up to heaven. And I do not believe that the heavens were empty. I firmly believe that her Savior appeared to her then in His tenderest glory. She called to Him and died. This is not the end for her, but the beginning.

WARWICK. I am afraid it will have a bad effect on the people.

LADVENU. It had, my lord, on some of them. I heard laughter. Forgive me for saying that I hope and believe it was English laughter.

THE CHAPLAIN (*rising frantically*). No: it was not. There was only one Englishman there that disgraced his country; and that was the mad dog, de Stogumber. (*He rushes wildly out, shrieking.*) Let them torture him. Let them burn him. I will go pray among her ashes. I am no better than Judas: I will hang myself.

WARWICK. Quick, Brother Martin: follow him: he will do himself some mischief. After him, quick.

(LADVENU *hurries out*, WARWICK *urging him. The* EXECUTIONER *comes in by the door behind the judges' chairs; and* WARWICK, *returning, finds himself face to face with him.*)

Well, fellow: who are you?

THE EXECUTIONER (*with dignity*). I am not addressed as fellow, my lord. I am the Master Executioner of Rouen: it is a highly skilled mystery. I am come to tell your lordship that your orders have been obeyed.

WARWICK. I crave your pardon, Master Executioner; and I will see that you lose nothing by having no relics to sell. I have your word, have I, that nothing remains, not a bone, not a nail, not a hair?

THE EXECUTIONER. Her heart would not burn, my lord; but everything that was left is at the bottom of the river. You have heard the last of her.

WARWICK (*with a wry smile, thinking of what* LADVENU *said*). The last of her? Hm! I wonder!

Epilogue

(*A restless fitfully windy night in June 1456, full of summer lightning after many days of heat. King* CHARLES *the Seventh of France, formerly Joan's Dauphin, now Charles the Victorious, aged 51, is in bed in one of his royal chateaux. The bed, raised on a dais of two steps, is towards the*

*side of the room so as to avoid blocking a tall lancet window in the middle.
Its canopy bears the royal arms in embroidery. Except for the canopy and
the huge down pillows there is nothing to distinguish it from a broad
settee with bed-clothes and a valance. Thus its occupant is in full view
from the foot.*

CHARLES *is not asleep: he is reading in bed, or rather looking at the
pictures in Fouquet's Boccaccio with his knees doubled up to make a
reading desk. Beside the bed on his left is a little table with a picture of
the Virgin, lighted by candles of painted wax. The walls are hung from
ceiling to floor with painted curtains which stir at times in the draughts.
At first glance the prevailing yellow and red in these hanging pictures is
somewhat flamelike when the folds breathe in the wind.*

The door is on CHARLES's *left, but in front of him close to the corner
farthest from him. A large watchman's rattle, handsomely designed and
gaily painted, is in the bed under his hand.*

CHARLES *turns a leaf. A distant clock strikes the half-hour softly.*
CHARLES *shuts the book with a clap; throws it aside; snatches up the
rattle; and whirls it energetically, making a deafening clatter.* LADVENU
*enters, 25 years older, strange and stark in bearing, and still carrying the
cross from Rouen.* CHARLES *evidently does not expect him; for he springs
out of bed on the farther side from the door.*)

CHARLES. Who are you? Where is my gentleman of the bedchamber?
What do you want?

LADVENU (*solemnly*). I bring you glad tidings of great joy. Rejoice,
O king; for the taint is removed from your blood, and the stain from
your crown. Justice, long delayed, is at last triumphant.

CHARLES. What are you talking about? Who are you?

LADVENU. I am Brother Martin.

CHARLES. And who, saving your reverence, may Brother Martin be?

LADVENU. I held this cross when The Maid perished in the fire.
Twenty-five years have passed since then: nearly ten thousand days. And
on every one of those days I have prayed God to justify His daughter on
earth as she is justified in heaven.

CHARLES (*reassured, sitting down on the foot of the bed*). Oh, I remember now. I have heard of you. You have a bee in your bonnet about
The Maid. Have you been at the inquiry?

LADVENU. I have given my testimony.

CHARLES. Is it over?

LADVENU. It is over.

CHARLES. Satisfactorily?

LADVENU. The ways of God are very strange.

CHARLES. How so?

LADVENU. At the trial which sent a saint to the stake as a heretic and
a sorceress, the truth was told; the law was upheld; mercy was shewn beyond all custom; no wrong was done but the final and dreadful wrong of
the lying sentence and the pitiless fire. At this inquiry from which I have

just come, there was shameless perjury, courtly corruption, calumny of the dead who did their duty according to their lights, cowardly evasion of the issue, testimony made of idle tales that could not impose on a ploughboy. Yet out of this insult to justice, this defamation of The Church, this orgy of lying and foolishness, the truth is set in the noonday sun on the hilltop; the white robe of innocence is cleansed from the smirch of the burning faggots; the holy life is sanctified; the true heart that lived through the flame is consecrated; a great lie is silenced for ever; and a great wrong is set right before all men.

CHARLES. My friend: provided they can no longer say that I was crowned by a witch and a heretic, I shall not fuss about how the trick has been done. Joan would not have fussed about it if it came all right in the end: she was not that sort: I knew her. Is her rehabilitation complete? I made it pretty clear that there was to be no nonsense about it.

LADVENU. It is solemnly declared that her judges were full of corruption, cozenage, fraud, and malice. Four falsehoods.

CHARLES. Never mind the falsehoods: her judges are dead.

LADVENU. The sentence on her is broken, annulled, annihilated, set aside as non-existent, without value or effect.

CHARLES. Good. Nobody can challenge my consecration now, can they?

LADVENU. Not Charlemagne nor King David himself was more sacredly crowned.

CHARLES (rising). Excellent. Think of what that means to me!

LADVENU. I think of what it means to her!

CHARLES. You cannot. None of us ever knew what anything meant to her. She was like nobody else; and she must take care of herself wherever she is; for I cannot take care of her; and neither can you, whatever you may think: you are not big enough. But I will tell you this about her. If you could bring her back to life, they would burn her again within six months, for all their present adoration of her. And you would hold up the cross, too, just the same. So (crossing himself) let her rest; and let you and I mind our own business, and not meddle with hers.

LADVENU. God forbid that I should have no share in her, nor she in me! (He turns and strides out as he came, saying) Henceforth my path will not lie through palaces, nor my conversation be with kings.

CHARLES (following him towards the door, and shouting after him). Much good may it do you, holy man! (He returns to the middle of the chamber, where he halts, and says quizzically to himself:) That was a funny chap. How did he get in? Where are my people? (He goes impatiently to the bed, and swings the rattle. A rush of wind through the open door sets the walls swaying agitatedly. The candles go out. He calls in the darkness.) Hallo! Someone come and shut the windows: everything is being blown all over the place.

(A flash of summer lightning shews up the lancet window. A figure is seen in silhouette against it.)

Who is there? Who is that? Help! Murder! (*Thunder. He jumps into bed, and hides under the clothes.*)

JOAN'S VOICE. Easy, Charlie, easy. What art making all that noise for? No one can hear thee. Thourt asleep. (*She is dimly seen in a pallid greenish light by the bedside.*)

CHARLES (*peeping out*). Joan! Are you a ghost, Joan?

JOAN. Hardly even that, lad. Can a poor burnt-up lass have a ghost? I am but a dream that thourt dreaming.

(*The light increases: they become plainly visible as he sits up.*)

Thou looks older, lad.

CHARLES. I am older. Am I really asleep?

JOAN. Fallen asleep over thy silly book.

CHARLES. That's funny.

JOAN. Not so funny as that I am dead, is it?

CHARLES. Are you really dead?

JOAN. As dead as anybody ever is, laddie. I am out of the body.

CHARLES. Just fancy! Did it hurt much?

JOAN. Did what hurt much?

CHARLES. Being burnt.

JOAN. Oh, *that!* I cannot remember very well. I think it did at first; but then it all got mixed up; and I was not in my right mind until I was free of the body. But do not thou go handling fire and thinking it will not hurt thee. How hast been ever since?

CHARLES. Oh, not so bad. Do you know, I actually lead my army out and win battles? Down into the moat up to my waist in mud and blood. Up the ladders with the stones and hot pitch raining down. Like you.

JOAN. No! Did I make a man of thee after all, Charlie?

CHARLES. I am Charles the Victorious now. I had to be brave because you were. Agnes put a little pluck into me too.

JOAN. Agnes? Who was Agnes?

CHARLES. Agnes Sorel. A woman I fell in love with. I dream of her often. I never dreamed of you before.

JOAN. Is she dead, like me?

CHARLES. Yes. But she was not like you. She was very beautiful.

JOAN (*laughing heartily*). Ha ha! I was no beauty: I was always a rough one: a regular soldier. I might almost as well have been a man. Pity I wasnt: I should not have bothered you all so much then. But my head was in the skies; and the glory of God was upon me; and, man or woman, I should have bothered you as long as your noses were in the mud. Now tell me what has happened since you wise men knew no better than to make a heap of cinders of me?

CHARLES. Your mother and brothers have sued the courts to have your case tried over again. And the courts have declared that your judges were full of corruption and cozenage, fraud and malice.

JOAN. Not they. They were as honest a lot of poor fools as ever burned their betters.

CHARLES. The sentence on you is broken, annihilated, annulled: null, non-existent, without value or effect.

JOAN. I was burned, all the same. Can they unburn me?

CHARLES. If they could, they would think twice before they did it. But they have decreed that a beautiful cross be placed where the stake stood, for your perpetual memory and for your salvation.

JOAN. It is the memory and the salvation that sanctify the cross, not the cross that sanctifies the memory and the salvation. (*She turns away, forgetting him.*) I shall outlast that cross. I shall be remembered when men will have forgotten where Rouen stood.

CHARLES. There you go with your self-conceit, the same as ever! I think you might say a word of thanks to me for having had justice done at last.

CAUCHON (*appearing at the window between them*). Liar!

CHARLES. Thank you.

JOAN. Why, if it isnt Peter Cauchon! How are you, Peter? What luck have you had since you burned me?

CAUCHON. None. I arraign the justice of Man. It is not the justice of God.

JOAN. Still dreaming of justice, Peter? See what justice came to with me! But what has happened to thee? Art dead or alive?

CAUCHON. Dead. Dishonored. They pursued me beyond the grave. They excommunicated my dead body: they dug it up and flung it into the common sewer.

JOAN. Your dead body did not feel the spade and the sewer as my live body felt the fire.

CAUCHON. But this thing that they have done against me hurts justice; destroys faith; saps the foundation of The Church. The solid earth sways like the treacherous sea beneath the feet of men and spirits alike when the innocent are slain in the name of law, and their wrongs are undone by slandering the pure of heart.

JOAN. Well, well, Peter, I hope men will be the better for remembering me; and they would not remember me so well if you had not burned me.

CAUCHON. They will be the worse for remembering me: they will see in me evil triumphing over good, falsehood over truth, cruelty over mercy, hell over heaven. Their courage will rise as they think of you, only to faint as they think of me. Yet God is my witness I was just: I was merciful: I was faithful to my light: I could do no other than I did.

CHARLES (*scrambling out of the sheets and enthroning himself on the side of the bed*). Yes: it is always you good men that do the big mischiefs. Look at me! I am not Charles the Good, nor Charles the Wise, nor Charles the Bold. Joan's worshippers may even call me Charles the Coward because I did not pull her out of the fire. But I have done less harm than any of you. You people with your heads in the sky spend all your time trying to turn the world upside down; but I take the world as it is, and say that top-side-up is right-side-up; and I keep my nose pretty close to the ground. And I ask you, what king of France has done better, or been a better fellow in his little way?

JOAN. Art really king of France, Charlie? Be the English gone?

DUNOIS (*coming through the tapestry on* JOAN's *left, the candles relighting themselves at the same moment, and illuminating his armor and surcoat cheerfully*). I have kept my word: the English are gone.

JOAN. Praised be God! now is fair France a province in heaven. Tell me all about the fighting, Jack. Was it thou that led them? Wert thou God's captain to thy death?

DUNOIS. I am not dead. My body is very comfortably asleep in my bed at Chateaudun; but my spirit is called here by yours.

JOAN. And you fought them my way, Jack: eh? Not the old way, chaffering for ransoms; but The Maid's way: staking life against death, with the heart high and humble and void of malice, and nothing counting under God but France free and French. Was it my way, Jack?

DUNOIS. Faith, it was any way that would win. But the way that won was always your way. I give you best, lassie. I wrote a fine letter to set you right at the new trial. Perhaps I should never have let the priests burn you; but I was busy fighting; and it was The Church's business, not mine. There was no use in both of us being burned, was there?

CAUCHON. Ay! put the blame on the priests. But I, who am beyond praise and blame, tell you that the world is saved neither by its priests nor its soldiers, but by God and His Saints. The Church Militant sent this woman to the fire; but even as she burned, the flames whitened into the radiance of the Church Triumphant.

(*The clock strikes the third quarter. A rough male voice is heard trolling an improvised tune.*)

        Rum tum trumpledum,
        Bacon fat and rumpledum,
        Old Saint mumpledum,
        Pull his tail and stumpledum
        O my Ma—ry Ann!

(*A ruffianly English soldier comes through the curtains and marches between* DUNOIS *and* JOAN.)

DUNOIS. What villainous troubadour taught you that doggerel?

THE SOLDIER. No troubadour. We made it up ourselves as we

marched. We were not gentlefolks and troubadours. Music straight out of the heart of the people, as you might say. Rum tum trumpledum, Bacon fat and rumpledum, Old Saint mumpledum, Pull his tail and stumpledum: that dont mean anything, you know; but it keeps you marching. Your servant, ladies and gentlemen. Who asked for a saint?

JOAN. Be you a saint?

THE SOLDIER. Yes, lady, straight from hell.

DUNOIS. A saint, and from hell!

THE SOLDIER. Yes, noble captain: I have a day off. Every year, you know. Thats my allowance for my one good action.

CAUCHON. Wretch! In all the years of your life did you do only one good action?

THE SOLDIER. I never thought about it: it came natural like. But they scored it up for me.

CHARLES. What was it?

THE SOLDIER. Why, the silliest thing you ever heard of. I —

JOAN (interrupting him by strolling across to the bed, where she sits beside CHARLES). He tied two sticks together, and gave them to a poor lass that was going to be burned.

THE SOLDIER. Right. Who told you that?

JOAN. Never mind. Would you know her if you saw her again?

THE SOLDIER. Not I. There are so many girls! and they all expect you to remember them as if there was only one in the world. This one must have been a prime sort; for I have a day off every year for her; and so, until twelve o'clock punctually, I am a saint, at your service, noble lords and lovely ladies.

CHARLES. And after twelve?

THE SOLDIER. After twelve, back to the only place fit for the likes of me.

JOAN (rising). Back there! You! that gave the lass the cross!

THE SOLDIER (excusing his unsoldierly conduct). Well, she asked for it; and they were going to burn her. She had as good a right to a cross as they had; and they had dozens of them. It was her funeral, not theirs. Where was the harm in it?

JOAN. Man: I am not reproaching you. But I cannot bear to think of you in torment.

THE SOLDIER (cheerfully). No great torment, lady. You see I was used to worse.

CHARLES. What! worse than hell?

THE SOLDIER. Fifteen years' service in the French wars. Hell was a treat after that.

(JOAN throws up her arms, and takes refuge from despair of humanity before the picture of the Virgin.)

Suits me somehow. The day off was dull at first, like a wet Sunday. I dont mind it so much now. They tell me I can have as many as I like as soon as I want them.

CHARLES. What is hell like?

THE SOLDIER. You wont find it so bad, sir. Jolly. Like as if you were always drunk without the trouble and expense of drinking. Tip top company too: emperors and popes and kings and all sorts. They chip me about giving that young judy the cross; but I dont care: I stand up to them proper, and tell them that if she hadnt a better right to it than they, she'd be where they are. That dumbfounds them, that does. All they can do is gnash their teeth, hell fashion; and I just laugh, and go off singing the old chanty: Rum tum trumple — Hullo! Who's that knocking at the door?

(*They listen. A long gentle knocking is heard.*)

CHARLES. Come in.

(*The door opens; and an old* PRIEST, *white-haired, bent, with a silly but benevolent smile, comes in and trots over to* JOAN.)

THE NEWCOMER. Excuse me, gentle lords and ladies. Do not let me disturb you. Only a poor old harmless English rector. Formerly chaplain to the cardinal: to my lord of Winchester. John de Stogumber, at your service. (*He looks at them inquiringly.*) Did you say anything? I am a little deaf, unfortunately. Also a little — well, not always in my right mind, perhaps; but still, it is a small village with a few simple people. I suffice: I suffice: they love me there; and I am able to do a little good. I am well connected, you see; and they indulge me.

JOAN. Poor old John! What brought thee to this state?

DE STOGUMBER. I tell my folks they must be very careful. I say to them, "If you only saw what you think about you would think quite differently about it. It would give you a great shock. Oh, a great shock." And they all say "Yes, parson: we all know you are a kind man, and would not harm a fly." That is a great comfort to me. For I am not cruel by nature, you know.

THE SOLDIER. Who said you were?

DE STOGUMBER. Well, you see, I did a very cruel thing once because I did not know what cruelty was like. I had not seen it, you know. That is the great thing: you must see it. And then you are redeemed and saved.

CAUCHON. Were not the sufferings of our Lord Christ enough for you?

DE STOGUMBER. No. Oh no: not at all. I had seen them in pictures, and read of them in books, and been greatly moved by them, as I thought. But it was no use: it was not our Lord that redeemed me, but a young woman whom I saw actually burned to death. It was dreadful: oh, most dreadful. But it saved me. I have been a different man ever since, though a little astray in my wits sometimes.

CAUCHON. Must then a Christ perish in torment in every age to save those that have no imagination?

JOAN. Well, if I saved all those he would have been cruel to if he had not been cruel to me, I was not burnt for nothing, was I?

DE STOGUMBER. Oh no; it was not you. My sight is bad: I cannot distinguish your features: but you are not she: oh no: she was burned to a cinder: dead and gone, dead and gone.

THE EXECUTIONER (*stepping from behind the bed curtains on* CHARLES'S *right, the bed being between them*). She is more alive than you, old man. Her heart would not burn; and it would not drown. I was a master at my craft: better than the master of Paris, better than the master of Toulouse; but I could not kill The Maid. She is up and alive everywhere.

THE EARL OF WARWICK (*sallying from the bed curtains on the other side, and coming to* JOAN's *left hand*). Madam: my congratulations on your rehabilitation. I feel that I owe you an apology.

JOAN. Oh, please dont mention it.

WARWICK (*pleasantly*). The burning was purely political. There was no personal feeling against you, I assure you.

JOAN. I bear no malice, my lord.

WARWICK. Just so. Very kind of you to meet me in that way: a touch of true breeding. But I must insist on apologizing very amply. The truth is, these political necessities sometimes turn out to be political mistakes; and this one was a veritable howler; for your spirit conquered us, madam, in spite of our faggots. History will remember me for your sake, though the incidents of the connection were perhaps a little unfortunate.

JOAN. Ay, perhaps just a little, you funny man.

WARWICK. Still, when they make you a saint, you will owe your halo to me, just as this lucky monarch owes his crown to you.

JOAN (*turning from him*). I shall owe nothing to any man: I owe everything to the spirit of God that was within me. But fancy me a saint! What would St Catherine and St Margaret say if the farm girl was cocked up beside them!

(*A clerical-looking* GENTLEMAN *in black frockcoat and trousers, and tall hat, in the fashion of the year 1920, suddenly appears before them in the corner on their right. They all stare at him. Then they burst into uncontrollable laughter.*)

THE GENTLEMAN. Why this mirth, gentlemen?

WARWICK. I congratulate you on having invented a most extraordinarily comic dress.

THE GENTLEMAN. I do not understand. You are all in fancy dress: I am properly dressed.

DUNOIS. All dress is fancy dress, is it not, except our natural skins?

THE GENTLEMAN. Pardon me: I am here on serious business, and cannot engage in frivolous discussions. (*He takes out a paper, and assumes a dry official manner.*) I am sent to announce to you that Joan of Arc, formerly known as The Maid, having been the subject of an inquiry instituted by the Bishop of Orleans —

JOAN (*interrupting*). Ah! They remember me still in Orleans.

THE GENTLEMAN (*emphatically, to mark his indignation at the in-*

terruption). — by the Bishop of Orleans into the claim of the said
Joan of Arc to be canonized as a saint —

JOAN (*again interrupting*). But I never made any such claim.

THE GENTLEMAN (*as before*). — The Church has examined the claim
exhaustively in the usual course, and, having admitted the said Joan suc-
cessively to the ranks of Venerable and Blessed, —

JOAN (*chuckling*). Me venerable!

THE GENTLEMAN. — has finally declared her to have been endowed
with heroic virtues and favored with private revelations, and calls the said
Venerable and Blessed Joan to the communion of the Church Triumphant as Saint Joan.

JOAN (*rapt*). Saint Joan!

THE GENTLEMAN. On every thirtieth day of May, being the anni-
versary of the death of the said most blessed daughter of God, there shall
in every Catholic church to the end of time be celebrated a special office
in commemoration of her; and it shall be lawful to dedicate a special
chapel to her, and to place her image on its altar in every such church.
And it shall be lawful and laudable for the faithful to kneel and address
their prayers through her to the Mercy Seat.

JOAN. Oh no. It is for the saint to kneel. (*She falls on her knees,
still rapt.*)

THE GENTLEMAN (*putting up his paper, and retiring beside the EX-
ECUTIONER*). In Basilica Vaticana, the sixteenth day of May, nineteen
hundred and twenty.

DUNOIS (*raising JOAN*). Half an hour to burn you, dear Saint; and
four centuries to find out the truth about you!

DE STOGUMBER. Sir: I was chaplain to the Cardinal of Winchester
once. They always would call him the Cardinal of England. It would
be a great comfort to me and to my master to see a fair statue to The
Maid in Winchester Cathedral. Will they put one there, do you think?

THE GENTLEMAN. As the building is temporarily in the hands of the
Anglican heresy, I cannot answer for that.

(*A vision of the statue in Winchester Cathedral is seen through the
window.*)

DE STOGUMBER. Oh look! look! that is Winchester.

JOAN. Is that meant to be me? I was stiffer on my feet.

(*The vision fades.*)

THE GENTLEMAN. I have been requested by the temporal authorities
of France to mention that the multiplication of public statues to The
Maid threatens to become an obstruction to traffic. I do so as a matter
of courtesy to the said authorities, but must point out on behalf of The
Church that The Maid's horse is no greater obstruction to traffic than any
other horse.

JOAN. Eh! I am glad they have not forgotten my horse.

(*A vision of the statue before Rheims Cathedral appears.*)
Is that funny little thing me too?

CHARLES. That is Rheims Cathedral where you had me crowned. It must be you.

JOAN. Who has broken my sword? My sword was never broken. It is the sword of France.

DUNOIS. Never mind. Swords can be mended. Your soul is unbroken; and you are the soul of France.

(*The vision fades. The* ARCHBISHOP *and the* INQUISITOR *are now seen on the right and left of* CAUCHON.)

JOAN. My sword shall conquer yet: the sword that never struck a blow. Though men destroyed my body, yet in my soul I have seen God.

CAUCHON (*kneeling to her*). The girls in the field praise thee; for thou hast raised their eyes; and they see that there is nothing between them and heaven.

DUNOIS (*kneeling to her*). The dying soldiers praise thee, because thou art a shield of glory between them and the judgment.

THE ARCHBISHOP (*kneeling to her*). The princes of The Church praise thee, because thou hast redeemed the faith their worldlinesses have dragged through the mire.

WARWICK (*kneeling to her*). The cunning counsellors praise thee, because thou hast cut the knots in which they have tied their own souls.

DE STOGUMBER (*kneeling to her*). The foolish old men on their deathbeds praise thee, because their sins against thee are turned into blessings.

THE INQUISITOR (*kneeling to her*). The judges in the blindness and bondage of the law praise thee, because thou hast vindicated the vision and the freedom of the living soul.

THE SOLDIER (*kneeling to her*). The wicked out of hell praise thee, because thou hast shewn them that the fire that is not quenched is a holy fire.

THE EXECUTIONER (*kneeling to her*). The tormentors and executioners praise thee, because thou hast shewn that their hands are guiltless of the death of the soul.

CHARLES (*kneeling to her*). The unpretending praise thee, because thou hast taken upon thyself the heroic burdens that are too heavy for them.

JOAN. Woe unto me when all men praise me! I bid you remember that I am a saint, and that saints can work miracles. And now tell me: shall I rise from the dead, and come back to you a living woman?

(*A sudden darkness blots out the walls of the room as they all spring to their feet in consternation. Only the figures and the bed remain visible.*)

What! Must I burn again? Are none of you ready to receive me?

CAUCHON. The heretic is always better dead. And mortal eyes cannot distinguish the saint from the heretic. Spare them. (*He goes out as he came.*)

DUNOIS. Forgive us, Joan: we are not yet good enough for you. I shall go back to my bed. (*He also goes*).

WARWICK. We sincerely regret our little mistake; but political necessities, though occasionally erroneous, are still imperative; so if you will be good enough to excuse me — (*he steals discreetly away*).

THE ARCHBISHOP. Your return would not make me the man you once thought me. The utmost I can say is that though I dare not bless you, I hope I may one day enter into your blessedness. Meanwhile, however — (*he goes*).

THE INQUISITOR. I who am of the dead, testified that day that you were innocent. But I do not see how The Inquisition could possibly be dispensed with under existing circumstances. Therefore — (*he goes*).

DE STOGUMBER. Oh, do not come back: you must not come back. I must die in peace. Give us peace in our time, O Lord! (*He goes.*)

THE GENTLEMAN. The possibility of your resurrection was not contemplated in the recent proceedings for your canonization. I must return to Rome for fresh instructions. (*He bows formally, and withdraws.*)

THE EXECUTIONER. As a master in my profession I have to consider its interests. And, after all, my first duty is to my wife and children. I must have time to think over this. (*He goes.*)

CHARLES. Poor old Joan! They have all run away from you except this blackguard who has to go back to hell at twelve o'clock. And what can I do but follow Jack Dunois' example, and go back to bed too? (*He does so.*)

JOAN (*sadly*). Goodnight, Charlie.

CHARLES (*mumbling in his pillows*). Goo ni. (*He sleeps. The darkness envelops the bed.*)

JOAN (*to the* SOLDIER). And you, my one faithful? What comfort have you for Saint Joan?

THE SOLDIER. Well, what do they all amount to, these kings and captains and bishops and lawyers and such like? They just leave you in the ditch to bleed to death; and the next thing is, you meet them down there, for all the airs they give themselves. What I say is, you have as good a right to your notions as they have to theirs, and perhaps better. (*Settling himself for a lecture on the subject.*) You see, it's like this. If — (*the first stroke of midnight is heard softly from a distant bell*). Excuse me: a pressing appointment — (*he goes on tiptoe*).

(*The last remaining rays of light gather into a white radiance descending on* JOAN. *The hour continues to strike.*)

JOAN. O God that madest this beautiful earth, when will it be ready to receive Thy saints? How long, O Lord, how long?

Curtain

The heroism of Shaw's Saint Joan is hardly typical of the drama that developed out of Naturalism and Realism. In the twentieth century, we have found it increasingly convenient to blame "society" or "the system" for man's failures, shortcomings, and crimes. The essential elements of confrontation in serious drama have often been reduced to heredity-and-environment as the villain, with the central character as the victim. In the words of John Gassner:

> The failure of modern plays as tragic art must have other causes than contemporaneity of substance. I would venture the view that a reason for failure will be found in the social dramatist's, let alone the propagandist's, failure to achieve a real tragic catharsis.
> . . . He neglects to effectuate the 'pity' and the 'fear' — that is, the tensions and the empathy implicit in these Aristotelian terms.[1]

Death of a Salesman (1949) is perhaps a good example of failure to achieve dramatic catharsis. Both reporters and scholars have questioned Arthur Miller (1915–   ) about what the play "means" and who its protagonist, Willy Loman, really represents. Once, when quizzed about Willy as a tragic hero, Miller made it clear that he saw Willy as an average American, at least when he wrote the play. He also suggested that he did not blame Willy for his delusive dreams, but the society which invented and encouraged them. Now, the American Dreams of success, possessions, power, and popularity still preoccupy millions of Americans like Willy, most of whom cannot hope to achieve them completely. What is crucial here, however, is not whether society has made a victim of Willy by teaching him to dream, but whether he had any means of fulfilling his dream, even in minor degree, and whether he had any awareness of what his real talents might be — and how to use them to acquire at least a few fragments of the Dream. Most rational men, even those dedicated to the pursuit of wealth and success — and happiness — finally have to have some honest realization of who they are and what they can do. Then they can scale their hopes more sensibly in terms of possibilities. Willy does not. He cannot.

Society — the American Dream — does not destroy Willy; he does that himself. It is the weaknesses of the man, not of the society, that are dramatically at issue in this play. A devastating indictment of the Dream could be written — quite a few attempts have been made — but the fact is that the Dream can actually be realized on various levels by able, ambitious men. That is what keeps the Dream alive. It is a different matter entirely to ask what their lives would be had they other dreams, other aims.

When *Death of a Salesman* first appeared, all but the cautious newspaper reviewers grandly called it tragedy. But Willy does not experience

[1] John Gassner, *The Theatre of Our Times* (New York: Crown, 1954), p. 63.

tragic enlightenment; no wisdom comes through his suffering. As we know through Willy's fantasies about his Uncle Ben and his lapses into private reminiscence, his mind is becoming deranged. In reliving the past, he is searching for an answer to his failures and mistakes — for classic self-recognition. But at the brink, he opts out. He kills himself in an apparent accident, an escape he has been subconsciously and consciously seeking with more fervor than knowing himself. As a result, there is no catharsis in the classic sense.

Neither insanity nor death offers a satisfactory purgation of the audience's pity and fear; the hero must *face* who he is and what he has become for a classic catharsis to be achieved. When this does not occur, the play might be called a "pathegy" instead of a tragedy — that is, the characters are pathetic, rather than tragic. One can feel sorry for them as helpless victims, but one also tends to feel contempt for them as weak, self-indulgent people. Willy, for example, is a habitual liar who wallows in self-pity. We are sorry he is weak, but we wish he were not stupid. It is difficult to empathize with him. This being so, the drama cannot hope to achieve tragic dimensions. If we must view Willy as less than an ordinary man — not quite admirable, not quite intelligent enough to distinguish the American Dream from the American Reality, a product of his own mistakes and not a deity's — then pathos is the most that can be hoped for. If, on the other hand, we view him as typical of the harried modern American man, then there is a possibility for empathy, and even for tragedy. But Miller has not allowed Willy Loman that moment of truth when he recognizes himself — the point of catharsis in classical tragedy. Willy chooses death instead.

By tacking the Requiem onto the end of the play, Miller indicates that he was unable to resolve the drama with Willy's off-stage death. Despite his repudiation of classic catharsis, he provides the opportunity for it through a surrogate, Willy's son, Biff. Miller has Biff state the meaning of Willy's life and death: "He never knew who he was." That is the crux of Willy Loman's pathos and Biff's tragedy, if it can be so called. Self-knowledge is achieved not by the father but by the son.

Biff's story, so closely intertwined with the lies and dreams and ambitions of his father, makes a sub- or mirror plot. Biff's disappointments and failures are a direct result of being fed by his father on impossible expectations, of being encouraged to cut corners, to cheat in small ways, to rely on attractiveness instead of ability. Biff's knowledge of who he is and what he is worth is hard won and not a little bitter to him. But it is what makes him more heroic than Willy. As he tells his brother Happy in his final rejection of the dream begun by his father and perpetuated by Happy: "I know who I am, kid." Those are the magic words that purge the pity and the fear.

G.L.

ARTHUR MILLER

Death of a Salesman

Certain Private Conversations in Two Acts and a Requiem

Characters

WILLY LOMAN
LINDA
BIFF
HAPPY
BERNARD
THE WOMAN (MISS FRANCIS)
CHARLEY
UNCLE BEN
HOWARD WAGNER
JENNY
STANLEY
MISS FORSYTHE
LETTA

(*The action takes place in Willy Loman's house and
yard and in various places he visits in the New York and
Boston of today.*

*Throughout the play, in the stage directions, left and
right mean stage left and stage right.*)

ACT ONE

(*A melody is heard, played upon a flute. It is small and fine, telling of
grass and trees and the horizon. The curtain rises.*

*Before us is the Salesman's house. We are aware of towering, angular
shapes behind it, surrounding it on all sides. Only the blue light of the
sky falls upon the house and forestage; the surrounding area shows an
angry glow of orange. As more light appears, we see a solid vault of
apartment houses around the small, fragile-seeming home. An air of the
dream clings to the place, a dream rising out of reality. The kitchen at
center seems actual enough, for there is a kitchen table with three chairs,
and a refrigerator. But no other fixtures are seen. At the back of the
kitchen there is a draped entrance which leads to the living-room. To the
right of the kitchen, on a level raised two feet, is a bedroom furnished*

538

only with a brass bedstead and a straight chair. On a shelf over the bed a silver athletic trophy stands. A window opens onto the apartment house at the side.

Behind the kitchen, on a level raised six and a half feet, is the boys' bedroom, at present barely visible. Two beds are dimly seen, and at the back of the room a dormer window. [*This bedroom is above the unseen living-room.*] At the left a stairway curves up to it from the kitchen.

The entire setting is wholly or, in some places, partially transparent. The roof-line of the house is one-dimensional; under and over it we see the apartment buildings. Before the house lies an apron, curving beyond the forestage into the orchestra. This forward area serves as the back yard as well as the locale of all WILLY's imaginings and of his city scenes. Whenever the action is in the present the actors observe the imaginary wall-lines, entering the house only through its door at the left. But in the scenes of the past these boundaries are broken and characters enter or leave a room by stepping "through" a wall onto the forestage.

From the right, WILLY LOMAN, the Salesman, enters, carrying two large sample cases. The flute plays on. He hears but is not aware of it. He is past sixty years of age, dressed quietly. Even as he crosses the stage to the doorway of the house, his exhaustion is apparent. He unlocks the door, comes into the kitchen, and thankfully lets his burden down, feeling the soreness of his palms. A word-sigh escapes his lips — it might be "Oh, boy, oh, boy." He closes the door, then carries his cases out into the living-room, through the draped kitchen doorway.

LINDA, his wife, has stirred in her bed at the right. She gets out and puts on a robe, listening. Most often jovial, she has developed an iron repression of her exceptions to WILLY's behavior — she more than loves him, she admires him, as though his mercurial nature, his temper, his massive dreams and little cruelties, served her only as sharp reminders of the turbulent longings within him, longings which she shares but lacks the temperament to utter and follow to their end.)

LINDA (*hearing* WILLY *outside the bedroom, calls with some trepidation*). Willy!

WILLY. It's all right. I came back.

LINDA. Why? What happened? (*Slight pause.*) Did something happen, Willy?

WILLY. No, nothing happened.

LINDA. You didn't smash the car, did you?

WILLY (*with casual irritation*). I said nothing happened. Didn't you hear me?

LINDA. Don't you feel well?

WILLY. I'm tired to the death.

(*The flute has faded away. He sits on the bed beside her, a little numb.*)

I couldn't make it. I just couldn't make it, Linda.

LINDA (*very carefully, delicately*). Where were you all day? You look terrible.

WILLY. I got as far as a little above Yonkers. I stopped for a cup of coffee. Maybe it was the coffee.

LINDA. What?

WILLY (*after a pause*). I suddenly couldn't drive any more. The car kept going off onto the shoulder, y'know?

LINDA (*helpfully*). Oh. Maybe it was the steering again. I don't think Angelo knows the Studebaker.

WILLY. No, it's me, it's me. Suddenly I realize I'm goin' sixty miles an hour and I don't remember the last five minutes. I'm — I can't seem to — keep my mind to it.

LINDA. Maybe it's your glasses. You never went for your new glasses.

WILLY. No, I see everything. I came back ten miles an hour. It took me nearly four hours from Yonkers.

LINDA (*resigned*). Well, you'll just have to take a rest, Willy, you can't continue this way.

WILLY. I just got back from Florida.

LINDA. But you didn't rest your mind. Your mind is over-active, and the mind is what counts, dear.

WILLY. I'll start out in the morning. Maybe I'll feel better in the morning. (*She is taking off his shoes.*) These goddam arch supports are killing me.

LINDA. Take an aspirin. Should I get you an aspirin? It'll soothe you.

WILLY (*with wonder*). I was driving along, you understand? And I was fine. I was even observing the scenery. You can imagine, me looking at scenery, on the road every week of my life. But it's so beautiful up there, Linda, the trees are so thick, and the sun is warm. I opened the windshield and just let the warm air bathe over me. And then all of a sudden I'm goin' off the road! I'm tellin' ya, I absolutely forgot I was driving. If I'd've gone the other way over the white line I might've killed somebody. So I went on again — and five minutes later I'm dreamin' again, and I nearly — (*he presses two fingers against his eyes*). I have such thoughts, I have such strange thoughts.

LINDA. Willy, dear. Talk to them again. There's no reason why you can't work in New York.

WILLY. They don't need me in New York. I'm the New England man. I'm vital in New England.

LINDA. But you're sixty years old. They can't expect you to keep traveling every week.

WILLY. I'll have to send a wire to Portland. I'm supposed to see Brown and Morrison tomorrow morning at ten o'clock to show the line. Goddammit, I could sell them! (*He starts putting on his jacket.*)

LINDA (*taking the jacket from him*). Why don't you go down to the place tomorrow and tell Howard you've simply got to work in New York? You're too accommodating, dear.

WILLY. If old man Wagner was alive I'd a been in charge of New York now! That man was a prince, he was a masterful man. But that boy of his, that Howard, he don't appreciate. When I went north the first time, the Wagner Company didn't know where New England was!

LINDA. Why don't you tell those things to Howard, dear?

WILLY (*encouraged*). I will, I definitely will. Is there any cheese?

LINDA. I'll make you a sandwich.

WILLY. No, go to sleep. I'll take some milk. I'll be up right away. The boys in?

LINDA. They're sleeping. Happy took Biff on a date tonight.

WILLY (*interested*). That so?

LINDA. It was so nice to see them shaving together, one behind the other, in the bathroom. And going out together. You notice? The whole house smells of shaving lotion.

WILLY. Figure it out. Work a lifetime to pay off a house. You finally own it, and there's nobody to live in it.

LINDA. Well, dear, life is a casting off. It's always that way.

WILLY. No, no, some people — some people accomplish something. Did Biff say anything after I went this morning?

LINDA. You shouldn't have criticized him, Willy, especially after he just got off the train. You mustn't lose your temper with him.

WILLY. When the hell did I lose my temper? I simply asked him if he was making any money. Is that a criticism?

LINDA. But, dear, how could he make any money?

WILLY (*worried and angered*). There's such an undercurrent in him. He became a moody man. Did he apologize when I left this morning?

LINDA. He was crestfallen, Willy. You know how he admires you. I think if he finds himself, then you'll both be happier and not fight any more.

WILLY. How can he find himself on a farm? Is that a life? A farm-hand? In the beginning, when he was young, I thought, well, a young man, it's good for him to tramp around, take a lot of different jobs. But it's more than ten years now and he has yet to make thirty-five dollars a week!

LINDA. He's finding himself, Willy.

WILLY. Not finding yourself at the age of thirty-four is a disgrace!

LINDA. Shh!

WILLY. The trouble is he's lazy, goddammit!

LINDA. Willy, please!

WILLY. Biff is a lazy bum!

LINDA. They're sleeping. Get something to eat. Go on down.

WILLY. Why did he come home? I would like to know what brought him home.

LINDA. I don't know. I think he's still lost, Willy. I think he's very lost.

WILLY. Biff Loman is lost. In the greatest country in the world a young man with such — personal attractiveness, gets lost. And such a hard worker. There's one thing about Biff — he's not lazy.

LINDA. Never.

WILLY (*with pity and resolve*). I'll see him in the morning; I'll have a nice talk with him. I'll get him a job selling. He could be big in no time. My God! Remember how they used to follow him around in high school? When he smiled at one of them their faces lit up. When he walked down the street . . . (*He loses himself in reminiscences.*)

LINDA (*trying to bring him out of it*). Willy, dear, I got a new kind of American-type cheese today. It's whipped.

WILLY. Why do you get American when I like Swiss?

LINDA. I just thought you'd like a change —

WILLY. I don't want a change! I want Swiss cheese. Why am I always being contradicted?

LINDA (*with a covering laugh*). I thought it would be a surprise.

WILLY. Why don't you open a window in here, for God's sake?

LINDA (*with infinite patience*). They're all open, dear.

WILLY. The way they boxed us in here. Bricks and windows, windows and bricks.

LINDA. We should've bought the land next door.

WILLY. The street is lined with cars. There's not a breath of fresh air in the neighborhood. The grass don't grow any more, you can't raise a carrot in the back yard. They should've had a law against apartment houses. Remember those two beautiful elm trees out there? When I and Biff hung the swing between them?

LINDA. Yeah, like being a million miles from the city.

WILLY. They should've arrested the builder for cutting those down. They massacred the neighborhood. (*Lost.*) More and more I think of those days, Linda. This time of year it was lilac and wisteria. And then the peonies would come out, and the daffodils. What fragrance in this room!

LINDA. Well, after all, people had to move somewhere.

WILLY. No, there's more people now.

LINDA. I don't think there's more people. I think —

WILLY. There's more people! That's what's ruining this country! Population is getting out of control. The competition is maddening! Smell the stink from that apartment house! And another one on the other side. . . . How can they whip cheese?

(*On* WILLY's *last line,* BIFF *and* HAPPY *raise themselves up in their beds, listening.*)

LINDA. Go down, try it. And be quiet.

WILLY (*turning to* LINDA, *guiltily*). You're not worried about me, are you, sweetheart?

BIFF. What's the matter?

HAPPY. Listen!

LINDA. You've got too much on the ball to worry about.

WILLY. You're my foundation and my support, Linda.

LINDA. Just try to relax, dear. You make mountains out of molehills.

WILLY. I won't fight with him any more. If he wants to go back to Texas, let him go.

LINDA. He'll find his way.

WILLY. Sure. Certain men just don't get started till later in life. Like Thomas Edison, I think. Or B. F. Goodrich. One of them was deaf. (*He starts for the bedroom doorway.*) I'll put my money on Biff.

LINDA. And Willy — if it's warm Sunday, we'll drive in the country. And we'll open the windshield, and take lunch.

WILLY. No, the windshields don't open on the new cars.

LINDA. But you opened it today.

WILLY. Me? I didn't. (*He stops.*) Now isn't that peculiar! Isn't that a remarkable — (*he breaks off in amazement and fright as the flute is heard distantly*).

LINDA. What, darling?

WILLY. That is the most remarkable thing.

LINDA. What, dear?

WILLY. I was thinking of the Chevvy. (*Slight pause.*) Nineteen twenty-eight . . . when I had that red Chevvy — (*breaks off*). That funny? I coulda sworn I was driving that Chevvy today.

LINDA. Well, that's nothing. Something must've reminded you.

WILLY. Remarkable. Ts. Remember those days? The way Biff used to simonize that car? The dealer refused to believe there was eighty thousand miles on it. (*He shakes his head.*) Heh! (*To* LINDA.) Close your eyes, I'll be right up. (*He walks out of the bedroom.*)

HAPPY (*to* BIFF). Jesus, maybe he smashed up the car again!

LINDA (*calling after* WILLY). Be careful on the stairs, dear! The cheese is on the middle shelf! (*She turns, goes over to the bed, takes his jacket, and goes out of the bedroom.*)

(*Light has risen on the boys' room. Unseen,* WILLY *is heard talking to himself, "Eighty thousand miles," and a little laugh.* BIFF *gets out of bed, comes downstage a bit, and stands attentively.* BIFF *is two years older than his brother* HAPPY, *well built, but in these days bears a worn air and seems less self-assured. He has succeeded less, and his dreams are stronger and less acceptable than* HAPPY'S. HAPPY *is tall, powerfully made. Sexuality is like a visible color on him, or a scent that many women have discovered. He, like his brother, is lost, but in a different way, for he has never allowed himself to turn his face toward defeat and is thus more confused and hard-skinned, although seemingly more content.*)

HAPPY (*getting out of bed*). He's going to get his license taken away if he keeps that up. I'm getting nervous about him, y'know, Biff?

BIFF. His eyes are going.

HAPPY. No, I've driven with him. He sees all right. He just doesn't keep his mind on it. I drove into the city with him last week. He stops at a green light and then it turns red and he goes. (*He laughs.*)

BIFF. Maybe he's color-blind.

HAPPY. Pop? Why he's got the finest eye for color in the business. You know that.

BIFF (*sitting down on his bed*). I'm going to sleep.

HAPPY. You're not still sour on Dad, are you, Biff?

BIFF. He's all right, I guess.

WILLY (*underneath them, in the living-room*). Yes, sir, eighty thousand miles — eighty-two thousand!

BIFF. You smoking?

HAPPY (*holding out a pack of cigarettes*). Want one?

BIFF (*taking a cigarette*). I can never sleep when I smell it.

WILLY. What a simonizing job, heh!

HAPPY (*with deep sentiment*). Funny, Biff, y'know? Us sleeping in here again? The old beds. (*He pats his bed affectionately.*) All the talk that went across those two beds, huh? Our whole lives.

BIFF. Yeah. Lotta dreams and plans.

HAPPY (*with a deep and masculine laugh*). About five hundred women would like to know what was said in this room.

(*They share a soft laugh.*)

BIFF. Remember that big Betsy something — what the hell was her name — over on Bushwick Avenue?

HAPPY (*combing his hair*). With the collie dog!

BIFF. That's the one. I got you in there, remember?

HAPPY. Yeah, that was my first time — I think. Boy, there was a pig!

(*They laugh, almost crudely.*)

You taught me everything I know about women. Don't forget that.

BIFF. I bet you forgot how bashful you used to be. Especially with girls.

HAPPY. Oh, I still am, Biff.

BIFF. Oh, go on.

HAPPY. I just control it, that's all. I think I got less bashful and you got more so. What happened, Biff? Where's the old humor, the old confidence?

(*He shakes* BIFF's *knee.* BIFF *gets up and moves restlessly about the room.*)

What's the matter?

BIFF. Why does Dad mock me all the time?

HAPPY. He's not mocking you, he —

BIFF.   Everything I say there's a twist of mockery on his face. I can't get near him.

HAPPY.   He just wants you to make good, that's all. I wanted to talk to you about Dad for a long time, Biff. Something's — happening to him. He — talks to himself.

BIFF.   I noticed that this morning. But he always mumbled.

HAPPY.   But not so noticeable. It got so embarrassing I sent him to Florida. And you know something? Most of the time he's talking to you.

BIFF.   What's he say about me?

HAPPY.   I can't make it out.

BIFF.   What's he say about me?

HAPPY.   I think the fact that you're not settled, that you're still kind of up in the air . . .

BIFF.   There's one or two other things depressing him, Happy.

HAPPY.   What do you mean?

BIFF.   Never mind. Just don't lay it all to me.

HAPPY.   But I think if you just got started — I mean — is there any future for you out there?

BIFF.   I tell ya, Hap, I don't know what the future is. I don't know — what I'm supposed to want.

HAPPY.   What do you mean?

BIFF.   Well, I spent six or seven years after high school trying to work myself up. Shipping clerk, salesman, business of one kind or another. And it's a measly manner of existence. To get on that subway on the hot mornings in summer. To devote your whole life to keeping stock, or making phone calls, or selling or buying. To suffer fifty weeks of the year for the sake of a two-week vacation, when all you really desire is to be outdoors, with your shirt off. And always to have to get ahead of the next fella. And still — that's how you build a future.

HAPPY.   Well, you really enjoy it on a farm? Are you content out there?

BIFF (*with rising agitation*).   Hap, I've had twenty or thirty different kinds of jobs since I left home before the war, and it always turns out the same. I just realized it lately. In Nebraska when I herded cattle, and the Dakotas, and Arizona, and now in Texas. It's why I came home now, I guess, because I realized it. This farm I work on, it's spring there now, see? And they've got about fifteen new colts. There's nothing more inspiring or — beautiful than the sight of a mare and a new colt. And it's cool there now, see? Texas is cool now, and it's spring. And whenever spring comes to where I am, I suddenly get the feeling, my God, I'm not gettin' anywhere! What the hell am I doing, playing around with horses, twenty-eight dollars a week! I'm thirty-four years old, I oughta be makin' my future. That's when I come running home. And now, I get here, and I don't know what to do with myself. (*After a pause.*)   I've always made a point of not wasting my life, and every time I come back here I know that all I've done is to waste my life.

HAPPY. You're a poet, you know that, Biff? You're a — you're an idealist!

BIFF. No, I'm mixed up very bad. Maybe I oughta get married. Maybe I oughta get stuck into something. Maybe that's my trouble. I'm like a boy. I'm not married, I'm not in business, I just — I'm like a boy. Are you content, Hap? You're a success, aren't you? Are you content?

HAPPY. Hell, no!

BIFF. Why? You're making money, aren't you?

HAPPY (moving about with energy, expressiveness). All I can do now is wait for the merchandise manager to die. And suppose I get to be merchandise manager? He's a good friend of mine, and he just built a terrific estate on Long Island. And he lived there about two months and sold it, and now he's building another one. He can't enjoy it once it's finished. And I know that's just what I would do. I don't know what the hell I'm workin' for. Sometimes I sit in my apartment — all alone. And I think of the rent I'm paying. And it's crazy. But then, it's what I always wanted. My own apartment, a car, and plenty of women. And still, goddammit, I'm lonely.

BIFF (with enthusiasm). Listen, why don't you come out West with me?

HAPPY. You and I, heh?

BIFF. Sure, maybe we could buy a ranch. Raise cattle, use our muscles. Men built like we are should be working out in the open.

HAPPY (avidly). The Loman Brothers, heh?

BIFF (with vast affection). Sure, we'd be known all over the counties!

HAPPY (enthralled). That's what I dream about, Biff. Sometimes I want to just rip my clothes off in the middle of the store and outbox that goddam merchandise manager. I mean I can outbox, outrun, and outlift anybody in that store, and I have to take orders from those common, petty sons-of-bitches till I can't stand it any more.

BIFF. I'm tellin' you, kid, if you were with me I'd be happy out there.

HAPPY (enthused). See, Biff, everybody around me is so false that I'm constantly lowering my ideals . . .

BIFF. Baby, together we'd stand up for one another, we'd have someone to trust.

HAPPY. If I were around you —

BIFF. Hap, the trouble is we weren't brought up to grub for money. I don't know how to do it.

HAPPY. Neither can I!

BIFF. Then let's go!

HAPPY. The only thing is — what can you make out there?

BIFF. But look at your friend. Builds an estate and then hasn't the peace of mind to live in it.

HAPPY. Yeah, but when he walks into the store the waves part in front of him. That's fifty-two thousand dollars a year coming through the revolving door, and I got more in my pinky finger than he's got in his head.

BIFF. Yeah, but you just said —

HAPPY. I gotta show some of those pompous, self-important executives over there that Hap Loman can make the grade. I want to walk into the store the way he walks in. Then I'll go with you, Biff. We'll be together yet, I swear. But take those two we had tonight. Now weren't they gorgeous creatures?

BIFF. Yeah, yeah, most gorgeous I've had in years.

HAPPY. I get that any time I want, Biff. Whenever I feel disgusted. The only trouble is, it gets like bowling or something. I just keep knockin' them over and it doesn't mean anything. You still run around a lot?

BIFF. Naa. I'd like to find a girl — steady, somebody with substance.

HAPPY. That's what I long for.

BIFF. Go on! You'd never come home.

HAPPY. I would! Somebody with character, with resistance! Like Mom, y'know? You're gonna call me a bastard when I tell you this. That girl Charlotte I was with tonight is engaged to be married in five weeks. (*He tries on his new hat.*)

BIFF. No kiddin'!

HAPPY. Sure, the guy's in line for the vice-presidency of the store. I don't know what gets into me, maybe I just have an overdeveloped sense of competition or something, but I went and ruined her, and furthermore I can't get rid of her. And he's the third executive I've done that to. Isn't that a crummy characteristic? And to top it all, I go to their weddings! (*Indignantly, but laughing.*) Like I'm not supposed to take bribes. Manufacturers offer me a hundred-dollar bill now and then to throw an order their way. You know how honest I am, but it's like this girl, see. I hate myself for it. Because I don't want the girl, and, still, I take it and — I love it!

BIFF. Let's go to sleep.

HAPPY. I guess we didn't settle anything, heh?

BIFF. I just got one idea that I think I'm going to try.

HAPPY. What's that?

BIFF. Remember Bill Oliver?

HAPPY. Sure, Oliver is very big now. You want to work for him again?

BIFF. No, but when I quit he said something to me. He put his arm on my shoulder, and he said, "Biff, if you ever need anything, come to me."

HAPPY. I remember that. That sounds good.

BIFF. I think I'll go to see him. If I could get ten thousand or even seven or eight thousand dollars I could buy a beautiful ranch.

HAPPY. I bet he'd back you. 'Cause he thought highly of you, Biff. I mean, they all do. You're well liked, Biff. That's why I say to come back here, and we both have the apartment. And I'm tellin' you, Biff, any babe you want . . .

BIFF. No, with a ranch I could do the work I like and still be something. I just wonder, though. I wonder if Oliver still thinks I stole that carton of basketballs.

HAPPY. Oh, he probably forgot that long ago. It's almost ten years. You're too sensitive. Anyway, he didn't really fire you.

BIFF. Well, I think he was going to. I think that's why I quit. I was never sure whether he knew or not. I know he thought the world of me, though. I was the only one he'd let lock up the place.

WILLY (*below*). You gonna wash the engine, Biff?

HAPPY. Shh!

(BIFF *looks at* HAPPY, *who is gazing down, listening.* WILLY *is mumbling in the parlor.*)

You hear that?

(*They listen.* WILLY *laughs warmly.*)

BIFF (*growing angry*). Doesn't he know Mom can hear that?

WILLY. Don't get your sweater dirty, Biff!

(*A look of pain crosses* BIFF'S *face.*)

HAPPY. Isn't that terrible? Don't leave again, will you? You'll find a job here. You gotta stick around. I don't know what to do about him, it's getting embarrassing.

WILLY. What a simonizing job!

BIFF. Mom's hearing that!

WILLY. No kiddin', Biff, you got a date? Wonderful!

HAPPY. Go on to sleep. But talk to him in the morning, will you?

BIFF (*reluctantly getting into bed*). With her in the house. Brother!

HAPPY (*getting into bed*). I wish you'd have a good talk with him.

(*The light on their room begins to fade.*)

BIFF (*to himself in bed*). That selfish, stupid . . .

HAPPY. Sh. . . . Sleep, Biff.

(*Their light is out. Well before they have finished speaking,* WILLY'S *form is dimly seen below in the darkened kitchen. He opens the refrigerator, searches in there, and takes out a bottle of milk. The apartment houses are fading out, and the entire house and surroundings become covered with leaves. Music insinuates itself as the leaves appear.*)

WILLY. Just wanna be careful with those girls, Biff, that's all. Don't make any promises. No promises of any kind. Because a girl, y'know, they always believe what you tell 'em, and you're very young, Biff, you're too young to be talking seriously to girls.

(*Light rises on the kitchen.* WILLY, *talking, shuts the refrigerator door and comes downstage to the kitchen table. He pours milk into a glass. He is totally immersed in himself, smiling faintly.*)

Too young entirely, Biff. You want to watch your schooling first. Then when you're all set, there'll be plenty of girls for a boy like you. (*He smiles broadly at a kitchen chair.*) That so? The girls pay for you? (*He laughs.*) Boy, you must really be makin' a hit. (*willy is gradually addressing — physically — a point offstage, speaking through the wall of the kitchen, and his voice has been rising in volume to that of a normal conversation.*) I been wondering why you polish the car so careful. Ha! Don't leave the hubcaps, boys. Get the chamois to the hubcaps. Happy, use newspaper on the windows, it's the easiest thing. Show him how to do it, Biff! You see, Happy? Pad it up, use it like a pad. That's it, that's it, good work. You're doin' all right, Hap. (*He pauses, then nods in approbation for a few seconds, then looks upward.*) Biff, first thing we gotta do when we get time is clip that big branch over the house. Afraid it's gonna fall in a storm and hit the roof. Tell you what. We get a rope and sling her around, and then we climb up there with a couple of saws and take her down. Soon as you finish the car, boys, I wanna see ya. I got a surprise for you, boys.

BIFF (*offstage*). Whatta ya got, Dad?

WILLY. No, you finish first. Never leave a job till you're finished — remember that. (*Looking toward the "big trees."*) Biff, up in Albany I saw a beautiful hammock. I think I'll buy it next trip, and we'll hang it right between those two elms. Wouldn't that be something? Just swingin' there under those branches. Boy, that would be . . .

(*young biff and young happy appear from the direction willy was addressing. happy carries rags and a pail of water. biff, wearing a sweater with a block "S," carries a football.*)

BIFF (*pointing in the direction of the car offstage*). How's that, Pop, professional?

WILLY. Terrific. Terrific job, boys. Good work, Biff.

HAPPY. Where's the surprise, Pop?

WILLY. In the back seat of the car.

HAPPY. Boy! (*He runs off.*)

BIFF. What is it, Dad? Tell me, what'd you buy?

WILLY (*laughing, cuffs him*). Never mind, something I want you to have.

BIFF (*turns and starts off*). What is it, Hap?

HAPPY (*offstage*). It's a punching bag!

BIFF. Oh, Pop!

WILLY. It's got Gene Tunney's signature on it!

(*happy runs onstage with a punching bag.*)

BIFF. Gee, how'd you know we wanted a punching bag?

WILLY. Well, it's the finest thing for the timing.

HAPPY (*lies down on his back and pedals with his feet*). I'm losing weight, you notice, Pop?

WILLY (*to* HAPPY). Jumping rope is good too.

BIFF. Did you see the new football I got?

WILLY (*examining the ball*). Where'd you get a new ball?

BIFF. The coach told me to practice my passing.

WILLY. That so? And he gave you the ball, heh?

BIFF. Well, I borrowed it from the locker room. (*He laughs confidentially*).

WILLY (*laughing with him at the theft*). I want you to return that.

HAPPY. I told you he wouldn't like it!

BIFF (*angrily*). Well, I'm bringing it back!

WILLY (*stopping the incipient argument, to* HAPPY). Sure, he's gotta practice with a regulation ball, doesn't he? (*To* BIFF.) Coach'll probably congratulate you on your initiative!

BIFF. Oh, he keeps congratulating my initiative all the time, Pop.

WILLY. That's because he likes you. If somebody else took that ball there'd be an uproar. So what's the report, boys, what's the report?

BIFF. Where'd you go this time, Dad? Gee, we were lonesome for you.

WILLY (*pleased, puts an arm around each boy and they come down to the apron*). Lonesome, heh?

BIFF. Missed you every minute.

WILLY. Don't say? Tell you a secret, boys. Don't breathe it to a soul. Someday I'll have my own business, and I'll never have to leave home any more.

HAPPY. Like Uncle Charley, heh?

WILLY. Bigger than Uncle Charley! Because Charley is not — liked. He's liked, but he's not — well liked.

BIFF. Where'd you go this time, Dad?

WILLY. Well, I got on the road, and I went north to Providence. Met the Mayor.

BIFF. The Mayor of Providence!

WILLY. He was sitting in the hotel lobby.

BIFF. What'd he say?

WILLY. He said, "Morning!" And I said, "You got a fine city here, Mayor." And then he had coffee with me. And then I went to Waterbury. Waterbury is a fine city. Big clock city, the famous Waterbury clock. Sold a nice bill there. And then Boston — Boston is the cradle of the Revolution. A fine city. And a couple of other towns in Mass., and on to Portland and Bangor and straight home!

BIFF. Gee, I'd love to go with you sometime, Dad.

WILLY. Soon as summer comes.

HAPPY. Promise?

WILLY. You and Hap and I, and I'll show you all the towns. America is full of beautiful towns and fine, upstanding people. And they know me, boys, they know me up and down New England. The finest people. And when I bring you fellas up, there'll be open sesame for all of us, 'cause one thing, boys: I have friends. I can park my car in any street in New England, and the cops protect it like their own. This summer, heh?

BIFF and HAPPY (*together*). Yeh! You bet!

WILLY. We'll take our bathing suits.

HAPPY. We'll carry your bags, Pop!

WILLY. Oh, won't that be something! Me comin' into the Boston stores with you boys carryin' my bags. What a sensation!

(BIFF *is prancing around, practicing passing the ball.*)

You nervous, Biff, about the game?

BIFF. Not if you're gonna be there.

WILLY. What do they say about you in school, now that they made you captain?

HAPPY. There's a crowd of girls behind him every time the classes change.

BIFF (*taking* WILLY's *hand*). This Saturday, Pop, this Saturday — just for you, I'm going to break through for a touchdown.

HAPPY. You're supposed to pass.

BIFF. I'm takin' one play for Pop. You watch me, Pop, and when I take off my helmet, that means I'm breakin' out. Then you watch me crash through that line!

WILLY (*kisses* BIFF). Oh, wait'll I tell this in Boston!

(BERNARD *enters in knickers. He is younger than* BIFF, *earnest and loyal, a worried boy.*)

BERNARD. Biff, where are you? You're supposed to study with me today.

WILLY. Hey, looka Bernard. What're you lookin' so anemic about, Bernard?

BERNARD. He's gotta study, Uncle Willy. He's got Regents next week.

HAPPY (*tauntingly, spinning* BERNARD *around*). Let's box, Bernard!

BERNARD. Biff! (*He gets away from* HAPPY.) Listen, Biff, I heard Mr. Birnbaum say that if you don't start studyin' math he's gonna flunk you, and you won't graduate. I heard him!

WILLY. You better study with him, Biff. Go ahead now.

BERNARD. I heard him!

BIFF. Oh, Pop, you didn't see my sneakers! (*He holds up a foot for* WILLY *to look at.*)

WILLY. Hey, that's a beautiful job of printing!

BERNARD (*wiping his glasses*). Just because he printed University of Virginia on his sneakers doesn't mean they've got to graduate him, Uncle Willy!

WILLY (*angrily*). What're you talking about? With scholarships to three universities they're gonna flunk him?

BERNARD. But I heard Mr. Birnbaum say ——

WILLY. Don't be a pest, Bernard! (*To his boys.*) What an anemic!

BERNARD. Okay, I'm waiting for you in my house, Biff.

(BERNARD *goes off. The Lomans laugh.*)

WILLY. Bernard is not well liked, is he?

BIFF. He's liked, but he's not well liked.

HAPPY. That's right, Pop.

WILLY. That's just what I mean. Bernard can get the best marks in school, y'understand, but when he gets out in the business world, y'understand, you are going to be five times ahead of him. That's why I thank Almighty God you're both built like Adonises. Because the man who makes an appearance in the business world, the man who creates personal interest, is the man who gets ahead. Be liked and you will never want. You take me, for instance. I never have to wait in line to see a buyer. "Willy Loman is here!" That's all they have to know, and I go right through.

BIFF. Did you knock them dead, Pop?

WILLY. Knocked 'em cold in Providence, slaughtered 'em in Boston.

HAPPY (*on his back, pedaling again*). I'm losing weight, you notice, Pop?

(LINDA *enters, as of old, a ribbon in her hair, carrying a basket of washing.*)

LINDA (*with youthful energy*). Hello, dear!

WILLY. Sweetheart!

LINDA. How'd the Chevvy run?

WILLY. Chevrolet, Linda, is the greatest car ever built. (*To the boys.*) Since when do you let your mother carry wash up the stairs?

BIFF. Grab hold there, boy!

HAPPY. Where to, Mom?

LINDA. Hang them up on the line. And you better go down to your friends, Biff. The cellar is full of boys. They don't know what to do with themselves.

BIFF. Ah, when Pop comes home they can wait!

WILLY (*laughs appreciatively*). You better go down and tell them what to do, Biff.

BIFF. I think I'll have them sweep out the furnace room.

WILLY. Good work, Biff.

BIFF (*goes through wall-line of kitchen to doorway at back and calls down*). Fellas! Everybody sweep out the furnace room! I'll be right down!

VOICES. All right! Okay, Biff.

BIFF. George and Sam and Frank, come out back! We're hangin' up the wash! Come on, Hap, on the double!

(*He and* HAPPY *carry out the basket.*)

LINDA. The way they obey him!

WILLY. Well, that's training, the training. I'm tellin' you, I was sellin' thousands and thousands, but I had to come home.

LINDA. Oh, the whole block'll be at that game. Did you sell anything?

WILLY. I did five hundred gross in Providence and seven hundred gross in Boston.

LINDA. No! Wait a minute, I've got a pencil. (*She pulls pencil and paper out of her apron pocket.*) That makes your commission . . . two hundred — my God! Two hundred and twelve dollars!

WILLY. Well, I didn't figure it yet, but . . .

LINDA. How much did you do?

WILLY. Well, I — I did — about a hundred and eighty gross in Providence. Well, no — it came to — roughly two hundred gross on the whole trip.

LINDA (*without hesitation*). Two hundred gross. That's . . . (*she figures*).

WILLY. The trouble was that three of the stores were half closed for inventory in Boston. Otherwise I woulda broke records.

LINDA. Well, it makes seventy dollars and some pennies. That's very good.

WILLY. What do we owe?

LINDA. Well, on the first there's sixteen dollars on the refrigerator —

WILLY. Why sixteen?

LINDA. Well, the fan belt broke, so it was a dollar eighty.

WILLY. But it's brand new.

LINDA. Well, the man said that's the way it is. Till they work themselves in, y'know.

(*They move through the wall-line into the kitchen.*)

WILLY. I hope we didn't get stuck on that machine.

LINDA. They got the biggest ads of any of them!

WILLY. I know, it's a fine machine. What else?

LINDA. Well, there's nine-sixty for the washing machine. And for the vacuum cleaner there's three and a half due on the fifteenth. Then the roof, you got twenty-one dollars remaining.

WILLY. It don't leak, does it?

LINDA. No, they did a wonderful job. Then you owe Frank for the carburetor.

WILLY. I'm not going to pay that man! That goddam Chevrolet, they ought to prohibit the manufacture of that car!

LINDA. Well, you owe him three and a half. And odds and ends, comes to around a hundred and twenty dollars by the fifteenth.

WILLY. A hundred and twenty dollars! My God, if business don't pick up I don't know what I'm gonna do!

LINDA. Well, next week you'll do better.

WILLY. Oh, I'll knock 'em dead next week. I'll go to Hartford. I'm very well liked in Hartford. (*Pause.*) You know, the trouble is, Linda, people don't seem to take to me.

(*They move onto the forestage.*)

LINDA. Oh, don't be foolish.

WILLY. I know it when I walk in. They seem to laugh at me.

LINDA. Why? Why would they laugh at you? Don't talk that way, Willy.

(WILLY *moves to the edge of the stage.* LINDA *goes into the kitchen and starts to darn stockings.*)

WILLY. I don't know the reason for it, but they just pass me by. I'm not noticed.

LINDA. But you're doing wonderful, dear. You're making seventy to a hundred dollars a week.

WILLY. But I gotta be at it ten, twelve hours a day. Other men — I don't know — they do it easier. I don't know why — I can't stop myself — I talk too much. A man oughta come in with a few words. One thing about Charley. He's a man of few words, and they respect him.

LINDA. You don't talk too much, you're just lively.

WILLY (*smiling*). Well, I figure, what the hell, life is short, a couple of jokes. (*To himself.*) I joke too much! (*The smile goes.*)

LINDA. Why? You're —

WILLY. I'm fat. I'm very — foolish to look at, Linda. I didn't tell you, but Christmas time I happened to be calling on F. H. Stewarts, and a salesman I know, as I was going in to see the buyer, I heard him say something about — walrus. And I — I cracked him right across the face. I won't take that. I simply will not take that. But they do laugh at me. I know that.

LINDA. Darling . . .

WILLY. I gotta overcome it. I know I gotta overcome it. I'm not dressing to advantage, maybe.

LINDA. Willy, darling, you're the handsomest man in the world —

WILLY. Oh, no, Linda.

LINDA. To me you are. (*Slight pause.*) The handsomest.

(*From the darkness is heard the laughter of a woman.* WILLY *doesn't turn to it, but it continues through* LINDA's *lines.*)

And the boys, Willy. Few men are idolized by their children the way you are.

(*Music is heard as behind a scrim, to the left of the house,* THE WOMAN, *dimly seen, is dressing.*)

WILLY (*with great feeling*). You're the best there is, Linda, you're a pal, you know that? On the road — on the road I want to grab you sometimes and just kiss the life outa you.

(*The laughter is loud now, and he moves into a brightening area at the left, where* THE WOMAN *has come from behind the scrim and is standing, putting on her hat, looking into a "mirror" and laughing.*)

'Cause I get so lonely — especially when business is bad and there's nobody to talk to. I get the feeling that I'll never sell anything again, that I won't make a living for you, or a business, a business for the boys.

(*He talks through* THE WOMAN'S *subsiding laughter;* THE WOMAN *primps at the "mirror."*)

There's so much I want to make for —

THE WOMAN. Me? You didn't make me, Willy. I picked you.

WILLY (*pleased*). You picked me?

THE WOMAN (*who is quite proper-looking,* WILLY'S *age*). I did. I've been sitting at that desk watching all the salesmen go by, day in, day out. But you've got such a sense of humor, and we do have such a good time together, don't we?

WILLY. Sure, sure. (*He takes her in his arms.*) Why do you have to go now?

THE WOMAN. It's two o'clock . . .

WILLY. No, come on in! (*He pulls her.*)

THE WOMAN. . . . my sisters'll be scandalized. When'll you be back?

WILLY. Oh, two weeks about. Will you come up again?

THE WOMAN. Sure thing. You do make me laugh. It's good for me. (*She squeezes his arm, kisses him.*) And I think you're a wonderful man.

WILLY. You picked me, heh?

THE WOMAN. Sure. Because you're so sweet. And such a kidder.

WILLY. Well, I'll see you next time I'm in Boston.

THE WOMAN. I'll put you right through to the buyers.

WILLY (*slapping her bottom*). Right. Well, bottoms up!

THE WOMAN (*slaps him gently and laughs*). You just kill me, Willy.

(*He suddenly grabs her and kisses her roughly.*)

You kill me. And thanks for the stockings. I love a lot of stockings. Well, good night.

WILLY. Good night. And keep your pores open!

THE WOMAN. Oh, Willy!

(THE WOMAN *bursts out laughing, and* LINDA'S *laughter blends in.* THE WOMAN *disappears into the dark. Now the area at the kitchen table brightens.* LINDA *is sitting where she was at the kitchen table, but now is mending a pair of her silk stockings.*)

LINDA. You are, Willy. The handsomest man. You've got no reason to feel that —

WILLY (*coming out of* THE WOMAN's *dimming area and going over to* LINDA). I'll make it all up to you, Linda, I'll —

LINDA. There's nothing to make up, dear. You're doing fine, better than —

WILLY (*noticing her mending*). What's that?

LINDA. Just mending my stockings. They're so expensive —

WILLY (*angrily, taking them from her*). I won't have you mending stockings in this house! Now throw them out!

(LINDA *puts the stockings in her pocket.*)

BERNARD (*entering on the run*). Where is he? If he doesn't study!

WILLY (*moving to the forestage, with great agitation*). You'll give him the answers!

BERNARD. I do, but I can't on a Regents! That's a state exam! They're liable to arrest me!

WILLY. Where is he? I'll whip him, I'll whip him!

LINDA. And he'd better give back that football, Willy, it's not nice.

WILLY. Biff! Where is he? Why is he taking everything?

LINDA. He's too rough with the girls, Willy. All the mothers are afraid of him!

WILLY. I'll whip him!

BERNARD. He's driving the car without a license!

(THE WOMAN's *laugh is heard.*)

WILLY. Shut up!

LINDA. All the mothers —

WILLY. Shut up!

BERNARD (*backing quietly away and out*). Mr. Birnbaum says he's stuck up.

WILLY. Get outa here!

BERNARD. If he doesn't buckle down he'll flunk math! (*He goes off.*)

LINDA. He's right, Willy, you've gotta —

WILLY (*exploding at her*). There's nothing the matter with him! You want him to be a worm like Bernard? He's got spirit, personality . . .

(*As he speaks,* LINDA, *almost in tears, exits into the living-room.* WILLY *is alone in the kitchen, wilting and staring. The leaves are gone. It is night again, and the apartment houses look down from behind.*)

Loaded with it. Loaded! What is he stealing? He's giving it back, isn't he? Why is he stealing? What did I tell him? I never in my life told him anything but decent things.

(HAPPY *in pajamas has come down the stairs;* WILLY *suddenly becomes aware of* HAPPY's *presence.*)

HAPPY. Let's go now, come on.

WILLY (*sitting down at the kitchen table*). Huh! Why did she have to wax the floors herself? Every time she waxes the floors she keels over. She knows that!

HAPPY. Shh! Take it easy. What brought you back tonight?

WILLY. I got an awful scare. Nearly hit a kid in Yonkers. God! Why didn't I go to Alaska with my brother Ben that time! Ben! That man was a genius, that man was success incarnate! What a mistake! He begged me to go.

HAPPY. Well, there's no use in —

WILLY. You guys! There was a man started with the clothes on his back and ended up with diamond mines!

HAPPY. Boy, someday I'd like to know how he did it.

WILLY. What's the mystery? The man knew what he wanted and went out and got it! Walked into a jungle, and comes out, the age of twenty-one, and he's rich! The world is an oyster, but you don't crack it open on a mattress!

HAPPY. Pop, I told you I'm gonna retire you for life.

WILLY. You'll retire me for life on seventy goddam dollars a week? And your women and your car and your apartment, and you'll retire me for life! Christ's sake, I couldn't get past Yonkers today! Where are you guys, where are you? The woods are burning! I can't drive a car!

(*CHARLEY has appeared in the doorway. He is a large man, slow of speech, laconic, immovable. In all he says, despite what he says, there is pity, and, now, trepidation. He has a robe over pajamas, slippers on his feet. He enters the kitchen.*)

CHARLEY. Everything all right?

HAPPY. Yeah, Charley, everything's . . .

WILLY. What's the matter?

CHARLEY. I heard some noise. I thought something happened. Can't we do something about the walls? You sneeze in here, and in my house hats blow off.

HAPPY. Let's go to bed, Dad. Come on.

(*CHARLEY signals to HAPPY to go.*)

WILLY. You go ahead, I'm not tired at the moment.

HAPPY (*to WILLY*). Take it easy, huh? (*He exits.*)

WILLY. What're you doin' up?

CHARLEY (*sitting down at the kitchen table opposite WILLY*). Couldn't sleep good. I had a heartburn.

WILLY. Well, you don't know how to eat.

CHARLEY. I eat with my mouth.

WILLY. No, you're ignorant. You gotta know about vitamins and things like that.

CHARLEY. Come on, let's shoot. Tire you out a little.

WILLY (*hesitantly*). All right. You got cards?

CHARLEY (*taking a deck from his pocket*). Yeah, I got them. Someplace. What is it with those vitamins?

WILLY (*dealing*). They build up your bones. Chemistry.

CHARLEY. Yeah, but there's no bones in a heartburn.

WILLY. What are you talkin' about? Do you know the first thing about it?

CHARLEY. Don't get insulted.

WILLY. Don't talk about something you don't know anything about.

(*They are playing. Pause.*)

CHARLEY. What're you doin' home?

WILLY. A little trouble with the car.

CHARLEY. Oh. (*Pause.*) I'd like to take a trip to California.

WILLY. Don't say.

CHARLEY. You want a job?

WILLY. I got a job, I told you that. (*After a slight pause.*) What the hell are you offering me a job for?

CHARLEY. Don't get insulted.

WILLY. Don't insult me.

CHARLEY. I don't see no sense in it. You don't have to go on this way.

WILLY. I got a good job. (*Slight pause.*) What do you keep comin' in here for?

CHARLEY. You want me to go?

WILLY (*after a pause, withering*). I can't understand it. He's going back to Texas again. What the hell is that?

CHARLEY. Let him go.

WILLY. I got nothin' to give him, Charley, I'm clean, I'm clean.

CHARLEY. He won't starve. None a them starve. Forget about him.

WILLY. Then what have I got to remember?

CHARLEY. You take it too hard. To hell with it. When a deposit bottle is broken you don't get your nickel back.

WILLY. That's easy enough for you to say.

CHARLEY. That ain't easy for me to say.

WILLY. Did you see the ceiling I put up in the living-room?

CHARLEY. Yeah, that's a piece of work. To put up a ceiling is a mystery to me. How do you do it?

WILLY. What's the difference?

CHARLEY. Well, talk about it.

WILLY. You gonna put up a ceiling?

CHARLEY. How could I put up a ceiling?

WILLY. Then what the hell are you bothering me for?

CHARLEY. You're insulted again.

WILLY. A man who can't handle tools is not a man. You're disgusting.

CHARLEY. Don't call me disgusting, Willy.

(UNCLE BEN, *carrying a valise and an umbrella, enters the forestage from around the right corner of the house. He is a stolid man, in his sixties, with a mustache and an authoritative air. He is utterly certain of his destiny, and there is an aura of far places about him. He enters exactly as* WILLY *speaks.*)

WILLY.   I'm getting awfully tired, Ben.

(BEN's *music is heard.* BEN *looks around at everything.*)

CHARLEY.   Good, keep playing; you'll sleep better. Did you call me Ben?

(BEN *looks at his watch.*)

WILLY.   That's funny. For a second there you reminded me of my brother Ben.

BEN.   I only have a few minutes.

(*He strolls, inspecting the place.* WILLY *and* CHARLEY *continue playing.*)

CHARLEY.   You never heard from him again, heh? Since that time?

WILLY.   Didn't Linda tell you? Couple of weeks ago we got a letter from his wife in Africa. He died.

CHARLEY.   That so.

BEN (*chuckling*).   So this is Brooklyn, eh?

CHARLEY.   Maybe you're in for some of his money.

WILLY.   Naa, he had seven sons. There's just one opportunity I had with that man . . .

BEN.   I must make a train, William. There are several properties I'm looking at in Alaska.

WILLY.   Sure, sure! If I'd gone with him to Alaska that time, everything would've been totally different.

CHARLEY.   Go on, you'd froze to death up there.

WILLY.   What're you talking about?

BEN.   Opportunity is tremendous in Alaska, William. Surprised you're not up there.

WILLY.   Sure, tremendous.

CHARLEY.   Heh?

WILLY.   There was the only man I ever met who knew the answers.

CHARLEY.   Who?

BEN.   How are you all?

WILLY (*taking a pot, smiling*).   Fine, fine.

CHARLEY.   Pretty sharp tonight.

BEN.   Is Mother living with you?

WILLY.   No, she died a long time ago.

CHARLEY. Who?

BEN. That's too bad. Fine specimen of a lady, Mother.

WILLY (*to* CHARLEY). Heh?

BEN. I'd hoped to see the old girl.

CHARLEY. Who died?

BEN. Heard anything from Father, have you?

WILLY (*unnerved*). What do you mean, who died?

CHARLEY (*taking a pot*). What're you talkin' about?

BEN (*looking at his watch*). William, it's half-past eight!

WILLY (*as though to dispel his confusion he angrily stops* CHARLEY'S *hand*). That's my build!

CHARLEY. I put the ace —

WILLY. If you don't know how to play the game I'm not gonna throw my money away on you!

CHARLEY (*rising*). It was my ace, for God's sake!

WILLY. I'm through, I'm through!

BEN. When did Mother die?

WILLY. Long ago. Since the beginning you never knew how to play cards.

CHARLEY (*picks up the cards and goes to the door*). All right! Next time I'll bring a deck with five aces.

WILLY. I don't play that kind of game!

CHARLEY (*turning to him*). You ought to be ashamed of yourself!

WILLY. Yeah?

CHARLEY. Yeah! (*He goes out.*)

WILLY (*slamming the door after him*). Ignoramus!

BEN (*as* WILLY *comes toward him through the wall-line of the kitchen*). So you're William.

WILLY (*shaking* BEN's *hand*). Ben! I've been waiting for you so long! What's the answer? How did you do it?

BEN. Oh, there's a story in that.

(LINDA *enters the forestage, as of old, carrying the wash basket.*)

LINDA. Is this Ben?

BEN (*gallantly*). How do you do, my dear.

LINDA. Where've you been all these years? Willy's always wondered why you —

WILLY (*pulling* BEN *away from her impatiently*). Where is Dad? Didn't you follow him? How did you get started?

BEN. Well, I don't know how much you remember.

WILLY. Well, I was just a baby, of course, only three or four years old —

BEN. Three years and eleven months.

WILLY. What a memory, Ben!

BEN. I have many enterprises, William, and I have never kept books.

WILLY. I remember I was sitting under the wagon in — was it Nebraska?

BEN. It was South Dakota, and I gave you a bunch of wild flowers.

WILLY. I remember you walking away down some open road.

BEN (*laughing*). I was going to find Father in Alaska.

WILLY. Where is he?

BEN. At that age I had a very faulty view of geography, William. I discovered after a few days that I was heading due south, so instead of Alaska, I ended up in Africa.

LINDA. Africa!

WILLY. The Gold Coast!

BEN. Principally diamond mines.

LINDA. Diamond mines!

BEN. Yes, my dear. But I've only a few minutes —

WILLY. No! Boys! Boys!

(YOUNG BIFF *and* HAPPY *appear.*)

Listen to this. This is your Uncle Ben, a great man! Tell my boys, Ben!

BEN. Why, boys, when I was seventeen I walked into the jungle, and when I was twenty-one I walked out. (*He laughs.*) And by God I was rich.

WILLY (*to the boys*). You see what I been talking about? The greatest things can happen!

BEN (*glancing at his watch*). I have an appointment in Ketchikan Tuesday week.

WILLY. No, Ben! Please tell about Dad. I want my boys to hear. I want them to know the kind of stock they spring from. All I remember is a man with a big beard, and I was in Mamma's lap, sitting around a fire, and some kind of high music.

BEN. His flute. He played the flute.

WILLY. Sure, the flute, that's right!

(*New music is heard, a high, rollicking tune.*)

BEN. Father was a very great and a very wild-hearted man. We would start in Boston, and he'd toss the whole family into the wagon, and then he'd drive the team right across the country; through Ohio, and Indiana, Michigan, Illinois, and all the Western states. And we'd stop in the towns and sell the flutes that he'd made on the way. Great inventor, Father. With one gadget he made more in a week than a man like you could make in a lifetime.

WILLY. That's just the way I'm bringing them up, Ben — rugged, well liked, all-around.

BEN. Yeah? (*To* BIFF.) Hit that, boy — hard as you can. (*He pounds his stomach.*)

BIFF. Oh, no, sir!

BEN (*taking boxing stance*).   Come on, get to me!   (*He laughs.*)

WILLY.   Go to it, Biff! Go ahead, show him!

BIFF.   Okay! (*He cocks his fists and starts in.*)

LINDA (*to* WILLY).   Why must he fight, dear?

BEN (*sparring with* BIFF).   Good boy! Good boy!

WILLY.   How's that, Ben, heh?

HAPPY.   Give him the left, Biff!

LINDA.   Why are you fighting?

BEN.   Good boy! (*Suddenly comes in, trips* BIFF, *and stands over him, the point of his umbrella poised over* BIFF'S *eye.*)

LINDA.   Look out, Biff!

BIFF.   Gee!

BEN (*patting* BIFF'S *knee*).   Never fight fair with a stranger, boy. You'll never get out of the jungle that way. (*Taking* LINDA'S *hand and bowing.*) It was an honor and a pleasure to meet you, Linda.

LINDA (*withdrawing her hand coldly, frightened*).   Have a nice — trip.

BEN (*to* WILLY).   And good luck with your — what do you do?

WILLY.   Selling.

BEN.   Yes. Well . . . (*he raises his hand in farewell to all*).

WILLY.   No, Ben, I don't want you to think . . . (*he takes* BEN'S *arm to show him*). It's Brooklyn, I know, but we hunt too.

BEN.   Really, now.

WILLY.   Oh, sure, there's snakes and rabbits and — that's why I moved out here. Why, Biff can fell any one of these trees in no time! Boys! Go right over to where they're building the apartment house and get some sand. We're gonna rebuild the entire front stoop right now! Watch this, Ben!

BIFF.   Yes, sir! On the double, Hap!

HAPPY (*as he and* BIFF *run off*).   I lost weight, Pop, you notice?

(CHARLEY *enters in knickers, even before the boys are gone.*)

CHARLEY.   Listen, if they steal any more from that building the watchman'll put the cops on them!

LINDA (*to* WILLY).   Don't let Biff . . .

(BEN *laughs lustily.*)

WILLY.   You shoulda seen the lumber they brought home last week. At least a dozen six-by-tens worth all kinds a money.

CHARLEY.   Listen, if that watchman —

WILLY.   I gave them hell, understand. But I got a couple of fearless characters there.

CHARLEY.   Willy, the jails are full of fearless characters.

BEN (*clapping* WILLY *on the back, with a laugh at* CHARLEY).   And the stock exchange, friend!

WILLY (*joining in* BEN'S *laughter*).   Where are the rest of your pants?

CHARLEY. My wife bought them.

WILLY. Now all you need is a golf club and you can go upstairs and go to sleep. (*To* BEN.) Great athlete! Between him and his son Bernard they can't hammer a nail!

BERNARD (*rushing in*). The watchman's chasing Biff!

WILLY (*angrily*). Shut up! He's not stealing anything!

LINDA (*alarmed, hurrying off left*). Where is he? Biff, dear! (*She exits.*)

WILLY (*moving toward the left, away from* BEN). There's nothing wrong. What's the matter with you?

BEN. Nervy boy. Good!

WILLY (*laughing*). Oh, nerves of iron, that Biff!

CHARLEY. Don't know what it is. My New England man comes back and he's bleedin', they murdered him up there.

WILLY. It's contacts, Charley, I got important contacts!

CHARLEY (*sarcastically*). Glad to hear it, Willy. Come in later, we'll shoot a little casino. I'll take some of your Portland money. (*He laughs at* WILLY *and exits.*)

WILLY (*turning to* BEN). Business is bad, it's murderous. But not for me, of course.

BEN. I'll stop by on my way back to Africa.

WILLY (*longingly*). Can't you stay a few days? You're just what I need, Ben, because I — I have a fine position here, but I — well, Dad left when I was such a baby and I never had a chance to talk to him and I still feel — kind of temporary about myself.

BEN. I'll be late for my train.

(*They are at opposite ends of the stage.*)

WILLY. Ben, my boys — can't we talk? They'd go into the jaws of hell for me, see, but I —

BEN. William, you're being first-rate with your boys. Outstanding, manly chaps!

WILLY (*hanging on to his words*). Oh, Ben, that's good to hear! Because sometimes I'm afraid that I'm not teaching them the right kind of — Ben, how should I teach them?

BEN (*giving great weight to each word, and with a certain vicious audacity*). William, when I walked into the jungle, I was seventeen. When I walked out I was twenty-one. And, by God, I was rich! (*He goes off into darkness around the right corner of the house.*)

WILLY. . . . was rich! That's just the spirit I want to imbue them with! To walk into a jungle! I was right! I was right! I was right!

(BEN *is gone, but* WILLY *is still speaking to him as* LINDA, *in nightgown and robe, enters the kitchen, glances around for* WILLY, *then goes to the door of the house, looks out and sees him. Comes down to his left. He looks at her.*)

LINDA. Willy, dear? Willy?

WILLY. I was right!

LINDA. Did you have some cheese? (*He can't answer.*) It's very late, darling. Come to bed, heh?

WILLY (*looking straight up*). Gotta break your neck to see a star in this yard.

LINDA. You coming in?

WILLY. Whatever happened to that diamond watch fob? Remember? When Ben came from Africa that time? Didn't he give me a watch fob with a diamond in it?

LINDA. You pawned it, dear. Twelve, thirteen years ago. For Biff's radio correspondence course.

WILLY. Gee, that was a beautiful thing. I'll take a walk.

LINDA. But you're in your slippers.

WILLY (*starting to go around the house at the left*). I was right! I was! (*Half to* LINDA, *as he goes, shaking his head.*) What a man! There was a man worth talking to. I was right!

LINDA (*calling after* WILLY). But in your slippers, Willy!

(WILLY *is almost gone when* BIFF, *in his pajamas, comes down the stairs and enters the kitchen.*)

BIFF. What is he doing out there?

LINDA. Sh!

BIFF. God Almighty, Mom, how long has he been doing this?

LINDA. Don't, he'll hear you.

BIFF. What the hell is the matter with him?

LINDA. It'll pass by morning.

BIFF. Shouldn't we do anything?

LINDA. Oh, my dear, you should do a lot of things, but there's nothing to do, so go to sleep.

(HAPPY *comes down the stair and sits on the steps.*)

HAPPY. I never heard him so loud, Mom.

LINDA. Well, come around more often; you'll hear him. (*She sits down at the table and mends the lining of* WILLY's *jacket.*)

BIFF. Why didn't you ever write me about this, Mom?

LINDA. How would I write to you? For over three months you had no address.

BIFF. I was on the move. But you know I thought of you all the time. You know that, don't you, pal?

LINDA. I know, dear, I know. But he likes to have a letter. Just to know that there's still a possibility for better things.

BIFF. He's not like this all the time, is he?

LINDA. It's when you come home he's always the worst.

BIFF. When I come home?

LINDA.   When you write you're coming, he's all smiles, and talks about the future, and — he's just wonderful. And then the closer you seem to come, the more shaky he gets, and then, by the time you get here, he's arguing, and he seems angry at you. I think it's just that maybe he can't bring himself to — to open up to you. Why are you so hateful to each other? Why is that?

BIFF (*evasively*).   I'm not hateful, Mom.

LINDA.   But you no sooner come in the door than you're fighting!

BIFF.   I don't know why. I mean to change. I'm tryin', Mom, you understand?

LINDA.   Are you home to stay now?

BIFF.   I don't know. I want to look around, see what's doin'.

LINDA.   Biff, you can't look around all your life, can you?

BIFF.   I just can't take hold, Mom. I can't take hold of some kind of a life.

LINDA.   Biff, a man is not a bird, to come and go with the springtime.

BIFF.   Your hair . . . (*he touches her hair*). Your hair got so gray.

LINDA.   Oh, it's been gray since you were in high school. I just stopped dyeing it, that's all.

BIFF.   Dye it again, will ya? I don't want my pal looking old. (*He smiles.*)

LINDA.   You're such a boy! You think you can go away for a year and . . . You've got to get it into your head now that one day you'll knock on this door and there'll be strange people here —

BIFF.   What are you talking about? You're not even sixty, Mom.

LINDA.   But what about your father?

BIFF (*lamely*).   Well, I meant him too.

HAPPY.   He admires Pop.

LINDA.   Biff, dear, if you don't have any feeling for him, then you can't have any feeling for me.

BIFF.   Sure I can, Mom.

LINDA.   No. You can't just come to see me, because I love him. (*With a threat, but only a threat, of tears.*) He's the dearest man in the world to me, and I won't have anyone making him feel unwanted and low and blue. You've got to make up your mind now, darling, there's no leeway any more. Either he's your father and you pay him that respect, or else you're not to come here. I know he's not easy to get along with — nobody knows that better than me — but . . .

WILLY (*from the left, with a laugh*).   Hey, hey, Biffo!

BIFF (*starting to go out after WILLY*).   What the hell is the matter with him?

(HAPPY *stops him.*)

LINDA.   Don't — don't go near him!

BIFF.   Stop making excuses for him! He always, always wiped the floor with you. Never had an ounce of respect for you.

HAPPY. He's always had respect for —

BIFF. What the hell do you know about it?

HAPPY (surlily). Just don't call him crazy!

BIFF. He's got no character — Charley wouldn't do this. Not in his own house — spewing out that vomit from his mind.

HAPPY. Charley never had to cope with what he's got to.

BIFF. People are worse off than Willy Loman. Believe me, I've seen them!

LINDA. Then make Charley your father, Biff. You can't do that, can you? I don't say he's a great man. Willy Loman never made a lot of money. His name was never in the paper. He's not the finest character that ever lived. But he's a human being, and a terrible thing is happening to him. So attention must be paid. He's not to be allowed to fall into his grave like an old dog. Attention, attention must be finally paid to such a person. You called him crazy —

BIFF. I didn't mean —

LINDA. No, a lot of people think he's lost his — balance. But you don't have to be very smart to know what his trouble is. The man is exhausted.

HAPPY. Sure!

LINDA. A small man can be just as exhausted as a great man. He works for a company thirty-six years this March, opens up unheard-of territories to their trademark, and now in his old age they take his salary away.

HAPPY (indignantly). I didn't know that, Mom.

LINDA. You never asked, my dear! Now that you get your spending money someplace else you don't trouble your mind with him.

HAPPY. But I gave you money last —

LINDA. Christmas time, fifty dollars! To fix the hot water it cost ninety-seven fifty! For five weeks he's been on straight commission, like a beginner, an unknown!

BIFF. Those ungrateful bastards!

LINDA. Are they any worse than his sons? When he brought them business, when he was young, they were glad to see him. But now his old friends, the old buyers that loved him so and always found some order to hand him in a pinch — they're all dead, retired. He used to be able to make six, seven calls a day in Boston. Now he takes his valises out of the car and puts them back and takes them out again and he's exhausted. Instead of walking he talks now. He drives seven hundred miles, and when he gets there no one knows him any more, no one welcomes him. And what goes through a man's mind, driving seven hundred miles home without having earned a cent? Why shouldn't he talk to himself? Why? When he has to go to Charley and borrow fifty dollars a week and pretend to me that it's his pay? How long can that go on? How long? You see what I'm sitting here and waiting for? And you tell me he has no character? The man who never worked a day but for your benefit? When does he get the medal for that? Is this his reward — to turn around at the

age of sixty-three and find his sons, who he loved better than his life, one
a philandering bum —

HAPPY. Mom!

LINDA. That's all you are, my baby! (*To* BIFF.) And you! What
happened to the love you had for him? You were such pals! How you
used to talk to him on the phone every night! How lonely he was till he
could come home to you!

BIFF. All right, Mom. I'll live here in my room, and I'll get a job. I'll
keep away from him, that's all.

LINDA. No, Biff. You can't stay here and fight all the time.

BIFF. He threw me out of this house, remember that.

LINDA. Why did he do that? I never knew why.

BIFF. Because I know he's a fake and he doesn't like anybody around
who knows!

LINDA. Why a fake? In what way? What do you mean?

BIFF. Just don't lay it all at my feet. It's between me and him —
that's all I have to say. I'll chip in from now on. He'll settle for half my
pay check. He'll be all right. I'm going to bed. (*He starts for the stairs.*)

LINDA. He won't be all right.

BIFF (*turning on the stairs, furiously*). I hate this city and I'll stay
here. Now what do you want?

LINDA. He's dying, Biff.

(HAPPY *turns quickly to her, shocked.*)

BIFF (*after a pause*). Why is he dying?

LINDA. He's been trying to kill himself.

BIFF (*with great horror*). How?

LINDA. I live from day to day.

BIFF. What're you talking about?

LINDA. Remember I wrote you that he smashed up the car again? In
February?

BIFF. Well?

LINDA. The insurance inspector came. He said that they have evidence. That all these accidents in the last year — weren't — weren't —
accidents.

HAPPY. How can they tell that? That's a lie.

LINDA. It seems there's a woman . . . (*she takes a breath*).

BIFF (*sharply but contained*). What woman?

LINDA (*simultaneously*). . . . and this woman . . .

LINDA. What?

BIFF. Nothing. Go ahead.

LINDA. What did you say?

BIFF. Nothing. I just said what woman?

HAPPY. What about her?

LINDA. Well, it seems she was walking down the road and saw his car. She says that he wasn't driving fast at all, and that he didn't skid. She says he came to that little bridge, and then deliberately smashed into the railing, and it was only the shallowness of the water that saved him.

BIFF.   Oh, no, he probably just fell asleep again.

LINDA.   I don't think he fell asleep.

BIFF.   Why not?

LINDA.   Last month . . . (*With great difficulty.*) Oh, boys, it's so hard to say a thing like this! He's just a big stupid man to you, but I tell you there's more good in him than in many other people. (*She chokes, wipes her eyes.*) I was looking for a fuse. The lights blew out, and I went down the cellar. And behind the fuse box — it happened to fall out — was a length of rubber pipe — just short.

HAPPY.   No kidding?

LINDA.   There's a little attachment on the end of it. I knew right away. And sure enough, on the bottom of the water heater there's a new little nipple on the gas pipe.

HAPPY (*angrily*).   That — jerk.

BIFF.   Did you have it taken off?

LINDA.   I'm — I'm ashamed to. How can I mention it to him? Every day I go down and take away that little rubber pipe. But, when he comes home, I put it back where it was. How can I insult him that way? I don't know what to do. I live from day to day, boys. I tell you, I know every thought in his mind. It sounds so old-fashioned and silly, but I tell you he put his whole life into you and you've turned your backs on him. (*She is bent over in the chair, weeping, her face in her hands.*) Biff, I swear to God! Biff, his life is in your hands!

HAPPY (*to* BIFF).   How do you like that damned fool!

BIFF (*kissing her*).   All right, pal, all right. It's all settled now. I've been remiss. I know that, Mom. But now I'll stay, and I swear to you, I'll apply myself. (*Kneeling in front of her, in a fever of self-reproach.*) It's just — you see, Mom, I don't fit in business. Not that I won't try. I'll try, and I'll make good.

HAPPY.   Sure you will. The trouble with you in business was you never tried to please people.

BIFF.   I know, I —

HAPPY.   Like when you worked for Harrison's. Bob Harrison said you were tops, and then you go and do some damn fool thing like whistling whole songs in the elevator like a comedian.

BIFF (*against* HAPPY).   So what? I like to whistle sometimes.

HAPPY.   You don't raise a guy to a responsible job who whistles in the elevator!

LINDA.   Well, don't argue about it now.

HAPPY.   Like when you'd go off and swim in the middle of the day instead of taking the line around.

BIFF (*his resentment rising*).   Well, don't you run off? You take off sometimes, don't you? On a nice summer day?

HAPPY.   Yeah, but I cover myself!

LINDA. Boys!

HAPPY. If I'm going to take a fade the boss can call my number where I'm supposed to be and they'll swear to him that I just left. I'll tell you something that I hate to say, Biff, but in the business world some of them think you're crazy.

BIFF (*angered*). Screw the business world!

HAPPY. All right, screw it! Great, but cover yourself!

LINDA. Hap, Hap!

BIFF. I don't care what they think! They've laughed at Dad for years, and you know why? Because we don't belong in this nuthouse of a city! We should be mixing cement on some open plain, or — or carpenters. A carpenter is allowed to whistle!

(WILLY *walks in from the entrance of the house, at left.*)

WILLY. Even your grandfather was better than a carpenter. (*Pause. They watch him.*) You never grew up. Bernard does not whistle in the elevator, I assure you.

BIFF (*as though to laugh* WILLY *out of it*). Yeah, but you do, Pop.

WILLY. I never in my life whistled in an elevator! And who in the business world thinks I'm crazy?

BIFF. I didn't mean it like that, Pop. Now don't make a whole thing out of it, will ya?

WILLY. Go back to the West! Be a carpenter, a cowboy, enjoy yourself!

LINDA. Willy, he was just saying —

WILLY. I heard what he said!

HAPPY (*trying to quiet* WILLY). Hey, Pop, come on now . . .

WILLY (*continuing over* HAPPY's *line*). They laugh at me, heh? Go to Filene's, go to the Hub, go to Slattery's, Boston. Call out the name Willy Loman and see what happens! Big shot!

BIFF. All right, Pop.

WILLY. Big!

BIFF. All right!

WILLY. Why do you always insult me?

BIFF. I didn't say a word. (*To* LINDA.) Did I say a word?

LINDA. He didn't say anything, Willy.

WILLY (*going to the doorway of the living-room*). All right, good night, good night.

LINDA. Willy, dear, he just decided . . .

WILLY (*to* BIFF). If you get tired hanging around tomorrow, paint the ceiling I put up in the living-room.

BIFF. I'm leaving early tomorrow.

HAPPY. He's going to see Bill Oliver, Pop.

WILLY (*interestedly*). Oliver? For what?

BIFF (*with reserve, but trying, trying*). He always said he'd stake me. I'd like to go into business, so maybe I can take him up on it.

LINDA.   Isn't that wonderful?

WILLY.   Don't interrupt. What's wonderful about it? There's fifty men in the City of New York who'd stake him. (*To* BIFF.) Sporting goods?

BIFF.   I guess so. I know something about it and —

WILLY.   He knows something about it! You know sporting goods better than Spaulding, for God's sake! How much is he giving you?

BIFF.   I don't know, I didn't even see him yet, but —

WILLY.   Then what're you talkin' about?

BIFF (*getting angry*).   Well, all I said was I'm gonna see him, that's all!

WILLY (*turning away*).   Ah, you're counting your chickens again.

BIFF (*starting left for the stairs*).   Oh, Jesus, I'm going to sleep!

WILLY (*calling after him*).   Don't curse in this house!

BIFF (*turning*).   Since when did you get so clean?

HAPPY (*trying to stop them*).   Wait a . . .

WILLY.   Don't use that language to me! I won't have it!

HAPPY (*grabbing* BIFF, *shouts*).   Wait a minute! I got an idea. I got a feasible idea. Come here, Biff, let's talk this over now, let's talk some sense here. When I was down in Florida last time, I thought of a great idea to sell sporting goods. It just came back to me. You and I, Biff — we have a line, the Loman Line. We train a couple of weeks, and put on a couple of exhibitions, see?

WILLY.   That's an idea!

HAPPY.   Wait! We form two basketball teams, see? Two waterpolo teams. We play each other. It's a million dollars' worth of publicity. Two brothers, see? The Loman Brothers. Displays in the Royal Palms — all the hotels. And banners over the ring and the basketball court: "Loman Brothers." Baby, we could sell sporting goods!

WILLY.   That is a one-million-dollar idea!

LINDA.   Marvelous!

BIFF.   I'm in great shape as far as that's concerned.

HAPPY.   And the beauty of it is, Biff, it wouldn't be like a business. We'd be out playin' ball again . . .

BIFF (*enthused*).   Yeah, that's . . .

WILLY.   Million-dollar . . .

HAPPY.   And you wouldn't get fed up with it, Biff. It'd be the family again. There'd be the old honor, and comradeship, and if you wanted to go off for a swim or somethin' — well, you'd do it! Without some smart cooky gettin' up ahead of you!

WILLY.   Lick the world! You guys together could absolutely lick the civilized world.

BIFF.   I'll see Oliver tomorrow. Hap, if we could work that out . . .

LINDA.   Maybe things are beginning to —

WILLY (*wildly enthused, to* LINDA).   Stop interrupting! (*To* BIFF.) But don't wear sport jacket and slacks when you see Oliver.

BIFF.   No, I'll —

WILLY. A business suit, and talk as little as possible, and don't crack any jokes.

BIFF. He did like me. Always liked me.

LINDA. He loved you!

WILLY (*to* LINDA). Will you stop! (*To* BIFF.) Walk in very serious. You are not applying for a boy's job. Money is to pass. Be quiet, fine, and serious. Everybody likes a kidder, but nobody lends him money.

HAPPY. I'll try to get some myself, Biff. I'm sure I can.

WILLY. I see great things for you kids, I think your troubles are over. But remember, start big and you'll end big. Ask for fifteen. How much you gonna ask for?

BIFF. Gee, I don't know —

WILLY. And don't say "Gee." "Gee" is a boy's word. A man walking in for fifteen thousand dollars does not say "Gee!"

BIFF. Ten, I think, would be top though.

WILLY. Don't be so modest. You always started too low. Walk in with a big laugh. Don't look worried. Start off with a couple of your good stories to lighten things up. It's not what you say, it's how you say it — because personality always wins the day.

LINDA. Oliver always thought the highest of him —

WILLY. Will you let me talk?

BIFF. Don't yell at her, Pop, will ya?

WILLY (*angrily*). I was talking, wasn't I?

BIFF. I don't like you yelling at her all the time, and I'm tellin' you, that's all.

WILLY. What're you, takin' over this house?

LINDA. Willy —

WILLY (*turning on her*). Don't take his side all the time, goddammit!

BIFF (*furiously*). Stop yelling at her!

WILLY (*suddenly pulling on his cheek, beaten down, guilt ridden*). Give my best to Bill Oliver — he may remember me. (*He exits through the living-room doorway.*)

LINDA (*her voice subdued*). What'd you have to start that for?

(BIFF *turns away.*)

You see how sweet he was as soon as you talked hopefully? (*She goes over to* BIFF.) Come up and say good night to him. Don't let him go to bed that way.

HAPPY. Come on, Biff, let's buck him up.

LINDA. Please, dear. Just say good night. It takes so little to make him happy. Come. (*She goes through the living-room doorway, calling upstairs from within the living-room.*) Your pajamas are hanging in the bathroom, Willy!

HAPPY (*looking toward where* LINDA *went out*). What a woman! They broke the mold when they made her. You know that, Biff?

BIFF. He's off salary. My God, working on commission!

HAPPY. Well, let's face it: he's no hot-shot selling man. Except that sometimes, you have to admit, he's a sweet personality.

BIFF (*deciding*). Lend me ten bucks, will ya? I want to buy some new ties.

HAPPY. I'll take you to a place I know. Beautiful stuff. Wear one of my striped shirts tomorrow.

BIFF. She got gray. Mom got awful old. Gee, I'm gonna go in to Oliver tomorrow and knock him for a —

HAPPY. Come on up. Tell that to Dad. Let's give him a whirl. Come on.

BIFF (*steamed up*). You know, with ten thousand bucks, boy!

HAPPY (*as they go into the living-room*). That's the talk, Biff, that's the first time I've heard the old confidence out of you! (*From within the living-room, fading off.*) You're gonna live with me, kid, and any babe you want just say the word . . .

(*The last lines are hardly heard. They are mounting the stairs to their parents' bedroom.*)

LINDA (*entering her bedroom and addressing* WILLY, *who is in the bathroom. She is straightening the bed for him*). Can you do anything about the shower? It drips.

WILLY (*from the bathroom*). All of a sudden everything falls to pieces! Goddam plumbing, oughta be sued, those people. I hardly finished putting it in and the thing . . . (*his words rumble off*).

LINDA. I'm just wondering if Oliver will remember him. You think he might?

WILLY (*coming out of the bathroom in his pajamas*). Remember him? What's the matter with you, you crazy? If he'd've stayed with Oliver he'd be on top by now! Wait'll Oliver gets a look at him. You don't know the average caliber any more. The average young man today — (*he is getting into bed*) — is got a caliber of zero. Greatest thing in the world for him was to bum around.

(BIFF *and* HAPPY *enter the bedroom. Slight pause.* WILLY *stops short, looking at* BIFF.)

Glad to hear it, boy.

HAPPY. He wanted to say good night to you, sport.

WILLY (*to* BIFF). Yeah. Knock him dead, boy. What'd you want to tell me?

BIFF. Just take it easy, Pop. Good night. (*He turns to go.*)

WILLY (*unable to resist*). And if anything falls off the desk while you're talking to him — like a package or something — don't you pick it up. They have office boys for that.

LINDA. I'll make a big breakfast —

WILLY. Will you let me finish? (*To* BIFF.) Tell him you were in the business in the West. Not farm work.

BIFF. All right, Dad.

LINDA. I think everything —

WILLY (*going right through her speech*). And don't undersell yourself. No less than fifteen thousand dollars.

BIFF (*unable to bear him*). Okay. Good night, Mom. (*He starts moving.*)

WILLY. Because you got a greatness in you, Biff, remember that. You got all kinds a greatness . . .

(*He lies back, exhausted.* BIFF *walks out.*)

LINDA (*calling after* BIFF). Sleep well, darling!

HAPPY. I'm gonna get married, Mom. I wanted to tell you.

LINDA. Go to sleep, dear.

HAPPY (*going*). I just wanted to tell you.

WILLY. Keep up the good work.

(HAPPY *exits.*)

God . . . remember that Ebbets Field game? The championship of the city?

LINDA. Just rest. Should I sing to you?

WILLY. Yeah. Sing to me.

(LINDA *hums a soft lullaby.*)

When that team came out — he was the tallest, remember?

LINDA. Oh, yes. And in gold.

(BIFF *enters the darkened kitchen, takes a cigarette, and leaves the house. He comes downstage into a golden pool of light. He smokes, staring at the night.*)

WILLY. Like a young god. Hercules — something like that. And the sun, the sun all around him. Remember how he waved to me? Right up from the field, with the representatives of three colleges standing by? And the buyers I brought, and the cheers when he came out — Loman, Loman, Loman! God Almighty, he'll be great yet. A star like that, magnificent, can never really fade away!

(*The light on* WILLY *is fading. The gas heater begins to glow through the kitchen wall, near the stairs, a blue flame beneath red coils.*)

LINDA (*timidly*). Willy dear, what has he got against you?

WILLY.   I'm so tired. Don't talk any more.

(BIFF *slowly returns to the kitchen. He stops, stares toward the heater.*)

LINDA.   Will you ask Howard to let you work in New York?
WILLY.   First thing in the morning. Everything'll be all right.

(BIFF *reaches behind the heater and draws out a length of rubber tubing. He is horrified and turns his head toward* WILLY'S *room, still dimly lit, from which the strains of* LINDA'S *desperate but monotonous humming rise.*)

(*Staring through the window into the moonlight.*) Gee, look at the moon moving between the buildings!

(BIFF *wraps the tubing around his hand and quickly goes up the stairs.*)

ACT TWO

(*Music is heard, gay and bright. The curtain rises as the music fades away.* WILLY, *in shirt sleeves, is sitting at the kitchen table, sipping coffee, his hat in his lap.* LINDA *is filling his cup when she can.*)

WILLY.   Wonderful coffee. Meal in itself.
LINDA.   Can I make you some eggs?
WILLY.   No. Take a breath.
LINDA.   You look so rested, dear.
WILLY.   I slept like a dead one. First time in months. Imagine, sleeping till ten on a Tuesday morning. Boys left nice and early, heh?
LINDA.   They were out of here by eight o'clock.
WILLY.   Good work!
LINDA.   It was so thrilling to see them leaving together. I can't get over the shaving lotion in this house!
WILLY (*smiling*).   Mmm —
LINDA.   Biff was very changed this morning. His whole attitude seemed to be hopeful. He couldn't wait to get downtown to see Oliver.
WILLY.   He's heading for a change. There's no question, there simply are certain men that take longer to get — solidified. How did he dress?
LINDA.   His blue suit. He's so handsome in that suit. He could be a — anything in that suit!

(WILLY *gets up from the table.* LINDA *holds his jacket for him.*)

WILLY.   There's no question, no question at all. Gee, on the way home tonight I'd like to buy some seeds.

LINDA (*laughing*). That'd be wonderful. But not enough sun gets back there. Nothing'll grow any more.

WILLY. You wait, kid, before it's all over we're gonna get a little place out in the country, and I'll raise some vegetables, a couple of chickens . . .

LINDA. You'll do it yet, dear.

(*WILLY walks out of his jacket. LINDA follows him.*)

WILLY. And they'll get married, and come for a weekend. I'd build a little guest house. 'Cause I got so many fine tools, all I'd need would be a little lumber and some peace of mind.

LINDA (*joyfully*). I sewed the lining . . .

WILLY. I could build two guest houses, so they'd both come. Did he decide how much he's going to ask Oliver for?

LINDA (*getting him into the jacket*). He didn't mention it, but I imagine ten or fifteen thousand. You going to talk to Howard today?

WILLY. Yeah. I'll put it to him straight and simple. He'll just have to take me off the road.

LINDA. And Willy, don't forget to ask for a little advance, because we've got the insurance premium. It's the grace period now.

WILLY. That's a hundred . . . ?

LINDA. A hundred and eight, sixty-eight. Because we're a little short again.

WILLY. Why are we short?

LINDA. Well, you had the motor job on the car . . .

WILLY. That goddam Studebaker!

LINDA. And you got one more payment on the refrigerator . . .

WILLY. But it just broke again!

LINDA. Well, it's old, dear.

WILLY. I told you we should've bought a well-advertised machine. Charley bought a General Electric and it's twenty years old and it's still good, that son-of-a-bitch.

LINDA. But, Willy —

WILLY. Whoever heard of a Hastings refrigerator? Once in my life I would like to own something outright before it's broken! I'm always in a race with the junkyard! I just finished paying for the car and it's on its last legs. The refrigerator consumes belts like a goddam maniac. They time those things. They time them so when you finally paid for them, they're used up.

LINDA (*buttoning up his jacket as he unbuttons it*). All told, about two hundred dollars would carry us, dear. But that includes the last payment on the mortgage. After this payment, Willy, the house belongs to us.

WILLY. It's twenty-five years!

LINDA. Biff was nine years old when we bought it.

WILLY. Well, that's a great thing. To weather a twenty-five year mortgage is —

LINDA.   It's an accomplishment.

WILLY.   All the cement, the lumber, the reconstruction I put in this house! There ain't a crack to be found in it any more.

LINDA.   Well, it served its purpose.

WILLY.   What purpose? Some stranger'll come along, move in, and that's that. If only Biff would take this house, and raise a family . . . (*he starts to go*). Good-by, I'm late.

LINDA (*suddenly remembering*).   Oh, I forgot! You're supposed to meet them for dinner.

WILLY.   Me?

LINDA.   At Frank's Chop House on Forty-eighth near Sixth Avenue.

WILLY.   Is that so! How about you?

LINDA.   No, just the three of you. They're gonna blow you to a big meal!

WILLY.   Don't say! Who thought of that?

LINDA.   Biff came to me this morning, Willy, and he said, "Tell Dad, we want to blow him to a big meal." Be there six o'clock. You and your two boys are going to have dinner.

WILLY.   Gee whiz! That's really somethin'. I'm gonna knock Howard for a loop, kid. I'll get an advance, and I'll come home with a New York job. Goddammit, now I'm gonna do it!

LINDA.   Oh, that's the spirit, Willy!

WILLY.   I will never get behind a wheel the rest of my life!

LINDA.   It's changing, Willy, I can feel it changing!

WILLY.   Beyond a question. G'by, I'm late. (*He starts to go again.*)

LINDA (*calling after him as she runs to the kitchen table for a handkerchief*).   You got your glasses?

WILLY (*feels for them, then comes back in*).   Yeah, yeah, got my glasses.

LINDA (*giving him the handkerchief*).   And a handkerchief.

WILLY.   Yeah, handkerchief.

LINDA.   And your saccharine?

WILLY.   Yeah, my saccharine.

LINDA.   Be careful on the subway stairs.

(*She kisses him, and a silk stocking is seen hanging from her hand.* WILLY *notices it.*)

WILLY.   Will you stop mending stockings? At least while I'm in the house. It gets me nervous. I can't tell you. Please.

(LINDA *hides the stocking in her hand as she follows* WILLY *across the forestage in front of the house.*)

LINDA.   Remember, Frank's Chop House.

WILLY (*passing the apron*).   Maybe beets would grow out there.

LINDA (*laughing*).   But you tried so many times.

WILLY. Yeah. Well, don't work hard today. (*He disappears around the right corner of the house.*)

LINDA. Be careful!

(*As* WILLY *vanishes,* LINDA *waves to him. Suddenly the phone rings. She runs across the stage and into the kitchen and lifts it.*)

Hello? Oh, Biff! I'm so glad you called. I just . . . Yes, sure, I told him. Yes, he'll be there for dinner at six o'clock, I didn't forget. Listen, I was just dying to tell you. You know that little rubber pipe I told you about? That he connected to the gas heater? I finally decided to go down the cellar this morning and take it away and destroy it. But it's gone! Imagine? He took it away himself, it isn't there! (*She listens.*) When? Oh, then you took it. Oh — nothing, it's just that I'd hoped he'd taken it away himself. Oh, I'm not worried, darling, because this morning he left in such high spirits, it was like the old days! I'm not afraid any more. Did Mr. Oliver see you? . . . Well, you wait there then. And make a nice impression on him, darling. Just don't perspire too much before you see him. And have a nice time with Dad. He may have big news too! . . . That's right, a New York job. And be sweet to him tonight, dear. Be loving to him. Because he's only a little boat looking for a harbor. (*She is trembling with sorrow and joy.*) Oh, that's wonderful, Biff, you'll save his life. Thanks, darling. Just put your arm around him when he comes into the restaurant. Give him a smile. That's the boy. . . . Good-by, dear. . . . You got your comb? . . . That's fine. Good-by, Biff dear.

(*In the middle of her speech,* HOWARD WAGNER, *thirty-six, wheels on a small typewriter table on which is a wire-recording machine and proceeds to plug it in. This is on the left forestage. Light slowly fades on* LINDA *as it rises on* HOWARD. HOWARD *is intent on threading the machine and only glances over his shoulder as* WILLY *appears.*)

WILLY. Pst! Pst!

HOWARD. Hello, Willy, come in.

WILLY. Like to have a little talk with you, Howard.

HOWARD. Sorry to keep you waiting. I'll be with you in a minute.

WILLY. What's that, Howard?

HOWARD. Didn't you ever see one of these? Wire recorder.

WILLY. Oh. Can we talk a minute?

HOWARD. Records things. Just got delivery yesterday. Been driving me crazy, the most terrific machine I ever saw in my life. I was up all night with it.

WILLY. What do you do with it?

HOWARD. I bought it for dictation, but you can do anything with it. Listen to this. I had it home last night. Listen to what I picked up. The first one is my daughter. Get this. (*He flicks the switch and "Roll out the Barrel" is heard being whistled.*) Listen to that kid whistle.

WILLY. That is lifelike, isn't it?

HOWARD. Seven years old. Get that tone.

WILLY. Ts, ts. Like to ask a little favor of you . . .

(*The whistling breaks off, and the voice of* HOWARD's *daughter is heard.*)

HIS DAUGHTER. "Now you, Daddy."

HOWARD. She's crazy for me! (*Again the same song is whistled.*) That's me! Ha! (*He winks.*)

WILLY. You're very good!

(*The whistling breaks off again. The machine runs silent for a moment.*)

HOWARD. Sh! Get this now, this is my son.

HIS SON. "The capital of Alabama is Montgomery; the capital of Arizona is Phoenix; the capital of Arkansas is Little Rock; the capital of California is Sacramento . . ." (*And on, and on.*)

HOWARD (*holding up five fingers*). Five years old, Willy!

WILLY. He'll make an announcer some day!

HIS SON (*continuing*). "The capital . . ."

HOWARD. Get that — alphabetical order! (*The machine breaks off suddenly.*) Wait a minute. The maid kicked the plug out.

WILLY. It certainly is a —

HOWARD. Sh, for God's sake!

HIS SON. "It's nine o'clock, Bulova watch time. So I have to go to sleep."

WILLY. That really is —

HOWARD. Wait a minute! The next is my wife.

(*They wait.*)

HOWARD'S VOICE. "Go on, say something." (Pause.) "Well, you gonna talk?"

HIS WIFE. "I can't think of anything."

HOWARD'S VOICE. "Well, talk — it's turning."

HIS WIFE (*shyly, beaten*). "Hello." (*Silence.*) "Oh, Howard, I can't talk into this . . ."

HOWARD (*snapping the machine off*). That was my wife.

WILLY. That is a wonderful machine. Can we —

HOWARD. I tell you, Willy, I'm gonna take my camera, and my band-saw, and all my hobbies, and out they go. This is the most fascinating relaxation I ever found.

WILLY. I think I'll get one myself.

HOWARD. Sure, they're only a hundred and a half. You can't do without it. Supposing you wanna hear Jack Benny, see? But you can't be at home at that hour. So you tell the maid to turn the radio on when Jack Benny comes on, and this automatically goes on with the radio . . .

WILLY. And when you come home you . . .

HOWARD. You can come home twelve o'clock, one o'clock, any time you like, and you get yourself a Coke and sit yourself down, throw the switch, and there's Jack Benny's program in the middle of the night!

WILLY.   I'm definitely going to get one. Because lots of time I'm on the road, and I think to myself, what I must be missing on the radio!

HOWARD.   Don't you have a radio in the car?

WILLY.   Well, yeah, but whoever thinks of turning it on?

HOWARD.   Say, aren't you supposed to be in Boston?

WILLY.   That's what I want to talk to you about, Howard. You got a minute? (*He draws a chair in from the wing.*)

HOWARD.   What happened? What're you doing here?

WILLY.   Well . . .

HOWARD.   You didn't crack up again, did you?

WILLY.   Oh, no. No . . .

HOWARD.   Geez, you had me worried there for a minute. What's the trouble?

WILLY.   Well, tell you the truth, Howard. I've come to the decision that I'd rather not travel any more.

HOWARD.   Not travel! Well, what'll you do?

WILLY.   Remember, Christmas time, when you had the party here? You said you'd try to think of some spot for me here in town.

HOWARD.   With us?

WILLY.   Well, sure.

HOWARD.   Oh, yeah, yeah. I remember. Well, I couldn't think of anything for you, Willy.

WILLY.   I tell ya, Howard. The kids are all grown up, y'know. I don't need much any more. If I could take home — well, sixty-five dollars a week, I could swing it.

HOWARD.   Yeah, but Willy, see, I —

WILLY.   I tell ya why, Howard. Speaking frankly and between the two of us, y'know — I'm just a little tired.

HOWARD.   Oh, I could understand that, Willy. But you're a road man, Willy, and we do a road business. We've only got a half-dozen salesmen on the floor here.

WILLY.   God knows, Howard, I never asked a favor of any man. But I was with the firm when your father used to carry you in here in his arms.

HOWARD.   I know that, Willy, but —

WILLY.   Your father came to me the day you were born and asked me what I thought of the name of Howard, may he rest in peace.

HOWARD.   I appreciate that, Willy, but there just is no spot here for you. If I had a spot I'd slam you right in, but I just don't have a single solitary spot.

(*He looks for his lighter.* WILLY *has picked it up and gives it to him. Pause.*)

WILLY (*with increasing anger*).   Howard, all I need to set my table is fifty dollars a week.

HOWARD. But where am I going to put you, kid?

WILLY. Look, it isn't a question of whether I can sell merchandise, is it?

HOWARD. No, but it's business, kid, and everybody's gotta pull his own weight.

WILLY (*desperately*). Just let me tell you a story, Howard —

HOWARD. 'Cause you gotta admit, business is business.

WILLY (*angrily*). Business is definitely business, but just listen for a minute. You don't understand this. When I was a boy — eighteen, nineteen — I was already on the road. And there was a question in my mind as to whether selling had a future for me. Because in those days I had a yearning to go to Alaska. See, there were three gold strikes in one month in Alaska, and I felt like going out. Just for the ride, you might say.

HOWARD (*barely interested*). Don't say.

WILLY. Oh, yeah, my father lived many years in Alaska. He was an adventurous man. We've got quite a little streak of self-reliance in our family. I thought I'd go out with my older brother and try to locate him, and maybe settle in the North with the old man. And I was almost decided to go, when I met a salesman in the Parker House. His name was Dave Singleman. And he was eighty-four years old, and he'd drummed merchandise in thirty-one states. And old Dave, he'd go up to his room, y'understand, put on his green velvet slippers — I'll never forget — and pick up his phone and call the buyers, and without ever leaving his room, at the age of eighty-four, he made his living. And when I saw that, I realized that selling was the greatest career a man could want. Cause what could be more satisfying than to be able to go, at the age of eighty-four, into twenty or thirty different cities, and pick up a phone, and be remembered and loved and helped by so many different people? Do you know? when he died — and by the way he died the death of a salesman, in his green velvet slippers in the smoker of the New York, New Haven and Hartford, going into Boston — when he died, hundreds of salesmen and buyers were at his funeral. Things were sad on a lotta trains for months after that. (*He stands up.* HOWARD *has not looked at him.*) In those days there was personality in it, Howard. There was respect, and comradeship, and gratitude in it. Today, it's all cut and dried, and there's no chance for bringing friendship to bear — or personality. You see what I mean? They don't know me any more.

HOWARD (*moving away, to the right*). That's just the thing, Willy.

WILLY. If I had forty dollars a week — that's all I'd need. Forty dollars, Howard.

HOWARD. Kid, I can't take blood from a stone, I —

WILLY (*desperation is on him now*). Howard, the year Al Smith was nominated, your father came to me and —

HOWARD (*starting to go off*). I've got to see some people, kid.

WILLY (*stopping him*). I'm talking about your father! There were promises made across this desk! You mustn't tell me you've got people to see — I put thirty-four years into this firm, Howard, and now I can't pay my insurance! You can't eat the orange and throw the peel away — a man is not a piece of fruit! (*After a pause.*) Now pay attention. Your father — in 1928 I had a big year. I averaged a hundred and seventy dollars a week in commissions.

HOWARD (*impatiently*). Now, Willy, you never averaged —

WILLY (*banging his hand on the desk.*) I averaged a hundred and seventy dollars a week in the year of 1928! And your father came to me — or rather, I was in the office here — it was right over this desk — and he put his hand on my shoulder —

HOWARD (*getting up*). You'll have to excuse me, Willy, I gotta see some people. Pull yourself together. (*Going out.*) I'll be back in a little while.

(*On* HOWARD's *exit, the light on his chair grows very bright and strange.*)

WILLY. Pull myself together! What the hell did I say to him? My God, I was yelling at him! How could I! (WILLY *breaks off, staring at the light, which occupies the chair, animating it. He approaches this chair, standing across the desk from it.*) Frank, Frank, don't you remember what you told me that time? How you put your hand on my shoulder, and Frank . . .

(*He leans on the desk and as he speaks the dead man's name he accidentally switches on the recorder, and instantly:*)

HOWARD'S SON. ". . . of New York is Albany. The capital of Ohio is Cincinnati, the capital of Rhode Island is . . ." (*The recitation continues.*)

WILLY (*leaping away with fright, shouting*). Ha! Howard! Howard! Howard!

HOWARD (*rushing in*). What happened?

WILLY (*pointing at the machine, which continues nasally, childishly, with the capital cities*). Shut it off! Shut it off!

HOWARD (*pulling the plug out*). Look, Willy . . .

WILLY (*pressing his hands to his eyes*). I gotta get myself some coffee. I'll get some coffee . . .

(WILLY *starts to walk out.* HOWARD *stops him.*)

HOWARD (*rolling up the cord*). Willy, look . . .

WILLY. I'll go to Boston.

HOWARD. Willy, you can't go to Boston for us.

WILLY. Why can't I go?

HOWARD. I don't want you to represent us. I've been meaning to tell you for a long time now.

WILLY. Howard, are you firing me?

HOWARD. I think you need a good long rest, Willy.

WILLY. Howard ——

HOWARD. And when you feel better, come back, and we'll see if we can work something out.

WILLY. But I gotta earn money, Howard. I'm in no position to ——

HOWARD. Where are your sons? Why don't your sons give you a hand?

WILLY. They're working on a very big deal.

HOWARD. This is no time for false pride, Willy. You go to your sons and you tell them that you're tired. You've got two great boys, haven't you?

WILLY. Oh, no question, no question, but in the meantime . . .

HOWARD. Then that's that, heh?

WILLY. All right, I'll go to Boston tomorrow.

HOWARD. No, no.

WILLY. I can't throw myself on my sons. I'm not a cripple!

HOWARD. Look, kid, I'm busy this morning.

WILLY (grasping HOWARD's arm). Howard, you've got to let me go to Boston!

HOWARD (hard, keeping himself under control). I've got a line of people to see this morning. Sit down, take five minutes, and pull yourself together, and then go home, will ya? I need the office, Willy. (He starts to go, turns, remembering the recorder, starts to push off the table holding the recorder.) Oh, yeah. Whenever you can this week, stop by and drop off the samples. You'll feel better, Willy, and then come back and we'll talk. Pull yourself together, kid, there's people outside.

(HOWARD exits, pushing the table off left. WILLY stares into space, exhausted. Now the music is heard — BEN's music — first distantly, then closer, closer. As WILLY speaks, BEN enters from the right. He carries valise and umbrella.)

WILLY. Oh, Ben, how did you do it? What is the answer? Did you wind up the Alaska deal already?

BEN. Doesn't take much time if you know what you're doing. Just a short business trip. Boarding ship in an hour. Wanted to say good-by.

WILLY. Ben, I've got to talk to you.

BEN (glancing at his watch). Haven't the time, William.

WILLY (crossing the apron to BEN). Ben, nothing's working out. I don't know what to do.

BEN. Now, look here, William. I've bought timberland in Alaska and I need a man to look after things for me.

WILLY. God, timberland! Me and my boys in those grand outdoors!

BEN. You've a new continent at your doorstep, William. Get out of these cities, they're full of talk and time payments and courts of law. Screw on your fists and you can fight for a fortune up there.

WILLY. Yes, yes! Linda, Linda!

(LINDA enters as of old, with the wash.)

LINDA. Oh, you're back?

BEN. I haven't much time.

WILLY. No, wait! Linda, he's got a proposition for me in Alaska.

LINDA. But you've got — (*To* BEN.) He's got a beautiful job here.

WILLY. But in Alaska, kid, I could —

LINDA. You're doing well enough, Willy!

BEN (*to* LINDA). Enough for what, my dear?

LINDA (*frightened of* BEN *and angry at him*). Don't say those things to him! Enough to be happy right here, right now. (*To* WILLY, *while* BEN *laughs.*) Why must everybody conquer the world? You're well liked, and the boys love you and someday — (*to* BEN) — why, old man Wagner told him just the other day that if he keeps it up he'll be a member of the firm, didn't he, Willy?

WILLY. Sure, sure. I am building something with this firm, Ben, and if a man is building something he must be on the right track, mustn't he?

BEN. What are you building? Lay your hand on it. Where is it?

WILLY (*hesitantly*). That's true, Linda, there's nothing.

LINDA. Why? (*To* BEN.) There's a man eighty-four years old —

WILLY. That's right, Ben, that's right. When I look at that man I say, what is there to worry about?

BEN. Bah!

WILLY. It's true, Ben. All he has to do is go into any city, pick up the phone, and he's making his living and you know why?

BEN (*picking up his valise*). I've got to go.

WILLY (*holding* BEN *back*). Look at this boy!

(BIFF, *in his high school sweater, enters carrying suitcase.* HAPPY *carries* BIFF'*s shoulder guards, gold helmet, and football pants.*)

Without a penny to his name three great universities are begging for him, and from there the sky's the limit, because it's not what you do, Ben. It's who you know and the smile on your face! It's contacts, Ben, contacts! The whole wealth of Alaska passes over the lunch table at the Commodore Hotel, and that's the wonder, the wonder of this country, that a man can end with diamonds here on the basis of being liked! (*He turns to* BIFF.) And that's why when you get out on that field today it's important. Because thousands of people will be rooting for you and loving you. (*To* BEN, *who has again begun to leave.*) And Ben! when he walks into a business office his name will sound out like a bell and all the doors will open to him! I've seen it, Ben, I've seen it a thousand times! You can't feel it with your hand like timber, but it's there!

BEN. Good-by, William.

WILLY. Ben, am I right? Don't you think I'm right? I value your advice.

BEN. There's a new continent at your doorstep, William. You could walk out rich. Rich! (*He is gone.*)

WILLY. We'll do it here, Ben! You hear me? We're gonna do it here!

(Young BERNARD *rushes in. The gay music of the* BOYS *is heard.*)

BERNARD. Oh, gee, I was afraid you left already!

WILLY. Why? What time is it?

BERNARD. It's half-past one!

WILLY. Well, come on, everybody! Ebbets Field next stop! Where's the pennants? (*He rushes through the wall-line of the kitchen and out into the living-room.*)

LINDA (*to* BIFF). Did you pack fresh underwear?

BIFF (*who has been limbering up*). I want to go!

BERNARD. Biff, I'm carrying your helmet, ain't I?

HAPPY. No, I'm carrying the helmet.

BERNARD. Oh, Biff, you promised me.

HAPPY. I'm carrying the helmet.

BERNARD. How am I going to get in the locker room?

LINDA. Let him carry the shoulder guards. (*She puts her coat and hat on in the kitchen.*)

BERNARD. Can I, Biff? 'Cause I told everybody I'm going to be in the locker room.

HAPPY. In Ebbets Field it's the clubhouse.

BERNARD. I meant the clubhouse. Biff!

HAPPY. Biff!

BIFF (*grandly, after a slight pause*). Let him carry the shoulder guards.

HAPPY (*as he gives* BERNARD *the shoulder guards*). Stay close to us, now.

(WILLY *rushes in with the pennants.*)

WILLY (*handing them out*). Everybody wave when Biff comes out on the field. (HAPPY *and* BERNARD *run off.*) You set now, boy?

(*The music has died away.*)

BIFF. Ready to go, Pop. Every muscle is ready.

WILLY (*at the edge of the apron*). You realize what this means?

BIFF. That's right, Pop.

WILLY (*feeling* BIFF'S *muscles*). You're comin' home this afternoon captain of the All-Scholastic Championship Team of the City of New York.

BIFF. I got it, Pop. And remember, pal, when I take off my helmet, that touchdown is for you.

WILLY. Let's go!

(*He is starting out, with his arm around* BIFF, *when* CHARLEY *enters, as of old, in knickers.*)

I got no room for you, Charley.

CHARLEY. Room? For what?

WILLY. In the car.

CHARLEY. You goin' for a ride? I wanted to shoot some casino.

WILLY (*furiously*). Casino! (*Incredulously.*) Don't you realize what today is?

LINDA. Oh, he knows, Willy. He's just kidding you.

WILLY. That's nothing to kid about!

CHARLEY. No, Linda, what's goin' on?

LINDA. He's playing in Ebbets Field.

CHARLEY. Baseball in this weather?

WILLY. Don't talk to him. Come on, come on! (*He is pushing them out.*)

CHARLEY. Wait a minute, didn't you hear the news?

WILLY. What?

CHARLEY. Don't you listen to the radio? Ebbets Field just blew up.

WILLY. You go to hell! (CHARLEY *laughs. Pushing them out.*) Come on, come on! We're late.

CHARLEY (*as they go*). Knock a homer, Biff, knock a homer!

WILLY (*the last to leave, turning to* CHARLEY). I don't think that was funny, Charley. This is the greatest day of his life.

CHARLEY. Willy, when are you going to grow up?

WILLY. Yeah, heh? When this game is over, Charley, you'll be laughing out of the other side of your face. They'll be calling him another Red Grange. Twenty-five thousand a year.

CHARLEY (*kidding*). Is that so?

WILLY. Yeah, that's so.

CHARLEY. Well, then, I'm sorry, Willy. But tell me something.

WILLY. What?

CHARLEY. Who is Red Grange?

WILLY. Put up your hands. Goddam you, put up your hands.

(CHARLEY, *chuckling, shakes his head and walks away, around the left corner of the stage.* WILLY *follows him. The music rises to a mocking frenzy.*)

Who the hell do you think you are, better than everybody else? You don't know everything, you big, ignorant, stupid . . . Put up your hands!

(*Light rises, on the right side of the forestage, on a small table in the reception room of* CHARLEY's *office. Traffic sounds are heard.* BERNARD, *now mature, sits whistling to himself. A pair of tennis rackets and an overnight bag are on the floor beside him.*)

(*Offstage.*) What are you walking away for? Don't walk away! If you're going to say something say it to my face! I know you laugh at me behind my back. You'll laugh out of the other side of your goddam face after this game. Touchdown! Touchdown! Eighty thousand people! Touchdown! Right between the goal posts.

(BERNARD *is a quiet, earnest, but self-assured young man.* WILLY'S *voice is coming from right upstage now.* BERNARD *lowers his feet off the table and listens.* JENNY, *his father's secretary, enters.*)

JENNY (*distressed*).　Say, Bernard, will you go out in the hall?

BERNARD.　What is that noise? Who is it?

JENNY.　Mr. Loman. He just got off the elevator.

BERNARD (*getting up*).　Who's he arguing with?

JENNY.　Nobody. There's nobody with him. I can't deal with him any more, and your father gets all upset every time he comes. I've got a lot of typing to do, and your father's waiting to sign it. Will you see him?

WILLY (*entering*).　Touchdown! Touch — (*he sees* JENNY). Jenny, Jenny, good to see you. How're ya? Workin'? Or still honest?

JENNY.　Fine. How've you been feeling?

WILLY.　Not much any more, Jenny. Ha, ha! (*He is surprised to see the rackets.*)

BERNARD.　Hello, Uncle Willy.

WILLY (*almost shocked*).　Bernard! Well, look who's here! (*He comes quickly, guiltily, to* BERNARD *and warmly shakes his hand.*)

BERNARD.　How are you? Good to see you.

WILLY.　What are you doing here?

BERNARD.　Oh, just stopped by to see Pop. Get off my feet till my train leaves. I'm going to Washington in a few minutes.

WILLY.　Is he in?

BERNARD.　Yes, he's in his office with the accountant. Sit down.

WILLY (*sitting down*).　What're you going to do in Washington?

BERNARD.　Oh, just a case I've got there, Willy.

WILLY.　That so? (*Indicating the rackets.*) You going to play tennis there?

BERNARD.　I'm staying with a friend who's got a court.

WILLY.　Don't say. His own tennis court. Must be fine people, I bet.

BERNARD.　They are, very nice. Dad tells me Biff's in town.

WILLY (*with a big smile*).　Yeah, Biff's in. Working on a very big deal, Bernard.

BERNARD.　What's Biff doing?

WILLY.　Well, he's been doing very big things in the West. But he decided to establish himself here. Very big. We're having dinner. Did I hear your wife had a boy?

BERNARD.　That's right. Our second.

WILLY.　Two boys! What do you know!

BERNARD.　What kind of a deal has Biff got?

WILLY.　Well, Bill Oliver — very big sporting-goods man — he wants Biff very badly. Called him in from the West. Long distance, carte blanche, special deliveries. Your friends have their own private tennis court?

BERNARD. You still with the old firm, Willy?

WILLY (after a pause). I'm — I'm overjoyed to see how you made the grade, Bernard, overjoyed. It's an encouraging thing to see a young man really — really — Looks very good for Biff — very — (He breaks off, then) Bernard — (He is so full of emotion, he breaks off again.)

BERNARD. What is it, Willy?

WILLY (small and alone). What — what's the secret?

BERNARD. What secret?

WILLY. How — how did you? Why didn't he ever catch on?

BERNARD. I wouldn't know that, Willy.

WILLY (confidentially, desperately). You were his friend, his boyhood friend. There's something I don't understand about it. His life ended after that Ebbets Field game. From the age of seventeen nothing good ever happened to him.

BERNARD. He never trained himself for anything.

WILLY. But he did, he did. After high school he took so many correspondence courses. Radio mechanics; television; God knows what, and never made the slightest mark.

BERNARD (taking off his glasses). Willy, do you want to talk candidly?

WILLY (rising, faces BERNARD). I regard you as a very brilliant man, Bernard. I value your advice.

BERNARD. Oh, the hell with the advice, Willy. I couldn't advise you. There's just one thing I've always wanted to ask you. When he was supposed to graduate, and the math teacher flunked him —

WILLY. Oh, that son-of-a-bitch ruined his life.

BERNARD. Yeah, but, Willy, all he had to do was go to summer school and make up that subject.

WILLY. That's right, that's right.

BERNARD. Did you tell him not to go to summer school?

WILLY. Me? I begged him to go. I ordered him to go!

BERNARD. Then why wouldn't he go?

WILLY. Why? Why? Bernard, that question has been trailing me like a ghost for the last fifteen years. He flunked the subject, and laid down and died like a hammer hit him!

BERNARD. Take it easy, kid.

WILLY. Let me talk to you — I got nobody to talk to. Bernard, Bernard, was it my fault? Y'see? It keeps going around in my mind, maybe I did something to him. I got nothing to give him.

BERNARD. Don't take it so hard.

WILLY. Why did he lay down? What is the story there? You were his friend!

BERNARD. Willy, I remember, it was June, and our grades came out. And he'd flunked math.

WILLY. That son-of-a-bitch!

BERNARD. No, it wasn't right then. Biff just got very angry, I remember, and he was ready to enroll in summer school.

WILLY (*surprised*). He was?

BERNARD. He wasn't beaten by it at all. But then, Willy, he disappeared from the block for almost a month. And I got the idea that he'd gone up to New England to see you. Did he have a talk with you then?

(WILLY *stares in silence.*)

Willy?

WILLY (*with a strong edge of resentment in his voice*). Yeah, he came to Boston. What about it?

BERNARD. Well, just that when he came back — I'll never forget this, it always mystifies me. Because I'd thought so well of Biff, even though he'd always taken advantage of me. I loved him, Willy, y'know? And he came back after that month and took his sneakers — remember those sneakers with "University of Virginia" printed on them? He was so proud of those, wore them every day. And he took them down in the cellar, and burned them up in the furnace. We had a fist fight. It lasted at least half an hour. Just the two of us, punching each other down the cellar, and crying right through it. I've often thought of how strange it was that I knew he'd given up his life. What happened in Boston, Willy?

(WILLY *looks at him as at an intruder.*)

I just bring it up because you asked me.

WILLY (*angrily*). Nothing. What do you mean, "What happened?" What's that got to do with anything?

BERNARD. Well, don't get sore.

WILLY. What are you trying to do, blame it on me? If a boy lays down is that my fault?

BERNARD. Now, Willy, don't get —

WILLY. Well, don't — don't talk to me that way! What does that mean, "What happened?"

(CHARLEY *enters. He is in his vest, and he carries a bottle of bourbon.*)

CHARLEY. Hey, you're going to miss that train. (*He waves the bottle.*)

BERNARD. Yeah, I'm going. (*He takes the bottle.*) Thanks, Pop. (*He picks up his rackets and bag.*) Good-by, Willy, and don't worry about it. You know, "If at first you don't succeed . . ."

WILLY. Yes, I believe in that.

BERNARD. But sometimes, Willy, it's better for a man just to walk away.

WILLY. Walk away?

BERNARD. That's right.

WILLY. But if you can't walk away?

BERNARD (*after a slight pause*). I guess that's when it's tough. (*Extending his hand.*) Good-by, Willy.

WILLY (*shaking BERNARD's hand*). Good-by, boy.

CHARLEY (*an arm on BERNARD's shoulder*). How do you like this kid? Gonna argue a case in front of the Supreme Court.

BERNARD (*protesting*). Pop!

WILLY (*genuinely shocked, pained, and happy*). No! The Supreme Court!

BERNARD. I gotta run. 'By, Dad!

CHARLEY. Knock 'em dead, Bernard!

(BERNARD *goes off.*)

WILLY (*as CHARLEY takes out his wallet*). The Supreme Court! And he didn't even mention it!

CHARLEY (*counting out money on the desk*). He don't have to — he's gonna do it.

WILLY. And you never told him what to do, did you? You never took any interest in him.

CHARLEY. My salvation is that I never took any interest in anything. There's some money — fifty dollars. I got an accountant inside.

WILLY. Charley, look . . . (*With difficulty.*) I got my insurance to pay. If you can manage it — I need a hundred and ten dollars.

(CHARLEY *doesn't reply for a moment; merely stops moving.*)

I'd draw it from my bank but Linda would know, and I . . .

CHARLEY. Sit down, Willy.

WILLY (*moving toward the chair*). I'm keeping an account of everything, remember. I'll pay every penny back. (*He sits.*)

CHARLEY. Now listen to me, Willy.

WILLY. I want you to know I appreciate . . .

CHARLEY (*sitting down on the table*). Willy, what're you doin'? What the hell is goin' on in your head?

WILLY. Why? I'm simply . . .

CHARLEY. I offered you a job. You can make fifty dollars a week. And I won't send you on the road.

WILLY. I've got a job.

CHARLEY. Without pay? What kind of a job is a job without pay? (*He rises.*) Now, look, kid, enough is enough. I'm no genius but I know when I'm being insulted.

WILLY. Insulted!

CHARLEY. Why don't you want to work for me?

WILLY. What's the matter with you? I've got a job.

CHARLEY. Then what're you walkin' in here every week for?

WILLY (*getting up*). Well, if you don't want me to walk in here —

CHARLEY. I am offering you a job.

WILLY.   I don't want your goddam job!

CHARLEY.   When the hell are you going to grow up?

WILLY (*furiously*).   You big ignoramus, if you say that to me again I'll rap you one! I don't care how big you are. (*He's ready to fight.*)

(*Pause.*)

CHARLEY (*kindly, going to him*).   How much do you need, Willy?

WILLY.   Charley, I'm strapped, I'm strapped. I don't know what to do. I was just fired.

CHARLEY.   Howard fired you?

WILLY.   That snotnose. Imagine that? I named him. I named him Howard.

CHARLEY.   Willy, when're you gonna realize that them things don't mean anything? You named him Howard, but you can't sell that. The only thing you got in this world is what you can sell. And the funny thing is that you're a salesman, and you don't know that.

WILLY.   I've always tried to think otherwise, I guess. I always felt that if a man was impressive, and well liked, that nothing —

CHARLEY.   Why must everybody like you? Who liked J. P. Morgan? Was he impressive? In a Turkish bath he'd look like a butcher. But with his pockets on he was very well liked. Now listen, Willy, I know you don't like me, and nobody can say I'm in love with you, but I'll give you a job because — just for the hell of it, put it that way. Now what do you say?

WILLY.   I — I just can't work for you, Charley.

CHARLEY.   What're you, jealous of me?

WILLY.   I can't work for you, that's all, don't ask me why.

CHARLEY (*angered, takes out more bills*).   You been jealous of me all your life, you damned fool! Here, pay your insurance. (*He puts the money in* WILLY'S *hand.*)

WILLY.   I'm keeping strict accounts.

CHARLEY.   I've got some work to do. Take care of yourself. And pay your insurance.

WILLY (*moving to the right*).   Funny, y'know? After all the highways, and the trains, and the appointments, and the years, you end up worth more dead than alive.

CHARLEY.   Willy, nobody's worth nothin' dead. (*After a slight pause.*) Did you hear what I said?

(WILLY *stands still, dreaming.*)

Willy!

WILLY.   Apologize to Bernard for me when you see him. I didn't mean to argue with him. He's a fine boy. They're all fine boys, and they'll end up big — all of them. Someday they'll all play tennis together. Wish me luck, Charley. He saw Bill Oliver today.

CHARLEY. Good luck.

WILLY (*on the verge of tears*). Charley, you're the only friend I got. Isn't that a remarkable thing? (*He goes out.*)

CHARLEY. Jesus!

(CHARLEY *stares after him a moment and follows. All light blacks out. Suddenly raucous music is heard, and a red glow rises behind the screen at right.* STANLEY, *a young waiter, appears, carrying a table, followed by* HAPPY, *who is carrying two chairs.*)

STANLEY (*putting the table down*). That's all right, Mr. Loman, I can handle it myself. (*He turns and takes the chairs from* HAPPY *and places them at the table.*)

HAPPY (*glancing around*). Oh, this is better.

STANLEY. Sure, in the front there you're in the middle of all kinds a noise. Whenever you got a party, Mr. Loman, you just tell me and I'll put you back here. Y'know, there's a lotta people they don't like it private, because when they go out they like to see a lotta action around them because they're sick and tired to stay in the house by theirself. But I know you, you ain't from Hackensack. You know what I mean?

HAPPY (*sitting down*). So how's it coming, Stanley?

STANLEY. Ah, it's a dog's life. I only wish during the war they'd a took me in the Army. I coulda been dead by now.

HAPPY. My brother's back, Stanley.

STANLEY. Oh, he come back, heh? From the Far West.

HAPPY. Yeah, big cattle man, my brother, so treat him right. And my father's coming too.

STANLEY. Oh, your father too!

HAPPY. You got a couple of nice lobsters?

STANLEY. Hundred per cent, big.

HAPPY. I want them with the claws.

STANLEY. Don't worry, I don't give you no mice.

(HAPPY *laughs.*)

How about some wine? It'll put a head on the meal.

HAPPY. No. You remember, Stanley, that recipe I brought you from overseas? With the champagne in it?

STANLEY. Oh, yeah, sure. I still got it tacked up yet in the kitchen. But that'll have to cost a buck apiece anyways.

HAPPY. That's all right.

STANLEY. What'd you, hit a number or somethin'?

HAPPY. No, it's a little celebration. My brother is — I think he pulled off a big deal today. I think we're going into business together.

STANLEY. Great! That's the best for you. Because a family business, you know what I mean? — that's the best.

HAPPY. That's what I think.

STANLEY. 'Cause what's the difference? Somebody steals? It's in the family. Know what I mean? (*Sotto voce.*) Like this bartender here. The boss is goin' crazy what kinda leak he's got in the cash register. You put it in but it don't come out.

HAPPY (*raising his head*). Sh!

STANLEY. What?

HAPPY. You notice I wasn't lookin' right or left, was I?

STANLEY. No.

HAPPY. And my eyes are closed.

STANLEY. So what's the — ?

HAPPY. Strudel's comin'.

STANLEY (*catching on, looks around*). Ah, no, there's no —

(*He breaks off as a furred, lavishly dressed girl enters and sits at the next table. Both follow her with their eyes.*)

Geez, how'd ya know?

HAPPY. I got radar or something. (*Staring directly at her profile.*) Oooooooo . . . Stanley.

STANLEY. I think that's for you, Mr. Loman.

HAPPY. Look at that mouth. Oh, God. And the binoculars.

STANLEY. Geez, you got a life, Mr. Loman.

HAPPY. Wait on her.

STANLEY (*going to the* GIRL'S *table*). Would you like a menu, ma'am?

GIRL. I'm expecting someone, but I'd like a —

HAPPY. Why don't you bring her — excuse me, miss, do you mind? I sell champagne, and I'd like you to try my brand. Bring her a champagne, Stanley.

GIRL. That's awfully nice of you.

HAPPY. Don't mention it. It's all company money. (*He laughs.*)

GIRL. That's a charming product to be selling, isn't it?

HAPPY. Oh, gets to be like everything else. Selling is selling, y'know.

GIRL. I suppose.

HAPPY. You don't happen to sell, do you?

GIRL. No, I don't sell.

HAPPY. Would you object to a compliment from a stranger? You ought to be on a magazine cover.

GIRL (*looking at him a little archly*). I have been.

(STANLEY *comes in with a glass of champagne.*)

HAPPY. What'd I say before, Stanley? You see? She's a cover girl.

STANLEY. Oh, I could see. I could see.

HAPPY (*to the* GIRL). What magazine?

GIRL. Oh, a lot of them. (*She takes the drink.*) Thank you.

HAPPY. You know what they say in France, don't you? "Champagne is the drink of the complexion." — Hya, Biff!

(BIFF *has entered and sits with* HAPPY.)

BIFF.   Hello, kid. Sorry I'm late.

HAPPY.   I just got here. Uh, Miss — ?

GIRL.   Forsythe.

HAPPY.   Miss Forsythe, this is my brother.

BIFF.   Is Dad here?

HAPPY.   His name is Biff. You might've heard of him. Great football player.

GIRL.   Really? What team?

HAPPY.   Are you familiar with football?

GIRL.   No, I'm afraid I'm not.

HAPPY.   Biff is quarterback with the New York Giants.

GIRL.   Well, that is nice, isn't it? (*She drinks.*)

HAPPY.   Good health.

GIRL.   I'm happy to meet you.

HAPPY.   That's my name. Hap. It's really Harold, but at West Point they called me Happy.

GIRL (*now really impressed*).   Oh, I see. How do you do? (*She turns her profile.*)

BIFF.   Isn't Dad coming?

HAPPY.   You want her?

BIFF.   Oh, I could never make that.

HAPPY.   I remember the time that idea would never come into your head. Where's the old confidence, Biff?

BIFF.   I just saw Oliver —

HAPPY.   Wait a minute. I've got to see that old confidence again. Do you want her? She's on call.

BIFF.   Oh, no. (*He turns to look at the* GIRL.)

HAPPY.   I'm telling you. Watch this. (*Turning to the* GIRL.) Honey? (*She turns to him.*) Are you busy?

GIRL.   Well, I am . . . but I could make a phone call.

HAPPY.   Do that, will you, honey? And see if you can get a friend. We'll be here for a while. Biff is one of the greatest football players in the country.

GIRL (*standing up*).   Well, I'm certainly happy to meet you.

HAPPY.   Come back soon.

GIRL.   I'll try.

HAPPY.   Don't try, honey, try hard.

(*The* GIRL *exits.* STANLEY *follows, shaking his head in bewildered admiration.*)

Isn't that a shame now? A beautiful girl like that? That's why I can't get married. There's not a good woman in a thousand. New York is loaded with them, kid!

BIFF.   Hap, look —

HAPPY.   I told you she was on call!

BIFF (*strangely unnerved*).   Cut it out, will ya? I want to say something to you.

HAPPY.   Did you see Oliver?

BIFF.   I saw him all right. Now look, I want to tell Dad a couple of things and I want you to help me.

HAPPY.   What? Is he going to back you?

BIFF.   Are you crazy? You're out of your goddam head, you know that?

HAPPY.   Why? What happened?

BIFF (breathlessly).   I did a terrible thing today, Hap. It's been the strangest day I ever went through. I'm all numb, I swear.

HAPPY.   You mean he wouldn't see you?

BIFF.   Well, I waited six hours for him, see? All day. Kept sending my name in. Even tried to date his secretary so she'd get me to him, but no soap.

HAPPY.   Because you're not showin' the old confidence, Biff. He remembered you, didn't he?

BIFF (stopping HAPPY with a gesture).   Finally, about five o'clock, he comes out. Didn't remember who I was or anything. I felt like such an idiot, Hap.

HAPPY.   Did you tell him my Florida idea?

BIFF.   He walked away. I saw him for one minute. I got so mad I could've torn the walls down! How the hell did I ever get the idea I was a salesman there? I even believed myself that I'd been a salesman for him! And then he gave me one look and — I realized what a ridiculous lie my whole life has been! We've been talking in a dream for fifteen years. I was a shipping clerk.

HAPPY.   What'd you do?

BIFF (with great tension and wonder).   Well, he left, see. And the secretary went out. I was all alone in the waiting-room. I don't know what came over me, Hap. The next thing I know I'm in his office — paneled walls, everything. I can't explain it. I — Hap, I took his fountain pen.

HAPPY.   Geez, did he catch you?

BIFF.   I ran out. I ran down all eleven flights. I ran and ran and ran.

HAPPY.   That was an awful dumb — what'd you do that for?

BIFF (agonized).   I don't know, I just — wanted to take something, I don't know. You gotta help me, Hap, I'm gonna tell Pop.

HAPPY.   You crazy? What for?

BIFF.   Hap, he's got to understand that I'm not the man somebody lends that kind of money to. He thinks I've been spiting him all these years and it's eating him up.

HAPPY.   That's just it. You tell him something nice.

BIFF.   I can't.

HAPPY.   Say you got a lunch date with Oliver tomorrow.

BIFF.   So what do I do tomorrow?

HAPPY.   You leave the house tomorrow and come back at night and say Oliver is thinking it over. And he thinks it over for a couple of weeks, and gradually it fades away and nobody's the worse.

BIFF.   But it'll go on forever!

HAPPY. Dad is never so happy as when he's looking forward to something!

(WILLY *enters.*)

Hello, scout!

WILLY. Gee, I haven't been here in years!

(STANLEY *has followed* WILLY *in and sets a chair for him.* STANLEY *starts off but* HAPPY *stops him.*)

HAPPY. Stanley!

(STANLEY *stands by, waiting for an order.*)

BIFF (*going to* WILLY *with guilt, as to an invalid*). Sit down, Pop. You want a drink?

WILLY. Sure, I don't mind.

BIFF. Let's get a load on.

WILLY. You look worried.

BIFF. N-no. (*To* STANLEY.) Scotch all around. Make it doubles.

STANLEY. Doubles, right. (*He goes.*)

WILLY. You had a couple already, didn't you?

BIFF. Just a couple, yeah.

WILLY. Well, what happened, boy? (*Nodding affirmatively, with a smile.*) Everything go all right?

BIFF (*takes a breath, then reaches out and grasps* WILLY'*s hand*). Pal ... (*He is smiling bravely, and* WILLY *is smiling too.*) I had an experience today.

HAPPY. Terrific, Pop.

WILLY. That so? What happened?

BIFF (*high, slightly alcoholic, above the earth*). I'm going to tell you everything from first to last. It's been a strange day. (*Silence. He looks around, composes himself as best he can, but his breath keeps breaking the rhythm of his voice.*) I had to wait quite a while for him, and —

WILLY. Oliver?

BIFF. Yeah, Oliver. All day, as a matter of cold fact. And a lot of — instances — facts, Pop, facts about my life came back to me. Who was it, Pop? Who ever said I was a salesman with Oliver?

WILLY. Well, you were.

BIFF. No, Dad, I was a shipping clerk.

WILLY. But you were practically —

BIFF (*with determination*). Dad, I don't know who said it first, but I was never a salesman for Bill Oliver.

WILLY. What're you talking about?

BIFF. Let's hold on to the facts tonight, Pop. We're not going to get anywhere bullin' around. I was a shipping clerk.

WILLY (*angrily*). All right, now listen to me —

BIFF. Why don't you let me finish?

WILLY. I'm not interested in stories about the past or any crap of that kind because the woods are burning, boys, you understand? There's a big blaze going on all around. I was fired today.

BIFF (*shocked*). How could you be?

WILLY. I was fired, and I'm looking for a little good news to tell your mother, because the woman has waited and the woman has suffered. The gist of it is that I haven't got a story left in my head, Biff. So don't give me a lecture about facts and aspects. I am not interested. Now what've you got to say to me?

(STANLEY *enters with three drinks. They wait until he leaves.*)

Did you see Oliver?

BIFF. Jesus, Dad!

WILLY. You mean you didn't go up there?

HAPPY. Sure he went up there.

BIFF. I did. I — saw him. How could they fire you?

WILLY (*on the edge of his chair*). What kind of a welcome did he give you?

BIFF. He won't even let you work on commission?

WILLY. I'm out! (*Driving.*) So tell me, he gave you a warm welcome?

HAPPY. Sure, Pop, sure!

BIFF (*driven*). Well, it was kind of —

WILLY. I was wondering if he'd remember you. (*To* HAPPY.) Imagine, man doesn't see him for ten, twelve years and gives him that kind of a welcome!

HAPPY. Damn right!

BIFF (*trying to return to the offensive*). Pop, look —

WILLY. You know why he remembered you, don't you? Because you impressed him in those days.

BIFF. Let's talk quietly and get this down to the facts, huh?

WILLY (*as though* BIFF *had been interrupting*). Well, what happened? It's great news, Biff. Did he take you into his office or'd you talk in the waiting-room?

BIFF. Well, he came in, see, and —

WILLY (*with a big smile*). What'd he say? Betcha he threw his arm around you.

BIFF. Well, he kinda —

WILLY. He's a fine man. (*To* HAPPY.) Very hard man to see, y'know.

HAPPY (*agreeing*). Oh, I know.

WILLY (*to* BIFF). Is that where you had the drinks?

BIFF. Yeah, he gave me a couple of — no, no!

HAPPY (*cutting in*). He told him my Florida idea.

WILLY. Don't interrupt. (*To* BIFF.) How'd he react to the Florida idea?

BIFF. Dad, will you give me a minute to explain?

WILLY. I've been waiting for you to explain since I sat down here! What happened? He took you into his office and what?

BIFF. Well — I talked. And — and he listened, see.

WILLY. Famous for the way he listens, y'know. What was his answer?

BIFF. His answer was — (*he breaks off, suddenly angry*). Dad, you're not letting me tell you what I want to tell you!

WILLY (*accusing, angered*). You didn't see him, did you?

BIFF. I did see him!

WILLY. What'd you insult him or something? You insulted him, didn't you?

BIFF. Listen, will you let me out of it, will you just let me out of it!

HAPPY. What the hell!

WILLY. Tell me what happened!

BIFF (*to* HAPPY). I can't talk to him!

(*A single trumpet note jars the ear. The light of green leaves stains the house, which holds the air of night and a dream.* YOUNG BERNARD *enters and knocks on the door of the house.*)

YOUNG BERNARD (*frantically*). Mrs. Loman, Mrs. Loman!

HAPPY. Tell him what happened!

BIFF (*to* HAPPY). Shut up and leave me alone!

WILLY. No, no! You had to go and flunk math!

BIFF. What math? What're you talking about?

YOUNG BERNARD. Mrs. Loman, Mrs. Loman!

(LINDA *appears in the house, as of old.*)

WILLY (*wildly*). Math, math, math!

BIFF. Take it easy, Pop!

YOUNG BERNARD. Mrs. Loman!

WILLY (*furiously*). If you hadn't flunked you'd've been set by now!

BIFF. Now, look, I'm gonna tell you what happened, and you're going to listen to me.

YOUNG BERNARD. Mrs. Loman!

BIFF. I waited six hours —

HAPPY. What the hell are you saying?

BIFF. I kept sending in my name but he wouldn't see me. So finally he . . . (*he continues unheard as light fades low on the restaurant*).

YOUNG BERNARD. Biff flunked math!

LINDA. No!

YOUNG BERNARD. Birnbaum flunked him! They won't graduate him!

LINDA. But they have to. He's gotta go to the university. Where is he? Biff! Biff!

YOUNG BERNARD. No, he left. He went to Grand Central.

LINDA. Grand — You mean he went to Boston!

YOUNG BERNARD.   Is Uncle Willy in Boston?

LINDA.   Oh, maybe Willy can talk to the teacher. Oh, the poor, poor boy!

(*Light on house area snaps out.*)

BIFF (*at the table, now audible, holding up a gold fountain pen*).   . . . so I'm washed up with Oliver, you understand? Are you listening to me?

WILLY (*at a loss*).   Yeah, sure. If you hadn't flunked —

BIFF.   Flunked what? What're you talking about?

WILLY.   Don't blame everything on me! I didn't flunk math — you did! What pen?

HAPPY.   That was awful dumb, Biff, a pen like that is worth —

WILLY (*seeing the pen for the first time*).   You took Oliver's pen?

BIFF (*weakening*).   Dad, I just explained it to you.

WILLY.   You stole Bill Oliver's fountain pen!

BIFF.   I didn't exactly steal it! That's just what I've been explaining to you!

HAPPY.   He had it in his hand and just then Oliver walked in, so he got nervous and stuck it in his pocket!

WILLY.   My God, Biff!

BIFF.   I never intended to do it, Dad!

OPERATOR'S VOICE.   Standish Arms, good evening!

WILLY (*shouting*).   I'm not in my room!

BIFF (*frightened*).   Dad, what's the matter?

(*He and* HAPPY *stand up.*)

OPERATOR.   Ringing Mr. Loman for you!

WILLY.   I'm not there, stop it!

BIFF (*horrified, gets down on one knee before* WILLY).   Dad, I'll make good, I'll make good.

(WILLY *tries to get to his feet.* BIFF *holds him down.*)

Sit down now.

WILLY.   No, you're no good, you're no good for anything.

BIFF.   I am, Dad, I'll find something else, you understand? Now don't worry about anything. (*He holds up* WILLY'*s face.*) Talk to me, Dad.

OPERATOR.   Mr. Loman does not answer. Shall I page him?

WILLY (*attempting to stand, as though to rush and silence the* OPERATOR).   No, no, no!

HAPPY.   He'll strike something, Pop.

WILLY.   No, no . . .

BIFF (*desperately, standing over* WILLY).   Pop, listen! Listen to me! I'm telling you something good. Oliver talked to his partner about the

Florida idea. You listening? He — he talked to his partner, and he came to me . . . I'm going to be all right, you hear? Dad, listen to me, he said it was just a question of the amount!

WILLY. Then you . . . got it?

HAPPY. He's gonna be terrific, Pop!

WILLY (*trying to stand*). Then you got it, haven't you? You got it! You got it!

BIFF (*agonized, holds* WILLY *down*). No, no. Look, Pop. I'm supposed to have lunch with them tomorrow. I'm just telling you this so you'll know that I can still make an impression, Pop. And I'll make good somewhere, but I can't go tomorrow, see?

WILLY. Why not? You simply —

BIFF. But the pen, Pop!

WILLY. You give it to him and tell him it was an oversight!

HAPPY. Sure, have lunch tomorrow!

BIFF. I can't say that —

WILLY. You were doing a crossword puzzle and accidentally used his pen!

BIFF. Listen, kid, I took those balls years ago, now I walk in with his fountain pen? That clinches it, don't you see? I can't face him like that! I'll try elsewhere.

PAGE'S VOICE. Paging Mr. Loman!

WILLY. Don't you want to be anything?

BIFF. Pop, how can I go back?

WILLY. You don't want to be anything, is that what's behind it?

BIFF (*now angry at* WILLY *for not crediting his sympathy*). Don't take it that way! You think it was easy walking into that office after what I'd done to him? A team of horses couldn't have dragged me back to Bill Oliver!

WILLY. Then why'd you go?

BIFF. Why did I go? Why did I go! Look at you! Look at what's become of you!

(*Off left,* THE WOMAN *laughs.*)

WILLY. Biff, you're going to go to that lunch tomorrow, or —

BIFF. I can't go. I've got no appointment!

HAPPY. Biff, for . . . !

WILLY. Are you spiting me?

BIFF. Don't take it that way! Goddammit!

WILLY (*strikes* BIFF *and falters away from the table*). You rotten little louse! Are you spiting me?

THE WOMAN. Someone's at the door, Willy!

BIFF. I'm no good, can't you see what I am?

HAPPY (*separating them*). Hey, you're in a restaurant! Now cut it out, both of you!

(*The girls enter.*)

Hello, girls, sit down.

(THE WOMAN *laughs, off left.*)

MISS FORSYTHE. I guess we might as well. This is Letta.

THE WOMAN. Willy, are you going to wake up?

BIFF (*ignoring* WILLY). How're ya, miss, sit down. What do you drink?

MISS FORSYTHE. Letta might not be able to stay long.

LETTA. I gotta get up very early tomorrow. I got jury duty. I'm so excited! Were you fellows ever on a jury?

BIFF. No, but I been in front of them!

(*The girls laugh.*)

This is my father.

LETTA. Isn't he cute? Sit down with us, Pop.

HAPPY. Sit him down, Biff!

BIFF (*going to him*). Come on, slugger, drink us under the table. To hell with it! Come on, sit down, pal.

(*On* BIFF's *last insistence,* WILLY *is about to sit.*)

THE WOMAN (*now urgently*). Willy, are you going to answer the door!

(THE WOMAN's *call pulls* WILLY *back. He starts right, befuddled.*)

BIFF. Hey, where are you going?

WILLY. Open the door.

BIFF. The door?

WILLY. The washroom . . . the door . . . where's the door?

BIFF (*leading* WILLY *to the left*). Just go straight down.

(WILLY *moves left.*)

THE WOMAN. Willy, Willy, are you going to get up, get up, get up, get up?

(WILLY *exits left.*)

LETTA. I think it's sweet you bring your daddy along.

MISS FORSYTHE. Oh, he isn't really your father!

BIFF (*at left, turning to her resentfully*). Miss Forsythe, you've just seen a prince walk by. A fine, troubled prince. A hard-working, unappreciated prince. A pal, you understand? A good companion. Always for his boys.

LETTA. That's so sweet.

HAPPY. Well, girls, what's the program? We're wasting time. Come on, Biff. Gather round. Where would you like to go?

BIFF. Why don't you do something for him?

HAPPY. Me!

BIFF. Don't you give a damn for him, Hap?

HAPPY. What're you talking about? I'm the one who —

BIFF. I sense it, you don't give a good goddam about him. (*He takes the rolled-up hose from his pocket and puts it on the table in front of* HAPPY.) Look what I found in the cellar, for Christ's sake. How can you bear to let it go on?

HAPPY. Me? Who goes away? Who runs off and —

BIFF. Yeah, but he doesn't mean anything to you. You could help him — I can't! Don't you understand what I'm talking about? He's going to kill himself, don't you know that?

HAPPY. Don't I know it! Me!

BIFF. Hap, help him! Jesus . . . help him. . . . Help me, help me, I can't bear to look at his face! (*Ready to weep, he hurries out, up right.*)

HAPPY (*starting after him*). Where are you going?

MISS FORSYTHE. What's he so mad about?

HAPPY. Come on, girls, we'll catch up with him.

MISS FORSYTHE (*as* HAPPY *pushes her out*). Say, I don't like that temper of his!

HAPPY. He's just a little overstrung, he'll be all right!

WILLY (*off left, as* THE WOMAN *laughs*). Don't answer! Don't answer!

LETTA. Don't you want to tell your father —

HAPPY. No, that's not my father. He's just a guy. Come on, we'll catch Biff, and, honey, we're going to paint this town! Stanley, where's the check! Hey, Stanley!

(*They exit.* STANLEY *looks toward left.*)

STANLEY (*calling to* HAPPY *indignantly*). Mr. Loman! Mr. Loman!

(STANLEY *picks up a chair and follows them off. Knocking is heard off left.* THE WOMAN *enters, laughing.* WILLY *follows her. She is in a black slip; he is buttoning his shirt. Raw, sensuous music accompanies their speech.*)

WILLY. Will you stop laughing? Will you stop?

THE WOMAN. Aren't you going to answer the door? He'll wake the whole hotel.

WILLY. I'm not expecting anybody.

THE WOMAN. Whyn't you have another drink, honey, and stop being so damn self-centered?

WILLY. I'm so lonely.

THE WOMAN. You know you ruined me, Willy? From now on, whenever you come to the office, I'll see that you go right through to the buyers. No waiting at my desk any more, Willy. You ruined me.

WILLY. That's nice of you to say that.

THE WOMAN. Gee, you are self-centered! Why so sad? You are the saddest, self-centeredest soul I ever did see-saw.

(*She laughs. He kisses her.*)

Come on inside, drummer boy. It's silly to be dressing in the middle of the night. (*As knocking is heard.*) Aren't you going to answer the door?

WILLY. They're knocking on the wrong door.

THE WOMAN. But I felt the knocking. And he heard us talking in here. Maybe the hotel's on fire!

WILLY (*his terror rising*). It's a mistake.

THE WOMAN. Then tell him to go away!

WILLY. There's nobody there.

THE WOMAN. It's getting on my nerves, Willy. There's somebody standing out there and it's getting on my nerves!

WILLY (*pushing her away from him*). All right, stay in the bathroom here, and don't come out. I think there's a law in Massachusetts about it, so don't come out. It may be that new room clerk. He looked very mean. So don't come out. It's a mistake, there's no fire.

(*The knocking is heard again. He takes a few steps away from her, and she vanishes into the wing. The light follows him, and now he is facing* YOUNG BIFF, *who carries a suitcase.* BIFF *steps toward him. The music is gone.*)

BIFF. Why didn't you answer?

WILLY. Biff! What are you doing in Boston?

BIFF. Why didn't you answer? I've been knocking for five minutes, I called you on the phone —

WILLY. I just heard you. I was in the bathroom and had the door shut. Did anything happen home?

BIFF. Dad — I let you down.

WILLY. What do you mean?

BIFF. Dad . . .

WILLY. Biffo, what's this about? (*Putting his arm around* BIFF.) Come on, let's go downstairs and get you a malted.

BIFF. Dad, I flunked math.

WILLY. Not for the term?

BIFF. The term. I haven't got enough credits to graduate.

WILLY. You mean to say Bernard wouldn't give you the answers?

BIFF. He did, he tried, but I only got a sixty-one.

WILLY. And they wouldn't give you four points?

BIFF. Birnbaum refused absolutely. I begged him, Pop, but he won't give me those points. You gotta talk to him before they close the school. Because if he saw the kind of man you are, and you just talked to him in your way, I'm sure he'd come through for me. The class came right before practice, see, and I didn't go enough. Would you talk to him? He'd like you, Pop. You know the way you could talk.

WILLY. You're on. We'll drive right back.

BIFF. Oh, Dad, good work! I'm sure he'll change it for you!

WILLY. Go downstairs and tell the clerk I'm checkin' out. Go right down.

BIFF. Yes, sir! See, the reason he hates me, Pop — one day he was late for class so I got up at the blackboard and imitated him. I crossed my eyes and talked with a lithp.

WILLY (*laughing*). You did? The kids like it?

BIFF. They nearly died laughing!

WILLY. Yeah! What'd you do?

BIFF. The thquare root of thixthy-twee is . . .

(WILLY *bursts out laughing*; BIFF *joins him.*)

And in the middle of it he walked in!

(WILLY *laughs and* THE WOMAN *joins in offstage.*)

WILLY (*without hesitation*). Hurry downstairs and —

BIFF. Somebody in there?

WILLY. No, that was next door.

(THE WOMAN *laughs offstage.*)

BIFF. Somebody got in your bathroom!

WILLY. No, it's the next room, there's a party —

THE WOMAN (*enters, laughing. She lisps this*). Can I come in? There's something in the bathtub, Willy, and it's moving!

(WILLY *looks at* BIFF, *who is staring open-mouthed and horrified at* THE WOMAN.)

WILLY. Ah — you better go back to your room. They must be finished painting by now. They're painting her room so I let her take a shower here. Go back, go back . . . (*he pushes her*).

THE WOMAN (*resisting*). But I've got to get dressed, Willy, I can't —

WILLY. Get out of here! Go back, go back. . . . (*Suddenly striving for the ordinary.*) This is Miss Francis, Biff, she's a buyer. They're painting her room. Go back, Miss Francis, go back . . .

THE WOMAN. But my clothes, I can't go out naked in the hall!

WILLY (*pushing her offstage*). Get outa here! Go back, go back!

(BIFF *slowly sits down on his suitcase as the argument continues off-stage.*)

THE WOMAN. Where's my stockings? You promised me stockings, Willy!

WILLY. I have no stockings here!

THE WOMAN. You had two boxes of size nine sheers for me, and I want them!

WILLY. Here, for God's sake, will you get outa here!

THE WOMAN (*enters holding a box of stockings*). I just hope there's nobody in the hall. That's all I hope. (*To* BIFF.) Are you football or baseball?

BIFF. Football.

THE WOMAN (*angry, humiliated*). That's me too. G'night. (*She snatches her clothes from* WILLY, *and walks out.*)

WILLY (*after a pause*). Well, better get going. I want to get to the school first thing in the morning. Get my suits out of the closet. I'll get my valise.

(BIFF *doesn't move.*)

What's the matter?

(BIFF *remains motionless, tears falling.*)

She's a buyer. Buys for J. H. Simmons. She lives down the hall — they're painting. You don't imagine — (*He breaks off. After a pause.*) Now listen, pal, she's just a buyer. She sees merchandise in her room and they have to keep it looking just so. . . . (*Pause. Assuming command.*) All right, get my suits.

(BIFF *doesn't move.*)

Now stop crying and do as I say. I gave you an order. Biff, I gave you an order! Is that what you do when I give you an order? How dare you cry! (*Putting his arm around* BIFF.) Now look, Biff, when you grow up you'll understand about these things. You mustn't — you mustn't overemphasize a thing like this. I'll see Birnbaum first thing in the morning.

BIFF. Never mind.

WILLY (*getting down beside* BIFF). Never mind! He's going to give you those points. I'll see to it.

BIFF. He wouldn't listen to you.

WILLY. He certainly will listen to me. You need those points for the U. of Virginia.

BIFF. I'm not going there.

WILLY. Heh? If I can't get him to change that mark you'll make it up in summer school. You've got all summer to —

BIFF (*his weeping breaking from him*). Dad . . .

WILLY (*infected by it*). Oh, my boy . . .

BIFF. Dad . . .

WILLY. She's nothing to me, Biff. I was lonely, I was terribly lonely.

BIFF. You — you gave her Mama's stockings! (*His tears break through and he rises to go.*)

WILLY (*grabbing for* BIFF). I gave you an order!

BIFF. Don't touch me, you — liar!

WILLY. Apologize for that!

BIFF. You fake! You phony little fake! You fake!

(*Overcome, he turns quickly and weeping fully goes out with his suitcase.* WILLY *is left on the floor on his knees.*)

WILLY. I gave you an order! Biff, come back here or I'll beat you! Come back here! I'll whip you!

(STANLEY *comes quickly in from the right and stands in front of* WILLY.)

(*Shouts at* STANLEY.) I gave you an order . . .

STANLEY. Hey, let's pick it up, pick it up, Mr. Loman. (*He helps* WILLY *to his feet.*) Your boys left with the chippies. They said they'll see you home.

(*A second waiter watches some distance away.*)

WILLY. But we were supposed to have dinner together.

(*Music is heard,* WILLY's *theme.*)

STANLEY. Can you make it?

WILLY. I'll — sure, I can make it. (*Suddenly concerned about his clothes.*) Do I — I look all right?

STANLEY. Sure, you look all right. (*He flicks a speck off* WILLY's *lapel.*)

WILLY. Here — here's a dollar.

STANLEY. Oh, your son paid me. It's all right.

WILLY (*putting it in* STANLEY's *hand*). No, take it. You're a good boy.

STANLEY. Oh, no, you don't have to . . .

WILLY. Here — here's some more, I don't need it any more. (*After a slight pause.*) Tell me — is there a seed store in the neighborhood?

STANLEY. Seeds? You mean like to plant?

(*As* WILLY *turns,* STANLEY *slips the money back into his jacket pocket.*)

WILLY. Yes. Carrots, peas . . .

STANLEY. Well, there's hardware stores on Sixth Avenue, but it may be too late now.

WILLY (*anxiously*). Oh, I'd better hurry. I've got to get some seeds. (*He starts off to the right.*) I've got to get some seeds, right away. Nothing's planted. I don't have a thing in the ground.

(WILLY *hurries out as the light goes down.* STANLEY *moves over to the right after him, watches him off. The other waiter has been staring at* WILLY.)

STANLEY (*to the waiter*). Well, whatta you looking at?

(*The waiter picks up the chairs and moves off right.* STANLEY *takes the table and follows him. The light fades on this area. There is a long pause, the sound of the flute coming over. The light gradually rises on the kitchen, which is empty.* HAPPY *appears at the door of the house, followed by* BIFF. HAPPY *is carrying a large bunch of long-stemmed roses. He enters the kitchen, looks around for* LINDA. *Not seeing her, he turns to* BIFF, *who is just outside the house door, and makes a gesture with his hands, indicating "Not here, I guess." He looks into the living-room and freezes. Inside,* LINDA, *unseen, is seated,* WILLY'S *coat on her lap. She rises ominously and quietly and moves toward* HAPPY, *who backs up into the kitchen, afraid.*)

HAPPY. Hey, what're you doing up?

(LINDA *says nothing but moves toward him implacably.*)

Where's Pop?

(*He keeps backing to the right, and now* LINDA *is in full view in the doorway to the living-room.*)

Is he sleeping?

LINDA. Where were you?

HAPPY (*trying to laugh it off*). We met two girls, Mom, very fine types. Here, we brought you some flowers. (*Offering them to her.*) Put them in your room, Ma.

(*She knocks them to the floor at* BIFF'S *feet. He has now come inside and closed the door behind him. She stares at* BIFF, *silent.*)

Now what'd you do that for? Mom, I want you to have some flowers —

LINDA (*cutting* HAPPY *off, violently to* BIFF). Don't you care whether he lives or dies?

HAPPY (*going to the stairs*). Come upstairs, Biff.

BIFF (*with a flare of disgust, to* HAPPY). Go away from me! (*To* LINDA.) What do you mean, lives or dies? Nobody's dying around here, pal.

LINDA. Get out of my sight! Get out of here!

BIFF. I wanna see the boss.

LINDA. You're not going near him!

BIFF. Where is he? (*He moves into the living-room and* LINDA *follows.*)

LINDA (*shouting after* BIFF). You invite him for dinner. He looks forward to it all day —

(BIFF *appears in his parents' bedroom, looks around, and exits.*)

— and then you desert him there. There's no stranger you'd do that to!

HAPPY. Why? He had a swell time with us. Listen, when I —

(LINDA *comes back into the kitchen.*)

— desert him I hope I don't outlive the day!

LINDA. Get out of here!

HAPPY. Now look, Mom . . .

LINDA. Did you have to go to women tonight? You and your lousy rotten whores!

(BIFF *re-enters the kitchen.*)

HAPPY. Mom, all we did was follow Biff around trying to cheer him up! (*To* BIFF.) Boy, what a night you gave me!

LINDA. Get out of here, both of you, and don't come back! I don't want you tormenting him any more. Go on now, get your things together! (*To* BIFF.) You can sleep in his apartment. (*She starts to pick up the flowers and stops herself.*) Pick up this stuff, I'm not your maid any more. Pick it up, you bum, you!

(HAPPY *turns his back to her in refusal.* BIFF *slowly moves over and gets down on his knees, picking up the flowers.*)

You're a pair of animals! Not one, not another living soul would have had the cruelty to walk out on that man in a restaurant!

BIFF (*not looking at her*). Is that what he said?

LINDA. He didn't have to say anything. He was so humiliated he nearly limped when he came in.

HAPPY. But, Mom, he had a great time with us —

BIFF (*cutting him off violently*). Shut up!

(*Without another word,* HAPPY *goes upstairs.*)

LINDA. You! You didn't even go in to see if he was all right!

BIFF (*still on the floor in front of* LINDA, *the flowers in his hand; with self-loathing*). No. Didn't. Didn't do a damned thing. How do you like that, heh? Left him babbling in a toilet.

LINDA. You louse. You . . .

BIFF. Now you hit it on the nose! (*He gets up, throws the flowers in the wastebasket.*) The scum of the earth, and you're looking at him!

LINDA. Get out of here!

BIFF. I gotta talk to the boss, Mom. Where is he?

LINDA. You're not going near him. Get out of this house!

BIFF (*with absolute assurance, determination*). No. We're gonna have an abrupt conversation, him and me.

LINDA. You're not talking to him!

(*Hammering is heard from outside the house, off right.* BIFF *turns toward the noise.*)

(*Suddenly pleading.*) Will you please leave him alone?

BIFF. What's he doing out there?

LINDA. He's planting the garden!

BIFF (*quietly*). Now? Oh, my God!

(BIFF *moves outside,* LINDA *following. The light dies down on them and comes up on the center of the apron as* WILLY *walks into it. He is carrying a flashlight, a hoe, and a handful of seed packets. He raps the top of the hoe sharply to fix it firmly, and then moves to the left, measuring off the distance with his foot. He holds the flashlight to look at the seed packets, reading off the instructions. He is in the blue of night.*)

WILLY. Carrots . . . quarter-inch apart. Rows . . . one-foot rows. (*He measures it off.*) One foot. (*He puts down a package and measures off.*) Beets. (*He puts down another package and measures again.*) Lettuce. (*He reads the package, puts it down.*) One foot —

(*He breaks off as* BEN *appears at the right and moves slowly down to him.*)

What a proposition, ts, ts. Terrific, terrific. 'Cause she's suffered, Ben, the woman has suffered. You understand me? A man can't go out the way he came in, Ben, a man has got to add up to something. You can't, you can't.

(BEN *moves toward him as though to interrupt.*)

You gotta consider, now. Don't answer so quick. Remember, it's a guaranteed twenty-thousand-dollar proposition. Now look, Ben, I want you to go through the ins and outs of this thing with me. I've got nobody to talk to, Ben, and the woman has suffered, you hear me?

BEN (*standing still, considering*). What's the proposition?

WILLY. It's twenty thousand dollars on the barrelhead. Guaranteed, gilt-edged, you understand?

BEN. You don't want to make a fool of yourself. They might not honor the policy.

WILLY. How can they dare refuse? Didn't I work like a coolie to meet every premium on the nose? And now they don't pay off? Impossible!

BEN. It's called a cowardly thing, William.

WILLY. Why? Does it take more guts to stand here the rest of my life ringing up a zero?

BEN (*yielding*). That's a point, William. (*He moves, thinking, turns.*) And twenty thousand — that *is* something one can feel with the hand, it is there.

WILLY (*now assured, with rising power*). Oh, Ben, that's the whole beauty of it! I see it like a diamond, shining in the dark, hard and rough, that I can pick up and touch in my hand. Not like — like an appointment! This would not be another damned-fool appointment, Ben, and it changes all the aspects. Because he thinks I'm nothing, see, and so he spites me. But the funeral — (*straightening up*). Ben, that funeral will be massive! They'll come from Maine, Massachusetts, Vermont, New Hampshire! All the old-timers with the strange license plates — that boy will be thunder-struck, Ben, because he never realized — I am known! Rhode Island, New York, New Jersey — I am known, Ben, and he'll see it with his eyes once and for all. He'll see what I am, Ben! He's in for a shock, that boy!

BEN (*coming down to the edge of the garden*). He'll call you a coward.

WILLY (*suddenly fearful*). No, that would be terrible.

BEN. Yes. And a damned fool.

WILLY. No, no, he mustn't, I won't have that! (*He is broken and desperate.*)

BEN. He'll hate you, William.

(*The gay music of the* BOYS *is heard.*)

WILLY. Oh, Ben, how do we get back to all the great times? Used to be so full of light, and comradeship, the sleigh-riding in winter, and the ruddiness on his cheeks. And always some kind of good news coming up, always something nice coming up ahead. And never even let me carry the valises in the house, and simonizing, simonizing that little red car! Why, why can't I give him something and not have him hate me?

BEN. Let me think about it. (*He glances at his watch.*) I still have a little time. Remarkable proposition, but you've got to be sure you're not making a fool of yourself.

(BEN *drifts off upstage and goes out of sight.* BIFF *comes down from the left.*)

WILLY (*suddenly conscious of* BIFF, *turns and looks up at him, then begins picking up the packages of seeds in confusion*). Where the hell is that seed? (*Indignantly.*) You can't see nothing out here! They boxed in the whole goddam neighborhood!

BIFF. There are people all around here. Don't you realize that?

WILLY. I'm busy. Don't bother me.

BIFF (*taking the hoe from* WILLY). I'm saying good-by to you, Pop.

(WILLY *looks at him, silent, unable to move.*)

I'm not coming back any more.

WILLY. You're not going to see Oliver tomorrow?

BIFF. I've got no appointment, Dad.

WILLY. He put his arm around you, and you've got no appointment?

BIFF. Pop, get this now, will you? Every time I've left it's been a fight that sent me out of here. Today I realized something about myself and I tried to explain it to you and I — I think I'm just not smart enough to make any sense out of it for you. To hell with whose fault it is or anything like that. (*He takes* WILLY's *arm.*) Let's just wrap it up, heh? Come on in, we'll tell Mom. (*He gently tries to pull* WILLY *to left.*)

WILLY (*frozen, immobile, with guilt in his voice*). No, I don't want to see her.

BIFF. Come on! (*He pulls again, and* WILLY *tries to pull away.*)

WILLY (*highly nervous*). No, no, I don't want to see her.

BIFF (*tries to look into* WILLY's *face, as if to find the answer there*). Why don't you want to see her?

WILLY (*more harshly now*). Don't bother me, will you?

BIFF. What do you mean, you don't want to see her? You don't want them calling you yellow, do you? This isn't your fault; it's me, I'm a bum. Now come inside!

(WILLY *strains to get away.*)

Did you hear what I said to you?

(WILLY *pulls away and quickly goes by himself into the house.* BIFF *follows.*)

LINDA (*to* WILLY). Did you plant, dear?

BIFF (*at the door, to* LINDA). All right, we had it out. I'm going and I'm not writing any more.

LINDA (*going to* WILLY *in the kitchen*). I think that's the best way, dear. 'Cause there's no use drawing it out, you'll just never get along.

(WILLY *doesn't respond.*)

BIFF. People ask where I am and what I'm doing, you don't know, and you don't care. That way it'll be off your mind and you can start brightening up again. All right? That clears it, doesn't it?

(WILLY *is silent, and* BIFF *goes to him.*)

You gonna wish me luck, scout? (*He extends his hand.*) What do you say?

LINDA. Shake his hand, Willy.

WILLY (*turning to her, seething with hurt*). There's no necessity to mention the pen at all, y'know.

BIFF (*gently*). I've got no appointment, Dad.

WILLY (*erupting fiercely*). He put his arm around . . . ?

BIFF. Dad, you're never going to see what I am, so what's the use of arguing? If I strike oil I'll send you a check. Meantime forget I'm alive.

WILLY (*to* LINDA). Spite, see?

BIFF. Shake hands, Dad.

WILLY. Not my hand.

BIFF. I was hoping not to go this way.

WILLY. Well, this is the way you're going. Good-by.

(BIFF *looks at him a moment, then turns sharply and goes to the stairs.*)

(*Stops him.*) May you rot in hell if you leave this house!

BIFF (*turning*). Exactly what is it that you want from me?

WILLY. I want you to know, on the train, in the mountains, in the valleys, wherever you go, that you cut down your life for spite!

BIFF. No, no.

WILLY. Spite, spite, is the word of your undoing! And when you're down and out, remember what did it. When you're rotting somewhere beside the railroad tracks, remember, and don't you dare blame it on me!

BIFF. I'm not blaming it on you!

WILLY. I won't take the rap for this, you hear?

(HAPPY *comes down the stairs and stands on the bottom step, watching.*)

BIFF. That's just what I'm telling you!

WILLY (*sinking into a chair at the table, with full accusation*). You're trying to put a knife in me — don't think I don't know what you're doing!

BIFF. All right, phony! Then let's lay it on the line. (*He whips the rubber tube out of his pocket and puts it on the table.*)

HAPPY. You crazy —

LINDA. Biff! (*She moves to grab the hose, but* BIFF *holds it down with his hand.*)

BIFF. Leave it there! Don't move it!

WILLY (*not looking at it*). What is that?

BIFF. You know goddam well what that is.

WILLY (*caged, wanting to escape*). I never saw that.

BIFF. You saw it. The mice didn't bring it into the cellar! What is this supposed to do, make a hero out of you? This supposed to make me sorry for you?

WILLY. Never heard of it.

BIFF. There'll be no pity for you, you hear it? No pity!

WILLY (*to* LINDA). You hear the spite!

BIFF. No, you're going to hear the truth — what you are and what I am!

LINDA. Stop it!

WILLY. Spite!

HAPPY (*coming down toward* BIFF). You cut it now!

BIFF (*to* HAPPY). The man don't know who we are! The man is gonna know! (*To* WILLY.) We never told the truth for ten minutes in this house!

HAPPY. We always told the truth!

BIFF (*turning on him*). You big blow, are you the assistant buyer? You're one of the two assistants to the assistant, aren't you?

HAPPY. Well, I'm practically —

BIFF. You're practically full of it! We all are! And I'm through with it. (*To* WILLY.) Now hear this, Willy, this is me.

WILLY. I know you!

BIFF. You know why I had no address for three months? I stole a suit in Kansas City and I was in jail. (*To* LINDA, *who is sobbing.*) Stop crying. I'm through with it.

(LINDA *turns away from them, her hands covering her face.*)

WILLY. I suppose that's my fault!

BIFF. I stole myself out of every good job since high school!

WILLY. And whose fault is that?

BIFF. And I never got anywhere because you blew me so full of hot air I could never stand taking orders from anybody! That's whose fault it is!

WILLY. I hear that!

LINDA. Don't, Biff!

BIFF. It's goddam time you heard that! I had to be boss big shot in two weeks, and I'm through with it!

WILLY. Then hang yourself! For spite, hang yourself!

BIFF. No! Nobody's hanging himself, Willy! I ran down eleven flights with a pen in my hand today. And suddenly I stopped, you hear me? And in the middle of that office building, do you hear this? I stopped in the middle of that building and I saw — the sky. I saw the things that I love in this world. The work and the food and time to sit and smoke. And I looked at the pen and said to myself, what the hell am I grabbing this for? Why am I trying to become what I don't want to be? What am I doing in an office, making a contemptuous, begging fool of myself, when all I want is out there, waiting for me the minute I say I know who I am! Why can't I say that, Willy?

(*He tries to make* WILLY *face him, but* WILLY *pulls away and moves to the left.*)

WILLY (*with hatred, threateningly*). The door of your life is wide open!

BIFF.   Pop! I'm a dime a dozen, and so are you!

WILLY (*turning on him now in an uncontrolled outburst*).   I am not a dime a dozen! I am Willy Loman, and you are Biff Loman!

(BIFF *starts for* WILLY, *but is blocked by* HAPPY. *In his fury,* BIFF *seems on the verge of attacking his father.*)

BIFF.   I am not a leader of men, Willy, and neither are you. You were never anything but a hard-working drummer who landed in the ash can like all the rest of them! I'm one dollar an hour, Willy! I tried seven states and couldn't raise it. A buck an hour! Do you gather my meaning? I'm not bringing home any prizes any more, and you're going to stop waiting for me to bring them home!

WILLY (*directly to* BIFF).   You vengeful, spiteful mutt!

(BIFF *breaks from* HAPPY. WILLY, *in fright, starts up the stairs.* BIFF *grabs him.*)

BIFF (*at the peak of his fury*).   Pop, I'm nothing! I'm nothing, Pop. Can't you understand that? There's no spite in it any more. I'm just what I am, that's all.

(BIFF'S *fury has spent itself, and he breaks down, sobbing, holding on to* WILLY, *who dumbly fumbles for* BIFF'S *face.*)

WILLY (*astonished*).   What're you doing? What're you doing? (*To* LINDA.) Why is he crying?

BIFF (*crying, broken*).   Will you let me go, for Christ's sake? Will you take that phony dream and burn it before something happens? (*Struggling to contain himself, he pulls away and moves to the stairs.*) I'll go in the morning. Put him — put him to bed. (*Exhausted,* BIFF *moves up the stairs to his room.*)

WILLY (*after a long pause, astonished, elevated*).   Isn't that — isn't that remarkable? Biff — he likes me!

LINDA.   He loves you, Willy!

HAPPY (*deeply moved*).   Always did, Pop.

WILLY.   Oh, Biff! (*Staring wildly.*) He cried! Cried to me. (*He is choking with his love, and now cries out his promise.*) That boy — that boy is going to be magnificent!

(BEN *appears in the light just outside the kitchen.*)

BEN.   Yes, outstanding, with twenty thousand behind him.

LINDA (*sensing the racing of his mind, fearfully, carefully*).   Now come to bed, Willy. It's all settled now.

WILLY (*finding it difficult not to rush out of the house*).   Yes, we'll sleep. Come on. Go to sleep, Hap.

BEN.   And it does take a great kind of a man to crack the jungle.

(*In accents of dread,* BEN's *idyllic music starts up.*)

HAPPY (*his arm around* LINDA).   I'm getting married, Pop, don't forget it. I'm changing everything. I'm gonna run that department before the year is up. You'll see, Mom. (*He kisses her.*)

BEN.   The jungle is dark but full of diamonds, Willy.

(WILLY *turns, moves, listening to* BEN.)

LINDA.   Be good. You're both good boys, just act that way, that's all.

HAPPY.   'Night, Pop. (*He goes upstairs.*)

LINDA (*to* WILLY).   Come, dear.

BEN (*with greater force*).   One must go in to fetch a diamond out.

WILLY (*to* LINDA, *as he moves slowly along the edge of the kitchen, toward the door*).   I just want to get settled down, Linda. Let me sit alone for a little.

LINDA (*almost uttering her fear*).   I want you upstairs.

WILLY (*taking her in his arms*).   In a few minutes, Linda. I couldn't sleep right now. Go on, you look awful tired. (*He kisses her.*)

BEN.   Not like an appointment at all. A diamond is rough and hard to the touch.

WILLY.   Go on now. I'll be right up.

LINDA.   I think this is the only way, Willy.

WILLY.   Sure, it's the best thing.

BEN.   Best thing!

WILLY.   The only way. Everything is gonna be — go on, kid, get to bed. You look so tired.

LINDA.   Come right up.

WILLY.   Two minutes.

(LINDA *goes into the living-room, then reappears in her bedroom.* WILLY *moves just outside the kitchen door.*)

Loves me. (*Wonderingly.*) Always loved me. Isn't that a remarkable thing? Ben, he'll worship me for it!

BEN (*with promise*).   It's dark there, but full of diamonds.

WILLY.   Can you imagine that magnificence with twenty thousand dollars in his pocket?

LINDA (*calling from her room*). Willy! Come up!

WILLY (*calling into the kitchen*). Yes! Yes. Coming! It's very smart, you realize that, don't you, sweetheart? Even Ben sees it. I gotta go, baby. 'By! 'By! (*Going over to* BEN, *almost dancing.*) Imagine! When the mail comes he'll be ahead of Bernard again!

BEN. A perfect proposition all around.

WILLY. Did you see how he cried to me? Oh, if I could kiss him, Ben!

BEN. Time, William, time!

WILLY. Oh, Ben, I always knew one way or another we were gonna make it, Biff and I!

BEN (*looking at his watch*). The boat. We'll be late. (*He moves slowly off into the darkness.*)

WILLY (*elegiacally, turning to the house*). Now when you kick off, boy, I want a seventy-yard boot, and get right down the field under the ball, and when you hit, hit low and hit hard, because it's important, boy. (*He swings around and faces the audience.*) There's all kinds of important people in the stands, and the first thing you know . . . (*Suddenly realizing he is alone.*) Ben! Ben, where do I . . . ? (*He makes a sudden movement of search.*) Ben, how do I . . . ?

LINDA (*calling*). Willy, you coming up?

WILLY (*uttering a gasp of fear, whirling about as if to quiet her*). Sh! (*He turns around as if to find his way; sounds, faces, voices, seem to be swarming in upon him and he flicks at them, crying.*) Sh! Sh!

(*Suddenly music, faint and high, stops him. It rises in intensity, almost to an unbearable scream. He goes up and down on his toes, and rushes off around the house.*)

Shhh!

LINDA. Willy?

(*There is no answer.* LINDA *waits.* BIFF *gets up off his bed. He is still in his clothes.* HAPPY *sits up.* BIFF *stands listening.*)

(*With real fear.*) Willy, answer me! Willy!

(*There is the sound of a car starting and moving away at full speed.*)

No!

BIFF (*rushing down the stairs*). Pop!

(*As the car speeds off, the music crashes down in a frenzy of sound, which becomes the soft pulsation of a single cello string.* BIFF *slowly returns to his bedroom. He and* HAPPY *gravely don their jackets.* LINDA *slowly walks out of her room. The music has developed into a dead march. The leaves of day are appearing over everything.* CHARLEY *and* BERNARD, *somberly dressed, appear and knock on the kitchen door.* BIFF *and*

HAPPY *slowly descend the stairs to the kitchen as* CHARLEY *and* BERNARD *enter. All stop a moment when* LINDA, *in clothes of mourning, bearing a little bunch of roses, comes through the draped doorway into the kitchen. She goes to* CHARLEY *and takes his arm. Now all move toward the audience, through the wall-line of the kitchen. At the limit of the apron,* LINDA *lays down the flowers, kneels, and sits back on her heels. All stare down at the grave.*)

REQUIEM

CHARLEY.   It's getting dark, Linda.

(LINDA *doesn't react. She stares at the grave.*)

BIFF.   How about it, Mom? Better get some rest, heh? They'll be closing the gate soon.

(LINDA *makes no move. Pause.*)

HAPPY (*deeply angered*).   He had no right to do that. There was no necessity for it. We would've helped him.

CHARLEY (*grunting*).   Hmmm.

BIFF.   Come along, Mom.

LINDA.   Why didn't anybody come?

CHARLEY.   It was a very nice funeral.

LINDA.   But where are all the people he knew? Maybe they blame him.

CHARLEY.   Naa. It's a rough world, Linda. They wouldn't blame him.

LINDA.   I can't understand it. At this time especially. First time in thirty-five years we were just about free and clear. He only needed a little salary. He was even finished with the dentist.

CHARLEY.   No man only needs a little salary.

LINDA.   I can't understand it.

BIFF.   There were a lot of nice days. When he'd come home from a trip; or on Sundays, making the stoop; finishing the cellar; putting on the new porch; when he built the extra bathroom; and put up the garage. You know something, Charley, there's more of him in that front stoop than in all the sales he ever made.

CHARLEY.   Yeah. He was a happy man with a batch of cement.

LINDA.   He was so wonderful with his hands.

BIFF.   He had the wrong dreams. All, all, wrong.

HAPPY (*almost ready to fight* BIFF).   Don't say that!

BIFF.   He never knew who he was.

CHARLEY (*stopping* HAPPY'S *movement and reply. To* BIFF).   Nobody dast blame this man. You don't understand: Willy was a salesman. And for a salesman, there is no rock bottom to the life. He don't put a bolt to a nut, he don't tell you the law or give you medicine. He's a man way out there in the blue, riding on a smile and a shoeshine. And when they start not smiling back — that's an earthquake. And then you get yourself a couple of spots on your hat, and you're finished. Nobody dast blame this man. A salesman is got to dream, boy. It comes with the territory.

BIFF. Charley, the man didn't know who he was.

HAPPY (*infuriated*). Don't say that!

BIFF. Why don't you come with me, Happy?

HAPPY. I'm not licked that easily. I'm staying right in this city, and I'm gonna beat this racket! (*He looks at* BIFF, *his chin set.*) The Loman Brothers!

BIFF. I know who I am, kid.

HAPPY. All right, boy. I'm gonna show you and everybody else that Willy Loman did not die in vain. He had a good dream. It's the only dream you can have — to come out number-one man. He fought it out here, and this is where I'm gonna win it for him.

BIFF (*with a hopeless glance at* HAPPY, *bends toward his mother*). Let's go, Mom.

LINDA. I'll be with you in a minute. Go on, Charley.

(*He hesitates.*)

I want to, just for a minute. I never had a chance to say good-by.

(CHARLEY *moves away, followed by* HAPPY. BIFF *remains a slight distance up and left of* LINDA. *She sits there, summoning herself. The flute begins, not far away, playing behind her speech.*)

Forgive me, dear. I can't cry. I don't know what it is, but I can't cry. I don't understand it. Why did you ever do that? Help me, Willy, I can't cry. It seems to me that you're just on another trip. I keep expecting you. Willy, dear, I can't cry. Why did you do it? I search and search and I search, and I can't understand it, Willy. I made the last payment on the house today. Today, dear. And there'll be nobody home. (*A sob rises in her throat.*) We're free and clear. (*Sobbing more fully, released.*) We're free.

(BIFF *comes slowly toward her.*)

We're free. . . . We're free. . . .

(BIFF *lifts her to her feet and moves out up right with her in his arms.* LINDA *sobs quietly.* BERNARD *and* CHARLEY *come together and follow them, followed by* HAPPY. *Only the music of the flute is left on the darkening stage as over the house the hard towers of the apartment buildings rise into sharp focus, and*

The Curtain Falls.)

The novella *Billy Budd* (written *c.* 1889, published 1924) was the only major work distilled out of the barren final years between Herman Melville's active period as a novelist and his death. Both as man and author, Melville (1819–1891) had more than his share of disappointments. Most of his books did not sell well, and the later ones were not generally understood. The last twenty years of his life were spent as a customs inspector. Embittered and disillusioned, Melville had reason, by the time he wrote *Billy Budd*, to curse the world. But he did not. *Billy Budd* is perhaps affirmation of his acceptance of life on the terms it offered him.

In adapting Melville's story to the stage, Coxe and Chapman have effectively selected action from the novella for dramatic impact, and they have retained the subtlety of the characters' moral struggles. For the literary minded, it is tempting to criticize the play in terms of its success or failure in translating the novella to the stage. Certainly this is an interesting exercise, but it is basically not so significant as analyzing the play itself as an example of tragedy to discover how it operates in dramatic terms. In the theatre, playwright-adapters cannot count on — indeed, usually do not want — audiences who know the prose-fiction source by heart. A play is its own entity; it has form, effects, and identity separate from what may have inspired it.

Writing of the motives in the novella, Richard Harter Fogle sees *Billy Budd* as a nineteenth-century version of classical tragedy:

> . . . old forms revivified by new issues. According to Aristotelian prescription it portrays men as better than they are. The principals are exceptional: Billy, Captain Vere, and Claggart stand high in the hierarchy of natural man, above the limited comprehension of the worldly-wise. The last meeting of Vere and Budd is too sacred for the common view. . . . As to Claggart, his evil is an object of moral and aesthetic appreciation, a quality to be savored by connoisseurs.[1]

The authors of the play saw in *Billy Budd* a morality play, a story of "good, evil, and the way the world takes such absolutes."[2] The absolutes of good and evil are of course personified in Billy and Claggart, with Vere personifying the world. Billy is total goodness, an almost unbelievable combination of innocence, simplicity, kindness, guilelessness, forgiveness, and ignorance of evil. His physical perfection is marred only by his stutter. And it is that one imperfection that turns his action in the play into moral perfection: if he had been able to argue with Claggart, he would not have killed him. The act of striking him down is

[1] Richard Harter Fogle, "Billy Budd — Acceptance or Irony," *Tulane Studies in English*, VIII (1958), 110.

[2] Louis O. Coxe and Robert Chapman, "Notes on the Play," in *Billy Budd* (New York: Hill and Wang, 1962), p. 88.

morally righteous — good — under the circumstances. If he had been able to defend his action to Captain Vere on the spot, he might have justified it in Vere's eyes and saved his own life. But his inability to speak for himself again suits his action: in terms of morality, what is there to say when you have killed a man?

Claggart is an equally unbelievable combination of sadistic viciousness, brutality, heartlessness, and destructiveness. Ironically, what undermines his perfect badness is loquacity; if Billy's downfall comes because he cannot talk, Claggart's comes because he talks too much. All the sailors know him for what he is because he himself has told them. And finally, he gets it across even to Billy. Viewed as a balance, his garrulity is as righteous under the circumstances as Billy's silence: no amount of talk can justify destroying a fellow human being.

Captain Vere stands between angel and devil. He is a man, a believable combination of worldly good and evil, able to see both sides, a victim of choice. He believes in Billy's pure innocence and Claggart's pure wickedness, and must himself, in the play, choose between absolute good and evil: whether to hang a saint or save his life. However, Captain Vere lives by the laws of man, which are not necessarily good or evil. They are made to prevent chaos, to judge conflicts like that between Billy and Claggart. Vere's moral duty to them wins over his personal duty to save an innocent man. His choice becomes then not one between good and evil, but of expediency. By man's laws, he does the good and right thing.

Not one of these three characters could be called a classically tragic hero. Billy never achieves self-recognition; he accepts his fate with equanimity but never really understands it. Claggart knows himself but in the end is acted upon rather than acting. Vere misses his opportunity to rise above man's law and do what he believes to be right. But the play can still be called a tragedy, perhaps a moral tragedy of mankind. Absolute good and absolute evil are brought into conflict, and they explode. Each destroys the other, "for human life is a compromise that follows the middle way."[3] The tragedy of mankind is that it cannot brook the totalities, neither the angels nor the devils.

> The killing of Claggart is divine justice, but on the *Indomitable*, it is the murder of a superior officer under wartime conditions. . . . In *Billy Budd*, this tragic discrepancy is born of the dogma of the Fall of Man, which inevitably brings it into being. The law of the Mutiny Act is the law of a fallen world, in which an unfallen man like Billy cannot long exist. . . .[4]

G.L.

[3] Brooks Atkinson, Foreword to *Billy Budd* (New York: Hill and Wang, 1962), p. 5.

[4] Fogle, p. 111.

LOUIS O. COXE and
ROBERT CHAPMAN

Billy Budd

BASED ON A NOVEL BY HERMAN MELVILLE

Characters

EDWARD FAIRFAX VERE, *Captain, Royal Navy*
PHILIP MICHAEL SEYMOUR, *First Officer*
JOHN RATCLIFFE, *First Lieutenant*
BORDMAN WYATT, *Sailing Master*
GARDINER, *a Midshipman*
REA, *a Midshipman*
SURGEON
JOHN CLAGGART, *Master-at-Arms*
SQUEAK, *Master-at-Arms' man*
THE DANSKER, *Mainmast man*
JENKINS, *Captain of the Maintop*
PAYNE, *Maintopman*
KINCAID, *Maintopman*
O'DANIEL, *Maintopman*
BUTLER, *Maintopman*
TALBOT, *Mizzentopman*
JACKSON, *Maintopman*
BILLY BUDD, *Foretopman*
HALLAM, *a Marine*
MESSBOY
STOLL, *Helmsman*
DUNCAN, *Mate of the Main Deck*
BYREN, *Relief Helmsman*
DRUMMER
OTHER SAILORS, *crew of the* INDOMITABLE

(The entire action takes place aboard H.M.S.
INDOMITABLE *at sea, August, 1798, the year
following the Naval mutinies at Spithead and
the Nore.*)

ACT ONE

Scene 1

(*Although outside it is a fine morning in early August, the between-
decks compartment of the crew's quarters assigned to the maintopmen is*

dark and shadowy except for the light spilling down the companionway from above and, through the open gun-ports, the flicker of sunlight reflected on the water. The smoking-lamp burns feebly over a wooden mess table and two benches lowered for use.

JENKINS *sits at the table mending a piece of clothing. In the shadow* THE DANSKER *sits motionless on a low sea chest, smoking a pipe. Neither man speaks for a long minute.*

Then JACKSON *appears on deck at the top of the companionway and lurches down into the compartment. He is doubled up in pain.)*

CLAGGART (*off*). You there! Jackson!

JACKSON. Oh Christ, he's followed me!

JENKINS. Who?

JACKSON. Master-at-Arms. He'll send me aloft again sure, and I can't hang on . . .

JENKINS. What the devil's wrong with you, jack? Here, sit down.

CLAGGART (*entering down the companionway*). Why have you come down off the mainmast, Jackson? Your watch over?

JACKSON. Sick, Mister Claggart, I'm bloody sick, so I'm shaking up there on the yard till I near fell off.

JENKINS. Grab an arm, mate, I'll take you along to sick-bay.

CLAGGART. Stand away from him, Jenkins. (*To* JACKSON.) Just where does this sickness strike you, in the guts, or limbs? Or in the head? Does it exist at all?

JENKINS. You can see he's sick as a puking cat, plain as your stick.

CLAGGART. The role of Good Samaritan hardly fits you, Jenkins. (*To* JACKSON.) Now up, man. Turn topside.

JACKSON. I can't, I can't, I'm deathly sick, God help me, sir!

CLAGGART. That's hard. But this ship needs all hands. We're under-manned. The aches and pains of landsmen have their cures, but ours have none. You'll have to get aloft. Now move!

JACKSON. I ain't bluffing, sir, I swear I'm not! Please, Mister Claggart . . . I got Cooper's leave, he says all right, I can come down.

CLAGGART. You have not got my leave. Cooper is captain of the main-top and ought to know better. Four men to every spar, and no replacements. Now up. Back where you belong.

JACKSON (*starts up the ladder*). God, sir, I can't, I can't stand it! It'll be my death, sure!

CLAGGART. No more talk, man! Up you get! Start!

(JACKSON *goes painfully up the ladder and out of sight on deck.* CLAGGART *starts out after him.*)

JENKINS (*mutters*). God damn your bloody heart!

CLAGGART. Did you say something, Jenkins?

(JENKINS *does not answer.* CLAGGART *goes out, calling after* JACKSON.)

Now Jackson, get along. Up! Up!

JENKINS. I'll stick him one day before long! I will, if I hang for it.

(*Laughter and talk in the next compartment followed by entrance of* BUTLER, TALBOT *and* KINCAID.)

BUTLER. Messboy!

TALBOT. Haul in the slops!

KINCAID. Suppose we'll get the new man? The jack they 'pressed this morning off that merchantman? I see 'em come alongside just now.

TALBOT. I pity that poor bastard, so I do. I hear they get good pay on merchant ships. Eat good, too, and then treated like the God-damn Prince of Wales.

(MESSBOY *enters with an iron pot of food and spits on the deck.*)

Spit in it, damn you. Can't taste no worse.

MESSBOY. Ain't nobody making you eat it, mate. You can wash your feet in it if you like.

(O'DANIEL *and* PAYNE *enter.*)

TALBOT. What's eating you, Jenkins? Ain't you going to join the banquet?

JENKINS. By God, I seen a thing just now I won't stand for! I'm sitting here off watch, and I seen it all. That blacksnake Claggart kicked Jackson back aloft, and him sick as a pinkass baby in a cradle, as any fool could see.

PAYNE. He's the Master-at-Arms, ain't he?

JENKINS. Cooper sent him down. Who's captain of the starboard watch, him or Claggart? Cooper could have found him a relief. Plain murder, by God!

TALBOT. You think Claggart can get away with what he does without Captain Starry Vere knows what's going on? Him and that red snapper Seymour, and them other bloody officers!

JENKINS. Jackson'll fall. By God, no man can hang to a spar sick like that. He'll fall sure.

O'DANIEL. Tush, man, nobody falls in His Majesty's Navy. We lose our footing. 'Tis flying we do, to be sure.

TALBOT. I tell you it's Vere that's the cause of it! Our glorious fine Captain Vere, with a league of braid around his arm and a ramrod up his bum.

O'DANIEL. Vere, is it. As captains go, mate, let me tell you, he's an angel with a harp alongside of the skipper on the *Royal George*. Every day that one flogged a dozen men. Picked 'em by lottery, by God. Never took the gratings down till they was rusty with blood. Ho! This Vere's a saint in heaven after him.

JENKINS.   Ram the *Royal George* and everybody in her! Claggart's the man we want, and the sooner the better, say I!

O'DANIEL.   Ah, we'd had him puking his blood at Spithead, the devil rot his wick.

BUTLER.   You was there, O'Daniel? At Spithead?

O'DANIEL.   Aye. I was. Wherever you do find Englishmen doing a smart thing, you'll find an Irishman is at the bottom of it. Oho, fine it was, every day of it, with officers quaking in their cabins, spitting green, and the whole English government wetting their breeches from the fear of us! Ah, lovely it was, lovely!

TALBOT.   Belay your Irish noise, you fat-mouthed mackerel-snatcher. I'll tell you this, we need men on here is not afraid to use their knives if it come to that. And you can be bloody sure it will come to that, mind my word, Mickey Cork.

JENKINS.   What did you ever use your knife for, Talbot, but to scratch your lice? Ah, you're a dancing daredevil, you are for sure.

TALBOT.   I'll be happy to show you, if you like.

JENKINS.   Trouble will be hunting you out, mate, if you're not careful.

TALBOT.   Trouble! You whoreson cockney cullion! There's not a man aboard don't know you for a coward, you whining bitchboy!

JENKINS.   Get out.

TALBOT.   Damn your seed, I'm not afraid of you, or your sniveling hangbys, either!

JENKINS.   Move! Get out of it, or by God I'll run my knife to the hilts in you!

TALBOT.   You son of a whore! Pigsticker!

(*They attack one another with drawn knives,* JENKINS *reaching suddenly across the table to seize* TALBOT. *Silently they thrash around the compartment upsetting benches and food while the others look on unmoved.*)

O'DANIEL.   Ah, I do love to see two Englishmen fighting each other. It's fonder they are of killing themselves than fighting their proper foes. (*Laughs hoarsely.*)

PAYNE.   Tomorrow's rum on Jenkins. Any bets?

KINCAID.   He never lost one yet.

(JENKINS *throws* TALBOT *on the deck and holds the knife at his throat for a moment before letting him up, first taking his knife. He holds out his hand.*)

JENKINS.   I'm leading seaman in this compartment, mind that.

(TALBOT *hits* JENKINS' *hand and goes off angrily.*)

KINCAID.   You're captain, that's all right by me.

o'daniel. Eyes in the boat, lads. Here comes pfft-face.

(squeak, billy *and* gardiner *appear on deck and start down the companionway.*)

gardiner. Hang it, step lively, boy! Your ship is . . . Doff your hat to officers when they speak to you! By God, I'll teach you to touch your hat to a midshipman's coat, if it's only stuck on a broomstick to try!

billy. Aye, sir.

(*The men react to* gardiner *with yawns and gestures behind his back.*)

gardiner. Very well. Your ship is H.M.S. Indomitable now, and we sail her tautly, and we tolerate no nonsense. Is that clear?

billy. Aye, sir.

gardiner (*to* squeak). See this new man is assigned to a watch, and get him squared away. (*To* billy.) You're green, of course, I can see that. But I expect we'll ripen you. (*He trips going up the ladder and* squeak *tries to help him.*) Carry on. (gardiner *exits.*)

squeak. My name's Squeak. I'm the Master-at-Arms' man. Have you met the Master-at-Arms yet, Mister Claggart?

(billy *shakes his head.*)

Oh, you'll like him. He's a nice fellow.

(o'daniel *chokes on his pipe smoke and the other men react similarly.*)

Stow your gear along in there. This here's the larboard section of the maintop. Captain of the watch is Jenkins. Him, there. Report to him. (*He pats* billy *on the chest and grins before starting up the ladder.*)

jenkins. What's a green hand dumped in here for?

squeak. Complaining, Jenkins?

jenkins. I'm asking. What's wrong with that?

squeak. Mister Claggart wants him here, that's why. Maybe he wants Billy Boy to set you pigs an example. Refer any more complaints to the Master-at-Arms!

(*Exits.* billy *grins at the men, who return his look.*)

billy. My name is Budd. Billy, if you like.

kincaid. I'm Kincaid. This is where you swing your hammock. That's O'Daniel, this here's Payne, and Butler. This is Jenkins, captain of the watch, and that old jack's called the Dansker. Don't know why, unless maybe he's Danish. You never had a real name, Dansker?

the dansker. Not for many years.

BUTLER. You'd be the new impressed man?

BILLY. Aye, so I am. I just came off the *Rights of Man* this morning.

THE DANSKER. Forget about the *Rights of Man* now, lad.

JENKINS. How long you been going to sea, baby?

BILLY. About ten years, but in the merchant service.

O'DANIEL. Merchant service! Whissht! (*Laughs hoarsely.*)

BILLY. I know I'm new at Navy work, and probably there'll be some things I'll need help with.

JENKINS. No doubt, little boy.

BILLY. I'll learn fast, never fear. But she's a big old girl, this ship. I never was in a ship-of-the-line before. I'd have got lost trying to find the mess by myself. Maybe fallen in the magazine!

O'DANIEL. Ah, you get used to it. She's big, is this tub, but she's not so big you can get lost in her.

PAYNE. Sometimes I wish to God you could. Maybe we could lose O'Daniel.

(BILLY *laughs and the others join.*)

BILLY. You're Irish, aren't you? I like the Irish. There was an Irishman on the *Rights of Man*, with big red whiskers . . . when I came away, he gave me a silver knife. This is it.

O'DANIEL. It's a beauty. Mind you keep an eye on it.

BUTLER. What's the matter, boy?

BILLY. I was just thinking, maybe I won't ever see my friends again.

O'DANIEL. If they was Irish, don't you worry at all. The Irish is liable to turn up almost anywheres, excepting England and the fires of hell, which is much the same.

PAYNE. Danny, if it wasn't for the harps, the devil wouldn't have nothing to do. What was potato-eaters doing on a merchant ship?

BILLY. Just sailors, like me. Most of us had no other home, even the skipper. He was a kind old bloke. Looked fierce, but he always had a kind word. Used to keep a bird in a cage in his cabin. The skipper let me feed the bird sometimes. Worms right out of the ship's biscuit. That was mostly all the meat we got.

O'DANIEL. The bargemen is in Navy biscuit would eat the bird.

KINCAID. Sit down here, Bill. Maggots or not, this is what we get. You hungry?

BILLY. I'm always hungry.

KINCAID. Try your first sample of His Majesty's bounty. We don't know what it is, but we been eating it for a long time.

BUTLER. Here, eat mine. Tastes like it's been eat before, anyhow.

JENKINS. Give him more lobscouse, Butler. We got to keep the roses in his cheeks, ain't we, boy?

BILLY (*laughing*). I could eat anything right now. Even this.

O'DANIEL. Help you to forget about home and mother, lad.

JENKINS. Tell us about home and mother, Baby Budd.

BILLY. There's not much to tell. I've got no home, and never had a family to remember.

JENKINS. Ain't that too bad.

BILLY. Oh, I'd feel a lot worse if I'd been 'pressed with a wife and children.

KINCAID. That's the truth.

O'DANIEL. We're all patriotic volunteers.

KINCAID. Guano! Wait till my hitch is up, you won't see no more of me.

BUTLER. Three weeks drunk in Portsmouth, then back in the ruddy fleet.

THE DANSKER. Men like us got no other home.

O'DANIEL. No other home, is it? Ah, 'tis so thick the sweet thoughts is in here, I can scarce breathe.

PAYNE. Then you can strangle or get out.

JENKINS. Aye, get along, you lousy harp, give us some fresh air.

O'DANIEL. If you begged me to stay itself, I'd be off to where there's smarter lads. Boy, let you pay no heed to these white mice, mind what I say. And be hanged, the lot of yous! (*He starts up the ladder.*)

KINCAID. You'll catch it, Danny, if Captain holds an inspection.

O'DANIEL (*returning*). Ah whissht, I was forgetting that. And I do think that me figure shows up better here below than it does in the broad daylight.

BILLY. Inspection today?

PAYNE. Ah, the Old Man crawls over the ship from arsehole to appetite any time he ain't got nothing else to do. You never know when till you see him.

KINCAID. What the devil he wants to inspect this hooker for, I can't figure. He's seen it before.

BUTLER. He ain't seen Billy.

BILLY. What's the Captain like? On the *Rights of Man*, the captain . . .

JENKINS. You going to jaw some more about that rocking horse? I suppose you was at Spithead, too?

BILLY. Spithead? Where is that?

JENKINS. A little party the Navy had a year ago. A mutiny, Baby, a mutiny. Know what that is?

BILLY. Why did they mutiny?

O'DANIEL. Arra, it's easy to see you're new to the Navy.

JENKINS. Jimmy-Legs is ten good goddam reasons for it, himself.

BILLY. Who's Jimmy-Legs?

KINCAID. Master-at-Arms. We call him Jimmy-Legs.

BUTLER. Watch out for that one, Billy.

PAYNE. He's the devil himself between decks.

O'DANIEL. What d'you expect, the saints of heaven? Not in an English tub.

BILLY. Why don't you like the Master-at-Arms?

JENKINS.   You'll find out soon enough, Baby.

BUTLER.   Watch him, boy. Jenkins can tell you. He's had a time or two with Claggart.

JENKINS.   Aye, and I'll have another, one day before too long.

BUTLER.   Sure, Jenkins. You look after Bill.

JENKINS.   How old are you, kid? Sixteen?

BILLY.   I don't know, maybe . . . twenty.

JENKINS.   He don't even know how old he is! My guess is, too young to know what his parts are for.

O'DANIEL.   Is it anybody is that young?

KINCAID.   Stow it, Jenkins. Come on, don't pay no attention to him. He's feeling ugly today.

JENKINS.   Well now, ain't you getting holier than a bloody bishop. Let him talk up for himself, if he don't like it.

KINCAID.   Stow it, I say. You got no reason to crawl over Bill. Let him be.

BILLY.   That's all right, Tom. I don't mind a joke. Black's the white of me eye, mates!

(*All laugh except* JENKINS.)

JENKINS.   Mama taught you pretty manners, huh? Oh! Ain't got no mama, you say? Well now, think what that makes you! (*Laughs.*)

BILLY.   Tell me what you mean, Mister Jenkins.

PAYNE.   What's gnawing your arse, Jenkins? Can't you see the boy's trying to be friendly?

JENKINS.   You forgetting who's leading seaman here? Come on, Baby, talk back, why don't you? Scared?

BILLY.   N-no. Why do you think I'd be scared, M-M-Mister Jenkins?

JENKINS.   He stammers! What do you know! The little bastard's so scared he's stammering.

BILLY.   Don't call me that again.

JENKINS.   Sounds good, ha? Sounds fine. I like the way it rolls out your mouth. Bastard Baby Budd . . .

(BILLY *strikes him.* JENKINS *staggers and falls, pulls a knife and gets up, lunging at* BILLY. PAYNE, BUTLER *and* KINCAID *get up and stand close to* BILLY, *silently protecting him.*)

JENKINS.   Get away, God damn you! He's got to find out who gives orders here.

KINCAID.   Not this time, Jenkins. Lay off.

O'DANIEL.   Belay it. You're wearing me out, the pair of yous.

BUTLER.   Put away the knife.

(JENKINS *sees their determination and relaxes a little, uncertain what to do.*)

BILLY.   Will you shake hands? Or would you rather fight?

JENKINS.   You little bas . . .

(*Lunges forward.* BILLY *catches his arm and bends it, holding* JENKINS *cursing and powerless.*)

BILLY.   That's enough, mate. Pipe down and let us be.

O'DANIEL.   Good lad! Save the great strength is in you, Jenkins, for fighting the devil is after your soul.

JENKINS.   All right, all right. You can let me go now.

O'DANIEL.   Leave him go, lad. I won't hurt him at all.

BILLY.   You're like Red Whiskers on the *Rights*, he liked to fight too. (*Freeing him.*) Will you shake hands, mate?

JENKINS (*momentarily uncertain what to do*).   Shake hands, is it? . . . Well, you beat me fair. You got guts, which is more than I give you credit for. (*They shake hands.*)

KINCAID.   You're a hell of a peacemaker, Bill.

PAYNE.   That's the only time I ever hear Jenkins eating his own words.

O'DANIEL.   Ah, that's a terrible diet, would make any man puke.

JENKINS.   Don't you be getting any wrong ideas. I'm still a match for you!

KINCAID.   Better belay your mess gear, Bill.

JENKINS.   Where you come from, Baby?

PAYNE.   Stow it! Jimmy-Legs!

(BILLY *goes on talking as* CLAGGART *enters.*)

BILLY.   I don't know, I guess from Portsmouth. I never lived ashore, that I can remember. Where do you come from?

(*Drops a pot on deck.* CLAGGART *stands over him.*)

CLAGGART.   Handsomely done, young fellow, handsomely done. And handsome is as handsome did it, too. You can wipe that up, Jenkins. (*To* BILLY.) What is your name?

BILLY.   Budd, sir. William Budd, ship *Rights of Man*.

CLAGGART.   Your ship is *H.M.S. Indomitable* now.

BILLY.   Aye, sir.

CLAGGART.   You look sturdy. What was your station aboard the merchantman?

BILLY.   M-m-mizzentopman, sir.

CLAGGART.   You like that station?

BILLY.   Aye, sir, well enough.

CLAGGART.   How long have you been at sea?

BILLY.   Ten years, sir, near as I can tell.

CLAGGART.   Education?

BILLY. None, sir.

CLAGGART. So. You come aboard with nothing but your face to recommend you. Well, while beauty is always welcome, that alone may not avail us much against the French. There are other requirements in the service.

BILLY. I'll learn quickly, sir.

CLAGGART. The sea's a taskmaster, young fellow. It salts the sweetness out of boyish faces. You cannot tell what motion lies asleep in that flat water. Down where the manta drifts, and the shark and ray, storms wait for a wind while all the surface dazzles.

BILLY. I am a seaman, sir. I love the sea. I've hardly lived ashore.

CLAGGART. Then let the wind and sea have license to plunder at their will. As of today, a new maintopman swings between sky and water. (*He turns toward the ladder and notices the mess on deck.*) I thought I asked you to wipe that up, Jenkins.

JENKINS. That's the messboy's job.

CLAGGART. Clean up, Jenkins.

(*JENKINS hesitates.*)

That is an order. Turn to.

BILLY. I'll give you a hand, Jenkins. Come on.

CLAGGART. Ah, there. See how helpful Billy is. Why can't you take a leaf from this innocent young David's book, Jenkins?

(*Turns away.* JENKINS *accidentally brushes against him and receives a savage cut from* CLAGGART'S *rattan across his face.*)

Watch what you're doing, man!

JENKINS. I swear . . . !

CLAGGART. Yes, what is it that you swear? Well, speak. Nothing at all to say? Then hear me: I have my methods with unruly tempers.

(*On deck there is a loud crescendo scream and a crash. Running footsteps, shouts, voice calling for the* SURGEON. *The men surge toward the ladder.*)

CLAGGART. Stand fast!

(SQUEAK *enters down the hatchway, whispers to* CLAGGART.)

All right, I know.

(SQUEAK *comes down into the compartment and runs off.*)

JENKINS. It's Jackson! I knew it, by God, I told you so!

(*Men turn to stare at* CLAGGART *as several sailors enter down the companionway, bearing the body of* JACKSON, *inert and shattered. They carry him through the compartment and off to sick-bay.*)

SURGEON (*as he moves through the compartment*).   Clear the way, you men. Take him into the sick-bay, through here. Carry him gently. Easy, now. Easy. (*Exit.*)

JENKINS (*pointing to* CLAGGART).   He sent him back aloft. Killed him, he did!

O'DANIEL.   Might as well have knifed him.

CLAGGART.   Stand fast. Stop where you are. Your man Jackson is looked after.

O'DANIEL (*in a low voice*).   Then he's a dead man surely.

CLAGGART.   Who spoke?

JENKINS.   We'll have a showdown now! After him, mates! Cut into him!

(*The men move toward* CLAGGART *in a rush, drawing knives and cursing him, as* CAPTAIN VERE *appears in the companion hatchway.*)

VERE.   Stand fast! Hold where you are. Master-at-Arms, what is the matter here?

(*The men stop in their tracks and stare at* VERE, *who comes part way down the ladder.*)

CLAGGART.   These dogs are out of temper, sir.

VERE (*to men*).   You will come to attention when I address you! Let me remind you that this ship is at war. This is a wartime cruise, and this vessel sails under the Articles of War. Volunteer or 'pressed man, veteran seaman or recruit, you are no longer citizens, but sailors: a crew that I shall work into a weapon. One lawless act, one spurt of rebel temper from any man in this ship, high or low, I will pay out in coin you know of. You have but two duties: to fight and to obey, and I will bend each contumacious spirit, each stiff-necked prideful soul of you, or crush the spirit in you if I must. Abide by the Articles of War and my commands, or they will cut you down. Now: choose.

(*The men are silent.*)

Very well. Master-at-Arms, this accident on deck, the sailor fallen from the yardarm. Do you know how it occurred?

CLAGGART.   I do not, sir.

VERE.   You are his messmates. Does any man of you know how this occurred? (*To* BUTLER.) You?

BUTLER.   No, sir.

VERE. Jenkins, do you?

(JENKINS *hesitates a moment.* CLAGGART *moves slightly, tapping his hand with the rattan.*)

JENKINS. No, sir.

VERE (*notices the cut on* JENKINS' *face*). What's this, what's this? Speak up, man. I want no random bloodshed aboard this ship.

JENKINS. I . . . fell, Captain. Fell, and . . . and cut my cheek.

VERE. I see. You fell. Master-at-Arms, you will excuse this man from duty till the Surgeon tends him.

CLAGGART. Aye, aye, sir.

VERE. We must not wound ourselves, draining the blood from enterprise that takes a whole man. (*He turns to go up the ladder and sees* BILLY.) Well. This is a new face. Who are you, boy?

CLAGGART. Maintopman 'pressed from the *Rights of Man* this morning, sir. William Budd.

VERE. Let him speak for himself.

(BILLY *tries to speak but can only stammer incoherently.*)

That's all right, boy, take your time. No need to be nervous.

BILLY. I saw a man go aloft, sir, as I came on board just a while ago. He looked sick, sir, he did. This officer was there, too, he can tell you. (*To* CLAGGART.) Don't you remember, sir?

VERE. Did you send a sick man aloft, Master-at-Arms?

CLAGGART. I did not, sir.

VERE. Very well. (*To* BILLY.) Well, Budd, I hope you take to Navy life and duty without too much regret. We go to fight the French and shall need wits and hearts about us equal to the task.

BILLY. I'll do my best, sir.

VERE. I'm sure you will. We are all here to do our several duties, and though they may seem petty from one aspect, still they must all be done. The Admiral himself looks small and idle to the man like you who can see him from the maintop, threading his pattern on the quarterdeck. The Navy's only life.

(SURGEON *enters.*)

SURGEON. Captain — Jackson, the man who fell just now — he's dead, sir.

VERE (*after a pause*). Carry on, Master-at-Arms.

(*He goes out up the companionway.* SURGEON *exits.*)

CLAGGART. You've made a good impression on the Captain, Billy

Budd. You have a pleasant way with you. If you wish to make a good impression on me, you will need to curb your tongue. Jenkins, I thought you were ordered to sick-bay. Jump to it. And I suggest you change that shirt. See how fouled it is with a peculiar stain. Why can't you keep clean like Billy here?

(*He strikes* JENKINS *viciously on the arm with his rattan, smiles at him, and exits up the ladder.*)

JENKINS. God damn his flaming soul! I can't stand it no more!

BILLY. I don't see what you can do, mate. He didn't mean it when he hurt you then.

JENKINS. Listen boy, I know Jimmy-Legs. He lives on hurting people. Stay away from him, and keep your mouth shut, if you don't want trouble.

O'DANIEL. Did you hear the lad speak up to the skipper?

PAYNE. Aye, you watch your tongue, Bill. Claggart will be after you for talking up like that.

KINCAID. He's a cool one, Billy is. None of us got the nerve.

BUTLER. It's nerve gets a man in trouble in this tub.

THE DANSKER. Jimmy-Legs is down on you already, Billy.

BILLY. Down on me? Why, he's friendly to me.

JENKINS. Claggart don't make no friends.

O'DANIEL. You seen Jackson when they brought him below. That's how friendly he gets.

(*Bosun's pipe off.*)

DUNCAN (*off*). Relieve the watch!

KINCAID. First watch on the *Indomitable*, Bill. Better lay up to the mainmast and report. (*Exit.*)

BUTLER. Don't slip off the yardarm.

PAYNE. Watch your step.

BILLY. Not me. You watch for me. Got to find the mainmast, and I'm in a hurry.

O'DANIEL. You'll never find your way in this old tub. I'll come along and show you. If anybody comes calling for O'Daniel while I'm out, take the message.

PAYNE. O'Daniel couldn't find his breeches if they wasn't buttoned on. You come with me.

(BILLY *and* PAYNE *go off.*)

JENKINS. Poor bastard. I pity him, I do.

BUTLER. He's dead, ain't he? Better off than us.

JENKINS. Not Jackson. I mean the baby here. Billy.

BUTLER. We could have fared worse for a messmate.

JENKINS. Aye. He can take care of himself. Heave up the table.

Scene 2

(*In the early evening of the same day, the off-duty sections of the crew are mustered aft on the maindeck for* JACKSON's *funeral. Above them* CAPTAIN VERE *stands uncovered at the forward break of the quarterdeck, reading the Committal Prayer. The westward sky is bright yellow and red, but fades into darkness as the scene progresses.*

The men are uncovered and stand at attention.)

VERE.   Unto Almighty God we commend the soul of our brother departed and we commit his body to the deep, in sure and certain hope of the resurrection unto Eternal Life, through our Lord Jesus Christ, at whose coming in glorious majesty to judge the world, the sea shall give up her dead, and the corruptible bodies of those who sleep in Him shall be changed and made like unto His glorious body according to the mighty working whereby He is able to subdue all things unto Himself. Amen.

MEN.   Amen.

(*Short drum-roll followed by a muffled splash as* JACKSON's *body slips over the side. Then the bosun's pipe. Officers cover and march off.*)

CLAGGART.   Ship's company: Cover! Petty officers, dismiss your divisions.

VOICE (*off*).   Carpenters and gunners: Dismiss!

VOICE (*off*).   Afterguardsmen: Dismiss!

VOICE (*off*).   Fore, main, and mizzentopmen: Dismiss!

(*The men break formation and go off, excepting* BUTLER, JENKINS, PAYNE, KINCAID *and* BILLY, *who gather near the ratlines, at the rail.*)

BUTLER.   I suppose in this clear water you could see him go down for quite a way.

BILLY.   We're moving slow in this calm.

JENKINS.   There'll be wind enough before dawn.

BUTLER.   And that's the end of Enoch Jackson. Over the side he goes, and his mates forget him.

JENKINS.   Whatever's happened to Jackson, he ain't worried none. He's got a hundred fathoms over him to keep him warm and cosy.

BILLY.   I'd rather be buried at sea than on the beach, when I come to die. Will you stand by the plank, Tom, so I'll shake a friendly hand before I sink? Oh! But it's dead I'll be then, come to think!

(*All laugh.*)

PAYNE.   Don't you worry none. By that time, you won't give a sailmaker's damn.

KINCAID.   It's only living makes sense to me, anyhow.

BILLY.   Aye, I like to live. Even when it seems bad, there's a lot that's good in it.

JENKINS.   Maybe for you, Bill. You wouldn't know trouble if it come up and spit in your eye.

BILLY.   Don't you try now, mate! You might miss, and I got a clean jumper on!

PAYNE.   That's the way to be, if you ask me. There's always trouble, if you know where to look for it.

BUTLER.   You don't have to see nothing if you close your eyes.

KINCAID.   When I close my eyes I sleep sound as a drunk marine.

BILLY.   Aye, after I roll in my hammock, it's one, two, three, and I'm deep down under.

JENKINS.   Well, it's down under for me right now. Let's lay below.

KINCAID.   Aye, we'll be on watch before long. Coming, Bill?

BILLY.   I think I'll stay and watch the water for a while. I like to watch the sea at night.

JENKINS.   Aye. It's deep and silent, and it can drown a man before he knows it.

BILLY.   Sleep sound, mates.

(*All but* JENKINS *go down the companion hatchway.*)

JENKINS.   Billy: stay clear of Jimmy-Legs.

(JENKINS *exits down the hatchway.* BILLY *is left alone staring over the side until* CLAGGART *enters. He does not see* BILLY, *but stops near the quarterdeck ladder and gazes fixedly seaward.*)

BILLY.   Good evening, sir.

CLAGGART (*startled, then subtly sarcastic*).   Good evening.

BILLY.   Will it be all right if I stay topside a bit to watch the water?

CLAGGART.   I suppose the Handsome Sailor may do many things forbidden to his messmates.

BILLY.   Yes, sir. The sea's calm tonight, isn't it? Calm and peaceful.

CLAGGART.   The sea's deceitful, boy: calm above, and underneath, a world of gliding monsters preying on their fellows. Murderers, all of them. Only the sharpest teeth survive.

BILLY.   I'd like to know about such things, as you do, sir.

CLAGGART.   You're an ingenuous sailor, Billy Budd. Is there, behind that youthful face, the wisdom pretty virtue has need of? Even the gods must know their rivals, boy; and Christ had first to recognize the ills before he cured 'em.

BILLY.   What, sir?

CLAGGART.   Never mind. But tell me this: how have you stomach to stand here and talk to me? Are you so innocent and ignorant of what I am? You know my reputation. Jenkins and the rest are witnesses, and certainly you've heard them talking to me. Half of them would knife me in the back some night and do it gladly; Jenkins is thinking of it. Doubtless he'll try one day. How do you dare, then? Have you not intelligence enough to be afraid of me? To hate me as all the others do?

BILLY. Why should I be afraid of you, sir? You speak to me friendly when we meet. I know some of the men . . . are fearful of you, sir, but I can't believe they're right about it.

CLAGGART. You're a fool, fellow. In time, you'll learn to fear me like the rest. Young you are, and scarcely used to the fit of your man's flesh.

BILLY. I know they're wrong, sir. You aren't like they say. Nobody could be so.

CLAGGART. So . . . ? So what, boy? Vicious, did you mean to say, or brutal? But they aren't wrong, and you would see it, but for those blue eyes that light so kindly on your fellow men.

BILLY. Oh, I've got no education, I know that. There must be a lot of things a man misses when he's ignorant. But learning's hard. Must be sort of lonely, too.

CLAGGART. What are you prating of, half-man, half-child? Your messmates crowd around, admire your yellow hair and your blue eyes, do tricks and favors for you out of love, and you talk about loneliness!

BILLY. I just noticed the way you were looking off to leeward as I came up, sir. Kind of sad, you were looking.

CLAGGART. Not sadness, boy. Another feeling, more like . . . pleasure. That's it. I can feel it now, looking at you. A certain . . . pleasure.

BILLY (flattered). Thank you, sir.

CLAGGART (annoyed at BILLY's incomprehension). Pah.

BILLY. Just talking with you, sir, I can tell they're wrong about you. They're ignorant, like me.

CLAGGART. Compliment for compliment, eh, boy? Have you no heart for terror, fellow? You've seen this stick in use. Have you not got sense and spleen and liver to be scared, even to be cowardly?

BILLY. No, sir, I guess not. I like talking to you, sir. But please, sir, tell me something.

CLAGGART. I wonder if I can. Well, ask it.

BILLY. Why do you want us to believe you're cruel, and not really like everybody else?

CLAGGART. I think you are the only child alive who wouldn't understand if I explained; or else you'd not believe it.

BILLY. Oh, I'd believe you, sir. There's much I could learn from you: I never knew a man like you before.

CLAGGART (slowly). Do you — like me, Billy Budd?

BILLY. You've always been most pleasant with me, sir.

CLAGGART. Have I?

BILLY. Yes, sir. In the mess, the day I came aboard. And almost every day you have a pleasant word.

CLAGGART. And what I have said tonight, are these pleasant words?

BILLY. Yes, sir. I was wondering . . . could I talk to you between watches, when you've nothing else to do?

CLAGGART. You're a plausible boy, Billy. Aye, the nights are long, and talking serves to pass them.

BILLY. Thank you, sir. That would mean a lot to me.

CLAGGART. Perhaps to me as well.

(*Drops his rattan.* BILLY *picks it up and hands it back to him.* CLAGGART *stares at it a moment, then at* BILLY.)

No. No! Charm me, too, would you! Get away!

BILLY (*surprised and puzzled*). Aye, sir.

(*He exits down the hatchway. After a pause in which* CLAGGART *recovers his self-control* SQUEAK *appears.*)

CLAGGART (*without turning*). Come here. I thought I told you to put that new seaman Budd on report. Why was it not done?

SQUEAK. I tried, Mister Claggart, sir. I couldn't find nothing out of place. Gear all stowed perfect.

CLAGGART. Then disarrange it. You know the practice. I want him on report.

SQUEAK. Two of his messmates is ones nearly caught me at it before.

CLAGGART. Then be more careful. Now get along and see you make out something.

(SQUEAK *scurries off belowdecks as* VERE *comes into sight on the quarterdeck.*)

VERE. Master-at-Arms. What is that man doing above decks?

CLAGGART. Ship's corporal, sir. A routine report.

VERE. There is nothing in this ship of so routine a nature that I do not concern myself in it. Remember that.

CLAGGART. Aye, aye, sir. With your permission, sir.

(*Exit.* VERE *walks along the deck and scans the sails as* SEYMOUR *enters.*)

SEYMOUR. Fine evening, sir.

VERE. Yes, a fine evening, Seymour. How is the glass?

SEYMOUR. Falling, I believe, sir. I think we'll toss a little before morning. Well, I suppose I should be in my cabin inspecting the deck logs.

VERE. Stay for a moment, Seymour. In the days and nights to come, you and I will not often have an opportunity to stand easy and talk.

SEYMOUR. Aye, sir. I expect the French will put us to our stations any hour now.

VERE. Are you impressed by omens, Seymour? This seaman we've just buried: I think of him as an omen of some sort, a melancholy prologue to this voyage.

SEYMOUR. Aye, sir. Hard on the sailor, certainly, but that's the service. But we've been lucky in other ways. An accident, now, that's unavoidable.

VERE. It was more than an accident, Seymour.

SEYMOUR. This maintop sailor? How do you mean, sir?

VERE. The man was sent aloft sick, by the Master-at-Arms, contrary to my standing order. Budd, the new seaman, implied as much, and the maintop watch confirmed it. The Master-at-Arms lied to me.

SEYMOUR. What are you going to do, sir? What action can you take? He's a valuable man, one we can hardly do without as things are now.

VERE. I shall do nothing at present, only wait and observe him. No court-martial could do more than strip him of his rank for such misconduct. I will let him have his head until some act puts him squarely counter to the law, then let the law consume him.

SEYMOUR. Why trouble the natural order to no purpose? Shouldn't we let it be?

VERE. Must a man always shrug, let things alone and drift? Would to God I could take this power of mine and break him now, smash all the laws to powder and be a man again.

SEYMOUR. We must serve the law, sir, or give up the right and privilege of service. It's how we live.

VERE. Live? Oh, you're right. Below this deck are men who at a skip on the hurling spars against the wind, at Beat-to-quarters run as if they willed it. Yet each of us steps alone within this pattern, this formal movement centered on itself. Men live and die, taken by pattern, born to it, knowing nothing. No man can defy the code we live by and not be broken by it.

SEYMOUR. You are the Captain, sir. You maintain that code.

VERE. Keep an order we cannot understand. That's true. The world demands it: demands that at the back of every peacemaker there be the gun, the gallows and the gaol. I talk of justice, and would turn the law gentle for those who serve here; but a Claggart stands in my shadow, for I need him. So the world goes, wanting not justice, but order . . . to be let alone to hug its own iniquities. Let a man work to windward of that law and he'll be hove down. No hope for him, none.

(*Enter* WYATT.)

WYATT. Eight o'clock report, sir. Ship inspected and all in order.

SEYMOUR. Very well, carry on.

(WYATT *goes off.*)

By your leave, sir. Good night.

(*Exit.* VERE *remains, crosses to the hatch and looks down, then slowly upward at the set of the sails.*)

Scene 3

(*The maindeck several nights later.*
Four bells is struck offstage. A sailor climbs wearily down the ratlines,
drops to the deck and goes below. CLAGGART *stands by the larboard rail.*
As BILLY *enters from below decks, he sees the Master-at-Arms.*)

BILLY. Hello, sir.

(CLAGGART *looks at him without answering, then turns and goes off*
forward. THE DANSKER *follows* BILLY *up onto the deck.*)

Well, that's all there is to tell, Dansker. I always lash my hammock just
so, and stow my gear same as all the others. They don't get in trouble.

THE DANSKER. Mister Claggart is down upon you, Billy.

BILLY. Jimmy-Legs? Why, he calls me the sweet and pleasant fellow,
they tell me.

THE DANSKER. Does he so, Baby lad? Aye, a sweet voice has Mister
Claggart.

BILLY. For me he has. I seldom pass him but there comes a pleasant
word.

THE DANSKER. And that's because he's down upon you.

BILLY. But he's my friend. I know he talks a little strange, but he's
my friend.

THE DANSKER. Nobody's friend is Jimmy-legs. Yours the least of all,
maybe. Lay aloft, Baby. You'll be late to relieve your watch.

BILLY. Aye, Dansker.

(*He climbs up the ratlines out of sight.* THE DANSKER *watches him go.*
CLAGGART *appears, but* THE DANSKER *ignores him and goes off aft. As*
JENKINS *comes into view climbing down the ratlines,* CLAGGART *gestures*
off and fades into a shadowy corner of the deck near the quarterdeck
ladder. SQUEAK *enters as* JENKINS *drops to the deck, and intercepts him*
as he starts down the companionway.)

SQUEAK. It's all right, mate, slack off and stay a bit.

JENKINS. What do you want? I pick my own company.

SQUEAK. So does I, mate, so does I. And if I may make so bold to
say it, you'll be smarter to pick your company more careful.

JENKINS. If you got something to say to me, talk up, else I'll get below.

SQUEAK. Don't be hasty, now, mate, don't be in a sweat. It's haste
gets good men into trouble. What d'you think of our new hand here,
Billy Boy? Mister Claggart's taken with him, too. Fine young fellow, ha?

JENKINS. Talk plain. What d'you mean?

SQUEAK. I overheard him talking just this day. Would maybe surprise
you some, what he had to say about yourself and a few other lads.

JENKINS. What?

SQUEAK. Aoh, bit of talk about his messmates. He don't fancy us! Not like his feather boys aboard the merchantman.

JENKINS. You lying cut-throat, try something else! Billy's in my mess; since he come on board he's rare been out of my sight. You're lying, you bloody nark! I know you too well. You'll need to try some other way to get Bill into trouble. Get away, and don't come lying to me no more.

SQUEAK. Aoh, so it's that friendly you are! Well, now, ain't that sweet! You're not smart, Jenkins. Remember, man: I tried to help you out. When you're feeling the cat between your shoulders . . .

JENKINS (*seizing him*). Damn your lies! Get back to Jimmy-Legs and kiss his butt. And stay out of my way!

(*Throws* SQUEAK *down and exits.* SQUEAK *watches him go.* CLAGGART *steps out of the shadows.*)

CLAGGART. I heard your little talk. You lack subtlety; but I'm the greater fool to use you in these matters. You're inept.

SQUEAK. Aoh! Why don't you do it yourself, if you don't need me!

CLAGGART. I need nobody, least of all a rum-soaked footpad from the Old Bailey. If you wish to have free rein with your distasteful habits, mind your cockney manners! I stand between you and the flogging whip. Improve your style, or you stand tomorrow forenoon at the gratings!

SQUEAK. I only meant as you could do it better, Mister Claggart, I wouldn't say nothing to . . .

CLAGGART (*cuts him on the arm with his rattan*). Don't touch me! — Keep Budd in petty troubles, that you can do. Unlash his hammock. Keep him on report. In time I'll let you know what plans I have for him. Get aft!

(SQUEAK, *eager to get away, scuttles aft as* THE DANSKER *enters.*)

Well, old man. Moon's in and out tonight. There's weather somewhere.

(THE DANSKER *turns down the night lamp over the cabin door and starts off.*)

Stay and have a pipe.

THE DANSKER. I have the watch.

CLAGGART. You take your duties as seriously as ever.

THE DANSKER. Aye. They are all of life for an old seaman like me. (*Turns to go.*)

CLAGGART. You move away from me as though I were some kind of stalking beast. You avoid me, too.

THE DANSKER. Your word, John, "too."

CLAGGART. You know what I mean. The hands detest me. You are a hand, older than most, and older in your hatred, I have no doubt. But why, man? You at least should see me as I am, a man who knows how the world's made: made as I am.

THE DANSKER. How can I know what goes on in your head?

CLAGGART. The enigmatic Dansker. Come, it's dark, we can drop disguises when night serves to hold the disclosing soul apart.

THE DANSKER. You know who you remind me of . . . maintopman: Billy Budd.

CLAGGART. More enigmas! That sunny, smiling infant with no spleen nor knowledge in his head?

THE DANSKER. I'll leave you now.

CLAGGART. No, stay a while. This is a night for secrets and disclosures.

THE DANSKER. You have half the truth and Billy Budd the other. He can't see there's evil in the world, and you won't see the good.

CLAGGART. So. And I take it you come in between.

THE DANSKER. I keep outside. I am too old to stand between sky and water.

CLAGGART. And yet you hate me, too.

THE DANSKER. I hate an incomplete man.

CLAGGART. Damn all this talk. Hate me and have done. Let it alone, I say. Whatever else it is, this thing is Man, still!

THE DANSKER. I'll be off.

CLAGGART. Don't go. The moon's gone under. Let us talk this out. You are a wise man in your senile way.

THE DANSKER. Then take this for all my wisdom. You recognize the hatred of your shipmates as an honor paid to a soul they cannot understand. Your fine contempt for human love is nothing but regret.

CLAGGART. Stop there. I know the rest by heart. Nothing you say to me but clatters in my belly, watch on watch. Aye: when this arm moves out in gesture of love, it mocks me with a blow. Who lifts this arm? What officer commands this hireling flesh? Somewhere below the farthest marks and deeps, God anchors hearts, and his sea rusts mine hollow. The flukes break in the bottom, and I slack and stand, go in and out forever at God's humor. Look at this sea: for all her easy swell, who knows what bones, ribs and decay are fathomed at her base and move in her motion, so that on the flattest water, the very stricture of the dead can kill that beauty with a dance of death? — Here is a man. He holds, past fathom curves, drowned fleets of human agonies that gesture when the long tide pulls.

THE DANSKER. Aye, John. But you must know that other men are moved so. Look up some evening at the quarterdeck for another poor thoughtful devil like you, like me, pacing all night between his doubts.

CLAGGART. What, Vere? That fine-drawn manner doesn't deceive me. There's a whited sepulchre, like all soft-spoken charmers of this world.

THE DANSKER. You don't believe in anything besides yourself, eh John?

CLAGGART. I've said what I have said. I know myself, and look to that. You should try it. Go to your post, old man, and your everlasting duties.

(CLAGGART *turns away.* BILLY *scrambles into view down the ratlines and calls out excitedly.*)

BILLY.   Quarterdeck ho!
RATCLIFFE (*coming forward to the forward break of the quarterdeck*). Sound off!
BILLY.   Strange sail one mile off the larboard beam!
CLAGGART (*to* THE DANSKER).   A Frenchman! Get to your station.
RATCLIFFE (*on the quarterdeck ladder*).   Mister Duncan! Sound Beat-to-quarters! Clear for action!
DUNCAN (*offstage*).   Aye aye, sir!
RATCLIFFE.   Gardiner!

(*Enter* GARDINER.)

GARDINER.   Sir?
RATCLIFFE.   Report to the Captain, strange sail on the larboard beam. Then send Payne to the wheel.

(*Exit* GARDINER.)

Master-at-Arms, send a man to the mast to relay lookout's reports. Inspect battle stations and report to me when they are fully manned.
CLAGGART.   Aye aye, sir. (*Exit.*)
VOICE (*off*).   She's a French frigate! Steering east by south!

(*Enter* VERE *and* SEYMOUR.)

VERE.   Prepare to make chase. Have your quartermaster steer small.
RATCLIFFE.   Aye aye, sir.

(*Enter the* DRUMMER *and sound Beat-to-quarters. Men run on, to gun stations, rigging, crossing stage and off.*)

SEYMOUR.   She's too fast for us, sir. We'll never come up with her.
VERE.   We are bound to try, though we were sure to fail. And we may smell powder before this chase is over.
CLAGGART (*re-entering*).   Battle stations fully manned, sir!
SEYMOUR.   May we try a shot at her now?
VERE.   She's drawing south. Yes, commence firing, Mr. Seymour.
SEYMOUR.   Larboard battery, fire one!
DUNCAN.   Fire!

(*Fire one gun.*)

VERE.   Fire at will!
SEYMOUR.   Fire at will!

(*Guns fire dissynchronously.*)

ACT TWO

Scene 1

(*The quarterdeck and part of the maindeck a few minutes before 0800. A high wind. On the quarterdeck are* LIEUTENANT WYATT, MIDSHIPMAN REA *and the helmsman,* STOLL.)

REA. I'm glad this watch is over. I'm tired.

WYATT. Make your entry in the log before your relief comes up. Bring it out here and I'll sign it.

REA. Aye, sir. What was our last position, do you remember?

WYATT. Thirteen ten west, forty-three forty north.

REA. And an easterly breeze.

WYATT. Aye, make it so. That'll make Ratcliffe happy. Last time he had an east wind, she blew his hat over the side. And put down "Running ground swell."

REA. Aye aye, sir. (*Exits.*)

WYATT. Helmsman, keep her close-hauled.

STOLL. I can't sir. Too much cloth in the wind.

WYATT. Well, hold her close as you can, and let the next watch reef sail if they like.

STOLL. Aye aye, sir.

(*Enter* RATCLIFFE.)

WYATT. Morning, Johnny! You're on time!

RATCLIFFE. What's the course?

WYATT. Steady south. Wind's easterly. Glass is dropping.

RATCLIFFE. East wind? Damn it.

(*Enter* BYREN, *the relief helmsman.*)

By the way, you forgot to sign the order book.

WYATT. All right. Thanks.

STOLL. I've been relieved, sir. Byren has the helm.

WYATT. Very well.

(*Exit* STOLL.)

Who's mate of your watch?

RATCLIFFE. The Admiralty midshipman. That lobcock Gardiner, hang him.

(*Eight bells.*)

WYATT. Where the devil is he? It's eight.

(*Enter* REA *and* GARDINER *separately, meeting.*)

RATCLIFFE. There he comes. He looks happy. That means trouble for some poor devil.

(GARDINER *snatches the log out of* REA'S *hands and bounds up to the quarterdeck.*)

REA. I've been relieved, sir. Horatio, Lord Gardiner has the watch.

WYATT. Ah, Midshipman Gardiner. The backbone of the British Navy.

RATCLIFFE. The backside, if you ask me.

WYATT. All right, Rea. You can turn in.

(REA *exits.*)

RATCLIFFE. Pity we lost that Frenchman last night. A little action would season the monotony of these interminable watches.

WYATT. Did you ever hear of a ship-of-the-line running down a frigate, even with the wind? Ah, it's a magnificent morning! Thickening overcast, heavy ground swell, a fresh levanter breeze, and you, Johnny, are the Pride of the Morning!

RATCLIFFE. Mmm. Has the skipper been on deck yet?

WYATT. Not since sunrise. He came up then and paced the deck and stared off east like a sleepwalker. Then went below again without a word.

RATCLIFFE. He thinks too much.

WYATT. Well, if you ever make captain, your crew won't have that to complain of, anyway. Am I relieved?

RATCLIFFE. Yes, I relieve you. (*Tosses his cap to* WYATT.) Here. Take this below, will you?

WYATT. What? You'll be out of uniform, man. Mister Gardiner wouldn't approve of your standing watch without a hat, would you, Midshipman Gardiner?

GARDINER. Sir, the Articles state that officers on watch . . .

RATCLIFFE. Well, hang it, I lost twelve shillings the last time my hat went over the rail, and this is the only other one I've got. To hell with the Articles.

WYATT. Mind your language! It's downright mutinous. Well, don't expect me to stand your watches if you catch your death of cold. Good morning. (*Exit.*)

GARDINER. Midshipman Rea, sir, I don't like to say it, but his log entries are impossible.

RATCLIFFE. Then enter yourself, Mister Gardiner. So are you.

GARDINER. Yes sir. But I do think he ought to be told . . .

RATCLIFFE. Go find the Captain and report to him the wind's abeam. Respectfully suggest we ought to take in topsails.

GARDINER. Aye aye, sir. (*Goes down stairs.*)

RATCLIFFE. And don't forget to tell him I haven't got a hat.

GARDINER. What's that, sir?

RATCLIFFE. Nothing, sir! You got my order. Dump your ballast and shove off!

GARDINER. I thought you spoke to me, sir.

RATCLIFFE. I avoid that whenever possible. Move!

GARDINER. Yes, sir.

RATCLIFFE. Ye gods, what a brat. Nothing off, helmsman. She's well enough thus.

BYREN. Nothing off, sir.

GARDINER (*nearly bumping into* VERE *as he emerges from cabin, followed by* SEYMOUR *and* HALLAM). Atten-tion!

RATCLIFFE. Good morning, sir.

VERE. Morning, Mister Ratcliffe.

GARDINER (*starting after* VERE, *bumps into* HALLAM). Damn it, man, watch what you're doing!

VERE. Midshipman Gardiner.

GARDINER. Sir?

VERE. How long, pray, have you been in this ship, or any ship?

GARDINER. This is my first cruise, sir.

VERE. Your first cruise. A wartime cruise as well. And you are a midshipman. A midshipman, Mister Gardiner, let me tell you, is neither fish, flesh, nor fowl, and certainly no seaman. You're a salt-water hermaphrodite, Mister Gardiner. And unless you have a mind to be generally known as Spit-kit Gardiner, I recommend more tolerance toward the men. Now, is that clear?

GARDINER. Aye aye, sir!

VERE. Very well, you may carry on.

RATCLIFFE. We've a weather helm, sir, and bow seas.

VERE. Take in topsails, if you please, Mister Ratcliffe.

RATCLIFFE. Aye aye, sir. Mister Duncan!

DUNCAN (*enters*). Aye, sir?

RATCLIFFE. Douse your topsails and topgallants. Haul in the weather braces.

DUNCAN. Aye aye, sir. (*Exit.*) Away aloft! Hands by topgallant sheets and halyards!

GARDINER. Aloft there! Keep fast the weather sheets till the yards are down, da . . . if you please!

RATCLIFFE. Get aloft yourself, Mister Gardiner, see they do it right, since you're not satisfied.

GARDINER. Sir, the Articles state that . . .

RATCLIFFE. Did you hear me?

GARDINER. Aye aye, sir. (*Exits up ratlines.*)

DUNCAN (*off*). Haul taut!

VERE. You disapprove of Gardiner, Mister Ratcliffe?

RATCLIFFE. He seems to think he's the only midshipman aboard capable of doing anything properly. He's always looking at you as if your hat weren't squared.

VERE. That is an unfortunate simile under the present circumstances.

RATCLIFFE (*caught*). Oh, I — er — Keep her close to the wind, helmsman. Don't fall away!

DUNCAN (*off*). Let go topgallant bowlines!

VERE. I think Gardiner has had enough correction for one day. Call him down to our level, Mister Ratcliffe.

RATCLIFFE. Aye, sir. Mister Gardiner! You may come off your perch now!

(BILLY *descends rigging and starts offstage.*)

What do you think of our new man Budd, Captain?

SEYMOUR. That boy did a smart piece of work for us last night, sir. He's the nimblest man on the tops I've ever watched. Wyatt wants him for captain of the foretop.

VERE. Very well, let Budd take the post. He certainly deserves it for his actions last night during the chase. I'll speak to him myself.

SEYMOUR. He'll like hearing it from you, sir.

VERE. Hallam, go call Budd, the lad moving forward there.

(*Exit* HALLAM. GARDINER *appears, looking sick.*)

Well done, Gardiner. You may lay below and draw an extra tot of rum. You look . . . chilly.

GARDINER. Thank you, sir. (*Exit.*)

SEYMOUR. By the way, sir, Budd has been on the Master-at-Arms' report once or twice for some petty misdemeanor. Nothing serious.

(*Steps aside with* RATCLIFFE. BILLY *enters, followed by* HALLAM.)

BILLY. You sent for me, sir?

VERE. Yes, Budd. Your division officer recommends you for a post of more responsibility. He thinks you can perform duties of a higher station, and so do I, after last night. So I've agreed that you shall have Williams' place on the foretop.

BILLY. But — Williams is captain of the foretop, sir.

VERE. The station calls for a younger man. Lieutenant Wyatt asked for you, and the spirit you showed last night warrants it. That is a real honor for a man so new on board.

BILLY. The Navy's new to me, Captain, but I hardly know anything else but the sea and ships.

VERE. And how do you like us, now that the awesomeness has worn away a bit?

BILLY. The Navy's a bustling world, sir. Bigger than the *Rights of Man*, and I get lost sometimes. But my mates lend me a hand. Why even Jimmy-Legs — beg pardon, sir, the Master-at-Arms, I mean — he's good to me, too.

VERE. The sea and the Navy exact a discipline, but it need not be a harsh one. In some ways I envy the man who dances across the tops and seems to rule the ship and sea below. Up there is a pleach of ropes for you to make a world of. Though winds have their way with tackle of your world, you live at ease against your strength and the round bole of the mast in your back. You are a king up there, while the water curds and frolics at the forefoot. I envy you that stance.

BILLY. You can trust me, Captain.

VERE. I do, boy. Very well, that's all.

BILLY. Aye aye, sir. Thank you, sir, thank you! (*Runs off.*)

VERE. Hallam, find the Master-at-Arms and bid him report to me.

HALLAM. Aye aye, sir.

(*Exit.* SEYMOUR *joins* VERE.)

VERE. If I had a son, I'd hope for one like Budd.

SEYMOUR. Aye, sir. Fine boy. He's a force for order in this ship, certainly. I hope his charm's contagious.

VERE. One such is enough. Men cannot stand very much perfection. It's a disease that we stamp out at its first rash showing.

(*Enter* CLAGGART. SEYMOUR *withdraws.*)

Master-at-Arms, I want to make a change on the Watch, Quarter and Station Bill. I needn't have troubled you about it until later, but I am especially interested in this change.

CLAGGART. The time of day is indifferent to me, sir.

VERE. Williams, present captain of the foretop, is assigned to the afterguard. I am replacing him with Budd.

CLAGGART. William Budd, sir? You do not mean the so-called Handsome Sailor?

VERE. Aye, William Budd, the new seaman from the *Rights of Man*.

CLAGGART. I know him, sir.

VERE. Do you find anything unusual in this replacement?

CLAGGART. You must be aware, sir, that he is . . .

VERE. Well? That he is what? I know he's an able seaman.

CLAGGART. Nothing, sir. But I wondered if he were entirely trustworthy. He has been aboard such a brief time.

VERE. Long enough to prove himself to me, and to his shipmates.

CLAGGART. Very good, sir.

VERE. He is captain of the foretop. That is all.

CLAGGART. With your permission, sir. Will there not be some dissatisfaction among the foretopmen who have been aboard much longer than Budd?

VERE. Master-at-Arms: I concern myself with these matters. They are none of your function. Until such time as the senior topmen formally object to Budd for incapacity, he is captain of the foretop. Make it so on the Bill. (*Exit.*)

RATCLIFFE. What are you waiting for, man? Light to dawn? Promotion? You got the order.

CLAGGART. With your permission, sir.

(*As* CLAGGART *goes off,* RATCLIFFE *spits over the rail.*)

Scene 2

(*Forward part of the deck. Night. Eight bells. A man descends the rigging and goes off.* CLAGGART *enters, stands by the hatch for a moment, then exits forward.* BILLY *comes down off watch, drops to the deck and remains in shadow, leaning over the rail, looking seaward.* JENKINS *stealthily and silently comes up from below deck.*)

BILLY. Jenkins! What you doing topside . . .

(JENKINS *puts his hand over* BILLY'S *mouth.*)

JENKINS (*in a whisper*). Stow the noise! (*Releases* BILLY.)

BILLY. You're after Mister Claggart, like you said you would!

JENKINS. Well? What about it? You try and stop me?

BILLY. He knows, Jenkins! I tell you, he knows! He's ready for you!

JENKINS. Then by God, I'll oblige him! I been waiting up here every night, waiting for him to come by when it's dark. Now get away and let me do it!

BILLY. No! I won't let you hang yourself!

JENKINS. I don't give a fiddler's damn what happens to me! Move out of my way, mate!

BILLY. No! Give me the knife.

JENKINS. The knife's for Claggart. You're a nice boy, Bill, but I ain't playing with you. You get away below, quick. This game ain't for boys.

BILLY. Damme, no, Jenkins! You'll hang yourself!

JENKINS. Take your hands off! The moon's under, I can do it now! Oh, sweet mother of God, leave me go!

BILLY. No!

JENKINS. Yes, by God!

(JENKINS *strikes* BILLY; *struggle, in which* BILLY *wrests knife from* JENKINS, *and it falls on deck.* BILLY *knocks* JENKINS *down.*)

CLAGGART (*offstage*). What's that noise? Stand where you are!
(*Entering.*) You again! Well? Explain this pageant.

BILLY.   He . . . I had to hit him, sir. He struck at me.

CLAGGART.   Mm. And drew that knife on you, too, no doubt.

BILLY.   Yes, sir.

CLAGGART.   I have been waiting, forward there, for Jenkins. You in-
tercepted him, I take it.

BILLY.   I didn't know you were looking for him, sir.

CLAGGART.   You shouldn't meddle, my fine young friend, in matters
that don't concern you! I was expecting him.

(*Enter* THE DANSKER.)

There, help the body up. I do not thank you, boy, for cheating me of
the pleasure of his punishment.

WYATT (*offstage*).   What's the disturbance there? You, forward on
the spar-deck!

CLAGGART.   Master-at-Arms reports all in order, sir!

WYATT (*offstage*).   Stand where you are.

CLAGGART.   The sweet and pleasant fellow saved you, Jenkins. But
I reserve you still for my own justice in due time. Say nothing to this
officer.

(*Enter* WYATT.)

WYATT.   What's the matter, Master-at-Arms? It's an odd hour for
stargazing.

CLAGGART.   A slight matter, sir. I found these two men together here
on deck, contrary to the Captain's orders. I was sending them below when
you called out.

WYATT.   Oh, is that all. Carry on, then.

CLAGGART.   Aye aye, sir. Now then, get below, both of you.

(*Enter* VERE *followed by* HALLAM. THE DANSKER *goes off.*)

Attention!

VERE.   Wyatt, what's this mean?

WYATT.   Two men on deck without permission, sir.

VERE.   Is there no more to this? The story's lame, man. What occurred? (*Silence.*) Very well, then. Go along, both of you.

BILLY.   Aye aye, sir. Come along, mate. (*Exits with* JENKINS.)

VERE.   Your knife, Master-at-Arms?

CLAGGART.   William Budd's, sir, I believe.

VERE.   Return it to him. (*Exits with* HALLAM *and* WYATT.)

(CLAGGART *raps rail with rattan.* SQUEAK *approaches warily.*)

CLAGGART. Listen carefully; you may make up for your late mistakes if you do this smartly. Give Budd just time enough to get to sleep. At four bells wake him. Bring him to the lee forechains. You understand?

SQUEAK. Mister Claggart, sir . . . we done enough to him. He's a good lad, Mister Claggart. Couldn't it be somebody else? Jenkins, maybe?

CLAGGART. So. He's softened your heart too, eh? Do as you're ordered, man, or I'll see your back laid raw with a flogging whip! Remember: I will be watching you. Bring him to the lee forechains. And when you're there . . .

SQUEAK. Dansker. Moving forward.

CLAGGART. Step back, you fool. Wait for me.

(*Exit* SQUEAK. THE DANSKER *enters.*)

THE DANSKER. Baby saved you, eh? And you are angry.

CLAGGART. Saved me, you say? From what? I've tried to tempt Jenkins to this blow, so as to break his toplofty spirit with his neck; and I am "saved" by that guileless idiot! He'd turn the other cheek to me, in Christian kindness! Well: there's a second pleasure in striking that same face twice. I can destroy him, too, if I choose to do it!

THE DANSKER. Crazy, crazy!

CLAGGART. All right, old man, call it madness then. Whatever its name, it will plunder the sweetness from that face, or it will kill us both.

THE DANSKER. You are afraid of him.

CLAGGART. Afraid? Of Budd? What nonsense is that?

THE DANSKER. He usurps the crew; they turn from hating you to loving him, and leave you impotent.

CLAGGART. That bastard innocent frighten me! That witless kindness that spills from him has neither force nor aim. Stand out from between us, or you founder together, sink in five hundred fathoms with him, if I want it so!

THE DANSKER. Aye, then, if you take that tack, let it be both of us. You expect me to sit by and watch your deliberate arm seize him and force him under?

CLAGGART. Why not? You have always done that. I thought your practice was to stay outside. What breeds the saintly knight errant in you?

THE DANSKER. I am old, but I have some manhood left.

CLAGGART. What can you do? You've drifted with the tide too long, old one. You are as involved as I am now.

THE DANSKER. So you may say. In this ship a man lives as he can, and finds a way to make life tolerable for himself. I did so. That was a fault. But no longer.

CLAGGART. Stand clear. You haven't courage to cross me.

THE DANSKER. Eh, I'm not afraid of you; I see your scheme.

CLAGGART. Damn your feeble, ineffectual eyes!

(*Striking him;* THE DANSKER *falls.*)

You can see only what I let you see!

THE DANSKER.   Say what you like. I see your scheme; so will Captain if need be.

CLAGGART (*pulling him to his feet*).   Take a warning for yourself, old man. And keep away! You are on watch, eh? Well, go back to sleep again, or I'll report you.

(THE DANSKER *exits.* CLAGGART *watches him go, then violently breaks his rattan and throws the pieces over the side.*)

Scene 3

(*Forward part of the main deck. Four bells.* CLAGGART *stands with one hand on the rail, waiting. After a short pause, hearing a sound, he fades into shadow.* SQUEAK *enters, bending over and running.*)

SQUEAK.   Hsssssssssst!

(BILLY, *sleepy and rubbing his eyes, enters.*)

BILLY.   You brought me all the way up here, out of my hammock. Now what do you want?

SQUEAK.   I heard you're captain of the foretop, Bill. That right?

BILLY.   Aye. What's that to do with you?

SQUEAK.   Ah, now you can be more use to your shipmates than ever you was before.

BILLY.   What?

SQUEAK.   You was impressed, now, weren't you? Well, so was I. We're not the only impressed ones, Billy. There's a gang of us. Could you help . . . at a pinch?

BILLY.   What do you mean?

SQUEAK.   See here . . . (*holds up two coins*). Here's two gold guineas for you, Bill. Put in with us. Most of the men aboard are only waiting for a word, and they'll follow you. There's more for you where these come from. What d'you say? If you join us, Bill, there's not a man aboard won't come along! Are you with us? The ship'll be ours when we're ready to take it!

BILLY.   Damme, I don't know what you're driving at, but you had better go where you belong!

(SQUEAK, *surprised, does not move.* BILLY *springs up.*)

If you don't start, I'll toss you back over the rail!

(SQUEAK *decamps.* BILLY *watches him and starts off himself.* THE DANSKER, *offstage, calls out.*)

THE DANSKER. Hallo, what's the matter? (*Enters.*) Ah, Beauty, is it you again? Something must have been the matter, for you stammered.

(CLAGGART *appears and comes forward.*)

CLAGGART. You seem to favor the maindeck, Billy Budd. What brings you topside at this hour, man, against my orders and the Captain's?

BILLY. I . . . found an afterguardsman in our part of the ship here, and I bid him be off where he belongs.

THE DANSKER. And is that all you did about it, boy?

BILLY. Aye, Dansker, nothing more.

CLAGGART. A strange sort of hour to police the deck. Name the afterguardsman.

BILLY. I . . . can't say, Mister Claggart. I couldn't see him clear enough.

THE DANSKER. Don't be a fool, speak up, accuse him.

CLAGGART. Well?

BILLY. I can't say, sir.

CLAGGART. You refuse? Then get below, and stay where you belong.

BILLY. Aye aye, sir. Good night, sir. Good night, Dansker. (*Exits.*)

CLAGGART. I'm glad you saw this mutinous behavior.

THE DANSKER. Your crazy brain squeezes out false conclusions. He has done nothing except find you out, though he's too innocent to know it.

CLAGGART. I am not hoodwinked by his weak excuse. What else would he be doing at this hour, but fanning rebel tempers like his own?

THE DANSKER. I stood in the shadows forward when your pander Squeak slipped by me, running from this place. You set him on, on purpose to trap Billy.

CLAGGART. And I will do that, old man. But you will say nothing about it; see you don't.

(*Enter* VERE *followed by* HALLAM.)

VERE. Well, Master-at-Arms. You stand long watches.

CLAGGART. Sir. May I take the liberty of reserving my explanation for your private ear. I believe your interest in this matter would incline you to prefer some privacy.

VERE (*to* THE DANSKER *and* HALLAM). Leave us. Hallam, stand within hail.

(THE DANSKER *and* HALLAM *go off.*)

Well? What is it you wish to say, Master-at-Arms?

CLAGGART. During my rounds this night, I have seen enough to convince me that one man aboard, at least, is dangerous; especially in a ship which musters some who took a guilty part in the late serious uprisings . . .

VERE.   You may spare a reference to that.

CLAGGART.   Your pardon, sir. Quite lately I have begun to notice signs of some sort of movement secretly afoot, and prompted by the man in question. I thought myself not warranted, so long as this suspicion was only indistinct, in reporting it. But recently . . .

VERE.   Come to the point, man.

CLAGGART.   Sir, I deeply feel the cruel responsibility of making a report involving such serious consequences to the sailor mainly concerned. But God forbid, sir, that this ship should suffer the experience of the Nore.

VERE.   Never mind that! You say there is one dangerous man. Name him.

CLAGGART.   William Budd, the . . . captain of the foretop.

VERE.   William Budd?

CLAGGART.   The same, sir. But for all his youth and appealing manners, a secret, vicious lad.

VERE.   How, vicious?

CLAGGART.   He insinuates himself into the good will of his mates so that they will at least say a word for him, perhaps even take action with him, should it come to that. With your pardon, sir; you note but his fair face; under that there lies a man-trap.

VERE (*after a pause*).   Master-at-Arms, I intend to test your accusation here and now. Hallam!

(*Enter* HALLAM.)

HALLAM.   Aye, sir.

VERE.   Find Budd, the foretopman. Manage to tell him out of earshot that he is wanted here. Keep him in talk yourself. Go along.

HALLAM.   Aye aye, sir. (*Exits.*)

VERE (*angry and perturbed*).   Do you come to me with such a foggy tale, Master-at-Arms? As to William Budd, cite me an act, or spoken word of his, confirming what you here in general charge against him. Wait; weigh what you speak. Just now, and in this case, there is the yardarm end for false witness.

CLAGGART.   I understand, sir. Tonight, when on my rounds, discovering Budd's hammock was unused, I combed the ship, and found him in conclave with several growlers; men, who, like himself, spread unrest and rebellion in the crew. They were collected here, near the lee forechains, and when I ordered them below, young Budd and others threatened me, and swore they'd drop me, and some officers they hate, overboard, some misty night. Should you, sir, desire substantial proof, it is not far.

(*Enter* HALLAM, *followed by* BILLY.)

VERE.   Hallam, stand apart and see that we are not disturbed.

(HALLAM *exits*.)

And now, Master-at-Arms, tell this man to his face what you told me of him.

CLAGGART (*moving near to* BILLY, *and looking directly at him*).   Certainly, sir. I said this man, this William Budd, acting so out of angry resentment against impressment and his officers, against this ship, this Service, and the King, breeds in the crew a spirit of rebellion against the officers, the mates, and me, urging some outrage like the late revolt. I myself have seen and heard him speak with manifest malingerers and men who growl of mistreatment, harshness, unfair pay and similar complaints. I say this man threatened his officers with murder, and was bent tonight on urging other men to act concertedly in mutiny. I have nothing further to say, sir.

(BILLY *tries to speak, but can make only incoherent sounds. He seems to be in pain from the contortions of his face and the gurgling which is all he can effect for speech.*)

VERE.   Speak man, speak! Defend yourself! (*Remembering* BILLY'S *impediment, goes to him and puts a hand on his shoulder reassuringly.*) There is no hurry, boy. Take your time, take your time.

(*After agonized dumb gesturing and stammering, increased by* VERE'S *kindness,* BILLY'S *arm hits out at* CLAGGART. CLAGGART *staggers, falls, lies still.*)

VERE.   Stand back, man! It was a lie, then!

(BILLY, *shaking, only stares at the body.* VERE *raises the body to a sitting position. Since* CLAGGART *remains inert,* VERE *lowers him again slowly, then rises.* BILLY *tries again to speak, without success; he is crying and badly frightened.*)

No need to speak now, Billy. Hallam!

(*Enter* HALLAM.)

Tell the Surgeon I wish to see him here at once. And bid Mister Seymour report to my cabin without delay. (*To* BILLY.) Retire to the stateroom aft. Remain there till I summon you.

(BILLY *exits.* VERE *waits, turning once to stare at* CLAGGART'S *body. Enter the* SURGEON.)

Surgeon, tell me how it is with him.

(SURGEON *bends over* CLAGGART *briefly, then looks up in surprise.*)

Come, we must dispatch. Go now. I shall presently call a drumhead court to try the man who out of God's own instinct dropped him there. Tell the lieutenants that a foretopman has, in an accidental fury, killed this man. Inform the Captain of Marines as well, and charge them to keep the matter to themselves.

(surgeon *exits.*)

The divine judgment of Ananias! Struck dead by the Angel of God . . . and I must judge the Angel. Can I save him? Have I that choice?

ACT THREE

Scene 1

(*Captain* vere's *cabin, a quarter of an hour later.* vere *and* seymour.)

seymour.　Budd beat a man to death! What had he done?

vere.　Lied again: lied to Budd's face, hoping to kill him by it. Oh, the boy was tempted to it past endurance.

seymour.　False witness has its penalty, sir. Budd has set our justice right.

vere.　Aye, too right. This natural, right act, done in an instinct's fever of recognition, was late and fatal.

seymour.　What are you going to do, Captain? Isn't this last lie of the Master-at-Arms the very act you were waiting for, so as to let the law destroy him, as you said? He should have suffered at the yardarm if Billy hadn't killed him.

vere.　Yes. He should. But by fair process of authority. Budd has prevented that, and turned the law against himself.

seymour.　You can't condemn the boy for answering with his arm for lack of words! The motive was clearly justified.

vere.　Aye, but was the act? For God's sake try, try to convince me I am wrong!

seymour.　This Master-at-Arms, you knew him for a liar, a vicious dog.

vere.　A dog's obeyed in office. Claggart was authority.

seymour.　Then authority's an evil!

vere.　It often is. But it commands, and no man is its equal, not Billy, nor I. It will strike us down, and rightly, if we resist it.

seymour.　Rightly! What power gives evil its authority? We should thank God the man's dead, and the world well rid of that particular devil.

vere.　Our life has ways to hedge its evil in. No one must go above them; even innocents. Laws of one kind or other shape our course from birth to death. These are the laws pronouncing Billy's guilt; Admiralty codes are merely shadows of them.

SEYMOUR. That's tyranny, not law, forcing conformity to wrongs, giving the victory to the devil himself!

VERE. I thought so once. But without this lawful tyranny, what should we have but worse tyranny of anarchy and chaos? So aboard this man-of-war. Oh, if I were a man alone, manhood would declare for Billy.

SEYMOUR. Then do it. Put your strength and your authority behind Budd, and let him go.

VERE. When I think I could have watched him grow in comely wholeness of manhood . . . all lost now. What could have been, quenched in evil, swept out by that undertow.

SEYMOUR. It's more than anyone can have to answer for, Captain; to his peers, or to his God. Let him go free and try on mortal flesh! Will you urge a noose for him, marked like a common felon, and that devil still to have his wish, killing the boy at last?

VERE. Can I do otherwise? I'd give my life to save his, if I could.

SEYMOUR. It's in your hands, Captain. Only you can help him now.

VERE. Billy, Billy. What have we done to you? (*Knock.*) Yes, come in.

(*Enter* HALLAM.)

HALLAM. Lieutenants Ratcliffe and Wyatt, sir.

VERE. Let them come in.

(*Enter* RATCLIFFE *and* WYATT.)

SEYMOUR. You both know why you've been summoned hither?

WYATT. Yes, sir.

RATCLIFFE. Aye, sir, in a general sort of way.

SEYMOUR. Then take your chairs. Ratcliffe. You here, Wyatt. You are appointed members of a court-martial convened under extraordinary circumstances by Captain Vere. I am Senior Member, and I declare this court open.

(WYATT, RATCLIFFE, *and* SEYMOUR *sit.* VERE *remains standing, apart.*)

Sentry, bring the prisoner in.

(HALLAM *salutes and exits.*)

As you know, the Master-at-Arms has been killed by the foretopman, Budd. Whether by accident or by design, and whether the act shall carry the penalty of death or no, you are to decide. There is only one witness, Captain Vere. I shall call upon him to give his deposition as soon as the sentry brings in the prisoner.

(*An uneasy silence.*)

WYATT.   Budd wouldn't kill a minnow without good reason.

RATCLIFFE.   What did the . . .

SEYMOUR.   I had rather you did not express an opinion until after you have heard the evidence.

(*Another awkward silence.* HALLAM *finally enters with* BILLY.)

Sentry, stand outside.

(*Exit* HALLAM.)

You may sit down.

BILLY.   Th-th-thank you, sir.

SEYMOUR.   Captain: will you be good enough to give us your account?

VERE (*turning towards them*).   I speak not as your Captain, but as witness before this court. The Master-at-Arms early this morning detailed to me an account of mutinous sentiments expressed by Budd, and in particular, spoke of overhearing a specific conversation last night on the mid-watch. He alleged that Budd offered him violence and threatened further violence against the officers.

WYATT.   Budd a mutineer! That's absurd, he's the best-liked man . . .

SEYMOUR.   Lieutenant Wyatt. Please do not interrupt the witness.

RATCLIFFE.   Did the Master-at-Arms specify who the other malcontents were, sir?

VERE.   He did not. He said merely that he was in possession of substantial proof of his accusation.

SEYMOUR.   With your permission, sir . . . Budd, did you speak with anyone in the Master-at-Arms' hearing last night?

BILLY.   I . . . spoke a little . . . with the Dansker, sir.

WYATT.   Who is the Dansker?

BILLY.   He's just called the Dansker, sir. He's always called so.

RATCLIFFE.   I know him. A mainmast sailor.

SEYMOUR.   Sentry.

(*Enter* HALLAM.)

HALLAM.   Sir.

SEYMOUR.   Do you know a mainmast sailor referred to as "the Dansker"?

HALLAM.   Aye, sir.

SEYMOUR.   Go on deck and find him. Let him know apart that he is wanted here, and arrange it so that none of the other people notice his withdrawing. See you do it tactfully. I want no curiosity aroused among the men.

HALLAM.   Aye aye, sir. (*Exits.*)

SEYMOUR.   Please go on.

VERE.   I sent at once for Budd. I ordered the Master-at-Arms to be present at this interview, to make his accusation to Budd's face.

RATCLIFFE.   May I ask what was the prisoner's reaction on being confronted by the Master-at-Arms?

VERE.   I perceived no sign of uneasiness in his demeanor. I believe he smiled.

RATCLIFFE.   And for the Master-at-Arms?

VERE.   When I directed him to repeat his accusation, he faced Budd and did so.

WYATT.   Did Budd reply?

VERE.   He tried to speak, but could not frame his words.

SEYMOUR.   And then, sir?

VERE.   He answered with blows, and his accuser fell. . . . It was apparent at once that the attack was fatal, but I summoned the Surgeon to verify the fact. That is all. (*Turns away.*)

SEYMOUR (*to* BILLY).   You have heard Captain Vere's account. Is it, or is it not, as he says?

BILLY.   Captain Vere tells the truth. It is just as Captain Vere says, but it is not as the Master-at-Arms said. I have eaten the King's bread, and I am true to the King.

VERE.   I believe you, boy.

BILLY.   God knows . . . I . . . thank you, sir.

SEYMOUR.   Was there any malice between you and the Master-at-Arms?

BILLY.   I bore no malice against the Master-at-Arms. I'm sorry he is dead. I did not mean to kill him. If I'd found my tongue, I would not have struck him. But he lied foully to my face, and I . . . had to say . . . something . . . and I could only say it . . . with a blow. God help me.

SEYMOUR.   One question more — you tell us that what the Master-at-Arms said against you was a lie. Now, why should he have lied with such obvious malice, when you have declared that there was no malice between you?

(BILLY *looks appealingly at* VERE.)

Did you hear my question?

BILLY.   I . . . I . . .

VERE.   The question you put to him comes naturally enough. But can he rightly answer it? Or anyone else, unless, indeed, it be he who lies within there.

(*Knock and enter immediately* HALLAM.)

HALLAM.   The mainmast man, sir.

SEYMOUR.   Send him in.

(HALLAM *nods off and* THE DANSKER *enters.* HALLAM *withdraws, closing door.*)

State your name and station.

THE DANSKER. I have no name. I'm called the Dansker, that's all I know. Mainmast man.

SEYMOUR. You have been summoned in secrecy to appear as a witness before this court, of which I am Senior Member. I may not at this time disclose to you the nature of the offense being tried. However, the offender is William Budd, foretopman. (*Pause.*) Do you consent to give this court your testimony, though ignorant of the case at trial, and further, to keep in strictest confidence all that passes here?

THE DANSKER. Aye.

SEYMOUR (*pushes forward a Bible*). Do you so swear?

THE DANSKER (*touching the Bible*). I do.

SEYMOUR. Then this is my question. In your opinion, is there malice between Budd and the Master-at-Arms?

THE DANSKER. Aye.

VERE (*wheeling around*). How!

SEYMOUR. Explain your statement.

THE DANSKER. How should he not have hated him?

SEYMOUR. Be plain, man. We do not deal in riddles here.

THE DANSKER. Master-at-Arms bore malice towards a grace he could not have. There was no reason for it.

RATCLIFFE. In other words, this malice was one-sided?

THE DANSKER. Aye.

RATCLIFFE. And you cannot explain how it arose?

THE DANSKER. Master-at-Arms hated Billy . . .

SEYMOUR. One moment. I notice that you have been using the past tense in your testimony. Why?

THE DANSKER. I look around and sense finality here.

WYATT. You cannot explain further the cause of Claggart's hate for Budd?

THE DANSKER. Master-at-Arms made his world in his own image. Pride was his demon, and he kept it strong by others' fear of him. Billy could not imagine such a nature, saw nothing but a lonely man, strange, but a man still, nothing to be feared. So Claggart, lest his world be proven false, planned Billy's death. The final reason is beyond my thinking.

VERE. Aye, that is thoughtfully put. There is a mystery in iniquity. But it seems to me, Seymour, that the point we seek here is hardly material.

SEYMOUR. Aye, sir. Very well, you may go.

THE DANSKER. One thing more. Since this Master-at-Arms first came on board from God knows where, I have seen his shadow lengthen along the deck, and being under it, I was afraid. Whatever happened here, I am in part to blame — more than this lad. (*To* BILLY.) I am an old man, Billy. You — try to — forgive me. (*Exits.*)

SEYMOUR. Have you any further questions to put to the accused?

RATCLIFFE. No.

WYATT. None.

SEYMOUR. William Budd, if you have anything further to say for yourself, say it now.

BILLY (*after glance at* VERE). I have said all, sir.

SEYMOUR. Sentry.

(*Enter* HALLAM.)

Remove the prisoner to the after compartment.

(HALLAM *and* BILLY *exit. A long pause.*)

Have you anything to say, Ratcliffe?

RATCLIFFE. Yes, sir. Claggart was killed because Budd couldn't speak. In that sense, that he stammers, he's a cripple. You don't hang a man for that, for speaking the only way he could.

WYATT. If you condemn him, it's the same thing as condoning the apparent lie the Master-at-Arms clearly told. I'd have struck him, too. The boy is clearly innocent, struck him in self-defense.

RATCLIFFE. Aye. I'm ready to acquit him now.

SEYMOUR. Good. Then we can reach a verdict at once.

VERE. Hitherto I have been a witness at this trial, no more. And I hesitate to interfere, except that at this clear crisis you ignore one fact we cannot close our eyes to.

SEYMOUR. With your pardon, sir, as Senior Member of this court, I must ask if you speak now as our commanding officer or as a private man.

VERE. As convening authority, Seymour. I summoned this court, and I must review its findings and approve them before passing them on to the Admiralty.

SEYMOUR. Aye, sir, that is your right.

VERE. No right. Which of us here has rights? It is my duty, and I must perform it. Budd has killed a man — his superior officer.

SEYMOUR. We have found a verdict, sir.

VERE. I know that, Seymour. Your verdict sets him free, and so would I wish to do. But are we free to choose as we would do if we were private citizens? The Admiralty has its code. Do you suppose it cares who Budd is? Who you and I are?

SEYMOUR. We don't forget that, sir. But surely Claggart's tales were simply lies. We've established that.

VERE. Aye. But the Nore and Spithead were brute facts, and must not come again. The men were starved out before, but if they should think we are afraid . . .

RATCLIFFE. Captain, how could they? They certainly know Budd is no mutineer.

WYATT. Of course not. Since he came on board, he's done more to keep the crew in hand than any of us.

SEYMOUR. That's true. The men took naturally to him.

VERE. As officers we are concerned to keep this ship effective as a weapon. And the law says what we must do in such a case as this. Come now, you know the facts, and the Mutiny Act's provisions. At sea, in time of war, an impressed man strikes his superior officer, and the blow is fatal. The mere blow alone would hang him, at least according to the Act. Well then, the men on board know that as well as you and I. And we acquit him. They have sense, they know the proper penalty to follow, and yet it does not follow.

SEYMOUR. But they know Budd, sir, and Claggart too, I daresay. Would they not applaud the decision that frees Budd? They would thank us.

WYATT. String him to a yard, and they'll turn round and rescue him, and string us up instead!

RATCLIFFE. Aye, that's a point. It's twice as dangerous to hang the boy as it would be to let him go. If there's a mutinous temper in the crew, condemning Budd would surely set it off.

VERE. That is possible. Whatever step we take, the risk is great; but it is ours. That is what makes us officers. Yet if in fear of what our office demands we shirk our duty, we only play at war, at being men. If by our lawful rigor mutiny comes, there is no blame for us. But if in fear, miscalled a kind of mercy, we pardon Budd against specific order, and then the crew revolts, how culpable and weak our verdict would appear! The men on board know what our case is, how we are haunted by the Spithead risings. Have they forgotten how the panic spread through England? No. Your clemency would be accounted fear, and they would say we flinch from practicing a lawful rigor lest new outbreaks be provoked. What shame to us! And what a deadly blow to discipline!

RATCLIFFE. I concede that, sir. But this case is exceptional, and pity, if we are men, is bound to move us, Captain.

VERE. So am I moved. Yet we cannot have warm hearts betraying heads that should be cool. In such a case ashore, an upright judge does not allow the pleading tears of women to touch his nature. Here at sea, the heart, the female in a man, weeps like a woman. She must be ruled out, hard though it be. (*Pause.*) Still silent? Very well, I see that something in all your downcast faces seems to urge that not alone the heart moves hesitancy. Conscience, perhaps. The private conscience moves you.

WYATT. Aye, that's it, sir. How can we condemn this man and live at peace again within ourselves? We have our standards; ethics, if you like.

VERE. Challenge your scruples! They move as in a dusk. Come, do they import something like this: if we are bound to judge, regardless of palliating circumstances, the death of Claggart as the prisoner's deed, then does that deed appear a capital crime whereof the penalty is mortal? But can we adjudge to summary and shameful death a fellow creature innocent before God, and whom we feel to be so? Does that state the case rightly?

SEYMOUR. That is my feeling, sir.

VERE. You all feel, I am sure, that the boy in effect is innocent; that what he did was from an unhappy stricture of speech that made him speak with blows. And I believe that, too; believe as you do, that he struck his man down, tempted beyond endurance. Acquit him, then, you say, as innocent?

RATCLIFFE. Exactly! Oh, I know the Articles prescribe death for what Budd has done, but that . . .

WYATT. Oh, stow the Articles! They don't account for such a case as this. You yourself say Budd is innocent.

VERE. In intent, Wyatt, in intent.

WYATT. Does that count for nothing? His whole attitude, his motive, count for nothing? If his intent . . .

VERE. The intent or non-intent of Budd is nothing to the purpose. In a court more merciful than martial it would extenuate, and shall, at the last Assizes, set him free. But here we have these alternatives only: condemn or let go.

SEYMOUR. But it seems to me we've got to consider the problem as a moral one, sir, despite the fact that we're not moralists. When Claggart told you his lie, the case immediately went beyond the scope of military justice.

VERE. I, too, feel that. But do these gold stripes across our arms attest that our allegiance is to Nature?

RATCLIFFE. To our country, sir.

VERE. Aye, Ratcliffe; to the King. And though the sea, which is inviolate Nature primeval, though it be the element whereon we move and have our being as sailors, is our official duty hence to Nature? No. So little is that true that we resign our freedom when we put this on. And when war is declared, are we, the fighters commissioned to destroy, consulted first?

WYATT. Does that deny us the right to act like men? We're not trying a murderer, a dockside cut-throat!

VERE. The gold we wear shows that we serve the King, the Law. What does it matter that our acts are fatal to our manhood, if we serve as we are forced to serve? What bitter salt leagues move between our code and God's own judgments! We are conscripts, every one, upright in this uniform of flesh. There is no truce to war born in the womb. We fight at command.

WYATT. All I know is that I can't sit by and see Budd hanged!

VERE. I say we fight by order, by command of our superiors. And if our judgments approve the war, it is only coincidence. And so it is with all our acts. So now, would it be so much we ourselves who speak as judges here, as it would be martial law operating through us? For that law, and for its rigor, we are not responsible. Our duty lies in this: that we are servants only.

RATCLIFFE. The Admiralty doesn't want service like that. What good would it do? Who'd profit by Budd's death?

WYATT. You want to make us murderers!

SEYMOUR. Wyatt! Control yourself!

VERE. What is this vessel that you serve in, Wyatt, an ark of peace? Go count her guns; then tell your conscience to lie quiet, if you can.

RATCLIFFE. But that is war. This would be downright killing!

SEYMOUR. It's all war, Ratcliffe; war to the death, for all of us.

VERE. You see that, Seymour? That this war began before our time?

SEYMOUR. And will end long after it.

VERE. Here we have the Mutiny Act for justice. No child can own a closer tie to parent than can that Act to what it stems from: War. This is a wartime cruise and in this ship are Englishmen who fight against their wills, perhaps against their conscience, 'pressed by war into the service of the King. Though we as fellow creatures understand their lot, what does it matter to the officer, or to the enemy? The French will cut down conscripts in the same swath with volunteers, and we will do as much for them. War has no business with anything but surfaces. War's child, the Mutiny Act, is featured like the father.

RATCLIFFE. Couldn't we mitigate the penalty if we convict him?

VERE. No, Ratcliffe. The penalty is prescribed.

RATCLIFFE. I'd like to think it over, Captain. I'm not sure.

VERE. I repeat, then, that while we ponder and you hesitate over anxieties I confess to sharing, the enemy comes nearer. We must act, and quickly. The French close in on us; the crew will find out shortly what has happened. Our consciences are private matters, Ratcliffe. But we are public men, controlling life and death within this world at sea. Tell me whether or not in our positions we dare let our consciences take precedence of the code that makes us officers and calls this case to trial.

RATCLIFFE (*after a pause; quietly*). No, sir.

WYATT. Can you stand Budd's murder on your conscience?

SEYMOUR. Wyatt! Hold your tongue!

WYATT (*jumping up*). I say let him go!

SEYMOUR. Sit down, sir!

VERE. Let him speak.

WYATT. I won't bear a hand to hang a man I know is innocent! My blood's not cold enough. I can't give the kind of judgment you want to force on us! I ask to be excused from sitting upon this court.

SEYMOUR. Do you know what you're saying? Sit down and hold your tongue, man!

VERE. The kind of judgment I ask of you is only this, Wyatt: that you recognize your function in this ship. I believe you know it quite as well as we, yet you rebel. Can't you see that you must first strip off the uniform you wear, and after that your flesh, before you can escape the case at issue here? Decide you must, Wyatt. Oh, you may be excused and wash your hands of it, but someone must decide. We are the law; law orders us to act, and shows us how. Do you imagine Seymour, or Ratcliffe here, or I, would not save this boy if we could see a way consistent with our duties? Acquit Budd if you can. God knows I wish I could. If in your mind as well as in your heart, you can say freely that his life is not forfeit to the law we serve, reason with us! Show us how to save him without putting aside our function. Or if you can't do that, teach us to put by our responsibility and not betray ourselves. Can you do this? Speak, man, speak! Show us how! Save him, Wyatt, and you save us all.

(WYATT *slowly sits down.*)

You recognize the logic of the choice I force upon you. But do not think me pitiless in thus demanding sentence on a luckless boy. I feel as you do for him. But even more, I think there is a grace of soul within him that shall forgive the law we bind him with, and pity us, stretched on the cross of choice. (*Turns away.*)

SEYMOUR. Well, gentlemen. Will you decide.

(*Officers write their verdicts on paper before them, and hand them to* SEYMOUR, *who rises, draws his dirk and places it on the table, pointing forward.*)

He is condemned, sir. Shall we appoint the dawn?

Scene 2

(CAPTAIN VERE's *cabin, 0400. Ship's bell strikes offstage.* VERE *sitting alone at his desk. Knock at the door.*)

VERE. Come in.

(*Enter* SEYMOUR.)

Oh, it's you, Seymour.

SEYMOUR. It's eight bells, Captain.

VERE. What's the hour of sunrise?

SEYMOUR. Four fifty-two, sir.

VERE. Eight bells. And one bell at four-thirty. Odd and even numbers caught between two hands. Budd shall not live to hear the odd made even or wrong made right. — Call all hands to quarters at four-thirty.

SEYMOUR. Aye aye, Captain. (*Turns irresolutely.*)

VERE. The wind has slackened, I think. How is the glass?

SEYMOUR. It's risen slightly. Sea has flattened out.

VERE. Fair weather after foul . . . it's all nature, nature and law. How exigent are these Mediterranean climates of the heart, and temperate zones of mind!

SEYMOUR. Have you been here all night, sir?

VERE. All night, Seymour . . . all my life moving between dark and dark. It has been a long night, but day will be quick and deadly on the mainyard. D'you think, Seymour, a man can forgive a wrong done of the heart's own election?

SEYMOUR.   Most people are decent enough. You can forgive them trespasses.

VERE.   No, by God. There's wickedness alive. It's dead now in one man, but it's alive to feel and smell at night. . . . Seymour, go below. Get Budd and bring him here.

SEYMOUR.   But Captain . . .

VERE.   Do as you're told. Get Budd and bring him here.

(SEYMOUR *exits.* VERE *sits motionless for a few moments, then rises and goes to the cabin door.*)

Sentry.

HALLAM.   Yes, sir?

VERE.   Who has the deck this watch?

HALLAM.   Mister Ratcliffe, Captain.

VERE.   Very well. (*Pause.*) Sentry!

HALLAM.   Sir?

VERE.   When Mister Seymour has returned, admit him right away.

HALLAM.   Aye aye, Captain.

VERE.   The wind's still sharp. You must be cold there, Hallam. Go to the leeward side. I'll be responsible.

HALLAM.   Thank you, sir. This is the coldest hour now, just before sunrise.

VERE (*closes door, returns slowly to his desk*).   The lamp holds steady when the vessel heels. Does the law hang straight in crooked lives? It burns, and shapes nothing but shadows here, plumb in the twisting cabin of the mind.

(*Footsteps, voices,* VERE *turns to door. Enter* SEYMOUR, BILLY, *and* HALLAM.)

Take off the manacles.

(HALLAM *frees* BILLY.)

SEYMOUR (*to* HALLAM).   Outside, man. Bear a hand. (*Exits with* HALLAM.)

VERE.   Sit down. No, it's better that I stand.

BILLY.   I was thinking, locked up below there . . . the Captain knows the rights of all this. He'll save me if it's right. Then you sent for me. Is there hope for me, Captain?

VERE.   Billy, what hope is there?

BILLY.   Tell me why. I only want to understand.

VERE.   How young you still are, Billy! Oh, I can tell you this: nothing is lost of anything that happens. I have given you the judgment of the world . . . deadly constraint . . . a length of hemp and a yard-arm. I have done this to you, no one else.

BILLY. I can't get the rights of all that's happened.

VERE. There's not much right, Billy. Only necessity. You and Claggart broke man's compromise with good and evil, and both of you must pay the penalty.

BILLY. Penalty? What for? Would anyone make laws just to be broken by fellows like me?

VERE. Aye, boy. You have learned this late. Most of us find out early and trim to a middle course.

BILLY. Do you mean . . . it's better to be like that?

VERE. Better as this world goes. When a man is born, he takes a guilt upon him, I can't say how or why. And life takes its revenge on those who hurt its pride with innocence.

BILLY. Do you think Claggart knew it would come to this?

VERE. He knew he would kill you, and he died to gain that end. But if you trust me, he'll not win entirely.

BILLY. How could he hate me like that?

VERE. The world we breathe is love and hatred both, but hatred must not win the victory.

BILLY. Claggart is dead. Now I'm to hang. Doesn't that show the law is wrong, when it can't choose between him and me?

VERE. Yes, it's all wrong, all wrong.

BILLY. I don't know, Captain. I never was a hand to wonder about things, but now I think that maybe there's a kind of cruelty in people that's just as much a part of them as kindness, say, or honesty, or m-m-m . . . I can't find words, I guess, Captain.

VERE. There are no words. We are all prisoners of deadly forms that are made to break us to their measure. Nothing has power to overcome them, except forgiveness. . . . Can you forgive what I have done?

BILLY. I *can* trust you, can't I? *Can* you show me it's all right, my being . . .

VERE (*turns away; a long pause*). It's nearly dawn, lad. In the Spanish villages they're lighting fires.

BILLY. I'm not afraid, sir. (*Steps toward* VERE.) It's getting light.

VERE. There's no time for either of us left. Go, take the morning. God knows you have the right to it. And when you are on the mainyard, think of me, and pray for those who must make choices. Hallam.

(*Enter* HALLAM *in doorway.*)

Take Budd into your charge.

(BILLY *and* HALLAM *go out.*)

Time has run out.

Scene 3

(*Main deck aft. Drum-to-formation. Crew forming up.* WYATT, MID-
SHIPMEN GARDINER *and* REA.)

WYATT.   Bear a hand. Form the men up in ranks.

GARDINER.   Aye, sir. All right, you! Close ranks! Move up, Stoll.
That's better. Talbot, square your hat. Form up straight there, damn it!

(*Drum.* MEN *come to attention.*)

WYATT.   Division commanders report!

VOICE (*off*).   Carpenters and gunners, present or accounted for, sir!

VOICE (*off*).   Marine Detachment, present or accounted for, sir!

VOICE (*off*).   Afterguard, present or accounted for, sir!

GARDINER.   Fore, main and mizzentopmen . . . one absentee!

WYATT.   All hands will stand by to witness punishment! Stand easy.

VOICES (*off*).   Stand easy!

(WYATT *walks away from men. Murmur in ranks.*)

KINCAID.   Where the devil is Billy? He wasn't in his hammock when
they piped us up.

O'DANIEL.   He'll be getting himself in trouble if he don't fall in.

KINCAID.   Who the hell they punishing, and what for?

JENKINS.   It's got to be flogging, or they wouldn't have us all up here.

KINCAID.   Vere never flogs anybody. And there ain't no gratings up.

THE DANSKER.   They flog men at noon. The early morning's for hanging.

KINCAID.   Hanging!

(*The word travels back.*)

Who? What for?

O'DANIEL.   The skipper, he don't confide in me no more.

KINCAID.   I thought they waited till they got ashore before they hanged
a man.

THE DANSKER.   Not in wartime.

JENKINS.   He goes up them ratlines, out on the yard, they slips a noose
around his neck, and then he jumps and hangs himself.

O'DANIEL.   They'd have the devil's work getting O'Daniel to jump.

KINCAID.   It's jump, or get pushed.

JENKINS.   Where's Claggart? God, you don't suppose it's Claggart!
Oh, Judas, let it be that fishblooded nark!

KINCAID.   Not him. He's too smart, he is.

JENKINS.   Where is he, then? He ain't here.

THE DANSKER.   He is here.

KINCAID. Where? I don't see him.
THE DANSKER. He is here.
KINCAID. Ah ... you're balmy, old man.

(*Enter* VERE, SEYMOUR, RATCLIFFE *and the* SURGEON. *Drum sounds Attention.*)

WYATT (*to* SEYMOUR). Ship's company present to witness execution, sir.
SEYMOUR. Very well. (*To* VERE.) Ship's company present to witness execution, sir.

(VERE *nods.*)

SEYMOUR (*to* WYATT). Lieutenant Wyatt, have the prisoner brought forward.
WYATT. Aye aye, sir. (*Marches to wing.*) Sentries, bring forward the prisoner. (*Marches back to his post.*)

(*Enter* BILLY *with two sentries. Astonished murmur through the crew, who momentarily break ranks.*)

WYATT. No talking in ranks!

(*Continued restless movement and murmurings.*)

Form up!
GARDINER. You men are at attention!
WYATT (*over subdued muttering*). You hear me? Silence in ranks!

(*Silence.* SENTRIES *lead* BILLY *to the foot of the ropes.* SEYMOUR *looks at* VERE, *who nods.* SEYMOUR *steps forward and reads.*)

SEYMOUR. Proceedings of the court-martial held aboard H.M.S. *Indomitable* on the eighth August, 1798. Convened under the authority of Edward Fairfax Vere, Senior Captain, Royal Navy, and composed of the First Officer, the Sailing Master, and the First Lieutenant of said vessel. In the case of William Budd, foretopman, Royal Navy. While attached and so serving in the aforesaid vessel, he did, on the 8th day of August, 1798, strike and kill his superior officer, one John Claggart, Master-at-Arms, Royal Navy.

(*Crew breaks out uneasily, astonished, talking excitedly.*)

JENKINS ⎫   ⎧ Billy! Did you, boy?
VOICE ⎪ (*together*). ⎨ Good lad!
VOICE ⎬   ⎪ Serves him proper!
KINCAID ⎭   ⎩ Hi, Billy! Hurrah!
WYATT. Quiet! Silence, you men! Form up!

GARDINER. Stand at attention, hang you! Silence in the ranks!
WYATT. Do you hear?

(*Excited muttering, low voices.*)

SEYMOUR. You will be silent and remain at strict attention until dismissed. (*Silence.*) . . . Master-at-Arms, Royal Navy. Therefore, the court sentences the aforementioned William Budd, foretopman, Royal Navy, to die by hanging on the first watch of the day following these proceedings. By authority of his Gracious Majesty George Rex and Alan Napier, Viscount Kelsey, First Sea Lord. Signed, Philip Seymour, Senior Member.

(*During the last phrases of the reading, the crew, upon hearing the sentence, breaks out again, some stepping forward, shouting; they are in an ugly temper.*)

VOICES (*together*). — No he don't!
— Not if I know it!
— Hang the jemmies instead, I say!
— Not Billy, you bloody swineheads!
— Not him, by Christ!
— You ain't hanging Billy, damn your eyes!
— Let them dance on a rope's end!
WYATT. Stand back! Sentries, guard your prisoner, if you have to fire!
GARDINER. Stand back, you damned clods! Keep back!
SEYMOUR (*steps forward*). Silence there! You will resume discipline instantly! Be warned.

(*Waits a silent moment. Men stop in disordered formation.*)

Stand back into ranks.
GARDINER. Form up again, quick about it now!

(*There is a surly movement into irregular lines.*)

SEYMOUR (*warily resuming procedure*). Prisoner, have you anything to say?

(BILLY *shakes his head.*)

If you have nothing to say, when the drum roll is sounded, you will proceed to carry out the sentence of this court. (*Signals to* WYATT.)
WYATT. Sound off!

(*Drum roll.* BILLY *turns and starts up the ropes.*)

VOICES (*together*). — Get him! Now!
— Bill! Stay where you are, boy, don't do it!
— Wait, Billy! Wait!
— Rush the deck, mates! Don't let them do it!
— We're here, Bill, don't you worry!

BILLY (*stops, turns forward, looks at* VERE, *and shouts out loud and clear, without trace of stammer*). God bless Captain Vere!

(*A second's pause;* VERE *is profoundly shaken;* BILLY *goes quickly up the ropes and out of sight. The crew moves back a step, is silent; officers and men in deep breathless quiet watch him out of sight and are staring overhead as*

The Curtain Falls.)

Archibald MacLeish (1892–   ), in his poetic drama *J. B.* (1956, produced 1958), found a new framework for *The Book of Job* and a more human conclusion. His choice of a circus ring as a metaphor for the world is both apt and ironic, since the action is tragic, rather than comic: as Aristotle stipulated, it is an imitation of a serious action; it is clearly not the real thing. God and Satan, impersonated by Zuss and Nickles, may act on Job, but they are not the villains of melodrama, nor is J. B. a pure, put-upon hero. As in the Old Testament, he is an imperfect human being trying to be good and do right. When his trials come, he proves steadfast.

In the Old Testament, Job's sufferings come directly from Satan's hand, but at God's instance. He proudly holds Job's piety up for Satan's admiration. Satan will not take the bait and tempts God instead. If Job finds things are not going well for him, will he not curse his Maker? God, binding Satan not to take Job's life, gives his license for every other extravagance of abuse to prove Job's steadfast devotion to Him. The result is that Job is made a pawn in a game between God and Satan, with God's ego the stake. And yet, at the center of all this divine sadism is something undeniably mighty and mystic. It is not what a man deserves, what a man earns, what a man begs that counts. It is, finally, the absolute power and enigmatic activity of the Spirit that created and animated the universe which is paramount. This force — called God — is not to be explained, argued with, justified, or cursed. It is Itself, and It is sufficient unto Itself. Man must accept It and what It decrees.

What makes an individual more than a cipher in the universal equation is endurance, steadfastness, acceptance — as Job learns. After God, in a series of ringing poetic metaphors, amasses a catalogue of strengths, powers, and wisdoms calculated to make Job finally understand the overwhelming All of His majesty and dominion, Job meekly responds: "I know that thou canst do every thing, and that no thought can be withholden from thee. Who is he that hideth counsel without knowledge? therefore have I uttered that I understood not; things too wonderful for me, which I knew not."[1] That is a rather anticlimactic capitulation to God's will, but Job's burdens are then lifted.

In Zuss, Nickles, the Messengers, and the latter-day Job's Comforters MacLeish brings a modern cynicism — or so it at first appears — to the story. MacLeish's introduction of the pair of old actors, commenting on J. B.'s tale like end-men in a minstrel show, may be a theatrical gimmick, but it does permit him, the omniscient poet, to provide surrogates for his own theories and doubts. It also introduces at least a surface complexity into the details of the plot action by providing a contrapuntal line. Zuss and Nickles give a brisk workout to some of the theological questions MacLeish and today's readers raise about the Old Testa-

[1] *Job* XLII: 2–3.

ment legend. Still, a sense of the inscrutability of the future — the unfathomable and unpredictable operation of the universe — lurks in the shadows. Job, in the person of J. B., cries out for justice, but of course there is no justice in cosmic terms, let alone in man's limited terms. At the Creation of Man and on each occasion of the conception of a new man, no promises were or are made which bind God or the universe for all eternity. All man can do is to live, work, and suffer. His heroism is to endure, to remain steadfast in what he believes, to keep his integrity, no matter how many insidious or vicious assaults are made on it. What can sustain him in this dark night of the body and soul? MacLeish suggests what the tellers of the Old Testament tales do not; human love. There is no justice for man. God — or the universe — simply IS. All man can hope for to help him endure is love.

The disasters which befall Job may seem too much to believe, or they may seem petty compared with the actual horrors thousands have undergone in recent wars. But they are crushing J. B. and they make him cry out for death as a welcome reprieve from life. He has not brought the disasters on himself; he has not been trying to destroy himself. Nor will he: if death comes, it must come from outside, the ultimate disaster. J. B. discovers that death, after all, is not the worst thing that can happen to a man; continuing to live is. In a punning sense, this is a life sentence instead of a death sentence. In *Job*, the rewards which come after the tests are earned by Job's endurance and unwavering faith. In *J. B.*, they are — if this exchange is to be credited — not rewards at all, but a continuation of the varied burdens of existence. The emphasis on human love as the means of bearing those burdens is a unique divergence from the biblical text, but it gives a modern validity to the fable. In MacLeish's own imagery, it blows on the coal of the heart. J. B. achieves his tragic stature not in facing the necessity of death, but in enduring the reality of life.

Whether MacLeish has written an ambiguous, parodic piece of poetic nonsense, as some insist, or whether he has illuminated the enigma of human existence with rare insight and beauty may well depend on how much illumination the reader or the viewer is able to perceive. Whatever the judgment, it cannot be said that MacLeish has hidden *his* light under a bushel.

G.L.

ARCHIBALD MacLEISH

J. B.

A *Play in Verse*

Characters

Mr. Zuss ⎱ *old actors, now circus vendors*
Nickles ⎰

A Distant Voice

J. B., *a banker*

Sarah, *his wife*

David ⎫
Mary ⎪
Jonathan ⎬ *their children*
Ruth ⎪
Rebecca ⎭

Two Maids

Two Messengers

Girl

Mrs. Adams

Jolly Adams

Mrs. Lesure

Mrs. Murphy

Mrs. Botticelli

Zophar ⎫
Eliphaz ⎬ *The Three Comforters*
Bildad ⎭

(The scene throughout is a corner inside an enormous circus tent where a sideshow of some kind has been set up. There is a rough stage across the corner, on the left of which a wooden platform has been built at a height of six or seven feet. A wooden ladder leans against it. To the right is a deal table with seven straight chairs. There is a door-shaped opening in the canvas to the right rear. Above, a huge, slanted pole thrusts the canvas out and up to make the peak of the corner. Clothes that have the look of vestments of many churches and times have been left about at one side and the other of the stage and the light at the beginning — such light as there is — is provided by bulbs dangling from hanks of wire.

672

The feel is of a public place at late night, the audience gone, no one about but maybe a stagehand somewhere cleaning up, fooling with the lights.)

The Prologue

(MR. ZUSS, *followed by* NICKLES, *enters from the dimness off to the left. They stop at the edge of the sideshow stage. Both wear the white caps and jackets of circus vendors. Both are old.* MR. ZUSS, *who has a bunch of balloons hitched to his belt, is large, florid, deep-voiced, dignified, imposing.* NICKLES *is gaunt and sardonic; he has a popcorn tray slung from straps across his shoulders. Both betray in carriage and speech the broken-down actor fallen on evil days but nevertheless and always actor. Throughout the Prologue, from the moment when they mount the sideshow stage, they jockey for position, gesture, work themselves up into theatrical flights and rhetorical emotions, play to each other as though they had an actual audience before them in the empty dark.*)

MR. ZUSS. This is it.
NICKLES.   This is what?
MR. ZUSS. Where they play the play, Horatio!
NICKLES. Bare stage?
MR. ZUSS.   Not in the least.
Heaven and earth. That platform's Heaven.

(*They step up onto the stage together.*)

NICKLES. Looks like Heaven!
MR. ZUSS.   As you remember it?
NICKLES. Somebody's got to. You weren't there.
They never sold balloons in Heaven —
Not in my time.
MR. ZUSS. Only popcorn.

(NICKLES *shrugs a shudder of disgust, heaving his tray.*)

NICKLES. The two best actors in America
Selling breath in bags . . .
MR. ZUSS.   and bags
To butter breath with . . .
NICKLES.   when they sell.
MR. ZUSS. Merchandise not moving, Nickles?
NICKLES. Moves whenever I do — all of it.
No rush to buy your worlds, I notice.
MR. ZUSS. I could sell one to a . . .
NICKLES.   . . . child!
You told me. Where's the earth?

MR. ZUSS.   Earth?
Earth is where that table is:
That's where Job sits — at the table.
God and Satan lean above. (*Peers anxiously up into the canvas sky.*)
I wonder if we'd better?
    NICKLES.   What?
    MR. ZUSS.   Play it.
    NICKLES.   Why not? Who cares? They don't.
    MR. ZUSS.   At least we're actors. They're not actors.
Never acted anything.
    NICKLES.   That's right.
They only own the show.
    MR. ZUSS.   I wonder . . .
    NICKLES.   They won't care and they won't know. (*His eyes follow*
      MR. ZUSS's *up to the dangling bulbs.*)
Those stars that stare their stares at me —
Are those the staring stars I see
Or only lights . . . not meant for me?
    MR. ZUSS.   What's that got to do with anything?
    NICKLES.   Very little. Shall we start?
    MR. ZUSS.   You think we ought to?
    NICKLES.   They won't care.
    MR. ZUSS.   Let's start . . . What staring stars?
    NICKLES.   They aren't.
They're only lights. Not meant.
    MR. ZUSS.   Why don't we
Start?
    NICKLES.   You'll play the part of . . .
    MR. ZUSS.   Naturally!
    NICKLES.   Naturally! And your mask?
    MR. ZUSS.   Mask!
    NICKLES.   Mask. Naturally. You wouldn't play God in your
Face, would you?
    MR. ZUSS.   What's the matter with it?
    NICKLES.   God the Creator of the Universe?
God who hung the world in time?
You wouldn't hang the world in time
With a two-days' beard on your chin or a pinky!
Lay its measure! Stretch the line on it!

(MR. ZUSS *stares coldly at* NICKLES, *unhitches his balloon belt with magnificent deliberation, drops it, steps forward to the front of the wooden stage, strikes an attitude.*)

    MR. ZUSS.   Whatsoever is under the whole
Heaven is mine!

NICKLES.   That's what I mean.
You need a mask.

MR. ZUSS (*heavy irony*).   Perhaps a more
Accomplished actor . . .

NICKLES.   Kiss your accomplishments!
Nobody doubts your accomplishments — none of them —
The one man for God in the theater!
They'd all say that. Our ablest actor.
Nobody else for the part, they'd say.

MR. ZUSS.   You make me humble.

NICKLES.   No! I'm serious.
The part was written for you.

MR. ZUSS (*gesture of protest*).   Oh!

NICKLES.   But this is God in *Job* you're playing:
God the Maker: God Himself!
Remember what He says? — the hawk
Flies by His wisdom! And the goats —
Remember the goats? He challenges Job with them:
Dost thou know the time of the wild goats?
What human face knows time like that time?
You'd need a face of fur to know it.
Human faces know too much too little.

MR. ZUSS (*suspiciously*).   What kind of mask?

NICKLES.   You'll find one somewhere.
They never play without the masks.

MR. ZUSS.   It's God the Father I play — not
God the boiling point of water!

NICKLES.   Nevertheless the mask is imperative.
If God should laugh
The mare would calf
The cow would foal:
Diddle my soul . . .

MR. ZUSS (*shocked*).   God never laughs! In the whole Bible!

NICKLES.   That's what I say. We do.

MR. ZUSS.   I don't.

NICKLES.   *Job* does. He covers his mouth with his hand.

MR. ZUSS.   Job is abashed.

NICKLES.   He says he's abashed.

MR. ZUSS.   He should be abashed: it's rank irreverence —
Job there on the earth . . .

NICKLES.   On his dung heap . . .

MR. ZUSS.   Challenging God!

NICKLES.   Crying to God.

MR. ZUSS.   Demanding *justice* of God!

NICKLES.   Justice!
No wonder he laughs. It's ridiculous. All of it.

God has killed his sons, his daughters,
Stolen his camels, oxen, sheep,
Everything he has and left him
Sick and stricken on a dung heap —
Not even the consciousness of crime to comfort him —
The rags of reasons.

    MR. ZUSS.   God is reasons.

    NICKLES.   For the hawks, yes. For the goats. They're grateful.
Take their young away they'll sing
Or purr or moo or splash — whatever.
Not for Job though.

    MR. ZUSS.   And that's why.

    NICKLES.   Why what?

    MR. ZUSS.   He suffers.

    NICKLES.   Ah? Because he's . . .
Not a bird you mean?

    MR. ZUSS.   You're frivolous . . .

    NICKLES.   That's precisely what you do mean!
The one thing God can't stomach is a man,
That scratcher at the cracked creation!
That eyeball squinting through into His Eye,
Blind with the sight of Sight! (*Tugs himself free of his tray.*) Blast
    this . . .

    MR. ZUSS.   God created the whole world.
Who is Job to . . .

    NICKLES.   Agh! the world!
The dirty whirler! The toy top!

    MR. ZUSS (*kicking savagely at the popcorn tray and the balloon belt to
    shove them under the platform*).   What's so wrong with the world?

    NICKLES.   Wrong with it!
Try to spin one on a dung heap!

(MR. ZUSS *does not answer. He goes on kicking at the tray.* NICKLES
*sits on a rung of the ladder. After a time he begins to sing to himself in
a kind of tuneless tune.*)

> I heard upon his dry dung heap
> That man cry out who cannot sleep:
> "If God is God He is not good,
> If God is good He is not God;
> Take the even, take the odd,
> I would not sleep here if I could
> Except for the little green leaves in the wood
> And the wind on the water."

(*There is a long silence.*)

MR. ZUSS. You are a bitter man.

NICKLES (*pompously*).   I taste of the world!
I've licked the stick that beat my brains out:
Stick that broke my father's bones!

MR. ZUSS. Our modern hero! Our Odysseus
Sailing sidewalks toward the turd
Of truth and touching it at last in triumph!
The honest, disillusioned man!
You sicken me.

NICKLES (*hurt*). All right, I sicken you.
No need to be offensive, is there?
If you would rather someone else . . .

MR. ZUSS. Did what?

NICKLES.   Played Job.

MR. ZUSS.   What's Job to do with it?

NICKLES. Job was honest. He saw God —
Saw him by that icy moonlight,
By that cold disclosing eye
That stares the color out and strews
Our lives . . . with light . . . for nothing.

MR. ZUSS.   Job!
I never thought of you for Job.

NICKLES. You never thought of me for Job!
What did you think of?

MR. ZUSS.   Oh, there's always
Someone playing Job.

NICKLES.   There must be
Thousands! What's that got to do with it?
Thousands — not with camels either:
Millions and millions of mankind
Burned, crushed, broken, mutilated,
Slaughtered, and for what? For thinking!
For walking round the world in the wrong
Skin, the wrong-shaped noses, eyelids:
Sleeping the wrong night wrong city —
London, Dresden, Hiroshima.
There never could have been so many
Suffered more for less. But where do
I come in?

(MR. ZUSS *shuffles uncomfortably.*)

        Play the dung heap?

MR. ZUSS. All we have to do is start.
Job will join us. Job will be there.

NICKLES. I know. I know. I know. I've seen him.

Job is everywhere we go,
His children dead, his work for nothing,
Counting his losses, scraping his boils,
Discussing himself with his friends and physicians,
Questioning everything — the times, the stars,
His own soul, God's providence.
What do *I* do?

MR. ZUSS. What do you do?
NICKLES. What do I do? You play God.
MR. ZUSS. I play God. I think I mentioned it.
NICKLES. You play God and I play . . . (*He lets himself down heavily on the rung of the ladder.*) Ah!
MR. ZUSS (*embarrassed*). I had assumed you knew.

(NICKLES *looks up at him, looks away.*)

                                                              You see,
I think of you and me as . . . opposites.

NICKLES. Nice of you.
MR. ZUSS.   I didn't mean to be nasty.
NICKLES. Your opposite! A demanding role!
MR. ZUSS.   I know.
NICKLES. But worthy of me? Worthy of me!
MR. ZUSS. I have offended you. I didn't mean to.
NICKLES. Did I say I was offended?

(*There is an awkward silence.* NICKLES, *his face in his hands, begins to hum the tune to his little song.* MR. ZUSS *looks up and around into the corners of the sky, his head moving cautiously. At length* NICKLES *begins to sing the words.*)

> I heard upon his dry dung heap
> That man cry out who cannot sleep:
> "If God is God He is not good,
> If God is good He is not God;
> Take the even, take the odd,
> I would not sleep here if I could . . . " (*Silence.*)

So I play opposite to God! (*Silence.*)
Father of Lies they call me, don't they?

(MR. ZUSS *does not answer. He is still searching the dark above. Silence.* NICKLES *goes back to the song.*)

> "I would not sleep here if I could
> Except for the little green leaves in the wood
> And the wind on the water."

(*Silence. Then suddenly, theatrically, on his feet.*) Who knows enough
  to know they're lies?
Show me the mask!
  MR. ZUSS.   What mask?
  NICKLES (*attitude*).   My mask!
  MR. ZUSS.   Are you sure you wear a mask?
  NICKLES.   Meaning only God should wear one?
  MR. ZUSS.   Meaning are you sure it's there.
  NICKLES.   *They* never play without them.
  MR. ZUSS.   Yes but
Where?
  NICKLES.   Where? In Heaven probably:
Up on the platform there in Heaven!
  MR. ZUSS.   Yes . . . You wouldn't care to . . .
  NICKLES.   What?
  MR. ZUSS.   Find it for yourself?
  NICKLES.   In Heaven?
Heaven is your department, Garrick.
  MR. ZUSS.   My department! I suppose it is.
Here! Hold this! Hold it! Steady . . .

(NICKLES *steadies the ladder.* MR. ZUSS *climbs warily, keeping his eye
on the canvas darkness; heaves himself over the rail; rummages around
on the platform; turns, holding out a huge white, blank, beautiful expressionless mask with eyes lidded like the eyes of the mask in Michel-
angelo's Night.*)

  NICKLES.   That's not mine — not *his.* It's His.
I've known that face before. I've seen it.
They find it under bark of marble
Deep within the rinds of stone:
God the Creator . . . (*nastily*) of the animals!
  MR. ZUSS (*outraged*).   God of
Everything that is or can!
  NICKLES.   Is or can — but cannot know.
  MR. ZUSS.   There is nothing those closed eyes
Have not known and seen.
  NICKLES.   Except
To know they see: to know they've seen it.
Lions and dolphins have such eyes.
They know the way the wild geese know —
Those pinpoint travelers who go home
To Labradors they never meant to,
Unwinding the will of the world like string.
What would they make of a man, those eyelids?
  MR. ZUSS.   Make of him! They made him.

NICKLES.   Made him
Animal like any other
Calculated for the boughs of
Trees and meant to chatter and be grateful!
But womb-worm wonders and grows wings — (*Breaks off, struck by his
    own words; goes on.*)
It actually does! The cock-eyed things
Dream themselves into a buzz
And drown on windowpanes. He made them
Wingless but they learn to wish.
That's why He fumbles Job. Job wishes! —
Thinks there should be justice somewhere —
Beats his bones against the glass.
Justice! In this cesspool! Think of it!
Job knows better when it's over.
    MR. ZUSS.   Job knows justice when it's over.
Justice has a face like this.
    NICKLES.   Like blinded eyes?
    MR. ZUSS.   Like skies.
    NICKLES.   Of stone.
Show me the other.

(MR. ZUSS *ducks away, rummaging in the clutter on the platform; turns
again.*)

    MR. ZUSS.   You won't find it
Beautiful, you understand.
    NICKLES.   I know that.
Beauty's the Creator's bait,
Not the Uncreator's: his
Is Nothing, the no-face of Nothing
Grinning with its not-there eyes.
Nothing at all! Nothing ever! . . .
Never to have been at all!

(MR. ZUSS *turns, lifts the second mask above* NICKLES' *gesturing. This
is large as the first but dark to the other's white, and open-eyed where the
other was lidded. The eyes, though wrinkled with laughter, seem to stare
and the mouth is drawn down in agonized disgust.*)

    MR. ZUSS.   Well?

(NICKLES *is silent.*)

(*Cheerfully.*) That's it. (*Silence.*) You don't care for it?
It's not precisely the expression
Anyone would choose. I know that.

Evil is never very pretty:
Spitefulness either. Nevertheless it's
His — you'll grant that, won't you? — the traditional
Face we've always found for him anyway.
God knows where we go to find it:
Some subterranean memory probably.

(NICKLES *has approached the ladder, staring. He does not reply.*)

Well, if you won't you won't. It's your
Option. I can't say I blame you.
I wouldn't do it. Fit my face to
That! I'd scrub the skin off afterward!
Eyes to those eyes!
   NICKLES (*harshly*). You needn't worry.
Your beaux yeux would never bear that
Look of . . .
   MR. ZUSS (*smugly*). No. I know.
   NICKLES.   . . . of pity!
Let me have it.

(NICKLES *starts up the ladder, the mask in* MR. ZUSS's *hands above him.*)

         Evil you call it!
Look at those lips: they've tasted something
Bitter as a broth of blood
And spat the sup out. Was that evil? (*He climbs another rung.*)
Was it? (*Another rung.*) Spitefulness you say:
You call that grin of anguish spite? (*He pulls himself over the rail, takes
     the mask in his hands.*)
I'd rather wear this look of loathing
Night after night than wear that other
Once — that cold complacence . . .

(MR. ZUSS *has picked up the first mask again, lifts it.*)

         Horrible!
Horrible as a star above
A burning, murdered, broken city!
I'll play the part! . . . Put your mask on! . . .
Give me the lines! . . .
   MR. ZUSS.   What lines?
   NICKLES.   His!
Satan's!
   MR. ZUSS. They're in the Bible aren't they?
   NICKLES. We're supposed to speak the Bible?
   MR. ZUSS. They do . . .

(The light bulbs fade out, yellow to red to gone. A slow, strong glow spots the platform throwing gigantic shadows up across the canvas. Back to back the shadows of mr. zuss *and* nickles *adjust their masks. The masked shadows turn to each other and gravely bow. Their gestures are the stiff formal gestures of pantomime. Their voices, when they speak, are so magnified and hollowed by the masks that they scarcely seem their own.)*

godmask.   Whence comest thou?
satanmask.   From going to and fro in the earth *(there is a snicker of suppressed laughter)*
And from walking up and down in it . . . *(A great guffaw.)*
    mr. zuss *(tears off his mask, shouting).*   Lights!

(The spotlight fades out. The dangling bulbs come feebly on.)

Nobody told you to laugh like that.
What's so funny? It's irreverent. It's impudent.
After all, you are talking to God.
That doesn't happen every Saturday
Even to kitchen kin like you.
Take that face off! It's indecent!
Makes me feel like scratching somewhere!
    nickles *(painfully removes his mask).*   Do I look as though I'd laughed?
If you had seen what I have seen
You'd never laugh again! . . . *(He stares at his mask.)* Weep either . . .
    mr. zuss.   You roared. I heard you.
    nickles.   Those eyes see.
    mr. zuss.   Of course they see — beneath the trousers
Stalking up the pulpit stair:
Under the skirts at tea — wherever
Decent eyes would be ashamed to.
Why should you laugh at that?
    nickles.   It isn't
That! It isn't that at all!
They see the world. They do. They see it.
From going to and fro in the earth,
From walking up and down, they see it.
I know what Hell is now — to see.
Consciousness of consciousness . . .
    mr. zuss.   Now
Listen! This is a simple scene.
I play God. You play Satan.
God is asking where you've been.
All you have to do is tell him:
Simple as that. "In the earth," you answer.

NICKLES.   Satan answers.

MR. ZUSS.   All right — Satan.
What's the difference?

NICKLES.   Satan sees.
He sees the parked car by the plane tree.
He sees behind the fusty door,
Beneath the rug, those almost children
Struggling on the awkward seat —
Every impossible delighted dream
She's ever had of loveliness, of wonder,
Spilled with her garters to the filthy floor.
Absurd despair! Ridiculous agony! (*He looks at the mask in his hands.*)
What has any man to laugh at!
The panting crow by the dry tree
Drags dusty wings. God's mercy brings
The rains — but not to such as he.

MR. ZUSS.   You play your part, I'll say that for you.
In it or out of it, you play.

NICKLES.   You really think I'm playing?

MR. ZUSS.   Aren't you?
Somebody is. Satan maybe.
Maybe Satan's playing you.
Let's begin from the beginning.
Ready!

(*They take their places back to back.*)

Masks!

(*They raise their masks to their faces.*)

Lights!

(*The bulbs go out. Darkness. Silence.*)

A DISTANT VOICE (*in the silence*).   Whence comest thou?

MR. ZUSS.   That's my line.

NICKLES.   I didn't speak it.

MR. ZUSS.   You did. Stop your mischief, won't you?

NICKLES.   Stop your own! Laughing. Shouting.

MR. ZUSS.   Lights, I said!

(*The spotlight throws the enormous shadows on the canvas sky.*)

GODMASK.   Whence comest thou?

SATANMASK.   From going to and fro in the earth . . . (*a choked silence*)
And from walking up and down in it.

GODMASK.   Hast thou considered my servant Job
That there is none like him on the earth,
A perfect and an upright man, one
That feareth God and escheweth evil?

(*The platform lights sink, the masked shadows fading with them, as a
strong light comes on below isolating the table where* J.B. *stands with
his* WIFE *and* CHILDREN.)

Scene 1

(*The platform is in darkness, the table in light.* J.B., *a big, vigorous
man in his middle or late thirties, stands at one end. At the other stands
his wife,* SARAH, *a few years younger than her husband, a fine woman with
a laughing, pretty face but a firm mouth and careful eyes, all New England.
She is looking reprovingly but proudly at her five blond sons and daughters, who shift from foot to foot behind their chairs, laughing and nudging
each other:* DAVID, *13;* MARY, *12;* JONATHAN, *10;* RUTH, *8;* REBECCA, *6.
Two buxom, middle-aged* MAIDS *in frilly aprons stand behind with their
hands folded. The children subside under their mother's eyes.*)

SARAH.   J.B. . . .

(*The heads bow.*)

J.B.   Our Father which art in Heaven
Give us this day our daily bread.
   REBECCA *and* RUTH (*pulling their chairs out, clattering into them*).
      Amenamen.
   THE OLDER CHILDREN (*less haste but no less eagerness*).   Amen!
   THE MAIDS (*wheeling majestically but urgently to go out*).   Amen!
   SARAH (*to* J.B. *over the rattle of dishes and the clatter of talk as she sits
      down*).   That was short and sweet, my darling.
   J.B. (*sitting down*).   What was?
   SARAH.   Grace was.
   J.B. (*cheerfully*).   All the essentials.
   SARAH.   Give? Eat?
   J.B.   Besides they're hungry.
   SARAH.   That's what grace is for — the hunger.
Mouth and meat by grace amazed,
God upon my lips is praised.
   J.B.   You think they stand in need of it — grace?
Look at them!
   SARAH (*beaming*).   Yes! Look! Oh look!

(*The* MAIDS *parade in with a huge turkey on a silver platter, china serving dishes with domed, blue covers, a gravy boat, a bottle of wine in a napkin.*)

MARY.   Papá! Papá! He heard! He heard!

DAVID.   Who did?

RUTH.   Ourfatherwhichartinheaven.

J.B. (*nudging the bird gently with his finger*).   He did indeed. What a bird He sent us!
Cooked to a turn!

RUTH.   He heard! He heard!

JONATHAN.   He heard! He heard! He sent a bird!

SARAH.   That's enough now, children. Quiet!
Your father's counting.

J.B.   Not today.
Not this gobbler. Feed a regiment.
Know what I was thinking, Sally?

SARAH.   What?

J.B.   How beautiful you are.

SARAH.   With your eye on a turkey? I like that!

J.B.   Why not? It's an eye-filling bird. Just look at it.

SARAH.   Someday you might look at me.

J.B.   I'm always looking at you, Sarah. (*He rises, knife and steel in hand, clashing them against each other in a noble rhythm.*)
Everywhere I look I see you.

SARAH (*scornfully*).   You never even see my clothes.

J.B. (*a shout of laughter*).   It's true. I don't. But I see you.

SARAH (*mock indignation*).   J! B!

J.B.   And what's wrong with the turkey?
What's wrong with that bottle of wine, either —
Montrachet or I'll drink the whole of it!
What's wrong with the bird or the wine or with anything —
The day either — what's wrong with the day? (*He begins carving expertly and rapidly.*)
Tell me what day it is.

JONATHAN.   Turkey Day.

MARY.   Cranberry Day.

RUTH.   Succotash Day.

DAVID.   When we all can have white.

JONATHAN.   And giblets to bite.

RUTH.   And two kinds of pie.

JONATHAN.   And squash in your eye.

MARY.   And mashed potatoes with puddles of butter.

JONATHAN.   And gravy and such.

REBECCA.   . . . and . . . and . . .

(*The children are screaming with laughter.*)

SARAH.   Children!

JONATHAN (*gasping*).   And all eat too much.

SARAH.   Children!

Quiet! Quiet every one of you or
Kate will take it all — everything —
Knives, forks, turkey, glasses . . .

J.B.   Not the wine though.

SARAH.   Job, I'm serious.

Answer your father's question, Jonathan.
Tell him what day it is.

JONATHAN (*hushed*).   Thanksgiving.

SARAH.   What day is that?

JONATHAN.   Thanksgiving Day.

DAVID.   The Day we give thanks to God.

MARY.   For His goodness.

SARAH.   And did you, David? Did you, Mary?

Has any one of you thanked God?
Really thanked Him?

(*There is an awkward silence.*)

                    Thanked Him for everything?

(*The children's heads are down.* J.B. *busies himself with his carving.*)

(*Gently.*) God doesn't give all this for nothing:
A good home, good food,
Father, mother, brothers, sisters.
We too have our part to play.
If we do our part He does His,
He always has. If we forget Him
He will forget. Forever. In everything.
David!

(DAVID *raises his head reluctantly.*)

          Did you think of God?

(DAVID *does not reply.*)

Did you think, when you woke in your beds this morning,
Any one of you, of Him?

(*Silence.*)

J.B. (*uncomfortable*).   Of course they did. They couldn't have
     helped it . . .

— Bit of breast for you, Rebecca?

SARAH.   Please, Job. I want them to answer me.

J.B.   How can they answer things like that?
— Gravy? That's the girl. — They know though.
Gift of waking, grace of light,
You and the world brought back together,
You from sleep, the world from night,
By God's great goodness and mercy.
— Wing for Mary? Wing for Mary! —
They know all that. It's hard to talk about.

SARAH (*flushed, an edge to her voice*).   Even if it's hard we have to.
We can't just take, just eat, just — relish!
Children aren't animals.

J.B. (*he goes on with his serving*).   Sweet Sal! Sweet Sal!
Children know the grace of God
Better than most of us. They see the world
The way the morning brings it back to them,
New and born and fresh and wonderful . . .
— Ruth? She's always ravenous. — I remember . . .
— Jonathan? He never is. — when I was
Ten I used to stand behind
The window watching when the light began,
Hidden and watching. — That's for David —
Dark and thin.

MARY.   Why? Why hidden?

J.B.   Hidden from the trees of course.
I must have thought the trees would see me
Peeking at them and turn back.

REBECCA.   Back where?

J.B.   Back where they came from, baby.
— That's for your mother: crisp and gold.

RUTH.   Father, you'd be cold. You didn't.

SARAH (*the edge still there*).   He still does. He lies there watching
Long before I see the light —
Can't bear to miss a minute of it:
Sun at morning, moon at night,
The last red apple, the first peas!
I've never seen the dish he wouldn't
Taste and relish and want more of:
People either!

J.B. (*serving himself with heaping spoons*).   Come on, Sal!
Plenty of people I don't like. (*He sits down. Pours himself a glass of wine.*)
I like their being people though . . . (*sips his wine*).
Trying to be.

SARAH.   You're hungry for them —
Any kind. People and vegetables:
Any vegetables so long as

Leaves come out on them. He loves leaves!

    J.B.   You love them too. You love them better.
Just because you know their names
You think you choose among your flowers:
Well, you don't. You love the lot of them.

    SARAH.   I can't take them as a gift though:
I owe for them. We do. We owe.

    J.B.   Owe for the greening of the leaves?

    SARAH.   Please!
Please, Job. I want the children
Somehow to understand this day, this . . .
Feast . . . (*her voice breaks*).

    J.B.   Forgive me, Sal. I'm sorry — but they
Do. They understand. A little.
Look at me, all of you. Ruth, you answer:
Why do we eat all this, these dishes,
All this food?

(RUTH *twists her napkin.*)

                You say, Rebecca.
You're the littlest of us all.
Why?

    REBECCA.   Because it's good?

    SARAH.   Baby!
Ah, my poor baby!

    J.B.   Why your poor baby?
She's right, isn't she? It is. It's good.

    SARAH.   Good — and God has sent it to us!

    J.B.   She knows that.

    SARAH.   Does she? (*She raises her head sharply.*) Job!
. . . do you?

(*Their eyes meet; hers drop.*)

Oh, I think you do . . . but sometimes —
Times like this when we're together —
I get frightened, Job . . . We have so
Much!

    J.B. (*dead serious*).   You ought to think I do.
Even if no one else should, you should.
Never since I learned to tell
My shadow from my shirt, not once,
Not for a watch-tick, have I doubted
God was on my side, was good to me.
Even young and poor I knew it.
People called it luck: it wasn't.

I never thought so from the first
Fine silver dollar to the last
Controlling interest in some company
I couldn't get — and got. It isn't
Luck.
    MARY.   That's in the story.
    JONATHAN.   Tell the
Story.
    RUTH.   Tell the lucky story.
    REBECCA.   Lucky, lucky, tell the lucky.
    J.B. (*getting to his feet again to carve*).   Tell the story? — Drumstick,
    David?
Man enough to eat a drumstick?
You too, Jonathan?
    REBECCA.   Story, story.
    J.B.   Fellow came up to me once in a restaurant:
"J.B.," he says — I knew him . . .
— Mary, want the other wing? —
"Why do you get the best of the rest of us?"
Fellow named Foley, I think, or Sullivan:
New-come man he was in town.
    MARY.   Your turn, Mother.
    SARAH.   Patrick Sullivan.
    J.B. *and the* CHILDREN (*together in a shouted chant*).   Patrick Sulli-
    van, that's the man!
    J.B.   "Why do you get the best of the rest of us?
I've got as many brains as you.
I work as hard. I keep the lamp lit.
Luck! That's what it is," says Sullivan.
"Look!" I said. "Look out the window!"
"What do you see?" "The street," he tells me.
    J.B. *and the* CHILDREN (*as before*).   "The street?" says I. "The street,"
    says he.
    J.B.   "What do you want me to call it?" he asks me.
"What do I want you to call it?" says I.
"A road," says I. "It's going somewhere."
"Where?" says he. "You say," I said to him.
    J.B. *and the* CHILDREN.   "God knows!" says Mr. Sullivan.
    J.B.   "He does," says I. "That's where it's going.
That's where I go too. That's why."
"Why what?" says he. "I get the best of you:
It's God's country, Mr. Sullivan."
    J.B. *and the* CHILDREN.   "God forbid!" says Mr. Sullivan.
    J.B.   I laughed till I choked. He only looked at me.
"Lucky so-and-so," he yells.
    SARAH.   Poor Mr. Sullivan.
    J.B. (*soberly*).   He was wrong.

It isn't luck when God is good to you.
It's something more. It's like those dizzy
Daft old lads who dowse for water.
They feel the alder twig twist down
And know they've got it and they have:
They've got it. Blast the ledge and water
Gushes at you. And they knew.
It wasn't luck. They knew. They felt the
Gush go shuddering through their shoulders, huge
As some mysterious certainty of opulence.
They couldn't hold it. I can't hold it. (*He looks at Sarah.*)
I've always known that God was with me.
I've tried to show I knew it — not
Only in words.

    SARAH (*touched*). Oh, you have,
I know you have. And it's ridiculous,
Childish, and I shouldn't be afraid . . .
Not even now when suddenly everything
Fills to overflowing in me
Brimming the fulness till I feel
My happiness impending like a danger.
If ever anyone deserved it, you do.

    J.B. That's not true. I don't deserve it.
It's not a question of deserving.

    SARAH. Oh, it is. That's all the question.
However could we sleep at night . . .

    J.B. Nobody *deserves* it, Sarah:
Not the world that God has given us.

(*There is a moment's strained silence, then* J.B. *is laughing.*)

But I believe in it, Sal. I trust in it.
I trust my luck — my life — our life —
God's goodness to me.

    SARAH (*trying to control her voice*). Yes! You do!
I know you do! And that's what frightens me!
It's not so simple as all that. It's not.
They mustn't think it is. God punishes.
God rewards and God can punish.
God is just.

    J.B. (*easy again*). Of course He's just.
He'll never change. A man can count on Him.
Look at the world, the order of it,
The certainty of day's return
And spring's and summer's: the leaves' green —
That never cheated expectation.

    SARAH (*vehemently*). God can reward and God can punish.

Us He has rewarded. Wonderfully.
Given us everything. Preserved us.
Kept us from harm, each one — each one.
And why? Because of you . . .

(J.B. *raises his head sharply.*)

No!
Let me say it! Let me say it!
I need to speak the words that say it —
I need to hear them spoken. Nobody,
Nobody knows of it but me.
You never let them know: not anyone —
Even your children. They don't know.

(J.B. *heaves himself out of his chair, swings round the table, leans over*
SARAH, *his arms around her.*)

J.B.   Eat your dinner, Sal my darling.
We love our life because it's good:
It isn't good because we love it —
Pay for it — in thanks or prayers. The thanks are
Part of love and paid like love:
Free gift or not worth having.
You know that, Sal (*he kisses her*), better than anyone.
Eat your dinner, girl! There's not a
Harpy on the roof for miles.
    SARAH (*reaches up to touch his cheek with her hand*).   Nevertheless
        it's true, Job. You
Can trust your luck because you've earned the
Right to trust it: earned the right
For all of us to trust it.
    J.B. (*back at his own place, filling his glass again*).   Nonsense!
We get the earth for nothing, don't we?
It's given to us, gift on gift:
Sun on the floor, airs in the curtain.
We lie a whole day long and look at it
Crowing or crying in our cribs:
It doesn't matter — crow or cry
The sun shines, the wind blows . . .
— Rebecca! Back for more already?
    REBECCA.   I want the wishbone, please.
    J.B.   Whatever
For?
    REBECCA.   To wish.
    SARAH.   For what, my baby?
    REBECCA.   For the wishbone.
    SARAH (*pulling* REBECCA *into her lap*).   Little pig!
Wishing for wishes!

J.B. (*forking the wishbone onto* REBECCA's *plate*).   That's my girl!

SARAH.   She is! The spit and image of you!
Thinking she can eat the world
With luck and wishes and no thanks!

J.B.   That isn't fair. We're thankful, both of us.

SARAH (*cuddling* REBECCA).   Both! And both the same! Just look
    at you!
A child shows gratitude the way a woman
Shows she likes a pretty dress —
Puts it on and takes it off again —
That's the way a child gives thanks:
She tries the world on. So do you.

J.B.   God understands that language, doesn't He?
He should. He made the colts.

SARAH.   But you're not
Colts! You talk. With tongues. Or ought to.

J.B.   And we use them, don't we, baby?
We love Monday, Tuesday, Wednesday . . .

SARAH (*rocking* REBECCA *on her knees*).   We love Monday, Tuesday,
    Wednesday.
Where have Monday, Tuesday, gone?
Under the grass tree,
Under the green tree,
One by one.

JONATHAN.   Say it again, Mother . . . Mother!

SARAH.   I never said it before. I don't
Know . . . How would you think it would go?
How does it go, Job? You said it.

J.B.   I didn't. I said we loved the world:
Monday, Tuesday, Wednesday, all of it.

SARAH.   How would you think it would go, Jonathan?

(*The words fall into a little tune as she repeats them.*)

                I love Monday, Tuesday, Wednesday.
                Where have Monday, Tuesday, gone?
                Under the grass tree,
                Under the green tree,
                One by one.

                Caught as we are in Heaven's quandary,
                Is it they or we are gone
                Under the grass tree,
                Under the green tree?

                I love Monday, Tuesday, Wednesday
                One by one.

REBECCA (*drowsily*).   Say it again.
SARAH.   Say it again?
JONATHAN.   You say it, Father.
J.B.   To be, become, and end are beautiful.
REBECCA.   That's not what she said at all.
J.B.   Isn't it? Isn't it?
SARAH (*kissing her*).   Not at all.

(*The light fades, leaving the two shadows on the canvas sky.*)

Scene 2

(*The platform. As the platform light comes on, the figures fade from the canvas sky and* MR. ZUSS *and* NICKLES *straighten up, lifting their masks off, stretching, yawning.*)

MR. ZUSS.   Well, that's our pigeon.
NICKLES.   Lousy actor.
MR. ZUSS.   Doesn't really act at all.
NICKLES.   Just eats.
MR. ZUSS.   And talks.
NICKLES.   The love of life!
Poisoning their little minds
With love of life! At that age!
MR. ZUSS.   No!
Some of that, I thought, was beautiful.
NICKLES.   Best thing you can teach your children
Next to never drawing breath
Is choking on it.
MR. ZUSS.   Who said that?
Someone's spoiled philosophy, it sounds like:
Intellectual butter a long war
And too much talking have turned rancid.
I thought he made that small familiar
Feast a true thanksgiving . . . only . . .
NICKLES.   Only what?
MR. ZUSS.   Something went wrong.
NICKLES.   That's what I've been telling you.
MR. ZUSS.   He didn't
Act.
NICKLES.   He can't. He's not an actor.
MR. ZUSS.   I wonder if he knows?
NICKLES.   Knows what?
MR. ZUSS.   Knows that he's in it?
NICKLES.   Is he?

MR. ZUSS.   Certainly.

NICKLES.   How can you tell?

MR. ZUSS.   That's him. That's Job.

He has the wealth, the wife, the children,

Position in the world.

NICKLES.   The piety!

MR. ZUSS.   He loves God, if that's what you're saying.

A perfect and an upright man.

NICKLES.   Piety's hard enough to take

Among the poor who have to practice it.

A rich man's piety stinks. It's insufferable.

MR. ZUSS.   You're full of fatuous aphorisms, aren't you!

A poor man's piety is hope of having:

A rich man has his — and he's grateful.

NICKLES.   Bought and paid for like a waiter's smirk!

You know what talks when that man's talking?

All that gravy on his plate —

His cash — his pretty wife — his children!

Lift the lot of them, he'd sing

Another canticle to different music.

MR. ZUSS.   That's what Satan says — but better.

NICKLES.   It's obvious. No one needs to say it.

MR. ZUSS.   You don't like him.

NICKLES.   I don't have to.

You're the one who has to like him.

MR. ZUSS.   I thought you spoke of Job with sympathy.

NICKLES.   Job on his dung hill, yes. That's human.

That makes sense. But this world-master,

This pious, flatulent, successful man

Who feasts on turkey and thanks God! —

He sickens me!

MR. ZUSS.   Of course he sickens you,

He trusts the will of God and loves — (Swollen with indignation and

    rhetoric. Swoops his mask up from the rail with a magnificent

    gesture, holds it.)

Loves a woman who must sometime, somewhere,

Later, sooner, leave him; fixes

All his hopes on little children

One night's fever or a running dog

Could kill between the dark and day;

Plants his work, his enterprise, his labor,

Here where every planted thing

Fails in its time but still he plants it . . .

NICKLES (nastily).   God will teach him better, won't He?

God will show him what the world is like —

What man's like — the ignoble creature,

Victim of the spinning joke!

MR. ZUSS. Teach him better than he knows!
God will show him God!
   NICKLES (*shrugging*). It's the same
Thing. It hurts.
   MR. ZUSS (*gathering momentum*). God will teach him!
God will show him what God *is* —
Enormous pattern of the steep of stars,
Minute perfection of the frozen crystal,
Inimitable architecture of the slow,
Cold, silent, ignorant sea-snail:
The unimaginable will of stone:
Infinite mind in midge of matter!
   NICKLES. Infinite mush! Wait till your pigeon
Pecks at the world the way the rest do —
Eager beak to naked bum!
   MR. ZUSS. You ought to have your tongue torn out!
   NICKLES. All men should: to suffer silently.
   MR. ZUSS. Get your mask back on! I tell you
Nothing this good man might suffer,
Nothing at all, would make him yelp
As you do. He'd praise God no matter.
   NICKLES (*whispering*). Why must he suffer then?

(*The question catches* MR. ZUSS *with his mask halfway to his face. He lowers it slowly, staring into it as though the answer might be written inside.*)

   MR. ZUSS (*too loud*).   To praise!
   NICKLES (*softly*). He praises now. Like a canary.
   MR. ZUSS (*lifts his mask again*). Well, will you put it on or won't
     you?
   NICKLES. Shall I tell you why? (*Violently.*) To learn!
Every human creature born
Is born into the bright delusion
Beauty and loving-kindness care for him.
Suffering teaches! Suffering's good for us!
Imagine men and women dying
Still believing that the cuddling arms
Enclosed them! They would find the worms
Peculiar nurses, wouldn't they? Wouldn't they? (*He breaks off; picks
     his mask up; goes on in a kind of jigging chant half to himself.*)
What once was cuddled must learn to kiss
The cold worm's mouth. That's all the mystery.
That's the whole muddle. Well, we learn it.
God is merciful and we learn it . . .
We learn to wish we'd never lived!
   MR. ZUSS. This man will not.

NICKLES.   Won't he? Won't he?
Shall I tell you how it ends?
Shall I prophesy? I see our
Smug world-master on his dung heap,
Naked, miserable, and alone,
Pissing the stars. Ridiculous gesture! —
Nevertheless a gesture — meaning
All there is on earth to mean:
Man's last word . . . and worthy of him!

   MR. ZUSS. This man will not. He trusts God.
No matter how it ends, he trusts Him.

   NICKLES. Even when God tests him? — tortures him?

   MR. ZUSS. Would God permit the test unless
He knew the outcome of the testing?

   NICKLES. Then why test him if God knows?

   MR. ZUSS. So Job can see.

   NICKLES.   See what?

   MR. ZUSS.   See God.

   NICKLES. A fine sight from an ash heap, certainly!

   MR. ZUSS. Isn't there anything you understand?
It's from the ash heap God is seen
Always! Always from the ashes.
Every saint and martyr knew that.

   NICKLES. And so he suffers to see God:
Sees God because he suffers. Beautiful!

   MR. ZUSS. Put on your mask. I'd rather look at . . .

   NICKLES. I should think you would! A human
Face would shame the mouth that said that!

(*They put their masks on fiercely, standing face to face. The platform
light fades out. The spotlight catches them, throwing the two masked
shadows out and up. The voices are magnified and hollow, the gestures
formal, as at the end of the Prologue.*)

   GODMASK. Hast thou considered my servant *Job*
That there is none like him on the earth,
A perfect and an upright man, one
That feareth God and escheweth evil?

   SATANMASK (*sardonic*). Doth *Job* fear God for naught?

(*The* GOD-SHADOW *turns away in a gesture of anger.*)

(*Deprecatingly.*) Hast thou not made an hedge about him
And about his house
And about all that he hath on every side?
Thou hast blessed the work of his hands
And his substance is increased.

(*The voice drops.*) *But put forth thine hand now and touch*
All that he hath . . . (*the voice becomes a hissing whisper*) *and he will*
Curse thee to thy face!
    GODMASK (*in a furious, great voice, arm thrown out in a gesture of
        contemptuous commitment*). *Behold!*
All that he hath is in thy power!

(*The* SATAN-SHADOW *bows mockingly; raises its two arms, advancing
until the shadows become one shadow. The light fades. Suddenly, out
of the darkness the* DISTANT VOICE *of the Prologue.*)

    THE DISTANT VOICE. *Only . . .* (*Silence.*)
    GODMASK. *Only*
Upon himself
Put not forth thy hand!

(*Darkness. The crash of a drum; a single stroke. Silence.*)

(NOTE: *The play is conceived and written without breaks, but if re-
cesses in the action are desired one might well be made at this point.*)

Scene 3

(*The table. As the lights come on the two leaning shadows, one
thrown upon the other, are visible on the canvas sky. They fade as the
scene brightens. The table has been pushed to one side as though against
a window in a living room.* SARAH *stands before it arranging flowers in a
bowl.* J.B. *is straddling a chair, watching.*)

    SARAH. Look, Job! Look! Across the street.
Two soldiers.
    J.B.   What about them?
    SARAH.   Only they
Stare so.
    J.B. Stare at what?
    SARAH.   The house.
I think they're drunk . . . A little.
    J.B. (*rises, stands beside her, his arm around her waist*). Plastered!
    SARAH. One of them anyway. He wobbles.
    J.B. That's no wobble. That's a waltz step.
    SARAH. They're crossing over.
    J.B.   They sure are.
    SARAH. What do you think they . . .
    J.B.   Listen!
    SARAH.   Yes . . .
What do you think they want, two soldiers?

J.B. No idea. Johnson will tend to them.

SARAH. I've never seen such staring eyes.

J.B. Glazed. Just glazed.

SARAH. They keep on ringing.
I know what it is, J.B.,
They have some kind of message for us.
David has sent them with a message —
Something about his regiment. They're coming
Every day now, ship by ship.
I hear them in the harbor coming.
He couldn't write and so he sent them.

J.B. Pretty drunk for messengers, those soldiers.

SARAH. What does it matter? They're just boys.
They've just got home. It doesn't matter.

J.B. Johnson's a judge of drunks. He'll handle them.

SARAH. He mustn't send them off. Don't let him!

(There is a commotion outside the canvas door.)

VOICE (*off*). Two young . . . gentlemen to see you.
Friends, they say, of Mr. David.

SARAH. Oh, I knew! I knew! I knew!

VOICE (*off*). That's telling him, Puss-foot!

VOICE (*off*). Puss-face!

(The two MESSENGERS *enter, dressed as soldiers. The* FIRST *is flushed and loud; the* SECOND, *very drunk, pale as bone.)*

J.B. Come in, gentlemen. Come in. Come in.
David's friends are always welcome.
This is David's mother.

SARAH. Won't you sit
Down?

FIRST MESSENGER. What did I tell you, Punk!
Any friends of David's.

SECOND MESSENGER. Any at
All . . .

FIRST MESSENGER. I told you that boy meant it.
What did I say when I see the joint?
That's the number, Punk, I told you.
Old Ten Twenty: that's the number.
(He turns to SARAH.*)* Twenty if you're men, he told us —
Ten for horses' whatses. What the
Hell, he always said: we're friends.

SECOND MESSENGER. Any at all he always . . .

FIRST MESSENGER. Pardon the
Language, lady.

SECOND MESSENGER.   Any a' ...
SARAH.   There!
Sit down.
FIRST MESSENGER.   It's just, we saw the number.
SARAH.   And David asked you to drop in.
FIRST MESSENGER.   Any friend of his, he told us.
Any time.
SECOND MESSENGER.   And we were cold:
A cold, hard march ...
FIRST MESSENGER.   What the
Hell's the matter with you! You drunk?
SARAH.   Sit by the fire, both of you. Where was he?
FIRST MESSENGER.   Where was who?
SARAH.   David.
FIRST MESSENGER.   When?
J.B.   When he told you.
FIRST MESSENGER.   In the mess.
Any friend of his, he told us.
Any time at all. Why?
You think we're lying to you?
J.B.   Certainly
Not.
FIRST MESSENGER.   You think we never knew him?
SARAH.   Of course. Of course you do.
FIRST MESSENGER.   We knew him.
SECOND MESSENGER.   Fumbling among the faces . . . knew him . . .
Night . . . our fingers numb . . .
FIRST MESSENGER.   Will you shut
Up or will I clout you, Big Mouth!
(*To* SARAH.)   That's why we come: because we knew him.
To tell you how we knew him.
SARAH.   Thank you.

(*Silence.*)

SECOND MESSENGER.   How it was with him . . .
FIRST MESSENGER.   Listen, Punk!
SECOND MESSENGER.   How, by night, by chance, darkling . . .
By the dark of chance . . .
FIRST MESSENGER.   He's drunk.
SECOND MESSENGER.   How, the war done, the guns silent . . .
No one knows who gave the order.
FIRST MESSENGER (*raising his voice*).   Like I say, because he said to.
Any friend of his he said to.
Just to tell you we knew David:
Maybe drink to David maybe . . .
SARAH.   Yes! Oh yes! Let's drink to David!
J.B.!

J.B.   Bourbon? Scotch?

FIRST MESSENGER.   Now you're
Cooking! Take your pants off, Punk:
We're in.

SARAH.   That's right. Put your feet up.
Oh, they're not too dirty. David's are
Dirtier. I'm sure of that.

FIRST MESSENGER.   David's feet! I'll say they are.
Look! What's going on here! David's
Feet!

SARAH.   I meant — with all that marching.

FIRST MESSENGER.   I don't get it. Look, it's true
They didn't have the right length lumber:
We did the best we could . . .

J.B. (*starts to his feet*).   What in
God's name are you saying, soldier?

SARAH (*rising*).   What does he mean, the lumber?

(*Silence.*)

FIRST MESSENGER.   You don't
Know? Ain't that the army for you!
(*To the* SECOND MESSENGER.) They don't know. They never told them.

SARAH.   Told us what?

FIRST MESSENGER.   We better go.

SARAH.   No! Please! Please! No!

FIRST MESSENGER.   Come on, we're getting out, you lunkhead.

J.B.   Not until you've told me. Sarah!
Perhaps you'd better, Sarah . . .

SARAH.   Please,
I want to hear it.

FIRST MESSENGER.   Jesus! . . . Jesus! . . .

(*There is a long silence. The* SECOND MESSENGER *turns slowly to* J.B., *his face drunken white, his eyes blank.*)

SECOND MESSENGER.   *I only am escaped alone to tell thee . . .*

(*The focus of light opens to include the platform where* MR. ZUSS *and* NICKLES *stand staring down, their masks in their hands.* MR. ZUSS's *face is expressionless.* NICKLES *wears a twisted grin. The* SECOND MESSENGER's *head falls forward onto his knees.*)

. . . My tongue loosened by drink . . . my thought
Darkened as by wind the water . . .
That day is lost where it befell . . .

SARAH (*she is holding herself by the straining of her clenched hands*).
What is it we were never told?

    J.B.   It isn't
True, you little drunken liar!
It can't be true! It isn't possible! (*Silence. The passion ebbs from* J.B.'s
    voice.)
We had a letter from him. (*Silence. Then, uncertainly.*) After the
End of it we had a letter. . . .

    (NICKLES *jerks a crooked leg over the rail, starts awkwardly down the
ladder, watching intently, peering back up at* MR. ZUSS, *watching.*)

    SECOND MESSENGER.   What shall I say to you . . . ? What I saw . . . ?
What I believe I saw . . . ? Or what
I must have seen . . . and have forgotten?

    SARAH (*a cry*).   David is our son, our son, our son.

    NICKLES (*prompting her from his ladder in a harsh half-whisper*).
That's the tune. He's ours. Go on with it:
Can't be happening to us! Can't be!
God won't let it happen, not to
Our kind, God won't! (*He leers up at* MR. ZUSS.)

    J.B. (*turning* SARAH *away from the* SECOND MESSENGER *into his arms*).
                 Sarah! Sarah!
David's all right. He has to be. He is.
I know he is. The war is over.
It never could have happened — never —
Never in this world.

    NICKLES (*the whisper harsher*).   Couldn't it?
Ask him! Couldn't it? Suppose it did though:
What would the world be made of then?

    SECOND MESSENGER.   I only am escaped alone, companions
Fallen, fallen, fallen . . . the earth
Smell remembers that there was a man.

    SARAH.   Job! He's dead! God has taken him!

    (*The focus of light narrows, is extinguished.*)

Scene 4

    (*Darkness. Silence. Then the crash of a drum. Silence again. Then
two cigarettes are lighted, one high above the stage, one lower. Then
gradually the lights come on, making four circles across the front of the
stage like the circles of sidewalk brightness under street lamps. Where
the cigarettes were lighted* MR. ZUSS *and* NICKLES *are now visible on the
platform rail and the ladder, squatting there like two tramps on the stairs*

of a stoop, turning their heads together one way and then the other, watching, not speaking. After a time the FIRST MESSENGER *comes strolling in from their right, a news camera slung from his neck. The* SECOND *follows with a notebook. They wear battered felt hats with their khaki shirts and trousers. They are followed at a little distance by a stylishly dressed* GIRL.)

GIRL. I don't like it.

FIRST MESSENGER. You'll do fine.

GIRL. I wish I was home in bed with a good
Boy or something. I don't like it.

FIRST MESSENGER. You'll do fine.

GIRL. I won't do fine:
I'm frightened.

FIRST MESSENGER. All you do, you go up to them,
Get them talking, keep them looking.

GIRL. Go up to them yourselves, why don't you?

FIRST MESSENGER. Sure, and get the brush-off. Girl like
You can keep them talking; keep them
Looking, that is. Pretty girl.

GIRL. I don't like it.

SECOND MESSENGER. You'll get used to it.

GIRL. Not where I work. Not Society.
Society page they never die.
Girl gets asked. Girl gets married.
Girl gets photographed in night club.
Girl gets older. Girl gets off.
Never catch them dead on Society.

SECOND MESSENGER. Like the robins.

FIRST MESSENGER. Yeah, like robins.

GIRL. Why the robins?

SECOND MESSENGER. Never see one
Dead.

FIRST MESSENGER. Nor sparrows neither.

SECOND MESSENGER. Either.

FIRST MESSENGER. Never hardly. Must be millions.

SECOND MESSENGER. Hardly ever see one dead.

GIRL. What happens to them?

SECOND MESSENGER. They get over it.

GIRL. Over what?

SECOND MESSENGER. Over being there.

GIRL. All I know is I don't like it.
Keep them talking till a flash bulb
Smacks them naked in the face —
It's horrible!

FIRST MESSENGER. It's genius! Listen, lady!
How do I get the photograph without?

Answer me that. How do I get the
Look a mother's face has maybe
Once in a lifetime: just before
Her mouth knows, when her eyes are knowing?
    GIRL.　I can't do it.
    FIRST MESSENGER.　*She* can't do it!
All you got to do is walk.
Wiggle your can. Keep them looking.
Then he tells them. Then I take them.
Then you beat it. Then that's that.
Except the drink we're going to buy you
Payday evening if you're good —
And if you're not there's lots of liars.
    SECOND MESSENGER.　You don't have to tell them: I do.
    GIRL.　Why do you?
    SECOND MESSENGER.　Because I have to.
I'm the one that has to tell them.
    GIRL.　Why?
    SECOND MESSENGER (*shrugging*).　Oh . . .
    GIRL.　　　　　　　　　　　　Why?
    SECOND MESSENGER.　　　　　　　　　There's always
Someone has to tell them, isn't there?
    GIRL.　Someone else can.
    SECOND MESSENGER.　No. There's always . . . (*he is groping from
       word to word*)
Someone chosen by the chance of seeing,
By the accident of sight,
By stumbling on the moment of it,
Unprepared, unwarned, unready,
Thinking of nothing, of his drink, his bed,
His belly, and it happens, and he sees it . . . (*He winces his eyes shut.*)
Caught in that inextricable net
Of having witnessed, having seen . . .
He alone!
    GIRL (*gently*).　But you don't have to.
(*To the* FIRST MESSENGER.)　Why does he have to?
    SECOND MESSENGER.　　　　　　　　　It was I.
I only. I alone. The moment
Closed us together in its gaping grin
Of horrible incredulity. I saw their
Eyes see mine! We saw each other!
    FIRST MESSENGER.　He has to. He was there. He saw it.
Route Two. Under the viaduct.
Traveling seventy — seventy-five —
Kid was driving them was drunk,
Had to be drunk, just drove into it.
He was walking home. He saw it.

Saw it start to, saw it had to,
Saw it. J.B.'s son. His daughter.
Four in all and all just kids.
They shrieked like kids he said.
   SECOND MESSENGER.   Then silent.
Blond in all that blood that daughter.
   GIRL (*her voice rising*). He can't tell them *that!*
   FIRST MESSENGER.   He has to.
Someone has to. They don't know.
They been out all evening somewhere.
   GIRL (*hysterically*). They don't have to know!
   FIRST MESSENGER.   They have to.

(NICKLES and MR. ZUSS on their perches have seen something off to *their right. They turn their heads together.*)

   GIRL. No!
   FIRST MESSENGER (*looking right, pulling his camera around*). That's
      them. They're coming. Quiet.
   GIRL. I can't do it.
   FIRST MESSENGER (*brutally*). You can do it.

(J.B. and SARAH, *arm in arm, walk slowly into the first circle of light.*
NICKLES and MR. ZUSS *lean forward, their masks dangling from their*
hands.)

   SECOND MESSENGER (*under his breath, staring at them as they come*).
I only, I alone, to tell thee . . .
I who have understood nothing, have known
Nothing, have been answered nothing . . .

(GIRL crosses to meet them with an affected walk, the FIRST MESSENGER
screening himself behind her, the SECOND *following.*)

   GIRL.   Good
Evening! What a pleasant evening!
Back from the theatre so soon?
We're neighbors, don't you know? You've met my
Miffkin walking me each morning:
You know Muff, my purple poodle . . .
Isn't it a pleasant evening!
   SECOND MESSENGER. I'm from the press. There's been an accident
      . . . (*He falters.*)
   FIRST MESSENGER. Four kids in a car. They're dead.
Two were yours. Your son. Your daughter.
Cops have got them in a cab.

Any minute now they'll be here. (*He raises his camera over the* GIRL's
   shoulder.)
   GIRL (*in her own voice, screaming*).   Don't look! Cover your face!
   SARAH (*with scarcely the breath to say it*).   Mary . . . Jonathan . . .

(*The flash.* J.B. *throws his elbow up as if to ward off a blow.* SARAH
does not move.)

J.B.   You bastards!
I'll beat your god-damned brains out . . . (*He lunges after them blinded
   by the flash as they scatter.*) Where have you
Gone?

(SARAH *moves like a sleepwalker through the circles of light, one after
the other, touches a chair, goes down on her knees beside it, clinging to it.*)

Answer me! (*Silence.*) Answer me! (*Silence.*)
   SARAH (*her voice dead*).   It wasn't
They that did it . . .

(J.B. *comes slowly back out of the darkness, sees her, crosses to her.
There is a long silence,* J.B. *looking right and left along the street.*)

          Why did He do it to them?
What had they done to Him — those children . . .
What had they done to Him . . . and we —
What had we done? . . . What had we done?
   J.B.   Don't, Sarah. Don't!

(NICKLES *lights a cigarette, grins back over his shoulder to* MR. ZUSS *in
the handful of yellow glare.*)

               It doesn't
Help to think that.
   SARAH.   Nothing helps! . . .
Nothing can help them now.
   J.B. (*a clumsy gesture*).   It . . . happened . . .
   SARAH (*fiercely*).   Yes, and Who let it happen?
   J.B. (*awkwardly*).   Shall we . . .
Take the good and not the evil?
We have to take the chances, Sarah:
Evil with good. (*Then, in a desperate candor.*) It doesn't mean there
Is no good!
   NICKLES (*in his cracked whisper*).   Doesn't it? Doesn't it?
   MR. ZUSS (*silencing* NICKLES *with his hand, his whisper hardly heard*).
Go on! Go on! That path will lead you.

SARAH (*bitterly*).   When you were lucky it was God!
J.B.   Sticks and stones and steel are chances.
There's no will in stone and steel . . . (*his voice breaks*).
It happens to us . . . (*He drops on his knees beside her.*)
SARAH.   No! . . . Don't touch me!

(*She clings to the chair, motionless, not weeping. The circles of light
fade out.*)

Scene 5

(*The dark diminishes until the white coats of* MR. ZUSS *and* NICKLES *are
visible on the platform.* MR. ZUSS *lifts a padded drumstick.* NICKLES
balances on the rail and starts cautiously down the ladder.)

MR. ZUSS.   Ready?
NICKLES (*cheerfully*).   Got to be, don't they?
MR. ZUSS.   I meant
You.
NICKLES.   They've got no choice. Disaster —
Death — mankind are always ready —
Ready for anything that hurts.
MR. ZUSS.   And you?
NICKLES.   I too! I too!
MR. ZUSS.   Provided
Someone else will bleed the blood
And wipe the blinded eye?
NICKLES.   I watch
Your world go round!
MR. ZUSS.   It must be wearing.
NICKLES.   Oh, it has its compensations.
Even a perfect and an upright man
Learns if you keep turning long enough.
First he thought it wasn't happening —
Couldn't be happening — not to him —
Not with you in the stratosphere tooting the
Blue trombone for the moon to dance.
Then he thought it chanced by chance! (*A dry hiccup of laughter.*)
Childish hypothesis of course
But still hypothesis — a start —
A pair of tongs to take the toad by —
Recognition that it *is* a toad:
Not quite comfort but still comfortable,
Eases the hook in the gills a little:
He'll learn.
MR. ZUSS (*preoccupied*).   Learn what?

NICKLES. Your — purpose for him!

MR. ZUSS. Keep your tongue in your teeth, will you?
(*He notices* NICKLES' *descent on the ladder for the first time.*) Here!
Wait a minute! Wait a
Minute! Where are you off to?

NICKLES. Bit of a
Walk in the earth for my health — or somebody's.
(*Bitterly.*) Up and down in the earth, you know —
Back and forth in it . . .

MR. ZUSS. Leave him alone!

NICKLES. He needs a helping hand: you've seen that —
A nudge from an old professional.

MR. ZUSS. Leave him a'
Lone! He can't act and you know it.

NICKLES. He doesn't have to act. He suffers.
It's an old role — played like a mouth-organ.
Any idiot on earth
Given breath enough can breathe it —
Given tears enough can weep.
All he needs is help to see.

MR. ZUSS. See what?

NICKLES. That bloody drum-stick striking;
See Who lets it strike the drum!

(MR. ZUSS, *whose lifted arm has been slowly falling, raises it abruptly.*)

MR. ZUSS. Wait! (*He starts to strike the drum, stops the stroke in mid-air.*) Wait for me. I'm coming.
Down! Wait! Wait I tell you!

(*The stroke of the drum. The light fades out.*
Out of the dark two circles of light, one on the platform, one on the table. Behind the table are the two* MESSENGERS. *The* FIRST, *wearing a police sergeant's cap, sits on a chair. The* SECOND, *wearing a patrolman's cap, stands beside him.* J.B., *a raincoat over rumpled clothes, stands facing them. Above, on the platform, as on the landing of a stair,* SARAH *stands pulling a dressing gown around her shoulders.* NICKLES *and* MR. ZUSS, *their masks in their hands, straddle a couple of chairs beyond the circle of light which centers on the table.*)

FIRST MESSENGER. Sorry to question you like this.
We got to get the story.

J.B. (*impatiently*). Go on.

FIRST MESSENGER. Turning your house into a . . .

J.B. No. Go on.
It doesn't matter.

SARAH (*toneless*).   Nothing matters but to
Know.
FIRST MESSENGER.   How many children?

(*Silence.*)

J.B.   Two.
FIRST MESSENGER (*writing*).   Girls?
SARAH.   We had two boys.
FIRST MESSENGER (*writing*).   Girls.
Names?
J.B.   Ruth. Rebecca.
SARAH.   Ruth is the
Oldest . . . now.
FIRST MESSENGER.   And you last saw her?
J.B.   Ruth?
SARAH (*her voice rising*).   It's Rebecca is missing!
J.B. (*silencing her*).   He
Knows!
SARAH (*harshly*).   No, it's God that knows!

(*There is an awkward silence. When* SARAH *speaks again her voice is dead.*)

She's the littlest one. She's gone.
FIRST MESSENGER.   How long ago?
SARAH.   Oh . . . hours!
FIRST MESSENGER.   It's three in the morning now.
J.B.   Since seven.
FIRST MESSENGER (*writing*).   And you reported it?
J.B.   Yes.
FIRST MESSENGER.   When?
J.B.   One o'clock. A quarter after.
We looked for her everywhere, of course.
Then we thought — I thought — if somebody . . .
Maybe the telephone would ring.
FIRST MESSENGER.   And you'd do better on your own?
J.B. (*reluctantly*).   Yes.
SARAH (*with rising violence*).   Yes! Yes! Yes!
We believe in our luck in this house!
We've earned the right to! We believe in it . . .
(*Bitterly.*) All but the bad!
NICKLES (*rocking back on his chair*).   That's playing it!
That's playing it! (*He begins to sing in his cracked whisper, beating a
    jazzed rhythm on the back of his mask as though it were a banjo.*)

If God is Will
And Will is well
Then what is ill?
God still?
Dew tell!

(MR. ZUSS *does not seem to hear. He is listening intently to the scene at the table.*)

FIRST MESSENGER.   And nobody telephoned?
J.B.   Nobody telephoned.
FIRST MESSENGER (*writing*).   Dressed? How was she
Dressed?
J.B. (*turning for the first time to look up at* SARAH).   White?
SARAH.   White! You saw her
Glimmering in the twilight.
FIRST MESSENGER (*writing*).   White.
SARAH.   All but her
Shoes.
FIRST MESSENGER (*looks up at the* SECOND).   Her shoes were what?
SARAH.   Red.

(*The* FIRST MESSENGER *looks up again. The* SECOND *turns his face away.*)

FIRST MESSENGER.   Rebecca have a red umbrella?
SARAH.   Parasol.
FIRST MESSENGER.   Little toy umbrella.
SARAH (*startled*).   Parasol. Yes, she might have had one.
FIRST MESSENGER.   You mean she owned one?
SARAH.   Yes. It belonged to a
Big doll we bought her once.
Scarlet silk. It opens and closes.
She kept it when the doll gave out.
She used to take it to bed with her even —
Open and close it.

(*The* FIRST MESSENGER *looks up for the third time at the* SECOND, *whose face, still turned away, is like stone.*)

J.B. (*a step forward*).   You've found the parasol!
SECOND MESSENGER (*not looking at him; a voice without expression or tone*).   What will it tell you? Will it tell you why?
J.B. (*to* FIRST MESSENGER).   I asked you: have you found the parasol?
FIRST MESSENGER.   He's the one. Ask him. He'll tell you.
SECOND MESSENGER (*with difficulty, like a man speaking out of physical pain*).   Can the tooth among the stones make answer? . . .

Can the seven bones reply? . . .
Out in the desert in the tombs
Are potter's figures: two of warriors,
Two of worthies, two of camels,
Two of monsters, two of horses.
Ask them why. They will not answer you . . . (*He brushes his hand heavily
across his face.*)
Death is a bone that stammers . . . a tooth
Among the flints that has forgotten.

    j.b. (*violently*).   Ask him! Has he found the parasol!
    first messenger.   We don't know. He found an umbrella —
Doll's umbrella — red.
    sarah.   Oh, where?
    j.b.   Nothing else? Just the umbrella?
    first messenger (*to* second).   Tell them, will you!

(*The* second messenger *does not move or speak. The* first *shrugs,
looks down at his pencil, rattles it off in a matter-of-fact monotone.*)

                                  Just past midnight
Pounding his beat by the back of the lumberyard
Somebody runs and he yells and they stumble —
Big kid — nineteen maybe —
Hopped to the eyes and scared — scared
Bloodless he could barely breathe.
Constable yanks him up by the britches:
"All right! Take me to it!"
Just a shot in the dark, he was so
Goddam scared there had to be something . . .
Well . . . He took him to it . . . back of the
Lumber trucks beside the track.

    j.b.   Go on.
    first messenger.   She had a toy umbrella.
That was all she had — but shoes:
Red shoes and a toy umbrella.
It was tight in her fist when he found her — still.

    j.b.   Let me see it! The umbrella!
    first messenger.   Constable will show it to you.

(*The* second messenger *takes something wound in newspaper out of
his pocket. He does not look at it or them. The* first messenger *half
opens it, lays it on the table.*)

    sarah.   Oh, my baby! Oh, my baby!

(*The* first messenger *gets out of his chair, stands a moment, awkwardly, goes out. The* second *follows.* j.b. *stands motionless over the*

table. SARAH *hugs her dressing gown around her, rocking herself slowly, her head bowed.*)

NICKLES (*leaning forward toward* J.B., *a wheedling whisper*). Now's the time to say it, mister.

MR. ZUSS. Leave him alone!

J.B. (*touching the parasol*). The Lord giveth . . . (*his voice breaks*) the Lord taketh away!

MR. ZUSS (*rising, whispering*). Go on!
Go on! Finish it! Finish it!

NICKLES.   What should he
Finish when he's said it all?

MR. ZUSS.   Go on!

NICKLES. To what? To where? He's got there, hasn't he?
Now he's said it, now he knows.
He knows Who gives, he knows Who takes now.

(J.B. *stands silent over the parasol.*)

MR. ZUSS. Why won't he play the part he's playing?

NICKLES. Because he isn't.

MR. ZUSS.   Isn't what?

NICKLES. Isn't playing. He's not playing.
He isn't in the play at all.
He's where we all are — in our suffering.
Only . . . (*Turns savagely on* MR. ZUSS.) . . . Now he knows its Name!

(NICKLES *points dramatically toward the canvas sky.* MR. ZUSS's *head tilts back following the gesture. He freezes into immobility.*)

MR. ZUSS. Look! Look up!

NICKLES.   That's your direction.

MR. ZUSS. Look, I say! The staring stars!

NICKLES. Or only lights not meant . . .

(NICKLES *twists his crooked neck, looks sidewise upward. The canvas sky has disappeared into a profound darkness. There seem to be stars beyond it.*)

                            You're mad.
You've lost your mind. You're maundering . . .

(*They rise together, their heads back, peering into the darkness overhead.*)

                              . . . maundering.

MR. ZUSS. Let's get back where we belong.

NICKLES. Go on!
MR. ZUSS.   No; you.
NICKLES.   All right . . . together.

(*They take each other's arm as the light fades.*)

Scene 6

(*Darkness and silence as before. The drum — a great crash and a long roll fading out. A gray light which has no visible source drifts across the stage where tables and chairs are scattered and overturned.* MR. ZUSS *and* NICKLES *are huddled together on their platform peering down.* J.B., *his clothes torn and white with dust, faces what was once the door. The two* MESSENGERS, *wearing steel helmets and brassards, stand there, carrying* SARAH *between them.*)

FIRST MESSENGER.   She said she lived around here somewhere.
This is all there is.
J.B.   Sarah!
FIRST MESSENGER.   Where do you want her?
J.B.   Sarah! Sarah!
FIRST MESSENGER.   On the floor? You got a floor.
You're lucky if you got a floor.

(*They lay her carefully down.* J.B. *takes his torn coat off, rolls it into a pillow, kneels to put it under her head.*)

J.B.   Where was she?
FIRST MESSENGER.   Underneath a wall.
(*Indicating* SECOND MESSENGER.) He heard her underneath a wall
Calling. (*To* SECOND MESSENGER.) Tell him what you heard her . . .
SECOND MESSENGER (*imitating*).   Ruth! . . . Ruth!
FIRST MESSENGER.   Nobody answered:
Nobody could have.

(J.B. *does not look up or speak. The* FIRST MESSENGER *starts toward the door, kicking a fallen chair out of his way.*)

You been down there?
Whole block's gone. Bank block. All of it.
J.B.'s bank. You know. Just gone.
Nothing left to show it ever.
Just the hole.

(SARAH *stirs, opens her eyes.* J.B. *leans over her. She turns away.*)

J.B.'s millions!

That's a laugh now — J.B.'s millions!
All he's got is just the hole.
Plant went too — all of it — everything.
Ask him! Just the hole. He'll tell you.

SARAH (*faintly, her voice following the rhythm of the* SECOND MES-
SENGER). Ruth! . . . Ruth!

FIRST MESSENGER.   He can tell you.
He can tell you what he saw.

SARAH (*tonelessly like a voice counting*). David . . . Jonathan . . .
Mary . . . Ruth . . .
I cannot say the last.

J.B. (*his hand on hers*). Rebecca.

SARAH. David . . . Jonathan . . . Mary . . . Ruth . . .

J.B. (*looking up over his shoulder, to the* SECOND MESSENGER). You
didn't find . . . there wasn't . . .

FIRST MESSENGER.   Tell him.
Tell him what you heard.

SECOND MESSENGER. I heard
Two words. I don't know what they mean.
I have brought them to you like a pair of pebbles
Picked up in a path or a pair of
Beads that might belong to somebody.

J.B. There wasn't . . . anyone beside?

SECOND MESSENGER (*almost a whisper*).   *I only am escaped alone to
tell thee.*

SARAH. David . . . Jonathan . . . Mary . . . Ruth . . .

J.B. Sarah! (*Silence.*) Listen to me! (*Silence.*) Sarah!
Even desperate we can't despair —
Let go each other's fingers — sink
Numb in that dumb silence — drown there
Sole in our cold selves . . . We cannot! . . .
God is there too, in the desperation.
I do not know why God should strike
But God is what is stricken also:
Life is what despairs in death
And, desperate, is life still . . . Sarah!
Do not let my hand go, Sarah!
Say it after me: The Lord
Giveth . . . Say it.

SARAH (*mechanically*). The Lord giveth.

J.B. The Lord taketh away . . .

SARAH (*flinging his hand from hers, shrieking*). Takes!
Kills! Kills! Kills! Kills!

(*Silence.*)

J.B. Blessed be the name of the Lord.

(*The light fades.*)

Scene 7

(Darkness. Silence. Then, out of the dark, MR. ZUSS's voice. It has recovered its confidence and timbre.)

MR. ZUSS.   Well, my friend . . .

(The platform comes into light, MR. ZUSS and NICKLES are still where they were, leaning over, elbows on the rail. They straighten up, stretching.)

                         . . . you see the position.
You see how it all comes out in the end.
Your fears were quite unfounded, weren't they?
   NICKLES *(sourly)*.   My fears for you?
   MR. ZUSS.   For me? . . . For me!
Why should you fear for me?
   NICKLES.   I can't
Think!
   MR. ZUSS.   No, for him.
   NICKLES.   That ham!
   MR. ZUSS.   Ham?
   NICKLES.   Ham!
   MR. ZUSS *(pleasantly)*.   And you've been telling me
Over and over that he isn't in it —
Isn't acting even: only
Living — breathing . . .
   NICKLES.   Man can muff his
Life as badly as his lines and louder.
In it or out of it he's ham.
He wouldn't understand if twenty
Thousand suffocating creatures
Shrieked and tore their tongues out at him
Choking in a bombed-out town. He'd be
Thankful!
   MR. ZUSS *(stiffly)*.   I think he understands it
Perfectly! I think that great
Yea-saying to the world was wonderful —
That wounded and deliberate Amen —
That — affirmation!
   NICKLES.   Affirmation!
Ever watch the worms affirming?
Ever hear a hog's Amen
Just when the knife first hurt? Death is
Good for you! It makes you glisten!
Get the large economy container,

Five for the price of one! You think it's
Wonderful . . . (*He wheels on* MR. ZUSS *in a sudden fury.*) I think it
    stinks!
One daughter raped and murdered by an idiot,
Another crushed by stones, a son
Destroyed by some fool officer's stupidity,
Two children smeared across a road
At midnight by a drunken child —
And all with God's consent! — foreknowledge! —
And he blesses God! (*Points dramatically at the white, calm, uncon-
    cerned mask in* MR. ZUSS'S *hands.*) It isn't decent!
It isn't moral even! It's disgusting!
His weeping wife in her despair
And he beside her on his trembling ham-bones
Praising God! . . . It's nauseating!
    MR. ZUSS. You don't lose gracefully, do you?
    NICKLES (*snarling*).   I don't
Lose.
    MR. ZUSS. You have.
    NICKLES.   That's not the end of it.
    MR. ZUSS. No, but that's the way it ends.
    NICKLES. Could have ended.
    MR. ZUSS.   What do you mean?
    NICKLES. Would have, if God had been content
With this poor crawling victory. He isn't.
Still He must pursue, still follow —
Hunt His creature through his branching veins
With agony until no peace is left him —
All one blazing day of pain:
Corner him, compel the answer.
He cannot rest until He wrings
The proof of pain, the ultimate certainty.
God always asks the proof of pain.
    MR. ZUSS. And Job, in his affliction, gives it.
    NICKLES. No! God overreaches at the end —
Pursues too far — follows too fearfully.
He seals him in his sack of skin
And scalds his skin to crust to squeeze
The answer out, but Job evades Him.
    MR. ZUSS. Who can evade the will of God!
It waits at every door we open.
What does Dante say? His will . . .
    NICKLES. Don't chant that chill equation at me!
    MR. ZUSS. His will: our peace.
    NICKLES. Will was never peace, no matter
Whose will, whose peace.
Will is rule: surrender is surrender.

You make your peace: you don't give in to it.
Job will make his own cold peace
When God pursues him in the web too far —
Implacable, eternal Spider.
A man can always cease: it's something —
A judgment anyway: reject
The whole creation with a stale pink pill.
 MR. ZUSS. World is Will. Job can't reject it.
 NICKLES. God has forgotten what a man can do
Once his body hurts him — once
Pain has penned him in where only
Pain has room to breathe. He learns!
He learns to spit his broken teeth out —
Spit the dirty world out — spit!
 MR. ZUSS. And that's the end of everything — to spit?
 NICKLES. Better than that other end
Of pain, of physical agony, of suffering
God prepares for all His creatures.
 MR. ZUSS. Is it better? Is it better?
Job has suffered and praised God.
Would Job be better off asleep
Among the clods of earth in ignorance?
 NICKLES. Yes, when he suffers in his body:
Yes, when his suffering is him.
 MR. ZUSS. His suffering will praise.
 NICKLES.   It will not.
 MR. ZUSS.   Well,
We still have time to see.
 NICKLES.   Put on your
Mask! You'll see!

(The light has faded but the faces of the actors are still visible.)

MR. ZUSS *(raising his mask)*. Put on your own!

(NICKLES leans over to find it, searching the floor of the platform with his hands. A long silence.)

 THE DISTANT VOICE *(from the silence at length)*. Hast thou con-
  sidered my servant Job
*That there is none like him on the earth,
A perfect and an upright man, one
That feareth God and escheweth evil?*
 NICKLES. Wait a minute! I can't find . . .
 THE DISTANT VOICE *(louder)*. *And still he holdeth fast his integrity . . .*
 NICKLES. Wait a minute, can't you? What the . . .

THE DISTANT VOICE (*almost a whisper*). Although thou movedst me
   against him
To destroy him . . .

(NICKLES *rises, his mask in his two hands. He wheels on* MR. ZUSS *only
to see that* MR. ZUSS *also has his mask in his hands and stands staring up
into the canvas sky. The* DISTANT VOICE *is barely audible.*)

without cause . . .

(*Silence. The two old actors stand side by side, holding their masks,
their heads moving slowly together as they search the dark.*)

NICKLES.   Who said that?

(*Silence.*)

MR. ZUSS.   They want us to go on.
NICKLES.   Why don't you?
MR. ZUSS.   He was asking you.
NICKLES.   Who was?
MR. ZUSS.   He was.
NICKLES.   Prompter probably. Prompter somewhere.
Your lines he was reading, weren't they?
MR. ZUSS.   Yes but . . .
NICKLES (*shouting*).   Anybody there?

(*Silence.*)

MR. ZUSS.   They want us to go on. I told you.
NICKLES.   Yes. They want us to go on . . .
I don't like it.
MR. ZUSS.   We began it.

(*They put their masks on slowly. The lights fade out. The huge
shadows appear on the canvas sky, facing each other.*)

GODMASK.   . . . And still he holdeth fast his integrity
Although thou movedst me against him
To destroy him (*his voice breaks*) . . . without cause.
SATANMASK.   Skin for skin, yea, all that a man
Hath will he give for his life.
But put forth thine hand now and touch
His bone and his flesh
And he will curse thee to thy face.

(*The* GOD-SHADOW *raises its arm again in the formal gesture of contemptuous commitment.*)

GODMASK.   Behold he is in thine hand . . . (GOD-SHADOW *turns away.*
       Silence.) . . . but . . .
Save his life!

(*The two shadows lean together over the earth.*)

(NOTE: *A second break in the action may be made here if it is thought desirable.*)

Scene 8

(*There is no light but the glow on the canvas sky, which holds the looming, leaning shadows. They fade as a match is struck. It flares in* SARAH'S *hand, showing her face, and glimmers out against the wick of a dirty lantern. As the light of the lantern rises,* J.B. *is seen lying on the broken propped-up table, naked but for a few rags of clothing.* SARAH *looks at him in the new light, shudders, lets her head drop into her hands. There is a long silence and then a movement in the darkness of the open door where four women and a young girl stand, their arms filled with blankets and newspapers. They come forward slowly into the light.*)

NICKLES (*unseen, his cracked, cackling voice drifting down from the
       darkness of the platform overhead*).   Never fails! Never fails!
Count on you to make a mess of it!
Every blessed blundering time
You hit at one man you blast thousands.
Think of that Flood of yours — a massacre!
Now you've fumbled it again:
Tumbled a whole city down
To blister one man's skin with agony.

(NICKLES' *white coat appears at the foot of the ladder. The women, in the circle of the lantern, are walking slowly around* J.B. *and* SARAH, *staring at them as though they were figures in a show window.*)

Look at your works! Those shivering women
Sheltering under any crumbling
Heap to keep the sky out! Weeping!
   MRS. ADAMS.   That's him.
   JOLLY ADAMS.   Who's him?
   MRS. ADAMS.   Grammar, Jolly.
   MRS. LESURE.   Who did she say it was?
   MRS. MURPHY.   Him she said it was.
Poor soul!

MRS. LESURE.   Look at them sores on him!

MRS. ADAMS.   Don't look, child. You'll remember them.

JOLLY ADAMS (*proudly*).   Every sore I seen I remember.

MRS. BOTTICELLI.   Who did she say she said it was?

MRS. MURPHY.   Him.

MRS. ADAMS.   That's his wife.

MRS. LESURE.   She's pretty.

MRS. BOTTICELLI.   Ain't she.
Looks like somebody we've seen.

MRS. ADAMS (*snooting her*).   I don't believe you would have seen her:
Picture possibly — her picture
Posed in the penthouse.

MRS BOTTICELLI.   Puce with pants?

MRS. ADAMS.   No, the negligee.

MRS. BOTTICELLI.   The net?

MRS. ADAMS.   The simple silk.

MRS. BOTTICELLI.   Oh la! With sequins?

MRS. MURPHY.   Here's a place to park your poodle —
Nice cool floor.

MRS. LESURE.   Shove over, dearie.

(*The women settle themselves on their newspapers off at the edge of the circle of light. NICKLES has perched himself on a chair at the side. Silence.*)

J.B. (*a whisper*).   God, let me die!

(*NICKLES leers up into the dark toward the unseen platform.*)

SARAH (*her voice dead*).   You think He'd help you
Even to that?

(*Silence. SARAH looks up, turning her face away from J.B. She speaks without passion, almost mechanically.*)

          God is our enemy.

J.B.   No ... No ... No ... Don't
Say that, Sarah!

(*SARAH's head turns toward him slowly as though dragged against her will. She stares and cannot look away.*)

          God has something
Hidden from our hearts to show.

NICKLES.   She knows! She's looking at it!

J.B.   Try to.
Sleep.

SARAH (*bitterly*).   He should have kept it hidden.

J.B.   Sleep now.

SARAH.   You don't have to see it:
I do.

J.B.   Yes, I know.

NICKLES (*a cackle*).   He knows!
He's back behind it and he knows!
If he could see what she can see
There's something else he might be knowing.

J.B.   Once I knew a charm for sleeping —
Not as forgetfulness but gift,
Not as sleep but second sight,
Come and from my eyelids lift
The dead of night.

SARAH.   The dead . . . of night . . .
(*She drops her head to her knees, whispering.*)   Come and from my eye-
     lids lift
The dead of night.

(*Silence.*)

J.B.   Out of sleep
Something of our own comes back to us:
A drowned man's garment from the sea.

(SARAH *turns the lantern down. Silence. Then the voices of the
women, low.*)

MRS. BOTTICELLI.   Poor thing!

MRS. MURPHY.   Poor thing!
Not a chick nor a child between them.

MRS. ADAMS.   First their daughters. Then their sons.

MRS. MURPHY.   First son first. Blew him to pieces.
More mischance it was than war.
Asleep on their feet in the frost they walked into it.

MRS. ADAMS.   Two at the viaduct: that makes three.

JOLLY ADAMS (*a child's chant*).   Jolly saw the picture! the picture!

MRS. ADAMS.   Jolly Adams, you keep quiet.

JOLLY ADAMS.   Wanna know? The whole of the viaduct . . .

MRS. ADAMS.   Never again will you look at them! Never!

MRS. LESURE.   Them magazines! They're awful! Which?

MRS. MURPHY.   And after that the little one.

MRS. BOTTICELLI.   Who in the
World are they talking about, the little one?
What are they talking?

MRS. LESURE.   I don't know.
Somebody dogged by death it must be.

MRS. BOTTICELLI. Him it must be.

MRS. LESURE. Who's him?

MRS. ADAMS. You know who.

MRS. MURPHY. You remember the . . .

MRS. ADAMS. Hush! The child!

MRS. MURPHY. Back of the lumberyard.

MRS. LESURE. Oh! Him!

MRS. MURPHY. Who did you think it was —
Penthouse and negligees, daughters and dying?

MRS. BOTTICELLI. Him? That's him? That millionaire?

MRS. LESURE. Millionaires he buys like cabbages.

MRS. MURPHY. He couldn't buy cabbages now by the look of him:
The rags he's got on.

MRS. BOTTICELLI. Look at them sores!

MRS. MURPHY. All that's left him now is her.

MRS. BOTTICELLI. Still that's something — a good woman.

MRS. MURPHY. What good is a woman to him with that hide on
    him? —
Or he to her if you think of it.

MRS. ADAMS. Don't!

MRS. LESURE. Can you blame her?

MRS. MURPHY. I don't blame her.
All I say is she's no comfort.
She won't cuddle.

MRS. ADAMS. Really, Mrs. . . .

MRS. MURPHY. Murphy, call me. What's got into you? . . .
Nothing recently, I'd hazard.

MRS. ADAMS. You're not so young yourself, my woman.

MRS. MURPHY. Who's your woman? I was Murphy's.

MRS. LESURE. None of us are maids entirely.

MRS. MURPHY. Maids in mothballs some might be.

MRS. ADAMS. Who might?

MRS. MURPHY. You might.

MRS. ADAMS. You! you're . . . historical!

MRS. MURPHY. I never slept a night in history!

MRS. BOTTICELLI. *I* have. Oh, my mind goes back.

MRS. ADAMS. None of that! We have a child here! (*Silence.*)
How far back?

MRS. BOTTICELLI. I often wonder.
Farther than the first but . . . where?

MRS. MURPHY. What do you care? It's lovely country. (*Silence.*)

        Roll a little nearer, dearie,
        Me backside's froze.

MRS. LESURE. You smell of roses.

MRS. MURPHY. Neither do you but you're warm.

MRS. BOTTICELLI.   Well,
Good night, ladies. Good night, ladies.

(*Silence. Out of the silence, felt rather than heard at first, a sound of sobbing, a muffled, monotonous sound like the heavy beat of a heart.*)

J.B.   If you could only sleep a little
Now they're quiet, now they're still.
SARAH (*her voice broken*).   I try. But oh I close my eyes and . . .
Eyes are open there to meet me!
(*Silence. Then in an agony of bitterness.*)   My poor babies! Oh, my
      babies!

(J.B. *pulls himself painfully up, sits huddled on his table in the feeble light of the lamp, his rags about him.*)

J.B. (*gently*).   Go to sleep.
SARAH.   Go! Go where?
If there were darkness I'd go there.
If there were night I'd lay me down in it.
God has shut the night against me.
God has set the dark alight
With horror blazing blind as day
When I go toward it . . . close my eyes.
J.B.   I know. I know those waking eyes.
His will is everywhere against us —
Even in our sleep, our dreams . . .
NICKLES (*a snort of laughter up toward the dark platform*).   Your
will, his peace!
Doesn't seem to grasp that, does he?
Give him another needling twinge
Between the withers and the works —
He'll understand you better.
J.B.   If I
Knew . . . If I knew why!
NICKLES.   If he knew
Why he wouldn't be there. He'd be
Strangling, drowning, suffocating,
Diving for a sidewalk somewhere . . .
J.B.   What I can't bear is the blindness —
Meaninglessness — the numb blow
Fallen in the stumbling night.
SARAH (*starting violently to her feet*).   Has death no meaning? Pain
      no meaning?
(*She points at his body.*)   Even these suppurating sores —
Have they no meaning for you?

NICKLES.   Ah!
J.B. (*from his heart's pain*).   God will not punish without cause.

(NICKLES *doubles up in a spasm of soundless laughter.*)

God is just.
    SARAH (*hysterically*).   God is just!
If God is just our slaughtered children
Stank with sin, were rotten with it! (*She controls herself with difficulty,
    turns toward him, reaches her arms out, lets them fall.*)
Oh, my dear! my dear! my dear!
Does God demand deception of us? —
Purchase His innocence by ours?
Must we be guilty for Him? — bear
The burden of the world's malevolence
For Him who made the world?
    J.B.   *He*
Knows the guilt is mine. He must know:
Has He not punished it? He knows its
Name, its time, its face, its circumstance,
The figure of its day, the door,
The opening of the door, the room, the moment . . .
    SARAH (*fiercely*).   And you? Do you? You do not know it.
Your punishment is all you know. (*She moves toward the door, stops,
    turns.*)
I will not stay here if you lie —
Connive in your destruction, cringe to it:
Not if you betray my children . . .
I will not stay to listen . . . They are
Dead and they were innocent: I will not
Let you sacrifice their deaths
To make injustice justice and God good!
    J.B. (*covering his face with his hands*).   My heart beats. I cannot
        answer it.
    SARAH.   If you buy quiet with their innocence —
Theirs or yours . . . (*softly*) I will not love you.
    J.B.   I have no choice but to be guilty.
    SARAH (*her voice rising*).   We have the choice to live or die,
All of us . . . curse God and die . . .

(*Silence.*)

    J.B.   God is God or we are nothing —
Mayflies that leave their husks behind —
Our tiny lives ridiculous — a suffering
Not even sad that Someone Somewhere

Laughs at as we laugh at apes.
We have no choice but to be guilty.
God is unthinkable if we are innocent.

(SARAH *turns, runs soundlessly out of the circle of light, out of the door. The women stir.* MRS. MURPHY *comes up on her elbow.*)

MRS. MURPHY. What did I say? I said she'd walk out on him.
MRS. LESURE. She did.
MRS. BOTTICELLI. Did she?
MRS. MURPHY. His hide was too much for her.
MRS. BOTTICELLI. His hide or his heart.
MRS. MURPHY. The hide comes between.
MRS. BOTTICELLI. The heart is the stranger.
MRS. MURPHY. Oh, strange!
It's always strange the heart is: only
It's the skin we ever know.
J.B. (*raising his head*). Sarah, why do you not speak to me? . . .
Sarah!

(*Silence.*)

MRS. ADAMS. Now he knows.
MRS. MURPHY. And he's alone now.

(J.B.'s *head falls forward onto his knees. Silence. Out of the silence his voice in an agony of prayer.*)

J.B. *Show me my guilt, O God!*
NICKLES. His
Guilt! His! You heard that, didn't you?
He wants to feel the feel of guilt —
That putrid poultice of the soul
That draws the poison in, not out —
Inverted catheter! You going to show him? (*Silence. Rises, moves toward the ladder.*)
Well? You going to show him . . . Jahveh? (*Silence. Crosses to the ladder's foot.*)
Where are those cold comforters of yours
Who justify the ways of God to
Job by making Job responsible? —
Those three upholders of the world —
Defenders of the universe — where are they? (*Silence. Starts up the ladder. Stops. The jeering tone is gone. His voice is bitter.*)
Must be almost time for comfort! . . .

(NICKLES *vanishes into the darkness above. The light fades.*)

Scene 9

(*Darkness.*)

J.B.'s VOICE.   *If I had perished from the womb, not having
Been . . .*

(*A light without source rises slowly like the light at evening which en-
larges everything. The canvas walls dissolve into distance, the canvas sky
into endlessness. The platform has been pushed away to the side until
only the ladder is visible. The women and the child are huddled together
like sleeping figures on a vast plain.* J.B. *is alone in an enormous loneliness. Out of that seeming distance the Three Comforters come shuffling
forward dressed in worn-out clothing.* ZOPHAR, *a fat, red-faced man wears
the wreck of a clerical collar.* ELIPHAZ, *lean and dark, wears an intern's
jacket which once was white.* BILDAD *is a squat, thick man in a ragged
wind-breaker. The women do not see them, but* JOLLY ADAMS *sits suddenly up clapping her hands to her mouth.* J.B., *his head on his arms,
sees nothing.*)

J.B.   Death cannot heal me . . . Death
Will leave my having been behind it
Like a bear's foot festering in a trap . . .
    JOLLY ADAMS (*her voice rising word by word to a scream*).   Look!
      Look! Look! Look!
Mother! Mother!

(*The women pull themselves up. The Three Comforters shuffle on,
squat in the rubbish around* J.B.: ZOPHAR *lighting the stub of a fat,
ragged cigar;* ELIPHAZ *lighting a broken pipe;* BILDAD *lighting a crumpled
cigarette.*)

    MRS. MURPHY.   Agh, the scavengers!
    MRS. BOTTICELLI.   Three old pokey crows they look like.
    MRS. MURPHY.   They are, too. It's the smell of the suffering.
See that leather-backed old bucket? —
Kind of character you hear from
Sundays in a public park
Pounding the hell out of everything . . . you know.
    MRS. BOTTICELLI.   I know. Wall Street. Bakers. Bankers.
    MRS. LESURE.   All the answers in a book.
    MRS. BOTTICELLI.   Russkys got them all — the answers.
    MRS. MURPHY.   Characters like that, they smell the
Human smell of heartsick misery
Farther than a kite smells carrion.
    MRS. LESURE.   Who's the collar?

MRS. MURPHY.   Some spoiled priest.

MRS. BOTTICELLI.   They can smell it farther even.

MRS. LESURE.   Not as far as dead-beat doctors:
They're the nosies.

MRS. MURPHY.   Let them nose!
(*A tremendous yawn.*) Ohhh, I'm halfway over . . . drownding
Down and down . . . I hear the seagulls
Singing soundings in the sea . . .

(*She lets herself fall back on her newspapers. The others follow one
by one.*)

JOLLY ADAMS.   I don't hear them.

MRS. BOTTICELLI.   Pound your ears.

MRS. LESURE.   Slip your moorings . . . Oh, I'm numb.

MRS. MURPHY.   Come alongside, dear.

MRS. LESURE.   I'm coming.

MRS. BOTTICELLI.   That doctor one, he makes me creep.

MRS. MURPHY.   Keep your thumb on your thoughts or he'll diddle
them.

MRS. BOTTICELLI.   Let him pry: he'll lose an eyeball.

MRS. LESURE.   He's a peeper. Watch your sleep.

MRS. MURPHY.   Who was she, all gore, all story,
Dabbled in a deep blood sea,
And what she washed in, that was she?

MRS. LESURE (*from her dream*).   Some queen of Scotland . . .

MRS. MURPHY.   Queen of Scones . . .

(*A long silence. The Three Comforters squat smoking and waiting.
At length* J.B. *pulls himself painfully up to kneel on his table, his face
raised.*)

J.B. (*a whisper*).   God! My God! My God! What have I
Done?

(*Silence.*)

BILDAD (*removing his cigarette*).   Fair question, Big Boy.
Anyone answer you yet? No answer?

ZOPHAR (*removing his cigar*).   That was answered long ago —
Long ago.

ELIPHAZ (*knocking out his pipe*).   In dreams are answers.
How do your dreams go, Big Boy? Tell!

J.B. (*peering*).   Is someone there? Where? I cannot
See you in this little light;
My eyes too fail me . . . (*Silence.*) Who is there? (*Silence.*)
I know how ludicrous I must look,

Covered with rags, my skin pustulant . . . (*Silence.*)
I know . . . (*Silence.*) I know how others see me. (**A** *long silence.*)
Why have you come?

    BILDAD (*a coarse laugh*). For comfort, Big Boy.
Didn't you ring?

    ZOPHAR (*a fat laugh*). That's it: for comfort!

    ELIPHAZ (*a thin laugh*). All the comfort you can find.

    BILDAD. All the kinds of.

    ELIPHAZ.   *All* the comforts.

    ZOPHAR. You called us and we came.

    J.B.   I called
God.

    BILDAD. Didn't you!

    ELIPHAZ.   Didn't you just!

    ZOPHAR. Why should God reply to you
From the blue depths of His Eternity?

    ELIPHAZ. Blind depths of His Unconsciousness?

    BILDAD. Blank depths of His Necessity?

    ZOPHAR. God is far above in Mystery.

    ELIPHAZ. God is far below in Mindlessness.

    BILDAD. God is far within in History —
Why should God have time for you?

    J.B. The hand of God has touched me. Look at me!
Every hope I ever had,
Every task I put my mind to,
Every work I've ever done
Annulled as though I had not done it.
My trace extinguished in the land,
My children dead, my father's name
Obliterated in the sunlight everywhere . . .
Love too has left me.

    BILDAD.   Love! (*A great guffaw.*)
What's love to Him? One man's misery!

    J.B. (*hardly daring*). If I am innocent . . . ?

    BILDAD (*snort of jeering laughter*).   Innocent! Innocent!
Nations shall perish in their innocence.
Classes shall perish in their innocence.
Young men in slaughtered cities
Offering their silly throats
Against the tanks in innocence shall perish.
What's your innocence to theirs?
God is History. If you offend Him
Will not History dispense with you?
History has no time for innocence.

    J.B. God is just. We are not squeezed
Naked through a ridiculous orifice
Like bulls into a blazing ring

To blunder there by blindfold laws
We never learn or can, deceived by
Stratagems and fooled by feints,
For sport, for nothing, till we fall
We're pricked so badly.
    BILDAD (*all park-bench orator*).   Screw your justice!
History is justice! — time
Inexorably turned to truth! —
Not for one man. For humanity.
One man's life won't measure on it.
One man's suffering won't count, no matter
What his suffering; but All will.
At the end there will be justice! —
Justice for All! Justice for everyone!
(*Subsiding.*) On the way — it doesn't matter.
    J.B. Guilt matters. Guilt must always matter.
Unless guilt matters the whole world is
Meaningless. God too is nothing.
    BILDAD (*losing interest*).   You may be guiltier than Hell
As History counts guilt and not
One smudging thumbprint on your conscience.
Guilt is a sociological accident:
Wrong class — wrong century —
You pay for your luck with your licks, that's all.
    ELIPHAZ (*has been fidgeting. Now he breaks in like a professor in a seminar, poking a forefinger at the air*).   Come! Come! Come! Guilt
        is a
Psychophenomenal situation —
An illusion, a disease, a sickness:
That filthy feeling at the fingers,
Scent of dung beneath the nails . . .
    ZOPHAR (*outraged, flushed, head thrown back*).   Guilt is illusion?
        Guilt is reality! —
The one reality there is!
All mankind are guilty always!
    BILDAD (*jeering*).   The Fall of Man it felled us all!
    J.B. (*voice breaks through the squabbling with something of its old authority*).   No doubt ye are the people
And wisdom shall die with you! I am
Bereaved, in pain, desperate, and you mock me!
There was a time when men found pity
Finding each other in the night:
Misery to walk with misery —
Brother in whose brother-guilt
Guilt could be conceived and recognized.
We have forgotten pity.

ELIPHAZ.   No.
We have surmounted guilt. It's quite,
Quite different, isn't it? You see the difference.
Science knows now that the sentient spirit
Floats like the chambered nautilus on a sea
That drifts it under skies that drive:
Beneath, the sea of the subconscious;
Above, the winds that wind the world.
Caught between that sky, that sea,
Self has no will, cannot be guilty.
The sea drifts. The sky drives.
The tiny, shining bladder of the soul
Washes with wind and wave or shudders
Shattered between them.
        ZOPHAR.   Blasphemy!
        BILDAD.   Bullshit!
        ELIPHAZ (*oblivious*).   There is no guilt, my man. We all are
Victims of our guilt, not guilty.
We kill the king in ignorance: the voice
Reveals: we blind ourselves. At our
Beginning, in the inmost room,
Each one of us, disgusting monster
Changed by the chilling moon to child,
Violates his mother. Are we guilty?
Our guilt is underneath the Sybil's
Stone: not known.
        J.B. (*violently*).   I'd rather suffer
Every unspeakable suffering God sends,
Knowing it was I that suffered,
I that earned the need to suffer,
I that acted, I that chose,
Than wash my hands with yours in that
Defiling innocence. Can we be men
And make an irresponsible ignorance
Responsible for everything? I will not
Listen to you! (*Pulls his rags over his head.*)
        ELIPHAZ (*shrugging*).   But you will. You will.
        ZOPHAR.   Ah, my son, how well you said that!
How well you said it! Without guilt
What is a man? An animal, isn't he?
A wolf forgiven at his meat,
A beetle innocent in his copulation.
What divides us from the universe
Of blood and seed, conceives the soul in us,
Brings us to God, but guilt? The lion
Dies of death: we die of suffering.

The lion vanishes: our souls accept
Eternities of reparation.
But for our guilt we too would vanish,
Bundles of corrupting bones
Bagged in a hairless hide and rotting.
Happy the man whom God correcteth!
He tastes his guilt. His hope begins.
He is in league with the stones in certainty.

  J.B. (*pulls his rags from his head, drags himself around toward the voice*). *Teach me and I will hold my tongue.*
Show me my transgression.

  ZOPHAR (*gently*).   No.
No, my son. You show me.

(*He hunches forward dropping his voice.*)   Search your inmost heart!
  Question it!
Guilt is a deceptive secret,
The labor often of years, a work
Conceived in infancy, brought to birth
In unpredictable forms years after:
At twelve the palpable elder brother;
At seventeen, perhaps, the servant
Seen by the lamp by accident . . .

  J.B. (*urgently, the words forced from him*).   My
Sin! Teach me my sin! My wickedness!
Surely iniquity that suffers
Judgment like mine cannot be secret.
Mine is no childish fault, no nastiness
Concealed behind a bathroom door,
No sin a prurient virtue practices
Licking the silence from its lips
Like sugar afterwards. Mine is flagrant,
Worthy of death, of many deaths,
Of shame, loss, hurt, indignities
Such as these! Such as these!
Speak of the sin I must have sinned
To suffer what you see me suffer.

  ZOPHAR.   Do we need to name our sins
To know the need to be forgiven?
Repent, my son! Repent!

  J.B. (*an agony of earnestness*).   I sit here
Such as you see me. In my soul
I suffer what you guess I suffer.
Tell me the wickedness that justifies it.
Shall I repent of sins I have not
Sinned to understand it? Till I
Die I will not violate my integrity.

ZOPHAR (*a fat chuckle*). Your integrity! Your integrity!
What integrity have you? —
A man, a miserable, mortal, sinful,
Venal man like any other.
You squat there challenging the universe
To tell you what your crime is called,
Thinking, because your life was virtuous,
It can't be called. It can. Your sin is
Simple. You were born a man!

    J.B. What is my fault? What have I done?

    ZOPHAR (*thundering*). What is your fault? Man's heart is evil!
What have you done? Man's will is evil.
Your fault, your sin, are heart and will:
The worm at heart, the wilful will
Corrupted with its foul imagining.

    J.B. (*crouches lower in his rags. Silence*). Yours is the cruelest comfort of them all,
Making the Creator of the Universe
The miscreator of mankind —
A party to the crimes He punishes . . .
Making my sin . . . a horror . . . a deformity . . .

    ZOPHAR (*collapsing into his own voice*). If it were otherwise we could
not bear it . . .
Without the fault, without the Fall,
We're madmen: all of us are madmen . . . (*He sits staring at his hands,
then repeats the phrase.*)

	Without the Fall
	We're madmen all.
	We watch the stars
	That creep and crawl . . .
BILDAD.	Like dying flies
	Across the wall
	Of night . . .
ELIPHAZ.	and shriek . . .
	And that is all.
ZOPHAR.	Without the Fall . . .

(*A long silence.*)

    J.B. (*out of the silence at last, barely audible*). God, my God, my
God, answer me! (*Silence. His voice rises.*)
I cry out of wrong but I am not heard . . .
I cry aloud but there is no judgment.
(*Silence. Violently.*) Though He slay me, yet will I trust in Him . . .

(*Silence. His voice drops.*) But I will maintain my own ways before
    Him . . .
(*Silence. The ancient human cry.*) Oh, that I knew where I might find
    Him! —
That I might come even to His seat!
I would order my cause before Him
And fill my mouth with arguments.

    (*There is a rushing sound in the air.*)

                              Behold,
I go forward but He is not there,
Backward, but I cannot perceive Him . . .

    (*Out of the rushing sound, the* DISTANT VOICE; J.B. *cowers as he hears
it, his rags over his head.*)

    THE DISTANT VOICE.   Who is this that darkeneth counsel
By words without knowledge? . . . Where wast thou
When I laid the foundations of the earth . . .
When the morning stars sang together
And all the sons of God shouted for
Joy? Hast thou commanded the morning?
Hast thou entered into the springs of the sea
Or hast thou walked in the search of the depth?
Have the gates of death been opened unto thee?
Where is the way where light dwelleth?
And as for darkness, where is the place thereof?
Hast thou entered into the treasures of the snow?
By what way is the light parted
Which scattereth the east wind upon the earth?
Canst thou bind the sweet influences of the Pleiades?
Hast thou given the horse strength?
Hast thou clothed his neck with thunder?
He saith among the trumpets, Ha, ha;
He smelleth the battle afar off,
The thunder of the captains and the shouting.
Doth the eagle mount up at thy command?
Her eyes behold afar off.
Her young ones also suck up blood:
And where the slain are, there is she . . .

    (*The rushing sound dies away. The Three Comforters stir uneasily,
peering up into the darkness. One by one they rise.*)

BILDAD.   The wind's gone round.
ZOPHAR.   It's cold.

BILDAD.   I told you.

ELIPHAZ.   I hear the silence like a sound.

ZOPHAR.   Wait for me!

BILDAD.   The wind's gone round.

(*They go out as they came. Silence.* J.B. *sits motionless, his head covered. The rushing sound returns like the second, stronger gust of a great storm. The* VOICE *rises above it.*)

THE DISTANT VOICE.   *Shall he that contendeth with the Almighty instruct*
Him? . . .

(*The rushing sound dies away again. The women sit up, huddle together.*)

JOLLY ADAMS (*screaming*).   Mother! Mother! what was
That?

MRS. ADAMS.   The wind, child. Only the wind.
Only the wind.

JOLLY ADAMS.   I heard a word.

MRS. ADAMS.   You heard the thunder in the wind.

JOLLY ADAMS (*drowsy*).   Under the wind there was a word . . .

(MRS. ADAMS *picks her up. The women gather their newspapers and blankets and stumble out into the darkness through the door. For the third time the rushing sound returns.*)

THE DISTANT VOICE.   *He that reproveth God, let him answer it!*

J.B.   *Behold, I am vile; what shall I answer thee?*
I will lay mine hand upon my mouth.

THE DISTANT VOICE.   *Gird up thy loins like a man:*
I will demand of thee, and declare thou unto me.

(J.B. *pulls himself painfully to his knees.*)

Wilt thou disannul my judgment?

(J.B. *does not answer.*)

Wilt thou condemn
Me that thou mayest be righteous?
Hast thou an arm like God? Or canst thou
Thunder with a voice like Him?
Deck thyself now with majesty and excellency
And array thyself with glory and beauty . . .

Then will I also confess unto thee
That thine own right hand can save thee.
    J.B. (*raises his bowed head. Gently*). *I know that thou canst do
      everything . . .*

(*The rushing sound dies away.*)

*And that no thought can be withholden from thee.
Who is he that hideth counsel without knowledge?
Therefore have I uttered that I understood not:
Things too wonderful for me, which I knew not.
Hear, I beseech thee, and I will speak: . . .* (*Silence.*)
*I have heard of thee by the hearing of the ear . . .
But now . . .* (*his face is drawn in agony*) *. . . mine eye seeth thee!* (*He
    bows his head. His hands wring each other.*) *Wherefore
I abhor myself . . . and repent . . .*

(*The light fades.*)

Scene 10

(*The platform. As the lights come on the two actors turn violently
away from each other, tearing their masks off.*)

    NICKLES (*with a gesture of disgust, skims his into a corner*). Well,
      that's that!
    MR. ZUSS.   That's . . . that!

(*Silence.*)

    NICKLES (*looks cautiously around at* MR. ZUSS). What's the matter
      with you?
    MR. ZUSS.   Nothing.
    NICKLES.   You don't look pleased.
    MR. ZUSS.   Should I?
    NICKLES.   Well,
You were right, weren't you?
    MR. ZUSS (*too loud*).   Of course I was right.
    NICKLES (*too soft*).   Anyway, you were magnificent.
    MR. ZUSS.   Thank you. (*Looks
    at the mask in his hands: puts it down as though it had stung him.
    Silence. Pretends to be busy with a shoelace.*)
Why did you say that?
    NICKLES.   What did I say?
    MR. ZUSS.   Why did you say it like that?
    NICKLES.   Like what?

MR. ZUSS (*imitating*). "Anyway!" . . . "Anyway, you were magnificent!"

NICKLES. You know. "Anyway." Regardless.

MR. ZUSS.   Regardless of
What?

NICKLES. Now, wait a minute! Wait a
Minute! You were magnificent. I said so.

MR. ZUSS. Go on. Finish it.

NICKLES.   Finish what?

MR. ZUSS. Regardless of . . . ?

NICKLES. . . .   . . . being right, of course.
What's got into you, my friend? What's eating you?
Being magnificent and being right
Don't go together in this universe.
It's being wrong — a desperate stubbornness
Fighting the inextinguishable stars —
Excites imagination. You were
Right. And knew it. And were admirable.
Notwithstanding! (*snickering*) anyway! (*a snarl*) regardless!

MR. ZUSS. I knew you noticed.

NICKLES.   Of course I noticed.
What lover of the art could fail to! (*Something in* MR. ZUSS'S *expression stops him.*) Noticed
What?

MR. ZUSS. That tone! That look he gave me!

NICKLES. He misconceived the part entirely.

MR. ZUSS. Misconceived the world! Buggered it!

NICKLES. Giving in like that! Whimpering!

MR. ZUSS. Giving in! You call that arrogant,
Smiling, supercilious humility
Giving in to God?

NICKLES.   Arrogant!
His suppurating flesh — his children —
Let's not talk about those children —
Everything he ever had!
And all he asks is answers of the universe:
All he asks is reasons why —
Why? Why? And God replies to him:
God comes whirling in the wind replying —
What? That God knows more than he does.
That God's more powerful than he! —
Throwing the whole creation at him!
Throwing the Glory and the Power!
What's the Power to a broken man
Trampled beneath it like a toad already?
What's the Glory to a skin that stinks!
And this ham actor! — what does *he* do?

How does he play Job to that?
(*Attitude.*) "Thank you!" "I'm a worm!" "Take two!"
Plays the way a sheep would play it —
Pious, contemptible, goddam sheep
Without the spunk to spit on Christmas!

(MR. ZUSS *has watched* NICKLES' *mounting rage in silence, staring at him.* NICKLES *breaks off, shuffles, looks at* MR. ZUSS, *crosses to the ladder, swings a leg across the rail.*)

Well . . . (*he swings the other over*) . . . you said he would . . . (*He starts down.*) You're right. (*Another rung.*)
I'm wrong. (*Another.*) You win. (*Another.*) God always wins. (*He peers down into the dark under the platform.*)
Where did I put that . . . popcorn?
MR. ZUSS.   Win!
Planets and Pleiades and eagles —
Screaming horses — scales of light —
The wonder and the mystery of the universe —
The unimaginable might of things —
Immeasurable knowledge in the waters somewhere
Wandering their ways — the searchless power
Burning on the hearth of stars —
Beauty beyond the feel of fingers —
Marvel beyond the maze of mind —
The whole creation! And God showed him!
God stood stooping there to show him!
Last Orion! Least sea shell! . . .
And what did Job do? (*Has worked himself up into a dramatic fury equaling* NICKLES'.) Job . . . just . . . sat! (*Silence.*)
Sat there! (*Silence.*) Dumb! (*Silence.*) Until it ended!
Then! . . . you heard him! (*Chokes.*) Then, he calmed me!
Gentled me the way a farmhand
Gentles a bulging, bugling bull!
Forgave me! . . . for the world! . . . for everything!
    NICKLES (*poking around in the shadow under the platform*). Nonsense! He repented, didn't he —
The perfect and the upright man!
He repented!
    MR. ZUSS. That's just it!
He repented. It was him —
Not the fear of God but him!
    NICKLES. Fear? Of course he feared. Why wouldn't he?
God with all those stars and stallions!
He with little children's bones!
    MR. ZUSS (*pursuing his mounting indignation*). . . . As though Job's suffering were justified

Not by the Will of God but Job's
Acceptance of God's will . . .
    NICKLES.   Well,
What did you hope for? Hallelujahs?
    MR. ZUSS (*not hearing*).   . . . In spite of everything he'd suffered!
In spite of all he'd lost and loved
He understood and he forgave it! . . .
    NICKLES (*a contemptuous snort as he straightens to face* MR. ZUSS *on
        the platform*).   What other victory could God win?
The choice is swallowing this swill of world
Or vomiting in the trough. Job swallowed it,
That's your triumph! — that he swallowed it.
    MR. ZUSS.   . . . He'd heard of God and now he saw Him!
Who's the judge in judgment there?
Who plays the hero, God or him?
Is God to be *forgiven?*
    NICKLES.   Isn't he?
Job was innocent, you may remember . . .
(*Silence. A nasty singsong.*) The perfect and the upright man!
    MR. ZUSS (*deflated*).   Don't start that again! I'm sick of it.
    NICKLES.   You are!
    MR. ZUSS.   *I* am. Sick to death. (*Swinging his leg over the
    rail and starting down the ladder.*)
I'd rather sell balloons to children . . .
Lights! . . . (*He shouts.*) Turn those lights on, can't you?
Want to see me break my neck?

(*The platform lights go out. Total darkness.*)

(*Louder.*) Lights! Lights! That's not the end of it.
    NICKLES (*in the darkness*).   Why isn't that the end? It's over.
Job has chosen how to choose.
You've made your bow. You want another?

(*The dangling light bulbs come feebly on. By their light* J.B. *can still
be seen kneeling on his broken table.* MR. ZUSS *and* NICKLES *crawl under
the platform after their traps. Their voices come from the shadow,
punctuated by grunts and wheezes.*)

    MR. ZUSS.   You know as well as I there's more . . .
There's always one more scene no matter
Who plays Job or how he plays it . . .
God restores him at the end.
    NICKLES (*a snort*).   God restores us all. That's normal.
That's God's mercy to mankind . . .
We never asked Him to be born . . .
We never chose the lives we die of . . .

They beat our rumps to make us breathe . . .
But God, if we have suffered patiently,
Borne it in silence, stood the stench,
Rewards us . . . gives our dirty selves back.

MR. ZUSS (*emerges in his white jacket, adjusting his cap*). Souls back!

NICKLES. •Selves back! Dirty selves
We've known too well and never wanted.

MR. ZUSS. That's not this play.

NICKLES (*backs out with his jacket and cap and tray; puts them on*).
Hell it isn't.

MR. ZUSS (*tightens his balloon belt*). God restores him *here*. On earth.

NICKLES (*balancing his tray*). So Job gets his in cash. That's generous.
What percentage off for cash?

MR. ZUSS. Gets all he ever had and more —
Much more.

NICKLES (*cheerfully ironic*). Sure. His wife. His children!

MR. ZUSS (*embarrassed*). He gets his wife back, and the children . . .
Follow in nature's course.

NICKLES (*who has stooped to pick up a bag of popcorn, straightens
slowly, stares at* MR ZUSS. *Harshly*). You're lying.

MR. ZUSS. I'm not lying.

NICKLES. I say you're lying.

MR. ZUSS. Why should I lie? It's in the Book.

NICKLES (*jeering*). Wife back! Balls! He wouldn't touch her.
He wouldn't take her with a glove!
After all that filth and blood and
Fury to begin again! . . .
This fetid earth! That frightened Heaven
Terrified to trust the soul
It made with Its own hands, but testing it,
Tasting it, by trial, by torture,
Over and over till the last, least town
On all this reeling, reeking earth
Stinks with a spiritual agony
That stains the stones with excrement and shows
In shadow on each greasy curtain!
After life like his to take
The seed up of the sad creation
Planting the hopeful world again —
He can't! . . . he won't! . . . he wouldn't touch her!

MR. ZUSS. He does though.

NICKLES (*raging*). Live his life again? —
Not even the most ignorant, obstinate,
Stupid or degraded man
This filthy planet ever farrowed,
Offered the opportunity to live

His bodily life twice over, would accept it —
Least of all Job, poor, trampled bastard!

(MR. ZUSS *has finished fooling with his balloons. He straightens up
and marches off without a glance at* NICKLES.)

It can't be borne twice over! Can't be!
    MR. ZUSS.   It is though. Time and again it is —
Every blessed generation . . .
(*His voice drifts back as he disappears.*) Time and again . . . Time and
    again . . .

(NICKLES *starts to follow, looks back, sees* J.B. *kneeling in his rubble,
hesitates, crosses, squats behind him, his vendor's cap pushed back on his
head, his tray on his knees.*)

    NICKLES.   J.B.!
    J.B.   Let me alone.
    NICKLES.   It's me.

(J.B. *shrugs.*)

I'm not the Father. I'm the — Friend.
    J.B.   I have no friend.
    NICKLES.   Oh come off it.
You don't have to act with me.

(J.B. *is silent.*)

O.K. Carry on.
All I wanted was to help.
Professional counsel you might call it . . .

(J.B. *is silent.*)

Of course you know how all this ends? . . .

(J.B. *is silent.*)

I wondered how you'd play the end.
    J.B.   Who knows what the end is, ever?
    NICKLES.   I do. You do.
    J.B.   Then don't tell me.
    NICKLES.   What's the worst thing you can think of?
    J.B.   I have asked for death. Begged for it. Prayed for it.
    NICKLES.   Then the worst thing can't be death.
    J.B.   Ah!

NICKLES.   You know now.

J.B.   No. You tell me.

NICKLES.   Why should I tell you when you know?

J.B.   Then don't. I'm sick of mysteries. Sick of them.

NICKLES.   He gives it back to you.

J.B.   What back?

NICKLES.   All of it,
Everything He ever took:
Wife, health, children, everything.

J.B.   I have no wife.

NICKLES.   She comes back to you.

J.B.   I have no children.

NICKLES (a nasty laugh).   You'll have better ones.

J.B.   My skin is . . . (he breaks off, staring at the skin of his naked arms).

NICKLES.   Oh come on! I know the
Look of grease paint!

J.B.   . . . whole! It's healed!

NICKLES (heavily ironic).   You see? You see what I mean? What He
plans for you?

(J.B., staring at his arms, is silent.)

(Leaning forward, urgently.) Tell me how you play the end.
Any man was screwed as Job was! . . .

(J.B. does not answer.)

I'll tell you how you play it. Listen!
Think of all the mucked-up millions
Since this buggered world began
Said, No!, said, Thank you!, took a rope's end,
Took a window for a door,
Swallowed something, gagged on something . . .

(J.B. lifts his head: he is listening but not to NICKLES.)

None of them knew the truth as Job does.
None of them had his cause to know.

J.B.   Listen! Do you hear? There's someone . . .

NICKLES (violently).   Job won't take it! Job won't touch it!
Job will fling it in God's face
With half his guts to make it spatter!
He'd rather suffocate in dung —
Choke in ordure —

J.B. (rising).   There is someone —
Someone waiting at the door.

NICKLES (*pulling his cap down, rising slowly*).   I know.

(*The dangling lights dim out.*)

Scene 11

(*A light comes from the canvas door. It increases as though day were beginning somewhere.* NICKLES *has gone.*)

J.B.   Who is it? (*He crosses toward the door walking with his old ease. Stops.*)   Is there someone there?

(*There is no answer. He goes on. Reaches the door.*)

Sarah!

(*The light increases. She is sitting on the sill, a broken twig in her hand.*)

SARAH.   Look, Job: the forsythia,
The first few leaves . . . not leaves though . . . petals . . .
    J.B. (*roughly*).   Get up!
    SARAH.   Where shall I go?
    J.B.   Where you went!
Wherever!

(*She does not answer.*)

(*More gently.*)   Where?
    SARAH.   Among the ashes.
All there is now of the town is ashes.
Mountains of ashes. Shattered glass.
Glittering cliffs of glass all shattered
Steeper than a cat could climb
If there were cats still . . . And the pigeons —
They wheel and settle and whirl off
Wheeling and almost settling . . . And the silence —
There is no sound there now — no wind sound —
Nothing that could sound the wind —
Could make it sing — no door — no doorway . . .
Only this. (*She looks at the twig in her hands.*) Among the ashes!
I found it growing in the ashes,
Gold as though it did not know . . .
(*Her voice rises hysterically.*) I broke the branch to strip the leaves off —
Petals again! . . . (*She cradles it in her arms.*) But they so clung to it!
    J.B.   Curse God and die, you said to me.

SARAH.   Yes. (*She looks up at him for the first time, then down again.*)
    You wanted justice, didn't you?
There isn't any. There's the world . . . (*She begins to rock on the doorsill,
    the little branch in her arms.*)
Cry for justice and the stars
Will stare until your eyes sting. Weep,
Enormous winds will thrash the water.
Cry in sleep for your lost children,
Snow will fall . . . snow will fall . . .
    J.B.   Why did you leave me alone?
    SARAH.   I loved you.
I couldn't help you any more.
You wanted justice and there was none —
Only love.
    J.B.   He does not love. He
Is.
    SARAH.   But we do. That's the wonder.
    J.B.   Yet you left me.
    SARAH.   Yes, I left you.
I thought there was a way away . . .
Water under bridges opens
Closing and the companion stars
Still float there afterwards. I thought the door
Opened into closing water.
    J.B.   Sarah! (*He drops on his knees beside her in the doorway, his
        arms around her.*)
    SARAH.   Oh, I never could!
I never could! Even the forsythia . . . (*She is half laughing, half crying.*)
Even the forsythia beside the
Stair could stop me.

(*They cling to each other. Then she rises, drawing him up, peering at
the darkness inside the door.*)

    J.B.   It's too dark to see.

(*She turns, pulls his head down between her hands and kisses him.*)

    SARAH.   Then blow on the coal of the heart, my darling.
    J.B.   The coal of the heart . . .
    SARAH.   It's all the light now.

(SARAH *comes forward into the dim room,* J.B. *behind her. She lifts a
fallen chair, sets it straight.*)

Blow on the coal of the heart.
The candles in churches are out.

The lights have gone out in the sky.
Blow on the coal of the heart
And we'll see by and by . . .

(J.B. *has joined her, lifting and straightening the chairs.*)

We'll see where we are.
The wit won't burn and the wet soul smoulders.
Blow on the coal of the heart and we'll know . . .
We'll know . . .

(*The light increases, plain white daylight from the door, as they work.*)

Curtain

PART TWO

DRAMATIC CRITICISM

from **THE POETICS**

A Tragedy, then, is an artistic imitation of an action that is serious, complete in itself, and of an adequate magnitude; so much for the object which is imitated. As for the medium, the imitation is produced in language embellished in more than one way, one kind of embellishment being introduced separately in one part, and another kind in another part of the whole. As for the manner, the imitation is itself in the form of an action directly presented, not narrated. And as for the proper function resulting from the imitation of such an object in such a medium and manner, it is to arouse the emotions of pity and fear in the audience; and to arouse this pity and fear in such a way as to effect that special purging off and relief (*catharsis*) of these two emotions which is the characteristic of Tragedy.

By 'language embellished in more than one way' is meant language which is simply rhythmical or metrical, language which is delivered in recitative, and language which is uttered in song. And by the separate introduction of one kind of embellished language in one part, and of another kind in another part, is meant that some portions of the tragedy (*e.g.*, prologue and episode) are rendered in verse alone, without being sung or chanted, and other portions again (*e.g.*, parode and stasimon) in the form of singing or chanting.

[The several elements in Aristotle's definition of tragedy are gathered from his previous remarks, as he says; save that hitherto the only possible reference to the function of tragedy, its effect upon the audience, or reader, is contained in the opening words of the treatise, where he promises to discuss the specific function of each kind of poetry. In the definition, he implies that other forms of art — we might instance comedy — have as their special end or pleasure the relief of others of the general class of disturbing emotions to which pity and fear belong.

The effect of tragedy upon the emotions is not merely something that took place in a former age, or among the Greeks alone; it may be observed at all times, and in virtually all persons, including the reader of this sentence. However much the malign influence of a narrowly intellectual education may check the native motions of the heart, few indeed must be they who are hopelessly bereft of all pleasure in the tragic *cathar-sis*. For generations, it is true, there has been a debate over the precise meaning one should attach to Aristotle's phrase — a debate that frequently has turned upon the study of words apart from things, and on the whole has not been sufficiently concerned with the actual experience of audiences, or rather of specially qualified judges, during the presentation of good tragedy and immediately thereafter. But if the words of Aristotle describe an effect which really occurs, it must be that a person of intelligence and normal sympathies will undergo, and be able to mark, the experience, not only in witnessing the best tragedy, but even in reading it. The student of the *Poetics* might render his notion of the tragic *catharsis* more exact by an attempt to observe his own emotions when he reads, or re-reads, Sophocles' *Oedipus the King* or Shakespeare's *Othello*.

Furthermore, one might collect and examine the utterances of poets and other men of unusual sensibility on the feelings which tragic stories have aroused in them; — not primarily such conscious explanations of the Aristotelian *catharsis* as that of Milton in his preface to *Samson Agonistes*. This, though important, is a different kind of evidence from the lines in the first of Milton's Latin Elegies — thus translated by Cowper:

> I gaze, and grieve, still cherishing my grief;
> At times, e'en bitter tears yield sweet relief.

Similar spontaneous illustrations of the tragic pleasure have come from other English poets; for example, Wordsworth, in the Dedication preceding *The White Doe of Rylstone*:

> Pleasing was the smart,
> And the tear precious in compassion shed;

and Coleridge, in *Love*:

> She wept with pity and delight.

It is probable also that a study of emotional suspense and its relief in the audience, by an experimental psychologist, would throw light upon the passage in Aristotle. For the present, however, no explanation could prove more helpful to the general reader than a part of Bywater's note, his language being followed almost verbatim:

> In Greek physiology and pathology, *catharsis* is a very general term for a physical clearance or discharge, the removal by art or an effort of nature of some bodily product, which, if allowed to remain, would cause discomfort or harm. The *catharsis* of the soul as described in the *Politics* of Aristotle is a similar process in reference to certain emotions — the tacit assumption being apparently that the emotions in question are analogous to those peccant humors in the body which, according to the ancient humoral theory of medicine, have to be expelled from the system by the appropriate *catharsis*.

With some adaptation of the statements and hints in *Politics* 8. 7, as thus interpreted, it is not difficult to recover the outlines at any rate of the Aristotelian theory of the cathartic effect of tragedy: Pity and fear are elements in human nature, and in some men they are present in a disquieting degree. With these latter the tragic excitement is a necessity; but it is also in a certain sense good for all. It serves as a sort of medicine, producing a *catharsis* to lighten and relieve the soul of the accumulated emotion within it; and as the relief is wanted, there is always a harmless pleasure attending the process of relief.

It must be added that pleasure, to Aristotle, signifies, not a passive state of being, but a form of activity.

In his working definition he does not allude to the element of pleasure in the tragic relief. As he develops his thought, we become aware that the relief is itself a form of pleasure; so that the characteristic effect of tragedy may be referred to as either one or the other. We discover, too, that there are certain satisfactions contributory to the main effect; for example, the pleasure of discovery or recognition, when we learn the author of a deed or the upshot of an incident; the pleasure of astonishment, when the outcome of a series of events is unexpected, yet is seen to be inevitable; and the pleasure derived from 'embellished language,' that is, from the rhythm and music of tragedy. Furthermore, the pleasure is explained negatively: the play must not offend us with effects that are revolting, or with events that run counter to our sense of what is reasonable and likely.]

Advancing now from the synthetic definition of Tragedy, we proceed to analyze the elements that separately demand the attention of the tragic poet. Since there are *dramatis personae* who produce the author's imitation of an action, it necessarily follows that (1) everything pertaining to the appearance of the actors on the stage — including costume, scenery, and the like — will constitute an element in the technique of tragedy; and that (2) the composition of the music ('Melody'), and (3) the composition in words ('Diction'), will constitute two further elements, as Melody and Diction represent the medium in which the action is imitated. By Diction is meant, in this connection, the fitting together of the words in metre; as for Melody (= 'Song'), the meaning is too obvious to need explanation.

But furthermore, the original object of the imitation is an action of men. In the performance, then, the imitation, which is also an action, must be carried on by agents, the *dramatis personae*. And these agents must necessarily be endowed by the poet with certain distinctive qualities both of (4) Moral Character (*ethos*) and (5) Intellect (*dianoia*) — one might say, of heart and head; for it is from a man's moral bent, and from the way in which he reasons, that we are led to ascribe goodness or badness, success or failure, to his acts. Thus, as there are two natural causes, moral bent and thought, of the particular deeds of men, so there are the same two natural causes of their success or failure in life. And the tragic poet must take cognizance of this.

Finally, the action which the poet imitates is represented in the tragedy by (6) the Fable or Plot. And according to our present distinction, Plot means that synthesis of the particular incidents which gives form or being to the tragedy as a whole; whereas Moral Bent is that which leads us to characterize the agents as morally right or wrong in what they do; and Intellect (or 'Thought') is that which shows itself whenever they prove a particular point, or, it may be, avouch some general truth.

In every tragedy, therefore, there are six constitutive elements, according to the quality of which we judge the excellence of the work as a whole: Plot (6); Moral Disposition (4); Diction (3); Intellect (5); Spectacle (1); Melody (2). Two of them, Melody and Diction, concern the medium of imitation; one, Spectacle, the manner; and three, Plot, Moral Disposition, and Intellect, the objects. There can be no other elements. These constitutive elements, accordingly, not a few of the tragic poets, so to speak, have duly employed [in spite of what adverse critics may assert]; for, indeed, every drama must contain certain things that are meant for the eye, as well as the elements of Moral Disposition, Plot, Diction, Melody, and Intellect.

[That element of a drama which is here called moral bent or disposition (*ethos*) is often rendered into English by the word 'character.' There is a danger, which Aristotle himself does not always avoid, of confusing character in this narrower sense with personality, and hence of identifying character with agent. From this confusion there often results a misunderstanding of Aristotle's subsequent remarks upon the relative importance of plot and moral bent (character in the narrower sense). In dealing with this point it is undesirable to refer to the *dramatis personae* as 'characters'; one would do well to use the word 'agents' instead, and to bear in mind that the personality of the agents is divided by Aristotle into two separate elements, corresponding to qualities of heart and head respectively. If at first we make the most of this distinction, we shall not go far astray in later passages where it is not so carefully preserved. What Aristotle next specifically maintains is that, among the six elements, plot or action is of greater importance than the moral bent of the agents; he might equally well have said it was of greater importance than their faculty of reason, *i.e.*, than "Thought."]

The most important of the constitutive elements is the Plot, that is, the organization of the incidents of the story; for Tragedy in its essence is an imitation, not of men as such, but of action and life, of happiness and misery. And happiness and misery are not states of being, but forms of activity; the end for which we live is some form of activity, not the realization of a moral quality. Men are better or worse, according to their moral bent; but they become happy or miserable in their actual deeds. In a play, consequently, the agents do not perform for the sake of representing their individual dispositions; rather, the display of moral character is included as subsidiary to the things that are done. So that the incidents of the action, and the structural ordering of these incidents, constitute the end and purpose of the tragedy. Here, as elsewhere, the final purpose is the main thing.

Such is the importance of this element that, we may add, whereas Tragedy cannot exist without action, it is possible to construct a tragedy in which the agents have no distinctive moral bent. In fact, the works of most of the modern tragic poets, from the time of Euripides on, are lacking in the element of character. Nor is the defect confined to tragic poets: it is common among poets in general. And there is a similar defect among the painters — in Zeuxis, for example, as contrasted with Polygnotus; for Polygnotus excels in the representation of the ethical element, whereas the pictures of Zeuxis are in this respect wholly deficient. [In the same way, one might compare the vigorous delineation of ethical qualities in Rembrandt with the absence of this power in Rubens. Among English poets of all sorts, Chaucer, Shakespeare, Milton, and Wordsworth serve to exemplify the presence of this quality; it is relatively lacking in Dryden, Shelley, and Byron.]

Again, one may string together a series of speeches in which the moral bent of the agents is delineated in excellent verse and diction, and with excellent order in the thoughts, and yet fail to produce the essential effect of Tragedy as already described. One is much more likely to produce this effect with a tragedy, however deficient in these respects, if it has a plot — that is, an artistic ordering of the incidents. In addition to all this, the most vital features of Tragedy, by which the interest and emotions of the audience are most powerfully aroused — that is, reversals of fortune, and discoveries of the identity of agents — are parts of the plot or action. It is significant, too, that beginners in the art become proficient in versification and in the delineation of personal traits before they are able to combine the incidents of the action into an effective whole. Herein the progress of the individual dramatist repeats the history of the art; for almost all the early poets succeeded better with these two elements than in the formation of plots.

(1) The Plot, then, is the First Principle, and as it were the very Soul of Tragedy.

(2) And the element of Character is second in importance. — There is a parallel in the art of painting: the most beautiful colors, laid on with no order, will not give as much pleasure as the simplest figure done in outline. — Tragedy is an imitation of an action: mainly on account of this action does it become, in the second place, an imitation of personal agents.

(3) Third in importance comes the Intellectual element. This corresponds to the power of the agent to say what can be said, or what is fitting to be said, in a given situation. It is that element in the speeches of a drama which is supplied by the study of Politics and the art of Rhetoric; for the older tragic poets [e.g., Sophocles] made their heroes express themselves like statesmen, whereas the modern [including Euripides] make theirs use the devices of the rhetoricians. This Intellectual element must

be clearly distinguished from the Ethical element in the drama, for the latter includes only such things as reveal the moral bias of the agents — their tendency to choose or to avoid a certain line of action, in cases where the motive is not otherwise evident. And hence the poet has no call to employ the ethical element in speeches where the agent is neither choosing nor avoiding a line of action. The Intellectual element, on the other hand, is manifested in everything the agents say to prove or disprove a special point, and in every utterance they make by way of generalization.

(4) Next in importance among the four essential constituents comes the Diction. This, as has been explained, means the interpretation of the sentiments of the agents in the form of language, and is essentially the same thing whether the language is metrical or not.

(5) Of the two elements remaining, Melody is the more important, since it occupies the chief place among the accessory pleasures of Tragedy.

(6) The element of Spectacle, though it arouses the interest of the audience, is last in importance, since it demands the lowest order of artistic skill, and is least connected with the art of poetry as such. A tragedy can produce its effect independently of a stage-performance and actors — that is, when it is read; and besides, the business of preparing the stage and the actors is the affair of the costumer rather than of poets.

Having thus distinguished the six constitutive elements, we are now to discuss, as the first and most important consideration in the art of Tragedy, the proper organization of the incidents into a plot that will have the ideal tragic effect. According to the definition, a tragedy is an imitation of an action that is complete in itself, forming a whole of a sufficient magnitude or extent; for a thing may be a whole and yet wanting in magnitude.

Now a Whole is that which has (1) a Beginning, (2) a Middle, and (3) an End.

(1) A beginning (= X) is that which does not itself come after anything else in a necessary sequence, but after which some other thing (= Y) does naturally exist or come to pass.

(2) A Middle (= Y) is that which naturally comes after something else (= X), and is followed by a third thing (= Z).

(3) An End (= Z), on the contrary, is that which naturally comes after something else (= Y) in either a necessary or a usual sequence, but has nothing else following it.

A well-constructed plot, therefore, can neither begin nor end where and when the poet happens to like. It must conform to the principles just enunciated.

And further, as to Magnitude: to be beautiful, a living organism, or any other individual thing made up of parts, must possess not only an orderly arrangement of these parts, but also a proper magnitude; for beauty depends upon these two qualities, size and order. Hence an extremely minute creature cannot be beautiful to us; for we see the whole in an almost infinitesimal moment of time, and lose the pleasure that comes from a distinct perception of order in the parts. Nor could a creature of vast dimensions be beautiful to us — a beast, say, one thousand miles in length; for in that case the eye could not take all of the object in at once — we should see the parts, but not the unity of the whole. In the same way, then, as an inanimate object made up of parts, or a living creature, must be of such a size that the parts and the whole may be easily taken in by the eye, just so must the plot of a tragedy have a proper length, so that the parts and the whole may be easily embraced by the memory. The artificial limits, of course, as these are determined by the conditions of stage-presentation, and by the power of attention in an audience, do not concern the art of poetry as such. If it were necessary to present one hundred tragedies in succession [an exaggerated illustration], they would doubtless have to be timed with water-clocks — as some say was formerly the custom. The artistic limit, set by the nature of the thing itself, is this: So long as the plot is perspicuous throughout, the greater the length of the story, the more beautiful will it be on account of its magnitude. But to define the matter in a general way, an adequate limit for the magnitude of the plot is this: Let the length be such that the story may pass from happiness to misfortune, or from misfortune to happiness, through a series of incidents linked together in a probable or inevitable sequence.

The Unity of a Plot does not consist, as some suppose, in having one man as subject; for the number of accidents that befall the individual man is endless, and some of them cannot be reduced to unity. So, too, during the life of any one man, he performs many deeds which cannot be brought together in the form of a unified action. . . . For, as in the other imitative arts, painting and the rest, so in poetry, the object of the imitation in each case is a unit; therefore in an epic or a tragedy, the plot, which is an imitation of a dramatic action, must represent an action that is organically unified, the structural order of the incidents being such that transposing or removing any one of them will dislocate and disorganize the whole. Every part must be necessary, and in its place; for a thing whose presence or absence makes no perceptible difference is not an organic part of the whole.

FRIEDRICH NIETZSCHE

from **THE BIRTH OF TRAGEDY**

We have tried to illustrate by this historical example how tragedy, being a product of the spirit of music, must surely perish by the destruction of that spirit. In order to moderate the strangeness of such an assertion and at the same time to demonstrate how we arrived at it, we must now frankly confront certain analogues of our own day. We must step resolutely into the thick of those struggles which are being waged right now between the insatiable thirst for knowledge and man's tragic dependency on art. I will not speak in this connection of those lesser destructive instincts which have at all times opposed art, and especially tragedy, and which in our own day seem to triumph to such an extent that of all the theatrical arts only the farce and the ballet can be said to thrive, with a luxuriance which not all find pleasing. I shall deal here only with the distinguished enemies of the tragic view, that is to say with the exponents of science, all dyed-in-the-wool optimists like their archetype, Socrates. And presently I shall name those forces which seem to promise a rebirth of tragedy and who knows what other fair hopes for the German genius.

Before rushing headlong into the fight let us put on the armor of such perceptions as we have already won. In opposition to all who would derive the arts from a single vital principle, I wish to keep before me those two artistic deities of the Greeks, Apollo and Dionysos. They represent to me, most vividly and concretely, two radically dissimilar realms of art. Apollo embodies the transcendent genius of the *principium individuationis*; through him alone is it possible to achieve redemption in illusion. The mystical jubilation of Dionysos, on the other hand, breaks the spell of individuation and opens a path to the maternal womb of being. Among the great thinkers there is only one who has fully realized the immense discrepancy between the plastic Apollonian art and the Dionysiac art of music. Independently of Greek religious symbols, Schopenhauer assigned to music a totally different character and origin from all the other arts, because it does not, like all the others, represent appearance, but the will directly. It is the metaphysical complement to everything that is physical in the world; the thing-in-itself where all else is appearance (*The World as Will and Idea, I*). Richard Wagner set his seal of approval on this key notion of all esthetics when he wrote in his book on Beethoven that music obeys esthetic principles quite unlike those governing the visual arts and that the category of beauty is altogether inapplicable to it — although a wrongheaded esthetic based on a misguided and decadent art has attempted to make music answer to criteria of beauty proper only to the plastic arts, expecting it to generate *pleasure in beautiful forms.* Once I had become aware of this antinomy I felt strongly moved to explore the nature of Greek tragedy, the profoundest manifestation of Hellenic genius. For the first time I seemed to possess the key enabling me to inspect the problem of tragedy in terms that were no longer derived from conventional esthetics. I was given such a strange and unfamiliar glimpse into the essence of Hellenism that it seemed to me that our classical philology, for all its air of triumphant achievement, had only dealt with phantasmagorias and externals.

We might approach this fundamental problem by posing the following question: what esthetic effect is produced when the Apollonian and Dionysiac forces of art, usually separate, are made to work alongside each other? Or, to put it more succinctly, in what relation does music stand to image and concept? Schopenhauer, whose clarity and perspicuity on that point Wagner praises, has, in *The World as Will and Idea, I,* the following passage, which I shall quote entire: "According to all this, we may regard the phenomenal world, or nature, and music as two different expressions of the same thing, which is therefore itself the only medium of the analogy between these two expressions, so that a knowledge of this medium is required in order to understand that analogy. Music, therefore, if regarded as an expression of the world, is in the highest degree a universal language, which is related indeed to the universality of concepts, much as these are related to the particular things. Its universality, however, is by no means the empty universality of abstraction, but is of quite a different kind, and is united with thorough and distinct definiteness. In this respect it resembles geometrical figures and numbers, which are the universal forms of all possible objects of experience and applicable to them all *a priori*, and yet are not abstract but perceptible and thoroughly determinate. All possible efforts, excitements and manifestations of will, all that goes on in the heart of man and that reason includes in the wide, negative concept of feeling, may be expressed by the infinite number of possible melodies, but always in the universality of mere form, without the material; always according to the thing-in-itself, not the phenomenon — of which melodies reproduce the very soul and essence as it were, without the body. This deep relation which music bears to the true nature of all things also explains the fact that suitable music played to any event or surrounding seems to disclose to us its most secret meaning and appears as the most accurate and distinct commentary upon it; as also the fact that whoever gives himself up entirely to the impression of a symphony seems to see all the possible events of life and the world take place in himself. Nevertheless, upon reflection he can find no likeness between the music and the things that passed before his mind. For, as we have said, music is distinguished from all the other arts by the fact that it is not a copy of the phenomenon, or, more accurately, the adequate objectivity of the will, but is the direct copy of the will itself, and therefore represents the metaphysical of everything physical in the world, and the thing-in-itself of every phenomenon. We might, therefore, just as well call the world embodied music as embodied will: and this is the reason why music makes every picture, and indeed every scene of real life and of the world, at once appear with higher significance; all the more so, to be sure, in proportion as its melody is analogous to the inner spirit of the given phenomenon. It rests upon this that we are able to set a poem to music as a song, or a perceptible representation as a pantomime, or both as an opera. Such particular pictures of human life, set to the universal language of music, are never bound to it or correspond to it with stringent necessity, but stand to it only in the relation of an example chosen at will to a general concept. In the determinateness of the real they represent that which music expresses in the universality of mere form. For melodies are to a certain extent, like general concepts, an abstraction from the actual. This actual world, then, the world of particular things, affords the object of perception, the special and the individual, the particular case, both to the universality of concepts and to the universality of the melodies. But these two universalities are in a certain respect opposed to each other; for the concepts contain only the forms, which are first of all abstracted from perception—the separated outward shell of things, as it were—and hence they are, in the strictest sense of the term, *abstracta*; music, on the other hand, gives the inmost kernel which precedes all forms, or the heart of things. This relation may be very well expressed in the language of the schoolmen by saying: the concepts are the *universalia post rem*, but music gives the *universalia ante rem* and the real world the *universalia in re*. That a relation is generally possible between a composition and a perceptible representation rests, as we have said, upon the fact that both are simply different expressions of the same inner being of the world. When now, in the particular case, such a relation is actually given—that is to say, when the composer has been able to express in the universal language of music the emotions of will which constitute the heart of an event— then the melody of the song, the music of the opera, is expressive. But the analogy discovered by the composer between the two must have proceeded from the direct knowledge of the nature of the world unknown to his reason and must not be an imitation produced with conscious intention by means of conceptions; otherwise the music does not express the inner nature of the will itself, but merely gives an inadequate imitation of its phenomenon: all specially imitative music does this."

In accordance with Schopenhauer's doctrine, we interpret music as the immediate language of the will, and our imaginations are stimulated to embody that immaterial world, which speaks to us with lively motion and yet remains invisible. Image and concept, on the other hand, gain a heightened significance under the influence of truly appropriate music. Dionysiac art, then, affects the Apollonian talent in a twofold manner:

first, music incites us to a symbolic intuition of the Dionysiac universality; second, it endows that symbolic image with supreme significance. From these facts, perfectly plausible once we have pondered them well, we deduce that music is capable of giving birth to myth, the most significant of similitudes; and above all, to the tragic myth, which is a parable of Dionysiac knowledge. When I spoke earlier of the lyric poet I demonstrated how, through him, music strives to account for its own essence in Apollonian images. Once we grant that music raised to its highest power must similarly try to find an adequate embodiment, it stands to reason that it will also succeed in discovering a symbolic expression for its proper Dionysiac wisdom. And where should we look for that expression if not in tragedy and the tragic spirit?

It is vain to try to deduce the tragic spirit from the commonly accepted categories of art: illusion and beauty. Music alone allows us to understand the delight felt at the annihilation of the individual. Each single instance of such annihilation will clarify for us the abiding phenomenon of Dionysiac art, which expresses the omnipotent will behind individuation, eternal life continuing beyond all appearance and in spite of destruction. The metaphysical delight in tragedy is a translation of instinctive Dionysiac wisdom into images. The hero, the highest manifestation of the will, is destroyed, and we assent, since he too is merely a phenomenon, and the eternal life of the will remains unaffected. Tragedy cries, "We believe that life is eternal!" and music is the direct expression of that life. The aims of plastic art are very different: here Apollo overcomes individual suffering by the glorious apotheosis of what is eternal in appearance: here beauty vanquishes the suffering that inheres in all existence, and pain is, in a certain sense, glossed away from nature's countenance. That same nature addresses us through Dionysiac art and its tragic symbolism, in a voice that rings authentic: "Be like me, the Original Mother, who, constantly creating, finds satisfaction in the turbulent flux of appearances!"

Dionysiac art, too, wishes to convince us of the eternal delight of existence, but it insists that we look for this delight not in the phenomena but behind them. It makes us realize that everything that is generated must be prepared to face its painful dissolution. It forces us to gaze into the horror of individual existence, yet without being turned to stone by the vision: a metaphysical solace momentarily lifts us above the whirl of shifting phenomena. For a brief moment we become, ourselves, the primal Being, and we experience its insatiable hunger for existence. Now we see the struggle, the pain, the destruction of appearances, as necessary, because of the constant proliferation of forms pushing into life, because of the extravagant fecundity of the world-will. We feel the furious prodding of this travail in the very moment in which we become one with the immense lust for life and are made aware of the eternity and indestructibility of that lust. Pity and terror notwithstanding, we realize our great good fortune in having life—not as individuals, but as part of the life force with whose procreative lust we have become one.

Our study of the genesis of Greek tragedy has shown us clearly how that tragic art arose out of music, and we believe that our interpretation has for the first time done justice to the original and astounding meaning of the chorus. Yet we must admit that the significance of the tragic myth was never clearly conceptualized by the Greek poets, let alone philosophers. Their heroes seem to us always more superficial in their speeches than in their actions: the myth, we might say, never finds an adequate objective correlative in the spoken word. The structure of the scenes and the concrete images convey a deeper wisdom than the poet was able to put into words and concepts. (The same may be claimed for Shakespeare, whose Hamlet speaks more superficially than he acts, so that the interpretation of *Hamlet* given earlier had to be based on a deeper investigation of the whole texture of the play.) As for Greek tragedy, which we experience only through the printed word, I have already indicated that the incongruence between myth and word may lead us to think it more trivial than it actually is and to presume for it a more superficial effect than, according to the ancients, it must have had. It is so easy to forget that what the poet qua poet was unable to achieve, namely the supreme spiritualization of myth, might be achieved by him at any moment in his character of musician.

. . . .

Tragedy absorbs the highest orgiastic music and in so doing consummates music. But then it puts beside it the tragic myth and the tragic hero. Like a mighty titan, the tragic hero shoulders the whole Dionysiac world and removes the burden from us. At the same time, tragic myth, through the figure of the hero, delivers us from our avid thirst for earthly satisfaction and reminds us of another existence and a higher delight. For this delight the hero readies himself, not through his victories but through his undoing. Tragedy interposes a noble parable, *myth*, between the universality of its music and the Dionysiac disposition of the spectator and in so doing creates the illusion that music is but a supreme instrument for bringing to life the plastic world of myth. By virtue of this noble deception it is now able to move its limbs freely in dithyrambic dance and to yield without reserve to an orgiastic abandon, an indulgence which, without this deception, it could not permit itself. Myth shields us from music while at the same time giving music its maximum freedom. In exchange, music endows the tragic myth with a convincing metaphysical significance, which the unsupported word and image could never achieve, and, moreover, assures the spectator of a supreme delight — though the way passes through annihilation and negation, so that he is made to feel that the very womb of things speaks audibly to him.

Since, in this last passage, I have tentatively set forth a difficult notion, which may not be immediately clear to many, I would now invite my friends to consider a particular instance that is within our common experience and which may support my general thesis. I shall not address myself to those who use the scenic representation and the words and emotions of the actors to help them respond to the music. To none of these is music as a mother tongue, and, notwithstanding that help, they never penetrate beyond the vestibule of musical perception. Some, like Gervinus, do not even attain the vestibule by this means. I address myself only to those having immediate kinship with music, who communicate with things almost entirely through unconscious musical relations. To these genuine musicians I direct my question: "How can anyone experience the third act of Tristan and Isolde, apart from either word or image, simply as the movement of a mighty symphony, without exhausting himself in the overstretching of his soul's pinions?" How is it possible for a man who has listened to the very heartbeat of the world-will and felt the unruly lust for life rush into all the veins of the world, now as a thundering torrent and now as a delicately foaming brook — how is it possible for him to remain unshattered? How can he bear, shut in the paltry glass bell of his individuality, to hear the echoes of innumerable cries of weal and woe sounding out of the "vast spaces of cosmic night," and not wish, amidst these pipings of metaphysical pastoral, to flee incontinent to his primordial home? And yet the reception of such a work does not shatter the recipient, the creation of it the creator. What are we to make of this contradiction?

It is at this point that the tragic myth and the tragic hero interpose between our highest musical excitement and the music, giving us a parable of those cosmic facts of which music alone can speak directly. And yet, if we reacted wholly as Dionysiac beings, the parable would fail entirely of effect, and not for a single moment would it distract our attention from the reverberations of the universalia ante rem. But now the Apollonian power, bent upon reconstituting the nearly shattered individual, asserts itself, proffering the balm of a delightful illusion. Suddenly we see only Tristan, lying motionless and torpid, and hear him ask, "Why does that familiar strain waken me?" And what before had seemed a hollow sigh echoing from the womb of things now says to us simply, "Waste and empty the sea." And where, before, we had felt ourselves about to expire in a violent paroxysm of feeling, held by a most tenuous bond to this our life, we now see only the hero, mortally wounded yet not dying, and hear his despairing cry: "To long, even in death, and be unable to die for longing!" And where, before, the jubilation of the horn after such an excess of feeling and such consuming pains would have cut us to the quick, as though it had been the crowning pain, now there stands between us and this absolute jubilation the rejoicing Kurwenal, turned toward the ship which brings Isolde. No matter how deeply pity moves us, that pity saves us from the radical "pity of things," even as the parable of myth saves us from the direct intuition of the cosmic idea, as idea and word save us from the undammed pouring forth of the unconscious will. It is through the workings of that marvelous Apollonian illusion that even the realm of sound takes plastic shape before us, as though it were only a question of the destinies of Tristan and Isolde, molded in the finest, most expressive material.

Thus the Apollonian spirit rescues us from the Dionysiac universality and makes us attend, delightedly, to individual forms. It focuses our pity on these forms and so satisfies our instinct for beauty, which longs for great and noble embodiments. It parades the images of life before us and incites us to seize their ideational essence. Through the massive impact of image, concept, ethical doctrine, and sympathy, the Apollonian spirit wrests man from his Dionysiac self-destruction and deceives him as to the universality of the Dionysiac event. It pretends that he sees only the particular image, e.g., Tristan and Isolde, and that the music serves only to make him see it more intensely. What could possibly be immune from the salutary Apollonian charm, if it is able to create in us the illusion that Dionysos may be an aid to Apollo and further enhance his effects? that music is at bottom a vehicle for Apollonian representations? In the pre-established harmony obtaining between the consummate drama and its music, that drama reaches an acme of visual power unobtainable to the drama of words merely. As we watch the rhythmically moving characters of the stage merge with the independently moving lines of melody into a single curving line of motion, we experience the most delicate harmony of sound and visual movement. The relationships of things thus become directly available to the senses, and we realize that in these relationships the essence of a character and of a melodic line are simultaneously made manifest. And as music forces us to see more, and more inwardly than usual, and spreads before us like a delicate tissue the curtain of the scene, our spiritualized vision beholds the world of the stage at once infinitely expanded and illuminated from within. What analogue could the verbal poet possibly furnish — he who tries to bring about that inward expansion of the visible stage world, its inner illumination, by much more indirect and imperfect means, namely word and concept? But, once musical tragedy has appropriated the word, it can at the same time present the birthplace and subsoil of the word and illuminate the genesis of the word from within. And yet it must be emphatically stated that the process I have described is only a marvelous illusion, by whose effects we are delivered from the Dionysiac extravagance and onrush. For, at bottom, music and drama stand in the opposite relation: music is the true idea of the cosmos, drama but a reflection of that idea. The identity between the melodic line and the dramatic character, between relations of harmony and character, obtains in an opposite sense from what we experience when we witness a musical tragedy. However concretely we move, enliven, and illuminate the characters from within, they will always remain mere appearance, from which there is no gateway leading to the true heart of reality. But music addresses us from that center; and though countless appearances were to file past that same music, they would never exhaust its nature but remain external replicas only. Nothing is gained for the understanding of either music or drama by resorting to that popular and utterly false pair of opposites, body and soul. Yet this contrast, crude and unphilosophical as it is, seems to have developed among our estheticians into an article of faith. About the contrast between the phenomenon and the thing-in-itself, on the other hand, they have never learned anything nor, for some obscure reason, wanted to learn.

If our analysis has shown that the Apollonian element in tragedy has utterly triumphed over the Dionysiac quintessence of music, bending the latter to its own purposes — which are to define the drama completely — still an important reservation must be made. At the point that matters most the Apollonian illusion has been broken through and destroyed. This drama which deploys before us, having all its movements and characters illumined from within by the aid of music — as though we witnessed the coming and going of the shuttle as it weaves the tissue — this drama achieves a total effect quite beyond the scope of any Apollonian artifice. In the final effect of tragedy the Dionysiac element triumphs once again: its closing sounds are such as were never heard in the Apollonian realm. The Apollonian illusion reveals its identity as the veil thrown over the Dionysiac meanings for the duration of the play, and yet the illusion is so potent that at its close the Apollonian drama is projected into a sphere where it begins to speak with Dionysiac wisdom, thereby denying itself and its Apollonian concreteness. The difficult relations between the two elements in tragedy may be symbolized by a fraternal union between the two deities: Dionysos speaks the language of Apollo, but Apollo, finally, the language of Dionysos; thereby the highest goal of tragedy and of art in general is reached.

MURRAY KRIEGER

TRAGEDY AND THE TRAGIC VISION

> *If there were no eternal consciousness in a man, if at the foundation of all
> there lay only a wildly seething power which writhing with obscure passions
> produced everything that is great and everything that is insignificant, if a
> bottomless void never satiated lay hidden beneath all — what then would
> life be but despair?*
>
> — SØREN KIERKEGAARD, Fear and Trembling

Now of course the tragic is not the only vision projected by our serious
literature and philosophy, nor is it necessarily the profoundest vision. But
it is surely the most spectacular, and the most expressive of the crisis-
mentality of our time. Consequently, it has won for those works obsessed
with it the excited attention of our most stimulating critical minds. Perhaps in their excitement over the individual work they have neglected to
define in general terms what this vision is — which is probably as it ought
to be with the practicing critic. In any case there does not seem to be a
systematic effort to say what is meant by the phrase and what, given this
meaning, it has meant to recent writing.

It must be granted that, as with all terms of this kind, any meaning imposed upon it must be an arbitrary one that may or may not command
agreement. But, agreed upon or not, it is valuable critically as it throws a
consistently clear albeit diffuse light upon a broad enough and deep
enough area in our literature. I propose here to create for the term a
tentative definition that I have found most illuminating of modern literature and the modern mind, and in the balance of this volume to use it to
conduct exploratory operations on a certain few novels of the last hundred
or so years in order to demonstrate its incisive powers. Since I have some
idea about where I shall come out, I must admit that my explorations will
have all too much direction to them and that consequently they will somewhat mislead us about the total reality of the works in the interest of showing the widespread relevance of my definition. By way of defense I can
plead only that the definition was empirical in its origin and that it followed my probings into the individual novels rather than the other way
round; in other words, that the meaning I am trying to create for the term
is one that in my reading of these novels I feel that I have discovered.

It is surely needless to add that the act of enclosing a number of literary works within the limits of a given definition hardly passes any judgment upon works on either side of the boundary. For a work not to qualify as an example of the tragic vision is hardly a mark against it. Indeed, in the eyes of many, it may be quite the contrary. Of course, the meaning I want to establish for the tragic vision — indeed, any that would be worth very much — will be far more restrictive than the general lay usage of "tragedy" or "the tragic," which somehow broadens out to synonymity with catastrophe, the sorrowful, that which stems from or leads to "pessimism." But how, if we limit ourselves to technical literary definition, can we find for the tragic any meaning beyond that of Aristotle? The answer is, by moving from formalistic aesthetics to what I would term "thematics."

Thus it becomes necessary first to determine the extent to which we want the meaning of "the tragic vision" entangled with that of "tragedy," surely a term well enough defined in our critical tradition. The most obvious difference I would mark between the two is also a crucial one: "tragedy" refers to an object's literary form, "the tragic vision" to a subject's psychology, his view and version of reality. It is more than a difference between two extant approaches to the tragic. Rather, the second has usurped the very possibility of the first after having been born side by side with it. Perhaps it would be more accurate to say that the tragic vision was born inside tragedy, as a part of it: as a possession of the tragic hero, the vision was a reflection in the realm of thematics of the fully fashioned aesthetic totality which was tragedy. But fearful and even demoniac in its revelations, the vision needed the ultimate soothing power of the aesthetic form which contained it — of tragedy itself — in order to preserve for the world a sanity which the vision itself denied.

It is for these reasons that the reader who as a modern is obsessed with notions of the tragic ought in a way to find himself disappointed on turning for the first time to Aristotle's celebrated definition in the Poetics. We have been so accustomed to doing this treatise deference — and rightfully so from a formalistic point of view — that we can no longer approach it freshly and feel the letdown that should be ours as we glance over its superficial formal prescriptions that are to pass as a description of so sacred and reverenced a literary genre. All this about magnitude and completeness and catharsis — are these to do justice to the profound complex of metaphysical and psychological forces which the tragic unleashes? Or so, at least, we ought as moderns to say superciliously. But probably we should have expected no more than this from the Poetics. Perhaps it was not for the Greek theoretical consciousness — even in as late a representative as Aristotle — to be as self-consciously aware of the disturbing implications of the tragic mentality as it was of the formal requirements which transcended, or rather absorbed, this mentality and restored order to the universe threatened by it.

The cathartic principle itself, in maintaining that pity and fear are not merely to be aroused but to be purged, is evidence of the need in tragedy to have dissonance exploded, leaving only the serenity of harmony behind.

As has often been noted, the peace of cosmic reconciliation is most explicitly insisted upon in the concluding portion of the *Oresteia* — the sublime *Eumenides* — or in the magnificent end of Oedipus' story at *Colonus*. Here is the restorative spirit of superhuman purgation at its most refined. Even in the less exceptional tragedies which do not conclude in such thorough and profound tranquillity — in those, that is, which end more "tragically" in the lay sense — there is often the touch of transcendent grace which saves the cosmos for us in the midst of the irrevocable devastation of human resources. It may, on rare and splendid occasions, be the pure shining thing of *Lear*; it may more often be little more than the matter-of-fact re-establishment of political order — an order, however, that reflects and is sanctioned by the cosmic order — which may be one of the reasons that it is so helpful to have tragedy concern itself with the fortunes of ruling princes.

But even if there were none of these, so long as tragedy remained a defined literary form, the fearsome chaotic necessities of the tragic vision would have to surrender finally to the higher unity which contained them. It is perhaps in this sense that we can speak of the formally sustained literary work ultimately coming to terms with itself. And from the standpoint of the audience — or at least the trained and sophisticated audience — even if there were no thematic elements of release for the passions aroused by the tragic performers, the disciplining and restricting demands upon aesthetic contemplation made by the rounded aesthetic whole would effect the catharsis demanded by Aristotle. The purging of dangerously aroused emotions, following as it does upon the satisfaction, the soothing grace, bestowed upon wayward materials by aesthetic completeness, uses form to overcome the threat of these materials and, consequently, these emotions. This roundedness, this completeness, carrying "aesthetic distance" with it as it brings us the assurances of form, presents us its formal order as a token, a security — something given in hand — to guarantee the cosmic order beyond the turbulence it has conquered. Thus it is that the cathartic principle is ultimately a purely formalistic one, even as tragedy, despite its foreboding rumblings, can remain a force for affirmation through its formal powers alone. Thus it is too that in the *Poetics* Aristotle rightly limits himself to formal considerations, leaving to later and less solvent generations the thematic implications of the vision which, so long as it is aesthetically framed in tragedy, is denied in its very assertion.

It is finally Hegel who, after many centuries during which no radically new approaches are made to tragedy — or at least none that are relevant to my interests here — takes up the task of explaining tragedy and catharsis in the thematic terms that Aristotle could afford to take for granted. Although it must be conceded that Hegel's analysis is clearly indebted to his metaphysic and his general philosophic method and although he does not concern himself with purely formal considerations, it is just this notion of reconciliation, of a final uniting or reuniting, that he emphasizes as the conclusive power of tragedy.[1] His insistence on the absoluteness, the wholeness, the indivisibility of what A. C. Bradley translates as "the ethical substance" is clue to Hegel's attempt to create a metaphysical equivalent for the unity of the Greek world — the unity which, translated into form, allowed tragedy to overcome the heretical defiance of its hero.

For Hegel the *hamartia* that defines the tragic hero always arises from his exclusive identification with a single moral claim, a claim which, however, just within its own sphere, is, from the view of a total morality — that is, the ethical substance — merely partial, a too-assertive particular. Thus the hero's vision is necessarily destructive of the unity of the moral world, threatening with its monomaniac tendencies to produce an anarchy of unsupported metonymic leaps. And in defense of its absolute claims, the ethical substance must justly assert its oneness by ensuring the defeat of the hero whose nature it is, "at once his greatness and his doom, that he knows no shrinking or half heartedness, but identifies himself wholly with the power that moves him, and will admit the justification of no other power."[2]

But this assertion of the ultimate unity of the moral order is what for Hegel leaves Greek tragedy with a final affirmation that transcends the carnage, "an aspect of reconciliation" that authoritatively seals the moral universe for even the most harshly devastated of its sacrificial victims, the bearers of the tragic vision. Here is a significant attempt to account thematically for the catharsis principle, to bring tragedy — for all its deadly turbulence — to the very threshold of a Wordsworthian "tranquil restoration." And who is to say that this restoration is not part of what may seem to be implied by the Aristotelian concept of *dénouement* — a falling action which does not usually stop with the hero's final destruction but leads to a quiet beyond the grave: to a resettling of things in acceptance of this destruction?

Of course it is this final inhibition of the tragic vision, this imposition of formal and moral order upon that which threatens it, that allows these dramas to be properly called classical in the best sense. And when the embracing frame is lost, the romantic tragic vision bursts forth unencumbered — often in merely melodramatic splendor — in no longer reconcilable defiance of traditional aesthetic as well as ethical order. Thus it may seem that Hegel, in assuming the virtues of the Greek world to be those of his own philosophic construct, is hardly representative of the self-conscious modernism that has dominated the last century and a half of our psychological history; the modernism that is characterized by fragmentation rather than by the ever-uniting synthesis which Hegel tried valiantly, if

---

[1] For Hegel on tragedy, see his *The Philosophy of Fine Art*, tr. F. P. B. Osmaston (London, 1920), I, 272–313; II, 213–215; IV, 295–303, 308–326, 330–342. A. C. Bradley's is of course a brilliantly succinct and, by now, a classical summary of the Hegelian view ("Hegel's Theory of Tragedy," *Oxford Lectures on Poetry* [London, 1909], pp. 69–95).

[2] Bradley, p. 72.

vainly, to impose upon it as its salvation. Can his or can any all-resolving "ethical substance" have validity for us as an absolute and claim our allegiance accordingly? Can it now claim the all-commanding universality that justly, though ruthlessly, imposes itself on the subversive tragic hero in its midst? Or is the tragic hero, as modern, fulfilling a proper human function and even a proper human obligation in standing with his integrity as an individual outside the universal? Which is another way of suggesting that whatever universals we may be left with do not deserve the obedience of the most daring of us. Hegel created a system whose universals, like those of the Greek world or even of the Elizabethan world as we find it reflected in Shakespeare, have a metaphysical sanction; whose social and political institutions have a cosmic sanction. How accurate an account is this of the shabby, Babbitt-like arbitrary things that must — if anything does — pass with our world as universals, given our secularized, hand-to-mouth versions of the claims of religion, of politics, of social morality? Surely the absolute is not to be found immanently within such as these. Justice, then, has passed from the universal to the rebellious individual; accordingly, our appropriate spokesman on matters relating the individual to the universal and the absolute is not the anachronistic system builder, Hegel, but that heterodox and unprofessional wrecker of the Hegelian universe, Søren Kierkegaard.

> Faith is precisely this paradox, that the individual as the particular is higher than the universal, is justified over against it, is not subordinate but superior — yet in such a way, be it observed, that it is the particular individual who, after he has been subordinated as the particular to the universal, now through the universal becomes the individual who as the particular is superior to the universal, for the fact that the individual as the particular stands in an absolute relation to the absolute.[3]

At what is for Kierkegaard the most crucial moment of man's existence — the moment of the leap to faith — the absolute is attainable only through the individual, the particular, the purely personal. It is denied to the universal. Here, unhappily enough perhaps, is the answer of modernism's "isolato" to the Hegelian attempt to restore the union of men within a congenial universe that sanctioned, indeed commanded, and fixed its divine blessing upon, this union. For Kierkegaard, the ultimate act — the act of faith — cannot be mediated, since only universals can mediate. Consequently, the paradox of faith is "inaccessible to thought" and cannot be verbally communicated, both thought and language — like reason, on which they largely depend — necessarily expressing universals. Further, it is the inaccessibility of faith to mediation that makes the Abraham who intended to sacrifice Isaac either a murderer or a "true knight of faith"

[3] *Fear and Trembling*, by Søren Kierkegaard, tr. Walter Lowrie (Princeton, N.J.: Princeton University Press, 1941), p. 82.

— in my terminology, either a tragic visionary[4], or a religious visionary — but *not* the sacrificer of his individual self to the universal expressed in moral law. The latter individual would be the highest form of ethical man but, for Kierkegaard, something less than either visionary. And Kierkegaard's Abraham, whichever visionary he may be, repudiates the universal. Thus the "immediacy" of either the tragic or the religious vision eliminates the universal as a possible resting place for the errant, as a possible justification of what he has so privately dared to will. And we can never be sure which of the two visions he carries. Indeed, now beyond reason, how can he himself claim certainty? For the religious vision would be too easy for Kierkegaard if one could *know* its authenticity.

The categories which Kierkegaard can help us impose provide our insecure world with alternatives to the way of Greek tragedy as it is interpreted by Nietzsche as well as by Hegel. While Nietzsche is, like Kierkegaard, an unhappy epitome of modern man, an alienated creature who is close to being himself a tragic visionary, he is like Hegel in wistfully finding and admiring in early tragedy the elements of reconciliation that give order to elements of chaotic conflict. Nietzsche sees united in tragedy the Apollonian and Dionysian motives, appropriately named by him for their respective gods: the one the dreamlike, sublime, and gracefully measured order of the light principle, in the highest sense the civilizing principle; the other the primordial, orgiastic release of the natural principle — the "underground" reality probably related to Jung's "racial unconscious" or to Freud's "id" — the barbarizing principle.[5] Nietzsche sees these motives as akin to the forces represented by the creative and yet restrained Olympians and by the chaos-producing Titans, except, of course, that instead of the unreconcilable warfare between Olympians and Titans there is in Greek culture a perfect blending of the Apollonian and the Dionysian.

> The Greek knew and felt the terror and horror of existence. That he might endure this terror at all, he had to interpose between himself and life the radiant dream-birth of the Olympians. . . . out of the original Titan thearchy of terror the Olympian thearchy of joy gradually evolved through the Apollonian impulse towards beauty. . . . How else could this people, so sensitive, so vehement in its desires, so singularly constituted for *suffering*, how could they have endured existence, if it had not been revealed to them in their gods, surrounded with a higher glory?

[4] In light of the shriveling of the tragic concept in the modern world and the reduction of a total view to the psychology of the protagonist, I believe that this protagonist is now more appropriately designated "tragic visionary" than he is "tragic hero."

[5] For this entire discussion, see "The Birth of Tragedy," tr. C. P. Fadiman, *The Philosophy of Nietzsche* (New York: Modern Library, n.d.), especially pp. 951–969, 992–1017.

Thus the Apollonian can so transform Dionysian terror "that lamentation itself becomes a song of praise."

Here is another thematic rendering of the principle of catharsis. But in order to make the formula work properly, both motives have to be maintained and maintained in equal strength. The Dionysian must be there for the Apollonian to transform, so that Apollonian radiance can retain its brilliance only by continually illuminating the Dionysian abyss. But it is an abyss which must not be denied, indeed must be acknowledged for what it is. Without the Dionysian, the Apollonian would seem to reflect a shallow, unearned optimism, a misreading of life that leaves the inescapable terror out of it. Thus Nietzsche can scorn the bland interpretations of "the serious and significant idea of Greek cheerfulness": "no matter where we turn at the present time we encounter the false notion that this cheerfulness results from a state of unendangered comfort." For the Apollonian cannot sustain itself in isolation; it can exist only in counterposition to the Dionysian. Otherwise it becomes perverted — as Nietzsche tells us it was perverted through Euripides — into the merely "Socratic," that moralistic denier of the Dionysian and consequently the destroyer of tragedy.

But what if we should find the Dionysian without the Apollonian? Here we would have life unalleviated, endlessly and unendurably dangerous, finally destructive and self-destructive — in short, the demoniacal. In effect it would be like tragedy without that moment in which the play comes round and the cosmos is saved and returned to us intact. It would be, in other words, the tragic vision wandering free of its capacious home in tragedy. The therapy produced by catharsis, which allowed the subversive elements to be healthily exposed and aesthetically overcome, would no longer be available. And the alienated members, now unchallenged, would be free to turn inward upon themselves to nourish their indignation in the dark underground. Nietzsche himself has told us:

> The tradition is undisputed that Greek tragedy in its earliest form had for its sole theme the sufferings of Dionysus, and that for a long time the only stage-hero was simply Dionysus himself . . . until Euripides, Dionysus never once ceased to be the tragic hero . . . . in fact all the celebrated figures of the Greek Stage — Prometheus, Oedipus, etc. — are but masks of this original hero, Dionysus.

But picture a world into which Dionysus cannot be reabsorbed by way of the Apollonian with its final assertion of Greek "cheerfulness" and aesthetic form, a world in which the Apollonian and Dionysian — long since torn asunder — must live in a lasting separation that causes each to pervert its nature, the Apollonian becoming the superficial worship of happiness and the Dionysian the abandoned worship of demonism. Our modern tragic vision is the Dionysian vision still, except that the visionary is now utterly lost, since there is no cosmic order to allow a return to the world for him who has dared stray beyond.

The Kierkegaardian spirit would rather characterize the tragic vision as "despair," perhaps finally much the same thing. It is despair which for Kierkegaard is both the most wretched and the most hopeful stage of man's sub-Christian existence. With some interpolation and considerable simplification on my part, the phenomenological pattern one may draw from Kierkegaard for the tragic visionary may be seen as something like the following sketch.[6] A man lives his day-to-day existence below the religious level, either "aesthetically," as an amoral or submoral hedonist, or "ethically," by easily subscribing, consciously or unconsciously, but for the most part automatically, to that hierarchy of moral values which enables him comfortably to function. If he is a self-conscious moralist, he is concerned with the discovery of order in apparent disorder; concerned, that is, with universal principles, but principles that are discoverable in and referable to the world of human relations.

While the ethical level is certainly an advance over the mindless complacency in the midst of an unperceived chaos found on Kierkegaard's "aesthetic"[7] level, nevertheless this ethical level, because it sees values — and the order constructed in terms of values — as immanent rather than as transcendent, must itself remain pragmatic in its dictates for action. The orderly and abstract principles, bounded by the uses of this world and resting on rationality, must resist the paradox or absurdity which for Kierkegaard characterizes the immediacy and subjectivity of Christian consciousness. Thus finally common-sense pragmatism must inhere in the ethical level.[8] And our ethical man, assuming the validity of his ab-

[6] In the interest of accuracy it must be acknowledged that Kierkegaard himself explicitly defines what he calls the tragic hero very differently from the way I am attributing to his view here. In *Fear and Trembling* he specifically claims that "the tragic hero still remains within the ethical." He sees the tragic hero as allowing himself to be embraced by the universal, his most cherished interests to be sacrificed to it. Perhaps here, as in so many other instances, Kierkegaard finds himself borrowing from the very Hegelianism he is bent on destroying. I believe that, as part of his dissatisfaction with the aesthetic in general, he never took this matter of the tragic as seriously as he might have taken it, that he never realized the revolutionary treatment of it that is promised by his other philosophic claims. It is thus, I hope, in the Kierkegaardian spirit, that I use Kierkegaard to support my own claims about the tragic though they run counter to his own occasional declarations.

[7] Whenever I use this term in the very special way of Kierkegaard I shall set it in quotation marks. Where it appears without them, it is being used in its common sense that pertains primarily to works of art and to our proper and limited responses to them as art.

[8] It is here, in his insistence that religion has dimensions beyond morality, that Kierkegaard strikes at the roots of that naturalistic humanism which would identify the two. Of course one may claim that Kierkegaard rather overdoes their separation since for him, it seems, the one (religion) can begin only where the other (morality) leaves off. I must, however, make it clear that, whenever speaking here of Kierkegaard's concept of religion, I mean only his version of Christianity. It must be conceded that in many places he refers to a pre-Christian, almost naturalistic religion, one in which the absolute is still immanent in the universal

stract and universal principles inasmuch as they are conducive to order, can make decisions cleanly, can act in accordance with these principles — as if they were the absolute — since they blink the possible existence of a true moral dilemma characterized by endless ambiguity. This is the farthest reach of Hegelian man.

But our man can undergo a cosmic "shock": he can one day, to use Kafka's metaphor, wake up and find himself irrevocably arrested "without having done anything wrong." Or an Ahab, living until then by the proper laws of seamanship, can one day lose his leg to the leviathan; a Lord Jim, living until then by a schoolboy's code of honor, can one day be paralyzed into inaction and be made to play the coward's role. Melville's Pierre, having dedicated himself at all costs to absolute righteousness, can discover in his righteousness a lust that has led to incest; Conrad's Kurtz, having dedicated himself through altruism to a missionary zeal, can discover in his zeal a worship of self and of gold that has led to blood sacrifice. Perhaps this shattering seizure is precisely what ethical man has had coming for assuming, as fallible individual, his identification with an ethical absolute. For the ethical is, by definition, the universal. And, however well meaning, the individual may very well be doomed to pervert the absolute he claims to represent, since he comes to it as individual and particular, and thus as unsanctioned.

In any case, with the shock our man is jarred loose. For "aesthetic" man the oblivious evasions of hedonic existence will of course no longer do. And ethical man, confronted by a moral contradiction which resists the elimination of either pole as well as the synthesis of both, finds suddenly that the neatly ordered and easily enacted worldly rights and wrongs of his ethical assumptions are utterly inadequate to the data of his moral experience. Unless he yields to "infinite resignation" by blindly, if courageously, sacrificing himself to the implacable demands of ethical absoluteness — thus at all costs still remaining Hegelian man[9] — he must deny its authority forever. And then, hopelessly adrift from his or any other moorings, he can float into will-lessness and thus abdicate from tragic heroism, or he can surge toward the demoniac. If his rebellion has rendered him unfit for society and its necessary universals — its laws — it is because, at whatever price, he has seen beyond them. If his end, as tragic, must be condemned even as it is pitied by the trim categories of

---

and which, consequently, still falls within the ethical. But if this stoical kind of religion can produce "the knight of infinite resignation," in its security it of course cannot begin to reach toward "the true knight of faith," who is rather a product of the loneliness and daring, the absurdity and subjectivity of Christian consciousness. It is only his notion of Christianity — defiant as it is of the ethical — to which Kierkegaard attributes absolute value, so that, to simplify matters, I have felt justified in speaking of it informally as his notion of religion in general, to the neglect of his other, inferior kind of religion.

[9] This is in effect Kierkegaard's own definition of the tragic hero. He allows him to go no further; and this admission on my part indicates how far beyond him I have without authorization moved using his tools.

worldly morality, he may, prideful as he is, take further pride in the fact that he has defiantly looked upon those insoluble cosmic antinomies which have dictated his fall.

Someone like Conrad's Marlow, however — the sensible even if sensitive man — must, at whatever cost to his pride and his vision, finally rest in the ethical level, however sympathetic he may be to those who have renounced it to move into the realm of the tragic. Who is to say whether it is out of a "failure of nerve" or out of a special strength flowing from a profoundly tranquil vision, hardly known to us since the Greeks, that he has resisted the unmitigated tragic? It depends, very likely, on whether our view is Kierkegaard's or that of a less austere, less Protestant authority; on whether ours is the tragic vision or the classic vision.

On the other hand, our excommunicated ethical man, realizing the complete futility of human existence, cannot find a relationship with anything beyond it. His permanent forsaking of the universal seems to forbid it. This, the essence of the tragic vision, is "the sickness unto death," despair. It is the stage induced by the shock; the stage which, beyond the "aesthetic" and the ethical, yet falls short of Kierkegaard's version of the Christian. An advance over the first two, it is yet much more treacherous and, if one remains in it continually, far more miserable. If one can attain a break-through — a bravely irrational one unmediated by universals — he can reach the glories of transcendence; if he fails, he must live in the contemplation of nothingness. Or, to put it more specifically, at best he can become a Kierkegaard, if we grant that Kierkegaard ever, or for very long, accomplished the leap of faith; if not, he must remain in the torments of the Zarathustrian Nietzsche or of a more consistent Heidegger who constantly and unblinkingly dares encounter the nothingness that has capriciously hurled him into momentary existence. But he can never again rest in the self-deceptions of our John Deweys: those of our insistent naturalists who, for all the hardheadedness of their religious disbelief, are yet naively optimistic believers in a structured social morality and in social progress. These are, from the Kierkegaardian standpoint, the men of little heart; those who, evading the atheist's existential obligation to confront nothingness and its frighteningly empty consequences, construct elaborate rational structures based on nothing else: who whistle in the dark as if all were light.

One may prefer to say that it represents a supreme act of human courage to create meaningful communal structures of value on a substructure of acknowledged nothingness. Perhaps, as humanists say, man's creating God *is* a more sublime act than God's creating man. Perhaps. But the honest existentialist — anxious to confront his ontological status — would see the naturalist's structure in the void as an evasive act of bravado, not a closing act of bravery.

In the Kierkegaardian universe, then, there are two authentic visions — those I have termed the tragic and the religious — that can be earned through crisis by being forged in what Dostoevsky spoke of as the "great furnace of doubt." The other I have referred to is in this sense an illusory one. For the cheerfully naturalistic vision, which, pampering its security, denies itself nothing despite the fearsome implications of its own metaphysical denials, which existentially shirks the void it must rationally insist upon, is a precrisis vision, an illusion of ethical man demanded by his comfort, but one the stricken man can no longer afford. Like Kurtz, the tragic visionary may at the critical moment search within and find himself "hollow at the core," but only because he has suddenly been seized from without by the hollowness of his moral universe, whose structure and meaning have until then sustained him. What the shock reveals to its victim — the existential absurdity of the moral life — explodes the meaning of the moral life, its immanent god and ground. And there can be no postcrisis meaning and god except in defiance of reason, in acknowledgment of the impossibly paradoxical nature of moral existence. But this is to go beyond the despair that defines the tragic visionary and to make the leap to the transcendent subjectivity of the only kind of religious vision that the Kierkegaardian Protestant world leaves to the stricken.[10]

On the other hand, the tragic visionary, in taking the alternative of defiance and seizing upon nothingness, is alone bold enough to take the existential consequences of his godlessness; and he takes them with pride, the very *hybris* that, in its sinfulness, moved him to godlessness rather than to transcendence. But he does not, like the naturalist, try to play both sides of the street to earn the prize of an ungrounded something: a world philosophically negated which is somehow made to yield the existential ease that would come if there were a meaning and purpose to be grasped. Sick of his precrisis delusion, the tragic visionary is God's angry man who will take only the real thing. He will refuse any longer to fool himself with the comfortable communal halfway houses of good works as

[10] Although this issue may not seem germane to a discussion of the tragic vision, it is worth adding — in order to expose another favorite illusion of our naturalistic and antiexistential tradition — that the religious vision described here cannot in fairness be reduced to any so-called "failure of nerve." This phrase the Kierkegaardian would reserve for the ethical man who flees the impact of the shock, for the naturalist himself. The shock may indeed cause our nerves to quake, but they fail only with the failure of our inner strength to manage, from the depths of despair, the awesome leap that makes "the true knight of faith" — no easy accomplishment and hardly a soothing one. The earned religious vision must not be cheapened. It is a vision that runs quite counter to that implied by the Philistine claim that there were "no atheists on Bataan." No matter how devout the final protestations of these doomed souls, these protestations were all simply too comforting in their urgency, from the Kierkegaardian point of view, to have a claim to religious authenticity. Thus Kierkegaard comments on people who want to make an easy, escapist thing of faith:

> . . . these caricatures of faith are part and parcel of life's wretchedness, and the infinite resignation has already consigned them to infinite contempt. . . . They would suck worldly wisdom out of the paradox. Perhaps one or another may succeed in that, for our age is not willing to stop with faith, with its miracle of turning water into wine, it goes further, it turns wine into water. (*Fear and Trembling*, p. 50.)

a substitute for the absolute dedication of a religious faith which his inherited skepticism, issuing its curse, has denied him.

Of course, from a less severely Protestant point of view, other "authentic" visions would be sanctioned. One that concerned me earlier is what I called the classic vision, a vision that is of the world without being crass, that is universal and conducive to order without optimistically thinning moral reality as the superficially ethical man would. This vision is the all-embracing one of an older world and an older order. It is what I have tried to talk about in discussing the formal and thematic triumph of tragedy over the errant tragic vision it contained within it. It is as if the security of the older order wanted to test the profundity of its assurances, its capacity to account for the whole of human experience, and thus bred within itself the tragic vision as its *agent provocateur*. And by having the rebellion incarnate in the tragic visionary finally succumb to a higher order which absorbs but never denies the "destructive element," by purifying itself through the cathartic principle, tragedy is asserting the argument a fortiori for the affirmation of its humanistic and yet superhumanistic values. Consequently, it can witness all that befalls its hero without sharing in his disavowal of the meaning of our moral life; without denying, with him, the sensibleness of the universe and of life despite the explosive terrors they can hold in store.

But human possibilities, reduced as they are by disintegrations within the world that produced a Kierkegaard as its spokesman, no longer can reach to so inclusive a vision. If the only appeal to universals, to order, is prereligious as well as pretragic, then the path of the religious visionary is as solitary as the tragic visionary's. And the ethical once shattered, there is no higher return to community — although, of course, for the less daring there may always be a retreat. The tragic vision remains what it was, but it can no longer be made through tragedy to yield to an order and a shared religious vision. The ultimately absorbent power of tragedy, symbolic of the earned affirmation of universals, is gone, with the result that the solitary visionary is left unchallenged, except by the threats of uncomprehending and unsympathizing destruction at the hands of aroused ethical righteousness, the arm of social practicality. This is hardly the all-deserving antagonist the tragic vision once had, nor is it one that can command a satisfying aesthetic completeness any more than it can a moral-religious unity. Instead, in the Kierkegaardian universe, we now find for the aware and authentic existent an unresolvable disjunctive: either the way of nothingness or the way of transcendence, but both equally the way of utter solitude. The universals which must damn him have been left behind.

It is perhaps for these reasons that recent literature expressing an earned religious vision is hard to come by. For this kind of religious vision is primarily characterized by the fact that it cannot be shared. Equally subjective, the tragic as the demoniac vision can at least be dramatized by being contrasted to the ethical with which it is at war and which, in defense of society, must seek to punish it — for good reasons and for bad. We can be shown the ambiguous nature of the values at stake in this struggle: the need for the insights provided by the tragic to advance our understanding beyond the unaccommodating caution of social necessity as institutionalized in the ethical; and yet the need to strike out at the visionary, to cling to the props society provides, at whatever cost to insight, since, man being a social animal, his struggle through daily drudgeries is a crucial and ordering activity that must not be threatened.

To sustain a balance and, consequently, an aesthetic tension between these antagonists, the author must resist identifying himself too thoroughly either with the tragic visionary or with the representative of the ethical. If he becomes one with his ethical man, he must dismiss the tragic realm too summarily, without granting its power — however costly — of revealing the full density of moral experience and the shallowness of the reasonable order it has been forced to cast off. And he must sell the vision short as vision, however quick he is to see it as tragic, or anyway as doomed, if not as at worst merely execrable or at best pathetic. Or if, on the other hand, the author becomes one with his tragic visionary, he so cuts himself off from man's communal need that, in surrendering to moral chaos, he surrenders also the only possibility left him to impose aesthetic form. Further, he shows himself to be too sure of the vision to acknowledge it as really tragic, however quick he is — in contrast to our too ethical author — to grant its value as a vision. Only within the balance, and the mutual qualifications it provides, can the vision be maintained both as tragic and as a vision worthy of our concern and our wonder. Thus, at the one extreme, in *Heart of Darkness*, for example, Conrad, through his alter ego Marlow, rejects Kurtz — indeed is utterly offended by the man — only in continual acknowledgment that his rebellion against decency, however odious, renders him in some way superior even to Marlow. And, at the other extreme, close as Gide comes to embracing the reckless passions of his hero in *The Immoralist*, the classical artist in him maintains enough distance to reveal to us honestly, and even with some condemnation, their destructive and self-destructive consequences.

Even with the ethical and the tragic held in such balance, however, the ethical may seem finally to be treated superciliously and even as at least half blind to what really is going on. And since the tragic is from the ethical standpoint so dangerously evil, there would seem to be a need for some level beyond the ethical from which the tragic visionary would be judged absolutely — a level which would include his insight and with it soar beyond a parochial pragmatism, but one which would have passed beyond the rage of rebellion to a final, perhaps other worldly affirmation. But this is to call once again for what we no longer have — for the transformations that only tragedy can perform. For how are we now to distinguish outwardly between the religious and the tragic, between the angelic and the demoniac, when both equally transgress the ethical and the universal? As Kierkegaard in such brilliant detail asks, how shall we tell the Abraham among us from the self-deceived, maddened infanticide? To stop short of the religious insight is of course to rest in demonism; yet to leap to the religious vision, itself a perilous undertaking, is not to deny the temporal and, of course, the dramatic validity of the tragic. In neither instance is a retreat to the ethical possible. And the balance of necessities between the tragic and the ethical must continue as the primary mode of dramatic conflict, with the inherent weaknesses of each — the moral failing of the one and the visionary failing of the other — poised against each other to create the unresolvable tension that must now replace tragedy's more sublime catharsis as the principle of aesthetic control.

By now I hope I have clarified the sense in which I have been speaking of the unrelieved tragic vision as a modern vision, which is to claim also that it is a Protestant vision and, in an obvious sense, a romantic vision. Further, in its seizing upon the particular and its denial of any totality it is an heretical vision; and in its defiance of all rational moral order it is a demoniac vision. Finally, in a very special sense it is a casuistic vision; and it is this characteristic, perhaps, that makes it especially accessible to literary portrayal. The tragic vision, a product of crisis and of shock, is an expression of man only in an extreme situation, never in a normal or routine one. Literature dealing with it frequently dwells on the exceptional man; and when it does choose a normal man it does so only to convert him, by way of the extremity he lives through, into the exceptional man. The tragic vision is, by my definition, a vision of extreme cases, a distillate of the rebellion, the godlessness which, once induced by crisis, purifies itself by rejecting all palliatives. And the tragic visionary, by the stark austerity of his ontological position and of his dramatic position in the fable, is the extremist who — despite his rich intermingling with the stuff of experience — finds himself transformed from character to parable.

The literary obsession with extremity, with the exceptional, may represent an attempt at realism ultimately more sincere and more authentic than the cultivation of the norm, of what Lionel Trilling celebrates as "the common routine." If one wishes to assume the Kierkegaardian version of the human predicament, he will insist that it does and that at all times it has represented the only authentic attempt at realism. Even without Kierkegaardian psychoanalysis, however, we must admit that, at least in our time, driven as it is by crises and "arrests" and blind as it is to the healing power and saving grace of tragedy, the tragic has come, however unfortunately, to loom as a necessary vision and — or so it seems to the sadder of us — as one that can be neither reduced nor absorbed. Or is it, perhaps, that the Kierkegaardian version is right and that our world has itself become the tragic visionary, in its unbelief using self-destructive crises to force itself finally to confront the absurdities of earthly reality — those which have always been there lurking beneath for the visionary who would dare give up all to read them? Which is to ask, fearfully and even unwillingly, whether we have not been beguiled by aesthetic satisfactions and whether the utterly stripped tragic vision may not after all be less illusory than the fullness which shines through tragedy.

BASIC CHARACTERISTICS OF THE TRAGIC

The tragic looms before us as an event that shows the terrifying aspects of existence, but an existence that is still human. It reveals its entanglement with the uncharted background of man's humanity. Paradoxically, however, when man faces the tragic, he liberates himself from it. This is one way of obtaining purification and redemption.

Breakdown and failure reveal the true nature of things. In failure, life's reality is not lost; on the contrary, here it makes itself wholly and decisively felt. *There is no tragedy without transcendence.* Even defiance unto death in a hopeless battle against gods and fate is an act of transcending: it is a movement toward man's proper essence, which he comes to know as his own in the presence of his doom.

Where awareness of the tragic has become fundamental to man's awareness of reality, we speak of tragic readiness.[1] But we must distinguish between awareness of the transitoriness of things and genuine awareness of the tragic.

When he thinks of transitoriness, man views the actual events leading up to death, as well as the ephemeral character of all life, as parts of the natural cycle of growth, decay, and renewed growth. He recognizes himself as within nature and identifies himself with it. Here man comes upon a secret that makes him tremble. What is the soul which, independent of the flux of time, knows itself to be immortal, although aware of the finiteness of its worldly existence, aware that it is doomed to pass away in death? Yet, neither this fact of morality nor this secret of the soul can rightly be termed tragic.

Genuine awareness of the tragic, on the contrary, is more than mere contemplation of suffering and death, flux and extinction. If these things are to become tragic, man must act. It is only then, through his own actions, that man enters into the tragic involvement that inevitably must destroy him. What will be ruined here is not merely man's life as concrete existence, but every concrete embodiment of whatever perfection he

"Basic Characteristics of the Tragic," from *Tragedy Is Not Enough* by Karl Jaspers. Reprinted by permission of the Beacon Press, copyright © 1952 by the Beacon Press. [Translator's minor footnotes have been omitted and those remaining have been renumbered.]

[1] *Tragische Haltung*: This is the inner attitude of composure in the face of tragedy; it resembles Hamlet's "the readiness is all."

sought. Man's mind fails and breaks down in the very wealth of its potentialities. Every one of these potentialities, as it becomes fulfilled, provokes and reaps disaster.

A yearning for deliverance has always gone hand in hand with the
knowledge of the tragic. When man encounters the hard fact of tragedy,
he faces an inexorable limit. At this limit, he finds no guarantee of general salvation. Rather, it is in acting out his own personality, in realizing
his selfhood even unto death, that he finds redemption and deliverance.

He may find this deliverance through his sheer strength to bear the unknown without question, and to endure it with unshakable defiance. This,
however, is the mere seed of deliverance, its barest possible form. Or he
may find deliverance by opening his eyes to the nature of the tragic process
which, brought to light, can purify the mind. Finally, deliverance may
already have preceded contemplation of the tragic process in the case
where some faith has, from the outset, led life onto the road to salvation.
Then, tragedy appears as overcome from the beginning as man transcends
to the unseen, to God, the background of all backgrounds.

. . . .

GUILT

Tragedy becomes self-conscious by understanding the fate of its characters as the consequence of guilt, and as the inner working out of guilt itself.
Destruction is the atonement of guilt.

To be sure, the world is full of guiltless destruction. Hidden evil destroys without being seen; it acts without being heard; no worldly authority
so much as hears about it, any more than when someone was being tortured to death in the dungeon of a castle. Men die as martyrs without
being martyrs, in so far as no one is present to bear witness or to learn of
their martyrdom. Every day some defenseless creatures are being tortured
and destroyed on this earth. Ivan Karamazov flies into a mad rage at the
thought of the children killed for mere pleasure by the warring Turks.
But this whole heartrending, gruesome reality is not tragic, in so far as
disaster is not the atonement of a guilt and is unconnected with the meaning of this life.

The question of guilt, however, is not limited to the actions and lives of
individual men. Rather, it refers to humanity as a whole, of which every
one of us is a part. Where are we to look for the guilt that is responsible
for all this undeserved disaster? Where is the power that makes the innocent miserable?

Wherever men saw this question clearly, they conceived of the idea of
complicity in guilt. All men are jointly committed and jointly liable.
Their common origin and their common goal account for this. A token
of this, though not an explanation, is that we feel shaken and perplexed
at the following thought, which seems absurd to our limited understanding: I am responsible for all the evil that is perpetrated in the world,
unless I have done what I could to prevent it, even to the extent of sacri-

ficing my life. I am guilty because I am alive and can continue to live while this is happening. Thus criminal complicity takes hold of everyone for everything that happens.

We must therefore speak of guilt in the wider sense of a guilt of human existence as such, and of guilt in the narrower sense of responsibility for any particular action. Where our own guilt is not limited to certain specific wrongdoings but, in a deeper sense, is found in the very nature of human existence, there the idea of guilt becomes truly inclusive. Tragic knowledge, therefore, distinguishes these two kinds of guilt:

First: Existence is guilt. Guilt in the larger sense is identical with existence as such. The idea, already found in Anaximander, recurs in Calderón, although in a different sense — that man's greatest guilt is to have been born.

This is revealed also in the fact that my very existence causes misery. Indian thought has an image for this: with every step, with every breath, I destroy living beings. Whether I act or not, merely by existing I infringe upon the existence of others. Passive or active, I incur the guilt of existence.

A particular life is guilty through its origin. True, I did not desire this world nor my particular existence in it. But I am guilty against my will, simply because it is I myself who have this origin. My descent from guilty ancestors causes my own guilt.

Antigone is born contrary to the law as the daughter of Oedipus and his own mother. The curse of her descent is active within her. But her very exclusion from the norm of legitimate descent accounts for her singular depth and human feeling: she possesses the surest and most unshakable knowledge of the divine law. She dies because she is greater than the others, because her exceptional case embodies truth. And she dies gladly. Death to her means release; all along her road of action she is at one with herself.

A particular character is guilty because of what he is.[2] Character is itself a form of destiny — in so far as I detach myself from my own character and turn to look upon it.

What baseness there is in me, what desires to do evil, what unregenerate pride there is in my perversity — all this I myself have neither wanted nor created. Yet I am guilty of all this. And my guilt begets my destiny, whether I die unwillingly and unredeemed, or whether I am destroyed in trying to transcend my base nature by summoning up a deeper resource of my being — a resource which enables me to reject what I was, even though I cannot become what I long to be.

Second: Action is guilt. Guilt in the narrower sense is found in any distinct action I carry out freely in the sense that it need not occur and could also occur differently.

---

[2] This was the "Orphic" view of Rohde and Nietzsche, now generally abandoned on the basis of new manuscript evidence brought forward by Diels. See, e.g., Jaeger, Theology, pp. 34 ff.

Guilty action may consist in flouting the law; it is personal arbitrariness consciously opposing the universal for no other reason than its own arbitrariness. It is the consequence of culpable ignorance, of half-conscious transpositions and concealments of motives. Nothing else is involved in such wilfulness beyond the misery of meanness and evil.

The situation is different when tragic knowledge recognizes the guilt of an action. Truthful and morally necessary action, although springing from the foundation of freedom, may entail failure. Man cannot escape his guilt through right and truthful conduct: guilt itself seems incurred guiltlessly. Man takes this guilt upon himself. He does not try to evade it. He stands by his guilt, not out of personal stubbornness, but for the sake of the very truth, which is destined for failure in his necessary sacrifice.[3]

MAN'S GREATNESS IN FAILURE

Tragic knowledge cannot be extended and deepened without seeing in man the quality of greatness over and above his atonement of guilt.

That man is not God is the cause of his smallness and undoing. But that he can carry his human possibilities to their extreme and can be undone by them with his eyes open — that is his greatness.

What we essentially learn from tragic knowledge, therefore, is what makes man suffer and what makes him fail, what he takes upon himself in the face of which realities, and in what manner or form he sacrifices his existence.

The tragic hero — man heightened and intensified — is man himself in good and evil, fulfilling himself in goodness and canceling out his own identity in evil.[4] In each case his existence is shipwrecked by the consistency with which he meets some unconditional demand, real or supposed.

His resistance, stubbornness, and pride drive him into the "greatness" of evil. His endurance, his dauntlessness, his love, raise him up into the good. Always he grows in stature through the experience of life at its limits. The poet sees in him the bearer of something that reaches beyond individual existence, the bearer of a power, a principle, a character, a demon.

Tragedy depicts a man in his greatness beyond good and evil. The poet's view resembles that of Plato: "Or do you suppose that great crimes and unmixed wickedness spring from a slight nature and not from a vigorous one . . . while a weak nature will never be the cause of anything great, either for good or for evil?" It is from the most gifted type of man that "these spring who do the greatest harm to communities and individuals, and the greatest good . . . but a small nature never does anything great for a man or a city."[5]

---

[3] *Schuld des Soseins*: this is guilt, not of existence, origin, or action, but arising from the stubbornness and meanness in one's character.

[4] *Im Bösen, sich vernichtigend*: this implies both physical and spiritual self-destruction.

[5] Plato, *Republic*, VI, 491 e, 495 b. Shorey translation (Loeb Classical Library).

from **THE TRAGIC FALLACY**

Modern critics have sometimes been puzzled to account for the fact that the concern of ancient tragedy is almost exclusively with kings and courts. They have been tempted to accuse even Aristotle of a certain naïveté in assuming (as he seems to assume) that the "nobility" of which he speaks as necessary to a tragedy implies a nobility of rank as well as of soul, and they have sometimes regretted that Shakespeare did not devote himself more than he did to the serious consideration of those common woes of the common man which subsequent writers have exploited with increasing pertinacity. Yet the tendency to lay the scene of a tragedy at the court of a king is not the result of any arbitrary convention but of the fact that the tragic writers believed easily in greatness just as we believe easily in meanness. To Shakespeare, robes and crowns and jewels are the garments most appropriate to man because they are the fitting outward manifestation of his inward majesty, but to us they seem absurd because the man who bears them has, in our estimation, so pitifully shrunk. We do not write about kings because we do not believe that any man is worthy to be one and we do not write about courts because hovels seem to us to be dwellings more appropriate to the creatures who inhabit them. Any modern attempt to dress characters in robes ends only by making us aware of a comic incongruity and any modern attempt to furnish them with a language resplendent like Shakespeare's ends only in bombast.

True tragedy capable of performing its function and of purging the soul by reconciling man to his woes can exist only by virtue of a certain pathetic fallacy far more inclusive than that to which the name is commonly given. The romantics, feeble descendants of the tragic writers to whom they are linked by their effort to see life and nature in grandiose terms, loved to imagine that the sea or the sky had a way of according itself with their moods, of storming when they stormed and smiling when they smiled. But the tragic spirit sustains itself by an assumption much more far-reaching and no more justified. Man as it sees him lives in a world which he may not dominate but which is always aware of him. Occupying the exact center of a universe which would have no meaning except for him and being so little below the angels that, if he believes in God, he has no hesitation in imagining Him formed as he is formed and crowned with a crown like that which he or one of his fellows wears, he assumes that each of his acts reverberates through the universe. His passions are important to him because he believes them important throughout all time and all space; the very fact that he can sin (no modern can) means that this universe is watching his acts; and though he may perish, a God leans out from infinity to strike him down. And it is exactly because an Ibsen cannot think of man in any such terms as these that his persons have so shrunk and that his "tragedy" has lost that power which real tragedy always has of making that infinitely ambitious creature called man content to accept his misery if only he can be made to feel great enough and important enough. An Oswald is not a Hamlet chiefly because he has lost that tie with the natural and supernatural world which the latter had. No ghost will leave the other world to warn or encourage him, there is no virtue and no vice which he can possibly have which can be really important, and when he dies neither his death nor the manner of it will be, outside the circle of two or three people as unnecessary as himself, any more important than that of a rat behind the arras.

Perhaps we may dub the illusion upon which the tragic spirit is nourished the Tragic, as opposed to the Pathetic, Fallacy, but fallacy though it is, upon its existence depends not merely the writing of tragedy but the existence of that religious feeling of which tragedy is an expression and by means of which a people aware of the dissonances of life manages nevertheless to hear them as harmony. Without it neither man nor his passions can seem great enough or important enough to justify the sufferings which they entail, and literature, expressing the mood of a people, begins to despair where once it had exulted. Like the belief in love and like most of the other mighty illusions by means of which human life has been given a value, the Tragic Fallacy depends ultimately upon the assumption which man so readily makes that something outside his own being, some "spirit not himself" — be it God, Nature, or that still vaguer thing called a Moral Order — joins him in the emphasis which he places upon this or that and confirms him in his feeling that his passions and his opinions are important. When his instinctive faith in that correspondence between the outer and the inner world fades, his grasp upon the faith that sustained him fades also, and Love or Tragedy or what not ceases to be the reality which it was because he is never strong enough in his own insignificant self to stand alone in a universe which snubs him with its indifference.

In both the modern and the ancient worlds tragedy was dead long before writers were aware of the fact. Seneca wrote his frigid melodramas under the impression that he was following in the footsteps of Sophocles, and Dryden probably thought that his *All for Love* was an improvement upon Shakespeare, but in time we awoke to the fact that no amount of rhetorical bombast could conceal the fact that grandeur was not to be counterfeited when the belief in its possibility was dead, and turning from the hero to the common man, we inaugurated the era of realism.

For us no choice remains except that between mere rhetoric and the frank consideration of our fellow men, who may be the highest of the anthropoids but who are certainly too far below the angels to imagine either that these angels can concern themselves with them or that they can catch any glimpse of even the soles of angelic feet. We can no longer tell tales of the fall of noble men because we do not believe that noble men exist. The best that we can achieve is pathos and the most that we can do is to feel sorry for ourselves. Man has put off his royal robes and it is only in sceptered pomp that tragedy can come sweeping by.

KENNETH BURKE

ON TRAGEDY

Ambitious writers have selected the "death of tragedy" as an instance of science's destructive effect upon the highest poetry. Tragedy, they have observed, was developed out of a sense of theological or metaphysical stability; man was dignified; he had some direct or personal relationship with the forces of the cosmos; his problems were of vast importance in the universal scheme. But the "illusions" of tragedy are slain by the scientific point of view, which leaves us too humiliated for the noble, godlike posturings of tragedy, wherein man shares the "mystic participation" which M. Lévy-Bruhl attributes to the savage: that sense of the universe as being personally with him or against him. Tragedy is ruined, they say, when the "illusion" of man's personal connection with superhuman processes is lost, when he is looked upon as a mere species of animal that happens to inhabit a planet for a certain number of years between its birth and its extinction. This "death of tragedy" (and thus, the death of the very essence of poetry) is manifested already as an inability to write great tragedies — and in time it will even be manifested as an inability to appreciate the great tragedies already written. Such is, in essence, the position of those who hold to a fundamental opposition between poetry and science — and it has been stated with much fervour and fluency by Mr. Krutch in his volume *The Modern Temper*.

From *Counter-statement*, by Kenneth Burke, Hermes edition (1953), pp. 199–201. Reprinted by permission of Hermes Publications, Los Altos, California.

Mr. Krutch combines under his concept of tragedy both the tragic drama and the tragic spirit. Once a distinction is made between them, however, the issue may look less discouraging. The death of the tragic drama we should attribute to the crumbling of an ideology, as previously explained. The highly fluctuant nature of our thinking at the present time makes more naturally for the essayistic than the dramatic — and the death of tragedy is a natural corollary of this general situation. The question of "poetic illusions" need not enter.

In the matter of the tragic spirit, however, there seems to be no essential abatement at all. For if tragedy is a sense of man's intimate participation in processes beyond himself, we find that science has replaced the older metaphysical structure with an historical structure which gives the individual man ample grounds to feel such participation. What science has taken from us as a personal relationship to the will of Providence, it has re-given as a personal relationship to the slow, unwieldy movements of human society. It is to the greatest credit of Nietzsche that he made this readjustment so thoroughly, turning from the "tragic dignity" of theology to the "tragic dignity" of history, and showing that if there was something "poetic" in the sense of a stable metaphysical structure personally concerned with the fate of man, there can be something equally "poetic" constructed out of the "illusion" or belief now current, the sense of the individual's place in an historical process. In another way the same readjustment was made by Pater in his Marius the Epicurean, where the "tragic fallacy" arises from our sense of Marius' close personal relationship to deep alterations in the mentality of peoples. Mr. Krutch himself, had he admitted a distinction between the tragic drama and the tragic spirit, would not have become involved as he does in the task of disproving his own thesis at the close of his book. For having said that tragedy is dead, and that it is dead because the new scientific "truths" have destroyed the tragic "illusions," he ends: "Some small part of the tragic fallacy may be said indeed to be still valid for us, for if we cannot feel ourselves as great as Shakespeare did, if we no longer believe in either our infinite capacities or our importance in the universe, we know at least that we have discovered the trick which has been played upon us and that whatever else we may be we are no longer dupes." He will accept the full responsibilities of this "truth," though the "truth" deprive him of something so edifying, so necessary to the most wholesome human expansiveness, as tragedy: "If death for us and our kind is the inevitable result of our stubbornness, then we can only say, 'So be it.' Ours is a lost cause and there is no place for us in the natural universe, but we are not, for all that, sorry to be human. We should rather die as men than live as animals." He pictures those of his kind watching simpler men who, through having gone less far in their thinking, enjoy certain vital advantages (high among which is "tragic importance"). But though recognizing the advantages that lie with the simple, those of his kind will follow their thoughts even to disaster. Such are Mr. Krutch's obdurate conclusions.

Now, tragedy as a mechanism is based upon a calamitous persistence in one's ways. It is "nobler" when the persistence is due to a moral stability on the part of the hero than when it is due to a mere misunderstanding. What, then, if not the formula for tragedy is this position of Mr. Krutch? He will take a personal stand in relation to a *historic* process (the historic process being in this instance the loss of certain magical or theological or metaphysical "illusions" based upon "non-scientific" systems of causality) — and in this stand he will persist at all hazards. It is good to have a writer display so well the basic machinery for a modern tragedy in a book heralding the death of all tragedy.

ARTHUR MILLER

TRAGEDY AND THE COMMON MAN

In this age few tragedies are written. It has often been held that the lack is due to a paucity of heroes among us, or else that modern man has had the blood drawn out of his organs of belief by the skepticism of science, and the heroic attack on life cannot feed on an attitude of reserve and circumspection. For one reason or another, we are often held to be below tragedy — or tragedy above us. The inevitable conclusion is, of course, that the tragic mode is archaic, fit only for the very highly placed, the kings or the kingly, and where this admission is not made in so many words it is most often implied.

I believe that the common man is as apt a subject for tragedy in its highest sense as kings were. On the face of it this ought to be obvious in the light of modern psychiatry, which bases its analysis upon classic formulations, such as the Oedipus and Orestes complexes, for instances, which were enacted by royal beings, but which apply to everyone in similar emotional situations.

More simply, when the question of tragedy in art is not at issue, we never hesitate to attribute to the well-placed and the exalted the very same mental processes as the lowly. And finally, if the exaltation of tragic

"Tragedy and the Common Man," by Arthur Miller, *The New York Times*, February 27, 1949. Copyright © 1949 by Arthur Miller. Reprinted by permission of The Viking Press.

action were truly a property of the high-bred character alone, it is inconceivable that the mass of mankind should cherish tragedy above all other forms, let alone be capable of understanding it.

As a general rule, to which there may be exceptions unknown to me, I think the tragic feeling is evoked in us when we are in the presence of a character who is ready to lay down his life, if need be, to secure one thing — his sense of personal dignity. From Orestes to Hamlet, Medea to Macbeth, the underlying struggle is that of the individual attempting to gain his "rightful" position in his society.

Sometimes he is one who has been displaced from it, sometimes one who seeks to attain it for the first time, but the fateful wound from which the inevitable events spiral is the wound of indignity, and its dominant force is indignation. Tragedy, then, is the consequence of a man's total compulsion to evaluate himself justly.

In the sense of having been initiated by the hero himself, the tale always reveals what has been called his "tragic flaw," a failing that is not peculiar to grand or elevated characters. Nor is it necessarily a weakness. The flaw, or crack in the character, is really nothing — and need be nothing, but his inherent unwillingness to remain passive in the face of what he conceives to be a challenge to his dignity, his image of his rightful status. Only the passive, only those who accept their lot without active retaliation, are "flawless." Most of us are in that category.

But there are among us today, as there always have been, those who act against the scheme of things that degrades them, and in the process of action everything we have accepted out of fear or insensitivity or ignorance is shaken before us and examined, and from this total onslaught by an individual against the seemingly stable cosmos surrounding us — from this total examination of the "unchangeable" environment — comes the terror and the fear that is classically associated with tragedy.

More important, from this total questioning of what has previously been unquestioned, we learn. And such a process is not beyond the common man. In revolutions around the world, these past thirty years, he has demonstrated again and again this inner dynamic of all tragedy.

Insistence upon the rank of the tragic hero, or the so-called nobility of his character, is really but a clinging to the outward forms of tragedy. If rank or nobility of character was indispensable, then it would follow that the problems of those with rank were the particular problems of tragedy. But surely the right of one monarch to capture the domain from another no longer raises our passions, nor are our concepts of justice what they were to the mind of an Elizabethan king.

The quality in such plays that does shake us, however, derives from the underlying fear of being displaced, the disaster inherent in being torn away from our chosen image of what and who we are in this world. Among us today this fear is as strong, and perhaps stronger, than it ever was. In fact, it is the common man who knows this fear best.

Now, if it is true that tragedy is the consequence of a man's total compulsion to evaluate himself justly, his destruction in the attempt posits a wrong or an evil in his environment. And this is precisely the morality of tragedy and its lesson. The discovery of the moral law, which is what the enlightenment of tragedy consists of, is not the discovery of some abstract or metaphysical quantity.

The tragic right is a condition of life, a condition in which the human personality is able to flower and realize itself. The wrong is the condition which suppresses man, perverts the flowing out of his love and creative instinct. Tragedy enlightens — and it must, in that it points the heroic finger at the enemy of man's freedom. The thrust for freedom is the quality in tragedy which exalts. The revolutionary questioning of the stable environment is what terrifies. In no way is the common man debarred from such thoughts or such actions.

Seen in this light, our lack of tragedy may be partially accounted for by the turn which modern literature has taken toward the purely psychiatric view of life, or the purely sociological. If all our miseries, our indignities, are born and bred within our minds, then all action, let alone the heroic action, is obviously impossible.

And if society alone is responsible for the cramping of our lives, then the protagonist must needs be so pure and faultless as to force us to deny his validity as a character. From neither of these views can tragedy derive, simply because neither represents a balanced concept of life. Above all else, tragedy requires the finest appreciation by the writer of cause and effect.

No tragedy can therefore come about when its author fears to question absolutely everything, when he regards any institution, habit or custom as being either everlasting, immutable or inevitable. In the tragic view the need of man to wholly realize himself is the only fixed star, and whatever it is that hedges his nature and lowers it is ripe for attack and examination. Which is not to say that tragedy must preach revolution.

The Greeks could probe the very heavenly origin of their ways and return to confirm the rightness of laws. And Job could face God in anger, demanding his right and end in submission. But for a moment everything is in suspension, nothing is accepted, and in this stretching and tearing apart of the cosmos, in the very action of so doing, the character gains "size," the tragic stature which is spuriously attached to the royal or the highborn in our minds. The commonest of men may take on that stature to the extent of his willingness to throw all he has into the contest, the battle to secure his rightful place in his world.

There is a misconception of tragedy with which I have been struck in review after review, and in many conversations with writers and readers alike. It is the idea that tragedy is of necessity allied to pessimism. Even the dictionary says nothing more about the word than that it means a story with a sad or unhappy ending. This impression is so firmly fixed that I almost hesitate to claim that in truth tragedy implies more optimism in its author than does comedy, and that its final result ought to be the reinforcement of the onlooker's brightest opinions of the human animal.

For, if it is true to say that in essence the tragic hero is intent upon claiming his whole due as a personality, and if this struggle must be total and without reservation, then it automatically demonstrates the indestructible will of man to achieve his humanity.

The possibility of victory must be there in tragedy. Where pathos rules, where pathos is finally derived, a character has fought a battle he could not possibly have won. The pathetic is achieved when the protagonist is, by virtue of his witlessness, his insensitivity or the very air he gives off, incapable of grappling with a much superior force.

Pathos truly is the mode for the pessimist. But tragedy requires a nicer balance between what is possible and what is impossible. And it is curious, although edifying, that the plays we revere, century after century, are the tragedies. In them, and in them alone, lies the belief — optimistic, if you will, in the perfectibility of man.

It is time, I think, that we who are without kings, took up this bright thread of our history and followed it to the only place it can possibly lead in our time — the heart and spirit of the average man.